Sciences of the Mind

Sciences of the Mind

Compiled from:

Biological Psychology
Third Edition
Frederick Toates

Biopsychology
Seventh Edition
John P. J. Pinel

Cognition
Sixth Edition
Gabriel A. Radvansky and Mark H. Ashcraft

PEARSON

Harlow, England • London • New York • Boston • San Francisco • Toronto • Sydney • Auckland • Singapore • Hong Kong
Tokyo • Seoul • Taipei • New Delhi • Cape Town • Sao Paulo • Mexico City • Madrid • Amsterdam • Munich • Paris • Milan

Pearson Education Limited
Edinburgh Gate
Harlow
Essex CM20 2JE

And associated companies throughout the world

Visit us on the World Wide Web at:
www.pearson.com/uk

Compiled from:

Biological Psychology
Third Edition
Frederick Toates
ISBN 978-0-273-73499-4
© Pearson Education 2001, 2011

Biopsychology
Seventh Edition
John P. J. Pinel
ISBN 978-0-205-54892-7
© 2009, 2006, 2003, 2000, 1997, 1993, 1990 Pearson Education, Inc.

Cognition
Sixth Edition
Gabriel A. Radvansky and Mark H. Ashcraft
ISBN 978-0-205-98580-7
© 2014, 2010, 2006 by Pearson Education, Inc.

ISBN 978-1-78449-016-4

Printed and bound in Great Britain by Ashford Colour Press, Gosport, Hampshire.

Contents

Chapter 18
Drugs and addiction

Learning outcomes for Chapter 18

After studying this chapter, you should be able to:

1 Discuss some of the problems in trying to define the terms 'drug' and 'addiction', while relating this to an understanding of the brain and the social context.

2 Explain some of the processes that are thought to underlie the craving, seeking and taking of drugs in humans, while discussing animal models of these phenomena.

3 Describe the effects of some addictive and non-addictive drugs on the brain and explain what this tells us about the bases of addiction. Discuss addiction to non-chemical activities, noting similarities and differences with drug-based addictions.

4 Critically discuss models that have been advanced to explain addiction.

Scene-setting questions

1 Why do people keep on taking drugs – to escape from reality or because the body comes to need them?

2 Does the effect of a drug depend on social context and expectations?

3 Is love like being addicted to a drug? Can sex be addictive?

4 Can you get addicted to the Internet?

5 Which is more addictive, heroin or nicotine?

6 What effect does ecstasy have? What is an LSD trip like?

7 Why can't people 'just say no' to drugs?

8 What is the range of possible addictions?

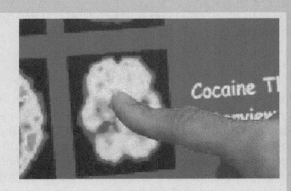

What is the range of possible addictions? Explore the video on the website accompanying this book at www.pearsoned.co.uk/toates

Why are warnings so often ineffective in countering drug-taking?

Source: Image courtesy of The Advertising Archives.

Introduction

When have you noticed 'drugs and addiction' discussed in the media? What was the context and what did these terms mean? The following reflects some typical items in the news.

'Agony of pop-star on entering rehabilitation – one more drink could be the last'.

'Police find drugs in football star's penthouse love-nest'.

'Yuppie weekend cocaine users are warned by police that they are not above the law'.

'Popular family vicar's life ruined by secret Internet sex addiction'.

By contrast, here are two imaginary headlines that you probably have never encountered but which reveal as much as those above.

'One-man drug-crazed crime-wave fuelled by need for mushrooms'.

'Housing estate ruled by fear of ecstasy gangs'.

These examples illustrate a number of points:

1 The criteria used to define the term 'drug' are as much legal, social and moral as they are psychological or biological. When you read about the footballer's 'drugs', you surely thought of heroin, cocaine or cannabis rather than tobacco or alcohol. The common expression 'drugs and alcohol' suggests that alcohol is not a drug. Yet it shows clear features in common with 'drugs', such as powerful mind-altering effects and a potential for addiction.

2 Some substances that are taken for their psychological effects are addictive whereas others are not. Some are normally discussed in the context of the social problems that they produce, associated with addiction. Are all drugs addictive? Certainly some, such as heroin, can be and they make the headlines. Nicotine is addictive but is perfectly legal and only rarely associated with crime, except smuggling.

3 Can you be addicted to something that is not a chemical? Since gambling and Internet sex can take control of a person's life and lead to ruin, we might include them under this heading. The challenge is to find features of addiction that are common across chemically related and non-chemically related activities.

4 Lots of people take ecstasy and magic mushrooms for their strong mind-altering effects. In the swinging 1960s, LSD was popular. Reports of addiction are extremely rare. So, there can be mind-altering drugs that have little or no addictive potential.

5 Some addictive substances are associated with serious crime and social disruption, whereas others are not. For some individuals, casual 'social use' of drugs is possible, whereas, for others, this switches to addiction. However, addiction is not intrinsic to the substance but is a complex property of the chemical and social context. Most of us drink socially but rather few become alcoholic. Some people manage to use 'hard drugs' only occasionally, e.g. the weekend (yuppie) cocaine user. What conditions tip only some individuals into addiction?

6 One feature that seems to cover all addiction is the notion of *conflict*. The pop-singer highlights the conflict involved with the addictive use of alcohol. A person can have conscious intentions to resist but finds him/herself pulled in the opposite direction. Someone engages in an activity to excess even though it brings serious problems, such as loss of job, home, family and health. The person might acknowledge this and wish to resist.

7 Certain drugs are associated with an aversive effect when they are no longer taken, termed **withdrawal**, the symptoms being **withdrawal symptoms**. The pop-singer was suffering from the pain of withdrawal.

The word 'drug' covers many substances taken, on the one hand, to counter and avoid disease, depressed mood or pain and, on the other, for a 'euphoric high' or spiritual enlightenment. This chapter is concerned with a group of **psychoactive drugs** taken to alter mood and cognition. It looks at their effects on the CNS and behaviour and the reasons people take them. Mood-altering drugs are not a heterogeneous class. They have different effects and people differ in their motivation to take them. However, there are some common features in the effects of a number of drugs (e.g. heroin, alcohol, caffeine, nicotine).

In each case, the drug can come to exert a strong motivational pull on the user, even though he or she acknowledges harmful effects. Drugs such as heroin, cocaine, alcohol and nicotine are taken for their rapid mood-altering properties. The enormous strength of motivation associated with taking some, e.g. heroin, is shown by the fact that people pay large sums and risk disease, loss of family, violence and death to obtain them.

Insight into drug-taking comes from at least three sources:

1 Behaviour of various species.

2 Subjective reports by humans.

3 Looking at the brains of humans and non-humans.

Biologically orientated research is directed to the neural basis of drug action, i.e. linking neurobiology to behavioural and experiential evidence. This involves trying to identify brain systems that have the following properties:

1 Their activity reflects motivation, is affected by conditional stimuli and is changed by the arrival of a drug.

2 The brain systems change with the development of drug-taking, e.g. a switch to addictive use.

3 Links between these regions and both sensory input and motor output can be identified.

4 They can be related to conventional motivation, such as feeding and sex.

Although, to understand drug effects, the drug's chemical properties are crucial, they cannot alone explain drug-taking behaviour (Peele, 1985). Environmental and personality factors are also involved. So, biological insight needs to interface with an understanding of social determinants. Explanations should be compatible with the vastly different levels of drug-taking that appear when comparing individuals or cultures or a given individual over the 'ups-and-downs' of life (Alexander, 2008; Peele and Alexander, 1985).

Humans provide subjective insight into the affective and cognitive events associated with seeking and taking drugs and withdrawal. Investigators relate these to psychological theory, but urge caution in the interpretation of subjective evidence. Verbal reports give unique insight into mood and the thoughts that occupy consciousness but, as discussed later, they might not always provide an infallible guide to the causes of behaviour (Robinson and Berridge, 1993).

Of course, evolution did not produce special processes dedicated to drug-taking. Drug-taking is best understood in a context of adaptive behaviour, such as sex, feeding and exploration, with which it shares properties. Drugs motivate in a way that has similarities with conventional rewards, e.g. pressing levers to obtain the reward of either food or injections of heroin intravenously (Chapter 15). Drugs exploit ('hijack') conventional motivational processes (e.g. mesolimbic dopamine system).

The following section looks at some characteristics of drug-taking.

Section summary

1 A number of psychoactive substances strongly attract people, associated with the risk of addiction.

2 Other psychoactive substances have a low addiction potential.

3 Some activities that are not associated with taking chemicals into the body also have the potential to develop addiction.

4 Addiction is characterized by compulsion even in the face of serious harm done by the activity.

 Test your knowledge

18.1 Which of the following has a low addiction potential? (i) Nicotine, (ii) heroin, (iii) LSD.

Answer on page 490

Characteristics of drug-taking

The motivation to take drugs is a complex function of the chemical properties of the drug as well as environmental factors, such as the location, the presence of other individuals and cues associated with drug-taking (Alexander, 2008). Motivation depends also upon a range of cognitive and emotional factors such as self-image and mood. Non-humans can provide models of features of drug-taking but they need to be considered in terms of some peculiarly human features.

The link to natural neurochemicals

By interacting with receptors on neurons, psychoactive drugs have psychological effects. Some drugs, such as the opiates, are chemically very similar to substances that the body produces naturally ('opioids'). These natural substances play a role in emotions, as in social bonding and distress calls (Chapters 12 and 15) and the inhibition of pain (Chapter 14). The body also contains its own source of cannabis-like chemicals (Chapter 14). This suggests that externally obtained chemicals influence those motivational and emotional processes that employ the natural equivalent. An understanding of the role of the natural chemicals (e.g. in social bonding) could provide valuable insight into why people are motivated to supplement them from outside, e.g. to reduce loneliness or alienation. The natural chemicals are evolutionarily old and this encourages the search for general principles applicable across species.

Withdrawal effects

Observable symptoms

In both humans and rats, if taking a drug such as heroin or alcohol is discontinued, observable withdrawal symptoms can occur (Wise, 1988). In humans, for opiates, these include aversive bodily signs, such as cramps, convulsions, sweating and a 'flu-like' condition (Koob, 1999). Rats shake their bodies (termed 'wet-dog shakes'), similar to a dog after it has got wet. Such withdrawal symptoms become paired with environmental cues and there can be 'conditional withdrawal symptoms', triggered by conditional stimuli paired with earlier withdrawal (Wikler, 1965). Withdrawal symptoms can also be triggered under normal conditions by injecting an opioid antagonist such as naloxone. Presumably this is due to blocking an endogenous opioid system and hence tilting the affect process in a negative direction.

An animal model of withdrawal from cocaine exists (Mutschler and Miczek, 1998): rats in withdrawal have elevated startle reflexes and a higher rate of ultrasonic vocalizations, both indices of negative affect (Chapter 12). In a **discrimination test** researchers can, in effect, ask the rat what the state feels like. For example, it can be rewarded with food for turning to the left when in drug withdrawal but to the right when not in withdrawal. Other states can be induced to see whether they are perceived as similar to withdrawal. Rats generalize between cocaine withdrawal and the state induced by the anxiogenic (anxiety-inducing) drug pentylenetetrazol (PTZ), i.e. they are perceived as similar.

Withdrawal symptoms are different according to the drug in question but what they all share is negative affect (Baker et al., 2004).

Unobserved signs

Psychologists cannot decide whether positive or negative affect is the most important for explaining the compulsive feature of drug-taking. It might well be naive to try to divide causes too neatly. However, negative affect is not necessarily always associated with observable signs of withdrawal (Baker et al., 2004). On being without a drug, e.g. cocaine, there can be an aversive state reported without external signs of withdrawal (Koob, 1999). Agony can be a private thing. In rats and humans, withdrawal signs are partly dependent upon social context (Alexander et al., 1985).

In any actions that are motivated to obtain drugs, the principles of conditioning are central, as described in the next two sections.

Classical conditioning

Classical conditioning plays an important role in various stages of drug-taking (Figure 18.1).

Motivational effects

Classical conditioning increases the motivation associated with drug-seeking and taking (Stewart et al., 1984) (Figure 18.1(a)). Let us assume that drugs are unconditional stimuli that elicit unconditional effects on the body. If neutral stimuli in the environment are repeatedly paired with drug-taking, they become conditional stimuli (CSs). For example, a syringe is a neutral stimulus prior to its being used to inject drugs. After this, it takes on new motivational properties: the sight of a syringe can evoke wanting a drug. Similarly, an open packet of cigarettes and lighter are CSs associated with nicotine (Thewissen et al., 2005). The term 'needle freak'

What is the role of context in drug-seeking and the effects of drugs?

Source: Janine Wiedel Photolibrary/Alamy.

refers to the ability of people addicted to heroin to experience something similar to the effect of a drug simply by going through the rituals of injection of a neutral substance.

By classical conditioning, a location associated with a drug can acquire incentive motivational properties (Chapter 15). For example, a rat prefers the side of a T-maze in which it received an injection of drug, a conditioned place preference (Bozarth, 1987). Given that classical conditioning underlies drug seeking and craving, it is logical to suppose that extinction procedures ('exposure') should be a therapeutic tool in combating drug-taking. Alas, exposure to drug-related cues in the absence of the drug has disappointing results (Marissen *et al.*, 2005).

Homeostatic reactions

Apart from psychoactive effects, drugs have other effects on the body. For example, heroin has effects on respiration. These are a disturbance to homeostasis and they trigger physiological counter-measures by the body. In this context, the drug is the unconditional stimulus (UCS) that triggers physiological compensation (UCR). Such counter-measures also occur within the person's

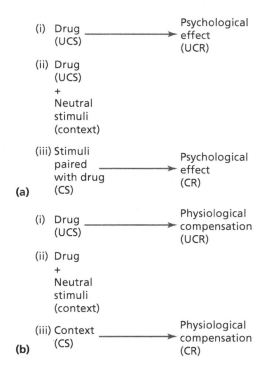

Figure 18.1 Conditioning of drug effects: (a) the motivational role, (b) role in compensation. (i) The unconditional role of a UCS triggering a UCR, (ii) pairing of drug-taking (UCS) with neutral stimuli and (iii) neutral stimuli become conditional stimuli (CS) having a capacity of their own (CR).

normal environment, which contains cues that can be conditioned, e.g. a particular room, friends and the sight of the syringe. Such conditional cues in the environment (CS) come to trigger some compensation (CR). See Figure 18.1(b).

Suppose that a person has a history of taking a drug in a particular context. Then, on one occasion, the drug is taken in a novel environment, not containing the familiar CSs. In the absence of the CR component of compensation, the counter-reaction would be expected to be weaker. Addicted people suffering or dying from an overdose commonly do so when injecting in an unfamiliar environment (Siegel, 1984). In fact, in purely chemical terms, the size of their dose might not appear excessive. However, in the absence of conditional counter-measures, the dose is, in effect, larger.

Instrumental conditioning

Introduction

In terms of instrumental conditioning, questions on drug-taking are framed around principles of reward and aversion, positive and negative reinforcement. Placed in an operant situation, animals can be persuaded to take drugs such as heroin by infusion through a cannula (Stewart *et al.*, 1984). It appears that different brain regions mediate the positive reinforcement (e.g. gain of pleasure) and negative reinforcement (e.g. loss of pain) aspects of drug-taking (Bechara *et al.*, 1998; Wise, 1988).

Negative reinforcement

Animals can be motivated to seek drugs because of a reduction that they cause in an aversive condition. Even though explicit physiological signs of withdrawal might not be evident, there can still be a CNS state of negative affect, the reduction of which by taking the drug constitutes negative reinforcement (Baker *et al.*, 2004). One might be able to infer an aversive state only from an animal's avoidance of external stimuli associated with being in the state. Soon after exposure to opiates, rats show avoidance of cues associated with their absence even though there are no observable physiological signs of withdrawal. Cocaine and amphetamine are not associated with aversive signs outside the nervous system but can be negatively reinforcing in alleviating a 'psychological distress syndrome' (see Robinson and Berridge, 1993).

The periaqueductal grey (Chapter 5) appears to be the site of negative reinforcement (Wise, 1988). Drugs that target receptors in this region seem to lower an aversive effect.

Animals seem to behave so as to maintain the level of natural opioids within limits. Isolated rats take more drugs than socially housed rats (Alexander *et al.*, 1985; Wolffgramm and Heyne, 1991). In laboratory rats, there may be something equivalent to a permanent withdrawal effect as a result of chronic low levels of endogenous opioids. This offers parallels with the suggestion that humans take drugs as self-medication for social alienation or other forms of psychological distress (Markou *et al.*, 1998). A negative mental state can be associated with cognitions about self-image and worthlessness (Peele, 1985). Cocaine use in humans tends to increase at times of perceived negative self-image (Singer, 1993).

Positive reinforcement

The *positive effect* of drugs refers to reward that can be induced even in the absence of a negative state. Its physical base is associated with the dopamine (DA) pathways ascending from the ventral tegmental area (Chapter 15) (Wise, 1988). In these terms, drugs form positive incentives to be pursued like sex or food (Robinson and Berridge, 1993; Stewart *et al.*, 1984). Activity at certain nuclei would tend to be rewarding in that it would move the animal to seek and 'consume' drugs. Rats can learn an operant task for drug reward, e.g. for microinjections into selected brain regions, even in the absence of any indices of withdrawal (Stewart *et al.*, 1984). Similarly, it seems that removal of withdrawal symptoms cannot explain how humans first move in a direction of addiction. People addicted to heroin commonly crave drugs when in the presence of drug-related cues.

In both humans and rats, presentation of small amounts of drug or cues associated with it triggers drug-seeking (Shaham and Stewart, 1995). For example, suppose a rat has learned an operant for intravenous drug reward but this has been extinguished by omission of drug. A small portion of drug is then injected 'free'. This is a cue to trigger re-arousal of the operant task. An arbitrary cue that had been paired with drug-delivery can maintain drug-seeking even in the absence of drug (Falk, 1994).

The factors of (i) reward and positive reinforcement and (ii) aversion and negative reinforcement cannot always be distinguished. A consensus view appears to be that, in a given individual, both types of process play a part in drug-taking with the relative weight shifting with circumstances (Bechara *et al.*, 1998; Koob, 1999; Wise, 1988).

Craving

As an example of subjective evidence, the term 'craving' (Chapter 16) describes an urge to take a drug and mental occupation with obtaining it (Franken, 2003; Markou *et al.*, 1993). Craving is associated with limbic system activation (Chapter 12; Childress *et al.*, 1999). Similarly, humans also report cravings for particular foods (Kassel and Shiffman, 1992). As a subjective state made available by verbal report, craving is a peculiarly human phenomenon. However, features of human craving can be modelled by non-humans (Chapter 15), e.g. lever-pressing by rats on extinction conditions in a task previously reinforced with drug. In humans, a lowering of the intensity of cocaine craving is caused by the agent desmethylimipramine. In rats, this also lowers responding in extinction, i.e. they tend to stop lever-pressing sooner (Fuchs *et al.*, 1998).

Defining addiction

Addiction refers to a person's abandonment to a pursuit, involving the neglect of other things and compromising the quality of life. After discontinuation of the addictive activity for short or long periods, there is a tendency to return to it ('relapse') (Peele and Degrandpre, 1998). There are a number of criteria that are employed to justify the term 'addiction' but not universal agreement on how many of these need to be present.

Link with withdrawal

To some experts, withdrawal symptoms offer a possible objective index of addiction (discussed by Wise, 1987). Their *presence* is certainly a useful pointer. However, some people described as addicted do not show physiological signs of withdrawal. It was once argued that cocaine is not addictive since there is not a pattern of associated ('extraneural') physiological withdrawal symptoms. However, this now seems an irrational criterion given the craving associated with the drug and its social and crime-related implications (Stolerman and Jarvis, 1995; Volkow *et al.*, 1997).

Curing withdrawal symptoms often has only a minimal effect in treating addiction (Wise, 1988). Subjective withdrawal symptoms do not correlate well with physiological signs of withdrawal (Henningfield *et al.*, 1987; Peele, 1985).

Other indices and criteria

Addiction is associated with **tolerance**, meaning that increasing amounts of drug need to be taken to obtain a given effect.

These days, 'addiction' is often used in non-chemical contexts, e.g. 'love addiction'. The broad usage points to important common features between drug and non-drug objects (Koob, 1999). However, it also raises a dilemma. If everything from praying and watching football to intravenous heroin use has the potential to be 'addictive', the word might appear to be devalued.

Alternatively, are there qualitatively different types of addiction? One way round this is to employ 'addiction' only where there are elements of danger, conflict and disruption to life involved.

A contemporary view is that all addictions have physical aspects and psychological aspects, as two sides of the same coin. That is to say, the psychological aspects are rooted in the brain. Thus, drugs and non-drug-related addictive behaviour would represent two different routes to tap a similar or identical underlying process. The motivation to take drugs might, like love, be based upon positive incentive motivational properties with the possibility of aversive effects of loss and abstinence.

Contextual factors

Contextual factors are important in drug-taking. For example, in humans, substances such as nicotine and caffeine presumably owe their high intake as much to their legality, relatively low cost, ready availability and compatibility with performing other tasks as to any intrinsic chemical properties.

This section looks at two examples of contextual factors.

The social dimension

A rat or non-human primate pressing a lever in a Skinner box might seem to exemplify the pure addictive potential of a drug, uncomplicated by cognition, social interaction and culture. However, experiments in which animals have worked for a drug at a very high rate (i) make the drug readily available by intravenous infusion

Rats housed in a rich physical and social context. Why are researchers interested in the effect of environmental enrichment on the tendency to drug-taking?

Source: courtesy of Bruce Alexander.

for minimal effort, (ii) have not allowed alternative sources of reward and (iii) involve a highly restrained physical context (Peele and Degrandpre, 1998). If availability is made more difficult, intake is lower.

Alexander *et al.* (1985) measured the oral intake of morphine solution by rats in a large social environment. Intake was only one-eighth that of isolated rats. Alexander and Hadaway (1982, p. 371) remark: 'The restrictive, isolated conditions of standard laboratory housing may be inherently stressful to mobile, social animals like rats and monkeys, and their self-administration of heroin could simply provide relief'. The presence of alternative sources of reward (e.g. social) offers effective competition to drug-taking in rats and humans (Peele, 1985).

In humans and non-humans, Peele and Degrandpre (1998) see a consistent pattern: cocaine has an addictive potential that is a function of both the chemical and the social context. Many humans can be described as 'occasional users', showing controlled use, e.g. monthly. Considerations of family and professional life are taken into account and restrain intake. Most American servicemen who employed opiates in Vietnam did not take this habit back to the United States with them at the end of the war (Robins *et al.*, 1975). Patients who self-administer narcotics for pain relief do not normally crave drugs when outside the clinical context (Chapter 14).

The dimension of control

The effects of a drug depend in part upon the nature of the *control* that the user is able to exert, which seems to be important for the addictive potential.

A rat pressing a lever in a Skinner box for drug reward is performing a particular behaviour, within a particular environment, under its own control. Effects of drugs taken under the animal's own control and their withdrawal effects are stronger than those experienced by a passive paired ('yoked') control receiving the same drug (MacRae and Siegel, 1997).

In humans, taking a drug involves performance of a procedure, a mechanical act or 'ritual', in a context of environmental and social cues. Changing the ability to control a situation can change the effect of the drug. If drugs are administered outside the control of the individual, they are perceived as being not so hedonically potent (Alexander and Hadaway, 1982). The particular route of administration can be important to some users (Peele, 1985). Control is qualified by history, context and goal.

Section summary

1   Some psychoactive drugs such as the opiates are very similar to natural neurochemicals.

2   Classical conditioning plays a role in drug-seeking and the effects of drugs.

3   Cessation of drug-taking can be associated with objective measures of withdrawal. Negative affect also follows.

4   The reinforcement for drug-taking appears to be both positive and negative.

5   Human craving can be modelled by animals placed on extinction conditions.

6   Context plays a crucial role in drug-seeking.

 ## Test your knowledge

18.2 Consider the phenomenon termed 'needle freak' and suppose that an addict is given a neutral substance, thinking that it is heroin. Using the terminology of classical conditioning, how would you describe (i) the injection and (ii) the effect of the injection?

 Answer on page 490   WEB

Drugs and drug-taking

This section looks at some of the activities that are related to drugs and addiction. It considers addictive drugs and also some drugs with little addictive potential.

Amphetamine and cocaine

The motivational potency of amphetamine and cocaine appears to depend mainly upon their ability to increase levels of dopamine (DA) at synapses (Pierce and Kalivas, 1997; Wang and McGinty, 1999). Cocaine blocks DA reuptake (Chapter 4). Amphetamine both blocks reuptake and triggers the release of DA into the synapse (Grace, 2001; Wise, 1988).

Amphetamine

In rats, microinjections of amphetamine into the nucleus accumbens (N.acc.) are rewarding in designs employing place preference and self-infusion by lever-pressing (Bardo, 1998) (Figure 18.2).

Human amphetamine users report increased attention and energy and changes in cognition (Ellinwood, 1967, 1968; Klee and Morris, 1997). An improvement in self-image is one of the first effects. Ordinary events take a heightened significance and the universe appears to 'make sense'. The drug gives novelty to an otherwise dull world, suggesting that it taps into an exploration process. Objects can (Ellinwood, 1968, p. 48): 'stimulate curiosity and a search for new categories and significance, or attempts to expand, change and distort the categories or unknown object for mutual reconciliation'. Users sometimes engage in mechanical manipulation of objects, e.g. repeated assembly and taking apart (Ellinwood and Kilbey, 1975). In distorting cognition, amphetamine has features in common with the hallucinogens (see later). On the negative side, humans can experience paranoia-inducing cognitive changes in their interpretation of the world.

Cocaine

See Figure 18.3. The N.acc. might be involved in cocaine reward (Maldonado *et al.*, 1993). However, evidence suggests that the primary site of action is outside the N.acc. For example, a conditioned place preference test is relatively insensitive to manipulation of the level of dopamine in the N.acc. (Baker *et al.*, 1996). Based on microinjection studies and conditioned place preference tests, a site of cocaine's action appears to be the DA projections to the prefrontal cortex (Bardo, 1998). However, its effect on behaviour seems to depend on connections from this region to the N.acc. (a glutamate-mediated link is shown). Why there is a difference in target neurons between amphetamine and cocaine is not clear.

In intravenous self-administration, DA antagonists sometimes increase the intake of cocaine and amphetamine, i.e. compensation occurs (Bardo, 1998). DA antagonists block a conditioned place preference. For humans, the power of cocaine to induce euphoria is reduced when DA receptors are blocked (Gunne *et al.*, 1972; Jönsson *et al.*, 1971).

Figures 18.4 and 18.5 show the level of cocaine in the brain following its injection intravenously. By comparison, the level of another substance, methylphenidate (also termed 'Ritalin'), is also shown. Like cocaine, this blocks reuptake of dopamine but it is less addictive. The subjective feeling of 'high' is also shown. In each case, you can see a sharp rise and fall of the 'high'. However, note that methylphenidate is broken down more slowly than cocaine. This suggests that cocaine's addictive potency is linked to the sharp onset and offset ('rise and fall') of its biological effect.

Try examining the diagram to see why bouts of cocaine taking, some 30 minutes or so apart, sometimes occur. You should see that by 30 minutes, there is a

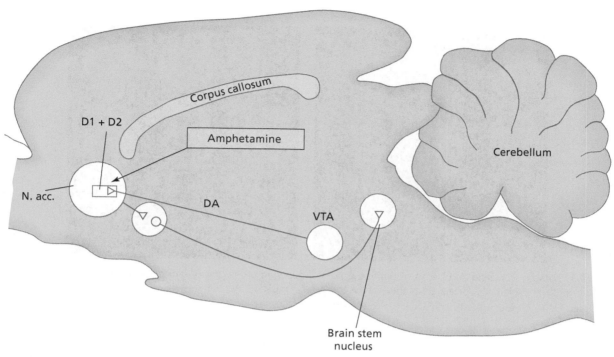

Figure 18.2 Suggested reward site of amphetamine in the rat brain. D$_1$ and D$_2$ are dopamine receptor subtypes.
Source: adapted from Bardo (1998, Fig. 1, p. 57).

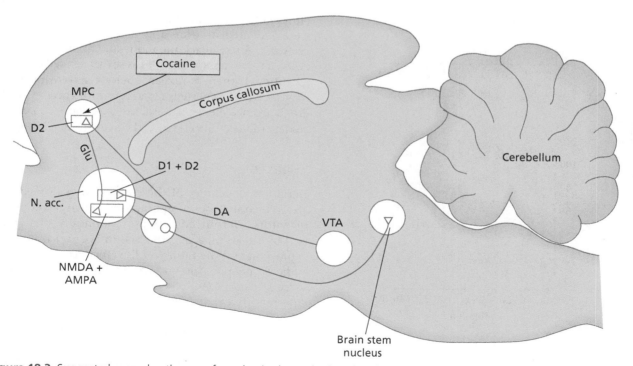

Figure 18.3 Suggested reward pathways of cocaine in the rat brain. Glu, glutamate; MPC, medial prefrontal cortex; NMDA, glutamate *N*-methyl-D-aspartate receptors.
Source: Bardo (1998, Fig. 2, p. 58).

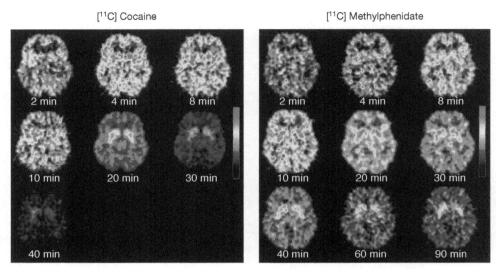

[¹¹C] Cocaine   [¹¹C] Methylphenidate

Figure 18.4 Comparison using a PET scan of the human brain following the taking of a drug: (a) labelled cocaine and (b) labelled methylphenidate. Scan taken at the level of the basal ganglia.
Source: Toates (2004, Book 6, Fig. 1.13), from Volkow, Fowler and Wang (2002, Fig. 1, page 356).

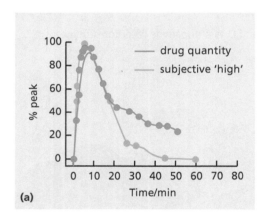

(a)

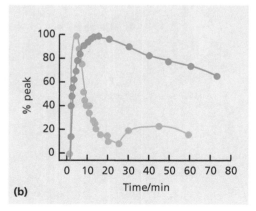

(b)

Figure 18.5 The presence of a drug in the brain and the subjective 'high' experienced by the user: (a) cocaine, (b) methylphenidate.
Source: Toates (2004, Book 6, Fig. 1.14), after Volkow, Fowler and Wang (2002, Fig. 2, page 357).

significant fall in receptor occupation. Hence more drug could give more occupation and an upswing in the 'high'.

Chapter 17 described a study on backward masking and the use of very brief sexual stimuli (Childress *et al.*, 2008). Now it is time to add that the researchers also employed drug-related stimuli and the participants under study were cocaine users. A similar set of brain regions (amygdala, ventral striatum and the orbitofrontal cortex) were activated by drug and sexual stimuli. This suggests that drugs hijack the motivational machinery that evolved to serve such activities as sexual behaviour.

Although there is not an obvious pattern of physiological withdrawal signs associated with cocaine, in the drug's absence the regular user can experience depression, anxiety (termed 'the crash') and craving (Koob, 1999).

Opiates

Heroin is a member of the class of drug termed opiates, which includes morphine, and which target opioid receptors. Heroin addicts are commonly characterized by isolation, a negative self-image and feelings of depression and the futility of life (Tokar *et al.*, 1975). To addicted people, opiates give happiness, an increased sense of detachment and a reduced sense of awareness. One reported that 'heroin does something for a sick ego'. The reports of addicted people suggest that drugs create a euphoria that is tied to altered perceptions of self and the world.

Opiates have both rewarding and aversion-removing effects. Figure 18.6 shows some brain sites of opiate reward. Among other sites, it appears that opiates either

A personal angle

Sigmund Freud

Early in his career, Freud's interest was attracted to cocaine (Clark, 1980). Dr Theodor Aschenbrandt had experimented on cocaine's effects on weary Bavarian soldiers, whose motivation and attention were revived. Freud tried the drug and reported: 'A few minutes after taking the cocaine one suddenly feels light and exhilarated' and he wrote to his wife in 1884: 'In my last severe depression I took coca again and a small dose lifted me to the heights in a wonderful fashion. I am just now busy collecting the literature for a song of praise to this magical substance' (Clark, 1980, p. 59).

Freud was criticized for his liberal attitudes but responded that he had never advocated injection, merely ingestion. That Freud did not develop an addiction to cocaine in spite of taking it for 10 years (Sulloway, 1979) exemplifies that addiction depends on the interaction of the drug with the whole person and environment. However, Freud was wrong to assume that he could harmlessly wean an addicted friend off morphine with the help of cocaine. One might expect cross-sensitization and indeed the friend became a cocaine addict (Gay, 1988).

excite neurons that form excitatory synapses upon DA neurons in the ventral tegmental area (VTA) or they inhibit neurons that inhibit DA neurons (Wise, 1988). In rats, minute local injections of opiates into the VTA are rewarding, an effect that is reduced or eliminated when the DA system is blocked (Wise and Bozarth, 1987). Also, microinjections of opiates in the N.acc. are rewarding (Bardo, 1998).

Evidence suggests that the rewarding effect of opiates is sufficient to motivate opiate intake (Wise, 1988). In rats, the first injection has some rewarding effect, when by definition there can be no withdrawal effect, at least as defined in terms of exogenous drug. Thus, if a naive rat is exposed to a particular environment during which it experiences a single morphine injection, it will subsequently show a preference for being in

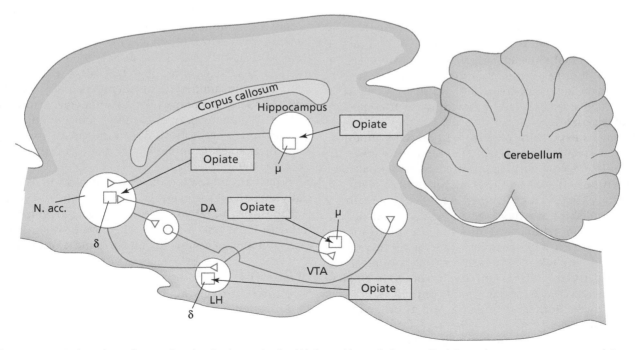

Figure 18.6 Opiate sites of reward action in the rat brain. LH, lateral hypothalamus; δ, delta opiate receptor; μ, mu opiate receptor.
Source: Bardo (1998, Fig. 3, p. 59).

that environment (Wise and Bozarth, 1987). However, we cannot ignore the suggestion that laboratory rats are permanently in a state similar to mild drug-withdrawal.

The periaqueductal grey (PAG) (Chapter 12) appears to be a principal site of aversion alleviation by opiates (Wise, 1988). Dependent rats, but not non-dependent ones, learn to press for infusion into the PAG (Wise and Bozarth, 1987). If specifically this region is first targeted with opiates and then an opiate antagonist is given, withdrawal symptoms are seen.

There are various bodily manifestations of opiate withdrawal, e.g. rats exhibit 'wet-dog shakes'. Also opiates might exert an aversion-alleviation effect outside the CNS, by, for example, removing gastrointestinal cramps (Wise, 1988).

Nicotine

Of all addictive substances, nicotine would probably rank worldwide as that causing the most harm to its users (Pomerleau and Pomerleau, 1984). However, it was only in the mid-1990s that its addictive potential was fully recognized. By comparison with opiates and cocaine, the subjective effects of cigarettes are more subtle, diffuse and hard to define.

Motivational mechanisms

Compared with opiates and cocaine, it is relatively difficult to establish nicotine as a reinforcer in an operant situation in non-humans (Donny *et al.*, 1998; Stolerman and Jarvis, 1995). Place preference conditioning is similarly more difficult (Rose and Corrigal, 1997). In rats, it is easier to obtain operant behaviour for nicotine (as for a variety of drugs) if the reward is associated with arbitrary extrinsic (i.e. 'contextual') cues such as a light or sound. Once established, omission of such a cue can lower responding.

Humans experience nicotine withdrawal symptoms, including irritability and depressed mood (Gilbert *et al.*, 1997). However, a positive incentive-motivational state is often suggested to be the principal factor underlying smoking (Pomerleau and Pomerleau, 1984), especially in first establishing the habit. Nicotine is associated with an increase in mental concentration. The motivational basis underlying a given smoker can vary, sometimes a cigarette being taken for relaxation and at other times to gain alertness (Gilbert *et al.*, 1997). This again emphasizes the importance of context and control.

The mechanical act of smoking and associated taste (e.g. of nicotine) form part of the attraction (Rose and Corrigal, 1997). For smokers, smoking-related cues are particularly strong in their ability to capture attention and increase the motivation to smoke (Hogarth *et al.*, 2003). When trying to quit, this points to the importance of avoiding smoking-related contexts, as is the case with other addictive drugs. The potent reinforcement potential in humans might, in addition to cross-species processes, depend upon the mechanical act of smoking (e.g. holding and puffing) and species-specific effects on cognitive processing.

The act of lighting is repeated regularly, specific to smoking and is stereotyped. It often tends to be a social activity and it might be expected that, when one smoker lights-up, this will trigger mirror neurons in another's brain (Iacoboni, 2008). Craving might owe something to such social facilitation. Indeed, some evidence suggests that in smokers, as compared with non-smokers, the mirror neuron system is relatively sensitive (Pineda and Oberman, 2006).

Neurochemistry

After inhaling, nicotine is taken into the blood and appears in the brain very rapidly. Within as little as seven seconds of puffing, 25% of inhaled nicotine has already crossed the blood–brain barrier (Pomerleau and Pomerleau, 1984). Nicotine leaves the brain rapidly after the cigarette has been smoked. These dynamics provide optimal conditions to associate the neurochemical changes with the sight of the cigarette, the action of smoking and the environmental context (i.e. classical conditioning). To make matters worse, nicotine is a special drug in combining universal availability and legality with a capacity to facilitate work!

Nicotine's motivational effects seem to depend upon actions on various neurochemicals, e.g. cholinergic, serotonergic and opioidergic, and hormonal systems (Dani and Heinemann, 1996; Koob, 1999). These neurochemical systems come together in influencing the mesolimbic dopaminergic pathway (Chiamulera, 2005). Nicotine shares the property of dopaminergic activation with other addictive drugs. Nicotine activates cholinergic (nicotinic) receptors on dopaminergic neurons, e.g. those that project from the VTA to the N.acc. (Rose and Corrigal, 1997).

In rats, a combination of stress and nicotine is especially effective in triggering DA activity in the N.acc. (Takahashi *et al.*, 1998). If this can be generalized to humans, it suggests a process whereby stress and nicotine combine to promote the intake of more nicotine.

Addictive potential

Nicotine is strongly addictive (Stolerman and Jarvis, 1995). Patients under treatment for addiction to hard drugs and who also smoked cigarettes ranked cigarettes as being more difficult to give up than the drug that was the target of treatment (Kozlowski *et al.*, 1989).

In Britain, the average male smoker smokes 17 cigarettes each day and the average female smoker 14 per day. Light smokers are rare. Craving is a common phenomenon in the absence of a cigarette and smokers generally rate their chances of giving up as low.

Alcohol

Acting on various neurotransmitters, alcohol has effects such as to lower anxiety, by which it can mediate negative reinforcement, and to induce mild euphoria (Chick and Erickson, 1996; Koob, 1999). Alcohol triggers activity in the body's natural opioid system, which might, in turn, promote craving for more (Mercer and Holder, 1997). Craving can be particularly exacerbated within certain external contexts (e.g. being in a bar) or internal contexts (e.g. stress or depression). The alcohol withdrawal effect has similarities with that of opiates and might also involve the PAG (Wise, 1988). Opiate agonists tend to increase alcohol consumption and antagonists tend to decrease it (Davidson and Amit, 1997). Wand et al. (1998) suggest that differences between individuals in tendency to alcoholism are mediated via different levels of endogenous opioid activity. Those prone to alcoholism appear to have an intrinsically low level of opioid activity.

Alcohol normally has relatively little reinforcement value to rats. However, strains of alcohol-preferring rats can be selectively bred (McBride and Li, 1998).

Marijuana

Marijuana has been used for more than 4000 years for therapeutic (Chapter 14) and recreational reasons (Stahl, 1998). The psychoactive ingredient of marijuana is delta-9-tetrahydrocannabinol (THC). The brain manufactures its own supply of a marijuana-like substance, termed anandamide, and contains cannabinoid (CB) receptors. A subtype, the CB1 receptor, is believed to mediate the rewarding effects of cannabinoid substances. Marijuana appears to act by boosting mesolimbic DA transmission and altering serotonergic neurotransmission (Gessa et al., 1998).

Can marijuana become addictive? Certainly there are people for whom its use is described as 'problematic' and the term 'cannabis dependence' has entered the clinical literature (Le Strat et al., 2009). To address the issue of addiction, researchers compare features of marijuana use with that of 'hard drugs'. Deprived of marijuana, heavy users crave the drug. Exposure to cues linked to marijuana use triggers activation in brain areas linked to addiction, such as the nucleus accumbens (Filbey et al., 2009). The degree of activation correlates with the extent of problems experienced.

Withdrawal symptoms associated with discontinuation of supply are sometimes experienced, consisting of anger and irritability, etc. (Haughey et al., 2008). That they are not more serious might be linked to the fact that there is not such a sharp onset–offset profile of effect as with other drugs; after appearing in the blood, cannabinoids are stored in body fats and then slowly released (Stahl, 1998) (which explains why some people take harder drugs, since their time-frame of detection is shorter). If there is receptor adaptation during the acute phase, the 'endogenous' source of drug from body fat might cushion the system against withdrawal effects for the time that it takes the receptor state to recover. Marijuana illustrates the earlier point about context-dependency of drug effects. People high in anxiety can find that this is increased by the drug (Szuster et al., 1988).

Caffeine

Regular users of relatively large amounts of caffeine (in the form of tea or coffee) report a withdrawal effect (e.g. headaches, sleepiness, irritability) when intake ceases (Griffiths and Woodson, 1988). A double-blind placebo-controlled study demonstrated that the effects are due to loss of the caffeine content of the beverage per se (Phillips-Bute and Lane, 1998). Caffeine does not reliably cause hedonic feelings in humans. Rather, it often induces anxiety. The fact that it is the world's most widely used psychoactive drug points to the inadequacy of hedonic explanations of drug-taking and suggests that wanting relates in no simple way to liking (Chapter 15).

How does caffeine act? There are receptors in the brain to the natural substance adenosine. Occupation by adenosine inhibits the activity of the neurons bearing these receptors. Dopaminergic neurons are among those having this type of receptor on their surface. Caffeine is similar to adenosine but, by occupying its receptors, caffeine prevents the action of adenosine. Hence, a source of inhibition on neurons involved in wanting and reward is lowered.

Dopaminergic drugs

So-called 'impulse control disorders', such as excessive buying, gambling and inappropriate sexual behaviour, sometimes emerge in Parkinson's disease patients as a result of dopaminergic medication (Chapter 10; Lim et al., 2008). Medication is designed to boost the level of dopaminergic activity in the affected brain region, so as to bring movement control nearer to normal. However, this inadvertently gives an over-dose of dopamine to the intact dopaminergic system involved with motivation (the mesolimbic dopaminergic pathway, introduced in Chapter 15). Some patients exhibit what is termed 'dopamine dysregulation syndrome' (DDS). This is a form of addiction to dopaminergic drugs, taking them in excess of what is optimal for the control of motor disorder. Such evidence lends support to the role of dopaminergic activation in addiction. It appears that drugs which give a steady long-acting boost to DA transmission provide less risk of addiction than those which trigger bursts of activation (Lawrence *et al.*, 2003). This would fit an understanding of the role of dopamine in motivation.

In terms of dopaminergic neurotransmission triggered by L-dopa in the ventral striatum, a study compared Parkinson's patients who showed DDS with those who did not (Evans *et al.*, 2006). It employed neuroimaging with positron emission tomography (PET) and ^{11}C-raclopride (RAC) (Chapter 5). Images were compared under the conditions when the patients were on and off L-dopa treatment.

Figure 18.7 compares Parkinson's patients who did not exhibit DDS (controls) with those who did exhibit it (DDS). The diagram might confuse you as much as it did me when I first saw it (through no fault of the authors). Note that the vertical axis shows the percentage *reduction* in RAC binding potential. RAC and dopamine released are in competition for occupation of receptors. So, the higher the vertical value, the less the occupation by the extraneous substance and the greater is the occupation of receptors by dopamine. Within the putamen, there is no difference between the two groups. The putamen is concerned with motor control (Chapter 10). By contrast, in the ventral striatum, a region concerned with

motivation (which includes the N.acc.), the DDS group showed a significantly higher reduction in RAC binding potential than did the control group. This points to a significantly higher occupation of receptors by dopamine in the ventral striatum in the DDS group. Figure 18.8 shows the localization in the brain, the ventral striatum, where there are significant differences between groups.

Are the effects of dopaminergic neurotransmission more closely associated with 'wanting' or 'liking' (Chapter 15)? In this case, wanting was for the dopaminergic drug L-dopa. Figure 18.9(a) shows a positive correlation between the reduction in RAC binding potential (i.e. increased occupation of ventral striatum with dopamine) and the individual's ranking of the degree of wanting. By contrast, there was a negative correlation between RAC binding potential and liking of the drug (Figure 18.9(b)).

Hallucinogens

The term **hallucinogen** refers to a class of drug for which the primary action is to change sensory perception (Aghajanian, 1994; Delgado and Moreno, 1998). It includes lysergic acid diethylamide (LSD), mescaline (from a type of cactus) and psilocybin (from a type of mushroom) and their effect in altering cognition is termed 'psychedelic' (Stahl, 1996). The person taking such a 'trip' might feel a sense of union with the universe or with God. Disorientation and panic are termed a 'bad trip', a state that can be characterized by paranoia and delusions.

It is difficult if not impossible to teach animals an operant task for hallucinogens and they have a low addictive potential in humans (Griffiths *et al.*, 1979). One special case is that monkeys in sensory isolation sometimes learn an operant task for them (Siegel and Jarvick, 1980). Monkeys exhibit orientation, tracking and startle responses, as if the drug is simulating external sensory stimulation. This might have features in common with animals kept in monotonous conditions working for a change in sensory stimulation (Chapter 15).

A common property of the substances just named is that their hallucinogenic potency is proportional to their ability to inhibit serotonergic neurons by acting at serotonin (5-HT$_2$) receptors (Aghajanian, 1994). In turn, the serotonin effect mediates changes at the locus coeruleus, which has broad noradrenergic projections throughout the brain.

Activity within the locus coeruleus appears to alter processing such that target neurons have a lower level of spontaneous activity and higher response to sensory stimulation. This seems to be the basis of distorted (e.g. heightened) perception and cognition induced by psychedelic drugs.

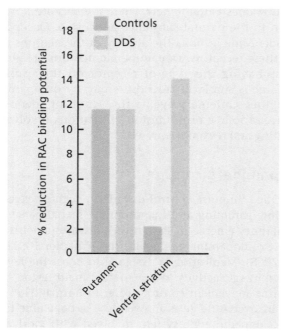

Figure 18.7 The percentage reduction in ^{11}C-raclopride (RAC) binding following administration of L-dopa, comparing two brain regions, the putamen and the ventral striatum.
Source: Evans *et al.* (2006) *Annals of Neurology*, 59, Fig. 1, p. 854.

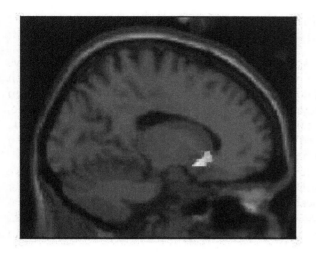

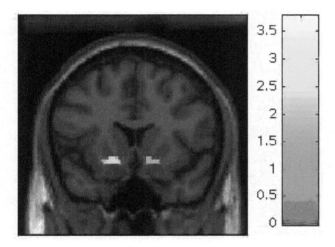

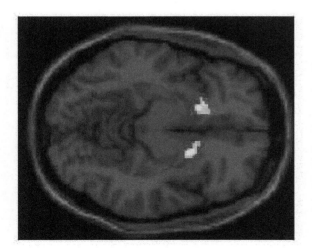

Figure 18.8 Sagittal (top), coronal (centre) and transaxial (lower) images showing in yellow/orange region of significant differences between groups.

Source: Evans *et al.* (2006) *Annals of Neurology*, 59, Fig. 2, p. 854.

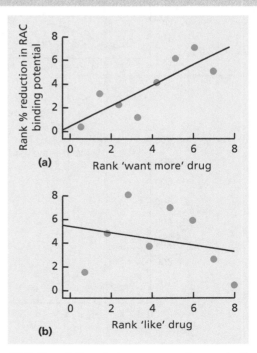

Figure 18.9 Correlations between percentage reduction in RAC binding potential and (a) wanting more drug and (b) liking the drug.

Source: Evans *et al.* (2006) *Annals of Neurology*, 59, Fig. 3, p. 855.

Ecstasy

Ecstasy, chemical name 3,4-methylenedioxymetham-phetamine (MDMA), became a popular recreational drug in the late 1980s (Steele *et al.*, 1994). It promotes the release and blocks reuptake of serotonin and dopamine, which mediates psychedelic effects. It is often taken at large social gatherings termed 'raves'. Ecstasy's effects include elevated mood, sensual awareness and a sense of 'awareness with others' (Stahl, 1996). On the negative side, there are reports of increased anxiety, panic attacks and psychosis (Steele *et al.*, 1994), as well as memory impairments and damage to the nervous system (Roberts *et al.*, 2009).

Similarities and differences among drug-related activities

In spite of diverse effects, a subgroup of psychoactive drugs activate some common neural systems. Activation of dopamine (e.g. at the N.acc.) appears to be a common factor in those that are addictive, e.g. amphetamine, cocaine, nicotine, morphine and alcohol (Everitt *et al.*, 2001). Non-addictive drugs, e.g. hallucinogens, have a primary site of action elsewhere in the brain.

In humans, there are similarities in the subjective effects of opiates, amphetamines and cocaine. A former cocaine addict can be at risk from relapse by an occasional use of heroin and the heroin addict is at risk from cocaine. In rats, an extinguished heroin habit can be reinstated by a 'free' priming delivery of cocaine and vice versa. This provides some rationale for the demand for total abstention from all drugs that is commonly made on rehabilitation programmes. Wise (1988,

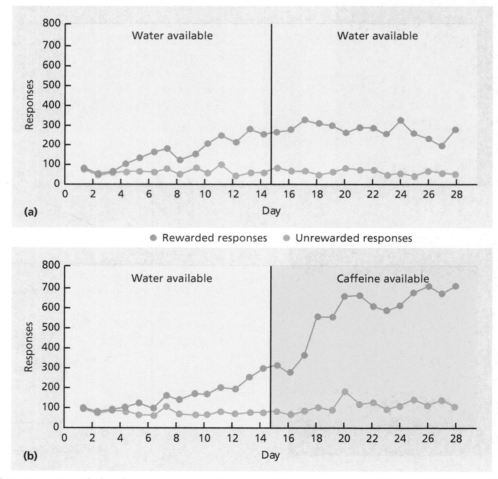

Figure 18.10 Responses rewarded with intravenous nicotine when (a) plain water is available and (b) when caffeine solution is available at day 14. The response was poking the nose into a hole (active). As a control, another hole was present into which a response did not trigger nicotine infusion (passive).

Source: Toates (2004, Figure 1.17), after Shoaib *et al.* (1999, Fig. 3).

p. 125) notes that nicotine and alcohol can activate DA neurons in the VTA:

> The possibility that nicotine, alcohol, and even caffeine may activate the same neural circuitry suggests other drug stimuli that may put an ex-addict at risk. Of these, smoking represents a potential stimulant to relapse that may be widely underestimated.

In people with a history of cocaine-taking, nicotine accentuates craving in the presence of cocaine-related cues (Reid *et al.*, 1998). Even caffeine might not be harmless in this regard. Evidence suggests that it can increase the tendency to take nicotine (Bernstein *et al.*, 2002). There is a possible rat model of this. Figure 18.10 shows the number of responses for intravenous nicotine by rats having available either plain water or water with caffeine added.

So much for this subgroup of drugs, which have the potential for addiction; let us now consider some non-drug-related activities that have similar properties.

Section summary

1. Amphetamine and cocaine increase levels of synaptic dopamine.

2. Opiates target opioid receptors and interact with dopaminergic neurotransmission. They have reward and aversion-alleviation effects.

3. Nicotine is rapidly absorbed into the bloodstream, enters the brain and affects a number of neurochemical activities, e.g. dopamine.

4. If operant behaviour for self-infusion of nicotine is associated with an arbitrary external cue, it is easier to produce.

5. Alcohol interacts with endogenous opioids.

6. People with Parkinson's disease and being treated with drugs that boost dopamine can develop an addiction to them.

7. Drugs such as LSD, termed hallucinogens, target serotonin.

☞ **Test your knowledge**

18.3 In the experiment shown in Figure 18.10, why have two holes and record nose-pokes in both (one connected to nicotine delivery and the other having no consequence)?

Answer on page 490   WEB

Non-drug-related activities

Introduction

Popular language refers to a number of non-chemical-related activities as being similar to drug-taking, including having the potential to become addictive. Does biological psychology offer any insights that would give a basis to such a description? As an example, playing video games can be highly engaging for some individuals. This activity is associated with activation of brain dopamine in the striatum (Koepp *et al.*, 1998).

Internet addiction

Adapting addiction to the 21st century, Griffiths (1999) identified Internet addiction, according to the core components of addiction. These are (i) salience, domination of thought processes by the target activity, (ii) a modification of mood when engaged in the activity, (iii) tolerance, increasing amounts of activity are required to achieve the same effect, (iv) withdrawal symptoms (mood lowering), (v) conflict, e.g. within the individual and with others over time and money spent, as well as disruption to life, and (vi) relapse.

All of the criteria listed can apply to any kind of Internet activity. However, specifically using the

Some activities that do not involve drug-taking nonetheless show addictive properties. Could there be any underlying similarities?
Source: Luca DiCecco/Alamy.

Internet to obtain sexual excitement can combine all of these features with social disapproval or in some cases strong legal sanctions against the activity (in the case of searching for under-age images). This use of the Internet is a well-recognized problem.

Sexual addiction

The term 'sexual addiction' refers to an element of conflict, in addition to excessive sexual activity (Goodman, 2008). Often sexual addiction arises at times of particular stress (Schneider and Weiss, 2001) – stress is known to exacerbate chemical addictions too. Addictive sexual behaviour could then be reinforced by anxiety reduction (Leiblum and Rosen, 2000, p. 471).

A treatment for sex addiction is the use of selective serotonin reuptake inhibitors (SSRIs) (Coleman, 2005). There are also reports of success in using the opioid antagonist naltrexone, thereby blocking the pleasure of engaging in the addictive activity (Bostwick and Bucci, 2008). Such treatments suggest the need for an integrative psychobiological approach to its understanding.

Sometimes addictions coexist. For example, the sex addict often has simultaneously an addiction to alcohol or illicit drugs. Cross-sensitization between activities might be expected on the basis of common underlying dopaminergic bases.

Gambling

Pathological gambling is recognized as an addictive activity, leading to severe financial difficulties and in the worst cases to suicide (Goudriaan *et al.*, 2004). It is associated with tolerance (need to increase the 'dose') and craving, suggesting the value of seeing common ground with drug-related addictions. It is often combined with addictions to chemicals. Withdrawal symptoms can include irritability and even such things as stomach upset, sweating and trembling (Cunningham-Williams *et al.*, 2009).

Resisting temptation involves exerting executive function to give weight to long-term negative consequences of gambling relative to its immediate pull. In laboratory tasks, pathological gamblers show deficits in executive function. This amounts to a deficiency in response inhibition. As a likely biological basis, some evidence points to deficits in functioning of the prefrontal cortex. There are leads pointing to possible genetic and neurochemical (e.g. dopamine) differences, comparing pathological gamblers and controls.

Having presented the evidence on chemical and non-chemical addictions, the discussion now uses this information for a more detailed look at explanations of drug-taking and addictive activities.

> ### Section summary
>
> 1 Certain non-drug-related activities exhibit properties similar to those associated with drugs.
> 2 Some non-drug-related activities have the potential to become addictive.
>
> ### Test your knowledge
>
> **18.4** When compulsive sexual behaviour is reinforced by anxiety reduction, what adjective qualifies such reinforcement?
>
> Answer on page 490

Trying to explain addiction

This section looks at some theories that attempt to give a broad explanation of drug-taking and addiction. Although the explanations sometimes seem to be in competition, the section will point to where their features can be reconciled.

Two orientations

In the context of opiate drugs, Alexander and Hadaway (1982) proposed a distinction between two explanatory frameworks: the **exposure orientation** and the **adaptive orientation**. According to the exposure orientation, addiction arises simply from exposure to drugs. Drugs irreversibly change the body so that, beyond a threshold, the individual wants and 'needs' more. However, according to the adaptive orientation, drugs are a support, chemotherapy for the mind, which allows the individual to function better at times of psychological need. Some people need such support ('a crutch'). The newly recognized non-chemical addictions such as to sex or the Internet appear also to provide a similar and temporary emotional support. You may feel that each perspective contains elements of the truth, possibly with the value of each differing between individuals and circumstances within an individual.

Affective states

Introduction

Taking drugs such as alcohol, heroin and cocaine has affective ('hedonic') consequences. It is therefore tempting to assume that the strength of motivation to take a drug correlates closely with the subjective euphoria obtained. Although an overall positive correlation exists, there is no simple equivalence (Robinson and Berridge, 1993), exemplified by Figure 18.9. With repeated drug use, subjectively reported hedonism can decline, whereas craving increases. In some cases, the first encounters with drugs (opiates, alcohol and nicotine) are unpleasant rather than euphoric and yet people are still moved to repeat the experience (Wise and Bozarth, 1987). Paranoia can result from amphetamine use but the habit persists (Ellinwood, 1967).

So, although affect plays an important role, it cannot fully explain addiction. Let us turn first to what might be explained by its role.

A model

Figure 18.11 represents positive and negative affective states with mutual inhibition, indicated by negative signs (Solomon and Corbit, 1974). A neutral affective state is the result of a balance between the two. These states depend in part upon stimuli, cognitions and goals, etc. Affect is closely related to cognition, e.g. negative affect biases towards experiencing negative thoughts and interpretations and triggering memories of negative events (Baker *et al.*, 2004). Negative cognition (e.g. from personal failure) tends to excite negative affect.

Given an appropriate social context, after entering the body drugs appear to tilt the balance temporarily in a positive direction. Thus, over a middle range, the distinction between gaining a positive effect and reducing a negative one becomes somewhat academic.

It appears that the normal balance giving life a slightly positive affect (if you are lucky!) is maintained by, among other things, a background level of endogenous opioid activity within the CNS (Skoubis *et al.*, 2005). See Figure 18.12(a). Opioid antagonists block the positive effect of natural opioids and thereby move the balance in a negative direction. This triggers or amplifies signs of social distress (Chapter 12). See Figure 18.12(b). Excessive stimulation in a positive direction by, say, opiate drugs (Figure 18.12(c)) would be followed by some neural adaptation of the system (Christie *et al.*, 1997). Adaptation would tend to tilt net affect in a negative direction by such means as loss of opioid receptors

(Figure 18.12(d)). Injection of an opioid antagonist would then shift it still further in a negative direction (Wise, 1988). It appears that an aversive state can arise either as a withdrawal reaction to the absence of the drug or from stress, depression, anxiety and, in addition in humans, personal life crises (Baker *et al.*, 2004; Singer, 1993). Drugs (and possibly some non-drug-based activities) then bring temporary relief.

Negative affect can be (but is not necessarily) associated with physiological signs of withdrawal outside the nervous system (Christie *et al.*, 1997; Koob, 1999). If drugs are readily available, their intake can be motivated by positive incentive processes. After they become unavailable, accompanied in some cases by explicit withdrawal, the control might shift to avoidance of negative affect (Baker *et al.*, 2004).

Automatic and controlled intake

As with other types of behaviour, that associated with drugs reflects processes organized at different levels of the CNS. These range from the controlled conscious choice to seek a drug for its anticipated beneficial effects to automatic responding to drug-related cues (Tiffany,

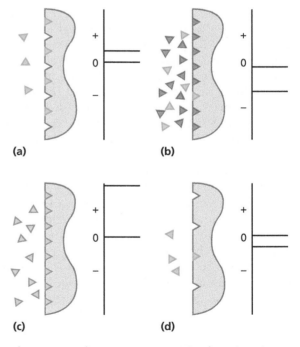

△ Opioid   ▲ Opioid–antagonist   △ Opiate drug

Figure 18.12 Suggested role of opioids, opioid antagonists and opiates and the associated level of affect. Neural events (left) and level of contribution to affect (graph to right). (a) Basal level in drug-free condition, (b) immediately after injection of opioid antagonist, (c) immediately after injection of opiate drug and (d) period after opiate drug has left the body.

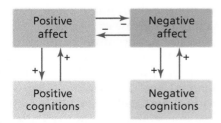

Figure 18.11 Model of affective states.

1990). Presumably, any instance of drug-seeking reflects a balance between these factors. It appears that drug-seeking starts in a conscious ('intentional') mode and then switches to a more automatic mode with experience. The addicted person becomes increasingly at the mercy of the pull of drug-related stimuli in the environment (Everitt *et al.*, 2001).

There is a rat model of this shift of weight (Vanderschuren and Everitt, 2004). Normally, activities such as feeding are inhibited by cues that signal aversive events. Lever-pressing in a Skinner box drops when such a cue is presented. Rats working for cocaine also exhibit such inhibition *early in their experience*. However, after extensive exposure, they cease to react to such cues and go on lever-pressing regardless. This might model the human addict's indifference to warning signs. Even after extensive exposure, not all rats switch to a compulsive pattern of use in which they are indifferent to such aversive cues (Deroche-Gamonet *et al.*, 2004). This points to individual differences, presumably in the sensitivity of dopaminergic pathways. Such differences might also be present between humans.

An addicted human is in a dilemma: a part of the mind seems to be offering restraint but another part, which mediates the compulsive pull, seems stronger. Which parts of the brain underlie these different tendencies? As noted, subcortical processes such as the N.acc. and PAG appear to be the primary bases of drug-seeking. It is especially the ventromedial prefrontal cortex (VMPFC) that mediates restraint and opposes the pull of lower brain regions. Activity in the VMPFC acts as the neural embodiment of processes termed 'self-directed' and 'willpower' (Bechara, 2005). With the help of this region, representations of harmful future consequences are retrieved as part of working memory and exploited in restraint. Individual differences in susceptibility to addiction could be embodied in different balances between mechanisms underlying impulsive reactivity (e.g. to drug-related cues) and restraint.

Once in the body, a drug itself might change weight between such levels. Consider, for example, alcohol. This would tend to lift the restraint that is normally offered on certain alcohol-related behaviour (e.g. seeking yet another drink) by higher-level cognitive controls (Chapter 15). Also drugs such as cocaine can damage the prefrontal cortex. This could thereby chronically weaken the role of restraint on drug-taking (or possibly any associated non-drug-based addictive activity).

Incentive sensitization theory

Introduction

A highly influential theory of drug-addiction with broad application across addictive substances is the **incentive sensitization theory** (Robinson and Berridge, 1993). It is based on three features of addiction: (i) craving, (ii) that craving and drug-taking can be reinstated long after drug use has ceased and (iii) 'as drugs come to be "wanted" more-and-more, they often come to be liked less-and-less' (p. 249). A rationale for the theory is summed up in a question posed by Ellinwood and Escalante (1970, p. 189): 'A puzzling, yet central, question in the study of the amphetamine psychosis is why individuals who are experiencing acute terror and other unpleasant effects continue to use amphetamines in large doses.'

Wanting and liking

Liking and wanting sometimes appear to increase in parallel (Willner *et al.*, 2005) but there is a paradox that drugs such as heroin can be liked less and less as they are sought more and more.

Some might explain the dissociation between wanting and liking by means of a switch from positive to negative reinforcement. Robinson and Berridge do not deny that this may capture part of the truth but suggest it is not the defining feature of the paradox, since wanting outlasts any withdrawal symptoms. Rather they argue that, with repeated use of drugs, there is sensitization of the neural system of wanting, which becomes uncoupled from liking. Only the wanting mechanism is sensitized. This causes a pathological focus of perception, attention and motivation upon drug-related stimuli and thoughts. The change in neural sensitivity is long-lasting and can be permanent, which renders addicts vulnerable to relapse even after years of abstinence. According to the theory, the mesolimbic DA system is the neural system that underlies the attribution of incentive value, termed **incentive salience**, and that is sensitized by drugs (Chapter 15). Of course, an explanation is needed as to why non-drug-related addictive activities can sometimes show similar properties to drug-related ones (Goodman, 2008). Presumably, dopaminergic activation must be intrinsically self-strengthening with repeated activation.

A lowering of DA activity is associated with a lowering of drug craving and a lowering of the strength with which drug-related cues capture attention (Leyton, 2010). However, it is not associated with a lowering of the pleasure derived from such drugs as nicotine, alcohol, amphetamine and cocaine (Leyton, 2010). Figure 18.13 shows this for the case of cocaine.

Further evidence on incentive sensitization includes the following. Withdrawal effects, unconditional or conditional, appear not to be able to explain relapse. Addicts commonly do not attribute relapse to withdrawal. Incentive sensitization can explain why addicts sometimes relapse to drug-taking years after quitting and even in the absence of negative affect (Robinson and Berridge, 2008).

Craving is often highest immediately after taking the drug, when presumably any aversive state has been partly if not wholly eliminated and withdrawal has not yet started. This provides a rationale for the advice of maintaining total abstinence. In rats, drug infusion into the brain can prime and reinstate drug-taking. Robinson and Berridge do not deny that increasing hedonism can result from drug use but merely that it alone cannot explain addiction (cf. Peele and Alexander, 1985). Nicotine is highly addictive and yet one imagines that few smokers would associate its use with unrestrained euphoria (see also earlier account of caffeine).

According to the theory, incentive salience and pleasure are not entirely separate processes. Indeed, applied to conventional motivational systems, it would be a maladaptive design feature if they were. Incentive salience is normally maintained in part by the pleasure that follows engagement with the incentive (Figure 18.14). For example, foods that evoke a positive affective rating are normally sought. However, in drug-taking some dissociation between wanting and liking is introduced. Increased sensitization is experienced subjectively as craving for drugs.

The environmental factor

The expression of incentive sensitization in behaviour is a function of the environment that has been associated with drug-taking (Robinson and Berridge, 2008). Drugs do not unconditionally sensitize a craving process divorced from the context in which the drug was taken. Hence, a drug-user might manifest the elevated craving and wanting associated with incentive sensitization only when in a drug-related environment. Incentive sensitization means that the amount of DA released in response to a given stimulus (taking a drug or an environmental cue paired in the past with drug-taking) increases (Robinson and Berridge, 2008). As noted, patients taking narcotics to counter pain do not usually crave drugs outside the clinical context (Chapter 14). Thus, particular cognitions, goals and strategies are part of the sensitization process.

Stress

Stress contributes to taking drugs. Since the drug takes away the sharp edge of stress, by implication, this seems to be a process of negative reinforcement. In addition, stress appears to increase the incentive salience attributed to drug-related stimuli. Both addictive drugs and stress sensitize DA activity (Robinson and Berridge, 1993). Stress-related sensitization of dopaminergic neurotransmission appears to act through CRF and corticosteroids (Goodman, 2008) (Chapter 13).

Therapy

As therapy, the theory gives a rationale for extinction procedures, i.e. repeated exposure to drug-related cues under guidance. However, clinically based extinction programmes might not generalize to the multitude of drug-related stimuli of the street. As noted earlier, results have been disappointing. DA antagonists would be a blunt instrument, reducing all of life's attractions. Perhaps the only effective treatment would be a chemical to undo sensitization, but there is no immediate prospect of that (Robinson and Berridge, 1993).

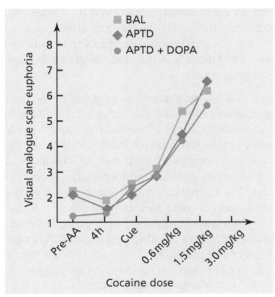

Figure 18.13 The effect of dose of cocaine on euphoria, as measured on a visual analogue scale. BAL = control condition, APTD = dopamine depletion by means of APTD; APTD + DOPA = combination of APTD plus L-dopa.

Source: Leyton (2010, Fig. 13.5, p. 229).

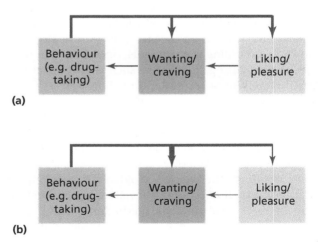

Figure 18.14 Situation (a) before and (b) after sensitization. States of positive affect ('hedonism') increase incentive salience. However, with experience, wanting/craving increases but liking/pleasure sometimes decreases.

Source: Toates (1998b, Fig. 2.25, p. 55).

A challenge to be met

It would be surprising if everything fitted neatly to a given theory. One result which appears to sit uncomfortably alongside incentive sensitization theory is that cocaine addiction is associated with a reduction in the number of DA D_2 receptors in the striatum (the region containing the N.acc.) (see Robinson and Berridge, 2008). Intuitively, one might have expected an increased number. Similarly, Chapter 16 (Figure 16.20, p. 429) showed a negative correlation between the degree of obesity and the number of D_2 receptors. This leads some to suggest that increased drug-taking or eating represents an attempt to compensate for this reduction. Can this effect be accommodated within incentive sensitization theory?

DA activation might be sufficiently intense to cause 'down-regulation' of DA receptors (loss of a number of DA receptors as a result of the impact of the transmitter). Yet still the release rate of DA might be so high that there is a net increase in DA activity over the course of addiction. There is some evidence that D_2 receptors can exist in more than one form, showing either high or low affinity for DA (Robinson and Berridge, 2008). Drug sensitization appears to cause (i) an increase in density of the high-affinity type, associated with (ii) a decrease in density of the low-affinity type. It might be that the effect of (i) far outweighs any effect of (ii).

Integration

This section will put the incentive-sensitization theory into a broader context.

A change of weight

Bechara *et al.* (1998) and Wise (1988) present models in which opiate addiction is explained by two distinct processes. First, there is an incentive motivational process. However, according to this model, once addiction develops, the weighting can change such that motivation is based largely on a second and distinct process: avoidance of aversive effects of withdrawal. Fewer 'highs' are reported and larger and larger doses are required to sustain avoidance of aversion. Craving can be based upon either process. According to this model, the role of positive incentive motivation becomes masked when control shifts to the aversion avoidance system. Suppose that withdrawal effects are alleviated, e.g. by prescription of the substitute drug methadone. The positive incentive motivational system then dominates intake.

The role of the insula

Having been largely ignored historically, the insular cortex ('insula') (Chapter 12) is now attracting interest in the study of drug addiction (Naqvi and Bechara, 2009). It might provide an integrative link for theories of drug-taking. Brain imaging has shown this structure to be activated during the experience of conscious drug urges. So, is its activity part of the causal sequence leading to drug-taking? Naqvi *et al.* (2007) compared smokers who had suffered damage to the insula or to other brain structures. Those with damage to the insula showed a disruption to their addiction in the sense that quitting was relatively easy. One reported (p. 534) that his 'body forgot the urge to smoke'. A study in rats pointed to a similar involvement of the insula: its temporary inactivation by injection of the local anaesthetic lidocaine temporarily abolished a conditioned place preference for drug administration (Contreras *et al.*, 2007).

The insula is involved in a number of functions concerned with the internal state of the body. For example, the insula receives visceral sensations from the organs such as the gut, the oesophagus and the heart. Information from the internal organs is processed and, reciprocally, output from the insula influences these organs. The insula also receives information on touch, taste and temperature. According to a contemporary understanding, the insula is the biological basis of the conscious experience of the body (Naqvi and Bechara, 2009).

Based on an understanding of the insula and its interconnections with other brain structures, Naqvi and Bechara propose a model that can integrate incentive models and withdrawal models. They suggest (p. 60):

> internal factors associated with deprivation states (such as withdrawal) are viewed as a 'gate' that determines how effective the incentive input is in exciting the motivational circuits that 'pull' and 'steer' the animal (or human) towards the appropriate goal object.

Naqvi and Bechara note that all drugs have characteristic immediate effects on the 'peripheral regions' of the body, in addition to their chemical effects on the brain. Snorted cocaine has a bitter taste and increases blood pressure and heart-rate. Each puff of cigarette smoke affects the respiratory tract, while nicotine affects the circulation. The influence on the respiratory tract triggers the insula and is perceived as pleasurable. Hence, the ritual of drug use (e.g. lighting up, puffing) plays a vital role in the motivation of drug-seeking and addiction.

The insula could integrate internal body states and external drug-related events. The insula projects to the N.acc. By this means, bodily states such as those of withdrawal could increase the wanting of drugs. The sight of another individual performing the act of injection or lighting could similarly increase wanting via the insula and N.acc.

Evolutionary considerations

So far, we have looked at the causal processes underlying drug-taking but it is useful to reconsider evolutionary aspects (Chapter 2). By directly acting on the brain, drugs have psychoactive effects. This is in contrast to, say, food or sex. In such conventional systems, rewarding effects are first mediated via sensory systems and subsequently activate the brain. Thus, drugs appear to short-circuit part of the system that underlies interaction with conventional incentives and to tap directly into reward systems.

Evolutionary psychology

A false signal

From an evolutionary perspective, taking addictive drugs can be understood by their ability to stimulate and overwhelm processes of natural reward that underlie conventional interactions, e.g. to approach food (Nesse and Berridge, 1997). As Nesse and Berridge note (p. 64): 'Drugs of abuse create a signal in the brain that indicates, falsely, the arrival of a huge fitness benefit'. (They use fitness here in the ethological sense: an increase in reproductive potential.)

Section summary

1 The exposure and adaptive orientations can each explain some features of drug-taking.
2 The incentive sensitization theory distinguishes between wanting and liking.
3 There is evidence that the insula has a role in addictive activities.

Test your knowledge

18.5 With reference to Figure 18.12, suppose that the same quantity of opiate drug as represented in part (c) were to be injected under the conditions of part (d). Which of the following would be the expected outcome in terms of affect? (i) A level the same as part (c), (ii) the same as before, i.e. as shown in part (d), (iii) somewhere between the situations shown in parts (c) and (d).

Answer on page 490

Bringing things together

To return to the contrast between the exposure orientation and the adaptive orientation, much evidence favours the latter. As a general principle, people seem to take drugs as part of a 'problem-solving exercise', to improve their cognitive and affective states. This may be in desperation, in a state of existential angst or as part of spiritual enlightenment. Both chemical and non-chemical-based activities can be recruited to such ends.

Rat models tend to support the adaptive orientation. The amount of drug that a rat takes is heavily dependent upon social context and other available rewards. The fact that nicotine is such a potent reinforcer for humans and relatively weak for rats might be explained in terms of the kinds of peculiarly human problems that it helps to solve, e.g. vigilance and promoting social interaction. However, somewhat in favour of the exposure orientation, it seems that the drug-related solution to a problem is more probable as a result of exposure, as suggested by the incentive sensitization theory. Also,

the move from controlled to automatic processes underlying intake highlights that exposure and repetition increase the tendency to take a drug.

Drug-taking appears to be motivated by positive and negative affect. A number of features are common with conventional motivations (e.g. craving and the role of classical conditioning) and non-chemical-related behaviours can take on addictive features. Drugs such as nicotine and heroin tap into conventional incentive motivational processes involving dopamine and opioids and appear to sensitize them. Such processes are clearly of adaptive value in a conventional context. For example, fitness maximization requires us to be pulled towards mates and sources of food at times of energy deficiency. Pavlovian conditioning between neutral cues and biological incentives is clearly adaptive and a conscious mind might adaptively be occupied by thoughts of biological incentives. However, this adaptive principle can break down when encountering a drug that taps into such a pathway, grossly sensitizes it and yet creates little in the way of negative feedback. Drugs that have a primary action not on dopaminergic and opioidergic systems, such as ecstasy and LSD, do not have this addictive potential (but that, of course, does not make them safe).

Although animal models might capture features of human behaviour, we need to consider the more complex cognitive and cultural context of human drug-taking. Humans start to take drugs for various reasons that seem peculiarly human, such as peer pressure. A contribution to, say, alcohol or heroin consumption may arise from a combination of chemical effects experienced within a context of a peer-group and social approval (Peele, 1985). We are reminded of the

cognitive interpretation that can be attached to various bodily sensations (Chapter 12). Drug-takers sometimes need to be instructed by peers in how to interpret drug-induced changes in sensation. Once initiated, it might be that features of human drug-taking can be captured by animal models.

 See the video coverage for this chapter and get a feel for what addiction is like.

Summary of Chapter 18

1 Some psychoactive chemicals have addictive properties, as do certain activities not related to obtaining chemicals.

2 The motivation to take a drug and the effect of the drug depend on the drug's chemical properties and contextual factors such as control, conditional stimuli and social factors.

3 Drugs that can become addictive have the common property of targeting the brain's mesolimbic dopamine system.

4 Other activities, not drug-related, can become addictive in ways similar to drugs, probably based on dopamine activation.

5 Various theories attempt to explain addiction. It is possible to see some compatible features between them.

Further reading

For theoretical aspects of addiction, see West (2006). For the underlying neurobiology, see Koob and Le Moal (2006) and Robbins *et al.* (2010). For a challenging account of addiction that links it to a political dimension, see Alexander (2008). For a classical text that takes a broad integrative overview of addictions, chemical-based and non-chemical-based, see Orford (2001).

18.3 This demonstrates selectivity of choice and that the behaviour is controlled by its consequences (gaining nicotine). Otherwise, if there were only one hole, any such increase in responding over time might simply reflect heightened activity.

18.4 Negative

18.5 (iii) Somewhere between the situations shown in parts (c) and (d).

Answers

Explanations for answers to 'test your knowledge' questions can be found on the website **www.pearsoned.co.uk/toates**

18.1 (iii) LSD

18.2 (i) Conditional stimulus (CS); (ii) conditional response (CR)

Visit www.pearsoned.co.uk/toates
for a range of resources to support study.
Test yourself with multiple choice questions and access a bank of over 100 videos that will bring the topics to life.

Chapter 13
Stress and coping

Learning outcomes for Chapter 13

After studying this chapter, you should be able to:

1 State what is meant by 'stress', while linking this to physiology, psychology and homeostasis.

2 Identify the criteria that point to the existence of stress. Relate these to measures of stress.

3 Describe features of the two principal neurohormonal systems that are stretched excessively under stress. Explain why they have a defining role in stress.

4 Explain why stress cannot simply be defined in terms of the potential stressors present in a situation. Outline the role of contextual factors such as coping.

5 Describe some of the basic features of the immune system and how the system can be affected by stress. Suggest how stress might have a part in exacerbating disorders that involve suppression of the immune system.

6 Identify some of the principal brain regions that are implicated in 'stress'. Relate their role under stress-free conditions to their performance in stress.

7 Show where understanding stress can help to explain the bases of a number of disorders: depression, coronary heart disease, post-traumatic stress disorder, irritable bowel syndrome and ulcers.

8 Outline how understanding the psychobiology of stress can give pointers as to reducing stress and can thereby make a positive contribution to health.

Scene-setting questions

1 Can someone actually enjoy stress?
2 Is stress invariably harmful to health?
3 Are stress-related diseases 'psychosomatic'?
4 How can the gut be sensitive to stress?
5 Can you die from a 'broken heart'?
6 Can science show how to live with stress or how to beat it?
7 Can self-harm serve as a coping strategy in response to insufferable stress?

 WEB

Can self-harm serve as a coping strategy in response to insufferable stress? Explore the video on the website accompanying this book at www.pearsoned.co.uk/toates

Stress in such an extreme situation is triggered by the failure to resolve a pressing problem over a period of time. How good is this as a general criterion of stress?
Source: Getty Images/Workbook Stock.

Introduction

Many of us know **stress** through personal experience. Think of some situations that you would describe as stressful. (An unexplained water leak in our house first springs to my mind. It feels that I am eminently qualified to write this chapter.) People report such things as isolation, being under siege, anticipation of exams, chronic ill-health, loss or breakdown of a close relationship and unemployment as being stressful. Is there a common feature that characterizes these situations?

They all engage our attention, pose demands for action and change, are largely uncontrollable and, in most cases, arrive against our wishes. They tend to leave us feeling helpless and a failure and they occur over periods of weeks or months. We cannot *cope*, sometimes expressed as not having a **coping strategy** or 'coping resources'. Stimuli that cause stress are termed **stressors**. In non-humans, these are often such things as prolonged exposure to noise or social conflict.

Stressors tend to add their effects. You hear comments such as, 'I might just have coped with the divorce *on its own* but not with that and the unemployment'. So, we are looking for neuropsychological processes that tend to cumulate negative effects.

In everyday use, stress mostly refers to psychologically disturbing events or events with psychological associations, involving long-term overload (Ursin and Olff, 1993). A challenge is to try to define common biological and psychological features of stressful situations.

Most would argue that stress is always negative and predisposes to illness but some suggest that mild stress can be exhilarating and only severe stress is bad. The workaholic entrepreneur is driven by the 'adrenalin rush' of stress. Such people may indeed be stimulating their adrenalin secretion but it is likely that they have considerable control over the situations in which they *willingly* engage. They are not stressed in the sense of being helpless and chronically beset by circumstances not of their choosing. Hormonal reactions do not always tell the whole story: as will be described shortly, they need to be seen in context.

To understand stress, let us consider homeostasis. The body is constructed so as to keep certain important parameters within close limits. When they shift from these, action is taken to bring them back. If something such as body temperature were to shift far from its norm, death would follow. A similar notion can be applied to stress. We try to protect our 'psychological homeostasis' by taking various actions, such as avoiding psychological overload, seeking comfort from others, finding prediction and control in our lives and avoiding conflict, etc. Stress represents a chronic disturbance to such *psychological* homeostasis. Disturbances to physiology, such as high blood pressure and adrenalin levels, are associated with this (Gianaros and Sheu, 2009).

Although we normally think of stressors as being psychological, two things need to be emphasized: (i) through the CNS, psychological stressors exert wide-ranging effects on the physiology of the body and (ii) some of these same effects on the body can be triggered by physiological stressors, i.e. deviations from physiological homeostasis, as in loss of blood (Selye, 1973). See Figure 13.1.

The term 'stress' can be used to cover the response to both psychological and physiological triggers (Ursin and Olff, 1993) and it thereby points to common reactions in the body. Physiological and behavioural mechanisms that are adaptive within a range (Chapter 12) can be stretched beyond this. Over a prolonged period, such

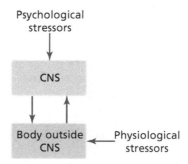

Figure 13.1 Stress, as determined by physiological and psychological stressors.

stretching is associated with psychological and physiological disruption described as 'stress' (Archer, 1979).

Of course, evolution did not produce systems that are intrinsically geared to produce pathology. Rather, stress is the pathological stretching of behavioural systems to beyond their adaptive range. For example, an elevated heart-rate and blood pressure can be adaptive in the short term in facing natural threats, such as bears. They can become seriously maladaptive if they are chronically activated day-after-day with little escape from the triggers to stress.

Awareness of stress is an important health issue. Stress can sometimes be better managed. We can direct attention to psychological states that are opposite to stress, as aspects of physical and psychological health.

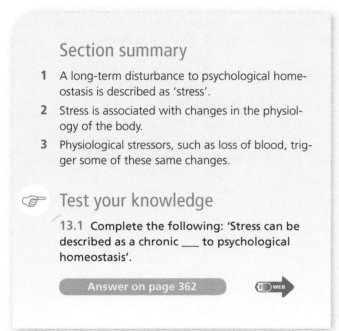

Section summary

1 A long-term disturbance to psychological homeostasis is described as 'stress'.

2 Stress is associated with changes in the physiology of the body.

3 Physiological stressors, such as loss of blood, trigger some of these same changes.

☞ Test your knowledge

13.1 Complete the following: 'Stress can be described as a chronic ___ to psychological homeostasis'.

Answer on page 362   ◖ WEB ▶

Characterizing stress

This section considers starting points for understanding stress.

Signs of stress: arousal

Confronted with a stressor, an animal shows EEG **arousal**, also termed 'activation' (Chapter 5; Ursin and Olff, 1993). Protracted arousal gives a possible indication of stress. Although there can be arousal without stress there cannot be stress without arousal (Pfaff *et al.*, 2007).

In stress, animals take both behavioural and physiological (e.g. autonomic) action. The sympathetic nervous system is usually excited and thereby adrenalin

(epinephrine) and noradrenalin (norepinephrine) are released into the bloodstream in increased amounts. Hormones termed corticosteroids (Chapter 6) are usually secreted at a high rate and they mobilize metabolic resources in the body. The set of reactions is termed the 'emergency reaction'. Long-term excitation of these hormonal systems gives an indication of stress.

Types of stressor

External stimuli

Consider an animal that is exposed to 'potential stressors', e.g. (i) confrontation with predators, (ii) dealing with dominants of the group or (iii) competing for food and reacting to rivals in overcrowded conditions. As a reaction, heart-rate accelerates. The animal might have a coping strategy available that reliably corrects the situation, such as to avoid, make an appeasement gesture or flee. Suppose it suffers no ill effects; after each contact, heart-rate rapidly returns to normal. Lengthy confrontation is avoided and the notion of stress would seem inappropriate. This is coping, by the criteria of the success of behaviour and the relatively light demands on the corticosteroid system and the autonomic nervous system (ANS).

The chapter concerns where a coping strategy is unavailable, the challenge cannot be countered and the animal is stressed. For example, it might take evasive action with autonomic activation but repeatedly fails to get away from a dominant animal.

Typically, secretion of corticosteroids and sympathetic activation with heart-rate acceleration would occur over long periods (von Holst, 1986). The persistence of arousal and failure to resolve the situation are associated with a range of characteristic pathology, such as ulcers and blocking of arteries. The coexistence of behavioural and physiological indices encourages use of the term 'stress'.

Cognitive processes

Some potential stressors, e.g. loud sounds, can be defined in terms of their physical properties. However, many situations that cause stress are not so easily defined (Ursin and Olff, 1993). Rather, what evokes stress is an event placed in the *context of earlier experiences*.

Corticosteroid secretion is sensitive to situations placed in context. For example, novelty can trigger it. Novelty is not some intrinsic property of an environment. Rather, the environment is novel in the context of previously experienced environments. Similarly, loss of control in a previously instrumental situation (i.e. extinction in a Skinner box) triggers release of corticosteroids. Earning a reward smaller than expectation is another trigger that can only be understood in terms of what was expected (Chorpita and Barlow, 1998), i.e. frustration is a trigger. This implies comparison of expected and actual events and a triggering by the difference.

In humans, loss of something such as a job is a stressor but this is not a physical stimulus comparable to a loud noise. We might stress ourselves through endless problem-solving, as in trying to balance dubious financial accounts, or by engaging in 'inner dialogues' on personal failure (Burell, 1996). In this case, stressors are characterized by such features as 'informational discrepancy', e.g. reality differs from expectations (Ursin and Olff, 1993), or there is an inability to solve a problem (Gianaros and Sheu, 2009). Attempts to cope with cognitive challenges are associated with sympathetic activation (Steptoe, 1993). In trying to define stress, a measure in such a case might be a verbal report, e.g. 'I feel that I cannot cope any longer'.

In social species, isolation from conspecifics causes stress, the 'isolation syndrome' (Chapter 12; Greenough, 1976). Evidence of stress is provided by a comparison with the unstressed behaviour and the hormonal profile of a stable socially housed animal.

Physiological stimuli

Physiological disturbances, e.g. blood loss or stretch of the bladder (Selye, 1973), trigger activation and corticosteroid release. The mobilization of resources in this 'general emergency reaction' supports any specific action also triggered. For example, a physiological challenge such as loss of blood triggers specific behavioural homeostatic actions such as seeking water and salt to correct the disturbance (Chapter 16).

Behavioural indices

Confronted with a stressor we might flee or fight, and activate the sympathetic system, and these actions might or might not be successful. Another strategy is passivity, with parasympathetic activation and inhibition of the sympathetic system (Fowles, 1982). Confronted with a dominant animal, a subordinate sometimes reacts in this way. Typically, when an active strategy fails, an animal switches to the passive mode. According to the definition suggested here, a failure of strategy over long periods constitutes stress.

Four criteria of stress

Four criteria characterize stress and can be applied across species, as follows (Toates, 1995)

1 Over time, action occurs in response to a situation but it fails to correct this situation.

2 There is excessive and protracted activity in neurohormonal systems. Typically, this would be the sympathetic branch and the system that secretes

corticosteroids from the adrenal gland (Selye, 1973; von Holst, 1986) or both.

3 There is vulnerability to certain pathology (e.g. gastric ulceration, hypertension, depression and disorders associated with suppression of the immune system) (Moberg, 1985).

4 There is a tendency to show apparently pointless behaviours such as stereotypies or inflicting self-harm (Mason, 1991).

In our case, to lower stress we might target voluntary behaviour. There could be some choice, e.g. we might readjust priorities and work less. We might be able to change how we interpret and react to events. Interventions might target the physiology of the body, e.g. drugs to lower the vigour of the heart's pumping.

The following section looks at the two neurohormonal systems that are involved in stress.

Section summary

1 External stimuli, defined as stressors, trigger behavioural and physiological activation.

2 The stress-evoking capacity of external events can often be understood only by taking account of their context and interpretation.

3 Humans can stress themselves by cognitive triggers such as protracted and unsuccessful problem-solving.

4 A capacity for coping reduces the impact of potential stressors.

5 An animal is stressed when coping resources are inadequate for the task.

6 Other criteria of stress are increases in (a) activity by neurohormonal systems, (b) the tendency to certain pathology and (c) the tendency to perform stereotypies.

7 Stress can be associated with (a) active strategies and sympathetic domination or (b) passive strategies with a bias towards parasympathetic activity.

☞ Test your knowledge

13.2 Apart from catecholamines, increased release of what other class of substance occurs in stress?

Answer on page 362

Two neurohormonal systems

Introduction

The perspective introduced here corresponds to the 'classical stress story' (Pfaff *et al.*, 2007). The focus is on two neurohormonal systems (Chapters 3 and 6): (i) the sympathetic branch of the ANS and (ii) the sequence CRF → ACTH → corticosteroids. Prolonged activation of these two systems can be used as one index of stress and it plays a role in disorders characterized as 'stress-related'.

The autonomic nervous system

Stress is associated with altered activity throughout the ANS, affecting its various outputs, such as the stomach and intestine. A principal concern is with parts that affect the circulatory system. We address this first.

Sympathetic branch

Emergencies activate the sympathetic branch of the ANS (SNS), especially when action appears possible. SNS activation triggers changes in the body, e.g. increased heart-rate. Also, a number of blood vessels are constricted but those in active skeletal muscles are dilated, facilitating blood flow.

SNS activation releases catecholamines: (i) noradrenalin from sympathetic neurons and (ii) adrenalin (A) and noradrenalin (NA) from the adrenal gland. In humans, most noradrenalin in the blood originates from the terminals of neurons of the SNS, some at the inner region of the adrenal gland, the **adrenal medulla**. Plasma adrenalin originates in the adrenal medulla (Musselman *et al.*, 1998).

Within the circulatory system, adrenalin and noradrenalin occupy two types of receptor: alpha adrenergic and beta adrenergic. For example, when these catecholamines occupy beta receptors at cardiac muscle, the frequency of the heartbeat is increased. The therapeutic drug class termed 'beta blockers' acts at this site (Scheidt, 1996). Cardiac muscle is excited by (1) direct sympathetic input via neurons and (2) noradrenalin and adrenalin from the bloodstream (Dampney, 1994). In response to sympathetic activation, blood flow through the heart can increase by a factor of 5. Occupation of catecholamine receptors on the smooth muscles that govern the diameter of blood vessels adjusts blood flow such that working skeletal muscle receives adequate blood (Vander *et al.*, 1994).

Parasympathetic branch

Parasympathetic activity is seen in day-to-day maintenance, e.g. promoting digestion, involving restraint on the heart. However, increased activation can occur in emergencies when no active strategy is perceived as possible (Bohus and Koolhaas, 1993).

The hypothalamic pituitary adrenocortical system

Introduction

Corticosteroids are secreted from the outer layer of the adrenal gland, the **adrenal cortex** (Figure 13.2). There are different corticosteroids having similar properties. In rats, the principal one is corticosterone (Bohus and de Kloet, 1981). In humans, it is cortisol (Baxter and Rousseau, 1979). Corticosteroids act throughout the

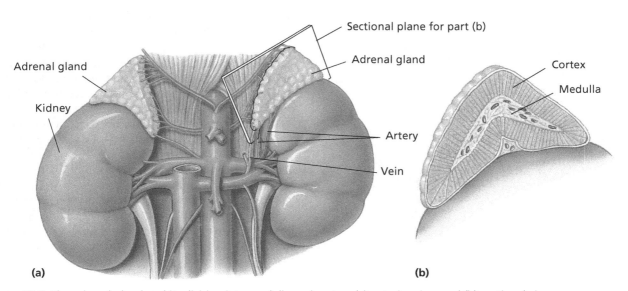

Figure 13.2 The adrenal gland and its division into medulla and cortex: (a) anterior view and (b) sectional view.
Source: Martini *et al.* (2000, Fig. 19-10, p. 510). Copyright © 2000, 1997 by Frederic H. Martini, Inc. and Michael J. Timmons. Reprinted by permission of Pearson Education, Inc.

body, e.g. at times of threat to mobilize energy and, at the brain, to alter arousal and cognitive and emotional processing (Erikson *et al.*, 2003). In primates, receptors for corticosteroids are found in the hippocampus, amygdala and regions of prefrontal cortex.

Consider Figure 13.3. At the first stage of the system, neurons with cell bodies at the paraventricular nucleus of the hypothalamus (PVN) (Chapter 5, Figure 5.31, p. 128) secrete corticotropin releasing factor (CRF), sometimes termed 'corticotropin releasing hormone' (Dunn and Berridge, 1990). At the pituitary, occupation of receptors by CRF releases adrenocorticotrophic hormone (ACTH). The sequence of hormones, CRF → ACTH → corticosteroids, is called the **pituitary adrenocortical system** (or pituitary adrenocortical axis). Since activity in the hypothalamus is the trigger for CRF secretion, this sometimes gives the axis the title 'hypothalamic pituitary adrenocortical system'. Mercifully, this is commonly abbreviated to 'HPA system' or 'HPA axis'.

Corticosteroids inhibit their own secretion (Figure 13.3). If such negative feedback is functioning optimally, when a stressor is terminated there is a prompt shut-down of the HPA axis and corticosteroid level quickly falls (Cullinan *et al.*, 1995). Malfunction can arise from inadequate negative feedback, in which case hormonal activation can long outlive the stressor. For example, excessive levels of corticosteroids can be toxic to neural tissue, e.g. in the hippocampus (Bremner, 1999). This can have negative effects on memory (Kim and Diamond, 2002).

Triggers

Acting via CNS processing, what triggers the set of hypothalamic neurons to release CRF? The HPA system is sensitive to (i) events in the internal environment (e.g. blood loss) and (ii) analysis by other parts of the brain that a challenge is arising in the external environment (Chorpita and Barlow, 1998). Psychological stimuli to stress are characterized by the common property of *uncertainty, challenge or threat and the possible need to take action.*

A long-term elevation of corticosteroid levels points to stress, since (i) this occurs at times of threat or challenge, (ii) it is associated with failure to resolve the problem and (iii) it has pathological consequences. However, brief activation of the HPA system does not indicate a stressor (Willner, 1993). Brief activation is a response to uncertainty (e.g. novelty, aversive stimulus) or arousal, whereas chronic activation reflects an inability to resolve uncertainty. From a functional perspective, triggering of corticosteroids by novelty makes adaptive sense since this represents a situation in which an animal might be called upon to fight, flee or freeze.

Where a well-tried strategy is available, there is little excitation of the HPA axis, even though a potential stressor is present. For example, if a tone is presented just before shock, the tone comes to evoke HPA activation. However, suppose that the animal successfully learns to perform an avoidance response by reacting quickly to the tone. Over this period, there is a gradual diminution in HPA activation until it returns to near baseline (Coover *et al.*, 1973).

Activation of the two systems

Successful action

To return to our favourite example (well, my favourite, at least), suppose that we meet a bear and run. The threat triggers SNS activation, which, among other things increases heart-rate. It also triggers HPA activation, which increases the supply of glucose to the blood. Both effects aid survival. Increased secretion of adrenalin and corticosteroid makes fuels such as glucose available from reserves. Fats are mobilized and their concentration in the blood increases (Guyton, 1991). Fats are metabolized (i.e. chemically converted to provide the fuel for action) as part of the physical exertion in running.

Assuming that one escapes, activity in the two neurohormonal systems might normally return to near baseline. If this happens the system is working optimally, i.e. the challenge promotes behavioural and neurohormonal actions that serve to resolve the challenge.

Stress and some consequences

Stress occurs when neurohormonal systems are excited in a way that is unjustified by the associated behaviour.

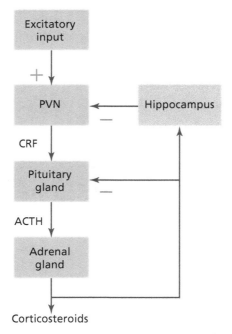

Figure 13.3 The system involved in the release of corticosteroids and their feedback effect.

A classic example consists of exciting these systems while in a sedentary situation, e.g. internal turmoil caused by anger directed at the boss but where neither fighting nor fleeing is advised.

Why is stress damaging to health? Among other reasons, fatty substances termed lipids are brought into the bloodstream in large amounts. If they are not metabolized, they tend to gather on the walls of arteries. This is termed **atherosclerosis** (or arteriosclerosis) (Scheidt, 1996). A long-term elevation of lipid levels, associated with them not being metabolized (e.g. during stressful inactivity), risks the health of the circulation.

A similar argument can be applied to the HPA system. Activation of this system followed by a quick return to a basal level characterizes an efficient response (Dienstbier, 1989). Excessive levels of corticosteroids over a protracted period are damaging, e.g. to the immune and nervous systems (Seeman and Robbins, 1994). If corticosteroid level declines only slowly, this indicates a continued excitation of the HPA system, an inefficient function. Ageing can be associated with excessive boosting of the HPA system with an associated weakening of negative feedback.

We now look at some of the situations that trigger stress.

Section summary

1 Stress is associated with an identifiable pattern of physiological changes.

2 Stressors commonly cause activation of the sympathetic system and a lowering of activity within the parasympathetic system.

3 Stress is sometimes associated with activation of the parasympathetic system.

4 Stressors trigger the hypothalamic pituitary adrenocortical system.

5 A healthy profile consists of a rapid activation of sympathetic and HPA systems and then a quick return to baseline.

6 One risk associated with stress is the deposition of lipids on the walls of the arteries.

 Test your knowledge

13.3 With respect to Figure 13.3, what would be the effect of injecting (i) a CRF antagonist, (ii) corticosteroids?

 Answer on page 362

Stressors, contexts and reactions

Introduction

Whether a potential stressor becomes an actual stressor can depend on context, e.g. (i) the capacity to predict when the stressor will occur, (ii) opportunities for action and (iii) what the animal does in response to the potential stressor and the outcome. Other factors include the history of the animal. Exposure to a stressor can change the animal, so that the future reaction to stressors is different. This section also considers that, confronted with a stressor, there can be more than one strategy.

Predictability and controllability

The consequences of exposure to a stressor vary with **controllability**. If an animal can exert control to terminate a stressor, indices of stress are lower, as compared with a passive ('yoked') control exposed to the same stressor (Weiss, 1972). Chronic lack of control is a developmental precursor of adult anxiety and depression (Chorpita and Barlow, 1998).

Weiss (1971) subjected yoked pairs of rats to electric shock to the tail. Both received identical shocks but, whereas one could exert control, the other ('control rat') could not. The active rat could terminate shock *for both rats* by turning a wheel, a coping strategy. The passive (control) rat also had access to a wheel but its actions were ineffective as far as the shock was concerned. Active rats showed greater weight gains and less gastric ulceration than did yoked controls. This experiment has proved to be a model of wide application, pointing to the importance of control. In humans, the impact of potential stressors is ameliorated by gaining control (Allan and Scheidt, 1996b). For example, a high pressure of work becomes less stressful if the person has capacity to make decisions on how the work is done.

Even in the absence of control, an animal that has some **predictability** of potential stressors shows fewer signs of stress compared with one without predictability, as indexed by gastric ulceration (Weiss, 1971). For example, predictability can be obtained where a warning sound occurs before shock.

Exposure to inescapable shock can lead to **learned helplessness**: an animal appears to learn that it has no agency and gives up. Following this, if a contingency of escape or avoidance is introduced, the animal fails to take appropriate action (Seligman, 1975). Learned helplessness is not 'non-behaving'. Rather, it exemplifies emotional-biasing of behaviour towards passivity, mediated via active inhibition of skeletal muscles. Experience with inescapable shock increases a rat's tendency to freeze in other situations, e.g. after shock in a novel environment. Passivity in the face of uncertain threat has some of the hallmarks of anxiety. This offers possible links with theorists who see anxiety as a precursor to depression (Chorpita and Barlow, 1998).

Sensitization

Exposure to a stressor can sensitize the nervous system such that the future behavioural and hormonal reaction to a stressor is increased (Sorg and Kalivas, 1995). Sensitization can be very long-lasting, even for a lifetime. In rats, exposure to an inescapable stressor can trigger a long-term increase in the tendency to immobility, a reduction in social interaction and increased HPA response to novelty (van Dijken *et al.*, 1993).

Developmental and age factors

Suppose that infant rats are briefly handled by the experimenter, involving separation from the mother. This intervention has a protective ('inoculating') effect regarding the impact of subsequent stressors. As an adult, the rat has a more healthy profile of HPA activity and an increased tendency to explore a novel environment (Castanon and Mormède, 1994). A capacity for control in the face of stressors when young gives rise to adult resilience, 'toughening-up' (Dienstbier, 1989), indexed by a greater density of corticosteroid receptors and lower levels of corticosteroids. Conversely, extended periods of separation from the mother have a detrimental effect upon later functioning of the HPA system.

Ageing is normally associated with some loss of corticosteroid receptors in the brain, reduced negative feedback and increasing levels of corticosteroids (Anisman *et al.*, 1998).

Active and passive strategies

Introduction

Related to the strategy that an animal adopts on confrontation with a stressor, Henry (1982) described two types of stress, which differ in the hormonal axis that is most activated:

1 The sympathetic system is associated with the behaviour of fight and flight and is activated when the power to gain access to such things as food or a mate is challenged: '. . . and the subject perceives that an adequate response is feasible'.

2 The HPA axis is strongly activated by: 'adverse conditions, such as immobilization, in which the animal is helpless'.

For various species (e.g. mice, rats and possibly humans), individuals have a bias towards either an active or a passive reaction (Castanon and Mormède, 1994), each with its characteristic hormonal profile. Genetic differences are associated with different biases. This difference in strategy suggests the application of the term 'personality' also to non-humans. However, the two behavioural options are not entirely distinct hormonally. Thus, a strategy of fight or flight with sympathetic activation also involves HPA activation. Henry suggests that there is an adaptive advantage in having the facility to inhibit behavioural tendencies to fight or flee. If an animal is confronted by regular challenges for which neither option is viable, there could be advantages in staying still.

An animal can be biased towards one strategy but have the facility for showing the other, albeit at a higher threshold. For instance, it might learn that one strategy has failed and then switch to the other. However, in stress either strategy can 'get stuck' outside its adaptive range. This leads to the notion of different kinds of stress, arising from a failure of one strategy or the other.

The next two sections review some classical studies of reaction to stressors in different species, looking for general principles.

Tree shrews

Von Holst (1986) placed a tree shrew (*Tupaia belangeri*; Figure 13.4) into a cage where a resident conspecific was already housed. A fight followed, the outcome of which established a victor (i.e. dominant) and a defeated animal ('vanquished'). According to their behaviour, the 'vanquished' group could be further divided into 'subdominants' and 'submissives'. Subdominants took active steps to avoid dominants. Submissives, by contrast, were passive and unresponsive, sitting in the corner in a way characterized as 'apathetic' or 'depressive'. In response to the threats of the dominant, they neither fled nor attempted to defend themselves.

Figure 13.4 Tree shrew.
Source: © Rod Williams/naturepl.com

Subdominants and submissives gradually lost weight. After 10 days of the encounter, testosterone concentration fell by 30% in subdominants and 60% in submissives. After 20 days, blood testosterone level doubled in dominants.

Corticosteroid concentration was elevated for the first three days in all animals, though more so in submissives than in dominants or subdominants. Following the establishment of a dominance relationship, this fell to its initial value in both dominants and subdominants. In the submissives, by contrast, corticosteroid levels were elevated dramatically (by 300%) and remained so throughout.

Von Holst looked at the level of tyrosine hydroxylase, a chemical in the synthetic pathway for catecholamines, in the adrenal glands. Following the encounter, this was not significantly changed in dominants and decreased by about 30% in submissives. It increased by more than 100% in subdominants, suggestive of sympathetic activation. The fact that their adrenal noradrenalin content increases by about 30% also points to this.

Figure 13.5 compares heart-rates for representative dominants and subdominants. In both cases, there is a sharp elevation on first meeting. In dominants, this soon returns to normal, whereas that of the subdominants remains elevated throughout. Note the near disappearance of the normal day–night rhythm in the magnitude of heart-rate in subdominants.

Dominants seemed to suffer no ill effects from the confrontation. Weight and testosterone levels were well maintained. Their heart-rate was restrained, in spite of the fact that they were required to exert authority in the occasional fight. According to the criteria proposed here, dominants were not stressed. They had a coping strategy. By contrast, both subgroups of vanquished animals were stressed. They lost weight and showed lowered reproductive capacity. Neither strategy, active or passive, seemed to work. The elevated heart-rate of subdominants would have been appropriate for a short-term fight or flight strategy with a high energy requirement. However, over long periods such elevation indicates that the underlying problem has not been

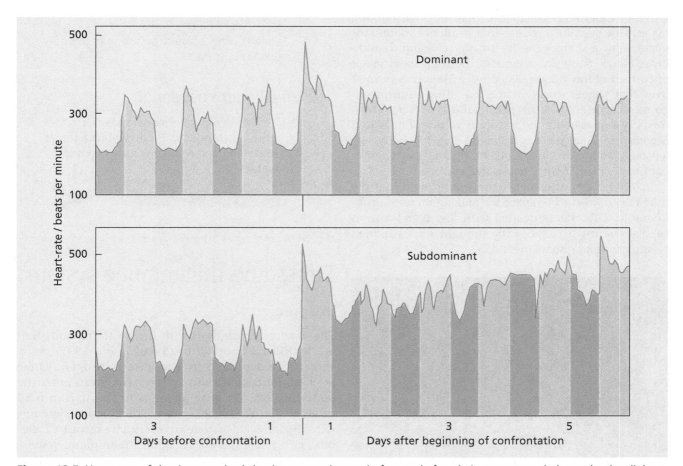

Figure 13.5 Heart-rate of dominant and subdominant tree shrews, before and after their encounter: dark purple, day; light purple, night.
Source: von Holst (1986, Fig. 3, p. 665).

solved. The physiological profile is inappropriate to behaviour. By the criterion of chronic elevated cortico-steroids, submissives were also stressed. Such elevation is appropriate for increased activity. However, their behaviour was that of passivity, a situation in which elevated HPA activity would seem inappropriate.

Primates

Sapolsky (1990a,b) studied wild olive baboons (*Papio anubis*) living in social troops of 50–200 animals, in East Africa (Figure 13.6). Sapolsky (1990a, p. 863) notes that olive baboons have little threat from predators which 'leaves them hours each day to devote to generating social stressors for each other'. Thus, they might provide a model of some stresses of humans in affluent societies. Baboon society is hierarchical with dominants gaining most desirable resources, e.g. food and resting sites. Fights over dominance are frequent and often with serious injury. Riddled with cunning and deception, the worst aspects of baboon society appear to be as Machiavellian as those of humans.

In a stable hierarchy, low-ranking baboon males have a higher basal level of cortisol than do high-ranking males. However, in response to a challenge, dominant males show a sharper rise in cortisol secretion than do lower ranks. Sapolsky associates the high basal levels of cortisol of low-ranking baboons with events in their lives that trigger the HPA axis, e.g. disruption of on-going activities, lack of predictability and control, frustration and being the innocent victim of displaced aggression. When there is instability in a hierarchy, e.g. a baboon equivalent of an impending *coup d'etat*, dominant males exhibit chronic elevated cortisol.

In 1984, East Africa experienced a drought and the time that needed to be spent in foraging increased considerably. This was associated with less aggression: as Sapolsky terms it (p. 865) the drought was 'a hidden blessing for subordinate individuals'.

Figure 13.6 Olive baboons.
Source: Gerry Ellis/Minden/FLPA

Sapolsky (1990a, p. 874) speculates: 'If one were giving stress management courses to baboons . . . ', and his advice is little different from that applicable to humans. Emphasis would be on acquiring predictability and control, forming reliable alliances, gaining skill at assessing social situations and finding suitable outlets for frustration. Success involves picking few fights and winning these.

The chapter now turns to the role of the immune system in stress.

Section summary

1 The impact of a stressor can be reduced by predictability and control.

2 In a situation of inescapable shock, learned helplessness can develop.

3 Exposure to a stressor can sensitize subsequent reactions to stressors.

4 There can be a bias towards either active or passive coping strategies.

5 Failure of either active or passive strategies corresponds to stress.

 ## Test your knowledge

13.4 Which neurohormonal system is particularly triggered at times when a threat is presented and *active* steps are taken to counter it?

Answer on page 362

Stress and the immune system

Introduction

The *immune system* deals with threats to the body that are within its boundaries (Evans *et al.*, 1997). Such threats are described by the term **pathogen**. These are harmful bacteria and viruses, which can enter the body through, for example, cuts to the skin or food eaten or during sexual contact. The immune system is our defence against these invaders and against cancerous cells. Stress has effects upon the immune system. Reciprocally, events within the immune system affect the brain processes associated with stress. This section considers these interacting factors.

The interaction between psychological states, as embodied in the nervous system, and the endocrine and immune systems is summarized in such terms as 'psychoneuroimmunology' or 'psychoendoimmunology' (Ader and Cohen, 1985). If this book had been written in the 1970s or 1980s, it is very unlikely it would have had any mention of the immune system. It is relatively recently that the interactions between (i) the nervous and endocrine systems and (ii) the immune system have been formally recognized. Links from psychological states to immune activity provide a framework for understanding how stress can increase proneness to infection (Cohen, 1996).

Some details of the immune system

Consider the cells (Chapter 1) that make up the immune system: many millions of them, termed white cells or **leucocytes**. They are stored at certain 'depots' in the body, such as the spleen, from which, they are supplied to the body fluids. Leucocytes are carried in the body fluids (e.g. blood) to all parts of the body. They patrol, being, metaphorically speaking, on the look-out for invasion. Detection of pathogens activates the immune system. Immune cells launch an attack, which, if successful, destroys the invader. Our principal concern is with one class of leucocyte, known as the **lymphocyte**. When the body is invaded by bacteria or viruses, lymphocytes multiply ('proliferate') and go on the offensive (Evans *et al.*, 1997). In launching an attack, chemicals termed **cytokines** are released from cells of the immune system.

Interactions between immune and nervous systems

The immune system influences the brain and the endocrine system and also it is influenced by them. This section looks at each of these directions of influence.

The effects of the immune system

The immune activation in response to infection has consequences for nervous and endocrine systems. For example, cells of the immune system release hormones that affect the CNS. Cytokines, released as part of the immune response, influence the activity of the nervous system (Viamontes, 2009). Thereby, the CNS is informed of the activity of the immune system. The cytokine interleukin-1 (IL-1), which is released from activated immune cells, plays an important role here. Cytokines injected into the cerebrospinal fluid (Chapter 5) have a potent effect on behaviour, which leads to the suggestion that, under natural conditions,

central cytokines influence behaviour (Chapter 12). Injection of IL-1 produces a 'sickness reaction' of fever, withdrawal from social contact and reduction of exploration, etc. (Larson, 2002).

Information on immune cell activity from the periphery to the brain is conveyed in part by means of neural links (Viamontes, 2009). A major part of the effect of IL-1 on the brain is mediated via the vagus nerve (Figure 3.30, p. 76). Neurons within this nerve are triggered by IL-1 detected at their tips and they convey this information to the brain.

Interleukin-1 (IL-1) causes the release of CRF from the hypothalamus (Sapolsky *et al.*, 1987), suggesting the appropriateness of the term 'stressor'. In turn, the CRF excites ACTH and corticosteroid release.

Following infection by a virus, the body is not in a condition to be active and typically the animal curls up in a lethargic ball until recovery (Hart, 1988). This exemplifies coordination between behaviour and physiology. In humans, activation of the immune system can contribute towards a depressed mood (Viamontes, 2009).

That the brain is sensitive to these signals has led to the notion that the immune system can be considered to be an internal sensory organ, i.e. one responsible for detecting bacteria and viruses, etc. Maier and Watkins (1998) suggest that we underestimate the importance of the immune system for psychological state. Day-to-day fluctuations in mood might depend at least in part upon changes within the immune system.

Effects on the immune system

The nervous system affects the activity of the immune system, this being mediated directly and through the endocrine system. At times the nervous system excites the immune system and at other times inhibition is exerted (O'Leary, 1990). Cells of the immune system have receptors for substances on their walls, which, in the nervous and endocrine systems, constitute neurotransmitters and hormones. In this way, the nervous and endocrine systems can influence the activity of the immune system.

Sympathetic neurons innervate the organs that constitute part of the immune system (Ballieux and Heijnen, 1987), organs that would normally be packed with leucocytes. The leucocytes contain receptors for the transmitter released by these neurons, suggesting that nervous system activity can excite or inhibit the release of leucocytes into the body fluids. Activation of the immune system appears to be specifically by the sympathetic branch.

Stress can inhibit, or 'down-regulate', the activity of the immune system (Evans *et al.*, 1997). For example, the human immune response is down-regulated by such chronic stressors as divorce, bereavement, sleep deprivation and war (Maier *et al.*, 1994). Down-regulation means a less effective defence against challenges.

Rats that have been exposed to stressors have a decreased activity of immune cells. Placing a rat in a situation of helplessness has a detrimental effect upon the immune system and the ability to reject a tumour (Laudenslager *et al.*, 1983). To have some coping capacity, e.g. the capacity to terminate shock by lever-pressing, is of benefit. It is not easy to generalize from this to humans.

Cohen (1996) asked volunteers to fill in stress- and life-events questionnaires and then exposed them to the common cold virus by nasal drops. They were then quarantined. Blood samples were taken to assess infection. Would stress increase the risk of an upper respiratory illness? There was a significant effect in this direction. Even where people did not subjectively feel that they were stressed, life-events normally termed 'stressful' were associated with increased susceptibility to illness.

Some cells of the immune system, a type of lymphocyte termed 'natural killer' (NK) cells, target cancerous cells and destroy them. However, the relationship between stress and the onset and development of cancer in humans is, at the time of writing, still controversial. The link between depression and health as mediated by the immune system is also not entirely clear (Stein *et al.*, 1991). There are indications that cervical cancer is more likely in women who report hopelessness and that cancer patients with social support are better able to survive (Edelman and Kidman, 1997). Optimism appears to speed wound-healing after surgery, an effect that is mediated, it would appear, in part via an enhanced immune activity (Kiecolt-Glaser *et al.*, 1998).

The *acute* application of some stressors, i.e. a change over minutes rather than hours or days (e.g. a public speaking task), can trigger *up*-regulation (Evans *et al.*, 1997). The acute phase of up-regulation might be due to sympathetic activity.

Stressors can exert effects through routes other than those nervous and endocrine system processes described so far. For example, divorce or bereavement might mean less sleep and exercise and an increase in alcohol and cigarette consumption, with independent effects on disease. Also by changes in physiology (e.g. blood flow), stressors might influence disease through routes other than the immune system (Maier *et al.*, 1994). Some stressors lower the production of saliva, probably with a reduction in protection of the oral cavity (Evans *et al.*, 1997). In stress, people might be more inclined to seek the company of others, with increased risk of such things as the common cold and influenza.

Function

Consider first that events in the immune system affect the nervous system. Suppose that an animal is suffering an infection. It could be in its interests to rest and sleep, to allow recovery to occur (Hart, 1988). Therefore, it could be advantageous for chemical messengers that are secreted by activated cells of the immune system to steer behaviour in this direction.

Why should the nervous and endocrine systems influence the immune system? Why does stress tend to lower the activity of the system? It might prove crucial to distinguish two phases of stress: (i) an acute phase, during which the immune system seems to be excited, and (ii) a chronic phase, during which it seems to be inhibited (Maier and Watkins, 1998). A time of sympathetic activation might well correspond to fight or flight, when presumably there is a risk of injury and infection (O'Leary, 1990) and to boost immune activity could make adaptive sense. On the other hand, suppression of immune function during chronic stress might be a means of restraining the activity of the (already excited) system at a time when infection might be less likely.

At first sight, it might seem logical to play safe; surely the bigger the immune response, the better. However, there are costs attached to immune activity, e.g. an energy cost (Sapolsky, 1992). Also, an activated immune system can launch an attack against parts of the 'self' (Råberg *et al.*, 1998), the so-called autoimmune disorders. So, under some conditions, there could be an adaptive advantage in restraining the immune system.

A caution

Psychoneuroimmunology (PNI) gives a scientific basis to folk wisdom on the capacity of the 'mind to affect the body' (Evans *et al.*, 1997). PNI evokes reactions ranging from scepticism to unqualified acceptance. To sceptics, the effects seem fragile and offer little clinical hope. To some of those into 'alternative approaches', it is attractive to attribute ills to a psychological construct, stress. However, we must avoid exaggerated claims of the kind that psychological factors are all-important and the causation of, say, cancer lies 'all in the mind'.

A critical approach recognizes interacting factors in disease onset and development. The psychological effect is only one factor among many that influence the immune system and might thereby influence disease. We need more cautious claims of the kind that, under some conditions, certain stressors can affect parts of the immune system and probably disease onset and development.

Having looked at the more peripheral parts of the picture we now look at the brain mechanisms that underlie stress.

Brain mechanisms

Introduction

We now consider those brain processes that are the neuropsychological embodiment of stress. There are some closely related leads in this investigation (Figure 13.7):

1   In stress, the neural mechanisms underlying such emotions as fear or anger (Chapter 12) are activated over long periods of time (Rosen and Schulkin, 1998).

2   The two hormonal systems described earlier (the sympathetic and HPA systems) are triggered by activity in particular parts of the brain. Therefore, psychologists can look at release of these hormones and trace the causal links back into the brain.

We shall now examine these sources of insight.

Initial triggers to emotion and stress

The amygdala is a site where emotional significance is attached to events. Some stimuli, such as loud sounds, evoke emotion simply by virtue of their sensory properties (Chapter 12). This draws attention to neurons within sensory pathways having collaterals that project to brain regions (e.g. amygdala) underlying stress. By contrast, other triggers such as frustration cannot be defined by sensory events per se but only by the comparison of sensory events with memories. Such 'cognitive input' suggests the involvement of the hippocampus and cortical processing (Glue *et al.*, 1993). Certain products of the immune system affect regions of brain underlying stress, as represented by 'physiological' in Figure 13.7.

Corticotropin releasing factor

Introduction

A neurochemical of the brain that plays a central role in emotional processing is corticotropin releasing factor (CRF) (Dunn and Berridge, 1990; Pfaff *et al.*, 2007). CRF was described earlier as a hormone, part of the HPA axis (Figure 13.3). At the pituitary gland, it plays this *peripheral* role (peripheral, that is, relative to regions deep in the brain). However, CRF also acts as a neurotransmitter or neuromodulator deep in the CNS, a *central* role. Stressors trigger coordinated CRF activity in both central and peripheral roles (Pfaff *et al.*, 2007). First, we look at the controls of CRF secretion when it acts as a hormone and we then consider its role as a neurotransmitter.

Hormonal role

CRF-containing neurons with cell bodies in the hypothalamus form the start of the HPA axis (Figure 13.3). These neurons receive inputs from various regions, e.g. other hypothalamic regions, brain stem, hippocampus and the central nucleus of the amygdala (Chapter 12; Amaral and Sinnamon, 1977). These neurons therefore form a common focus for various sources of information, conveying, in functional terms, 'challenge and the need to take action'.

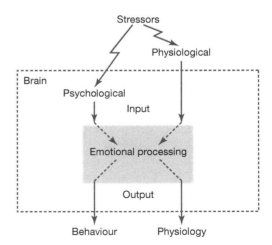

Figure 13.7 The brain is put into states of stress by means of stressors and their interpretation (the 'input'). In turn, the brain provides signals to the neurohormonal systems of stress (the 'output').

Neurotransmitter roles

Now we need to change hats, or, to be precise, roles of CRF and switch attention to a different role of the same substance.

CRF-containing neurons convey emotion-related information between various parts of the brain. Cell bodies of CRF-containing neurons are found in the amygdala (Bohus and Koolhaas, 1993). CRF's wide representation throughout the limbic system and in structures concerned with autonomic control suggests a coordinated role in autonomic and behavioural outputs, which is stretched excessively in stress.

Intracerebral CRF injection leads to EEG arousal and to an increase in the acoustic startle response (Chapter 12), an index of stress and anxiety (Dunn and Berridge, 1990). In exciting the locus coeruleus, CRF activates noradrenergic transmission over large areas of brain, discussed next.

Noradrenergic systems and the locus coeruleus

In reaction to stressors, noradrenalin (NA) acts peripherally as both neurotransmitter and hormone (Chapters 3 and 12). It is broadcast widely, attaches to a broad distribution of receptors and thereby influences diverse organs (e.g. cardiac muscle and smooth muscle in blood vessel walls). The same chemical is used in the CNS, where it is also widely distributed and serves a

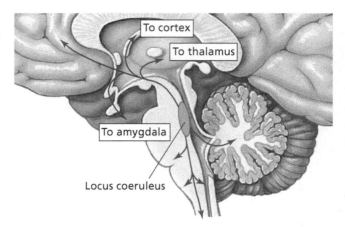

Figure 13.8 The human locus coeruleus and projections. Descending projections influence the ANS.

Source: Martin, J.H. (1996). *Neuroanatomy: Text and Atlas*, 2nd edition, Figure 3.17 p. 87. Reprinted with permission of The McGraw-Hill Companies, Inc.

neuromodulatory role at diverse targets (Zigmond *et al.*, 1995). The functional coherence of noradrenalin's dual role in periphery and CNS points to interesting evolutionary roots. That is to say, in both cases stressors trigger its release.

Activity within noradrenergic neurons that project from the locus coeruleus appears to be an important feature of stress, associated with both behavioural and sympathetic activity (Dampney, 1994; Pfaff *et al.*, 2007). See Figure 13.8.

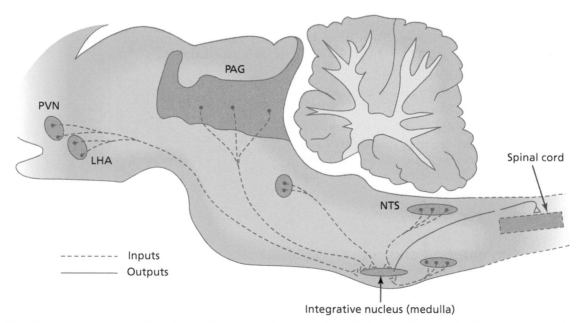

Figure 13.9 Some connections with an integrative nucleus in the medulla. LHA, lateral hypothalamic area; NTS, nucleus of the solitary tract; PAG, periaqueductal grey; PVN, paraventricular nucleus of hypothalamus.

Source: adapted from Dampney (1990, Fig. 3, p. 65).

Triggers to the sympathetic system

Moving to the output side of the brain, a nucleus that integrates information ('integrative nucleus') and controls sympathetic activity is located in the medulla (Figure 13.9; Dampney, 1994). Neurons project from here to sympathetic preganglionic neurons with cell bodies in the spinal cord and controlling the circulatory system (in Figure 13.8, note the link to the spinal cord). Figure 13.9 shows inputs to the 'integrative nucleus' from the lateral hypothalamus, nucleus of the solitary tract, paraventricular nucleus of the hypothalamus and the periaqueductal grey (Chapter 5). These brain regions are involved in recruiting defensive behaviours in response to threats. Considering adaptive functioning, the link with the sympathetic system points to coherence between behaviour (fight and flight) and physiology. In stress, these systems show elevated activity over long periods of time.

Following sections look at disorders associated with stress and, in so doing, further insight into the brain mechanisms that have been discussed in this section can be gained.

Section summary

1 Looking at the basic brain mechanisms of emotion and their protracted activation gives a lead to understanding stress.

2 In actions within the CNS and in triggering the HPA axis, corticotropin releasing factor (CRF) appears to play functionally coherent roles in its behavioural, autonomic and hormonal effects.

3 In stress, noradrenalin activation occurs in the periphery and CNS, indicating functional coherence.

4 Central noradrenergic systems trigger behavioural and autonomic activation.

5 The locus coeruleus and NA neurons that project from it have a pivotal role in activation at times of stress.

 ### Test your knowledge

13.6 CRF acts as (i) a hormone, (ii) a neurotransmitter or (iii) both. Justify your answer.

 Answer on page 362

Depression

Stress and depression can usefully be studied together, since stress is a risk factor for depression (Bremner, 1999). This section looks at areas of overlap in the two conditions.

The HPA axis

Increased HPA axis activity appears to be a major causal factor in depression (Bao *et al.*, 2008). Depression is associated with enlargement of the adrenal gland and elevated levels of cortisol in the blood (Holsboer and Barden, 1996). What triggers this activation? The drive from CRF-containing neurons at the start of the HPA axis is increased (Keller *et al.*, 2006). Increased drive might arise from the increased activity of noradrenergic neurons of the locus coeruleus that is observed in depression (Ur *et al.*, 1992).

An important factor in depression appears to be weakened negative feedback of corticosteroids in the brain. By reducing this inhibitory effect, the excitatory link is less opposed and thereby this contributes to HPA excitation (Holsboer and Barden, 1996). See Figure 13.3. Major depression is associated with some loss of tissue at the hippocampus, which could be the product of the toxicity of excessive corticosteroid levels (Bremner, 1999). This appears to be reflected in some deterioration of cognitive capacity, e.g. working memory (Hinkelmann *et al.*, 2009). A range of antidepressants tend to lower activity in the HPA axis (Mitchell, 1998) and an interesting idea is that antidepressants exert some effect by increasing corticosteroid feedback on the HPA axis (Barden *et al.*, 1995). Increasing age appears to lower the efficacy of corticosteroid feedback at the hippocampus (Seeman and Robbins, 1994) and might be a contributory factor to depression. Cushing's disease, which involves excessive secretion of corticosteroids, is commonly followed by depression (Holsboer and Barden, 1996).

The CNS affects the HPA axis and, reciprocally, the HPA axis (e.g. elevated corticosteroids) affects the CNS. Disturbances within these interactions appear to be fundamental to depression. By their actions at the brain, corticosteroids appear to bias towards negative emotion (Schulkin, 1994), vigilance and avoidance of conflict (van Honk *et al.*, 1998). Of course, in small doses and over a limited time period such changes could be adaptive.

Breier *et al.* (1988) found a tendency for people who had experienced separation from a parent in childhood to be predisposed to develop psychopathology when adult. Their cortisol levels were higher than controls.

In depression, there is increased blood flow to the amygdala and medial orbitofrontal cortex, both regions having a high density of corticosteroid receptors

(Erikson *et al.*, 2003). Thereby, elevated levels of corticosteroids appear to contribute to the negative bias to cognition in depression.

Role of CRF

The activity of CRF in the brains of people suffering depression is elevated (Bao *et al.*, 2008; Mitchell, 1998), i.e. there is a higher release level. This plays a role in increased activity in brain areas concerned with processing negative emotion, e.g. regions of the amygdala. In depression, increased activity of the locus coeruleus and the associated NA systems appears to be due to increased CRF-mediated input to the locus coeruleus. It might constitute an important biological basis of depression (Curtis and Valentino, 1994; Ur *et al.*, 1992). A number of effective treatments for depression lower CRF levels (Bao et al., 2008; Markou *et al.*, 1998), e.g. some antidepressant drugs oppose the excitatory effects of CRF in the locus coeruleus (Curtis and Valentino, 1994). New CRF antagonists are being sought as treatments (Keller *et al.*, 2006). Increased CRF activity in the brain is observed during withdrawal from drugs, pointing to common features between this state and depression (Markou *et al.*, 1998). Suicide victims show down-regulation (Chapter 4) of CRF receptors in their frontal cortex, suggestive of hyper-secretion of CRF (Markou *et al.*, 1998).

Section summary

1   In depression there is activation of the HPA axis.

2   Elevated corticosteroids appear to give a negative bias to mood.

3   Injection of CRF into the brain triggers features of depression and there is evidence of CRF activation in depression.

4   On balance, evidence suggests noradrenergic activation in depression.

Test your knowledge

13.7 Complete the following: 'A decrease in corticosteroid feedback action in the brain causes ___ activity in the HPA system'.

13.8 In what way could the material in this section make any sense in terms of the functional type of explanation?

 Answers on page 362

Stress and the cardiovascular system

Background

Associations between mental state and the heart have been observed for some 4500 years (Williams, 1989) and stress is central to the relationship.

What is termed **coronary heart disease (CHD)** is a disorder of the vessels that supply blood to the heart, in almost all cases consisting of atherosclerosis within the coronary arteries (Scheidt, 1996). CHD is the biggest killer in Western countries. This section explores the link between stress, personality and the health of the circulatory system.

Type A and Type B personalities

Early research identified **Type A behaviour**, particularly associated with CHD, the person who exhibits it being termed a 'Type A' (Friedman and Rosenman, 1959). Type A behaviour consists of being under excessive time-pressure, aggressively competitive, over-ambitious and easily aroused to hostility by situations judged as trivial by non-Type As. Billings *et al.* (1996) observe that CHD patients appear to be (p. 244): 'especially prone to the cultural emphasis on individualism and accomplishment, characteristics that promote isolation rather than interpersonal connection'.

The SNS is hyper-reactive in Type As, with the para-sympathetic under-active (Friedman, 1996). There is high secretion of corticosteroids and (usually, though not always) a high blood level of cholesterol and a tendency to heart attacks (Williams, 1989). The cause of the problem appears to lie in a chronic tilting of the sympathetic–parasympathetic balance towards the sympathetic (Roberts, 1996). So what tilts the balance? Friedman (1996) incriminates covert features of the Type A personality, consisting of insecurity and a low value of self-esteem. The perfectionist goals of self-esteem through achievement are never reached.

Type B behaviour is the opposite of the Type A, i.e. relaxed and without hostility and competitiveness (Friedman, 1996). The 'Type B' has a relatively high level of self-esteem and feelings of security and can tolerate the mistakes of others. Type Bs do not exhibit the neurohormonal abnormalities of Type As. Blood cholesterol is relatively low.

Although we are all probably familiar with some 'textbook' Type As and Type Bs, it is wrong to think in terms of an absolute bimodal distinction. Rather, a person might lie somewhere between the two or show a mixture of the two according to context.

The role of hostility

B.G., a businessman, aged 44, enjoyed getting his own way (Williams, 1989). B.G. would threaten others into surrender. (You might know a 'B.G.' or two!) One day, B.G. was driving his car when another motorist had the audacity to overtake. Normally, B.G. would 'pay the bastard back', by accelerating and emitting a warning blast on the horn. However, this time, just as B.G. was getting into attack mode, he had an experience as 'though a red-hot poker was being driven into the centre of his chest'. B.G. had his first heart attack.

The electrical activity of the heart, recorded by an electrocardiogram, was normal. B.G.'s pain went away and he was free of symptoms for several days. Alas, on the day scheduled for discharge from hospital, as a blood sample was being taken, B.G. switched into the anger mode. Whereupon, 'the red-hot poker hit his chest again'. The electrocardiogram indicated that the blood supply to B.G.'s heart was inadequate. Arteriosclerosis had almost completely blocked one of the arteries. Surgeons removed a vein from B.G.'s leg and transplanted it to the heart.

Williams employed therapy to target B.G.'s hostility and lack of trust. B.G. lived in a world populated by people whose incompetence demanded eternal vigilance. Williams prescribed behaviour modification in the hope that B.G. could alter his behaviour and cognitions. B.G. is not an isolated case. A positive correlation is found between hostility score and magnitude of arteriosclerosis of the coronary arteries.

Rather than personality, could some other factor correlate with Type A behaviour and contribute to the effects on the coronary condition (Steptoe, 1993)? For example, Type As probably smoke or drink more alcohol than Type Bs. However, personality is an independent factor that contributes in interaction with other factors such as smoking (Williams, 1989). There is disagreement as to whether all the characteristics of the Type A are equally toxic, with some theorists placing a particular blame on hostility.

B.G. illustrates two aspects of coronary heart disease: (i) the chronic background state of hostility and atherosclerosis that sets the scene and (ii) that in some cases, but not all, an emotional incident is the immediate trigger to a heart attack (Allan and Scheidt, 1996b).

There is a clear link between low socio-economic status (SES) and poor health (Gallo and Matthews, 2003). Numerous factors mediate this link but one is central to the present chapter: low SES is associated with a high frequency of negative cognitive and emotional reactions and low coping resources. The link appears to be mediated in part by the SNS and HPA systems.

Negative emotion does not necessarily have to be expressed in overt behaviour to influence the ANS. By the use of the imagination and sub-vocal speech, people mentally re-run, and ruminate on, perceived injustices and personal insults (Allan and Scheidt, 1996b). Therapy for cardiac health counters covert 'behaviour': it monitors the 'inner dialogue' for the appearance of hostile thoughts and challenges them (Burell, 1996).

By neuroimaging, researchers can look in the brain for the basis of the exaggerated response to threat that forms a contribution to CHD (the link between a challenge and the trigger to the peripheral reaction). Regions known to be involved in emotion are implicated, i.e. high activity by the amygdala, anterior cingulate cortex and insula correlates with strong peripheral reactions as measured by increased blood pressure (Gianaros and Sheu, 2009).

Section summary

1. Among the factors that determine coronary health is personality.

2. A distinction is drawn between Type A and Type B behaviours, corresponding to Type A and Type B people.

3. Early studies found Type As to be more prone to coronary disease.

4. In Type As, there is excessive reactivity by the SNS.

Test your knowledge

13.9 You are devising a drug to assist Type As with lowering the effects of their overreactivity on the circulatory system but not setting out to target the CNS. Your first thought would probably be antagonists to which kind of hormones/neurochemicals?

Answer on page 362

Post-traumatic stress disorder

The phenomenon

The condition termed **post-traumatic stress disorder (PTSD)** seriously disrupts many lives, e.g. war veterans (Richardson *et al.*, 2010). It follows trauma in which there is actual or threatened death or serious injury to the sufferer or another person. Some core symptoms of PTSD are regular activation of memories relating to the incident, nightmares and high SNS arousal (Davis *et al.*, 1997). In addition to core symptoms, depression, aggression, irritability and impulsiveness are common. PTSD is associated with a heightened magnitude of the startle response (Orr *et al.*, 1995) and increased heart-rate acceleration to sounds (Pallmeyer *et al.*, 1986).

Only a fraction of people exposed to trauma develop the disorder, which raises issues concerning the characteristics of sufferers (Yehuda *et al.*, 1995). Over one-third of the US soldiers who served in Vietnam have experienced PTSD (Davis *et al.*, 1997).

Biological bases

Pitman *et al.* (1993) refer to 'emotive biasing' in PTSD and suggest that its embodiment could be sensitization of links from the basal amygdala to the ventromedial hypothalamus, a form of long-term potentiation (Chapter 11; Adamec, 1997). Artificial stimulation of the amygdala is associated with 'memory flashback', suggesting that it triggers a search for emotionally tagged material that is brought into conscious awareness (Charney *et al.*, 1995). A range of stimuli might come to activate the amygdala and thereby retrieve traumatic memories (Le Doux, 1998). There is evidence suggesting damage to hippocampal tissue, in the cases of combat-related and childhood-abuse related PTSD. This is manifest as some loss of volume of this structure, particularly in certain subregions of the hippocampus (e.g. the dentate) that would normally exhibit neurogenesis (Wang *et al.*, 2010). This structure contains a high density of corticosteroid receptors and could be particularly vulnerable to an elevation in corticosteroid level. Given the role of the hippocampus in memory, early harm to this structure could have enormous implications for the recall of childhood memories (or a failure to do so).

One's intuitive guess would be that the HPA axis would also be chronically activated in this condition. Since the hippocampus is damaged and excessive corticosteroid levels are toxic to this structure, elevated levels of corticosteroids would be expected to accompany PTSD. However, there is some controversy on whether this is the case (Bremner, 1999; Yehuda *et al.*, 1995).

Section summary

1 Trauma, where there is actual or threatened death or serious injury, can trigger post-traumatic stress disorder (PTSD).

2 The hallmarks of PTSD are regular activation of traumatic memories, nightmares and SNS activation. Depression, aggressivity, irritability and impulsivity are often also shown.

 ## Test your knowledge

13.10 In PTSD, evidence points to a toxic effect of corticosteroids on the hippocampus. Not everyone subject to trauma suffers from PTSD, so is there any other possible explanation for why sufferers from PTSD might have a lower than normal volume of hippocampus?

Answer on page 362

Influence of stress on the gut

Introduction

Common sayings point to a belief that there exist causal links between mental states and gastrointestinal function. A link between stress and gastrointestinal disorders is indicated by (i) 'nervous irritation' and (ii) peptic ulceration, in the stomach and part of the small intestine, the duodenum (Levenstein, 1998). This section looks at these two examples of brain → gut links.

Irritable bowel syndrome

A disorder of the gut is the **irritable bowel syndrome** (**IBS**) (Stam *et al.*, 1997). It involves abdominal distension and pain, with abnormal patterns of defecation. Stressful events commonly precede an episode of IBS. IBS is associated with psychiatric illnesses, e.g. anxiety, depression and PTSD. Targeting depression or anxiety often alleviates it (Meyer and Gebhart, 1994).

The enteric nervous system (ENS) stimulates coordinated patterns of gastrointestinal activity (termed 'motility') involving waves of contraction (Chapter 3). The ANS modulates activity within the ENS. In IBS, it appears that activity is abnormal as a result of increased sensitivity somewhere within these networks of neurons (Stam *et al.*, 1997). Transit of material through the small intestine is slowed but large intestine transit is accelerated (Williams *et al.*, 1988). IBS patients show a higher than normal sensitivity to gut distension. There could be abnormal modulation of the link between the sensory detection of material in the gut and motor action by the smooth muscles. The modulatory signal would be sensitive to stress.

Figure 13.10 summarizes signals involved in gut motility and sensation. Disturbances within any of these could underlie IBS. Note the route from the external world to the CNS, then through the ANS to the enteric nervous system (ENS) and hence to smooth muscles of the gut wall. Abnormal activity in this pathway is assumed to underlie the stress-mediated contribution to IBS. Activity by CRF in the brain is implicated in this and CRF antagonists offer promise of help (Taché and Brunnhuber, 2008). Sensory neurons in the gut wall feed back through the pathway ENS → ANS → CNS (Zhou *et al.*, 2010). Abnormal sensitivity of this route or abnormal gut contents could set up disturbances in the feedback pathway, which might in turn influence motor outflow to the gut (Meyer and Gebhart, 1994).

IBS should not be seen simply as a brain-driven ('psychological') disorder. Such factors as a gut infection can also trigger it (Stam *et al.*, 1997). It is an interaction of local and central factors. Thus, an infection is more likely to trigger IBS in patients having prior stressful experiences.

Ulcers

Animal models show that **ulcers** can be triggered by several stressors. In baboons, gastric ulceration is highest in subordinates, who are subject to most social stress (Uno *et al.*, 1989). Increased risk of ulceration in people under stress (e.g. economic collapse) implicates psychosomatic disorders (Levenstein, 1998). As noted earlier, animals exposed to an uncontrollable aversive situation tend to develop gastric ulcers ('peptic ulcers'). Amelioration of the impact of stressors can be obtained by allowing the animal some facility for control (Weiss *et al.*, 1976).

There are neural and hormonal links between CNS and stomach (e.g. the vagus nerve), which could mediate causal links between psychological states and stomach pathology. However, a sensational discovery by the Australian doctor, B.J. Marshall, moved attention away from psychological factors: a microorganism, the bacterium *Helicobacter pylori*, is involved in peptic ulcers (Marshall, 1995). Targeting this with antibiotics led to a cure in many cases, which caused some to dismiss psychosomatic causes. In 1998, Levenstein wrote (p. 538):

> When *H. pylori* burst on the scene a few years ago, it revolutionised views on the aetiology and treatment of peptic ulcer. Psychosocial factors were quietly but firmly escorted off the stage, and gastroenterologists in particular banished psychological considerations with something approaching relief.

However, the world does not divide into neat physical versus psychological categories. Most people have the microorganism in their stomachs but do not develop peptic ulcers (Weiner, 1996). Some are not infected but still develop them. Antibiotic medication is not effective for all patients. Recognition of the role of a microorganism does not lower the importance of stress. There is the

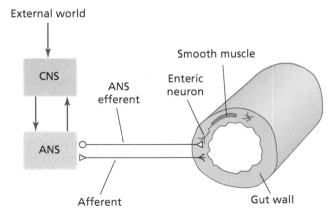

Figure 13.10 Some flows of information underlying gut motility.
Source: based on McKee and Quigley (1993).

possibility of interaction between them. For example, stress can probably increase the vulnerability of the stomach wall to bacterial infection (Overmier and Murison, 1997). The immune system normally mounts an attack against bacteria but might be compromised in stress.

Section summary

1   The enteric nervous system organizes contractions of the gut. The irritable bowel syndrome (IBS) is a disturbance to this.

2   Stress, the effects of which are mediated via the CNS and ANS, is a causal factor implicated in IBS.

3   Peptic ulcers can be caused jointly by psychological factors and bacterial infection.

☞ Test your knowledge

13.11 What type of muscle is involved in the irritable bowel syndrome? It is innervated by neurons of which system?

    Answer on page 362   ⬛ WEB ➤

Positive action for health

A better understanding of stress can not only alert us to avoid stressful situations but also to try to maximize situations that are low on stress or can counter stress. It is unfortunate that, in the history of psychology, most emphasis has been on negative emotions. However, there is a growing recognition of the role of positive emotions (Burgdorf and Panksepp, 2006; Ganzel et al., 2010), as reflected in the term 'positive psychology'. We can promote good health and happiness rather than simply the reduction of negative indices. Optimism can be good for health, with the possibility that part of the effect is mediated via the immune system (Taylor et al., 2000). Optimistic expectancies and positive affect are associated with elevated reaction by the immune system (Segerstrom and Sephton, 2010). This can give a rationale for cognitive interventions designed to cultivate optimism. fMRI studies of the brain reveal that so-called 'resilient' individuals show relatively low levels of carry-over of negative emotion after brief exposure to aversive images (Waugh et al., 2008). Their closer study might be useful in devising cognitive interventions that can exploit positive emotions to overcome the effects

of negative emotions. The presence of positive affect is associated with recovery of blood pressure to normal levels after a stress challenge (Steptoe et al., 2009).

Social contact

Introduction

Concerning the role of maladaptive social reactions in coronary disease, action can be taken to undermine toxic Type A effects (Williams, 1989). Since learning seems to be involved in the acquisition of a hostile way of reacting, relearning might help to change behaviour and cognitions. Psychologists emphasize that, for healthy development, it is important for a child to be able to trust another human.

For several disorders, people who are socially isolated run a greater risk than those who are happily socially integrated (Allan and Scheidt, 1996b; Grant et al., 2009). A caring social relationship seems to offer defence against stress. The presence of a friendly other person can moderate the effect of a stressor, as indexed by heart-rate or the rise in fatty acid levels in the blood (Bovard, 1985; Steptoe, 1993) or length of recovery following surgery (Kiecolt-Glaser et al., 1998).

Support groups for patients with coronary heart disease attempt to counter isolation and alienation and boost self-esteem (Billings et al., 1996). The term **belonging** refers to a particular lifestyle, social context and way of reacting. The individual forms part of a harmonious network, with meaning and purpose, and has a capacity for prediction, control and coping. Goals are acceptable and attainable within a social network and the person values friendship above the acquisition of material resources (Allan and Scheidt, 1996b).

Comparing cultures

Japanese culture emphasizes good interpersonal skills, social interaction and trusting interdependence, stability, cohesion and achievement by the common group more than do Western cultures. Japanese show lower hostility scores than Americans. By contrast, Marmot and Syme (1976, p. 246) suggest that people in American and Northern European cultures:

> display almost opposite characteristics to the protective features described, i.e. lack of stability, accent on the individual rather than the group, and a high likelihood of an individual finding himself in a situation for which his world-view has left him unprepared.

The United States has one of the highest rates of heart attacks in the developed world (Marmot and Syme, 1976). By contrast, the Japanese have one of the lowest. Comparing Japanese living in Japan and

California, the Californians have a much higher rate than those in Japan. Again, diet and smoking apparently can account for only part of the effect. Thus, comparing Japanese males eating a similar diet in Japan or California, the Californians had higher levels of blood cholesterol.

Explaining the effects

What could link social factors and the circulatory system? The effect appears to be mediated by what are termed 'lipoproteins'. Lipids (fats) such as cholesterol are found in the bloodstream in two forms, high-density lipoproteins (HDL) and low-density lipoproteins (LDL) (Scheidt, 1996). The ratio LDL/HDL gives an index of the risk of atherosclerosis, a high ratio being associated with a high risk (Roberts, 1996). As this ratio decreases, there is a decrease in the frequency of heart attacks. Could psychological factors be one determinant of this ratio? Looking at a group of 17-year-old Israelis, the ratio was higher in the non-religious than in the religious (Friedlander *et al.*, 1987). This could reflect differences in belonging and social cohesion.

What influences differences in circulatory systems between individuals? In early childhood, the Type B, in contrast to the Type A, was typically exposed to affection and admiration (Friedman, 1996). There might also be a role for genetic differences. How can positive social bonds with other humans influence the system? Psychobiological theories (Bovard, 1985) relate to the idea that humans have evolved as part of a social matrix. Presumably, brain processes of motivation and emotion (Panksepp, 1982) play a role in seeking and maintaining social bonds and have links to the ANS.

Trusting social contact moderates SNS activity (Bovard, 1985) and buffers against the stressors that will almost invariably arise (Ganzel *et al.*, 2010).

Meditation

Meditation, when a person sits relaxed, with closed eyes, and performs a repeated simple mental activity, triggers the 'relaxation response' that counters trends towards SNS domination and hyper-arousal (Bracke and Thoresen, 1996). Simultaneously, the parasympathetic contribution is strengthened (Sakakibara *et al.*, 1994). Group meetings for coronary heart disease patients involve meditation on feeling states and use of self-control in such forms as guided imagery (Billings *et al.*, 1996).

Section summary

1 Belonging (e.g. having a social bond) seems to benefit coronary health.

2 The effect of positive social contact seems to be mediated via the CNS restraining the SNS.

☞ Test your knowledge

13.12 Therapeutic interventions such as meditation tilt the ANS which way?

 Answer on page 362

Bringing things together

A protracted disturbance to psychological homeostasis, associated with unsuccessful attempts to counter this, constitute stress. Neurohormonal systems that are triggered by stressors serve a useful function when activated *under appropriate conditions*. For example, when confronted with a bear and having a capacity to escape, accelerated heart-rate and a high rate of secretion of cortisol are appropriate. Such reactions are not to our advantage when we are stuck for hours in a traffic-jam or endlessly chewing-over our rejection for promotion. These days, at least among readers of the present text, stress hormones are more likely to be triggered by traffic jams than bears.

Psychological states such as depression and anxiety have a basis in the brain, which has effects outside the nervous system, e.g. in the accumulation of deposits on blood vessels or forming lesions in the walls of the stomach. Such phenomena illustrate the shortcomings of logic based upon 'either/or', e.g. a disorder is either somatic or psychological. For example, gastric ulceration appears to reflect interaction between bacterial infection and CNS-mediated events. Similarly, cardiovascular disease is the result of interactions between (i) such things as diet and smoking and (ii) psychological states, not to forget the possible role of genetic differences underlying nervous system differences.

Figure 13.11 develops a diagram shown in Chapter 3 (Figure 3.36, p. 81) and will help to consolidate your understanding. Included now is the immune system.

Note the ANS links to endocrine and immune systems and the influence of the immune system on the brain.

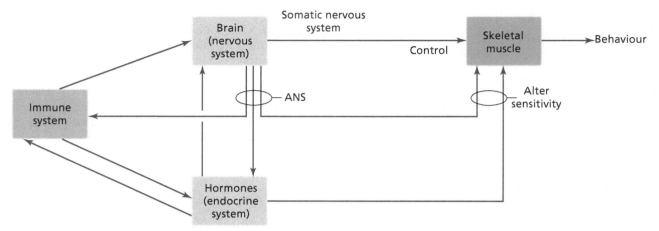

Figure 13.11 Nervous, endocrine and immune systems.

Summary of Chapter 13

1   The term 'stress' describes a long-term disturbance to psychological homeostasis.

2   Stress is associated with unsuccessful attempts to cope, excessive activity within certain neurohormonal systems and proneness to several disorders.

3   The sympathetic branch of the ANS and the pituitary adrenocortical system, involving corticosteroids, form a principal focus for understanding stress.

4   The level of stress depends on context, e.g. (i) the capacity to predict when a stressor will occur, (ii) opportunities for action and (iii) what is done in response to the potential stressor and the outcome of this action.

5   Stress reactions within the CNS can have effects on the immune system. Reciprocally, activity in the immune system has effects on the CNS and thereby stress-related behaviour.

6   Identifiable brain regions form the neural basis of stress and convey information to the neurohormonal systems that are activated under stress.

7   Stress increases the tendency to suffer from depression.

8   Stress has important implications for the health of the circulatory system.

9   Post-traumatic stress disorder (PTSD) follows trauma in which there is actual or threatened death or serious injury to the sufferer or another person

10   Stress can manifest as pathology of the stomach and intestine.

11   Interventions designed to lower the harmful effects of stress are based on lowering negative emotion and excessive sympathetic activity.

 See the video coverage for this chapter and experience something of the good and bad aspects of emotions.

Further reading

For classical writing, see Selye (1973). Sapolsky (2004) is also something of a classic, now in its 3rd edition. An account written by an eminent researcher is McEwen (2004). For theoretical and historical aspects, see Cooper and Dewe (2004). The link between stress and poverty is explored by Sapolsky (2005). For a (somewhat heavy-going) account, see Toates (1995). For applied ethology and stress, see Moberg and Mench (2000). For stress and the immune system, see Evans *et al.* (2000) and Clow and Hucklebridge (2002). For an integrative psychobiological account, see Ganzel *et al.* (2010). For positive emotions and health, see Post (2007).

Answers

Explanations for answers to 'test your knowledge' questions can be found on the website **www.pearsoned.co.uk/toates**

13.1   Disturbance (or, say, 'challenge')
13.2   Corticosteroids
13.3   (i) Lowered levels of ACTH and corticosteroids, increased levels of CRF; (ii) lowered levels of CRF and ACTH and a lowered rate of release of corticosteroids.

13.4   That involving the sympathetic nervous system.
13.5   It conveys information in the bloodstream to a location where it influences neural processing.
13.6   Both. As a hormone in the link to ACTH secretion; as a neurotransmitter in communication within the CNS.
13.7   Increased
13.8   That prolonged depression could reflect an exaggeration of a strategy that is adaptive in the short term, e.g. increased vigilance and temporary withdrawal from confrontation.
13.9   Adrenalin and noradrenalin
13.10 There could be a genetic/developmental influence leading to (1) lower than normal hippocampal volume and (2) increased tendency to PTSD.
13.11 Smooth, enteric nervous system
13.12 To activate the parasympathetic and inhibit the sympathetic nervous system.

Visit www.pearsoned.co.uk/toates
for a range of resources to support study.
Test yourself with multiple choice questions and access a bank of over 100 videos that will bring the topics to life.

Chapter 14
Pain

Learning outcomes for Chapter 14

After studying this chapter, you should be able to:

1 Describe what is meant by nociception and anti-nociception, while linking this to subjective pain.

2 Apply a functional explanation to nociception and anti-nociception. Give examples of pain that cannot be explained in adaptive terms and speculate why not.

3 Describe the route that nociceptive information takes from periphery to brain, while relating this to the observation that there is not a one-to-one link between the magnitude of the noxious stimulus and the intensity of pain.

4 Outline the principles of the gate theory of pain and what it can explain.

5 Identify the principal brain regions involved in pain and describe the link between them and the associated ascending and descending neural pathways.

6 Describe some forms of analgesia and the sites in the nociceptive system with which they are associated. Link analgesia to an understanding of the bases of pain.

7 State what is meant by the terms 'referred pain' and 'phantom pain' and explain how knowledge of the basics of pain allows us to understand them better.

8 Justify the claim that cognitive factors, such as expectations, play a part in pain. Link the role of cognitive factors to the biological bases of pain.

Scene-setting questions

1 How can something so debilitating as pain be said to be adaptive?
2 Why do we rub sore eyes?
3 Can you really suffer the pain of a broken heart?
4 What is it like to experience a phantom limb?
5 What is a placebo? Does it suggest 'mind over matter'?
6 Can you 'feel' the pain being suffered by another person?
7 What is the link between attention and pain?

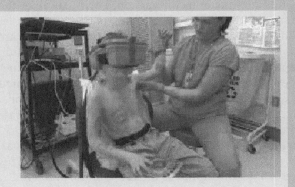

What is the link between attention and pain? Explore the video on the website accompanying this book at **www.pearsoned.co.uk/toates**

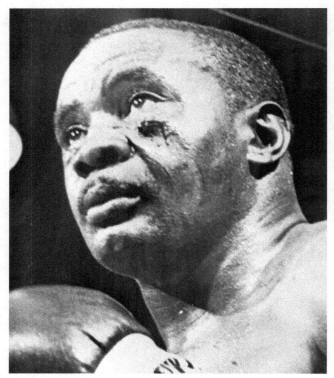

Under which circumstances can a person suffer injury but feel little pain?

Source: Topham Picturepoint/TopFoto.co.uk

Introduction

What is pain? It must be the exceedingly rare individual who cannot recall some experience of pain. Subjectively, pain is an unpleasant feeling that is usually caused by damage to the body and from which we try to escape. Pain, as from a toothache or a gut infection, takes command of attention (Eccleston and Crombez, 1999). We might be indifferent to certain stimuli but those triggering pain are different: pain poses overwhelming demands and moves us into action. People speak of the pain of rejection in love, something that also will not let go, and the pain of seeing someone else in distress. Are these just examples of the use of a colourful metaphor, or can we feel real pain from a broken heart or empathy?

People behave in ways characterized as pain-related and offer verbal reports on their inner experience. They describe their pain in terms of intensity, say, mild or excruciating, and can usually locate its source. Sometimes it is also possible to describe the pain's quality, e.g. gnawing, grinding, sharp, dull or stabbing. This suggests different stimuli as the cause of the problem.

Pain has a quality of intense *negative affect*, meaning that it feels bad. Do non-human animals suffer a similar affective experience? Of course, we do not know what subjective states they experience, if any. However, most of us would probably accept that they can suffer in this way. Their behaviour (e.g. writhing, squealing or jumping) suggests it. It forms a clear pattern associated with tissue damage and threat of such damage.

The term **nociception** refers to the detection of tissue damage or threatened damage. A **nociceptive system** is one that responds to tissue damage or potential damage (Melzack and Wall, 2008). The nociceptive system triggers action in an attempt to minimize the offending stimulation. Looking at the nervous system, there are close similarities in the nociceptive systems of humans and such species as rats. Therefore, the present chapter assumes that we and non-humans (or, at least, the more complex ones such as rats) share similar aversive experiences.

There is also a system of **anti-nociception**, which reduces nociceptive input to brain regions that underlie pain. For example, suppose that someone is engaged in competitive sport (e.g. the boxing champion Sonny Liston, who reputedly carried on fighting once even with a broken jaw) or escape from a battlefield. Activity of the anti-nociceptive system means that they are less likely even to notice wounds that they suffered (Melzack and Wall, 2008).

The medical profession and the lay public try to alleviate pain, a process termed **analgesia**. Substances that alleviate pain are known as **analgesics**. Analgesia can correspond to either a direct reduction of activity in the nociceptive system or an increase in activity of the anti-nociceptive system, which in turn blocks nociceptive activity.

The next section takes a functional perspective on nociception and anti-nociception.

Section summary

1   In response to tissue damage, a nociceptive system produces pain and triggers behaviour of a kind that tends to minimize this pain.

2   There exists also an anti-nociceptive system, which counters pain and the tendency to show pain-related behaviour.

☞ Test your knowledge

14.1 Agonists and antagonists acting where would be suggested as analgesics?

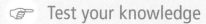
Answer on page 382

WEB

Adaptive value of pain

Introduction

The adaptive value of a nociceptive system and pain is that this permits flexible solutions to the problem of tissue damage and the threat of it. For example, we can move our bodies around until we happen upon a position that minimizes pain or we can remove a thorn from the foot. We can recruit social help: caregivers can help to remove thorns, empathize with us and bring comfort. Suppose that an animal injures a limb. If pain then triggers rest, this increases the recovery chances. Surely, most of us have taken to bed in pain, e.g. a severe headache or general discomfort caused by influenza. Rest improves our chances of recovery.

Pain-related behaviour has a layer of cultural relativity in its expression. Different cultures show different pain-related strategies of reacting, e.g. stoicism or expression of distress (Craig, 1995). In some cultures, rituals that seem to be excruciatingly painful to outsiders are engaged in voluntarily in religious causes.

There are some very rare humans who are born with an inability to experience pain in response to tissue damage. Studying them can give useful insight into the adaptive value of pain.

A personal angle

F.C.

F.C., a Canadian university student, did not exhibit the reactions to tissue damage that are normal and necessary for self-preservation and she suffered serious damage to her body (Baxter and Olszewski, 1960; McMurray, 1950). For example, she repeatedly bit the tip of her tongue. She burned herself by kneeling on a radiator, oblivious to tissue damage. F.C. did not turn over in bed and did not move her weight around while standing. These reactions would have helped to protect from damage to joints and skin, etc. Neither did F.C. show the autonomic reaction of increased heart-rate in response to what would normally be painful stimuli. The study of F.C. confirms the importance of pain in protecting against tissue damage by not only *reacting* to such damage but also by *pre-empting* it. F.C. died in 1955, aged 29. At autopsy, she was found to possess the sensory neurons that detect tissue damage and her brain appeared normal. This was of course before the days of neuroimaging. It is highly likely that abnormalities in information processing and activation of key brain regions in F.C. would be identified these days.

Why has an anti-nociceptive system evolved? A possibility is as follows (Bolles and Fanselow, 1980). Pain triggers adaptive behaviour such as licking wounds and resting until recovery. However, this has a net adaptive value only when there is no greater immediate threat. At times, fighting or fleeing might have to take precedence and would require resisting the tendency to engage in pain-related behaviour. Thus, it might have proven useful to inhibit the activity of the nociceptive system, e.g. when fleeing injured from a predator. In humans, anecdotal evidence suggests that even serious injury incurred, for instance, on a battlefield is sometimes only associated with pain when the victim is away from danger (Bromm, 1995).

Why so intense and pervasive?

An attention-grabbing system means that cognitive and behavioural resources are directed to reducing the input from tissue damage. Why though, from a functional viewpoint, does intense pain create *so strong* a negative emotion, which has consequences that are often debilitating? It is perhaps possible to see an adaptive significance of the intensity of pain, as follows.

Pain commands our attention but also *forces* us to take particular adaptive actions, such as staying still or favouring a damaged ankle by not putting too much pressure on it. From the viewpoint of evolution, it could even be argued, 'no pain, then no pleasure'. Pleasure encourages us to engage in activities such as eating, pursuing a mate or exploring a new environment. However, to follow the guide of pleasure would not always be to our benefit. Pain counters the lure of pleasure, as in getting up too soon from the sick bed.

The use of 'cold cognition' or even 'slightly warm cognition' would be unable to counter the pull of pleasurable activities. Without persuasion by pain, humans might not be able to make rational choices to protect the body (cf. Ainslie, 1975). Even when we could understand the source of our pain, cold reasoning might have little effect. It would be no match for the temptation to 'get up and go' in the present. For some people, the pain of a headache from the occasional hangover is even *too little* to deter over-drinking except for a short period. It would surely be to our detriment to take a 'morning-after superdrug' to eliminate such headaches since the pain is 'motivating us not to do something'.

Some pains have adaptive value and need to be intense, e.g. those of a sprained ankle or a hangover headache. By keeping weight off the ankle, we speed its recovery. However, you might wonder how, say, the pain of childbirth or the severe and chronic pain of cancer could possibly reflect an adaptive process. A possible explanation has two parts, described next.

Although of general adaptive value, of course, we normally attempt to minimize pain. In so doing, we often pay lip-service to its value; the next-day hangover can be treated with aspirin and the good resolution not to drink to excess again.

Evolutionary psychology

What is adaptive?

For pain to be adaptive overall does not require every instance to be precisely appropriate in intensity. Indeed, evolution could only have provided solutions that *on average* worked to our ancestors' advantage (Sufka and Turner, 2005). As a general solution, we are equipped to feel pain in response to damage in most parts of our body. Given this basic 'design', inevitably there will be situations in which pains arise that are not obviously to our advantage. Chronic pain appears to represent a stretching of otherwise adaptive systems to outside their adaptive range.

The second aspect is that many of the chronic pains, such as those associated with cancer, appear most commonly in later years. At this stage, humans are past the age at which reproduction could normally have taken place in early evolution. Indeed, in our evolutionary history few might even have reached this age. Hence, such pains would not necessarily have been experienced sufficiently often to have been a disadvantage.

We now turn to considering the nervous system processes that embody the nociceptive and anti-nociceptive systems.

Section summary

1 Pain has adaptive value in allowing flexible solutions to protect against tissue damage.

2 At times it could be adaptive not to react to tissue damage and this provides the likely reason for the evolution of an anti-nociceptive system.

3 Chronic pain appears to be an exaggerated activation of otherwise adaptive processes.

☞ Test your knowledge

14.2 Rats exhibit the response of freezing in certain situations of fear. What could be the relevance of the anti-nociception system to such freezing and its functional significance?

Answer on page 382

Tissue damage and the sensory input side

Introduction

This section describes the properties of the specialized neurons that detect tissue damage and convey information on this to the CNS. It asks how the signal that they produce contributes to pain. A later section describes what happens to this information when it reaches the brain. The chapter will discuss the limitations of trying to understand pain simply in terms of the input side.

Initial stage of a nociceptive pathway

Neurons that are activated by tissue damage are termed 'nociceptive neurons' (Chapter 3). In Figure 14.1, note the representative nociceptive neuron, by which information is transmitted from the periphery to the dorsal horn of the spinal cord. Tissue damage has a particular ability to trigger activity in these neurons, though some other stimuli have a limited capacity to do so.

At the tip of the axon of the nociceptive neuron, there is a free nerve ending sensitive to tissue damage. The tips of nociceptive neurons are termed **nociceptors** (detectors of 'noxious' stimulation). The branching of the tip defines the neuron's receptive field. Nociceptive neurons come in different forms corresponding to different types of stimuli that best activate them, e.g. 'sharp' or 'burning'. Nociceptive neurons have a high threshold: only strong stimulation will significantly excite them. In Figure 14.1, note also the other type of neuron, the large-diameter neuron. This type is sensitive to harmless touch but it also plays a role in pain, as discussed later.

The neurons in the spinal cord with which nociceptive neurons form synapses are termed **T cells** (Figure 14.1), meaning transmission cells (as distinct from immunological T cells). Nociceptive neurons release neurotransmitter that activates T cells. It appears that nociception employs more than one type of neurotransmitter, the principal ones being glutamate and substance P (Jessell and Kelly, 1991). T cells convey nociceptive information to the brain, e.g. in the **spinothalamic tract (STT)** (Figure 14.1).

The STT is not the only ascending pathway involved in pain but it can be used to exemplify the principles. Electrical stimulation of the STT results in the conscious sensation of pain. Surgical lesions of the tract can reduce pain but this is not always so.

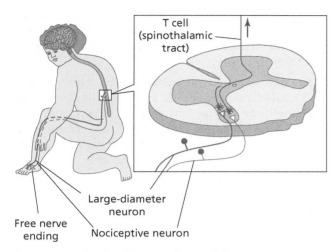

Figure 14.1 Sketch of body and part of the nervous system showing section of spinal cord. Also shown are a nociceptive neuron and a large-diameter neuron, sensitive to harmless touch.

Source: Toates (1997c, Fig. 4.2, p. 70).

Tissue damage, either to the tip itself or in its immediate vicinity, is normally the necessary stimulus to excite nociceptive neurons. When a neighbouring cell is damaged, chemicals are released and come into contact with nociceptors. This increases the chances that action potentials will arise. The high threshold of nociceptive neurons is due to the fact that their axons are of small diameter and are often termed 'small-diameter fibres'.

Since nociceptive neurons are particularly sensitive to noxious information, they are often termed 'pain receptors'. However, to be precise, they detect tissue damage rather than pain. Pain is not like light, a physical quality able to be detected. It is a complex sensation and emotion organized by the brain, and tissue damage does not invariably trigger pain. So the terms 'nociceptor' and 'nociceptive neuron' are preferred.

In Figure 14.1, imagine a region of body surface and the tips of nociceptive neurons located there. Typically, as shown, there are also other neurons with tips in the same area and with axons projecting to the spinal cord in parallel with those of nociceptive neurons. These axons are of larger diameter, have a lower threshold of activation and are often termed 'large-diameter neurons'. They can be triggered by nociceptive stimulation but even harmless stimuli, such as gentle touch, are sufficient. Both types of neuron make synapses in the dorsal horn of the spinal cord, though at slightly different locations (Figure 14.1). Thereby, they trigger activity in other neurons which then convey messages up the spinal cord to the brain. However, information derived from both types of neuron is also processed locally at the spinal cord location shown and this forms a focus in trying to understand pain.

No simple through-line

At one time it was thought that a simple one-to-one 'through-line' links activity in nociceptive neurons and the intensity of pain. Thus, patients who reported pain where no tissue damage (no 'organic disorder') could be identified were highly problematic. They might be referred to psychiatrists and/or labelled as malingerers (Melzack, 1993). Their pain, if it existed at all, was thought to have a quality different from 'real pain' and to be the business of the social, rather than biological, sciences. We now know that there is no *simple* through-line; the magnitude of pain sometimes does not reflect tissue damage. This provides one rationale for the study of the *psychology* of pain.

Suppose, for the sake of argument, that there were a direct link. Presumably, a surgical lesion at some point in the pathway would cure pain. By comparison, a lesion anywhere in the optic nerve would destroy vision. Indeed, surgery for chronic pain was once guided by making lesions in the so-called pain pathway. Again pointing to the true complexity, in many cases pain unfortunately returned after surgery (Melzack, 1993).

Today theorists and clinicians appreciate the complexity of pain. There can be intense pain with little evidence of tissue damage. Even after removing the initial trigger to pain, e.g. a tumour, the pain sometimes persists (Keefe *et al.*, 2005). There can be a relief of pain as a result simply of taking medicine of completely arbitrary content provided that the patient has a belief in its efficacy. So, we have a complex system with interacting factors, only one of which is the nociceptive sensory input. The biopsychosocial model of pain (Campbell and Edwards, 2009) has now largely replaced the older biomedical ('disease') model, which saw pain as a simple reflection of tissue damage. Of course, tissue damage often plays a crucial role but it is not a necessary or even sufficient condition for pain. Rather, social and cognitive factors can also play a significant role.

The next section looks at an influential theory of pain, which attempts to account for a range of phenomena partly in terms of events at the input side.

action potentials in small-diameter neurons trigger action potentials in T cells. When it is closed, activity in small-diameter neurons fails to instigate as much activity in T cells.

2 The ratio of activity in large-diameter neurons to that in small-diameter neurons, arising in the same region of the body (Figure 14.1 and 14.2(c)) is one factor that determines opening and closing of the gate. Active large-diameter neurons are good news for the sufferer since this tends to close the gate.

3 Activity in descending neural pathways also tends to close the gate (Figure 14.2(c)). Note the inhibitory synapse from neuron (1) onto the nociceptive neuron and the inhibitory link through what is termed a 'small neuron' (S).

4 Cognitive processes organized in the brain influence gating, by their input to descending pathways described in (3).

Section summary

1 Nociceptive neurons have small-diameter axons and a relatively high threshold of stimulation. They detect tissue damage by means of free-nerve endings at their tips.

2 Neurons with larger diameter axons are sensitive to non-noxious stimuli, i.e. have a lower threshold.

3 Both types of neuron form synapses in the dorsal horn of the spinal cord, where information processing occurs.

4 Pain commonly, but *not always*, corresponds to tissue damage and activity in nociceptive neurons.

☞ ## Test your knowledge

14.3 Consider a site in the spinal cord where a set of nociceptive neurons form synapses. What would be the expected effect of injecting a glutamate agonist into this region?

Answer on page 382 ◁💻WEB ➔

The gate theory

Basics of theory

In 1965, a new theory of pain, termed the **gate theory** appeared (Melzack and Wall, 1965). Its authors acknowledged that the details might be wrong but they were convinced that the important principles would stand the test of time. Gate theory offered explanations for a number of phenomena, such as (i) why pain does not bear a simple relationship to tissue damage and (ii) how the CNS could produce an anti-nociceptive effect. The theory proposed two processes of anti-nociception, both of which involve the site in the spinal cord where nociceptive neurons form synapses. First, there is the role of activity in large-diameter neurons (Figure 14.1). Second, there are pathways of neurons that descend from the brain. The ideas are summarized in Figure 14.2 and the assumptions of gate theory are as follows:

1 The capacity of nociceptive neurons to excite T cells (Figure 14.1) is not constant. There is, metaphorically speaking, a gate which determines this capacity (Figure 14.2(a) and (b)). When the gate is open,

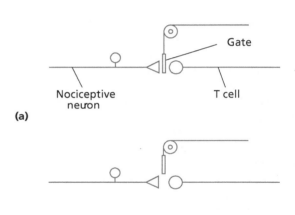

(a)

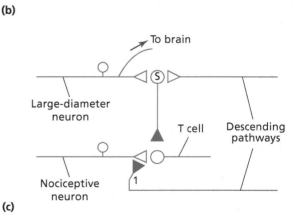

(b)

(c)

Figure 14.2 Gate theory expressed (a–b) by the analogy of a real gate: (a) closed, (b) open and (c) a more realistic representation, showing neurons. Open triangles, excitation; closed triangles, inhibition. S = small (local) neuron within spinal cord. 1 = neuron descending from brain.

Consider the local region of spinal cord where nociceptive and other neurons from a particular small region of the body make synapses (Figures 14.1 and 14.2(c)). Small neurons (S) within this local region exert an influence in controlling the opening and closing of the gate (Figure 14.2(c)). Activity in S inhibits the nociceptive pathway ('closes the gate'). So, the more the activity in S, the greater is the inhibition on the nociceptive pathway. What determines activity of neuron S? It is excited by activity in either large-diameter neurons or descending pathways from the brain, or both. This is represented by the two open triangles adjacent to S in Figure 14.2(c). Note also neuron 1 which represents another route of descending inhibition on the nociceptive pathway.

Concerning the neurochemistry of anti-nociception, a principal focus in gate theory is opioids (Chapter 12). Opioids are a class of natural anti-nociceptive (analgesic) substances, e.g. the natural enkephalins.

Figure 14.3 shows some of the synaptic processes that appear to be implicated in gating. An opioid termed enkephalin appears to be the chemical released by neurons of type S. The precise form of inhibition exerted by such neurons is uncertain. However, there are opioid receptors at the terminals of nociceptive neurons and at the T cells (Benedetti and Amanzio, 1997). By occupying receptors at the terminal of nociceptive neurons, enkephalin seems to reduce the amount of excitatory neurochemical that is released. By occupying sites at the T cell, enkephalin opposes the excitation of this cell. Figure 14.3 also shows an inhibitory link from the brain synapsing directly onto the nociceptive neuron. Elsewhere, there are also opioid receptors in the brain at regions where descending inhibitory pathways arise (Harris, 1996). Acting on neurons in the brain, opioids excite these descending pathways.

Functional significance

From a functional perspective, what advantage is there for the nervous system to be constructed in the manner suggested by gate theory? Why do large-diameter neurons inhibit the effect of activity in nociceptive neurons and thereby give anti-nociception? A possibility is as follows. The reduction of pain would encourage animals to lick their wounds (a reinforcement process), which would cleanse the wounds. Why is there descending inhibition? The possible logic was advanced earlier, i.e. an anti-nociceptive system is activated when the animal is engaging in such defensive behaviour as fighting or fleeing.

Opening the gate

As well as processes that close the gate, other processes appear to open it (Benedetti and Amanzio, 1997). The neurochemical cholecystokinin (CCK) 'opens the gate'. CCK is found at spinal sites (Figure 14.4) and in various brain regions. Like opioid receptors, CCK receptors are both pre- and postsynaptic. In causing an increase in pain, termed **hyperalgesia**, the sites of action of CCK might act in a functionally related way and be symmetrical with the role of opioids in analgesia. Analgesia induced by opioids is inhibited by CCK and enhanced by CCK antagonists. Opening the gate would appear to be a means of accentuating the role of the nociceptive system, e.g. when attention to wounds is especially important.

The value of the gate theory

A gate that is influenced in part by psychological ('cognitive') factors is of great significance for an integrative biological psychology. The theory provided a broad framework for considering how interventions to control pain might work (described later).

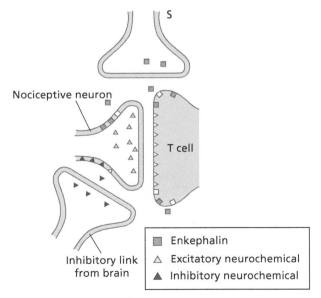

Figure 14.3 Representation of the possible mode of action of enkephalin released from neuron S and that of another (unspecific) inhibitory neurochemical, labelled simply as 'inhibitory neurochemical'.

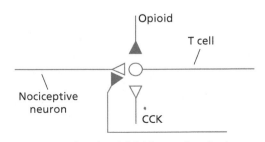

Figure 14.4 Gate showing inhibition and excitation.

Next we need to look at some brain processes involved in pain and thereby give further embodiment to the theory.

Brain processes

Introduction

Figure 14.5 summarizes both what has been described so far and the contents of the present section. In the spinal cord, sensory information ('Nociceptive input') ascends to the brain, conveying information on tissue damage. Information also descends in the spinal cord and it influences the ascending information. At the brain, pain arises from the activity in circuits of interacting brain regions, which are triggered by, among other things, the sensory input. This central 'computation' of pain then plays a role in pain-related behaviours such as yelling or resting. It also plays a role in ANS reactions such as sweating and heart-rate acceleration.

Terminations of ascending pathways

Figure 14.6 shows ascending nociceptive information arriving at various sites in the brain, via the spinothalamic tract. Synapses are formed in the midbrain, including the periaqueductal grey (labelled 'Homeostatic regions'), as well as with nuclei in the thalamus (MDvc and VMpo). This ascending information will have been already modulated at sites in the spinal cord, as described by gate theory.

The pain neuromatrix

Processing in the brain underlies (1) the affective quality of pain, i.e. its emotional value, and (2) the discriminative quality, e.g. where in the body the pain appears to be located.

Ascending information arrives at various identifiable brain regions that form part of the biological bases of pain, e.g. two nuclei of the thalamus (Figure 14.6). Further neurons then convey information from there to other regions, such as the anterior cingulate cortex (ACC) and the 'interoceptive cortex' ('insula cortex'). The collection of interacting brain regions that forms the biological basis of pain is termed the **pain neuromatrix**. It is assumed that chronic pain arises in part from increased sensitivity of interactions ('enhanced synaptic efficacy') between these brain regions (Moseley, 2003). Once sensitized, various inputs, e.g. cognitive, are sufficient to trigger reverberation between the parts.

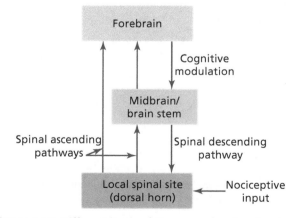

Figure 14.5 Different levels of the nervous system involved in pain.

In humans, some neurons of the primary and secondary somatosensory cortex, among other cortical regions, respond specifically to nociceptive stimuli, mainly on the contralateral side of the body (Area 3a in Figure 14.6). There is some topographic organization of neurons sensitive to nociceptive stimuli, comparable to that of neurons responsive to harmless somatosensory stimuli. This suggests that such neurons extract sensory and discriminative aspects of nociceptive stimuli (Kenshalo and Douglass, 1995; Rainville et al., 1997).

The anterior cingulate cortex (ACC) and insula cortex appear to be closely involved in the affective aspect of pain (Oshiro et al., 2009). In humans, positron emission tomography (PET) reveals an increase in regional cerebral blood flow in the ACC produced by nociceptive stimuli, whereas harmless stimuli do not have this effect. Nociceptive input to the ACC on one side of the brain tends to activate the ACC on both sides. This points to the role of the ACC in affective rather than sensory discriminative processing. For patients with chronic pain, surgical lesions of the ACC reduce the emotional ('affective') but not sensory aspects of pain. Patients having such lesions sometimes report that, although they still feel pain, it bothers them less (Rainville et al., 1997).

Rainville et al. (1997) investigated the effect of hypnosis on pain and blood flow to selected brain regions. Hypnotic suggestion was given that the patient would experience either increased or decreased strength of pain, while the actual nociceptive stimulus was held constant. Such suggestion changed pain's actual affective rating and blood flow to the ACC but not to the somatosensory cortex. A positive correlation emerged between the unpleasantness rating and activation of the ACC, as indexed by blood flow. Only the ACC showed changes consistent with different affective values, which Rainville et al. interpreted to mean that it is involved in affective rating. Anatomical connections between ACC and somatosensory cortex suggest that there is integration of these regions in determining the normal experience of pain.

The pain of social rejection is also associated with activation of the ACC (Chapter 1; Eisenberger et al., 2003). This cause is termed a 'psychogenic trigger', meaning that it lies in psychological processing as distinct from tissue damage. Yet this result gives psychogenically triggered pain a sound biological basis in the brain that is very similar to the basis of that triggered by a noxious stimulus.

There is a strong co-occurrence of pain and depression (Robinson et al., 2009). That pain should lead to depression makes intuitive sense, whereas to understand that depression can sensitize pain requires insight from neuroscience. There is considerable overlap in the profile of regions of brain, neurotransmitters and hormones involved in pain and depression. Thereby, depression can sensitize the pain neuromatrix.

Descending pathways

Electrical and chemical stimulation of descending pathways from brain to spinal cord can reduce pain. Areas of the midbrain, e.g. the periaqueductal grey (PAG) (Fields and Basbaum, 1994), are a source of the descending signals. There is a cortical input to the PAG, e.g. from the ACC, by which cognitive information appears to modulate the activity of the PAG (Figure 14.5). The PAG projects to other axons in the midbrain, which in turn project downwards to the spinal cord and to the region of the terminals of nociceptive neurons in the dorsal horn (Mason, 1999).

We now consider analgesia.

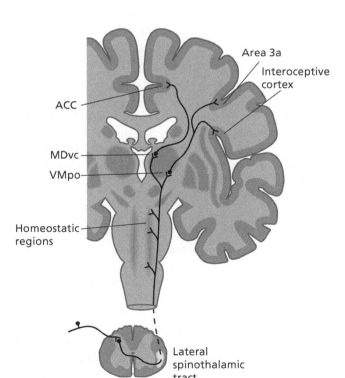

Figure 14.6 Neural processes involved in pain. MDvc and VMpo are two nuclei of the thalamus.
Source: Craig (2003, Figure 2, page 11).

Section summary

1   Nociceptive information arrives in the brain stem and thalamus. Information arriving at the thalamus is projected to cortical sites.

2   Neurons in regions of the somatosensory cortex encode the sensory properties of pain. Those in the anterior cingulate cortex and insula cortex encode its affective properties.

3   Information descends from the brain and influences activity in ascending pathways.

 ## Test your knowledge

14.6 Over weeks, a person in pain is said to show enhanced synaptic efficacy within the pain matrix. How might this be expected to reveal its effects in neuroimaging?

 Answer on page 382

Analgesia

This section gives examples of where an understanding of biological processes is relevant to analgesia.

The role of large-diameter neurons

According to gate theory, gentle stimulation of low-threshold large-diameter neurons tends to close the gate. Most people know that rubbing a painful site tends to reduce pain (e.g. the sore eyes of hayfever sufferers), at least in the short term. Rubbing stimulates the large-diameter neurons, the tips of which are at the site of irritation alongside the nociceptors. Various therapeutic techniques, e.g. electrical stimulation, involve, in effect, massaging the skin. The technique termed **transcutaneous electrical nerve stimulation (TENS)** (Meissner, 2009) involves applying weak electrical stimulation at the skin corresponding to an affected area. This is of sufficient intensity to generate activity in large-diameter neurons but not sufficient to trigger (high-threshold) nociceptive neurons.

Acupuncture

Gate theory might help us to understand the traditional Chinese technique of acupuncture: it is possible that its pain-relieving effects correspond to closing the gate (Filshie and Morrison, 1988). Acupuncture is often, but not always, effective in treating pain. It appears to cause the release of opioids, involving the PAG (Murotani *et al.*, 2010). Such factors as expectation (described shortly) can play an important role in its efficacy (Liu, 2009).

Analgesic chemicals

Introduction

Analgesics can act either peripherally or centrally and can be swallowed, injected or applied locally to the skin. Antagonists to neurotransmitters involved in pain might seem an obvious candidate for analgesia. If there were a neurotransmitter employed only in the nociceptive system, then we might have optimism for the development of a safe and targeted antagonist (Jessell and Kelly, 1991). Alas, nature is not usually so kind. Neurotransmitters tend to be multi-purpose, acting at different sites in the CNS and serving different roles. Any neurotransmitter involved in pain will probably also form part of non-pain-related systems. Targeting this transmitter in sufficient strength to reduce pain might create new problems at other parts of the CNS. For example, glutamate is employed in the nociceptive system but also more widely in the CNS.

Aspirin

Prostaglandins and other substances are released from damaged cells. They sensitize any nociceptors that are in the vicinity of the damage. This increases the chances that tissue damage will initiate action potentials. Aspirin is a peripherally acting analgesic that blocks the synthesis of prostaglandins. Thereby, aspirin lowers the frequency with which action potentials are generated (compare Figures 14.7(a) and (b)).

Lignocaine

The passage of action potentials depends on the movement of sodium into the neuron. Lignocaine blocks sodium channels in the membrane of neurons of all kinds. In Figure 14.7(c), suppose that an injection of lignocaine is given at a location between 2 and 3. If, within a length of axon, sodium channels are blocked, the action potential is unable to pass the affected region and comes to an end on reaching it. Lignocaine does not discriminate in favour of neurons carrying nociceptive information. If you have been injected with it at the dentist, you will know that you tend to feel numb in the mouth as a result of blocking sensory information. You have difficulty initiating movements at the mouth as a result of blocking motor neurons.

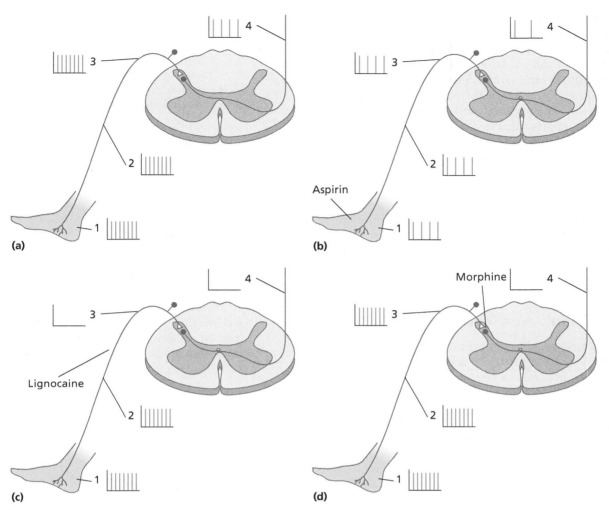

Figure 14.7 Action potentials arising at the tip of a nociceptive neuron (1) and monitored at two points along the axon (2 and 3) and in the T cell (4): (a) control, (b) with aspirin, (c) with lignocaine, injected between locations 2 and 3, and (d) with opiates. *Source:* after Toates (1997c, Fig. 4.6, p. 77).

Centrally acting drugs

A class of analgesics, termed opiates, e.g. heroin and morphine, act upon the CNS (Figure 14.7(d)). Years before the role of natural endogenous opioids (e.g. enkephalin) was established, it was of course known that opiate drugs have analgesic qualities. There are opioid receptors at the terminal of nociceptive neurons and at T cells (Figures 14.3 and 14.4). These are occupied by, say, morphine. This lowers the chances that action potentials arriving at the terminal are able to release sufficient neurotransmitter to stimulate activity in T cells. In addition, opioid receptors in the brain are occupied and this activates descending inhibitory pathways. Both sites of action have a mutually reinforcing action in triggering analgesic effects, 'closing the gate'.

Melzack (1988) reported that many people are denied narcotic (opiate) treatment for pain, since it is feared that they might become addicted. He argues that the risk is minimal and the reason for misunderstanding is simple: an unwarranted generalization from addicts to the person suffering from pain. Melzack suggests that morphine could alleviate the pain of cancer in between 80% and 90% of patients.

Comparing addicts and people in pain, the motivation of why people seek narcotics is quite different. Psychologically healthy people without a history of drug abuse do not usually become addicts on exposure to narcotics. One study looked at 11 882 patients, without a history of drug abuse. Of these, only four later showed abuse and for only one was abuse described as 'major' (Melzack, 1988). The Yom Kippur war resulted in thousands of Israeli casualties and these were treated with morphine but not one case of addiction was reported. An explanatory factor might well be an absence of classical conditioning: the environment of the hospital is very different from home or work.

Rather as with opiates and opioids, for some time anecdotal reports suggested a role for cannabis in pain relief. Only later was it realized that the body produces its own cannabis-like substances ('cannabinoids'), which have a role in anti-nociception. There are receptors for cannabinoids at various sites within the CNS (Rahn and Hohmann, 2009). Evidence points to a combined action of opioids and cannabinoids in anti-nociception. More recently, synthetic versions of cannabis have been tested and shown to have potent analgesic effects. The potential for pain therapy, for example, combined opiate–cannabinoid treatment, is under investigation.

Use of additional feedback

Feedback is an intrinsic part of the nociceptive system, e.g. pain causes a person to take action to try to lower pain. If the action is successful, it is likely to be repeated when in pain in the future. Note that the only measure normally involved is the perceived unpleasantness of the pain and its reduction. Investigators speculate: could there be some additional form of feedback that might improve things? For example, could patients monitor some biological correlate of pain and learn to alter this, thereby reducing their pain? Attempts have been made to monitor a correlate of pain, such as EEG activity, and reward patients if they are able to lower this. This amounts to instrumental conditioning with a lowering of pain as reinforcement (Flor *et al.*, 2002).

Although still at the experimental stage, neuroimaging of activity in the pain neuromatrix offers the possibility of using feedback to control pain. By fMRI neuroimaging, deCharms *et al.* (2005) gave participants feedback on the activity within the rostral ACC, while asking them to lower this level. Success was reported. As the authors noted (p. 18630):

> pain patients already have continuously available sensory feedback of their own pain level, they already have a strong motivation to learn to control their pain, and they typically have tried and practiced many strategies to alleviate their pain over many years.

There appears to be something special about adding the neuroimage of a key part of the pain neuromatrix to the feedback. Its visual aspect could prove to be of crucial significance.

Section summary

1 Aspirin lowers the frequency with which action potentials arise in nociceptive neurons and thereby has an analgesic effect.

2 Lignocaine blocks sodium channels in neurons including those in nociceptive neurons.

3 Opiates act on the CNS. They (a) block the capacity of nociceptive-neurons to trigger T cell activity and (b) activate a descending inhibitory pathway.

 Test your knowledge

14.7 Complete the following: 'The threshold of activation of nociceptive neurons is relatively ___ , whereas that of large-diameter neurons is relatively ___ '.

14.8 Which of the following has a broad effect on neurons, whether involved in nociception or not? (i) aspirin, (ii) lignocaine, or (iii) opiates.

Answers on page 382

Some unusual types of pain

This section considers some examples of phenomena that might be termed anomalous by the criterion of not fitting common-sense understanding. They start to make sense in light of understanding the neural systems that form the biological basis of pain.

Neuropathic pain

The term **neuropathic pain** describes pain that arises intrinsically as a result of damage to, or malfunction within, the nervous system (Seifert and Maihöfner, 2009). Neuropathic pain becomes chronic as a result of, for example, increases in activity within the pain neuromatrix or an expansion of the neuromatrix to take over other brain regions. The phenomenon of **wind-up** describes increased sensitivity of synapses in the nociceptive pathway (e.g. in the spinal cord), something like long-term potentiation (Sufka and Turner, 2005). Thereby, activity in the nociceptive pathway could be self-reinforcing, resulting in increased activity in the pain neuromatrix.

Referred pain

Suppose that there is tissue damage at a localized site. At times, pain is felt to be associated not with this site but with (i.e. 'referred to') some other site (Vahle-Hinz *et al.*, 1995). There exist some striking examples of such **referred pain**. Pain arising from tissue damage at the heart can be experienced at the left shoulder and arm. A kidney stone can trigger pain that is referred to the genitals. The pattern of referral is not haphazard but can be understood in terms of the developmental origin of the neurons involved (Chapter 6). For example, nociceptive neurons with their tips at an internal organ (e.g. the heart) can trigger the same T cells as those with their tips at the skin (e.g. left shoulder and arm) (Figure 14.8) (Pomeranz *et al.*, 1968). Note that neurons from both an internal organ and a region of skin make synaptic contact on the T cell in the spinal cord.

Why should tissue damage at, say, the heart, be perceived as arising at the skin? Why are pains having their origin at the skin not referred to the heart? The answer might lie in our relative familiarity with experiencing pain. Presumably, most of us know pain arising from tissue damage or threatened damage at our skin (e.g. banging a toe against a door) and such pain usually makes sense. For tactile stimulation, there is a relationship between the body region stimulated and the area of somatosensory cortex activated, i.e. the sensory homunculus (Chapter 5). Possibly, when nociceptive messages from the heart arrive at such brain regions, we interpret them in terms of the more familiar stimuli.

Functional chronic pain symptoms

Functional chronic pain symptoms are those in which (Harris *et al.*, 2009, p. 3146): 'patients paradoxically report frequent pain symptoms in the absence of anatomic injury or objective pathological findings'. An

example is fibromyalgia, which affects up to 4% of the population, and is associated with pains in the muscles and tendons throughout the body. Evidence points to activation of the pain neuromatrix (Derbyshire *et al.*, 2009). Glutamate is involved in transmission within the pain neuromatrix and it is activated in fibromyalgia, as indexed by its cerebrospinal levels (Peres *et al.*, 2004). The level of glutamate in parts of the insula is higher in fibromyalgia patients than controls, while successful treatment with acupuncture is associated with reduced levels (Harris *et al.*, 2008, 2009). Ketamine blocks the NMDA receptor to glutamate and reduces fibromyalgia pain levels (Graven-Nielsen *et al.*, 2000). The suggestion of changes in pain level (up or down) (e.g. by hypnosis) is associated with corresponding changes in patients' subjective pain and activation within the pain neuromatrix, as measured by fMRI (Derbyshire *et al.*, 2009).

Phantom pain

Introduction

People with a part of the body (e.g. a limb) amputated often still feel pain, apparently 'in' the missing part, termed **phantom pain** (Melzack, 1993). Melzack (1989, p. 2) describes reports from amputees, for example: 'I continue to feel my leg as vividly as I felt my real leg and I often feel a burning pain in my foot'. It is not just limbs that are felt as phantoms; following their surgical removal, the rectum, breasts, bladder and penis can all be experienced much as before. Even after seven years following amputation, some 60% of people suffer phantom pain related to a lost limb. Phantom pains can be similar to pains that were felt much earlier, i.e. when the missing part was still present. This suggests that specific memories play a role. However, such memories are not always essential. For example, people born without a limb can still suffer phantom sensations 'in' the missing limb.

Amputees use such expressions as sweaty, cold or itchy to describe the phantom limb. The feeling of the presence of a missing limb can be so real that amputees have difficulty, e.g., in not getting out of bed 'onto' the missing limb. Points of reference that helped to define the limb when it was intact, e.g. the tightness of a ring on a finger or the pain of a sore on the foot, can persist in vivid detail.

In three situations, phantom pain can be experienced apparently in the absence of corresponding sensory input to the brain (Melzack, 1989): (i) after amputation, (ii) when a body region remains but its sensory input to the spinal cord has been lost or (iii) where a break in the spinal cord occurs. In (iii), the feeling corresponds to a body region below the break. For paraplegics, where a total section of the spinal cord has been suffered, there

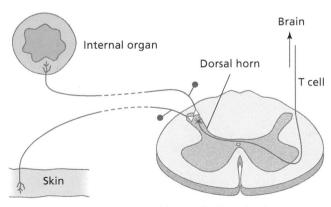

Figure 14.8 A possible neural basis of referred pain.
Source: after Toates (1997c, Fig. 4.5, p. 75).

can still be the experience of severe pain relating to a location below the break. This is referred to body sites for which, it appears, no neural communication with the brain is possible.

Explaining phantom pain

Theorists now view the brain as an active processor of sensory information, rather than a passive receiver. Melzack (1989) made the following points:

1 Patterns of activity in neural networks in the brain encode both nociceptive and harmless events in the world. Such patterns would normally be triggered by sensory inputs but do not always depend on them.

2 The sensation of a phantom body part feels like a real part. This suggests that brain processes activated are those that would, under normal circumstances, be triggered by afferent information arising from the lost part.

3 During the phantom experience, certain brain processes are active autonomously and 'revive' experiences associated with the part before there was a break in its connection with the brain.

A personal angle

Tom Sorenson

Aged 17 and being only three months from high school graduation, Tom Sorenson was involved in a traffic accident, in which he lost part of his left arm (Figure 14.9). Tom experienced a phantom hand, including itching and pain (Ramachandran and Blakeslee, 1998). Ramachandran placed a blindfold over Tom's eyes and proceeded to touch parts of his body. On touching Tom's cheek he correctly identified the location of the stimulus. Prompted with 'anything else'?, Tom replied that his missing 'phantom' thumb was also being touched. On touching the upper lip, Tom reported feeling touch both in the lip and in the index finger. A map of Tom's phantom hand could be drawn on his face. A similar map was constructed on his left arm (Figure 14.9).

How is the effect in people like Tom explained? Plasticity of neural connections is central to this (Ramachandran and Blakeslee, 1998). Consider the sensory homunculus in Figure 5.18 (p. 117) and look at the area of cortex devoted to analysing sensations from the fingers. This is surrounded by areas which analyse sensations from (on the one side) the face and (on the other)

the arm. When the region of cortex devoted to analysing the hand is lacking its normal input, neighbouring neurons (normally triggered by the face and arm) take over control. How does this occur? Neurons appear to sprout links and invade the hand area of cortex (Figure 14.10). Another process appears to be that the links (arm → finger area and face → finger area) are there all the time but are inhibited. Removing the normal sensory input from the fingers unmasks the links. Stimulation of either face or arm evokes the sensations of (i) the appropriate touch and (ii) touch on the phantom hand (by exciting neurons in the hand area of cortex). Tom only has to move his upper arm or face to trigger sensations in the phantom hand. Such cortical reorganization only occurs in those patients in whom amputation is associated with phantom limb pain (Flor and Diers, 2009).

Basic insights derived from treatment

To treat phantom limb pain, Ramachandran devised a simple piece of apparatus that was intended to fool the brain into perceiving movement in the non-existent arm. Figure 14.11 shows the situation for a patient who

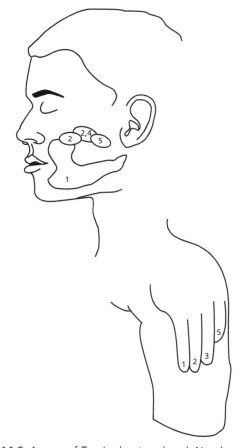

Figure 14.9 A map of Tom's phantom hand. Numbers correspond to the number of the digit associated with each region.

Source: Ramachandran and Hirstein, (1998, Fig. 4(B), (C), p. 1612).

has lost part of the right arm. A box contains a mirror at the midline. There are holes on one side for the patient to insert the stump (to the right) and the intact arm (to the left). The patient sees his/her intact left arm as normal and, on looking in the mirror, the image of this left arm, which appears to be a now intact right arm. On giving commands to both arms to move in synchrony, this is exactly what appears to happen. When the patient's right arm was previously felt to be frozen, it now feels as unfrozen. Visual feedback now matches the commands sent out to move the phantom right arm and thereby unfreezes it.

Regular practice with this apparatus is sometimes effective in eliminating the pain of the phantom limb. Why should pain abate as a result of seeing an intact limb? It appears to be due in part to reorganization (back to nearer normal) of the abnormal connections (Flor *et al.*, 2006). However, reorganization takes time and yet some reduction in pain can be immediate. Harris (1999) suggests that an important component of phantom limb pain arises from incongruity between (i) the commands to move the limb and (ii) the lack of appropriate tactile, proprioceptive and visual feedback that the limb has actually moved. The mirror apparatus lowers the incongruity. Ramachandran and Altschuler (2009) suggest that the false visual perception that the arm is intact enables the brain to interpret the pain message as spurious and thereby reject it. The visual sense appears to dominate.

In one study, patterns of stimulation were triggered at the stump and patients given the task of discriminating them (Flor *et al.*, 2001). Over days, patients got better

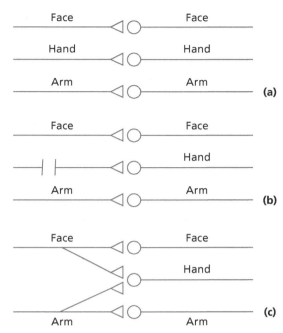

Figure 14.10 Possible plasticity of neural connections underlying phantom effects: (a) before injury showing specificity of connections from the periphery to sensory perception systems of brain; (b) breaking of input from hand; (c) loss of input from hand and sprouting of new links from neurons detecting touch at face and arm. Touch at face or arm could trigger phantom sensation of hand.

at this discrimination. In parallel, the pain reduced and there was reorganization of the somatosensory cortex in the direction of a more normal sensory homunculus.

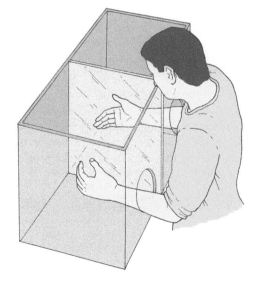

Figure 14.11 Mirror apparatus. (a) The view from above showing position of patient's arm intact (left) and amputated (right), (b) The view to one side showing something of the patient's perspective. Note the mirror image of intact left arm, appearing to be an intact right arm.

Within the secondary somatosensory cortex (Figure 9.19, p. 239), there is a form of mirror neuron (Ramachandran and Brang, 2009). These are activated either when (i) a person is touched or (ii) (s)he watches another individual being touched. Ramachandran and Brang studied individuals with an amputated arm and the experience of a phantom arm. When they watched the arm of another individual being touched, they felt a localized sensation in their phantom arm corresponding to the precise stimulus applied to the other individual. At the time of writing, the potential of this observation for the relief of pain has yet to be found. However, it is tantalizing that one patient reported that watching his wife massage her hand lowered the phantom pain that he felt.

The following section looks at other effects that also challenge any simple view of pain.

Section summary

1 Neuropathic pain arises within the nervous system.

2 In fibromyalgia, there is pain without tissue damage.

3 Tissue damage at one body region can trigger pain that is referred to a different region, termed 'referred pain'.

4 Pain associated with a missing body part is known as phantom pain.

5 Phantom pain provides further evidence that pain is the product of an active process organized by the brain.

 Test your knowledge

14.9 With regard to Figure 14.8 suppose that there is tissue damage at the internal organ and that this is felt as coming from the skin. What would be the expected effect of, in addition to this, activity in the nociceptive neuron that projects from the skin?

 Answer on page 382

Cognitive and social factors: theory and therapy

This section considers a cognitive approach to pain and links it to social factors. In these terms, therapies that address such things as goals, expectancies, attitudes and attention are given a rationale.

Cognitive interventions and basic understanding of pain

Cognitive interventions for pain tend to focus upon how patients interpret their pain in terms of its implications (Weisenberg, 1994). Therapeutic techniques used include relaxation, trying to divert attention and the forming of positive images. Therapists attempt to teach patients to see themselves as active agents who have some control, i.e. self-efficacy, rather than being hopeless and helpless victims. One theoretical rationale for the efficacy of such interventions is the gate theory, where cognitive factors influence the descending pathway. Indeed, the perception of self-efficacy in the face of pain is associated with triggering both opioid and non-opioid analgesia (Bandura *et al.*, 1987).Therapies give insights into the bases of pain.

Distraction

Presenting a 'distracting cognitive task' that draws on attention reduces the perceived intensity of pain. Bantick *et al.* (2002) applied a painful thermal stimulus to participants' left hands and, by fMRI, monitored brain activation in regions of the pain neuromatrix. The distraction by cognitive task was compared with a less demanding ('neutral') task.

Increased activation was recorded in the orbitofrontal cortex under the distraction condition. The authors suggest that this inhibits the pain neuromatrix. Distraction during a painful stimulus is associated with activation of the PAG (Tracey *et al.*, 2002). Distraction is a cognitive process, which engages forebrain processes (Figure 14.5). Via 'Cognitive modulation', this excites the PAG (part of the 'Midbrain/brain stem'), which then activates the 'Spinal descending pathway' and blocks the nociceptive messages. Hence, less afferent input from nociceptors gets to the brain. In addition, there appears to be a direct inhibition of activity in the pain neuromatrix.

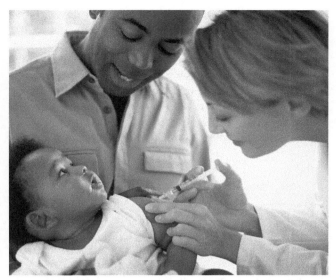

What might be going on in such situations apart from the arrival of a chemical in the body?

Source: Ian Hooton/Science Photo Library

Catastrophizing

Evidence suggests that the psychological process of 'catastrophizing' makes pain worse (Craig, 1994). This consists of focusing intense negative evaluation on the pain, rumination (mental 'chewing-over') and a perception of helplessness and hopelessness. Associated with this psychological state, there is increased activation of parts of pain neuromatrix involved with attentional and emotional processing, e.g. the anterior cingulate cortex (Gracely *et al.*, 2004). In pain, it seems that a role of regions of prefrontal cortex is to assess the controllability of the situation (Salomons *et al.*, 2007). Descending pathways then recruit lower brain regions, e.g. insula and PAG, in modulating pain. Such control appears to be deficient in patients who catastrophize their pain (Seminowicz and Davis, 2006).

Placebo effects

Introduction

The term 'placebo effect' applies to several areas of experience (Chapter 10), including pain (Beecher, 1955). In the case of pain, a placebo is an intervention (by substance or other procedure) that appears to have no *intrinsic* capacity to lower pain but, because of its context, has an analgesic capacity. For example, an injection *procedure* itself (even in the absence of a known analgesic substance) can trigger an analgesic ('placebo') effect. This capacity is demonstrated when injection of a chemically inert substance subsequently lowers pain.

In part, the effect can be the outcome of classical conditioning (Zubieta and Stohler, 2009). Suppose that there

is a history of an injection (e.g. of morphine) causing pain relief. Hence, by association, the syringe and the context of the injection can acquire some pain-relieving capacity, i.e. an association between the procedure (conditional stimulus), the drug (unconditional stimulus) and the pain relief (unconditional response). However, conditioning is not the whole explanation of the placebo effect (Stewart-Williams and Podd, 2004). It does not always require a history of associations. Thus, if a person is simply told that pain-relief is to be expected, there can be some tendency for it to be experienced.

Less well known than the placebo effect, is the symmetrical effect, the **nocebo effect**: an aversive state induced by the expectation of something aversive (Benedetti and Amanzio, 1997). An *increase* in pain can result from a contextual factor that has been associated with an increase in pain.

Examples of the placebo effect

Perhaps the best-known examples of the placebo effect concern inert chemicals. In order of increasing placebo efficacy, there is (i) a tablet, (ii) intramuscular injection (e.g. mild saline) and (iii) intravenous injection of the same substance (Wall, 1993).

There exists a surgical placebo (Cobb *et al.*, 1959). For instance, for patients suffering from angina pectoris, an inadequate supply of blood to the cardiac muscle causes pain. Most patients in one study were seriously disabled by their condition and unable to work. An operation consisted of tying arteries that run near to the heart. The rationale was that the disturbance of blood flow would stimulate sprouting of some new blood vessels through the heart muscle. Many patients were happy with the outcome. However, investigators were unable to find any sprouting of new vessels. This prompted a **double-blind study** (i.e. one in which neither patient nor therapist knows into which group a patient has been allocated) into the possibility that the benefit reflected a placebo effect.

For a control group, surgery was done only to the extent that the arteries were temporarily exposed. This gave the patient the impression that the full operation had been performed, whereas no tying of arteries was made. A serious ethical problem arises here: in the interests of research, some patients had to be told lies. This would probably mean that a similar study could not be performed these days. For both experimental and control groups there was a significant reduction in pain.

Placebo effects and the brain

In terms of an integrative biological psychology, a biological basis of the placebo must exist. Otherwise, we have inescapable mystery. Indeed, in fMRI studies, regions of the pain neuromatrix (Figure 14.6), such as the anterior

Patrick Wall's experience

The personal experience of the placebo effect by the eminent London pain researcher, Patrick Wall (one of the authors of 'gate theory'), is revealing. Wall (1993, p. 192) writes:

> When doctors who are not involved in a therapy under trial learn that it turns out to be a placebo, they howl with laughter. When you are the subject in a trial and discover that you have reacted to a placebo, as I have, you feel a fool. When you are the proponent or inventor of a therapy, whether based on contemporary rationale or old-fashioned faith, you are resentful of the need for placebo testing. If the test reveals a substantial placebo component in the response, diversions are created to eliminate consideration of the placebo effect.

cingulate cortex (ACC), insula and thalamus, exhibit lower activity following a placebo treatment (Petrovic *et al.*, 2002; Wager *et al.*, 2004).

The ACC has subdivisions that exhibit different properties: activity of the caudal region is associated with pain as such, whereas the rostral region is excited by opioids. This suggests that the rostral region could be a site of anti-nociception that opposes the caudal region (Petrovic, 2010). The placebo condition is associated with activation of the rostral region, as is the case with hypnotic suggestion.

Increased activity in regions of the orbitofrontal cortex (OFC) is observed during analgesia triggered by a placebo (Zubieta and Stohler, 2009). In humans, the OFC is a region associated with the formation of goals and expectations. The placebo seems to be an example of such cognitive processing. The OFC has connections with the ACC and with the brain stem and it appears to be associated with pain reduction based on cognitive processing (Petrovic, 2010).

The role of opioids in the placebo effect was established by the observation that, under some conditions, the effect is abolished by prior injection of the opioid antagonist naloxone (Levine *et al.*, 1978). If you like more detail, specifically the μ-opioid type of receptor is involved (Zubieta and Stohler, 2009). In the placebo effect, dopamine and opioids are activated in various brain regions (e.g. nucleus accumbens), corresponding to the *expectation* of beneficial effects. Comparing different people, high placebo responsiveness is associated with high activation of these neurochemicals. Opioid

receptors are found in regions of the pain neuromatrix which are reduced in activation corresponding to the placebo effect, e.g. the ACC and the insula (Petrovic, 2010). By contrast, the nocebo effect is based upon inhibition of activity in these same neurochemical systems (Scott *et al.*, 2008). The involvement of dopamine in the nucleus accumbens in pain relief by placebo suggests that this system underlies the expectation of reward (a similar message comes from Chapters 10, 11 and 15).

A pain shared?

'I feel your suffering.'

'My heart aches for you.'

'Your pain is shared with us all.'

These are expressions not just of sympathy but of **empathy**, which refers to a capacity for a person to put themselves in another's place and to experience something of what it is like. Theorists suggest that, for empathy, the observation of the emotional state of another (e.g. pain) triggers features of this same state in the brain of the observer. Brain neuroimaging permits researchers to put this to the test. They give a glimpse of what regions of the brain are doing when someone professes empathy for the pain of another (Singer *et al.*, 2004). Using an fMRI technique, women's brains were examined while their male partners were subject to painful stimulation to the hand.

Observing the partner in pain triggered parts of the brain of the observer that are normally triggered by painful stimuli, the pain neuromatrix. However, not all of the neuromatrix was triggered. Rather, only those parts

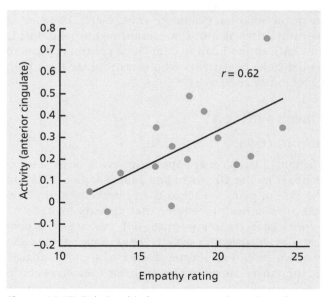

Figure 14.12 Relationship between empathy rating of individuals and the associated activation of the ACC.
Source: From Singer *et al.* (2004 Fig. 4A p.1161) Reprinted with permission from AAAS.

associated with the quality of *affect*, e.g. anterior cingulate cortex, were excited. Somatosensory cortex was not activated in empathy, again suggesting a role of this region in sensory and discriminative aspects of nociception, rather than affective aspects. Interestingly, as Figure 14.12 shows, there is a positive correlation between the score on an empathy scale and the degree of excitation of the ACC in response to the pain of the partner. (We can only imagine the breakfast table conversation that this study later triggered among the participants and the degree of marital empathy that was produced!)

What could be the functional significance of empathy? We are a social species and we have adapted to a life of bonding with others. To share the emotion of someone close to us would tend to move us into action in response to their pain. For this, we only need to trigger the affective parts of the pain neuromatrix rather than the sensory-discriminative parts. Indeed, we need to be able to discriminate pain in another person from pain that is endogenous to us (i.e. based on our own tissue damage). If too much of the pain neuromatrix were activated, we might mistake the source of pain. The sensory side of another's suffering is detected through our eyes and ears, etc., which labels it as primarily theirs in its origin.

Section summary

1 Cognition (e.g. catastrophizing) has an influence on pain.

2 A placebo is an intervention (e.g. substance or procedure) that can lower pain as a result of conditioning or a belief as to its efficacy.

3 The placebo effect has a biological basis in inhibiting parts of the pain neuromatrix.

4 A biological basis of empathy consists of the activation of regions of the observer's pain neuromatrix.

 ## Test your knowledge

14.10 Of the regions shown in Figure 14.6, which appear to be activated and which not activated during the experience of empathy for a pain sufferer?

Answer on page 382

Bringing things together

Pain is enigmatic and its study reveals anomalies. Pain is often overwhelming in its attention-grabbing capacity and the potency with which it can take control of consciousness and behaviour. Yet, it can sometimes be reduced by diverted and focused attention, as in competitive sport, or even by nothing more than taking a sugar pill in expectation of relief. We now understand pain better in terms of the contribution of types of neurons, routes of information transmission to and from the brain and brain mechanisms. Some factors can be defined at the neural level, e.g. (i) the properties of peripheral neurons, i.e. small- and large-diameter neurons and (ii) connections that neurons make within the spinal cord.

A pain neuromatrix of interacting brain regions forms the biological basis of pain but does not respond in a one-to-one fashion to nociceptive stimuli. Rather, such input is only one contributory factor to the neuromatrix. Such things as motivation, attention, mood, expectations and memories also play a part in determining pain. These involve (i) a gate mechanism at the spinal level and (ii) some active participation of the brain in pain and antinociception. Involvement of regions of prefrontal cortex in pain can be interpreted in terms of their general role in the control of emotion, expectation and decision-making.

The placebo effect can be better understood now in terms of its biological roots. Insights into the processes underlying the effect (e.g. expectation) reinforce our basic understanding of pain. For example, parts of the pain neuromatrix are affected by placebo treatments. Taking a biopsychosocial perspective, such observations offer the possibility of explaining a range of phenomena within a single integrative framework.

Viewing pain from a functional perspective also gives useful insights that can be linked to the neural processes. The evolution of an anti-nociceptive system in addition to the nociceptive systems raises issues on the adaptive value of such joint control. The observation that the anti-nociceptive system is recruited at times when it would be maladaptive to react to tissue damage, as in focused fight or flight, gives an indicator of function. Such considerations could provide a functional context in which to view the clinical role of distraction and positive expectation in bringing pain relief.

 See the video coverage for this chapter which shows how psychology can help people who are in pain.

Summary of Chapter 14

1 A nociceptive system underlies pain, whereas activity within an anti-nociceptive system lowers pain.

2 Pain has adaptive value in protecting animals from tissue damage and keeping them out of harm until recovery. At times it could be adaptive to inhibit pain and this seems to be the reason for the evolutionary appearance of an anti-nociceptive system.

3 Nociceptive neurons detect tissue damage and this leads normally to the sensation of pain. However, pain is not simply a one-to-one reflection of their activity.

4 As a metaphor, the spinal cord is the location of a 'gate'. As the gate opens, so nociceptive information passes, on its way to the brain. When the gate is closed information does not pass further.

5 It is possible to identify brain regions that have distinct roles in the discriminative and affective aspects of pain.

6 The role of different analgesics (pain-reducing substances) can be understood in terms of their actions at various sites in the nociceptive system.

7 Referred pain and phantom limb pain are two phenomena that challenge any simple interpretation of pain.

8 The placebo effect and pain triggered by witnessing another person in pain point to the complex cognitive processing that also forms part of the causation of pain.

Further reading

Pain is viewed in a psychological and philosophical context in Aydede (2006). For a biopsychosocial perspective on pain, see Gatchel *et al.* (2007). For the work of the pioneers of gate theory, see Melzack and Wall (2008) and Wall (2002). For hypnosis and its relation to gate theory, see Chaves and Dworkin (1997). Cognitive therapy and pain is described by Thorn (2004). For the placebo effect, see Petrovic (2010). For neuropathic pain, see Bennett (2010). For chronic pain, see Dickman and Simpson (2008). For phantom effects, see Ramachandran and Blakeslee (1998).

Answers

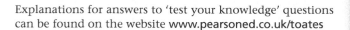

Explanations for answers to 'test your knowledge' questions can be found on the website **www.pearsoned.co.uk/toates**

14.1 An antagonist to the nociceptive system; an agonist to the anti-nociceptive system.

14.2 Freezing is adaptive, since by remaining motionless an animal tends to avoid detection. If it were to respond to tissue damage by, for example, licking a wound this would act counter to the effect.

14.3 An increase in pain.

14.4 The large-diameter neuron and the two neurons labelled 'Descending pathways'.

14.5 (i) The inhibitory neurochemical and (ii) enkephalin

14.6 Functional neuroimaging would be expected to show increased activity in brain regions forming the pain neuromatrix.

14.7 High; low

14.8 (ii) Lignocaine

14.9 Increased pain felt as coming from the skin.

14.10 Activated anterior cingulate cortex (and possibly interoceptive cortex); Area 3a not activated.

14 Sleep, Dreaming, and Circadian Rhythms

How Much Do You Need to Sleep?

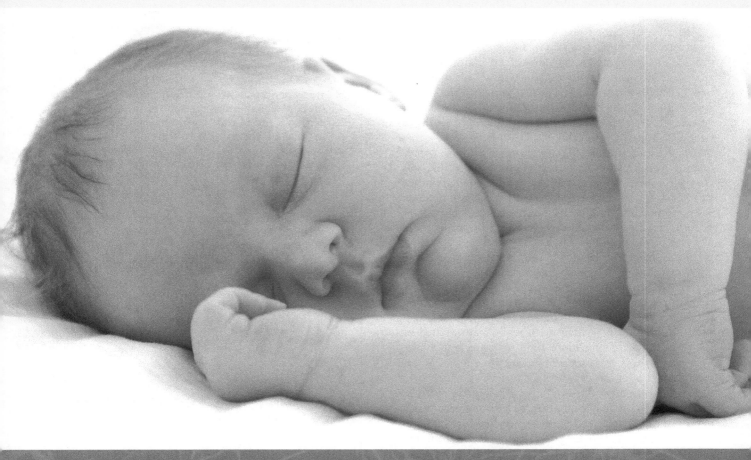

Most of us have a fondness for eating and sex—the two highly esteemed motivated behaviors discussed in Chapter 12 and 13. But the amount of time devoted to these behaviors by even the most amorous gourmands pales in comparison to the amount of time spent sleeping: Most of us will sleep for well over 175,000 hours in our lifetimes. This extraordinary commitment of time implies that sleep fulfills a critical biological function. But what is it? And what about dreaming: Why do we spend so much time dreaming? And why do we tend to get sleepy at about the same time every day? Answers to these questions await you in this chapter.

Almost every time I give a lecture about sleep, somebody asks "How much sleep do we need?" and each time, I provide the same unsatisfying answer. I explain that there are two fundamentally different answers to this question, but that neither has emerged a clear winner. One answer stresses the presumed health-promoting and recuperative powers of sleep and suggests that people need as much sleep as they can comfortably get. The other answer is that many of us sleep more than we need to and are consequently sleeping part of our lives away. Just think how your life could change if you slept 5 hours per night instead of 8. You would have an extra 21 waking hours each week, a mind-boggling 10,952 hours each decade.

As I prepared to write this chapter, I began to think of some of the personal implications of the idea that we get more sleep than we need. That is when I decided to do something a bit unconventional. While I write this chapter, I am going to be your subject in a sleep-reduction experiment. I am going to try to get no more than 5 hours of sleep per night—11:00 p.m. to 4:00 a.m.—until this chapter is written. As I begin, I am excited by the prospect of having more time to write, but a little worried that this extra time might be obtained at a personal cost that is too dear.

It is now the next day—4:50 Saturday morning to be exact—and I am just beginning to write. There was a party last night, and I didn't make it to bed by 11:00; but considering that I slept for only 3 hours and 35 minutes, I feel quite good. I wonder what I will feel like later in the day. In any case, I will report my experiences to you at the end of the chapter.

The following case study challenges several common beliefs about sleep. Ponder its implications before proceeding to the body of the chapter.

The Case of the Woman Who Wouldn't Sleep

Miss M . . . is a busy lady who finds her ration of twenty-three hours of wakefulness still insufficient for her needs. Even though she is now retired she is still busy in the community, helping sick friends whenever requested. She is an active painter and . . . writer. Although she becomes tired physically, when she needs to sit down to rest her legs, she does not ever report feeling sleepy. During the night she sits on her bed . . . reading, writing, crocheting or painting. At about 2:00 a.m. she falls asleep without any preceding drowsiness often while still holding a book in her hands. When she wakes about an hour later, she feels as wide awake as ever. . . .

We invited her along to the laboratory. She came willingly but on the first evening we hit our first snag. She announced that she did not sleep at all if she had interesting things to do, and by her reckoning a visit to a university sleep laboratory counted as very interesting. Moreover, for the first time in years, she had someone to talk to for the whole of the night. So we talked.

In the morning we broke into shifts so that some could sleep while at least one person stayed with her and entertained her during the next day. The second night was a repeat performance of the first night. . . .

In the end we prevailed upon her to allow us to apply EEG electrodes and to leave her sitting comfortably on the bed in the bedroom. She had promised that she would co-operate by not resisting sleep although she claimed not to be especially tired. . . . At approximately 1:30 a.m., the EEG record showed the first signs of sleep even though . . . she was still sitting with the book in her hands. . . .

The only substantial difference between her sleep and what we might have expected from any other . . . lady was that it was of short duration. . . . [After 99 minutes], she had no further interest in sleep and asked to . . . join our company again.

("The Case of the Woman Who Wouldn't Sleep," from *The Sleep Instinct* by R. Meddis. Copyright © 1977, Routledge & Kegan Paul, London, pp. 42–44. Reprinted by permission of the Taylor & Francis Group.)

14.1

The Psychophysiological Measures and Stages of Sleep

Many changes occur in the body during sleep. This section introduces you to the major ones.

The Three Standard Psychophysiological Measures of Sleep

There are major changes in the human EEG during the course of a night's sleep (Loomis, Harvey, & Hobart, 1936). Although the EEG waves that accompany sleep are generally high-voltage and slow, there are periods throughout the night that are dominated by low-voltage, fast waves similar to those in nonsleeping subjects. In 1953, Aserinsky and Kleitman discovered that *rapid eye movements (REMs)* occur under the closed eyelids of sleeping subjects during these periods of low-voltage, fast EEG activity. And in 1962, Berger and Oswald discovered that there is also a loss of electromyographic activity in the neck muscles during these same sleep periods. Subsequently, the **electroencephalogram (EEG)**, the **electro-oculogram (EOG)**, and the neck **electromyogram (EMG)** became the three standard psychophysiological bases for defining stages of sleep (Rechtschaffen & Kales, 1968)—see Chapter 5.

Figure 14.1 depicts a subject participating in a sleep experiment. A subject's first night's sleep in a sleep laboratory is often fitful. That's why it is the usual practice to have each subject sleep several nights in the laboratory before commencing a study. The disturbance of sleep observed during the first night in a sleep laboratory is called the *first-night phenomenon*. It is well known to graders of introductory psychology examinations because of the creative definitions of it that are offered by students who forget that it is a sleep-related, rather than a sex-related, phenomenon.

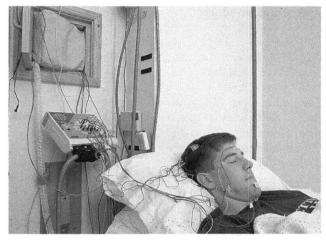

FIGURE 14.1   A subject participating in a sleep experiment.

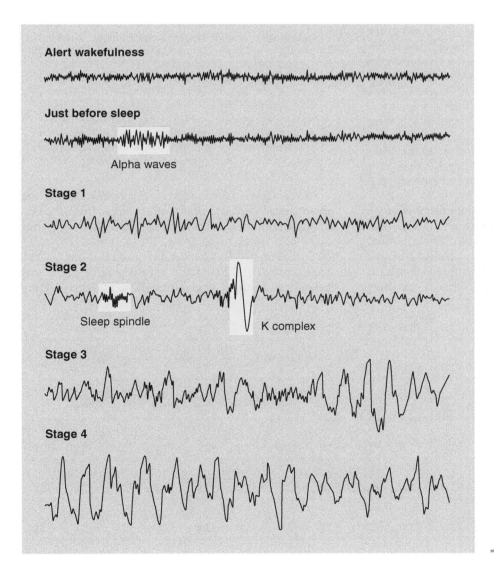

Four Stages of Sleep EEG

There are four stages of sleep EEG: stage 1, stage 2, stage 3, and stage 4. Examples of these are presented in Figure 14.2.

After the eyes are shut and a person prepares to go to sleep, **alpha waves**—waxing and waning bursts of 8- to 12-Hz EEG waves—begin to punctuate the low-voltage, high-frequency waves of active wakefulness. Then, as the person falls asleep, there is a sudden transition to a period of stage 1 sleep EEG. The stage 1 sleep EEG is a low-voltage, high-frequency signal that is similar to, but slower than, that of active wakefulness.

There is a gradual increase in EEG voltage and a decrease in EEG frequency as the person progresses from stage 1 sleep through stages 2, 3, and 4. Accordingly, the stage 2 sleep EEG has a slightly higher amplitude and a lower frequency than the

FIGURE 14.2   The EEG of alert wakefulness, the EEG that precedes sleep onset, and the four stages of sleep EEG. Each trace is about 10 seconds long.

stage 1 EEG; in addition, it is punctuated by two characteristic wave forms: K complexes and sleep spindles. Each *K complex* is a single large negative wave (upward deflection) followed immediately by a single large positive wave (downward deflection). Each *sleep spindle* is a 1- to 2-second waxing and waning burst of 12- to 14-Hz waves. The stage 3 sleep EEG is defined by the occasional presence of **delta waves**—the largest and slowest EEG waves, with a frequency of 1 to 2 Hz—whereas the stage 4 sleep EEG is defined by a predominance of delta waves.

Once subjects reach stage 4 EEG sleep, they stay there for a time, and then they retreat back through the stages of sleep to stage 1. However, when they return to stage 1, things are not at all the same as they were the first time through. The first period of stage 1 EEG during a night's sleep (**initial stage 1 EEG**) is not marked by any striking electromyographic or electrooculographic changes, whereas subsequent periods of stage 1 sleep EEG (**emergent stage 1 EEG**) are accompanied by REMs and by a loss of tone in the muscles of the body core.

After the first cycle of sleep EEG—from initial stage 1 to stage 4 and back to emergent stage 1—the rest of the night is spent going back and forth through the stages. Figure 14.3 illustrates the EEG cycles of a typical night's sleep and the close relation between emergent stage 1 sleep, REMs, and the loss of tone in core muscles. Notice that each cycle tends to be about 90 minutes long and that, as the night progresses, more and more time is spent in emergent stage 1 sleep, and less and less time is spent in the other stages, particularly stage 4. Notice also that there are brief periods during the night when the subject is awake; the subject usually does not remember these periods of wakefulness in the morning.

Let's pause here to get some sleep-stage terms straight. The sleep associated with emergent stage 1 EEG is usually called **REM sleep**, (pronounced "rehm"), after the associated rapid eye movements; whereas all other stages of sleep together are called *NREM sleep* (non-REM sleep). Stages 3 and 4 together are referred to as **slow-wave sleep (SWS)**, after the delta waves that characterize them.

REMs, loss of core-muscle tone, and a low-amplitude, high-frequency EEG are not the only physiological correlates of REM sleep. Cerebral activity (e.g., oxygen consumption, blood flow, and neural firing) increases to waking levels in many brain structures, and there

is a general increase in autonomic nervous system activity (e.g., in blood pressure, pulse, and respiration). Also, the muscles of the extremities occasionally twitch, and there is always some degree of clitoral or penile erection.

14.2
REM Sleep and Dreaming

Nathaniel Kleitman's laboratory was an exciting place in 1953. Kleitman's students had just discovered REM sleep, and they were driven by the fascinating implication of their discovery. With the exception of the loss of tone in the core muscles, all of the other measures suggested that REM sleep episodes were emotion-charged. Could REM sleep be the physiological correlate of dreaming? Could it provide researchers with a window into the subjective inner world of dreams? The researchers began by waking a few subjects in the middle of REM episodes:

> The vivid recall that could be elicited in the middle of the night when a subject was awakened while his eyes were moving rapidly was nothing short of miraculous. It [seemed to open] . . . an exciting new world to the subjects whose only previous dream memories had been the vague morning-after recall. Now, instead of perhaps some fleeting glimpse into the dream world each night, the subjects could be tuned into the middle of as many as ten or twelve dreams every night. (From *Some Must Watch While Some Must Sleep* by William C. Dement, Portable Stanford Books, Stanford Alumni Association, Stanford University, 1978, p. 37. Used by permission of William C. Dement.)

Strong support for the theory that REM sleep is the physiological correlate of dreaming came from the observation that 80% of awakenings from REM sleep but only 7% of awakenings from NREM (non-REM) sleep led to dream recall. The dreams recalled from NREM sleep tended to be isolated experiences (e.g., "I was falling"), while those associated with REM sleep took the

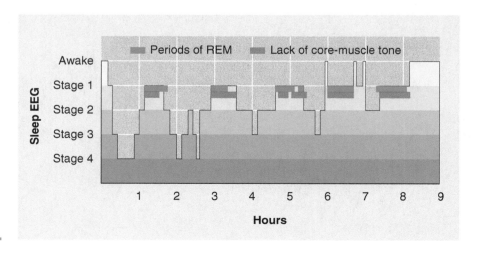

FIGURE 14.3 The course of EEG stages during a typical night's sleep and the relation of emergent stage 1 EEG to REMs and lack of tone in core muscles.

form of stories, or narratives. The phenomenon of dreaming, which for centuries had been the subject of wild speculation, was finally rendered accessible to scientific investigation.

Testing Common Beliefs about Dreaming

The high correlation between REM sleep and dream recall provided an opportunity to test some common beliefs about dreaming. The following are five such beliefs that were among the first to be addressed.

- Many people believe that external stimuli can become incorporated into their dreams. Dement and Wolpert (1958) sprayed water on sleeping subjects after they had been in REM sleep for a few minutes, and a few seconds after the spray, each subject was awakened. In 14 of 33 cases, the water was incorporated into the dream report. The following narrative was reported by a subject who had been dreaming that he was acting in a play:

  > I was walking behind the leading lady when she suddenly collapsed and water was dripping on her. I ran over to her and water was dripping on my back and head. The roof was leaking. . . . I looked up and there was a hole in the roof. I dragged her over to the side of the stage and began pulling the curtains. Then I woke up. (p. 550)

- Some people believe that dreams last only an instant, but research suggests that dreams run on "real time." In one study (Dement & Kleitman, 1957), subjects were awakened 5 or 15 minutes after the beginning of a REM episode and asked to decide on the basis of the duration of the events in their dreams whether they had been dreaming for 5 or 15 minutes. They were correct in 92 of 111 cases.
- Some people claim that they do not dream. However, these people have just as much REM sleep as normal dreamers. Moreover, they report dreams if they are awakened during REM episodes (Goodenough et al., 1959), although they do so less frequently than do normal dreamers.
- Penile erections are commonly assumed to be indicative of dreams with sexual content. However, erections are no more complete during dreams with frank sexual content than during those without it (Karacan et al., 1966). Even babies have REM-related penile erections.
- Most people believe that sleeptalking (*somniloquy*) and sleepwalking (*somnambulism*) occur only during dreaming. This is not so (see Dyken, Yamada, & Lin-Dyken, 2001). Sleepwalking usually occurs during stage 3 or 4 sleep, and it never occurs during dreaming, when core muscles tend to be totally relaxed. Sleeptalking has no special association with REM sleep—it can occur during any stage but often occurs during a transition to wakefulness.

The Interpretation of Dreams

The idea that dreams are disguised messages has a long history. For example, the Bible describes how a dream of seven lean cattle following and devouring seven fat cattle warned that seven years of famine would follow seven years of plenty. It was Freud's theory of dreams that refined this view of dreams and gave it legitimacy.

Freud believed that dreams are triggered by unacceptable repressed wishes, often of a sexual nature. He argued that because dreams represent unacceptable wishes, the dreams we experience (our *manifest dreams*) are merely disguised versions of our real dreams (our *latent dreams*): An unconscious censor disguises and subtracts information from our real dreams so that we can endure them. Freud thus concluded that one of the keys to understanding people and dealing with their psychological problems is to expose the meaning of their latent dreams through the interpretation of their manifest dreams.

There is no convincing evidence for the Freudian theory of dreams; indeed, the brain science of the 1890s, which served as its foundation, is now obsolete. Nevertheless, the Freudian theory of dreams has been the basis for many interesting stories; as a result, it continues to be widely disseminated to the general public through the entertainment and communication media as if it were fact. Many accept the notion that dreams bubble up from a troubled subconscious and that they represent repressed thoughts and wishes.

The modern alternative to the Freudian theory of dreams is Hobson's (1989) activation-synthesis theory (see Eiser, 2005). It is based on the observation that, during REM sleep, many brain-stem circuits become active and bombard the cerebral cortex with neural signals. The essence of the **activation-synthesis theory** is that the information supplied to the cortex during REM sleep is largely random and that the resulting dream is the cortex's effort to make sense of these random signals. Activation-synthesis theory does not deny that dreams have meaning, but it differs from Freudian theory in terms of where that meaning lies. Hobson's dreamers reveal themselves by what they add to the random jumble of brain-stem signals in order to create a coherent story.

14.3

Why Do We Sleep, and Why Do We Sleep When We Do?

Now that you have been introduced to the properties of sleep and its various stages, the focus of this chapter shifts to a consideration of two fundamental questions about sleep: Why do we sleep? And why do we sleep when we do?

Two kinds of theories for sleep have been proposed: *recuperation theories* and *circadian theories*. The differences between these two theoretical approaches are revealed by the answers they offer to the two fundamental questions about sleep.

The essence of **recuperation theories of sleep** is that being awake disrupts the *homeostasis* (internal physiological stability) of the body in some way and sleep is required to restore it. Various recuperation theories differ in terms of the particular physiological disruption they propose as the trigger for sleep—for example, it is commonly believed that the function of sleep is to restore energy levels. However, regardless of the particular function postulated by restoration theories of sleep, they all imply that sleepiness is triggered by a deviation from homeostasis caused by wakefulness and that sleep is terminated by a return to homeostasis.

The essence of **circadian theories of sleep** is that sleep is not a reaction to the disruptive effects of being awake but the result of an internal 24-hour timing mechanism (*circadian* means "lasting about 1 day")—that is, we humans are all programmed to sleep at night regardless of what happens to us during the day. According to these theories, we have evolved to sleep at night because sleep protects us from accident and predation during the night. (Remember that humans evolved long before the advent of artificial lighting.)

Circadian theories of sleep focus more on when we sleep than on the function of sleep. However, one extreme  version of a circadian theory proposes that sleep plays no role in the efficient physiological functioning of the body. According to this theory, early humans had enough time to get their eating, drinking, and reproducing out of the way during the daytime, and their strong motivation to sleep at night evolved to conserve their energy resources and to make them less susceptible to mishap (e.g., predation) in the dark. This theory suggests that sleep is like reproductive behavior in the sense that we are highly motivated to engage in it, but we don't need it to stay healthy.

Some metaphors may help you think about the difference between the recuperation and circadian approaches to sleep. In essence, recuperation theories view sleep as a  nightly repair person who fixes damage produced by wakefulness, while circadian theories regard sleep as a strict parent who demands inactivity because it keeps us out of trouble. It seems that choosing between the recuperation and circadian approaches is the logical first step in the search for the physiological basis of sleep. Several lines of research that have a bearing on the question of which theories explain sleep most convincingly will be discussed in the sections that follow. Perhaps not surprisingly, evidence suggests that both recuperative and circadian factors play roles in sleep.

Comparative Analysis of Sleep

All mammals and birds sleep, and their sleep is much like ours—characterized by high-amplitude, low-frequency EEG waves punctuated by periods of low-amplitude, high-frequency waves (see Winson, 1993). Even fish, reptiles, amphibians, and insects go through periods of inactivity and unresponsiveness that are similar to mammalian sleep (e.g., Shaw et al., 2000). Table 14.1 gives the average number of hours per day that various mammalian species spend sleeping.

The comparative investigation of sleep has led to several important con- 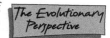 clusions. Let's consider four of these.

First, the fact that all mammals and birds sleep suggests that sleep serves some important physiological function, rather than merely protecting animals from mishap and conserving energy. The evidence is strongest in species that are at increased risk of predation when they sleep (e.g., antelopes) and in species that have evolved complex mechanisms that enable them to sleep. For example, some marine mammals, such as dolphins, sleep with only half of their brain at a time so that the other half can control resurfacing for air (see Rattenborg, Amlaner, & Lima, 2000). It is against the logic of natural selection for some animals to risk predation while sleeping and for others to

Mammalian Species	Hours of Sleep Per Day
TABLE 14.1	**The Average Number of Hours Slept per Day by Various Mammalian Species**
Giant sloth	20
Opossum, brown bat	19
Giant armadillo	18
Owl monkey, nine-banded armadillo	17
Arctic ground squirrel	16
Tree shrew	15
Cat, golden hamster	14
Mouse, rat, gray wolf, ground squirrel	13
Arctic fox, chinchilla, gorilla, raccoon	12
Mountain beaver	11
Jaguar, vervet monkey, hedgehog	10
Rhesus monkey, chimpanzee, baboon, red fox	9
Human, rabbit, guinea pig, pig	8
Gray seal, gray hyrax, Brazilian tapir	6
Tree hyrax, rock hyrax	5
Cow, goat, elephant, donkey, sheep	3
Roe deer, horse	2

have evolved complex mechanisms to permit them to sleep, unless sleep itself serves some critical function.

Second, the fact that all mammals and birds sleep suggests that the function of sleep is not some special, higher-order human function. For example, suggestions that sleep helps humans reprogram our complex brains or that it permits some kind of emotional release to maintain our mental health are improbable in view of the comparative evidence.

Third, the large between-species differences in sleep time suggest that although sleep may be essential for survival, it is not necessarily needed in large quantities (refer to Table 14.1). Horses and many other animals get by quite nicely on 2 or 3 hours of sleep per day.

Fourth, many studies have tried to identify some characteristic that identifies various species as long sleepers or short sleepers. Why do cats tend to sleep about 14 hours a day and horses only about 2? Under the influence of recuperation theories, researchers have focused on energy-related factors in their efforts. However, there is no strong relationship between a species' sleep time and its level of activity, its body size, or its body temperature (see Siegel, 2005). The fact that giant sloths sleep 20 hours per day is a strong argument against the theory that sleep is a compensatory reaction to energy expenditure—similarly, exercise has been shown to have little or no effect on subsequent sleep in humans (Youngstedt & Kline, 2006). In contrast, circadian theories correctly predict that the daily sleep time of each species is related to how vulnerable it is while it is asleep and how much time it must spend each day to feed itself and to take care of its other survival requirements. For example, zebras must graze almost continuously to get enough to eat and are extremely vulnerable to predatory attack when they are asleep—and they sleep only about 2 hours per day. In contrast, African lions often sleep more or less continuously for 2 or 3 days after they have gorged themselves on a kill. Figure 14.4 says it all.

FIGURE 14.4 After gorging themselves on a kill, African lions often sleep almost continuously for 2 or 3 days. And where do they sleep? Anywhere they want!

Circadian Sleep Cycles

The world in which we live cycles from light to dark and back again once every 24 hours, and most surface-dwelling species have adapted to this regular change in their environment by developing a variety of so-called **circadian rhythms** (see Foster & Kreitzman, 2004). For example, most species display a regular circadian sleep–wake cycle. Humans take advantage of the light of day to take care of their biological needs, and then they sleep for much of the night; *nocturnal animals*, such as rats, sleep for much of the day and stay awake at night.

Although the sleep–wake cycle is the most obvious circadian rhythm, it is difficult to find a physiological, biochemical, or behavioral process in animals that does not display some measure of circadian rhythmicity (Gillette & Sejnowski, 2005). Each day, our bodies adjust themselves in a variety of ways to meet the demands of the two environments in which we live: light and dark.

Our circadian cycles are kept on their once-every-24-hours schedule by temporal cues in the environment. The most important of these cues for the regulation of mammalian circadian rhythms is the daily cycle of light and dark. Environmental cues, such as the light–dark cycle, that can *entrain* (control the timing of) circadian rhythms are called **zeitgebers** (pronounced "ZITE-gay-bers"), a German word that means "time givers." In controlled laboratory environments, it is possible to lengthen or shorten circadian cycles by adjusting the duration of the light–dark cycle; for example, when exposed to alternating 10-hour periods of light and 10-hour periods of dark, subjects' circadian cycles begin to conform to a 20-hour day. In a world without 24-hour cycles of light and dark, other *zeitgebers* can entrain circadian cycles. For example, the circadian sleep–wake cycles of hamsters living in continuous darkness or in continuous light can be entrained by regular daily bouts of social interaction, hoarding, eating, or exercise (see Mistlberger et al., 1996; Sinclair & Mistlberger, 1997). Hamsters display particularly clear circadian cycles and thus are frequent subjects of research on circadian rhythms.

Free-Running Circadian Sleep–Wake Cycles

The study of sleep in the absence of *zeitgebers* provides a powerful method for studying regulation of the temporal pattern of sleep. What happens to sleep–wake cycles and other circadian rhythms in an environment that is devoid of *zeitgebers*? Remarkably, under conditions in which there are absolutely no temporal cues, humans and other animals maintain all of their circadian rhythms. Circadian rhythms in constant environments are said to be **free-running rhythms**, and their duration is called the **free-running period**. Free-running periods vary in length from subject to subject, are of relatively constant duration within a given subject, and are usually longer than 24 hours—about 25 hours in most humans (see Lavie, 2001). It seems that we all have an internal *biological clock* that habitually runs a little slow unless it is entrained by time-related cues in the environment. A typical free-running circadian sleep–wake cycle is illustrated in Figure 14.5. Notice its regularity. Without any external cues, this man fell asleep approximately every 25.3 hours for an entire month.

Perhaps the most remarkable characteristic of free-running circadian cycles is that they do not have to be learned. Even rats that are born and raised in an unchanging laboratory environment (in continuous light or in continuous darkness) display regular free-running sleep–wake cycles of about 25 hours (Richter, 1971).

Many animals display a circadian cycle of body temperature that is related to their circadian sleep–wake cycle: They tend to sleep during the falling phase of their circadian body temperature cycle and awaken during its rising phase. However, when subjects are housed in constant laboratory environments, their sleep–wake and body temperature cycles sometimes break away from one another. This phenomenon is called **internal desynchronization**. For example, in one case, the free-running periods of *both* the sleep–wake and body temperature cycles of a human subject were initially 25.7 hours; then, for some unknown reason, there was an increase in the free-running period of the sleep–wake cycle to 33.4 hours and a decrease in the free-running period of the body temperature cycle to 25.1 hours. The potential for the simultaneous existence of two different free-running periods suggests that there is more than one circadian timing mechanism, and that sleep is not causally related to the decreases in body temperature that are normally associated with it.

So, what has research on circadian sleep–wake cycles taught us about the function of sleep? The fact that the regularity of the free-running period of such cycles is maintained despite day-to-day variations in physical and mental activity provides strong support for the dominance of circadian factors over recuperative factors in the regulation of sleep. Indeed, there have been several attempts to change the timing of sleep in both human and nonhuman subjects by having them engage in intensive physical or mental activity or by exposing them to infectious agents, but these attempts have had little, if any, effect on the subjects' subsequent sleep (see Rechtschaffen, 1998).

There is another point about free-running circadian sleep–wake cycles that is incompatible with recuperative theories of sleep. On occasions when subjects stay awake longer than usual, the following sleep time is shorter rather than longer (Wever, 1979). Humans and other animals are programmed to have sleep–wake cycles of approximately 24 hours; hence, the more wakefulness there is during a cycle, the less time there is for sleep.

Jet Lag and Shift Work

People in modern industrialized societies are faced with two different disruptions of circadian rhythmicity: jet lag and shift work. **Jet lag** occurs when the *zeitgebers* that control the phases of various circadian rhythms are accelerated during east-bound flights (*phase advances*) or decelerated during west-bound flights (*phase delays*). In *shift work*, the *zeitgebers* stay the same, but workers are forced to adjust their natural sleep–wake cycles in order to meet the demands of changing work schedules. Both of these disruptions produce sleep disturbances, fatigue, general malaise, and deficits on tests of physical and cognitive function. The disturbances can last for many days; for example, it typically takes about 10 days to completely adjust to the phase advance of 10.5 hours that one experiences on a Tokyo-to-Boston flight.

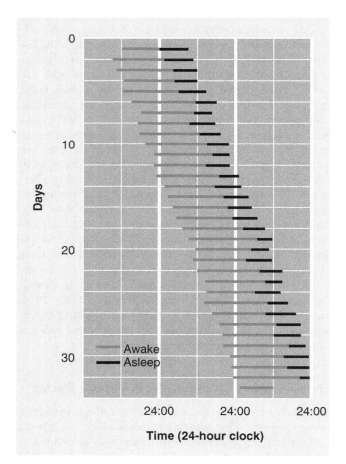

FIGURE 14.5 A free-running circadian sleep–wake cycle 25.3 hours in duration. Despite living in an unchanging environment with no time cues, the subject went to sleep each day approximately 1.3 hours later than he had the day before. (Adapted from Wever, 1979, p. 30.)

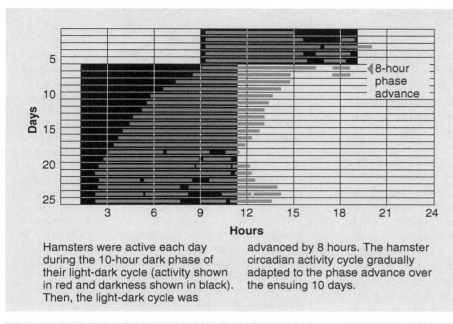

FIGURE 14.6 A period of forced exercise accelerates adaptation to an 8-hour phase advance in the circadian light–dark cycle. Daily activity is shown in red; periods of darkness are shown in black; and the period of forced exercise is shown in green. (Adapted from Mrosovsky & Salmon, 1987.)

Hamsters were active each day during the 10-hour dark phase of their light-dark cycle (activity shown in red and darkness shown in black). Then, the light-dark cycle was advanced by 8 hours. The hamster circadian activity cycle gradually adapted to the phase advance over the ensuing 10 days.

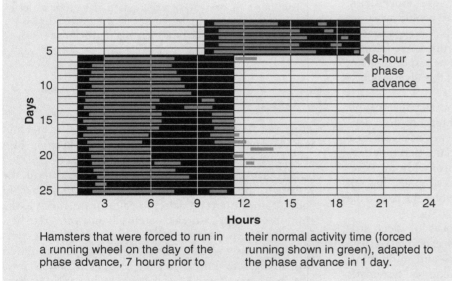

Hamsters that were forced to run in a running wheel on the day of the phase advance, 7 hours prior to their normal activity time (forced running shown in green), adapted to the phase advance in 1 day.

activity adapted quickly to an 8-hour advance in their light–dark cycle (see Figure 14.6).

Companies that employ shift workers have had great success in improving the productivity and job satisfaction of those workers by scheduling phase delays rather than phase advances; whenever possible, shift workers are transferred from their current schedule to one that begins later in the day. It is much more difficult to go to sleep 4 hours earlier and get up 4 hours earlier (a phase advance) than it is to go to sleep 4 hours later and get up 4 hours later (a phase delay). That is why east-bound flights tend to be more problematic for travelers than west-bound flights.

14.6

Effects of Sleep Deprivation

What can be done to reduce the disruptive effects of jet lag and shift work? Two behavioral approaches have been proposed for the reduction of jet lag. One is gradually shifting one's sleep–wake cycle in the days prior to the flight. The other is administering treatments after the flight that promote the required shift in the circadian rhythm. For example, exposure to intense light early in the morning following an east-bound flight accelerates adaptation to the phase advance. Similarly, the results of a study of hamsters (Mrosovsky & Salmon, 1987) suggest that a good workout early in the morning of the first day after an east-bound flight might accelerate adaptation to the phase advance; hamsters that engaged in one 3-hour bout of wheel running 7 hours before their usual period of

Recuperation theories of sleep make specific predictions about the effects of sleep deprivation. Because recuperation theories are based on the premise that sleep is a response to the accumulation of some debilitating effect of wakefulness, they predict (1) that long periods of wakefulness will produce physiological and behavioral disturbances (2) that these disturbances will grow steadily worse as the sleep deprivation continues, and (3) that after a period of deprivation has ended, much of the missed sleep will be regained. Have these predictions been confirmed?

This section begins with a cautionary note about the personal experience of sleep deprivation and a review of two classic sleep-deprivation case studies.

Personal Experience of Sleep Deprivation: A Cautionary Note

I am sure that you have experienced the negative effects of sleep loss. When you sleep substantially less than you are used to, the next day you feel crabby and unable to function as well as you usually do. Although such experiences of sleep deprivation are compelling, you need to be cautious in interpreting them. Let me illustrate this point by referring to a recurring news story.

Every few months, I see on the television news or read in the newspaper that people need more sleep. An "expert" explains that many people in *Thinking Clearly* modern society work such long, irregular hours that they do not sleep enough and suffer all kinds of adverse effects as a result. To make this point, there are typically interviews with people such as long-distance truck drivers and shift workers who describe their sleep-related problems. Two things never seem to occur to the news reporters or to the "expert." First, it never occurs to them that most people who sleep little or irregularly do so because they are under stress. Second, it never occurs to them that people who are forced to change their schedule of sleep also experience a major disruption of their circadian rhythms. Accordingly, stress and circadian disruptions might be responsible for, or at least might contribute to, many of the adverse effects commonly attributed to loss of sleep.

Further complicating matters is the fact that people have proven to be poor judges of the impact of sleep deprivation on their performance. Both types of errors have been reported: In some cases, people claim that they cannot function after sleep loss but perform without decrement; in other cases, people claim that sleep loss has not adversely affected their performance when the data tell a different story (see Durmer & Dinges, 2005).

Consequently, your own experiences of sleep loss and the testimonials of others who have experienced sleep loss need to be interpreted cautiously—and so do mine. Assessing the effects of sleep loss requires systematic research.

Two Classic Sleep-Deprivation Case Studies

Let's begin our consideration of the research on sleep deprivation by looking at two classic case studies. First is the case study of a group of sleep-deprived students, described by Kleitman (1963); second is the case of Randy Gardner, described by Dement (1978).

The Case of the Sleep-Deprived Students

While there were differences in the many subjective experiences of the sleep-evading persons, there were several features common to most. . . . [D]uring the first night the subject did not feel very tired or sleepy. He could read or study or do laboratory work, without much attention from the watcher, but usually felt an attack of drowsiness between 3 A.M. and 6 A.M. . . . Next morning the subject felt well, except for a slight malaise which always appeared on sitting down and resting for any length of time. However, if he occupied himself with his ordinary daily tasks, he was likely to forget having spent a sleepless night. During the second night . . . reading or study was next to impossible because sitting quietly was conducive to even greater sleepiness. As during the first night, there came a 2–3 hour period in the early hours of the morning when the desire for sleep was almost overpowering. . . . Later in the morning the sleepiness diminished once more, and the subject could perform routine laboratory work, as usual. It was not safe for him to sit down, however, without danger of falling asleep, particularly if he attended lectures. . . .

The third night resembled the second, and the fourth day was like the third. . . . At the end of that time the individual was as sleepy as he was likely to be. Those who continued to stay awake experienced the wavelike increase and decrease in sleepiness with the greatest drowsiness at about the same time every night. (Kleitman, 1963, pp. 220–221)

The Case of Randy Gardner

As part of a 1965 science fair project, Randy Gardner and two classmates, who were entrusted with keeping him awake, planned to break the then world record of 260 hours of consecutive wakefulness. Dement read about the project in the newspaper and, seeing an opportunity to collect some important data, joined the team, much to the comfort of Randy's worried parents. Randy proved to be a friendly and cooperative subject, although he did complain vigorously when his team would not permit him to close his eyes for more than a few seconds at a time. However, in no sense could Randy's behavior be considered abnormal or disturbed. Near the end of his vigil, Randy held a press conference attended by reporters and television crews from all over the United States, and he conducted himself impeccably. When asked how he had managed to stay awake for 11 days, he replied politely, "It's just mind over matter." Randy went to sleep exactly 264 hours and 12 minutes after his alarm clock had awakened him 11 days before. And how long did he sleep? Only 14 hours the first night, and thereafter he returned to his usual 8-hour schedule. Although it may seem amazing that Randy did not have to sleep longer to "catch up" on his lost sleep, the lack of substantial recovery sleep is typical of such cases.

(From *Some Must Watch While Some Must Sleep* by William C. Dement, Portable Stanford Books, Stanford Alumni Association, Stanford University, 1978, pp. 38–39. Used by permission of William C. Dement.)

Experimental Studies of Sleep Deprivation in Humans

Since the first studies of sleep deprivation by Dement and Kleitman in the mid-20th century, there have been hundreds of studies assessing the effects on human subjects of sleep-deprivation schedules ranging from a slightly reduced amount of sleep during one night to total sleep deprivation for several nights. The studies have assessed the effects of these schedules on dozens of different objective measures: measures of sleepiness, mood, cognition, motor performance, physiological function, and even molecular function (see Cirelli, 2006). Indeed, the literature on the effects of sleep deprivation is so immense and varied that it is particularly difficult to summarize.

Even moderate amounts of sleep deprivation—for example, 3 or 4 hours in one night—have been found to have three consistent effects. First, sleep-deprived subjects display an increase in sleepiness: They report being more sleepy, and they fall asleep more quickly if given the opportunity. Second, sleep-deprived subjects display disturbances on various written tests of mood. And third, they perform poorly on tests of vigilance, such as listening to a series of tones and responding when one differs slightly from the rest.

The effects of sleep deprivation on complex cognitive functions have been less consistent. One problem is that relatively few studies have assessed such effects of sleep deprivation—researchers have preferred to assess subjects' performance on the simple, dull, monotonous tasks most sensitive to the effects of sleep deprivation (see Harrison & Horne, 2000). Nevertheless, recent studies have been able to demonstrate disruption of the performance of complex cognitive tasks by sleep deprivation (see Durmer & Dinges, 2005), but in general at least 24 hours of total sleep deprivation have been required to produce consistent effects (e.g., Killgore, Balkin, & Wesensten, 2006; Strangman et al., 2005).

It has recently been suggested that only some kinds of complex cognitive abilities are negatively affected by sleep loss. Tasks that involve logical deduction or critical thinking are thought to be largely immune to the disruptive effects of sleep loss, whereas tests of executive function are thought to be less resistant. **Executive function** refers to a collection of cognitive abilities that appear to depend on the prefrontal cortex (see Nilsson et al., 2005). These abilities include assimilating changing information, updating plans and strategies, innovative thinking, lateral thinking, insightful thinking, and reference memory (memory for task-related general principles and skills). Consequently, recent studies have focused on the effects of sleep deprivation on prefrontal cortex function (e.g., Curcio, Ferrara, & De Gennaro, 2006).

The adverse effects of sleep deprivation on physical activity have been surprisingly slight and inconsistent in view of the general belief that a good night's sleep is essential for optimal motor performance. Here are three findings, which I selected because each study included many measures:

- Van Helder and Radomski (1989) found that periods of sleep deprivation of up to 72 hours had no effect on tests of strength or motor performance.
- Martin (1981) found that time to exhaustion was reduced in subjects who had endured 36 hours of sleep deprivation, but since no cardiovascular or metabolic measures were adversely affected, he attributed the finding to psychological factors.
- Meney and colleagues (1998) found no significant effect of 24 hours of sleep deprivation on measures of muscle strength, work rate, or heart rate.

After 2 or 3 days of continuous sleep deprivation, subjects experience microsleeps. **Microsleeps** are brief periods of sleep, typically about 2 or 3 seconds long, during which the eyelids droop and the subjects become less responsive to external stimuli, even though they remain sitting or standing. Microsleeps disrupt performance on passive tests, such as tests of vigilance, but such performance deficits can also occur in subjects who are not experiencing microsleeps (Dinges et al., 1997; Ferrara, De Gennaro, & Bertini, 1999).

To put sleep deprivation in context, I like to compare it to deprivation of the motivated behaviors discussed in Chapters 12 and 13. If subjects were deprived of the opportunity to eat or engage in sexual activity, the effects would be severe and unavoidable: In the first case, starvation *Thinking Clearly* and death would ensue; in the second, there would be a total loss of reproductive capacity. There have been no such dramatic effects reported in sleep-deprivation studies. This is puzzling.

Sleep-Deprivation Studies with Laboratory Animals

The **carousel apparatus** (see Figure 14.7 on page 358) has been used to deprive rats of sleep. Two rats, an experimental rat and its *yoked control*, are placed in separate chambers of the apparatus. Each time the EEG activity of the *The Evolutionary Perspective* experimental rat indicates that it is sleeping, the disk, which serves as the floor of half of both chambers, starts to slowly rotate. As a result, if the sleeping experimental rat does not awaken immediately, it gets shoved off the disk into a shallow pool of water. The yoked control is exposed to exactly the same pattern of disk rotations; but if it is not sleeping, it can easily avoid getting dunked by walking in the direction opposite to the direction of disk rotation. The experimental rats typically died after several days, while the yoked controls stayed reasonably healthy (see Rechtschaffen & Bergmann, 1995).

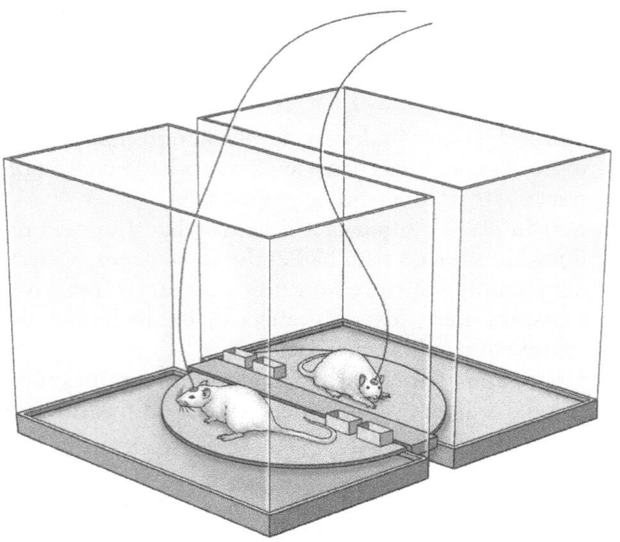

FIGURE 14.7 The carousel apparatus used to deprive an experimental rat of sleep while a yoked control rat is exposed to the same number and pattern of disk rotations. The disk on which both rats rest rotates every time the experimental rat has a sleep EEG. If the sleeping rat does not awaken immediately, it is deposited in the water. (Adapted from Rechtschaffen et al., 1983.)

The fact that human subjects have been sleep-deprived for similar periods of time without dire consequences argues for caution in interpreting the results of the carousel sleep-deprivation experiments. It may be that repeatedly being awakened by the moving platform or, worse yet, being plunged into water while sleeping kills the experimental rats not because it keeps them from sleeping but because it is stressful and physically damaging. This interpretation is consistent with the pathological symptoms that were revealed in the experimental rats by postmortem examination: swollen adrenal glands, gastric ulcers, and internal bleeding.

Thinking Clearly

You have already encountered many examples in this book of the value of the comparative approach. However, sleep deprivation may be one phenomenon that cannot be productively studied in nonhumans because of the unavoidable confounding effects of extreme stress (see Benington & Heller, 1999; D'Almeida et al., 1997; Horne, 2000).

REM-Sleep Deprivation

Because of its association with dreaming, REM sleep has been the subject of intensive investigation. In an effort to reveal the particular functions of REM sleep, sleep researchers have specifically deprived sleeping subjects of REM sleep by waking them up each time a bout of REM sleep begins.

REM-sleep deprivation has been shown to have two consistent effects (see Figure 14.8). First, with each successive night of deprivation, there is a greater tendency for subjects to initiate REM sequences. Thus, as REM-sleep deprivation proceeds, subjects have to be awakened more and more frequently to keep them from accumulating significant amounts of REM sleep. For example, during the first night of REM-sleep deprivation in one experiment (Webb & Agnew, 1967), the subjects had to be awakened 17 times to keep them from having extended periods of REM sleep; but during the seventh night of deprivation, they had to be awakened 67 times. Second, following REM-sleep deprivation, subjects display a *REM rebound;* that is, they have more than their usual amount of REM sleep for the first two or three nights (Brunner et al., 1990).

The compensatory increase in REM sleep following a period of REM-sleep deprivation suggests that the amount of REM sleep is regulated separately from the

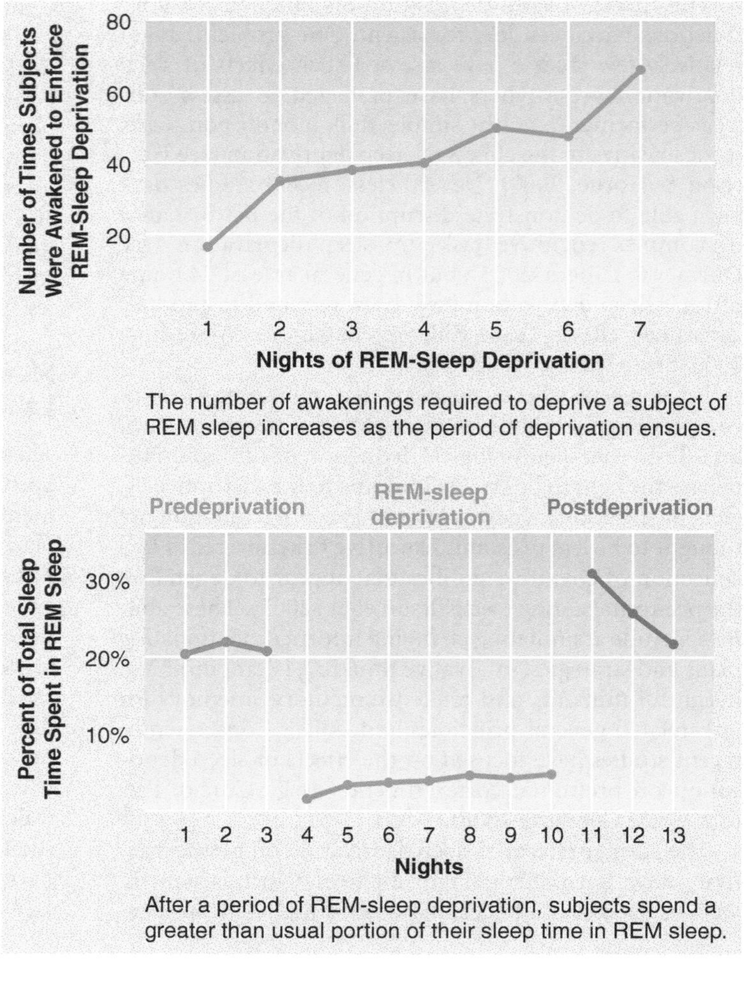
Number of Times Subjects Were Awakened to Enforce REM-Sleep Deprivation
80
60
40
20
1 2 3 4 5 6 7
Nights of REM-Sleep Deprivation
The number of awakenings required to deprive a subject of REM sleep increases as the period of deprivation ensues.
Predeprivation
REM-sleep deprivation
Postdeprivation
Percent of Total Sleep Time Spent in REM Sleep
30%
20%
10%
1 2 3 4 5 6 7 8 9 10 11 12 13
Nights
After a period of REM-sleep deprivation, subjects spend a greater than usual portion of their sleep time in REM sleep.

FIGURE 14.8 The two effects of REM-sleep deprivation.

amount of slow-wave sleep and that REM sleep serves a special function. This finding, coupled with the array of interesting physiological and psychological events that define REM sleep, has led to much speculation about its function.

Considerable attention has focused on the potential role of REM sleep in strengthening explicit memory (see Chapter 11). Many reviewers of the literature on this topic have treated the positive effect of REM sleep on the storage of existing memories as well established, and researchers have moved on to study the memory-promoting effects of other stages of sleep (e.g., Ellenbogen, Payne, & Stickgold, 2006; Stickgold, 2005; Stickgold & Walker, 2005) and the mechanisms of these memory-promoting effects (e.g., Rasch et al., 2007). However, two eminent sleep researchers, Robert Vertes and Jerome Seigel (2005), have argued that the evidence that REM sleep strengthens memory is unconvincing (see Vertes & Eastman, 2000). They point out, for example, that numerous studies failing to support a *mnemonic* (pertaining to memory) function of REM sleep have been ignored. They also question why the many patients who take certain antidepressant drugs that block REM sleep for months, or even years, experience no obvious memory problems.

The *default theory* is a different approach to REM sleep (Horne, 2000). According to this theory, it is difficult to stay continuously in NREM sleep, so the brain periodically switches to one of two other states. If there is any immediate bodily need to take care of (e.g., eating or drinking), the brain switches to wakefulness; if there are no immediate needs, it switches to the default state—REM sleep. According to the default theory, REM sleep and wakefulness are similar states, but REM sleep is more adaptive when there are no immediate bodily needs. Indirect support for this theory comes from the many similarities between REM sleep and wakefulness.

A study by Nykamp and colleagues (1998) supports the default theory of REM sleep. They awakened subjects every time they entered REM sleep, but instead of letting them go back to sleep immediately, they substituted a 15-minute period of wakefulness for each lost REM period. Under these conditions, the subjects, unlike the controls, were not tired the next day, despite getting only 5 hours of sleep, and they displayed no REM rebound. In other words, there seemed to be no need for REM sleep if periods of wakefulness were substituted for it. This is consistent with the finding that as antidepressants reduce REM sleep, the number of nighttime awakenings increases (see Horne, 2000).

Sleep Deprivation Increases the Efficiency of Sleep

One of the most important findings of human sleep-deprivation research is that individuals who are deprived of sleep become more efficient sleepers. In particular, their sleep has a higher proportion of slow-wave sleep (stages 3

and 4), which seems to serve the main restorative function. Because this is such an important finding, let's take a look at six major pieces of evidence that support it.

- Although subjects regain only a small proportion of their total lost sleep after a period of sleep deprivation, they regain most of their lost stage 4 sleep (e.g., Borbély et al., 1981; De Gennaro, Ferrara, & Bertini, 2000; Lucidi et al., 1997).
- After sleep deprivation, the slow-wave sleep EEG of humans is characterized by an even higher proportion than usual of slow waves (Borbély, 1981; Borbély et al., 1981).
- Short sleepers normally get as much slow-wave sleep as long sleepers do (e.g., Jones & Oswald, 1966; Webb & Agnew, 1970).
- If subjects take an extra nap in the morning after a full night's sleep, their naptime EEG shows few slow waves, and the nap does not reduce the duration of the following night's sleep (e.g., Åkerstedt & Gillberg, 1981; Hume & Mills, 1977; Karacan et al., 1970).
- Subjects who gradually reduce their usual sleep time get less stage 1 and stage 2 sleep, but the duration of their slow-wave sleep remains about the same as before (Mullaney et al., 1977; Webb & Agnew, 1975).
- Repeatedly waking subjects up during REM sleep produces little, if any, increase in the sleepiness they experience the next day, whereas repeatedly waking subjects up during slow-wave sleep has major effects (Nykamp et al., 1998).

mypsychkit

In the *Good Morning* module, the camera catches Pinel arriving at his office at 6:00 A.M. He discusses a common misconception about sleep.

The fact that sleep becomes more efficient in people who sleep less means that conventional sleep-deprivation studies are virtually useless for discovering how much sleep people need. The negative consequences of sleep loss in inefficient sleepers do not indicate whether the lost sleep was really needed; the true need for sleep can be assessed only by experiments in which sleep is regularly reduced for many weeks, to give the subjects the opportunity to adapt to getting less sleep by maximizing their sleep efficiency. Only when people are sleeping at their maximum efficiency is it possible to determine how much sleep they really need. Such sleep-reduction studies are discussed later in the chapter, but please pause here to think about this point—it is extremely important, and it is totally consistent with the growing appreciation of the plasticity and adaptiveness of the adult mammalian brain.

Thinking Clearly

Neuroplasticity

It is an appropriate time, here at the end of the section on sleep deprivation, for me to file a brief progress report. It has now been 2 weeks since I began my 5-hours-per-night sleep schedule. Generally, things are going well. My progress on this chapter has been faster than usual. I am not having any difficulty getting up on time or getting my work done, but I am finding that it takes a major effort to stay awake in the evening. If I try to read or watch a bit of television after 10:30, I experience microsleeps. My so-called friends delight in making sure that my transgressions last no more than a few seconds.

Scan Your Brain

Before continuing with this chapter, scan your brain by completing the following exercise to make sure you understand the fundamentals of sleep. The correct answers appear below. Before proceeding, review material related to your errors and omissions.

1. The three most commonly studied psychophysiological correlates of sleep are the EEG, EMG, and _____.
2. Stage 4 sleep EEG is characterized by a predominance of _____ waves.
3. _____ stage 1 EEG is accompanied by neither REM nor loss of core-muscle tone.
4. Dreaming occurs predominantly during _____ sleep.
5. The modern alternative to Freud's theory of dreaming is Hobson's _____ theory.
6. Environmental cues that can entrain circadian rhythms are called _____, or time givers.
7. In contrast to the prediction of the recuperation theories of sleep, when a subject stays awake longer than usual under free-running conditions, the following period of sleep tends to be _____.
8. The most convincing evidence that REM-sleep deprivation is not seriously debilitating comes from the study of patients taking certain _____ drugs.
9. After a lengthy period of sleep deprivation (e.g., several days), a subject's first night of sleep is only slightly longer than usual, but it contains a much higher proportion of _____ waves.
10. _____ sleep in particular, rather than sleep in general, appears to play the major recuperative role.

Scan Your Brain answers: (1) EOG, (2) delta, (3) Initial, (4) REM, (5) activation-synthesis, (6) *zeitgebers*, (7) shorter, (8) antidepressant, (9) slow (or delta), (10) Slow-wave (or stage 3 and 4).

14.7
Four Areas of the Brain Involved in Sleep

In this section, you will be introduced to four areas of the brain that are involved in sleep. You will learn more about them in the later section on sleep disorders.

Two Areas of the Hypothalamus Involved in Sleep

It is remarkable that two areas of the brain that are involved in the regulation of sleep were discovered early in the 20th century, long before the advent of modern behavioral neuroscience. The discovery was made by Baron Constantin von Economo, a Viennese neurologist (see Saper, Scammell, & Lu, 2005).

The Case of Constantin von Economo, the Insightful Neurologist

During World War I, the world was swept by a serious viral infection of the brain: *encephalitis lethargica*. Many of its victims slept almost continuously. Baron Constantin von Economo discovered that the brains of deceased victims who had problems with excessive sleep all had damage in the *posterior hypothalamus* and adjacent parts of the midbrain. He then turned his attention to the brains of a small group of victims of encephalitis lethargica who had had the opposite sleep-related problem: In contrast to most victims, they had difficulty sleeping. He found that the brains of the deceased victims in this minority always had damage in the *anterior hypothalamus* and adjacent parts of the basal forebrain. On the basis of these clinical observations, von Economo concluded that the posterior hypothalamus promotes wakefulness, whereas the anterior hypothalamus promotes sleep.

Since von Economo's discovery of the involvement of the posterior hypothalamus and the anterior hypothalamus in human wakefulness and sleep, respectively, that involvement has been confirmed by lesion studies in experimental animals (see Saper, Chou, & Scammell, 2001). The locations of the posterior and anterior hypothalamus are shown in Figure 14.9.

The Evolutionary Perspective

Reticular Activating System and Sleep

Another area involved in sleep was discovered through the comparison of the effects of two different brain-stem transections in cats. First, in 1936, Bremer severed the brain stems of cats between their *inferior colliculi* and *superior colliculi* in order to disconnect their forebrains from ascending sensory input (see Figure 14.10). This surgical preparation is called a **cerveau isolé preparation** (pronounced "ser-VOE ees-o-LAY"—literally, "isolated forebrain").

The Evolutionary Perspective

Bremer found that the cortical EEG of the isolated cat forebrains was indicative of almost continuous slow-wave sleep. Only when strong visual or olfactory stimuli were

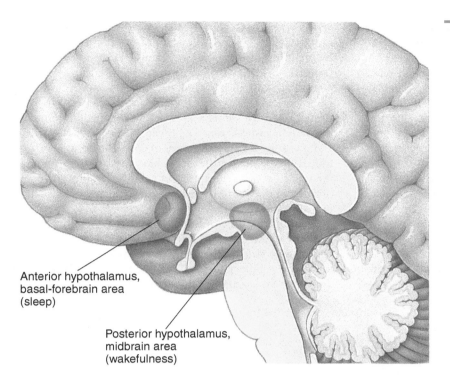

Anterior hypothalamus, basal-forebrain area (sleep)

Posterior hypothalamus, midbrain area (wakefulness)

presented (the cerveau isolé has intact visual and olfactory input) could the continuous high-amplitude, slow-wave activity be changed to a **desynchronized EEG**—a low-amplitude, high-frequency EEG. However, this arousing effect barely outlasted the stimuli.

Next, for comparison purposes, Bremer (1937) *transected* (cut through) the brain stems of a different group of cats. These transections were located in the caudal brain stem, and thus, they disconnected the brain from the rest of the nervous system (see Figure 14.10). This experimental preparation is called the **encéphale isolé preparation** (pronounced "on-say-FELL ees-o-LAY").

Although it cut most of the same sensory fibers as the cerveau isolé transection, the encéphale isolé transection did not disrupt the normal cycle of sleep EEG and wakefulness EEG. This suggested that a structure for maintaining wakefulness was located somewhere in the brain stem between the two transections.

Later, two important findings suggested that this wakefulness structure in the brain stem was the *reticular formation*. First, it was shown that partial transections at the cerveau isolé level disrupted normal sleep–wake cycles of cortical EEG only when they severed the reticular formation core of the brain stem; when the partial transections were restricted to more lateral areas, which contain the ascending sensory tracts, they had little effect on the cortical EEG (Lindsey, Bowden, & Magoun, 1949). Second, it was shown that electrical stimulation of the reticular formation of sleeping cats awakened them and produced a lengthy period of EEG desynchronization (Moruzzi & Magoun, 1949).

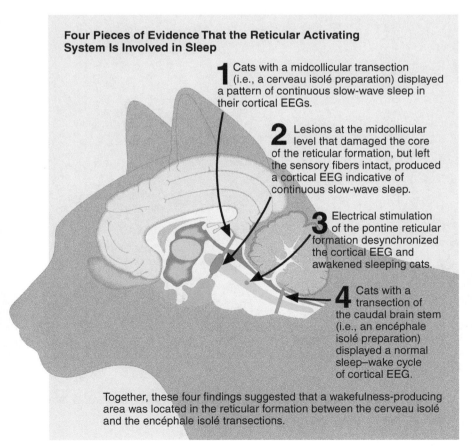

Four Pieces of Evidence That the Reticular Activating System Is Involved in Sleep

1 Cats with a midcollicular transection (i.e., a cerveau isolé preparation) displayed a pattern of continuous slow-wave sleep in their cortical EEGs.

2 Lesions at the midcollicular level that damaged the core of the reticular formation, but left the sensory fibers intact, produced a cortical EEG indicative of continuous slow-wave sleep.

3 Electrical stimulation of the pontine reticular formation desynchronized the cortical EEG and awakened sleeping cats.

4 Cats with a transection of the caudal brain stem (i.e., an encéphale isolé preparation) displayed a normal sleep–wake cycle of cortical EEG.

Together, these four findings suggested that a wakefulness-producing area was located in the reticular formation between the cerveau isolé and the encéphale isolé transections.

FIGURE 14.10 Four pieces of evidence that the reticular activating system is involved in sleep.

In 1949, Moruzzi and Magoun considered these four findings together: (1) the effects on cortical EEG of the cerveau isolé preparation, (2) the effects on cortical EEG of the encéphale isolé preparation, (3) the effects of reticular formation lesions, and (4) the effects on sleep of stimulation of the reticular formation. From these four key findings, Moruzzi and Magoun proposed that low levels of activity in the reticular formation produce sleep and that high levels produce wakefulness. Indeed, this theory is so widely accepted that the reticular formation is commonly referred to as the **reticular activating system**, even though maintaining wakefulness is only one of the functions of the many nuclei that it comprises.

Reticular REM-Sleep Nuclei

The fourth area of the brain that is involved in sleep controls REM sleep and is included in the brain area I have just described—it is part of the caudal reticular formation. It makes sense that an area of the brain involved in maintaining wakefulness would also be involved in the production of REM sleep because of the similarities between the two states. Indeed, REM sleep is controlled by a variety of nuclei scattered throughout the caudal reticular formation. Each site is responsible for controlling one of the major indices of REM sleep (Siegel, 1983; Vertes, 1983)—a site for the reduction of core-muscle tone, a site for EEG desynchronization, a site for rapid eye movements, and so on. The approximate location in the caudal brain stem of each of these REM-sleep nuclei is illustrated in Figure 14.11.

Please think for a moment about the broad implications of these various REM-sleep nuclei. In thinking about the brain mechanisms of behavior, many people assume that if there is one name for a behavior, there must be a

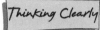

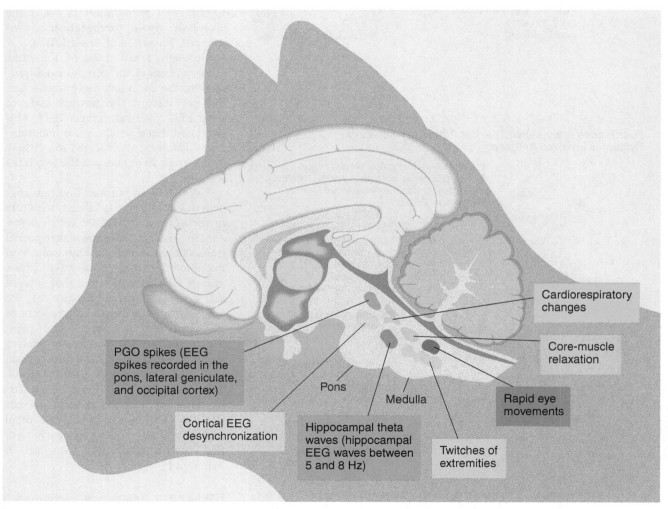

FIGURE 14.11   A sagittal section of the brain stem of the cat illustrating the areas that control the various physiological indices of REM sleep. (Adapted from Vertes, 1983.)

single structure for it in the brain: In other words, they assume that evolutionary pressures have acted to shape the human brain according to our current language and theories. Here we see the weakness of this assumption: The brain is organized along different principles, and REM sleep occurs only when a network of independent structures becomes active together. Relevant to this is the fact that the physiological changes that go together to define REM sleep sometimes break apart and go their separate ways—and the same is true of the changes that define slow-wave sleep. For example, during REM-sleep deprivation, penile erections, which normally occur during REM sleep, begin to occur during slow-wave sleep. And during total sleep deprivation, slow waves, which normally occur only during slow-wave sleep, begin to occur during wakefulness. This suggests that REM sleep, slow-wave sleep, and wakefulness are not each controlled by a single mechanism. Each state seems to result from the interaction of several mechanisms that are capable under certain conditions of operating independently of one another.

14.8

The Circadian Clock: Neural and Molecular Mechanisms

The fact that circadian sleep–wake cycles persist in the absence of temporal cues from the environment indicates that the physiological systems that regulate sleep are controlled by an internal timing mechanism—the **circadian clock**. The circadian clock has been the subject of such intensive investigation that it warrants its own section of this chapter.

Location of the Circadian Clock in the Suprachiasmatic Nuclei

The first breakthrough in the search for the circadian clock was Richter's 1967 discovery that large medial hypothalamic lesions disrupt circadian cycles of eating, drinking, and activity in rats. Next, specific lesions of the **suprachiasmatic nuclei (SCN)** of the medial hypothalamus were shown to disrupt various circadian cycles, including sleep–wake cycles. Although SCN lesions do not greatly affect the amount of time mammals spend sleeping, they do abolish the circadian periodicity of sleep cycles. Further support for the conclusion that the suprachiasmatic nuclei contain a circadian timing mechanism comes from the observation that the nuclei display circadian cycles of electrical, metabolic, and biochemical activity that can be entrained by the light–dark cycle (see Mistlberger, 2005; Saper et al., 2005).

If there was any lingering doubt about the location of the circadian clock, it was eliminated by the brilliant experiment of Ralph and his colleagues (1990). They removed the SCN from the fetuses of a strain of mutant hamsters that had an abnormally short (20-hour) free-running sleep–wake cycle. Then, they transplanted the SCN into normal adult hamsters whose free-running sleep–wake cycles of 25 hours had been abolished by SCN lesions. These transplants restored free-running sleep–wake cycles in the recipients; but, remarkably, the cycles were about 20 hours long rather than the original 25 hours. Transplants in the other direction—that is, from normal hamster fetuses to SCN-lesioned adult mutants—had the complementary effect: They restored free-running sleep–wake cycles that were about 25 hours long rather than the original 20 hours.

Although the suprachiasmatic nuclei are unquestionably the major circadian clocks in mammals, they are not the only ones. Three lines of experiments, largely conducted in the 1980s and 1990s, pointed to the existence of other circadian timing mechanisms in the body.

- Under certain conditions, bilateral SCN lesions have been shown to leave some circadian rhythms unaffected while abolishing others.
- Bilateral SCN lesions do not eliminate the ability of all environmental stimuli to entrain circadian rhythms; for example, SCN lesions can block entrainment by light but not by food or water availability.
- Just as suprachiasmatic neurons do, cells from other parts of the body display free-running circadian cycles of activity when maintained in tissue culture.

Mechanisms of Entrainment

How does the 24-hour light–dark cycle entrain the sleep–wake cycle and other circadian rhythms? To answer this question, researchers began at the obvious starting point: the eyes (see Morin & Allen, 2006). They tried to identify and track the specific neurons that left the eyes and carried the information about light and dark that entrained the biological clock. Cutting the *optic nerves* before they reached the *optic chiasm* eliminated the ability of the light–dark cycle to entrain circadian rhythms; however, when the *optic tracts* were cut at the point where they left the optic chiasm, the ability of the light–dark cycle to entrain circadian rhythms was unaffected. As Figure 14.12 illustrates, these two findings indicated that visual axons critical for the entrainment of circadian rhythms branch off from the optic nerve in the vicinity of the optic chiasm. This finding led to the discovery of the *retinohypothalamic tracts*, which leave the optic chiasm and project to the adjacent suprachiasmatic nuclei.

Surprisingly, although the retinohypothalamic tracts mediate the ability of light to entrain photoreceptors, neither rods nor cones are necessary for the entrainment. The mystery photoreceptors have proven to be neurons, a rare type of *retinal ganglion cells* with distinctive functional properties (see Berson, 2003; Hattar et al., 2002). During the course of evolution, these photoreceptors have

FIGURE 14.12   The discovery of the retino-hypothalamic tracts. Neurons from each retina project to both suprachiasmatic nuclei.

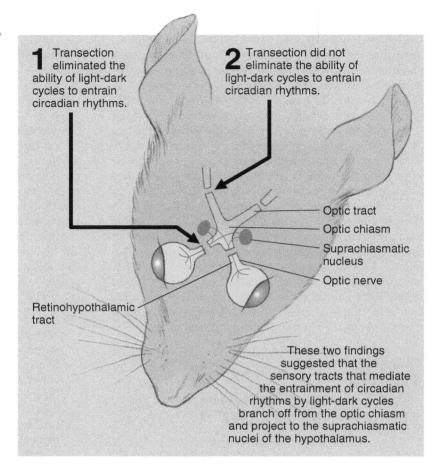

1 Transection eliminated the ability of light-dark cycles to entrain circadian rhythms.

2 Transection did not eliminate the ability of light-dark cycles to entrain circadian rhythms.

Optic tract

Optic chiasm

Suprachiasmatic nucleus

Optic nerve

Retinohypothalamic tract

These two findings suggested that the sensory tracts that mediate the entrainment of circadian rhythms by light-dark cycles branch off from the optic chiasm and project to the suprachiasmatic nuclei of the hypothalamus.

sacrificed the ability to respond quickly and briefly to rapid changes of light  in favor of the ability to respond consistently to slowly changing levels of background illumination. Their photopigment is *melanopsin* (Panda et al., 2005).

Genetics of Circadian Rhythms

An important breakthrough in the study of circadian rhythms came in 1988 when routine screening of a shipment of ham-  sters revealed that some of them had abnor- mally short 20-hour free-running circadian rhythms. Subse- quent breeding experiments showed that the abnormality was the result of a genetic mutation, and the gene that was found was named **tau** (Ralph & Menaker, 1988).

Although tau was the first mammalian circadian gene to be identified, it was not the first to have its molecular structure characterized. This honor went to *clock*, a mammalian circadian gene discov- ered in mice. The structure of the clock gene was charac- terized in 1997, and that of the tau gene was characterized in 2000 (Lowrey et al., 2000). The molecular structures of several other mammalian circadian genes have now been specified (see Morse & Sassone-Corsi, 2002).

The identification of circadian genes has led to three important discoveries.

- The same or similar circadian genes have been found in many species of different evolutionary ages (e.g., bacteria, flies, fish, frogs, mice, and humans), indicat- ing that circadian genes evolved early in evolutionary history and have been conserved in various descen- dant species (see Cermakian & Sassone-Corsi, 2002).
- Once the circadian genes were discovered, the funda- mental molecular mechanism of circadian rhythms was quickly clarified. The key mechanism seems to be the transcription of proteins by the circadian genes (see Dunlap, 2006; Hardin, 2006; Meyer, Saez, & Young, 2006). In some SCN cells, the expression of clock genes is on a circadian cycle; in other SCN cells, this expression is triggered by exposure to light (Antle & Silver, 2005).
- The identification of circadian genes provided a more direct method of exploring the circadian timing ca-

pacities of parts of the body other than the SCN. Mol- ecular circadian timing mechanisms similar to those in the SCN exist in most cells of the body (see Green & Menaker, 2003; Hastings, Reddy, & Maywood, 2003; Yamaguchi et al., 2003). Although most cells contain a genetic circadian clock, these cellular clocks are nor- mally entrained by neural and hormonal signals from the SCN.

14.9
Drugs That Affect Sleep

Most drugs that influence sleep fall into two different classes: hypnotic and antihypnotic. **Hypnotic drugs** are drugs that increase sleep; **antihypnotic drugs** are drugs that reduce sleep. A third class of sleep-influencing drugs comprises those that influence its circadian rhythmicity; the main drug of this class is **melatonin**.

Hypnotic Drugs

The **benzodiazepines** (e.g., Valium and Librium) were developed and tested for the treatment of anxiety, yet they are the most commonly prescribed hypnotic medications. In the short term, they increase drowsiness, decrease the time it takes to fall asleep, reduce the number of awakenings during a night's sleep, and increase total sleep time. Thus, they can be effective in the treatment of occasional difficulties in sleeping.

Although benzodiazepines can be effective therapeutic hypnotic agents in the short term, their prescription for the treatment of chronic sleep difficulties is ill-advised. Still, they are commonly prescribed for this purpose—primarily by general practitioners. Following are four complications associated with the chronic use of benzodiazepines as hypnotic agents:

- Tolerance develops to the hypnotic effects of benzodiazepines; thus, patients must take larger and larger doses to maintain the drugs' efficacy.
- Cessation of benzodiazepine therapy after chronic use causes *insomnia* (sleeplessness), which can exacerbate the very problem that the benzodiazepines were intended to correct.
- Chronic benzodiazepine use is addictive.
- Benzodiazepines distort the normal pattern of sleep; they increase the duration of sleep by increasing the duration of stage 2 sleep, while actually decreasing the duration of stage 4 and REM sleep.

Evidence that the raphé nuclei, which are serotonergic, play a role in sleep suggested that serotonergic drugs might be effective hypnotics. Efforts to demonstrate the hypnotic effects of such drugs have focused on **5-hydroxytryptophan (5-HTP)**—the precursor of serotonin—because 5-HTP, but not serotonin, readily passes through the blood–brain barrier. Injections of 5-HTP do reverse the insomnia produced in both cats and rats by the serotonin antagonist PCPA; however, they appear to be of no therapeutic benefit in the treatment of human insomnia (see Borbély, 1983).

Antihypnotic Drugs

There are two main classes of antihypnotic drugs: *stimulants* (e.g., cocaine and amphetamine) and *tricyclic antidepressants*. Both stimulants and antidepressants increase the activity of catecholamines (norepinephrine, epinephrine, and dopamine) by either increasing their release or blocking their reuptake from the synapse, or both.

From the perspective of the treatment of sleep disorders, the most important property of antihypnotic drugs is that they act preferentially on REM sleep. They can totally suppress REM sleep even at doses that have little effect on total sleep time.

Clinical Implications

Using stimulant drugs to treat chronic excessive sleepiness is a risky proposition. Most stimulants are highly addictive, and they produce a variety of adverse side effects, such as loss of appetite.

Melatonin

Melatonin is a hormone that is synthesized from the neurotransmitter serotonin in the **pineal gland** (see Moore, 1996). The pineal gland is an inconspicuous gland that René Descartes, whose dualistic philosophy was discussed in Chapter 2, once believed to be the seat of the soul. The pineal gland is located on the midline of the brain just ventral to the rear portion of the corpus callosum (see Figure 14.13 on page 366).

The pineal gland has important functions in birds, reptiles, amphibians, and fish (see Cassone, 1990). The pineal gland of these species has inherent timing properties and regulates circadian rhythms and seasonal changes in reproductive behavior through its release of melatonin. In humans and other mammals, however, the functions of the pineal gland and melatonin are not as apparent.

The Evolutionary Perspective

In humans and other mammals, circulating levels of melatonin display circadian rhythms under control of the suprachiasmatic nuclei (see Gillette & McArthur, 1996), with the highest levels being associated with darkness and sleep (see Foulkes et al., 1997). On the basis of this correlation, it has long been assumed that melatonin plays a role in promoting sleep or in regulating its timing in mammals.

In order to put the facts about melatonin in perspective, it is important to keep one significant point firmly in mind. In adult mammals, pinealectomy and the consequent elimination of melatonin appear to have little effect. The pineal gland plays a role in the development of mammalian sexual maturity, but its functions after puberty are not at all obvious.

Does *exogenous* (externally produced) melatonin improve sleep, as widely believed? The evidence is mixed (see van den Heuvel et al., 2005). However, a *meta-analysis* (a combined analysis of results of more than one study) of 17 studies indicated that exogenous melatonin has a slight, but statistically significant, *soporific* (sleep-promoting) effect (Brzezinski et al., 2005).

In contrast to the controversy over the soporific effects of exogenous melatonin in mammals, there is good evidence that it can shift the timing of mammalian circadian cycles. Indeed, several researchers have argued that melatonin is better classified as a **chronobiotic** (a substance that adjusts the timing of internal biological rhythms) than as a hypnotic (see Scheer & Czeisler, 2005). Arendt and Skene (2005) argue that administration of melatonin in the evening increases sleep by accelerating the start of the nocturnal phase of the circadian rhythm and that administration at dawn increases sleep by delaying the end of the nocturnal phase.

Exogenous melatonin has been shown to have a therapeutic potential in the treatment of two types of sleep problems (see Arendt & Skene, 2005). Melatonin before bedtime

Clinical Implications

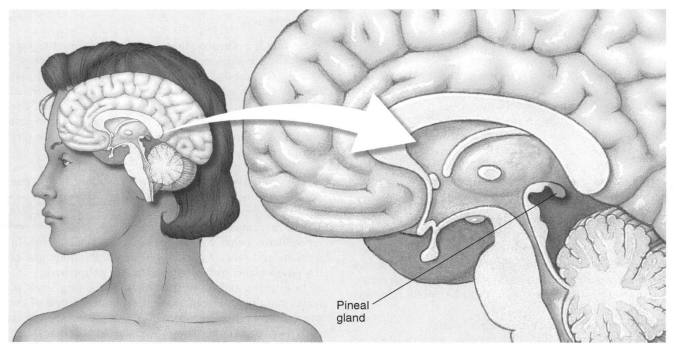

FIGURE 14.13 The location of the pineal gland, the source of melatonin.

has been shown to improve the sleep of those insomniacs who are melatonin-deficient and of blind people who have sleep problems attributable to the lack of the synchronizing effects of the light–dark cycle. Melatonin's effectiveness in the treatment of other sleep disorders remains controversial.

14.10
Sleep Disorders

Many sleep disorders fall into one of two complementary categories: insomnia and hypersomnia. **Insomnia** includes all disorders of initiating and maintaining sleep, *Clinical Implications* whereas **hypersomnia** includes disorders of excessive sleep or sleepiness. A third major class of sleep disorders includes all those disorders that are specifically related to REM-sleep dysfunction.

In various surveys, approximately 30% of the respondents report significant sleep-related problems. However, it is important to recognize that complaints of sleep problems often come from people whose sleep appears normal in laboratory sleep tests. For example, many people who complain of insomnia actually sleep a reasonable amount (e.g., 6 hours a night), but they believe that they should sleep more (e.g., 8 hours a night). As a result, they spend more time in bed than they should and have difficulty getting to sleep. Often, the anxiety associated with their inability to sleep makes it even more difficult for them to sleep (see Espie, 2002). Such patients can often be helped by counseling that convinces them to go to bed only when they are very sleepy (see Anch et al., 1988). Others with disturbed sleep have more serious problems (see Mahowald & Schenck, 2005).

Insomnia

Many cases of insomnia are **iatrogenic** (physician-created)—in large part because sleeping pills (e.g., benzodiazepines), which are usually prescribed by physicians, are a major cause of insomnia. At first, hypnotic drugs are effective in increasing sleep, but soon the patient is trapped in a rising spiral of drug use, as *tolerance* to the drug develops and progressively more of it is required to produce its original hypnotic effect. Soon, the patient cannot stop taking the drug without running the risk of experiencing *withdrawal symptoms*, which include insomnia. The case of Mr. B. illustrates this problem.

Mr. B., the Case of Iatrogenic Insomnia

Mr. B. was studying for a civil service exam, the outcome of which would affect his entire future. He was terribly worried about the test and found it difficult to get to sleep at night. Feeling that the sleep loss was affecting his ability to study, he consulted his physician. . . . His doctor prescribed a moderate dose of barbiturate at bedtime, and

Mr. B. found that this medication was very effective . . . for the first several nights. After about a week, he began having trouble sleeping again and decided to take two sleeping pills each night. Twice more the cycle was repeated, until on the night before the exam he was taking four times as many pills as his doctor had prescribed. The next night, with the pressure off, Mr. B. took no medication. He had tremendous difficulty falling asleep, and when he did, his sleep was terribly disrupted. . . . Mr. B. now decided that he had a serious case of insomnia, and returned to his sleeping pill habit. By the time he consulted our clinic several years later, he was taking approximately 1,000 mg sodium amytal every night, and his sleep was more disturbed than ever. . . . Patients may go on for years and years—from one sleeping pill to another—never realizing that their troubles are caused by the pills.

("Mr. B., the Case of Iatrogenic Insomnia," from *Some Must Watch While Some Must Sleep* by William C. Dement, Portable Stanford Books, Stanford Alumni Association, Stanford University, 1978, p. 80. Used by permission of William C. Dement.)

In one study, insomniacs claimed to take an average of 1 hour to fall asleep and to sleep an average of only 4.5 hours per night; but when they were tested in a sleep laboratory, they were found to have an average *sleep latency* (time to fall asleep) of only 15 minutes and an average nightly sleep duration of 6.5 hours. It used to be common medical practice to assume that people who claimed to suffer from insomnia but slept more than 6.5 hours per night were neurotic. However, this practice stopped when some of those diagnosed as *neurotic pseudoinsomniacs* were subsequently found to be suffering from sleep apnea, nocturnal myoclonus, or other sleep-disturbing problems. Insomnia is not necessarily a problem of too little sleep; it is often a problem of too little undisturbed sleep (Stepanski et al., 1987).

One of the most effective treatments for insomnia is *sleep restriction therapy* (Morin, Kowatch, & O'Shanick, 1990): First, the amount of time that an insomniac is allowed to spend in bed is substantially reduced. Then, after a period of sleep restriction, the amount of time spent in bed is gradually increased in small increments, as long as sleep latency remains in the normal range. Even severe insomniacs often benefit from this treatment

Some cases of insomnia have specific medical causes; **sleep apnea** is one such cause. The patient with sleep apnea stops breathing many times each night. Each time, the patient awakens, begins to breathe again, and drifts back to sleep. Sleep apnea usually leads to a sense of having slept poorly and is thus often diagnosed as insomnia. However, some patients are totally unaware of their multiple awakenings and instead complain of excessive sleepiness during the day, which leads to a diagnosis of *hypersomnia* (Stepanski et al., 1984).

Sleep apnea disorders are of two types: (1) *obstructive sleep apnea* results from obstruction of the respiratory passages by muscle spasms or *atonia* (lack of muscle

tone); (2) *central sleep apnea* results from the failure of the central nervous system to stimulate respiration. Sleep apnea is more common in males, in the overweight, and in the elderly (Villaneuva et al., 2005).

Two other specific causes of insomnia are related to the legs: periodic limb movement disorder and restless legs syndrome. **Periodic limb movement disorder** is disorder characterized by periodic, involuntary movements of the limbs, often involving twitches of the legs during sleep. Most patients suffering from this disorder complain of poor sleep and daytime sleepiness but are unaware of the nature of their problem. In contrast, people with **restless legs syndrome** are all too aware of their problem. They complain of a hard-to-describe tension or uneasiness in their legs that keeps them from falling asleep. Once established, both of these disorders are chronic (see Garcia-Borreguero et al., 2006). Much more research into their treatment is needed, although dopamine agonists are often prescribed (Hornyak et al., 2006; Lesage & Hening, 2004).

Hypersomnia

Narcolepsy is the most widely studied disorder of hypersomnia. It occurs in 1 out of 2000 individuals (Black, Brooks, & Nishino, 2004) and has two prominent symptoms (see Nishino & Kanbayashi, 2005). First, narcoleptics experience severe daytime sleepiness and repeated, brief (10- to 15-minute) daytime sleep episodes. Narcoleptics typically sleep only about an hour per day more than average; it is the inappropriateness of their sleep episodes that most clearly defines their condition. Most of us occasionally fall asleep on the beach, in front of the television, or in that most soporific of all daytime sites—the large, stuffy, dimly lit lecture hall. But narcoleptics fall asleep in the middle of a conversation, while eating, while scuba diving, or even while making love.

The second prominent symptom of narcolepsy is cataplexy (Houghton, Scammell, & Thorpy, 2004). **Cataplexy** is characterized by recurring losses of muscle tone during wakefulness, often triggered by an emotional experience. In its mild form, it may simply force the patient to sit down for a few seconds until it passes. In its extreme form, the patient drops to the ground as if shot and remains there for a minute or two, fully conscious.

In addition to the two prominent symptoms of narcolepsy (daytime sleep attacks and cataplexy), narcoleptics often experience two other symptoms: sleep paralysis and hypnagogic hallucinations. **Sleep paralysis** is the inability to move (paralysis) just as one is falling asleep or waking up. **Hypnagogic hallucinations** are dreamlike experiences during wakefulness. Many healthy people occasionally experience sleep paralysis and hypnagogic hallucinations. Have you experienced them?

Three lines of evidence suggested to early researchers that narcolepsy results from an abnormality in the mechanisms that trigger REM sleep. First, unlike normal people, narcoleptics often go directly into REM sleep when they fall asleep. Second and third, narcoleptics often experience dreamlike states and loss of muscle tone during wakefulness.

Some of the most exciting current research on the neural mechanisms of sleep in general and narcolepsy in particular began with the study of a strain of narcoleptic  dogs. After 10 years of studying the genetics of these narcoleptic dogs, Lin and colleagues (1999) finally isolated the gene that causes the disorder. The gene encodes a receptor protein that binds to a neuropeptide called **orexin** (sometimes called *hypocretin*), which exists in two forms: orexin-A and orexin-B (see Sakurai, 2005). Several studies have documented reduced levels of orexin in the cerebrospinal fluid of living narcoleptics and in the brains of deceased narcoleptics (see Nishino & Kanbayashi, 2005).

Where is orexin synthesized in the brain? Orexin is synthesized by neurons in the region of the hypothalamus that has been linked to the promotion of wakefulness: the posterior hypothalamus (mainly its lateral regions). The orexin-producing neurons project diffusely throughout the brain, but they show many connections with neurons of the other wakefulness-promoting area of the brain: the reticular formation. Currently, there is considerable interest in understanding the role of the orexin circuits in normal sleep–wake cycles (see Sakurai, 2007; Siegel, 2004).

When narcolepsy occurs in an identical twin, the probability that the other twin will be narcoleptic is only 25%. This finding suggests that environmental factors normally play a major role in the brain dysfunction associated with narcolepsy (Raizen, Mason, & Pack, 2006).

Narcolepsy has traditionally been treated with stimulants (e.g., amphetamine, methylphenidate), but these have substantial addiction potential and produce many undesirable side effects. A newly available stimulant, *modafil*, acts more specifically to reduce sleepiness and has been shown to be effective in the treatment of narcolepsy (see Banerjee, Vitiello, & Grunstein, 2004).

REM-Sleep–Related Disorders

Several sleep disorders are specific to REM sleep; these are classified as *REM-sleep–related disorders*. Even narcolepsy, which is usually classified as a hypersomnic disorder, can reasonably be considered to be a REM-sleep–related disorder—for reasons you have just encountered.

Occasionally, patients are discovered who have little or no REM sleep. Although this disorder is rare, it is important because of its theoretical implications. Lavie and others (1984) described a patient who had suffered a brain injury that presumably involved damage to the REM-sleep controllers in the caudal reticular formation. The most important finding of this case study was that the pa-

tient did not appear to be adversely affected by his lack of REM sleep. After receiving his injury, he completed high school, college, and law school and established a thriving law practice.

Some patients experience REM sleep without core-muscle atonia. It has been suggested that the function of REM-sleep atonia is to prevent the acting out of dreams. This theory receives support from case studies of people who suffer from this disorder—case studies such as the following one.

The Case of the Sleeper Who Ran Over Tackle

I was a halfback playing football, and after the quarterback received the ball from the center he lateraled it sideways to me and I'm supposed to go around end and cut back over tackle and—this is very vivid—as I cut back over tackle there is this big 280-pound tackle waiting, so I, according to football rules, was to give him my shoulder and bounce him out of the way. . . . [W]hen I came to I was standing in front of our dresser and I had [gotten up out of bed and run and] knocked lamps, mirrors and everything off the dresser, hit my head against the wall and my knee against the dresser. (Schenck et al., 1986, p. 294)

Presumably, REM sleep without atonia is caused by damage to the nucleus magnocellularis or to an interruption of its output. The **nucleus magnocellularis** is a structure of the caudal reticular formation that controls muscle relaxation during REM sleep. In normal dogs, it is active only during REM sleep; in narcoleptic dogs, it is also active during their narcoleptic attacks.

14.11
The Effects of Long-Term Sleep Reduction

You have already learned in this chapter that when people sleep less than they are used to sleeping, they do not feel or function well. I am sure that you have experienced these effects. But what do they mean? Most people—nonexperts and experts alike—believe that the adverse effects of sleep loss indicate that we need the sleep we typically get. However, there is an alternative interpretation, one that is consistent with the new awareness of the plasticity of the adult human brain. Perhaps the brain slowly adapts to the amount of sleep it usually gets—even though this amount may be far more than it needs—and is disturbed when there is a sudden reduction in the expected amount of sleep.

Fortunately, there is a way to determine which of these two interpretations of the effects of sleep loss is correct and to find out how much sleep people really need. The key is to study the effects of systematic programs of long-term sleep reduction. For example, if you reduced your regular amount of sleep from 8.5 hours per night to 6.5 hours per night, you would initially have some problems. But if you regularly slept 6.5 hours per night for a couple of months, would you eventually become comfortable with sleeping 6.5 hours each night? And what if you then further reduced your nightly sleep time to 6.0 hours? If it is possible for a person to adapt to a regular schedule of 6 hours of sleep per night without adverse consequences, then there would seem little reason for assuming a need for 8.5 hours.

Let's see what has happened in studies of long-term sleep reduction. Because they are so time-consuming, few of these critical studies have been conducted; but there have been enough of them for a clear pattern of results to have emerged. I think you will by amazed by the results.

There have been two kinds of long-term sleep-reduction studies: studies in which the subjects sleep nightly and studies in which subjects sleep by napping. Following a brief discussion of these two kinds of studies and my own personal experience of long-term sleep reduction, the chapter concludes with an important, and somewhat disturbing, recent finding that is sure to challenge your thinking about sleep.

Long-Term Reduction of Nightly Sleep

There have been two studies in which healthy subjects have reduced their nightly sleep for several weeks or longer. In one (Webb & Agnew, 1974), a group of 16 subjects slept for only 5.5 hours per night for 60 days, with only one detectable deficit on an extensive battery of mood, medical, and performance tests: a slight deficit on a test of auditory vigilance.

In the other systematic study of long-term nightly sleep reduction (Friedman et al., 1977; Mullaney et al., 1977), 8 subjects reduced their nightly sleep by 30 minutes every 2 weeks until they reached 6.5 hours per night, then by 30 minutes every 3 weeks until they reached 5 hours, and then by 30 minutes every 4 weeks thereafter. After a subject indicated a lack of desire to reduce sleep further, the person spent 1 month sleeping the shortest duration of nightly sleep that had been achieved, then 2 months sleeping the shortest duration plus 30 minutes. Finally, each subject slept however long was preferred each night for 1 year. The minimum duration of nightly sleep achieved during this experiment was 5.5 hours for 2 subjects, 5.0 hours for 4 subjects, and an impressive 4.5 hours for 2 subjects. In each of the subjects, a reduction in sleep time was associated with an increase in sleep efficiency: a decrease in the amount of time it took the subjects to fall asleep after going to bed, a decrease in the

number of nighttime awakenings, and an increase in the proportion of stage 4 sleep. After the subjects had reduced their sleep to 6 hours per night, they began to experience daytime sleepiness, and this became a problem as sleep time was further reduced. Nevertheless, there were no deficits on any of the mood, medical, or performance tests given to the subjects throughout the experiment. The most encouraging result was that a follow-up 1 year later found that all subjects were sleeping less than they had previously—between 7 and 18 hours less each week—with no excessive sleepiness.

Long-Term Sleep Reduction by Napping

Most mammals and human infants display **polyphasic sleep cycles**; that is, they regularly sleep more than once per day. In contrast, most adult humans display **monophasic sleep cycles**; that is, they sleep once per day. Nevertheless, most adult humans do display polyphasic cycles of sleepiness, with periods of sleepiness occurring in late afternoon and late morning (Stampi, 1992a). Have you ever experienced them?

Do adult humans need to take sleep in one continuous period per day, or can they sleep effectively in several naps as human infants and other mammals do? Which of the two sleep patterns is more efficient? Research has shown that naps have recuperative powers out of proportion with their brevity (e.g., Gillberg et al., 1996; Horne & Reyner, 1996; Naitoh, 1992; Smith et al., 2007), suggesting that polyphasic sleep might be particularly efficient.

Interest in the value of polyphasic sleep was stimulated by the legend that Leonardo da Vinci managed to generate a steady stream of artistic and engineering accomplishments during his life by napping for 15 minutes every 4 hours, thereby limiting his sleep to 1.5 hours per day. As unbelievable as this sleep schedule may seem, it has been replicated in several experiments (see Stampi, 1992b). Here are the main findings of these truly mind-boggling experiments. First, the subjects required a long time, about 2 weeks, to adapt to a polyphasic sleep schedule. Second, once adapted to polyphasic sleep, the subjects were content and displayed no deficits on the performance tests that they were given. Third, Leonardo's 4-hour schedule works quite well, but in unstructured working situations (e.g., as in around-the-world solo sailboat races), subjects often vary the duration of the cycle without feeling negative consequences. Fourth, most subjects display a strong preference for particular sleep durations (e.g., 25 minutes) and refrain from sleeping too little, which leaves them unrefreshed, or too much, which leaves them groggy for several minutes when they awake—an effect called *sleep inertia*. Fifth, at first most of the sleep is slow-wave sleep, but eventually the subjects return to their usual relative proportions of REM and slow-wave sleep; however, REM and slow-wave sleep seldom occur during the same nap.

The following are the words of artist Giancarlo Sbragia, who adopted Leonardo's sleep schedule:

> This schedule was difficult to follow at the beginning. . . . It took about 3 wk to get used to it. But I soon reached a point at which I felt a natural propensity for sleeping at this rate, and it turned out to be a thrilling and exciting experience.
>   . . . How beautiful my life became: I discovered dawns, I discovered silence, and concentration. I had more time for studying and reading—far more than I did before. I had more time for myself, for painting, and for developing my career. (Sbragia, 1992, p. 181)

Long-Term Sleep Reduction: A Personal Case Study

I began this chapter 4 weeks ago with both zeal and trepidation. I was fascinated by the idea that I could wring 2 or 3 extra hours of living out of each day by sleeping less, and I hoped that adhering to a sleep-reduction program while writing about sleep would create an enthusiasm for the subject that would color my writing and be passed on to you. On the other hand, I was more than a little concerned about the negative effect that losing 3 hours of sleep per night might have on me.

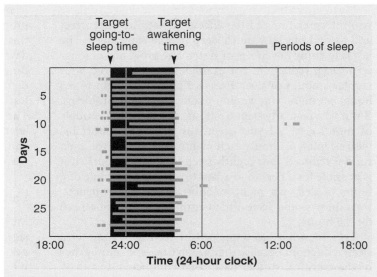

FIGURE 14.14   Sleep record of Pinel during a 4-week sleep-reduction program.

The Case of the Author Who Reduced His Sleep

Rather than using the gradual stepwise reduction method of Friedman and his colleagues, I jumped directly into my 5-hours-per-night sleep schedule. This proved to be less difficult than you might think. I took advantage of a trip to the East Coast from my home on the West Coast to reset my circadian clock. While I was in the East, I got up at 7:00 A.M., which is 4:00 A.M. on the West Coast, and I just kept on the same schedule when I got home. I decided to add my extra waking hours to the beginning of my day rather than to the end so there would be no temptation for me to waste them; there are not too many distractions around this university at 5:00 A.M.

Figure 14.14 is a record of my sleep times for the 4-week period that it took me to write a first draft of this chapter. I didn't quite meet my goal of sleeping less than 5 hours every night, but I didn't miss by much: My overall mean was 5.05 hours per night. Notice that in the last week, there was a tendency for my circadian clock to run a bit slow; I began sleeping in until 4:30 A.M. and staying up until 11:30 P.M.

What were the positives and negatives of my experience? The main positive was the added time to do things: Having an extra 21 hours per week was wonderful. Furthermore, because my daily routine was out of synchrony with everybody else's, I spent little time sitting in rush-hour traffic. The only negative of the experience was sleepiness. It was no problem during the day, when I was active. However, staying awake during the last hour before I went to bed—an hour during which I usually engaged in sedentary activities, such as reading—was at times a problem. This is when I became personally familiar with the phenomenon of microsleeps, and it was then that I required some assistance in order to stay awake. Going to bed and falling asleep each night became a fleeting but satisfying experience.

I began this chapter with this question: How much sleep do we need? Then, I gave you my best professorial it-could-be-this, it-could-be-that answer. However, that was a month ago. Now, after experiencing sleep reduction firsthand, I am less inclined toward wishy-washiness on the topic of sleep. The fact that most committed subjects who are active during the day can reduce their sleep to about 5.5 hours per night without great difficulty or major adverse consequences suggested to me that the answer is 5.5 hours of sleep. But that was before I reviewed the research on napping and polyphasic sleep schedules. Now, I must revise my estimate downward—substantially.

Effects of Shorter Sleep Times on Health

Earlier, I said that this chapter would end with an important new finding about sleep that would challenge your thinking on this topic. Here it is.

For decades, it has been reported that *Thinking Clearly* sleeping 8 hours or more per night is associated with health and longevity. Now a series of large-scale studies conducted in both the United States and Japan tell a different story (e.g., Ayas et al., 2003; Kripke et al., 2002; Patel et al., 2003; Tamakoshi

& Ohno, 2004). Unlike older studies, these new studies did not include subjects who were a potential source of bias, for example, people who slept little because they were ill, depressed, or under stress. These studies started with a sample of healthy subjects and studied those people's health for several years.

The results of these new studies are remarkably uniform (Kripke, 2004). For example, Figure 14.15 presents data from Tamakoshi and Ohno (2004), who followed 104,010 subjects for 10 years. You will immediately see *Clinical Implications* that sleeping 8 hours per night is not the healthy ideal that it has been assumed to be: The fewest deaths occurred among people sleeping between 5 and 7 hours per night, far fewer than among those who slept 8 hours.

Because these data are correlational, it is important not to interpret them causally. The researchers do not suggest

that sleeping 8 or more hours a night causes health problems: There is just *Thinking Clearly* something about the people who do so that leads them to die sooner than healthy people who sleep less. Although these studies do not prove that reducing your sleep will cause you to live longer, they do provide strong evidence that sleeping less than 8 hours is not a risk to one's health.

Conclusion

In this section, you have learned that people can reduce their sleep time substantially without any apparent ill effects—and that they can reduce their sleep time even further if they adhere to a polyphasic sleep regimen. You also learned that the health of people who sleep between 5 and 7 hours a night does not suffer; indeed, they are the most healthy and live the longest. Admittedly, more of these key long-term studies are required, but they are difficult and expensive to conduct. However, the results of existing studies, though incompatible with popular belief, are consistent and convey a clear message: There is good reason to *Thinking Clearly* question the assumption that the human species has a fundamental need for at least 8 hours of sleep per night.

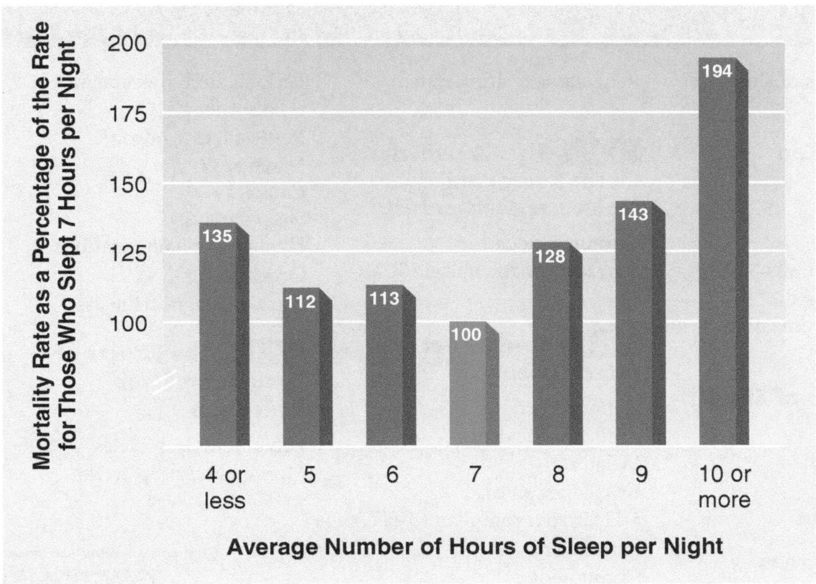

FIGURE 14.15 The mortality rates associated with different amounts of sleep, based on 104,010 subjects followed over 10 years. The mortality rate at 7 hours of sleep per night has been arbitrarily set at 100%, and the other mortality rates are presented in relation to it. (Adapted from Tamakoshi & Ohno, *Sleep* 2004, 27(1): 51–4.)

Bar chart — Mortality Rate as a Percentage of the Rate for Those Who Slept 7 Hours per Night vs. Average Number of Hours of Sleep per Night: 4 or less = 135; 5 = 112; 6 = 113; 7 = 100; 8 = 128; 9 = 143; 10 or more = 194.

Themes Revisited

The thinking clearly theme pervaded this chapter. The major purpose of the chapter was to encourage you to reevaluate conventional ideas about sleep. Has this chapter changed your thinking about sleep? Writing it changed mine.

The evolutionary perspective theme also played a prominent role in this chapter. You learned how thinking about the adaptive function of sleep and comparing sleep in different species have led to interesting insights. Also, you saw how research into the physiology and genetics of sleep has been conducted on nonhuman species.

The clinical implications theme received emphasis in the section on sleep disorders. Perhaps most exciting and interesting were the recent breakthroughs in the understanding of the genetics and physiology of narcolepsy.

Finally, the neuroplasticity theme arose in a fundamental way. The fact that the adult human brain has the capacity to change and adapt raises the possibility that it might successfully adapt to consistent long-term schedules of sleep reduction.

See Hard Copy for additional readings for Chapter 14.

Think about It

1. Do you think your life could be improved by changing when or how long you sleep each day? In what ways? What negative effects do you think such changes might have on you?

2. Some people like to stay up late, some people like to get up early, others like to do both, and still others like to do neither. Design a sleep-reduction program that is tailored to your own preferences and lifestyle and that is consistent with the research literature on circadian cycles and sleep deprivation. The program should produce the greatest benefits for you with the least discomfort.

3. How has reading about sleep research changed your views about sleep? Give three specific examples.

4. Given the evidence that the long-term use of benzodiazepines actually contributes to the problems of insomnia, why are they so commonly prescribed for its treatment?

5. Your friend tells you that everybody needs 8 hours of sleep per night; she points out that every time she stays up late to study, she feels lousy the next day. Convince her that she does not need 8 hours of sleep per night.

> **mypsychkit**
> Studying for an exam? Try the Practice Tests for Chapter 14.

Key Terms

14.1 **The Psychophysiological Measures and Stages of Sleep**

Electroencephalogram (EEG)
Electrooculogram (EOG)
Electromyogram (EMG)
Alpha waves
Delta waves
Initial stage 1 EEG
Emergent stage 1 EEG
REM sleep
Slow-wave sleep (SWS)

14.2 **REM Sleep and Dreaming**

Activation-synthesis theory

14.3 **Why Do We Sleep, and Why Do We Sleep When We Do?**

Recuperation theories of sleep

Circadian theories of sleep

14.5 **Circadian Sleep Cycles**

Circadian rhythms
Zeitgebers
Free-running rhythms
Free-running period
Internal desynchronization
Jet lag

14.6 **Effects of Sleep Deprivation**

Executive function
Microsleeps
Carousel apparatus

14.7 **Four Areas of the Brain Involved in Sleep**

Cerveau isolé preparation
Desynchronized EEG
Encéphale isolé preparation

Reticular activating system

14.8 **The Circadian Clock: Neural and Molecular Mechanisms**

Circadian clock
Suprachiasmatic nuclei (SCN)
Tau

14.9 **Drugs That Affect Sleep**

Hypnotic drugs
Antihypnotic drugs
Melatonin
Benzodiazepines
5-Hydroxytryptophan (5-HTP)
Pineal gland
Chronobiotic

14.10 **Sleep Disorders**

Insomnia
Hypersomnia
Iatrogenic
Sleep apnea

Periodic limb movement disorder
Restless legs syndrome
Narcolepsy
Cataplexy
Sleep paralysis
Hypnagogic hallucinations
Orexin
Nucleus magnocellularis

14.11 **The Effects of Long-Term Sleep Reduction**

Polyphasic sleep cycles
Monophasic sleep cycles

> **mypsychkit**
> Need some help studying the key terms for this chapter? Check out the electronic flash cards for Chapter 14.

12 Hunger, Eating, and Health
Why Do Many People Eat Too Much?

Eating is a behavior that is of interest to virtually everyone. We all do it, and most of us derive great pleasure from it. But for many of us, it becomes a source of serious personal and health problems.

Most eating-related health problems in industrialized nations are associated with eating too much—the average American consumes 3,800 calories per day, about twice the average daily requirement (see Kopelman, 2000). For example, by one estimate, well over half of the adult U.S. population meets the current criteria for clinical obesity, qualifying this problem for epidemic status (see Abelson & Kennedy, 2004). The resulting financial and personal costs are huge. Each year in the United States, about $100 billion is spent treating obesity-related disorders (see Olshansky et al., 2005). Moreover, each year an estimated 300,000 U.S. citizens die from disorders caused by their excessive eating (e.g., diabetes, hypertension, cardiovascular diseases, and some cancers). Although the United States is the trend-setter when it comes to overeating and obesity, many other countries are not far behind.

Ironically, as overeating and obesity have reached epidemic proportions, there has been a related increase in disorders associated with eating too little (see Polivy & Herman, 2002). For example, almost 3% of U.S. adolescents currently suffer from *anorexia nervosa* or *bulimia nervosa*, which can be life-threatening in extreme cases. The message of these statistics is clear. At some time in your life, you or somebody you care about will almost certainly suffer from a life-shortening, eating-related disorder.

The massive increases in obesity and other eating-related disorders that have occurred over the last few decades in many countries stand in stark contrast to most people's thinking about hunger and eating. Most people—and I assume that this includes you—believe that hunger and eating are normally triggered when the body's energy resources fall below a prescribed optimal level, or **set point**. They appreciate that many factors influence hunger and eating, but they assume that the hunger and eating system has evolved to supply the body with just the right amount of energy.

This chapter explores the incompatibility of the set-point assumption with the current epidemic of eating disorders. If we all have hunger and eating systems whose primary function is to maintain energy resources at optimal levels, then eating disorders should be rare. The fact that they are so prevalent suggests that hunger and eating are regulated in some other way.

The first sections of this chapter examine some of the fundamental characteristics of hunger and eating. From this examination, you will emerge with a different way of thinking about hunger, eating, and health. Armed with this new perspective, we will reexamine the clinical problems of obesity and anorexia nervosa in the final sections. This chapter will provide you with new insights of major personal relevance—I guarantee it.

Before you move on to the body of the chapter, I would like you to pause to consider a case study. What would a severely amnesic patient do if offered a meal shortly after finishing one? If his hunger and eating were controlled by energy set points, he would refuse the second meal. Did he?

The Case of the Man Who Forgot Not to Eat

Clinical Implications

R.H. was a 48-year-old male whose progress in graduate school was interrupted by the development of severe amnesia for long-term explicit memory. His amnesia was similar in pattern and severity to that of H.M., whom you met in Chapter 11, and an MRI examination revealed bilateral damage to the medial temporal lobes.

The meals offered to R.H. were selected on the basis of interviews with him about the foods he liked: veal parmigiana (about 750 calories) plus all the apple juice he wanted. On one occasion, he was offered a second meal about 15 minutes after he had eaten the first, and he ate it. When offered a third meal 15 minutes later, he ate that, too. When offered a fourth meal he rejected it, claiming that his "stomach was a little tight."

Then, a few minutes later, R.H. announced that he was going out for a good walk and a meal. When asked what he was going to eat, his answer was "veal parmigiana." Clearly, R.H.'s hunger (i.e., motivation to eat) did not result from an energy deficit (Rozin et al., 1998).

12.1

Digestion, Energy Storage, and Energy Utilization

Before you can understand how hunger works, you will need to understand how your body processes the food you eat. The primary purpose of eating is to supply the body with the molecular building blocks and energy it needs to survive and function (see Blackburn, 2001). This section provides a brief overview of the processes by which food is digested, stored, and converted to energy.

Digestion

The *gastrointestinal tract* and the process of digestion are illustrated in Figure 12.1. **Digestion** is the gastrointestinal

---

mypsychkit

In the module *Thinking about Hunger*, Pinel welcomes you to this chapter and talks about a common misconception about meal-time hunger.

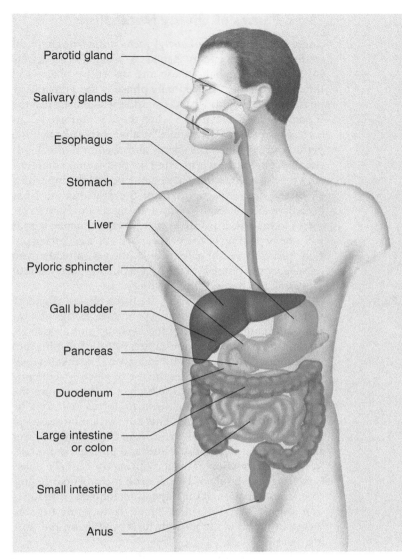

Steps in Digestion

1 Chewing breaks up food and mixes it with saliva.

2 Saliva lubricates food and begins its digestion.

3 Swallowing moves food and drink down the esophagus to the stomach.

4 The primary function of the stomach is to serve as a storage reservoir. The hydrochloric acid in the stomach breaks food down into small particles, and pepsin begins the process of breaking down protein molecules to amino acids.

5 The stomach gradually empties its contents through the pyloric sphincter into the duodenum, the upper portion of the intestine, where most of the absorption takes place.

6 Digestive enzymes in the duodenum, many of them from the gall bladder and pancreas, break down protein molecules to amino acids, and starch and complex sugar molecules to simple sugars. Simple sugars and amino acids readily pass through the duodenum wall into the bloodstream and are carried to the liver.

7 Fats are emulsified (broken into droplets) by bile, which is manufactured in the liver and stored in the gall bladder until it is released into the duodenum. Emulsified fat cannot pass through the duodenum wall and is carried by small ducts in the duodenum wall into the lymphatic system.

8 Most of the remaining water and electrolytes are absorbed from the waste in the large intestine, and the remainder is ejected from the anus.

Labels on figure: Parotid gland, Salivary glands, Esophagus, Stomach, Liver, Pyloric sphincter, Gall bladder, Pancreas, Duodenum, Large intestine or colon, Small intestine, Anus

FIGURE 12.1   The gastrointestinal tract and the process of digestion.

process of breaking down food and absorbing its constituents into the body. In order to appreciate the basics of digestion, it is useful to consider the body without its protuberances, as a simple living tube with a hole at each end. To supply itself with energy and other nutrients, the tube puts food into one of its two holes—typically the one with teeth—and passes the food along its internal canal so that the food can be broken down and partially absorbed from the canal into the body. The leftovers are jettisoned from the other end. Although this is not a particularly appetizing description of eating, it does serve to illustrate that, strictly speaking, food has not been consumed until it has been digested.

Energy Storage in the Body

As a consequence of digestion, energy is delivered to the body in three forms: (1) **lipids** (fats), (2) **amino acids** (the breakdown products of proteins), and (3) **glucose** (a simple sugar that is the breakdown product of complex *carbohydrates*, that is, complex starches and sugars).

The body uses energy continuously, but its consumption is intermittent; therefore, it must store energy for use in the intervals between meals. Energy is stored in three forms: *fats, glycogen*, and *proteins*. Most of the body's energy reserves are stored as fats, relatively little as glycogen and proteins (see Figure 12.2). Thus, changes in the body

Three Phases of Energy Metabolism

There are three phases of *energy metabolism* (the chemical changes by which energy is made available for an organism's use): the cephalic phase, the absorptive phase, and the fasting phase. The **cephalic phase** is the preparatory phase; it often begins with the sight, smell, or even just the thought of food, and it ends when the food starts to be absorbed into the bloodstream. The **absorptive phase** is the period during which the energy absorbed into the bloodstream from the meal is meeting the body's immediate energy needs. The **fasting phase** is the period during which all of the unstored energy from the previous meal has been used and the body is withdrawing energy from its reserves to meet its immediate energy requirements; it ends with the beginning of the next cephalic phase. During periods of rapid weight gain, people often go directly from one absorptive phase into the next cephalic phase, without experiencing an intervening fasting phase.

The flow of energy during the three phases of energy metabolism is controlled by two pancreatic hormones: insulin and glucagon. During the cephalic and absorptive phases, the pancreas releases a great deal of insulin into the bloodstream and very little glucagon. The **insulin** does three things: (1) It promotes the use of glucose as the primary source of energy by the body. (2) It promotes the conversion of bloodborne fuels to forms that can be stored: glucose to glycogen and fat, and amino acids to proteins. (3) It promotes the storage of glycogen in liver and muscle, fat in adipose tissue, and proteins in muscle. In short, the function of insulin during the cephalic phase is to lower the levels of bloodborne fuels, primarily glucose, in anticipation of the impending influx; and its function during the absorptive phase is to minimize the increasing levels of bloodborne fuels by utilizing and storing them.

In contrast to the cephalic and absorptive phases, the fasting phase is characterized by high blood levels of **glucagon** and low levels of insulin. Without high levels of insulin, glucose has difficulty entering most body cells; thus, glucose stops being the body's primary fuel. In effect, this saves the body's glucose for the brain, because insulin is not required for glucose to enter most brain cells. The low levels of insulin also promote the conversion of glycogen and protein to glucose. (The conversion of protein to glucose is called **gluconeogenesis**.)

On the other hand, the high levels of fasting-phase glucagon promote the release of **free fatty acids** from adipose tissue and their use as the body's primary fuel. The high glucagon levels also stimulate the conversion of free fatty acids to **ketones**, which are used by muscles as a source of energy during the fasting phase. After a prolonged period without food, however, the brain also starts to use ketones, thus further conserving the body's resources of glucose.

Figure 12.3 summarizes the major metabolic events associated with the three phases of energy metabolism.

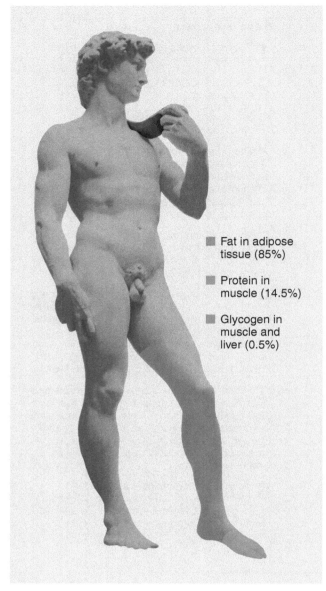

- Fat in adipose tissue (85%)
- Protein in muscle (14.5%)
- Glycogen in muscle and liver (0.5%)

FIGURE 12.2   Distribution of stored energy in an average person.

weights of adult humans are largely a consequence of changes in the amount of their stored body fat.

Because glycogen, which is largely stored in the liver, is readily converted to glucose—the body's main directly utilizable source of energy—one might expect that glycogen would be the body's preferred mode of energy storage. There are two main reasons why fat, rather than glycogen, is the primary mode of energy storage. One is that a gram of fat can store almost twice as much energy as a gram of glycogen; the other is that glycogen, unlike fat, attracts and holds substantial quantities of water. Consequently, if all your fat calories were stored as glycogen, you would likely weigh well over 275 kilograms (600 pounds)

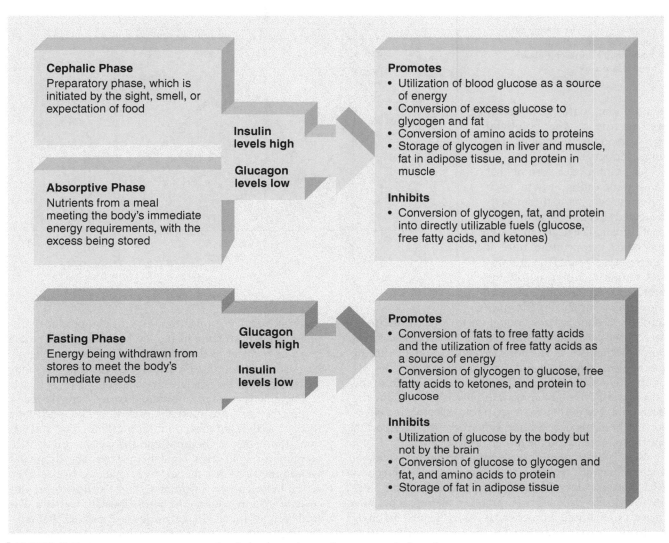

FIGURE 12.3 The major events associated with the three phases of energy metabolism: the cephalic, absorptive, and fasting phases.

12.2

Theories of Hunger and Eating: Set Points versus Positive Incentives

One of the main difficulties I have in teaching the fundamentals of hunger, eating, and body weight regulation is the **set-point assumption**. Although it dominates most people's thinking about hunger and eating (Assanand, Pinel, & Lehman, 1998a, 1998b), whether they realize it or not, it is inconsistent with the bulk of the evidence. What exactly is the set-point assumption?

Set-Point Assumption

Most people attribute *hunger* (the motivation to eat) to the presence of an energy deficit, and they view eating as the means by which the energy resources of the body are returned to their optimal level—that is, to the *energy set point*. Figure 12.4 on page 298 summarizes this set-point assumption. After a *meal* (a bout of eating), a person's energy resources are assumed to be near their set point and to decline thereafter as the body uses energy to fuel its physiological processes. When the level of the body's energy resources falls far enough below the set point, a person becomes motivated by hunger to initiate another meal. The meal continues, according to the set-point

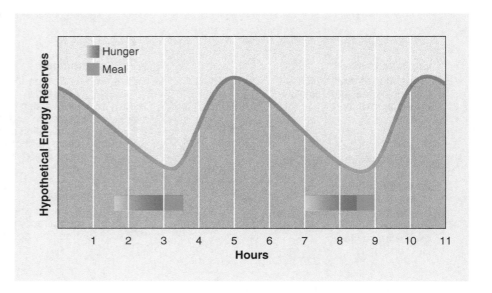

FIGURE 12.4 The energy set-point view that is the basis of many people's thinking about hunger and eating.

assumption, until the energy level returns to its set point and the person feels *satiated* (no longer hungry).

Set-point models assume that hunger and eating work in much the same way as a thermostat-regulated heating system in a cool climate. The heater increases the house temperature until it reaches its set point (the thermostat setting). This turns off the heat, and then the temperature of the house gradually declines until the decline is large enough to turn the heater back on. All set-point systems have three components: a set-point mechanism, a detector mechanism, and an effector mechanism. The *set-point mechanism* defines the set point, the *detector mechanism* detects deviations from the set point, and the *effector mechanism* acts to eliminate the deviations. For example, the set-point, detector, and effector mechanisms of a heating system are the thermostat, the thermometer, and the heater, respectively.

All set-point systems are **negative feedback systems**—systems in which feedback from changes in one direction elicit compensatory effects in the opposite direction. Negative feedback systems are common in mammals because they act to maintain **homeostasis**—a stable internal environment—which is critical for mammals' survival (see Wenning, 1999).

Glucostatic and Lipostatic Set-Point Theories of Hunger and Eating

In the 1940s and 1950s, researchers working under the assumption that eating is regulated by some type of set-point system speculated about the nature of the regulation. Several researchers suggested that eating is regulated by a system that is designed to maintain a blood glucose set point—the idea being that we become hungry when our blood glucose levels drop significantly below their set point and that we become satiated when eating returns our blood glucose levels to their set point. Various versions of this theory are referred to as the **glucostatic theory**. It seemed to make good sense that the main purpose of eating is to defend a blood glucose set point, because glucose is the brain's primary fuel.

The **lipostatic theory** is another set-point theory that was proposed in various forms in the 1940s and 1950s. According to this theory, every person has a set point for body fat, and deviations from this set point produce compensatory adjustments in the level of eating that return levels of body fat to their set point. The most frequently cited support for the theory is the fact that the body weights of adults stay relatively constant.

The glucostatic and lipostatic theories were viewed as complementary, not mutually exclusive. The glucostatic theory was thought to account for meal initiation and termination, whereas the lipostatic theory was thought to account for long-term regulation. Thus, the dominant view in the 1950s was that eating is regulated by the interaction between two set-point systems: a short-term glucostatic system and a long-term lipostatic system. The simplicity of these 1950s theories is appealing. Remarkably, they are still being presented as the latest word in some textbooks; perhaps you have encountered them.

Problems with Set-Point Theories of Hunger and Eating

Set-point theories of hunger and eating have several serious weaknesses (see de Castro & Plunkett, 2002). You have already learned one fact that undermines these theories: the current epidemic of obesity and other eating disorders. Let's look at three more.

- First, set-point theories of hunger and eating are inconsistent with basic eating-related evolutionary pressures as we understand them. The major eating-related problem faced by our ancestors was the inconsistency and unpredictability of the food supply. Thus, in order to survive, it was important for them to eat large quantities of good food when it was available so that calories could be banked in the form of body fat. Any ancestor—human or otherwise—that stopped feeling hungry as soon as immediate energy needs were met would not have survived the first hard winter or prolonged drought. For any warm-blooded species to survive under natural conditions, it needs a hunger and eating system that prevents energy deficits, rather than one that merely responds to them once they have developed. From this perspective, it is difficult to imagine how a set-point hunger and feeding system could have evolved in mammals (see Pinel, Assanand, & Lehman, 2000).

● Second, major predictions of the set-point theories of hunger and eating have not been confirmed. Early studies seemed to support the set-point theories by showing that large reductions in body fat, produced by starvation, or large reductions in blood glucose, produced by insulin injections, induce increases in eating in laboratory animals. The problem is that reductions in blood glucose of the magnitude needed to reliably induce eating rarely occur naturally. Indeed, as you have already learned in this chapter, over 50% of the U.S. adult population has a significant excess of fat deposits when they begin a meal. Conversely, efforts to reduce meal size by having subjects consume a high-calorie drink before eating have been largely unsuccessful; indeed, beliefs about the caloric content of a premeal drink often influence the size of a subsequent meal more than does its actual caloric content (see Lowe, 1993).

● Third, set-point theories of hunger and eating are deficient because they fail to recognize the major influences on hunger and eating of such important factors *Thinking Clearly* as taste, learning, and social influences. To convince yourself of the importance of these factors, pause for a minute and imagine the sight, smell, and taste of your favorite food. Perhaps it is a succulent morsel of lobster meat covered with melted garlic butter, a piece of chocolate cheesecake, or a plate of sizzling homemade french fries. Are you starting to feel a bit hungry? If homemade French fries—my personal weakness—were sitting in front of you right now, wouldn't you reach out and have one, or maybe the whole plateful? Have you not on occasion felt discomfort after a large main course, only to polish off a substantial dessert? The usual positive answers to these questions lead unavoidably to the conclusion that hunger and eating are not rigidly controlled by deviations from energy set points.

Positive-Incentive Perspective

The inability of set-point theories to account for the basic phenomena of eating and hunger has led to the development of an alternative theoretical perspective (see Berridge, 2004). The central assertion of this new theoretical perspective, commonly referred to as **positive-incentive theory**, is that humans and other animals are not normally driven to eat by internal energy deficits but are drawn to eat by the anticipated pleasure of eating—the anticipated pleasure of a behavior is called its **positive-incentive value** (see Bolles, 1980; Booth, 1981; Collier, 1980; Rolls, 1981; Toates, 1981). There are several different positive-incentive theories, and I refer generally to all of them as the *positive-incentive perspective*.

The major tenet of the positive-incentive perspective on eating is that eating is controlled in much the same way as sexual behavior: We engage in sexual behavior not because we have an internal deficit, but because we have evolved to crave it. The evolutionary pressures of unexpected food shortages have shaped us and all other warm-blooded animals, who need a continuous supply of energy to maintain their body temperatures, to take advantage of good food when it is present and eat it. According to the positive-incentive perspective, it is the presence of good food, or the anticipation of it, that normally makes us hungry, not an energy deficit.

According to the positive-incentive perspective, the degree of hunger you feel at any particular time depends on the interaction of all the factors that influence the positive-incentive value of eating. These include the following: the flavor of the food you are likely to consume, what you have learned about the effects of this food either from eating it previously or from other people, the amount of time since you last ate, the type and quantity of food in your gut, whether or not other people are present and eating, whether or not your blood glucose levels are within the normal range. This partial list illustrates one strength of the positive-incentive perspective. Unlike set-point theories, positive-incentive theories do not single out one factor as the major determinant of hunger and ignore the others; they acknowledge that many factors interact to determine a person's hunger at any time, and they suggest that this interaction occurs through the influence of these various factors on the positive-incentive value of eating (see Cabanac, 1971).

In this section, you learned that most people think about hunger and eating in terms of energy set points, and you were introduced to an alternative: the positive-incentive perspective. Which is correct? If you are like most people, you will have an attachment to familiar ways of thinking and a *Thinking Clearly* resistance to new ones. The principles of clear thinking, however, require that you put these tendencies aside and base your views about this important issue entirely on the evidence.

You have already learned about some of the major weaknesses of set-point theories of hunger and eating. In the next section, you will learn some of the things that biopsychological research has taught us about eating. As you progress through the section, notice the superiority of the positive-incentive theories over set-point theories in accounting for the basic facts of hunger and eating.

12.3

Factors That Determine What, When, and How Much We Eat

This section describes major factors that commonly determine what we eat, when we eat, and how much we eat. Notice that energy deficits are not included among these factors. Although major energy deficits clearly increase hunger and eating, they are not a common factor in the eating behavior of people like us, who live in food-replete societies. Although you may believe that your body is short of energy just before a meal, it is not. This misconception is one that is addressed in this section. Also, notice how research on nonhumans has played an important role in furthering understanding of eating by our species.

Factors That Determine What We Eat

Certain tastes have a high positive-incentive value for virtually all members of a species. For example, most humans have a special fondness for sweet, fatty, and salty tastes. This species-typical pattern of human taste preferences is adaptive because in nature sweet and fatty tastes are typically characteristic of high-energy foods that are rich in vitamins and minerals, and salty tastes are characteristic of sodium-rich foods. In contrast, bitter tastes, for which most humans have an aversion, are often associated with toxins. Superimposed on our species-typical taste preferences and aversions, each of us has the ability to learn specific taste preferences and aversions (see Rozin & Shulkin, 1990).

Learned Taste Preferences and Aversions Animals learn to prefer tastes that are followed by an infusion of calories, and they learn to avoid tastes that are followed by illness (e.g., Baker & Booth, 1989; Lucas & Sclafani, 1989; Sclafani, 1990). In addition, humans and other animals learn what to eat from their conspecifics. For example, rats learn to prefer flavors that they experience in mother's milk and those that they smell on the breaths of other rats (see Galef, 1995, 1996; Galef, Whishkin, & Bielavska, 1997). Similarly, in humans, many food preferences are culturally specific—for example, in some cultures, various nontoxic insects are considered to be a delicacy. Galef and Wright (1995) have shown that rats reared in groups, rather than in isolation, are more likely to learn to eat a healthy diet.

Learning to Eat Vitamins and Minerals How do animals select a diet that provides all of the vitamins and minerals they need? To answer this question, researchers have studied how dietary deficiencies influence diet selec-

tion. Two patterns of results have emerged: one for sodium and one for the other essential vitamins and minerals. When an animal is deficient in sodium, it develops an immediate and compelling preference for the taste of sodium salt (see Rowland, 1990). In contrast, an animal that is deficient in some vitamin or mineral other than sodium must learn to consume foods that are rich in the missing nutrient by experiencing their positive effects; this is because vitamins and minerals other than sodium normally have no detectable taste in food. For example, rats maintained on a diet deficient in *thiamine* (vitamin B1) develop an aversion to the taste of that diet; and if they are offered two new diets, one deficient in thiamine and one rich in thiamine, they often develop a preference for the taste of the thiamine-rich diet over the ensuing days, as it becomes associated with improved health.

If we, like rats, are capable of learning to select diets that are rich in the vitamins and minerals we need, why are dietary deficiencies so prevalent in our society? One reason is that, in order to maximize profits, manufacturers produce foods with the tastes that we prefer but with most of the essential nutrients extracted from them. (Even rats prefer chocolate chip cookies to nutritionally complete rat chow.) The second reason is illustrated by the classic study of Harris and associates (1933). When thiamine-deficient rats were offered two new diets, one with thiamine and one without, almost all of them learned to eat the complete diet and avoid the deficient one. However, when they were offered ten new diets, only one of which contained the badly needed thiamine, few developed a preference for the complete diet. The number of different substances, both nutritious and not, consumed each day by most people in industrialized societies is immense, and this makes it difficult, if not impossible, for their bodies to learn which foods are beneficial and which are not.

There is not much about nutrition in this chapter: Although it is critically important to eat a nutritious diet, nutrition seems to have little direct effect on our feelings of hunger. However, while I am on the topic, I would like to direct you to a good source of information about nutrition that could have a positive effect on your health: Some 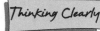 popular books on nutrition are dangerous, and even governments, inordinately influenced by economic considerations and special-interest groups, often do not provide the best nutritional advice (see Nestle, 2003). For sound research-based advice on nutrition, check out an article by Willett and Stampfer (2003) and the book on which it is based (Willett, Skerrett, & Giovannucci, 2001).

Factors That Influence When We Eat

Collier and his colleagues (see Collier, 1986) found that most mammals choose to eat many small meals (snacks) each

day if they have ready access to a continuous supply of food. Only when there are physical costs involved in initiating meals—for example, having to travel a considerable distance—does an animal opt for a few large meals.

The number of times humans eat each day is influenced by cultural norms, work schedules, family routines, personal preferences, wealth, and a variety of other factors. However, in contrast to the usual mammalian preference, most people, particularly those living in family groups, tend to eat a few large meals each day at regular times. Interestingly, each person's regular mealtimes are the very same times at which that person is likely to feel most hungry; in fact, many people experience attacks of malaise (headache, nausea, and an inability to concentrate) when they miss a regularly scheduled meal.

Premeal Hunger   I am sure that you have experienced attacks of premeal hunger. Subjectively, they seem to provide compelling support for set-point theories. Your body seems to be crying out: "I need more energy. I cannot function without it. Please feed me." But things are not always the way they seem. Woods has straightened out the confusion (see Woods, 1991; Woods & Ramsay, 2000; Woods & Strubbe, 1994).

According to Woods, the key to understanding hunger is to appreciate that eating meals stresses the body. Before a meal, the body's energy reserves are in reasonable homeostatic balance; then, as a meal is consumed, there is a homeostasis-disturbing influx of fuels into the bloodstream. The body does what it can to defend its homeostasis. At the first indication that a person will soon be eating—for example, when the usual mealtime approaches—the body enters the cephalic phase and takes steps to soften the impact of the impending homeostasis-disturbing influx by releasing insulin into the blood and thus reducing blood glucose. Woods's message is that the strong, unpleasant feelings of hunger that you may experience at mealtimes are not cries from your body for food; they are the sensations of your body's preparations for the expected homeostasis-disturbing meal. Mealtime hunger is caused by the expectation of food, not by an energy deficit.

Thinking Clearly   As a high school student, I ate lunch at exactly 12:05 every day and was overwhelmed by hunger as the time approached. Now, my eating schedule is different, and I never experience noontime hunger pangs; I now get hungry just before the time at which I usually eat. Have you had a similar experience?

Pavlovian Conditioning of Hunger   In a classic series of Pavlovian conditioning experiments on laboratory rats, Weingarten (1983, 1984, 1985) provided strong support for the view that hunger is often caused by the expectation of food, not by an energy deficit. During the conditioning phase of one of his experiments, Weingarten

presented rats with six meals per day at irregular intervals, and he signaled the impending delivery of each meal with a buzzer-and-light conditional stimulus. This conditioning procedure was continued for 11 days. Throughout the ensuing test phase of the experiment, the food was continuously available. Despite the fact that the subjects were never deprived during the test phase, the rats started to eat each time the buzzer and light were presented—even if they had recently completed a meal.

Factors That Influence How Much We Eat

The motivational state that causes us to stop eating a meal when there is food remaining is **satiety**. Satiety mechanisms play a major role in determining how much we eat.

Satiety Signals   As you will learn in the next section of the chapter, food in the gut and glucose entering the blood can induce satiety signals, which inhibit subsequent consumption. These signals depend on both the volume and the **nutritive density** (calories per unit volume) of the food.

The effects of nutritive density have been demonstrated in studies in which laboratory rats have been maintained on a single diet. Once a stable baseline of consumption has been established, the nutritive density of the diet is changed. Some rats learn to adjust the volume of food they consume to keep their caloric intake and body weights relatively stable. However, there are major limits to this adjustment: Rats rarely increase their intake sufficiently to maintain their body weights if the nutritive density of their conventional laboratory feed is reduced by more than 50% or if there are major changes in the diet's palatability.

The Evolutionary Perspective

Sham Eating   The study of **sham eating** indicates that satiety signals from the gut or blood are not necessary to terminate a meal. In sham-eating experiments, food is chewed and swallowed by the subject; but rather than passing down the subject's esophagus into the stomach, it passes out of the body through an implanted tube (see Figure 12.5 on page 302).

Because sham eating adds no energy to the body, set-point theories predict that all sham-eaten meals should be huge. But this is not the case. Weingarten and Kulikovsky (1989) sham fed rats one of two differently flavored diets: one that the rats had naturally eaten many times before and one that they had never eaten before. The first sham meal of the rats that had previously eaten the diet was the same size as the previously eaten meals of that diet; then, on ensuing days they began to sham eat more and more (see Figure 12.6 on page 302). In contrast, the rats that were presented with the unfamiliar diet sham ate large quantities right from the start. Weingarten and Kulikovsky concluded that the amount we eat is influ-

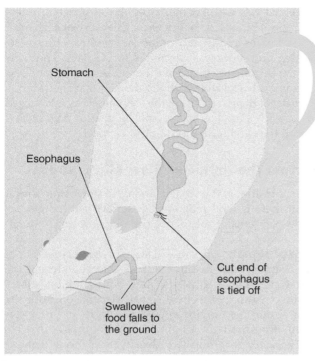

FIGURE 12.5   The sham-eating preparation.

Serving Size and Satiety   Many experiments have shown that the amount of consumption is influenced by serving size (Geier, Rozin, & Doros, 2006). The larger the servings, the more we tend to eat. There is even evidence that we tend to eat more when we eat with larger spoons.

Social Influences and Satiety   Feelings of satiety may also depend on whether we are eating alone or with others. Redd and de Castro (1992) found that their subjects consumed 60% more when eating with others. Laboratory rats also eat substantially more when fed in groups.

In humans, social factors have also been shown to reduce consumption. Many people eat less than they would like in order to achieve their society's ideal of slenderness, and others refrain from eating large amounts in front of others so as not to appear gluttonous. Unfortunately, in our culture, females are greatly influenced by such pressures, and, as you will learn later in the chapter, some develop serious eating disorders as a result.

Sensory-Specific Satiety   The number of different tastes available at each meal has a major effect on meal size. For example, the effect of offering a laboratory rat a varied diet of highly palatable foods—a **cafeteria diet**—is dramatic. Adults rats that were offered bread and chocolate in addition to their usual laboratory diet increased their average intake of calories by 84%, and after 120 days they had increased their average body weights by 49% (Rogers & Blundell, 1980). The spectacular effects of cafeteria diets on consumption and body weight clearly run

enced largely by our previous experience with the particular food's physiological effects, not by the immediate effect of the food on the body.

Appetizer Effect and Satiety   The next time you attend a dinner party, you may experience a major weakness of the set-point theory of satiety. If appetizers are served, you will experience the fact that small amounts of food consumed before a meal actually increase hunger rather than reducing it. This is the **appetizer effect**. Presumably, it occurs because the consumption of a small amount of food is particularly effective in eliciting cephalic-phase responses.

Thinking Clearly

FIGURE 12.6   Change in the magnitude of sham eating over repeated sham-eating trials. The rats in one group sham ate the same diet they had eaten before the sham-eating phase; the rats in another group sham ate a diet different from the one they had previously eaten. (Adapted from Weingarten, 1990.)

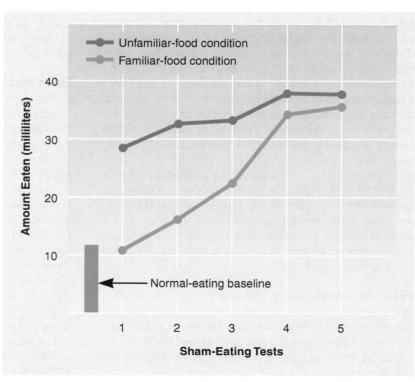

counter to the idea that satiety is rigidly controlled by internal energy set points.

The effect on meal size of cafeteria diets results from the fact that satiety is to a large degree taste-specific. As you eat one food, the positive-incentive value of all foods declines slightly, but the positive-incentive value of that particular food plummets. As a result, you soon become satiated on that food and stop eating it. However, if another food is offered to you, you will often begin eating again.

In one study of **sensory-specific satiety** (Rolls et al., 1981), human subjects were asked to rate the palatability of eight different foods, and then they ate a meal of one of them. After the meal, they were asked to rate the palatability of the eight foods once again, and it was found that their rating of the food they had just eaten had declined substantially more than had their ratings of the other seven foods. Moreover, when the subjects were offered an unexpected second meal, they consumed most of it unless it was the same as the first.

Booth (1981) asked subjects to rate the momentary pleasure produced by the flavor, the smell, the sight, or just the thought of various foods at different times after consuming a large, high-calorie, high-carbohydrate liquid meal. There was an immediate sensory-specific decrease in the palatability of foods of the same or similar flavor as soon as the liquid meal was consumed. This was followed by a general decrease in the palatability of all substances about 30 minutes later. Thus, it appears that signals from taste receptors produce an immediate decline in the positive-incentive value of similar tastes and that signals associated with the postingestive consequences of eating produce a general decrease in the positive-incentive value of all foods.

Rolls (1990) suggested that sensory-specific satiety has two kinds of effects: relatively brief effects that influence the selection of foods within a single meal and relatively enduring effects that influence the selection of foods from meal to meal. Some foods seem to be relatively immune to long-lasting sensory-specific satiety; foods such as rice, bread, potatoes, sweets, and green salads can be eaten almost every day with only a slight decline in their palatability (Rolls, 1986).

The phenomenon of sensory-specific satiety has two adaptive consequences. First, it encourages the consumption of a varied diet. If there were *The Evolutionary Perspective* no sensory-specific satiety, a person would tend to eat her or his preferred food and nothing else, and the result would be malnutrition. Second, sensory-specific satiety encourages animals that have access to a variety of foods to eat a lot; an animal that has eaten its fill of one food will often begin eating again if it encounters a different one (Raynor & Epstein, 2001). This encourages animals to take full advantage of times of abundance, which are all too rare in nature.

Scan Your Brain

Are you ready to move on to the discussion of the physiology of hunger and satiety in the following section? Find out by completing the following sentences with the most appropriate terms. The correct answers are provided below. Before proceeding, review material related to your incorrect answers and omissions.

1. The primary function of the _____ is to serve as a storage reservoir for undigested food.
2. Most of the absorption of nutrients into the body takes place through the wall of the _____, or upper intestine.
3. The phase of energy metabolism that is triggered by the expectation of food is the _____ phase.
4. During the absorptive phase, the pancreas releases a great deal of _____ into the bloodstream.
5. During the fasting phase, the primary fuels of the body are _____.
6. During the fasting phase, the primary fuel of the brain is _____.
7. The three components of a set-point system are a set-point mechanism, a detector, and an _____.
8. The theory that hunger and satiety are regulated by a blood glucose set point is the _____ theory.
9. Evidence suggests that hunger is greatly influenced by the current _____ value of food.
10. Most humans have a preference for sweet, fatty, and _____ tastes.
11. There are two mechanisms by which we learn to eat diets containing essential vitamins and minerals: one mechanism for _____ and another mechanism for the rest.
12. Satiety that is specific to the particular foods that produce it is called _____ satiety.

Scan Your Brain answers: (1) stomach, (2) duodenum, (3) cephalic, (4) insulin, (5) free fatty acids, (6) glucose, (7) effector, (8) glucostatic, (9) positive-incentive, (10) salty, (11) sodium, (12) sensory-specific.

12.4

Physiological Research on Hunger and Satiety

Now that you have been introduced to set-point theories, the positive-incentive perspective, and some basic factors that affect why, when, and how much we eat, this section introduces you to five prominent lines of research on the physiology of hunger and satiety.

Role of Blood Glucose Levels in Hunger and Satiety

As I have already explained, efforts to link blood glucose levels to eating have been largely unsuccessful. However, there was a renewed interest in the role of glucose in the regulation of eating in the 1990s, following the development of methods of continually monitoring blood glucose levels. In the classic experiment of Campfield and Smith (1990), rats were housed individually, with free access to a mixed diet and water, and their blood glucose levels were continually monitored via a chronic intravenous catheter (i.e., a hypodermic needle located in a vein). In this situation, baseline blood glucose levels rarely fluctuated more than 2%. However, about 10 minutes before a meal was initiated, the levels suddenly dropped about 8% (see Figure 12.7).

Do the observed reductions in blood glucose before a meal lend support to the glucostatic theory of hunger? I think not, for five reasons.

- It is a simple matter to construct a situation in which drops in blood glucose levels do not precede eating (e.g., Strubbe & Steffens, 1977)—for example, by unexpectedly serving a food with a high positive-incentive value.
- The usual premeal decreases in blood glucose seem to be a response to the intention to start eating, not the other way round. The premeal decreases in blood glucose are typically preceded by increases in blood insulin levels, which indicates that the decreases do not reflect gradually declining energy reserves but are actively produced by an increase in blood levels of insulin (see Figure 12.7).
- If an expected meal is not served, blood glucose levels soon return to their previous homeostatic level.
- The glucose levels in the extracellular fluids that surround CNS neurons stay relatively constant, even when blood glucose levels drop (see Seeley & Woods, 2003).
- Injections of insulin do not reliably induce eating unless the injections are sufficiently great to reduce blood glucose levels by 50% (see Rowland, 1981), and

large premeal infusions of glucose do not suppress eating (see Geiselman, 1987).

Myth of Hypothalamic Hunger and Satiety Centers

In the 1950s, experiments on rats seemed to suggest that eating behavior is controlled by two different regions of the hypothalamus: satiety by the **ventromedial hypothalamus (VMH)** and feeding by the **lateral hypothalamus (LH)**—see Figure 12.8. This theory turned out to be wrong, but it stimulated several important discoveries.

VMH Satiety Center   In 1940, it was discovered that large bilateral electrolytic lesions to the ventromedial hypothalamus produce **hyperphagia** (excessive eating) and extreme obesity in rats (Hetherington & Ranson, 1940). This *VMH syndrome* has two different phases: dynamic and static. The **dynamic phase**, which begins as soon as the subject regains consciousness after the operation, is characterized by several weeks of grossly excessive eating and rapid weight gain. However, after that, consumption gradually declines to a level that is just sufficient to maintain a stable level of obesity; this marks the beginning of the **static phase**. Figure 12.9 illustrates the weight gain and food intake of an adult rat with bilateral VMH lesions.

The most important feature of the static phase of the VMH syndrome is that the animal maintains its new body weight. If a rat in the static phase is deprived of food until it has lost a substantial amount of weight, it will regain the lost weight once the deprivation ends; conversely, if it is made to gain weight by forced feeding, it will lose the excess weight once the forced feeding is curtailed.

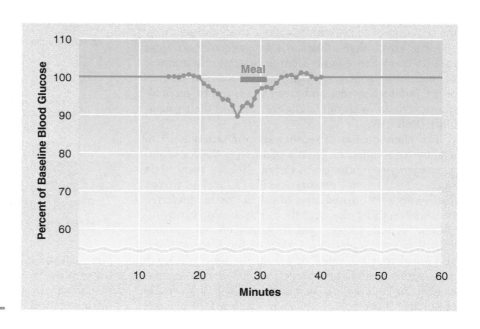

FIGURE 12.7   The meal-related changes in blood glucose levels observed by Campfield and Smith (1990).

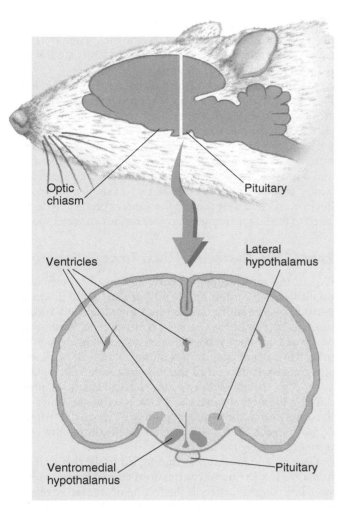

FIGURE 12.8 The locations in the rat brain of the ventromedial hypothalamus and the lateral hypothalamus.

Paradoxically, despite their prodigious levels of consumption, VMH-lesioned rats in some ways seem less hungry than unlesioned controls. Although VMH-lesioned rats eat much more than normal rats when palatable food is readily available, they are less willing to work for it (Teitelbaum, 1957) or to consume it if it is slightly unpalatable (Miller, Bailey, & Stevenson, 1950). Weingarten, Chang, and Jarvie (1983) showed that the finicky eating of VMH-lesioned rats is a consequence of their obesity, not a primary effect of their lesion; they are no less likely to consume unpalatable food than are unlesioned rats of equal obesity.

LH Feeding Center   In 1951, Anand and Brobeck reported that bilateral electrolytic lesions to the *lateral hypothalamus* produce **aphagia**—a complete cessation of eating. Even rats that were first made hyperphagic by

VMH lesions were rendered aphagic by the addition of LH lesions. Anand and Brobeck concluded that the lateral region of the hypothalamus is a feeding center. Teitelbaum and Epstein (1962) subsequently discovered two important features of the *LH syndrome*. First, they found that the aphagia was accompanied by **adipsia**—a complete cessation of drinking. Second, they found that LH-lesioned rats partially recover if they are kept alive by tube feeding. First, they begin to eat wet, palatable foods, such as chocolate chip cookies soaked in milk, and eventually they will eat dry food pellets if water is concurrently available.

Reinterpretation of the Effects of VMH and LH Lesions   The theory that the VMH is a satiety center crumbled in the face of two lines of evidence. One of these lines showed that the primary role of the hypothalamus is the regulation of energy metabolism, not the regulation of eating. The initial interpretation was that VMH-lesioned animals become obese because they overeat; however, the evidence suggests the converse—that they overeat because they become obese. Bilateral VMH lesions increase blood insulin levels, which

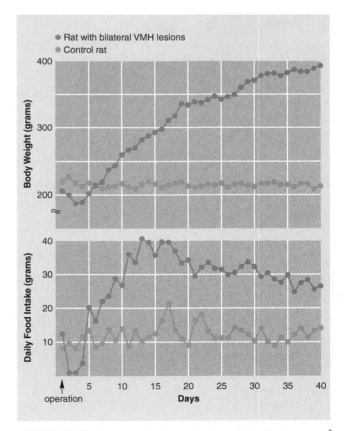

FIGURE 12.9 Postoperative hyperphagia and obesity in a rat with bilateral VMH lesions. (Adapted from Teitelbaum, 1961.)

increases **lipogenesis** (the production of body fat) and decreases **lipolysis** (the breakdown of body fat to utilizable forms of energy)—see Powley et al. (1980). Both are likely to be the result of the increases in insulin levels that occur following the lesion. Because the calories ingested by VMH-lesioned rats are converted to fat at a high rate, the rats must keep eating to ensure that they have enough calories in their blood to meet their immediate energy requirements (e.g., Hustvedt & Løvø, 1972); they are like misers who run to the bank each time they make a bit of money and deposit it in a savings account from which withdrawals cannot be made.

The second line of evidence that undermined the theory of a VMH satiety center has shown that many of the effects of VMH lesions are not attributable to VMH damage. A large fiber bundle, the *ventral noradrenergic bundle*, courses past the VMH and is thus inevitably damaged by large electrolytic VMH lesions; in particular, fibers that project from the nearby **paraventricular nuclei** of the hypothalamus are damaged (see Figure 12.10). Bilateral le-

sions of the noradrenergic bundle (e.g., Gold et al., 1977) or the paraventricular nuclei (Leibowitz, Hammer, & Chang, 1981) produce hyperphagia and obesity similar to those produced by VMH lesions.

Most of the evidence against the notion that the LH is a feeding center has come from a thorough analysis of the effects of bilateral LH lesions. Early research focused exclusively on the aphagia and adipsia that are produced by LH lesions, but subsequent research has shown that LH lesions produce a wide range of severe motor disturbances and a general lack of responsiveness to sensory input (of which food and drink are but two examples). Consequently, the idea that the LH is a center specifically dedicated to feeding no longer warrants serious consideration.

Role of the Gastrointestinal Tract in Satiety

One of the most influential early studies of hunger was published by Cannon and Washburn in 1912. It was a perfect collaboration: Cannon had the ideas, and Washburn had the ability to swallow a balloon. First, Washburn swallowed an empty balloon tied to the end of a thin tube. Then, Cannon pumped some air into the balloon and connected the end of the tube to a water-filled glass U-tube so that Washburn's stomach contractions produced a momentary increase in the level of the water at the other end of the U-tube. Washburn reported a "pang" of hunger each time that a large stomach contraction was recorded (see Figure 12.11).

Cannon and Washburn's finding led to the theory that hunger is the feeling of contractions caused by an empty stomach, whereas satiety is the feeling of stomach distention. However, support for this theory and interest in the role of the gastrointestinal tract in hunger and satiety quickly waned with the discovery that human patients whose stomachs had been surgically removed and whose esophaguses had been hooked up directly to their **duodenums** continued to report feelings of hunger and satiety and continued to maintain their normal body weights by eating more meals of smaller size.

In the 1980s, there was a resurgence of interest in the role of the gastrointestinal tract in eating. It was stimulated by a series of experiments that indicated that the gastrointestinal tract is the source of satiety signals. For example, Koopmans (1981) transplanted an extra stomach and length of intestine into rats and then joined the major arteries and veins of the implants to the recipients' circulatory systems (see Figure 12.12 on page 308). Koopmans found that food injected into the transplanted stomach and kept there by a noose around the *pyloric sphincter* decreased eating in proportion to both its caloric content and volume. Because the transplanted stomach had no functional nerves, the gastrointestinal satiety signal had to be reaching the brain through the blood. And because nutrients are not absorbed from the stomach, the bloodborne satiety signal could not have

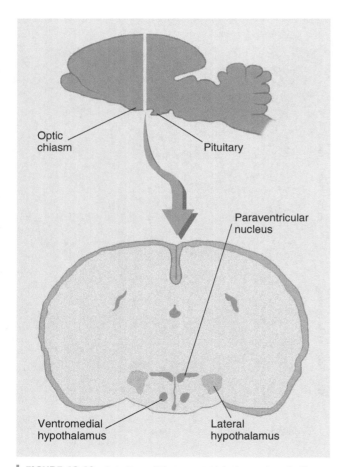

FIGURE 12.10 Location of the paraventricular nucleus in the rat hypothalamus. Note that the section through the hypothalamus is slightly different than the one in Figure 12.8.

Optic chiasm

Pituitary

Paraventricular nucleus

Ventromedial hypothalamus

Lateral hypothalamus

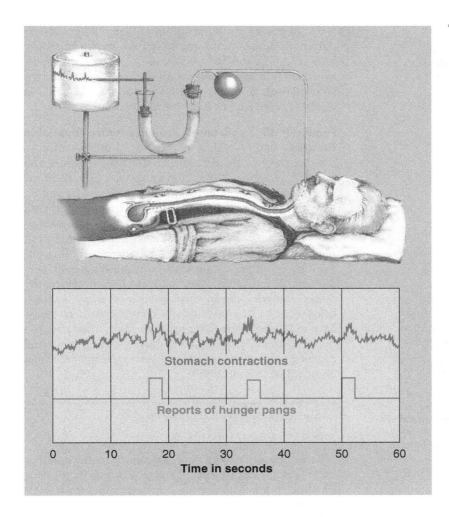

FIGURE 12.11 The system developed by Cannon and Washburn in 1912 for measuring stomach contractions. They found that large stomach contractions were related to pangs of hunger.

There has been considerable support for the hypothesis that peptides can function as satiety signals (see Ritter, 2004). Several gut peptides have been shown to bind to receptors in the brain, particularly in the hypothalamus, and a dozen or so (e.g., CCK, bombesin, glucagon, alpha-melanocyte-stimulating hormone, and somatostatin) have been reported to reduce food intake (see Batterham et al., 2006; Strubbe & van Dijk, 2002; Zhang et al., 2005). These have become known as *satiety peptides* (peptides that decrease appetite).

In studying the appetite-reducing effects of peptides, researchers had to rule out the possibility that these effects are not merely the consequence of illness (see Moran, 2004). Indeed, there is evidence that one peptide in particular, CCK, induces illness: CCK administered to rats after they have eaten an unfamiliar substance induces a *conditioned taste aversion* for that substance, and CCK induces nausea in human subjects. However, CCK reduces appetite and eating at doses substantially below those that are required to induce taste aversion in rats, and thus it qualifies as a legitimate *satiety peptide* (a peptide that decreases appetite).

Several *hunger peptides* (peptides that increase appetite) have also been discovered. These peptides tend to be synthesized in the brain, particularly in the hypothalamus. The most widely studied of these are neuropeptide Y, galanin, orexin-A, and ghrelin (e.g., Baird, Gray, & Fischer, 2006; Williams et al., 2004).

The discovery of the hunger and satiety peptides has had two major effects on the search for the neural mechanisms of hunger and satiety. First, the sheer number of these hunger and satiety peptides indicates that the neural system that controls eating likely reacts to many different signals (see Berthoud, 2002; Nogueiras & Tschöp, 2005; Schwartz & Azzara, 2004), not just to one or two (e.g., not just to glucose and fat). Second, the discovery that many of the hunger and satiety peptides have receptors in the hypothalamus has renewed interest in the role of the hypothalamus in hunger and eating (Horvath & Diano, 2004; Lam, Schwartz, & Rossetti, 2006; Luquet et al., 2005; Mercer & Speakman, 2001). This interest was further stimulated by the discovery that microinjection of

been a nutrient. It had to be some chemical or chemicals that were released from the stomach in response to the caloric value and volume of the food—which leads us nicely into the next subsection.

Hunger and Satiety Peptides

Soon after the discovery that the stomach and other parts of the gastrointestinal tract release chemical signals to 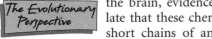 the brain, evidence began to accumulate that these chemicals were *peptides*, short chains of amino acids that can function as hormones and neurotransmitters. Ingested food interacts with receptors in the gastrointestinal tract and in so doing causes the tract to release peptides into the bloodstream. In 1973, Gibbs, Young, and Smith injected one of these gut peptides, **cholecystokinin (CCK)**, into hungry rats and found that they ate smaller meals. This led to the hypothesis that circulating gut peptides provide the brain with information about the quantity and nature of food in the gastrointestinal tract and that this information plays a role in satiety (see Badman & Flier, 2005; Flier, 2006).

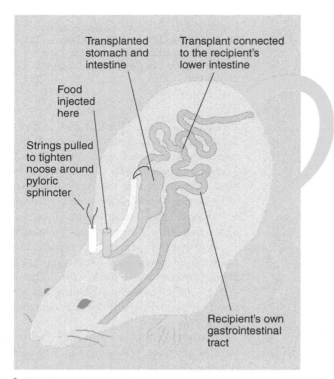

FIGURE 12.12 Transplantation of an extra stomach and length of intestine in a rat. Koopmans (1981) implanted an extra stomach and length of intestine in each of his experimental subjects. He then connected the major blood vessels of the implanted stomachs to the circulatory systems of the recipients. Food injected into the extra stomach and kept there by a noose around the pyloric sphincter decreased eating in proportion to its volume and caloric value.

gut peptides into some sites in the hypothalamus can have major effects on eating. Still, there is a general acceptance that hypothalamic circuits are only one part of a much larger system (see Cone, 2005).

Serotonin and Satiety

The monoaminergic neurotransmitter serotonin seems to play a role in satiety. The initial evidence for this role  came from a line of research on rats that was initiated in the 1970s. In these studies, serotonin agonists consistently reduced rats' food intake.

In rats, the satiety-inducing effects of serotonin have three major characteristics (see Blundell & Halford, 1998).

- They can even overcome the powerful attraction of highly palatable cafeteria diets.
- They reduce the amount of food that is consumed during each meal rather than reducing the number of meals (see Clifton, 2000).
- They are associated with a shift in food preferences away from fatty foods.

In humans, serotonin agonists (e.g., fenfluramine, dexfenfluramine, fluoxetine) have been shown to reduce hunger, eating, and body weight under a variety of conditions (see Blundell & Halford, 1998). Later in this chapter, you will learn about the use of serotonin in the treatment of obesity (see De Vry & Schreiber, 2000).

Prader-Willi Syndrome: Patients with Insatiable Hunger Prader-Willi syndrome could prove critical in the discovery of the neural mechanisms of hunger and satiety (Goldstone, 2004). Individuals with this syndrome experience insatiable hunger, little or no satiety, and an exceptionally slow metabolism. In short, the Prader-Willi patient acts as though he or she is starving. Other common physical and neurological symptoms include weak muscles, small hands and feet, stubbornness, feeding difficulties in infancy, tantrums, compulsivity, and skin picking. If untreated, most patients become extremely obese, and they die in early adulthood from diabetes, heart disease, or other obesity-related disorders. Some have even died from gorging until their stomachs split open. Fortunately, Miss A. was diagnosed in infancy and received excellent care, which kept her from becoming obese (Martin et al., 1998).

Prader-Willi Syndrome: The Case of Miss A.

Miss A. was born with little muscle tone. Because her sucking reflex was so weak, she was tube fed. By the time she was 2 years old, her *hypotonia* (below-normal muscle tone) had resolved itself, but a number of characteristic deformities and developmental delays began to appear.

At 3½ years of age, Miss A. suddenly began to display a voracious appetite and quickly gained weight. Fortunately, her family maintained her on a low-calorie diet and kept all food locked away.

Miss A. is moderately retarded, and she suffers from psychiatric problems. Her major problem is her tendency to have tantrums any time anything changes in her environment (e.g., a substitute teacher at school). Thanks largely to her family and pediatrician, she has received excellent care, which has minimized the complications that arise with Prader-Willi syndrome—most notably those related to obesity and its pathological effects.

Although the study of Prader-Willi syndrome has yet to provide any direct evidence about the neural mechanisms of hunger and eating, there has been a marked surge in its investigation. This increase has been stimulated by the recent identification of the genetic cause of the condition: an accident of reproduction that deletes or disrupts a section of chromosome 15 coming from the father. This information has provided clues about genetic factors in appetite.

12.5

Body Weight Regulation: Set Points versus Settling Points

One strength of set-point theories of eating is that they explain body weight regulation. You have already learned that set-point theories are largely inconsistent with the facts of eating, but how well do they account for the regulation of body weight? Certainly, most people in our culture believe that body weight is regulated by a body-fat set point (Assanand, Pinel, & Lehman, 1998a, 1998b). They believe that when fat deposits are below a person's set point, a person becomes hungrier and eats more, which results in a return of body-fat levels to that person's set point; and, conversely, they believe that when fat deposits are above a person's set point, a person becomes less hungry and eats less, which results in a return of body-fat levels to their set point.

Set-Point Assumptions about Body Weight and Eating

You have already learned that set-point theories do a poor job of explaining the characteristics of hunger and eating. Do they do a better job of accounting for the facts of body weight regulation? Let's begin by looking at three lines of evidence that challenge fundamental aspects of many set-point theories of body weight regulation.

Variability of Body Weight   The set-point model was expressly designed to explain why adult body weights remain constant. Indeed, a set-point mechanism should make it virtually impossible for an adult to gain or lose large amounts of weight. Yet, many adults experience large and lasting changes in body weight (see Booth, 2004). Moreover, set-point thinking crumbles in the face of the epidemic of obesity that is currently sweeping fast-food societies.

Set-point theories of body weight regulation suggest that the best method of maintaining a constant body weight is to eat each time there is a motivation to eat, because, according to the theory, the main function of hunger is to defend the set point. However, as I am sure many of you know from personal experience, many people avoid obesity only by resisting their urges to eat.

Set Points and Health   One implication of set-point theories of body weight regulation is that each person's set point is optimal for that person's health—or at least not incompatible with good health. This is why popular psychologists commonly advise people to "listen to the wisdom of their bodies" and eat as much as they need to satisfy their hunger. Experimental results indicate that

this common prescription for good health could not be further from the truth.

Two kinds of evidence suggest that typical *ad libitum* (free-feeding) levels of consumption are unhealthy (see Brownell & Rodin, 1994). First are the results of studies of humans who consume fewer calories than others. For example, people living on the Japanese island of Okinawa seemed to eat so few calories that their eating habits became a concern of health officials. When the health officials took a closer look, here is what they found (see Kagawa, 1978). Adult Okinawans were found to consume, on average, 20% fewer calories than other adult Japanese, and Okinawan school children were found to consume 38% fewer calories than recommended by public health officials. It was somewhat surprising then that rates of morbidity and mortality and of all aging-related diseases were found to be substantially lower in Okinawa than in other parts of Japan, a country in which overall levels of caloric intake and obesity are far below Western norms. For example, the death rates from stroke, cancer, and heart disease in Okinawa were only 59%, 69%, and 59%, respectively, of those in the rest of Japan. Indeed, the proportion of Okinawans living to be over 100 years of age was up to 40 times greater than that of inhabitants of various other regions of Japan.

The Okinawan study and the other studies that have reported major health benefits in humans who eat less (e.g., Manson et al., 1995; Meyer et al., 2006; Walford & Walford, 1994) are not controlled experiments; therefore, they must be interpreted with caution. For example, perhaps it is not the consumption of fewer calories per se that leads to health and longevity; perhaps people who eat less tend to eat healthier diets.

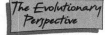
Thinking Clearly

Controlled experimental demonstrations in over a dozen different mammalian species, including monkeys (see Roth et al., 2002), of the beneficial effects of calorie restriction constitute the second kind of evidence that *ad libitum* levels of consumption are unhealthy. Fortunately, the results of such controlled experiments do not present the same problems of interpretation as do the findings of the Okinawa study and other similar correlational studies in humans. In typical *calorie-restriction experiments*, one group of subjects is allowed to eat as much as they choose, while other groups of subjects have their caloric intake of the same diets substantially reduced (by between 25% and 65% in various studies). Results of such experiments have been remarkably consistent (see Bucci, 1992; Masoro, 1988; Weindruch, 1996; Weindruch & Walford, 1988): In experiment after experiment, substantial reductions in the caloric intake of balanced diets have improved numerous indices of health and increased longevity. For example, in one experiment (Weindruch et al., 1986), groups of mice had their caloric intake of a well-balanced commercial diet reduced by either 25%, 55%, or 65% after weaning.

The Evolutionary Perspective

All levels of dietary restriction substantially improved health and increased longevity, but the benefits were greatest in the mice whose intake was reduced the most.

 Those mice that consumed the least had the lowest incidence of cancer, the best immune responses, and the greatest maximum life span—they lived 67% longer than mice that ate as much as they liked. Evidence suggests that dietary restriction can have beneficial effects even if it is not initiated until later in life (Mair et al., 2003; Vaupel, Carey, & Christensen, 2003).

One surprising point about the results of the calorie-restriction experiments: They suggested that the health benefits of the restricted diets may not be entirely attributable to loss of body fat (see Weindruch, 1996). The subjects in these experiments were not obese when they commenced their calorie-reduced diets, and thus they did not lose a lot of weight; moreover, there was no correlation between the amount of weight loss and degree of improved health. The current thinking is that some by-product of energy consumption accumulates in cells and accelerates aging with all its attendant health problems (Lane, Ingram, & Roth, 2002; Prolla & Mattson, 2001).

Thinking Clearly Please stop and think about the implications of these amazing calorie restriction experiments. How much do you eat?

Regulation of Body Weight by Changes in the Efficiency of Energy Utilization

Implicit in many set-point theories is the premise that body weight is largely a function of how much a person eats. Of course, how much someone eats plays a role in his or her body weight, but it is now clear that the body controls its fat levels, to a large degree, by changing the efficiency with which it uses energy. As a person's level of body fat declines, that person starts to use energy resources more efficiently, which limits further weight loss (see Martin, White, & Hulsey, 1991); conversely, weight gain is limited by a progressive decrease in the efficiency of energy utilization. Rothwell and Stock (1982) created a group of obese rats by maintaining them on a cafeteria

diet, and they found that the resting level of energy expenditure in these obese rats was 45% greater than in control rats.

This point is illustrated by the progressively declining effectiveness of weight-loss programs. Initially, low-calorie diets produce substantial weight loss. But the rate of weight loss diminishes with each successive week on the diet, until an equilibrium is achieved and little or no further weight loss occurs. Most dieters are familiar with this disappointing trend. A similar effect occurs with weight-gain programs (see Figure 12.13).

The mechanism by which the body adjusts the efficiency of its energy utilization in response to its levels of body fat has been termed **diet-induced thermogenesis**. Increases in the levels of body fat produce increases in body temperature, which require additional energy to maintain them—and decreases in the level of body fat have the opposite effects.

There are major differences among subjects both in their **basal metabolic rate** (the rate at which they utilize energy to maintain bodily processes when resting) and in their ability to adjust their metabolic rate in response to changes in the levels of body fat. We all know people who remain slim even though they eat gluttonously. However, the research on calorie-restricted diets suggests that these people may not eat with impunity: There may be a health cost to pay for overeating even in the absence of obesity.

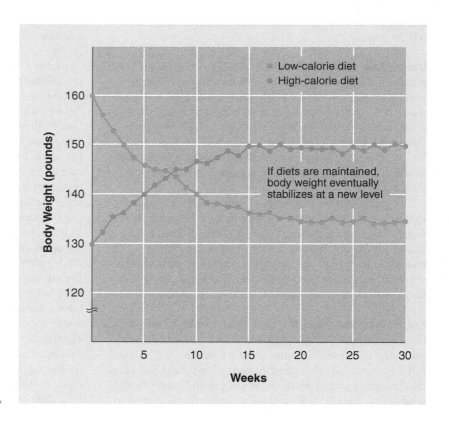

FIGURE 12.13 The diminishing effects on body weight of a low-calorie diet and a high-calorie diet.

Set Points and Settling Points in Weight Control

The theory that eating is part of a system designed to defend a body-fat set point has long had its critics (see Booth, Fuller, & Lewis, 1981; Wirtshafter & Davis, 1977); but for many years their arguments were largely ignored and the set-point assumption ruled. This situation has been changing: Several prominent reviews of research on hunger and weight regulation generally acknowledge that a strict set-point model cannot account for the facts of weight regulation, and they argue for a more flexible model (see Berthoud, 2002; Mercer & Speakman, 2001; Woods et al., 2000). Because body-fat set points still dominate the thinking of most people, I want to review the main advantages of one such flexible regulatory model: the settling-point model.

According to the settling-point model, body weight tends to drift around a natural **settling point**—the level at which the various factors that influence body weight achieve an equilibrium. The idea is that as body-fat levels increase, changes occur that tend to limit further increases until a balance is achieved between all factors that encourage weight gain and all those that discourage it.

The settling-point model provides a loose kind of homeostatic regulation, without a set-point mechanism or mechanisms to return body weight to a set point. According to the settling-point model, body weight remains stable as long as there are no long-term changes in the factors that influence it; and if there are such changes, their impact is limited by negative feedback. In the settling-point model, the feedback merely limits further changes in the same direction, whereas in the set-point model, negative feedback triggers a return to the set point. A neuron's resting potential is a well-known biological settling point—see Chapter 4.

The seductiveness of the set-point mechanism is attributable in no small part to the existence of the thermostat model, which provides a vivid means of thinking about it. Figure 12.14 presents an analogy I like to use to

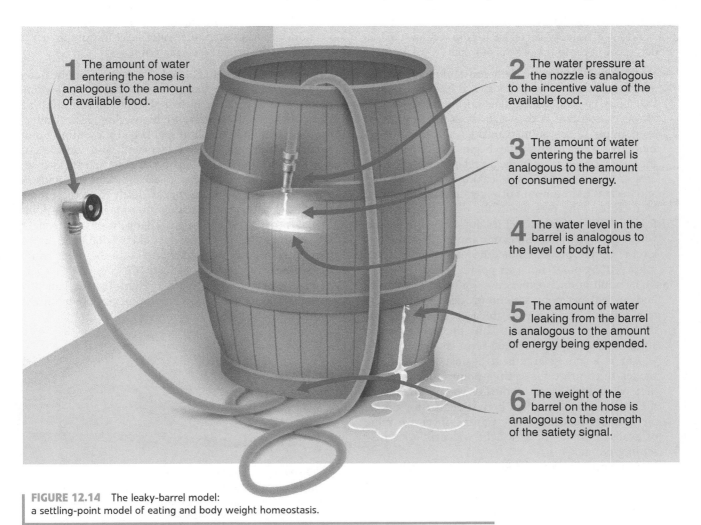

1 The amount of water entering the hose is analogous to the amount of available food.

2 The water pressure at the nozzle is analogous to the incentive value of the available food.

3 The amount of water entering the barrel is analogous to the amount of consumed energy.

4 The water level in the barrel is analogous to the level of body fat.

5 The amount of water leaking from the barrel is analogous to the amount of energy being expended.

6 The weight of the barrel on the hose is analogous to the strength of the satiety signal.

FIGURE 12.14 The leaky-barrel model: a settling-point model of eating and body weight homeostasis.

think about the settling-point mechanism. I call it the **leaky-barrel model**: (1) The amount of water entering the hose is analogous to the amount of food available to the subject; (2) the water pressure at the nozzle is analogous to the positive-incentive value of the available food; (3) the amount of water entering the barrel is analogous to the amount of energy consumed; (4) the water level in the barrel is analogous to the level of body fat; (5) the amount of water leaking from the barrel is analogous to the amount of energy being expended; and (6) the weight of the barrel on the hose is analogous to the strength of the satiety signal.

The main advantage of the settling-point model of body weight regulation over the body-fat set-point model is that it is more consistent with the data. Another advantage is that in those cases in which both models make the same prediction, the settling-point model does so more parsimoniously—that is, with a simpler mechanism that requires fewer assumptions. Let's use the leaky-barrel analogy to see how the two models account for four key facts of weight regulation.

- Body weight remains relatively constant in many adult animals. On the basis of this fact, it has been argued that body fat must be regulated around a set point. However, constant body weight does not require, or even imply, a set point. Consider the leaky-barrel model. As water from the tap begins to fill the barrel, the weight of the water in the barrel increases. This increases the amount of water leaking out of the barrel and decreases the amount of water entering the barrel by increasing the pressure of the barrel on the hose. Eventually, this system settles into an equilibrium where the water level stays constant; but because this level is neither predetermined nor actively defended, it is a settling point, not a set point.

- Many adult animals experience enduring changes in body weight. Set-point systems are designed to maintain internal constancy in the face of fluctuations of the external environment. Thus, the fact that many adult animals experience long-term changes in body weight is a strong argument against the set-point model. In contrast, the settling-point model predicts that when there is an enduring change in one of the parameters that affect body weight—for example, a major increase in the positive-incentive value of available food—body weight will drift to a new settling point.

- If a subject's intake of food is reduced, metabolic changes that limit the loss of weight occur; the opposite happens when the subject overeats. This fact is often cited as evidence for set-point regulation of body weight; however, because the metabolic changes merely limit further weight changes rather than elimi-

nating those that have occurred, they are more consistent with a settling-point model. For example, when water intake in the leaky-barrel model is reduced, the water level in the barrel begins to drop; but the drop is limited by a decrease in leakage and an increase in inflow attributable to the falling water pressure in the barrel. Eventually, a new settling point is achieved, but the reduction in water level is not as great as one might expect because of the loss-limiting changes.

- After an individual has lost a substantial amount of weight (by dieting, exercise, or the surgical removal of fat), there is a tendency for the original weight to be regained once the subject returns to the previous eating- and energy-related lifestyle. Although this finding is often offered as irrefutable evidence of a body-weight set point, the settling-point model readily accounts for it. When the water level in the leaky-barrel model is reduced—by temporarily decreasing input (dieting), by temporarily increasing output (exercising), or by scooping out some of the water (surgical removal of fat)—only a temporary drop in the settling point is produced. When the original conditions are reinstated, the water level inexorably drifts back to the original settling point.

Does it really matter whether we think about body weight regulation in terms of set points or settling points—or is making such a distinction just splitting hairs? It certainly matters to biopsychologists: Understanding that body weight is regulated by a settling-point system helps them better understand, and more accurately predict, the changes in body weight that are likely to occur in various situations; it also indicates the kinds of physiological mechanisms that are likely to mediate these changes. And it should matter to you. If the set-point model is correct, attempting to change your body weight would be a waste of time; you would inevitably be drawn back to your body-weight set point. On the other hand, the leaky-barrel model suggests that it is possible to permanently change your body weight by permanently changing any of the factors that influence energy intake and output.

Scan Your Brain

Are you ready to move on to the final two sections of the chapter, which deal with eating disorders? This is a good place to pause and scan your brain to see if you understand the physiological mechanisms of eating and weight regulation. Complete the following sentences by filling in the blanks. The correct answers are provided below. Before proceeding, review material related to your incorrect answers and omissions.

1. The expectation of a meal normally stimulates the release of _____ into the blood, which reduces blood glucose.
2. In the 1950s, the _____ hypothalamus was thought to be a satiety center.
3. A complete cessation of eating is called _____.
4. _____ is the breakdown of body fat to create usable forms of energy.
5. The classic study of Washburn and Cannon was the perfect collaboration: Cannon had the ideas, and Washburn could swallow a _____.
6. CCK is a gut peptide that is thought to be a _____ peptide.
7. _____ is the monoaminergic neurotransmitter that seems to play a role in satiety.
8. Okinawans eat less and live _____.
9. Experimental studies of _____ have shown that typical *ad libitum* (free-feeding) levels of consumption are unhealthy in many mammalian species.
10. As an individual grows fatter, further weight gain is minimized by diet-induced _____.
11. _____ models are more consistent with the facts of body-weight regulation than are set-point models.
12. _____ are to set points as leaky barrels are to settling points.

Scan Your Brain answers: (1) insulin, (2) ventromedial, (3) aphagia, (4) lipolysis, (5) balloon, (6) satiety, (7) serotonin, (8) longer, (9) calorie restriction, (10) thermogenesis, (11) settling-point, (12) thermostats.

12.6

Human Obesity: Causes, Treatments, and Mechanisms

You have already learned that obesity is currently a major health problem in many parts of the world. What is more alarming is the rate at which the problem is growing; in the United States, for example, the incidence of obesity has doubled in the last 20 years and continues to increase. The health implications are distressing. For example, it has been estimated that over one-third of the children born in the United States in 2000 will develop diabetes, and 10% of these will develop related life-threatening conditions by early adulthood (see Haslam, Sattar, & Lean, 2006; Olshansky et al., 2005).

Are obese people more susceptible to health problems even if their blood pressure and blood cholesterol levels are within the healthy range? Yes: A recent study of over 17,000 people found that those who are obese have a significantly higher risk of mortality even if their blood pressure and blood cholesterol levels are normal (Yan et al., 2006).

Why Is There an Epidemic of Obesity?

Let's begin our analysis of obesity by considering the pressures that are likely to have led to the evolution of our eating and weight-regulation systems (see Lazar, 2005; Pinel et al., 2000). During the course of evolution, inconsistent 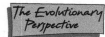 food supplies were one of the main threats to survival. As a result, the fittest individuals were those who preferred high-calorie foods, ate to capacity when food was available, stored as many excess calories as possible in the form of body fat, and used their stores of calories as efficiently as possible. Individuals who did not have these characteristics were unlikely to survive a food shortage, and so these characteristics were passed on to future generations.

The development of numerous cultural practices and beliefs that promote consumption has augmented the effects of evolution. For example, in my culture, it is commonly believed that one should eat three meals per day at regular times, whether one is hungry or not; that food should be the focus of most social gatherings; that meals should be served in courses of progressively increasing palatability; and that salt, sweets (e.g., sugar), and fats (e.g., butter) should be added to foods to improve their flavor and thus increase their consumption.

Each of us possesses an eating and weight-regulation system that evolved to deal effectively with periodic food shortages, and many of us live in cultures whose eating-related practices evolved for the same purpose. However, our current environment differs from our "natural" environment in critical food-related ways. We live in an environment in which an endless variety of foods of the highest positive-incentive value are readily and continuously available. The consequence is an appallingly high level of consumption.

Why Do Some People Become Obese While Others Do Not?

Why do some people become obese while others living under the same obesity-promoting conditions do not? At a superficial level, the answer is obvious: Those who are obese are those whose energy intake has grossly exceeded their energy output; those who are slim are those whose energy intake has not grossly exceeded their energy output. Although this answer provides little insight, it does serve to emphasize that two kinds of individual differences play a role in obesity: those that lead to differences in energy input and those that lead to differences in energy output. Let's consider examples of each kind.

There are many factors that lead some people to eat more than others who have comparable access to food. For example, some people consume more energy because they have strong preferences for the taste of high-calorie foods (see Blundell & Finlayson, 2004); some consume more because they were raised in families and/or cultures that promote excessive eating; and some consume more because they have particularly large cephalic-phase responses to the sight or smell of food (Rodin, 1985).

With respect to energy output, people differ markedly from one another in the degree to which they can dissipate excess consumed energy. The most obvious difference is that people differ substantially in the amount of exercise they get; however, there are others. You have already learned about two of them: differences in *basal metabolic rate* and in the ability to react to fat increases by *diet-induced thermogenesis*. The third factor is called **NEAT**, or *nonexercise activity thermogenesis*, which is generated by activities such as fidgeting and the maintenance of posture and muscle tone (Ravussin & Danforth, 1999) and can play a role in dissipating excess energy (Levine, Eberhardt, & Jensen, 1999; Ravussin, 2005).

Given the number of factors that can influence the accumulation of body fat, it is not surprising that genetics also plays a role. Many genes have been linked to obesity (see Rankinen et al., 2006). However, because there are so many of these genes, it is virtually impossible to sort out their effects, their interactions with one another, and their interactions with experience.

Why Are Weight-Loss Programs Typically Ineffective?

Figure 12.15 describes the course of the typical weight-loss program. Most weight-loss programs are unsuccessful in the sense that, as predicted by the settling-point model, most of the lost weight is regained once the dieter stops following the program and the original conditions are reestablished. The key to permanent weight loss is a permanent lifestyle change: Any healthy person who consistently eats a nutritional low-calorie diet will have no problems with obesity.

Exercise has many health-promoting effects; however, despite the general belief that exercise is the most effective method of losing weight, several studies have shown that it often contributes little to weight loss (e.g., Sweeney et al., 1993). One reason is that physical exercise normally accounts for only a small proportion of total energy expenditure: About 80% of the energy you expend is used to maintain the resting physiological processes of your body and to digest your food (Calles-Escandon & Horton, 1992). Another reason is that after exercise, many people

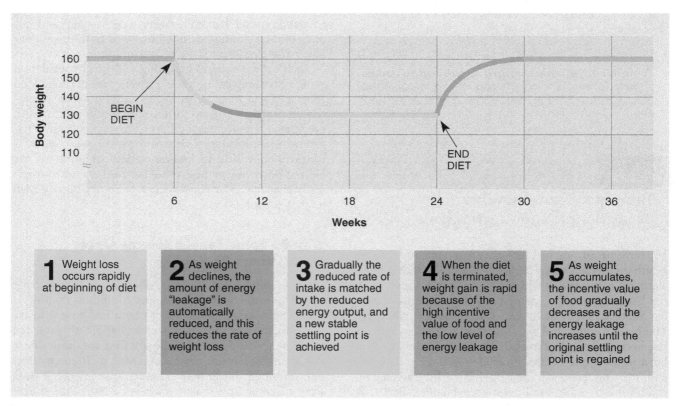

FIGURE 12.15   The five stages of a typical weight-loss program.

consume extra drinks and foods that contain more calories than the relatively small number that were expended during the exercise.

Severe cases of obesity sometimes warrant extreme treatment. The grossly obese are sometimes treated by wiring the jaw shut to limit consumption to liquids, stapling part of the stomach together to reduce the size of meals, cutting out a section of the duodenum to reduce the absorption of nutrients from the gastrointestinal tract, or implanting a band around the duodenum to restrict the flow of nutrients from the stomach. Unfortunately, jaw wiring has proven ineffective because some patients do not lose weight on a liquid diet, and those who do typically regain it once the wires are removed. The other methods are effective in promoting substantial weight loss, but they are often associated with diarrhea, flatulence, and vitamin and mineral deficiencies (Singh & Kumar, 2007).

Leptin and the Regulation of Body Fat

Fat is more than a passive storehouse of energy; it actively releases a peptide hormone called **leptin**. The discovery of leptin has been extremely influential (see Elmquist & Flier, 2004). The following three subsections describe (1) the discovery of leptin, (2) how its discovery has fueled the development of a new approach to the treatment of human obesity, and (3) how the understanding that leptin (and insulin) are feedback signals led to the discovery of a hypothalamic nucleus that plays an important role in the regulation of body fat.

Obese Mice and the Discovery of Leptin   In 1950, a spontaneous genetic mutation occurred in the mouse colony being maintained in the Jackson Laboratory at Bar Harbor, Maine. The mutant mice were *homozygous* for the gene (ob), and they were grossly obese, weighing up to three times as much as typical mice. These mutant mice are commonly referred to as **ob/ob mice**. See Figure 12.16.

FIGURE 12.16   An ob/ob mouse and a control mouse.

Ob/ob mice eat more than control mice; they convert calories to fat more efficiently; and they use their calories *The Evolutionary Perspective* more efficiently. Coleman (1979) hypothesized that ob/ob mice lack a critical hormone that normally inhibits fat production and maintenance.

In 1994, Friedman and his colleagues characterized and cloned the gene that is mutated in ob/ob mice (Zhang et al., 1994). They found that this gene is *expressed* only in fat cells, and they characterized the protein that it normally encodes, a peptide hormone that they named leptin. Because of their mutation, ob/ob mice lack leptin. This finding led to an exciting hypothesis: Perhaps leptin is a negative feedback signal that is normally released from fat stores to decrease appetite and increase fat metabolism. Could leptin be administered to obese humans to reverse the current epidemic of obesity?

Leptin as a Treatment for Human Obesity   The early studies of leptin seemed to confirm the hypothesis that it could function as an effective treatment for obesity. Receptors for leptin were found in the brain, and injecting it into ob/ob mice reduced both their eating and their body fat (see Seeley & Woods, 2003). All that remained was to prove leptin's effectiveness in human patients.

However, when research on leptin turned from ob/ob mice to obese humans, the program ran into two major snags. First, obese humans—unlike ob/ob mice—were found to have high, rather than low, levels of leptin (see Münzberg & Myers, 2005). Second, injections of leptin did not reduce either the eating or the body fat of obese humans (see Heymsfield et al., 1999).

Why the actions of leptin are different in humans and ob/ob mice has yet to *Clinical Implications* be explained. Nevertheless, efforts to use leptin in the treatment of human obesity have not been a total failure. Although few obese humans have a genetic mutation to the ob gene, leptin is a panacea for those few who do. Consider the following case.

The Case of the Child with No Leptin

The patient was of normal weight at birth, but her weight soon began to increase at an excessive rate. She demanded food continually and was disruptive when denied food. As a result of her extreme obesity, deformities of her legs developed, and surgery was required.

She was 9 when she was referred for treatment. At this point, she weighed 94.4 kilograms (about 210 pounds), and her weight was still increasing at an alarming rate. She was found to be homozygous for the ob gene and had no detectable leptin. Thus, leptin therapy was commenced.

The leptin therapy immediately curtailed the weight gain. She began to eat less, and she lost weight steadily over the 12-month period of the study, a total of 16.5 kilograms (about 36 pounds), almost all in the form of fat. There were no obvious side effects (Farooqi et al., 1999).

Leptin, Insulin, and the Arcuate Melanocortin System There was great fanfare when leptin was discovered. However, it was not the first peptide hormone to be discovered that seems to function as a negative feedback signal in the regulation of body fat (see Schwartz, 2000; Woods, 2004). More than 25 years ago, Woods and colleagues (1979) suggested that the pancreatic peptide hormone insulin serves such a function.

At first, the suggestion that insulin serves as a negative feedback signal for body fat regulation was viewed with skepticism. After all, how could the level of insulin in the body, which goes up and then comes back down to normal following each meal, provide the brain with information about gradually changing levels of body fat? It turns out that insulin does not readily penetrate the blood–brain barrier, and its levels in the brain were found to stay relatively stable. More importantly, brain levels of insulin were found to be positively correlated with levels of body fat (Seeley et al., 1996); receptors for insulin were found in the brain (Baura et al., 1993); and infusions of insulin into the brains of laboratory animals were found to reduce eating and body weight (Campfield et al., 1995; Chavez, Seeley, & Woods, 1995).

Why are there two fat feedback signals? One reason may be that leptin levels are more closely correlated with **subcutaneous fat** (fat stored under the skin), whereas insulin levels are more closely correlated with **visceral fat** (fat stored around the internal organs of the body cavity)—see Hug & Lodish (2005). Thus, each fat signal provides different information. Visceral fat is more common in males than females and poses the greater threat to health (Wajchenberg, 2000). Insulin, but not leptin, is also involved in glucose regulation (see Schwartz & Porte, 2005).

The discovery that leptin and insulin are signals that provide information to the brain about fat levels in the body provided a means for discovering the neural circuits that participate in fat regulation. Receptors for both peptide hormones are located in many parts of the nervous system, but most are in the hypothalamus, particularly in one area of the hypothalamus: the **arcuate nucleus**.

A closer look at the distribution of leptin and insulin receptors in the arcuate nucleus indicated that these receptors are not randomly distributed throughout the nucleus. They are located in two classes of neurons: neurons that release **neuropeptide Y** (the gut hunger peptide that you read about earlier in the chapter), and neurons that release **melanocortins**, a class of peptides that includes the gut satiety peptide α-*melanocyte-stimulating hormone*

(alpha-melanocyte-stimulating hormone). Attention has been mostly focused on the melanocortin-releasing neurons in the arcuate nucleus (often referred to as the **melanocortin system**) because injections of α-melanocyte-stimulating hormone have been shown to suppress eating and promote weight loss (see Horvath, 2005; Seeley & Woods, 2003). It seems, however, that the melanocortin system is only a minor component of a much larger system: Elimination of leptin receptors in the melanocortin system produces only a slight weight gain (see Münzberg & Myers, 2005)

Serotonergic Drugs and the Treatment of Obesity

Because—as you have already learned—serotonin agonists have been shown to reduce food consumption in both human and nonhuman subjects, they have considerable potential in the treatment of obesity (Halford & Blundell, 2000a). Serotonin agonists seem to act by a mechanism different from that for leptin and insulin, which produce long-term satiety signals based on fat stores. Serotonin agonists seem to increase short-term satiety signals associated with the consumption of a meal (Halford & Blundell, 2000b).

Serotonin agonists have been found in various studies of obese patients to reduce the following: the urge to eat high-calorie foods, the consumption of fat, the subjective intensity of hunger, the size of meals, the number of between-meal snacks, and bingeing. Because of this extremely positive profile of effects and the severity of the obesity problem, serotonin agonists (fenfluramine and dexfenfluramine) were rushed into clinical use. However, they were subsequently withdrawn from the market because chronic use was found to be associated with heart disease in a small, but significant, number of users. Currently, the search is on for serotonergic weight-loss medications that do not have dangerous side effects.

Clinical Implications

12.7

Anorexia and Bulimia Nervosa

In contrast to obesity, **anorexia nervosa** is a disorder of under-consumption (see Klein & Walsh, 2004). Anorexics eat so little that they experience health-threatening weight loss; and despite their grotesquely emaciated appearance, they often perceive themselves as fat (see Benninghoven et al., 2006). Anorexia nervosa is a very serious condition because it can lead to death—in approximately 10% of diagnosed cases, complications from starvation result in death (Birmingham et al., 2005), and there is a particularly high rate of suicide among anorexics (Pompili et al., 2004).

Clinical Implications

Anorexia nervosa is related to bulimia nervosa. **Bulimia nervosa** is a disorder characterized by periodic *bingeing* (eating huge amounts of food in short periods of time) followed by efforts to immediately eliminate the consumed calories from the body: by voluntary *purging* (vomiting); by excessive use of laxatives, enemas, or diuretics; or by extreme exercise. Bulimics may be obese or of normal weight. If they are underweight, they are diagnosed as *bingeing anorexics*.

The Relation between Anorexia and Bulimia

Are anorexia nervosa and bulimia nervosa really different disorders, as current convention dictates? The answer to this question depends on one's perspective. From the perspective of a physician, it is important to distinguish between these disorders because starvation produces different health problems than does repeated bingeing and purging. For example, anorexics often require treatment for reduced metabolism, *bradycardia* (slow heart rate), *hypotension* (low blood pressure), *hypothermia* (low body temperature), and *anemia* (deficiency of red blood cells) (Miller et al., 2005). In contrast, bulimics often require treatment for irritation and inflammation of the esophagus, vitamin and mineral deficiencies, electrolyte imbalance, dehydration, and acid reflux.

Although anorexia and bulimia nervosa may seem like very different disorders from a physician's perspective, scientists often find it more appropriate to view them as variations of the same disorder. According to this view, both anorexia and bulimia begin with an obsession about body image and slimness and extreme efforts to lose weight. Both anorexics and bulimics attempt to lose weight by strict dieting, but bulimics are less capable of controlling their appetites and thus enter into a cycle of starvation, bingeing, and purging (see Russell, 1979). The following are other similarities that support the view that anorexia and bulimia are variants of the same disorder (see Kaye et al., 2005):

- Both anorexics and bulimics have a distorted body image, seeing themselves as much fatter and less attractive than they are in reality (see Grant et al., 2002).
- In practice, many patients seem to straddle the two diagnoses and cannot readily be assigned to one or the other categories; moreover, many patients flip-flop between the two diagnoses as their circumstances change (Lask & Bryant-Waugh, 2000; Santonastaso et al., 2006; Tenconi et al., 2006).
- Anorexia and bulimia show the same pattern of distribution in the population. Although their overall incidence in the population is low (lifetime incidence estimates for American adults are 0.6% and 1.0% for anorexia and bulimia, respectively; Hudson et al., 2007), both conditions occur more commonly among educated females in affluent cultural groups (Lindberg & Hjern, 2003).

- Both anorexia and bulimia are highly correlated with obsessive-compulsive disorder and depression (Kaye et al., 2004; O'Brien & Vincent, 2003).
- Neither disorder responds well to existing therapies. Short-term improvements are common, but relapse is usual.

Anorexia and Positive Incentives

The positive-incentive perspective on eating suggests that the decline in eating that defines anorexia nervosa is likely a consequence of a corresponding decline in the positive-incentive value of food. However, the positive-incentive value of food for anorexia patients has received little attention—in part, because anorexic patients often display substantial interest in food. The fact that many anorexic patients are obsessed with food—continually talking about it, thinking about it, and preparing it for others (Crisp, 1983)—seems to suggest that food still holds a high positive-incentive value for them. However, to avoid confusion, it is necessary to keep in mind that the positive-incentive value of *interacting* with food is not necessarily the same as the positive-incentive value of *eating* food—and it is the positive-incentive value of eating food that is critical when considering anorexia nervosa.

A few studies have examined the positive-incentive value of various tastes in anorexic patients (see, e.g., Drewnowski et al., 1987; Roefs et al., 2006; Sunday & Halmi, 1990). In general, these studies have found that the positive-incentive value of various tastes is lower in anorexic patients than in control participants. However, these studies grossly underestimate the importance of reductions in the positive-incentive value of food in the etiology of anorexia nervosa, because the anorexic participants and the normal-weight control participants were not matched for weight.

Starvation normally triggers a radical increase in the positive-incentive value of food. This has been best documented by the descriptions and behavior of participants voluntarily undergoing experimental semistarvation. When asked how it felt to starve, one participant replied:

> I wait for mealtime. When it comes I eat slowly and make the food last as long as possible. The menu never gets monotonous even if it is the same each day or is of poor quality. It is food and all food tastes good. Even dirty crusts of bread in the street look appetizing. (Keys et al., 1950, p. 852)

Anorexia Nervosa: A Hypothesis

The dominance of set-point theories in research into the regulation of hunger and eating has resulted in widespread inattention to one of the major puzzles of

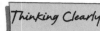

Thinking Clearly anorexia: Why does the adaptive massive increase in the positive-incentive value of eating that occurs in victims of starvation not occur in starving anorexics? Under conditions of starvation, the positive-incentive value of eating normally increases to such high levels that it is difficult to imagine how anybody who is starving—no matter how controlled, rigid, obsessive, and motivated—could refrain from eating in the presence of palatable food. Why this protective mechanism is not activated in severe anorexics is a pressing question about the etiology of anorexia nervosa. The answer will have to explain how anyone can overcome food's attraction enough to reach the level of starvation characteristic of extreme anorexia.

I believe that part of the answer lies in the research of Woods and his colleagues on the aversive physiological effects of meals. At the beginning of meals, people are normally in reasonably homeostatic balance, and this homeostasis is disrupted by the sudden infusion of calories. The other part of the answer lies in the finding that the aversive effects of meals are much greater in people who have been eating little (Brooks & Melnik, 1995). Meals, which produce adverse, but tolerable, effects in healthy individuals, may be extremely aversive for individuals who have undergone food deprivation. Evidence for the extremely noxious effects that eating meals has on starving humans is found in the reactions of World War II concentration camp victims to refeeding—many were rendered ill and some were even killed by the very food given to them by their liberators (Keys et al., 1950; see also Soloman & Kirby, 1990).

So why do severe anorexics not experience a massive increase in the positive-incentive value of eating, similar to the increase experienced by other starving individuals? The answer may be *meals*—meals forced on these patients as a result of the misconception of our society that meals are the healthy way to eat. Each meal consumed by an anorexic may produce a variety of conditioned taste aversions that reduce the motivation to eat. This hypothesis needs to be addressed because of its implication for treatment: Anorexic patients—or anybody else who is severely undernourished—should not be encouraged, or even permitted, to eat meals. They should be fed—or infused with—small amounts of food intermittently throughout the day.

I have described the preceding hypothesis to show you the value of the new ideas that you have encountered in this chapter: The major test of a new theory is whether it leads to innovative hypotheses. A few *Thinking Clearly* months ago, as I was perusing an article on global famine and malnutrition, I noticed an intriguing comment: One of the clinical complications that results from feeding meals to famine victims is anorexia (Blackburn, 2001). What do you make of this?

The Case of the Anorexic Student

In a society in which obesity is the main disorder of consumption, anorexics are out of step. People who are struggling to eat less have difficulty understanding those who have to struggle to eat. Still, when you stare anorexia in the face, it is difficult not to be touched by it. *Clinical Implications*

She began by telling me how much she had been enjoying the course and how sorry she was to be dropping out of the university. She was articulate and personable, and her grades were high—very high. Her problem was anorexia; she weighed only 82 pounds, and she was about to be hospitalized.

"But don't you want to eat?" I asked naively. "Don't you see that your plan to go to medical school will go up in smoke if you don't eat?"

"Of course I want to eat. I know I am terribly thin—my friends tell me I am. Believe me, I know this is wrecking my life. I try to eat, but I just can't force myself. In a strange way, I am pleased with my thinness."

She was upset, and I was embarrassed by my insensitivity. "It's too bad you're dropping out of the course before we cover the chapter on eating," I said, groping for safer ground.

"Oh, I've read it already," she responded. "It's the first chapter I looked at. It had quite an effect on me; a lot of things started to make more sense. The bit about positive incentives and learning was really good. I think my problem began when eating started to lose its positive-incentive value for me—in my mind, I kind of associated eating with being fat and all the boyfriend problems I was having. This made it easy to diet, but every once in a while I would get hungry and binge, or my parents would force me to eat a big meal. I would eat so much that I would feel ill. So I would put my finger down my throat and make myself throw up. This kept me from gaining weight, but I think it also taught my body to associate my favorite foods with illness—kind of a conditioned taste aversion. What do you think of my theory?"

Her insightfulness impressed me; it made me feel all the more sorry that she was going to discontinue her studies. How could such a bright, personable young woman knowingly risk her health and everything that she had worked for?

After a lengthy chat, she got up to leave, and I walked her to the door of my office. I wished her luck and made her promise to come back for a visit. I never saw her again. The image of her emaciated body walking down the hallway from my office has stayed with me.

Themes Revisited

Thinking Clearly Three of the book's four themes played prominent roles in this chapter. The thinking clearly theme was common as you were challenged to critically evaluate your own beliefs and ambiguous research findings, to consider the scientific implications of your own experiences, and to think creatively about the personal and clinical implications of the new ideas you encountered. The chapter ended by using these new ideas to develop a potentially important hypothesis about the etiology of anorexia nervosa. Because of its emphasis on thinking, this chapter is my personal favorite.

Both aspects of the evolutionary theme were emphasized repeatedly. First, you saw how thinking about hunger and eating from an evolutionary perspective leads to important insights. Second, you saw how controlled research on nonhuman species has contributed to our current understanding of human hunger and eating.

Finally, the clinical implications theme was featured in the cases of the man who forgot not to eat, the child with Prader-Willi syndrome, the child with no leptin, and the anorexic student.

The Evolutionary Perspective

mypsychkit
See Hard Copy for additional readings for Chapter 12.

Clinical Implications

Think about It

1. Set-point theories suggest that attempts at permanent weight loss are a waste of time. On the basis of what you have learned in this chapter, design an effective weight-loss program.
2. Most of the eating-related health problems of people in our society occur because the conditions in which we live are different from those in which our species evolved. Discuss.
3. On the basis of what you have learned in this chapter, develop a feeding program for laboratory rats that would lead to obesity. Compare this program with the eating habits prevalent in those cultures in which obesity is a serious problem.
4. What causes anorexia nervosa? Summarize the evidence that supports your view.

mypsychkit
Studying for an exam? Try the Practice Tests for Chapter 12.

Key Terms

Set point

12.1 Digestion, Energy Storage, and Energy Utilization

Digestion
Lipids
Amino acids
Glucose
Cephalic phase
Absorptive phase
Fasting phase
Insulin
Glucagon
Gluconeogenesis
Free fatty acids
Ketones

12.2 Theories of Hunger and Eating: Set Points versus Positive Incentives

Set-point assumption
Negative feedback systems

Homeostasis
Glucostatic theory
Lipostatic theory
Positive-incentive theory
Positive-incentive value

12.3 Factors That Determine What, When, and How Much We Eat

Satiety
Nutritive density
Sham eating
Appetizer effect
Cafeteria diet
Sensory-specific satiety

12.4 Physiological Research on Hunger and Satiety

Ventromedial hypothalamus (VMH)
Lateral hypothalamus (LH)
Hyperphagia

Dynamic phase
Static phase
Aphagia
Adipsia
Lipogenesis
Lipolysis
Paraventricular nuclei
Duodenum
Cholecystokinin (CCK)

12.5 Body Weight Regulation: Set Points versus Settling Points

Diet-induced thermogenesis
Basal metabolic rate
Settling point
Leaky-barrel model

12.6 Human Obesity: Causes, Treatments, and Mechanisms

NEAT
Leptin
Ob/ob mice

Subcutaneous fat
Visceral fat
Arcuate nucleus
Neuropeptide Y
Melanocortins
Melanocortin system

12.7 Anorexia and Bulimia Nervosa

Anorexia nervosa
Bulimia nervosa

mypsychkit
Need some help studying the key terms for this chapter? Check out the electronic flash cards for Chapter 12.

Hormones and Sex
What's Wrong with the Mamawawa?

This chapter is about hormones and sex, a topic that some regard as unfit for conversation but that fascinates many others. Perhaps the topic of hormones and sex is so fascinating because we are intrigued by the fact that our sex is so greatly influenced by the secretions of a small pair of glands. Because we each think of our gender as fundamental and immutable, it is a bit disturbing to think that it could be altered with a few surgical snips and some hormone injections. And there is something intriguing about the idea that our sex lives might be enhanced by the application of a few hormones. For whatever reason, the topic of hormones and sex is always a hit with my students. Some remarkable things await you in this chapter; let's go directly to them.

The Developmental and Activational Effects of Sex Hormones

Hormones influence sex in two ways: (1) by influencing the development from conception to sexual maturity of the anatomical, physiological, and behavioral characteristics that distinguish one as female or male; and (2) by activating the reproduction-related behavior of sexually mature adults. Both the *developmental* (also called *organizational*) and *activational* effects of sex hormones are discussed in this chapter. Although the distinction between the developmental and activational effects of sex hormones is not as clear as it was once assumed to be—for example, because the brain continues to develop into the late teens, adolescent hormone surges can have both

effects—it is still useful (Cohen-Bendahan, van de Beek, & Berenbaum, 2005).

The Men-Are-Men-and-Women-Are-Women Assumption

Almost everybody brings to the topic of hormones and sex a piece of excess baggage: the men-are-men-and-women-are-women assumption—or the "mamawawa." This assumption is seductive; it seems so right that we are continually drawn to it without considering alternative views. Unfortunately, it is fundamentally flawed.

The men-are-men-and-women-are-women assumption is the tendency to think about femaleness and maleness as discrete, mutually exclusive, complementary categories. In thinking about hormones and sex, this general attitude leads one to assume that females have female sex hormones that give them female bodies and make them do "female" things, and that males have male sex hormones that give them male bodies and make them do "male" things, opposite of females. Despite the fact that this approach to hormones and sex is totally wrong, its simplicity, symmetry, and comfortable social implications draw us to it. That's why this chapter grapples with it throughout.

13.1
The Neuroendocrine System

This section introduces the general principles of neuroendocrine function. It introduces these principles by focusing on the glands and hormones that are directly involved in sexual development and behavior.

The endocrine glands are illustrated in Figure 13.1. By convention, only the organs whose primary function appears to be the release of hormones are referred to as *endocrine glands*. However, other organs (e.g., the stomach, liver, and intestine) and body fat also release hormones into general circulation (see Chapter 12), and they are thus, strictly speaking, also part of the endocrine system.

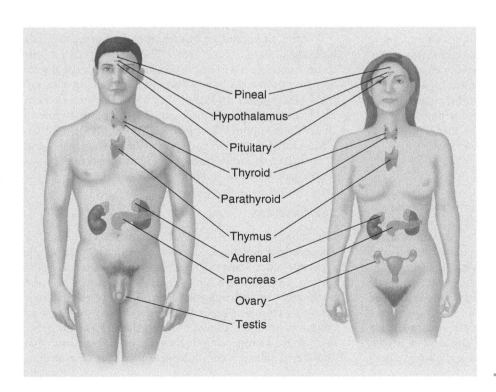

Pineal
Hypothalamus
Pituitary
Thyroid
Parathyroid
Thymus
Adrenal
Pancreas
Ovary
Testis

FIGURE 13.1 The endocrine glands.

Glands

There are two types of glands: exocrine glands and endocrine glands. **Exocrine glands** (e.g., sweat glands) release their chemicals into ducts, which carry them to their targets, mostly on the surface of the body. **Endocrine glands** (ductless glands) release their chemicals, which are called **hormones**, directly into the circulatory system. Once released by an endocrine gland, a hormone travels via the circulatory system until it reaches the targets on which it normally exerts its effect (e.g., other endocrine glands or sites in the nervous system).

Classes of Hormones

Most hormones fall into one of three classes: (1) amino acid derivatives, (2) peptides and proteins, and (3) steroids. **Amino acid derivative hormones** are hormones that are synthesized in a few simple steps from an amino acid molecule; an example is *epinephrine*, which is released from the *adrenal medulla* and synthesized from *tyrosine*. **Peptide hormones** and **protein hormones** are chains of amino acids—peptide hormones are short chains, and protein hormones are long chains. **Steroid hormones** are hormones that are synthesized from *cholesterol*, a type of fat molecule.

Steroid hormones play the major role in sexual development and behavior. Most other hormones produce their effects by binding to receptors in cell membranes. Steroid molecules can influence cells in this fashion; however, because they are small and fat-soluble, they can readily penetrate cell membranes and often affect cells in a second way. Once inside a cell, the steroid molecules can bind to receptors in the cytoplasm or nucleus and, by so doing, directly influence gene expression (amino acid derivative hormones and peptide hormones can also affect gene expression, but they do so less commonly and by less direct mechanisms because they cannot penetrate cell membranes). Consequently, of all the hormones, steroid hormones tend to have the most diverse and long-lasting effects on cellular function (Brown, 1994).

Gonads

Central to any discussion of hormones and sex are the **gonads**—the male **testes** (pronounced TEST-eez) and the female **ovaries** (see Figure 13.1). As you learned in Chapter 2, the primary function of the testes and ovaries is the production of *sperm cells* and *ova*, respectively. After **copulation** (sexual intercourse), a single sperm cell may *fertilize* an *ovum* to form one cell called a **zygote**, which contains all of the information necessary for the normal growth of a complete adult organism in its natural environment (see Primakoff & Myles, 2002). With the exception of ova and sperm cells, each cell of the human body has 23 pairs of chromosomes. In contrast, the ova and sperm cells contain only half that number, one member of each of the 23 pairs. Thus, when a sperm cell fertilizes an ovum, the resulting zygote ends up with the full complement of 23 pairs of chromosomes, one of each pair from the father and one of each pair from the mother.

Of particular interest in the context of this chapter is the pair of chromosomes called the **sex chromosomes**, so named because they contain the genetic programs that direct sexual development. The cells of females have two large sex chromosomes, called *X chromosomes*. In males, one sex chromosome is an X chromosome, and the other is called a *Y chromosome*. Consequently, the sex chromosome of every ovum is an X chromosome, whereas half the sperm cells have X chromosomes and half have Y chromosomes. Your gender with all its social, economic, and personal ramifications was determined by which of your father's sperm cells won the dash to your mother's ovum. If a sperm cell with an X sex chromosome won, you are a female; if one with a Y sex chromosome won, you are a male.

You might reasonably assume that X chromosomes are X-shaped and Y chromosomes are Y-shaped, but this is incorrect. Once a chromosome has duplicated, the two products remain joined at one point, producing an X shape. This is true of all chromosomes, including Y chromosomes. Because the Y chromosome is much smaller than the X chromosome, early investigators failed to discern one small arm and thus saw a Y. In humans, Y-chromosome genes encode only 27 proteins, in comparison to about 1,500 proteins encoded by X chromosome genes (see Arnold, 2004).

Writing this section reminded me of my seventh-grade basketball team, the "Nads." The name puzzled our teacher because it was not at all like the names usually favored by pubescent boys—names such as the "Avengers," the "Marauders," and the "Vikings." Her puzzlement ended abruptly at our first game as our fans began to chant their support. You guessed it: "Go Nads, Go! Go Nads, Go!" My 14-year-old spotted-faced teammates and I considered this to be humor of the most mature and sophisticated sort. The teacher didn't.

Sex Steroids

The gonads do more than create sperm and egg cells; they also produce and release steroid hormones. Most people are surprised to learn that the testes and ovaries release the very same hormones. The two main classes of gonadal hormones are **androgens** and **estrogens**; **testosterone** is the most common androgen, and **estradiol** is the most common estrogen. The fact that adult ovaries tend to release more estrogens than they do androgens and that adult testes release more androgens than they do estrogens has led to the common, but misleading, practice of referring to androgens as "the *male* sex hormones" and to estrogens as "the *female* sex hormones." This practice should be avoided because of its men-are-men-and-women-are-women implication that androgens produce maleness and estrogens produce femaleness. They don't.

The ovaries and testes also release a third class of steroid hormones called **progestins**. The most common progestin is **progesterone**, which in women prepares the uterus and the breasts for pregnancy. Its function in men is unclear.

Because the primary function of the **adrenal cortex**—the outer layer of the *adrenal glands* (see Figure 13.1)—is the regulation of glucose and salt levels in the blood, it is not generally thought of as a sex gland. However, in addition to its principal steroid hormones, it does release small amounts of all of the sex steroids that are released by the gonads.

Hormones of the Pituitary

The pituitary gland is frequently referred to as the *master gland* because most of its hormones are tropic hormones. *Tropic hormones* are hormones whose primary function is to influence the release of hormones from other glands (*tropic* is an adjective that describes things that stimulate or change other things). For example, **gonadotropin** is a pituitary tropic hormone that travels through the circulatory system to the gonads, where it stimulates the release of gonadal hormones.

The pituitary gland is really two glands, the posterior pituitary and the anterior pituitary, which fuse during the course of embryological development. The **posterior pituitary** develops from a small outgrowth of hypothalamic tissue that eventually comes to dangle from the *hypothalamus* on the end of the **pituitary stalk** (see Figure 13.2). In contrast, the **anterior pituitary** begins as part of the same embryonic tissue that eventually develops into the roof of the mouth; during the course of development, it pinches off and migrates upward to assume its position next to the posterior pituitary. It is the anterior pituitary that releases tropic hormones; thus, it is the anterior pituitary in particular, rather than the pituitary in general, that qualifies as the master gland.

Female Gonadal Hormone Levels Are Cyclic; Male Gonadal Hormone Levels Are Steady

Although men and women possess the same hormones, these hormones are not present at the same levels, and they do not necessarily perform the same functions. The major difference between the endocrine function of women and men is that in women the levels of gonadal and gonadotropic hormones go through a cycle that repeats itself every 28 days or so. It is these more-or-less regular hormone fluctuations that control the female **menstrual cycle**. In contrast, human males are, from a neuroendocrine perspective, rather dull creatures; males' levels of gonadal and gonadotropic hormones change little from day to day.

Because the anterior pituitary is the master gland, many early scientists assumed that an inherent difference between the male and female anterior pituitary was the basis for the difference in male and female patterns of gonadotropic and gonadal hormone release. However, this hypothesis was discounted by a series of clever transplant studies conducted by Geoffrey Harris in the 1950s (see Raisman, 1997). In these studies, a cycling pituitary removed from a mature female rat became a steady-state

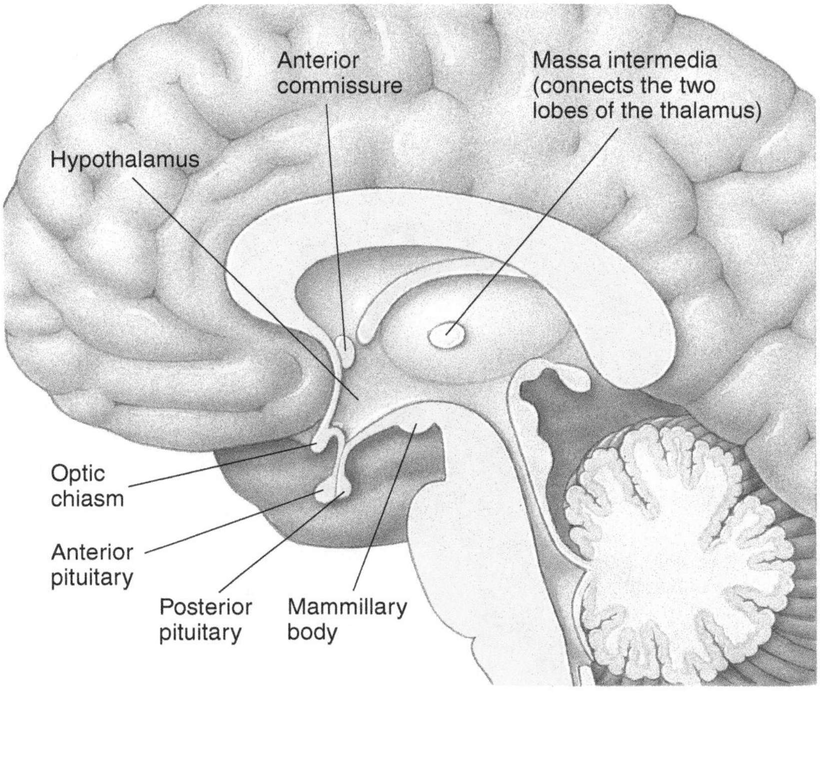

The Evolutionary Perspective

FIGURE 13.2 A midline view of the posterior and anterior pituitary and surrounding structures.

pituitary when transplanted at the appropriate site in a male, and a steady-state pituitary removed from a mature male rat began to cycle once transplanted into a female. What these studies established was that anterior pituitaries are not inherently female (cyclical) or male (steady-state); their patterns of hormone release are controlled by some other part of the body. The master gland seemed to have its own master. Where was it?

Neural Control of the Pituitary

The nervous system was implicated in the control of the anterior pituitary by behavioral research on birds and other animals that breed only during a specific time of the year. It was found that the seasonal variations in the light-dark cycle triggered many of the breeding-related changes in hormone release. If the lighting conditions under which the animals lived were reversed, for example, by having the animals transported across the equator, the breeding seasons were also reversed. Somehow, visual input to the nervous system was controlling the release of tropic hormones from the anterior pituitary.

The Evolutionary Perspective

The search for the particular neural structure that controlled the anterior pituitary turned, naturally enough, to the *hypothalamus*, the structure from which the pituitary is suspended. Hypothalamic stimulation and lesion experiments quickly established that the hypothalamus is the regulator of the anterior pituitary, but how the hypothalamus carries out this role remained a mystery. You see, the anterior pituitary, unlike the posterior pituitary, receives no neural input whatsoever from the hypothalamus, or from any other neural structure (see Figure 13.3).

Control of the Anterior and Posterior Pituitary by the Hypothalamus

There are two different mechanisms by which the hypothalamus controls the pituitary: one for the posterior pituitary and one for the anterior pituitary. The two major hormones of the posterior pituitary, **vasopressin** and **oxytocin**, are peptide hormones that are synthe-

sized in the cell bodies of neurons in the **paraventricular nuclei** and **supraoptic nuclei** of the hypothalamus (see Figure 13.3). They are then transported along the axons of these neurons to their terminals in the posterior pituitary and are stored there until the arrival of action potentials causes them to be released into the bloodstream. (Neurons that release hormones into general circulation are called *neurosecretory cells*.) Oxytocin stimulates contractions of the uterus during labor and the ejection of milk during suckling. Vasopressin (also called *antidiuretic hormone*) facilitates the reabsorption of water by the kidneys.

The means by which the hypothalamus controls the release of hormones from the neuron-free anterior pituitary was more difficult to explain. Harris (1955) suggested that the release of hormones from the anterior pituitary was itself regulated by hormones released from the hypothalamus. Two findings provided early support for this hypothesis. The first was the discovery of a vascular network, the **hypothalamopituitary portal system**, that seemed well suited to the task of carrying hormones from the hypothalamus to the anterior pituitary. As Figure 13.4 illustrates, a network of hypothalamic capillaries feeds a bundle of portal veins that carries blood down the pituitary stalk into another network of capillaries in the anterior pituitary. (A *portal vein* is a vein that connects one capillary network with another.) The second finding was the discovery that cutting the portal veins of the pituitary stalk disrupts the release of anterior pituitary hormones until the damaged veins regenerate (Harris, 1955).

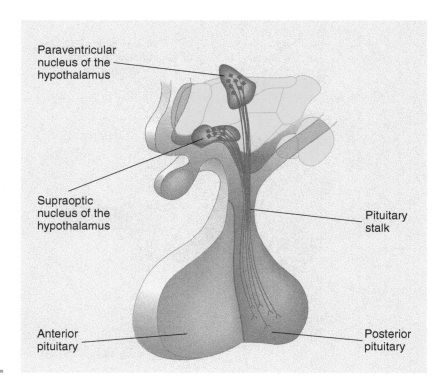

FIGURE 13.3 The neural connections between the hypothalamus and the pituitary. All neural input to the pituitary goes to the posterior pituitary; the anterior pituitary has no neural connections.

Paraventricular nucleus of the hypothalamus

Supraoptic nucleus of the hypothalamus

Anterior pituitary

Pituitary stalk

Posterior pituitary

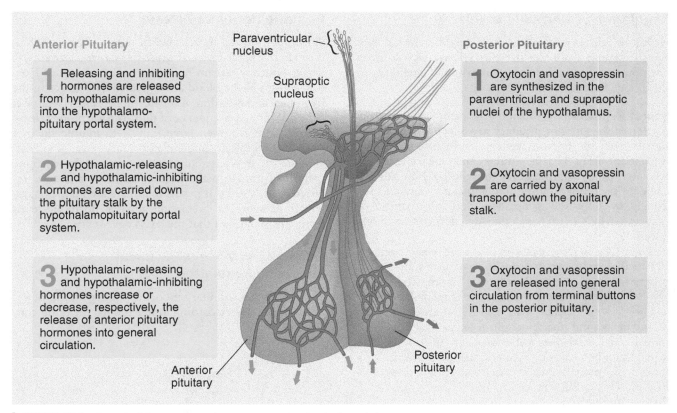

Anterior Pituitary

1 Releasing and inhibiting hormones are released from hypothalamic neurons into the hypothalamo-pituitary portal system.

2 Hypothalamic-releasing and hypothalamic-inhibiting hormones are carried down the pituitary stalk by the hypothalamopituitary portal system.

3 Hypothalamic-releasing and hypothalamic-inhibiting hormones increase or decrease, respectively, the release of anterior pituitary hormones into general circulation.

Paraventricular nucleus

Supraoptic nucleus

Anterior pituitary

Posterior pituitary

Posterior Pituitary

1 Oxytocin and vasopressin are synthesized in the paraventricular and supraoptic nuclei of the hypothalamus.

2 Oxytocin and vasopressin are carried by axonal transport down the pituitary stalk.

3 Oxytocin and vasopressin are released into general circulation from terminal buttons in the posterior pituitary.

FIGURE 13.4   Control of the anterior and posterior pituitary by the hypothalamus.

Discovery of Hypothalamic Releasing Hormones

It was hypothesized that the release of each anterior pituitary hormone is controlled by a different hypothalamic hormone. The hypothalamic hormones that were thought to stimulate the release of an anterior pituitary hormone were referred to as **releasing hormones**; those thought to inhibit the release of an anterior pituitary hormone were referred to as **release-inhibiting factors**.

Efforts to isolate the putative (hypothesized) hypothalamic releasing and inhibitory factors led to a major breakthrough in the late 1960s. Guillemin and his colleagues isolated **thyrotropin-releasing hormone** from the hypothalamus of sheep, and Schally and his colleagues isolated the same hormone from the hypothalamus of pigs. Thyrotropin-releasing hormone triggers the release of **thyrotropin** from the anterior pituitary, which in turn stimulates the release of hormones from the *thyroid gland.*

It is difficult to appreciate the effort that went into the initial isolation of thyrotropin-releasing hormone. Releasing and inhibiting factors exist in such small amounts that a mountain of hypothalamic tissue was required to extract even minute quantities. Schally reported that the

The Evolutionary Perspective

work of his group required over 1 million pig hypothalami. And where did Schally get such a quantity of pig hypothalami? From Oscar Mayer & Company—where else?

Why would two research teams dedicate over a decade of their lives to accumulate a pitifully small quantity of thyrotropin-releasing hormone? The reason was that it enabled both Guillemin and Schally to determine the chemical composition of thyrotropin-releasing hormone and then to develop methods of synthesizing larger quantities of the hormone for research and clinical use. For their efforts, Guillemin and Schally were awarded Nobel Prizes in 1977.

Schally's and Guillemin's isolation of thyrotropin-releasing hormone confirmed that hypothalamic releasing hormones control the release of hormones from the anterior pituitary and thus provided the major impetus for the isolation and synthesis of several other releasing hormones. Of direct relevance to the study of sex hormones was the subsequent isolation of **gonadotropin-releasing hormone** by Schally and his group (Schally, Kastin, & Arimura, 1971). This releasing hormone stimulates the release of both of the anterior pituitary's gonadotropins: **follicle-stimulating hormone** (**FSH**) and **luteinizing hormone** (**LH**). All hypothalamic releasing hormones, like all tropic hormones, have proven to be peptides.

Regulation of Hormone Levels

Hormone release is regulated by three different kinds of signals: signals from the nervous system, signals from hormones, and signals from nonhormonal chemicals in the blood (Brown, 1994).

Neural Regulation All endocrine glands, with the exception of the anterior pituitary, are directly regulated by signals from the nervous system. Endocrine glands located in the brain (i.e., the pituitary and pineal glands) are regulated by cerebral neurons; those located outside the CNS are innervated by the *autonomic nervous system*—usually by both the *sympathetic* and *parasympathetic* branches, which often have opposite effects on hormone release.

The effects of experience on hormone release are usually mediated by signals from the nervous system. It is

Thinking Clearly

extremely important to remember that hormone release is regulated by experience. This means that an explanation of any behavioral phenomenon in terms of a hormonal mechanism does not necessarily rule out an explanation in terms of an experiential mechanism. Indeed, hormonal and experiential explanations may merely be different aspects of the same hypothetical mechanism.

Hormonal Regulation Signals from the hormones themselves also influence hormone release. You have already learned, for example, that the tropic hormones of the anterior pituitary influence the release of hormones from their respective target glands. However, the regulation of endocrine function by the anterior pituitary is not a one-way street. Circulating hormones often provide feedback to the very structures that influence their release: the pituitary gland, the hypothalamus, and other sites in the brain. The function of most hormonal feedback is the maintenance of stable blood levels of the hormones. Thus, high gonadal hormone levels usually have effects on the hypothalamus and pituitary that decrease subsequent gonadal hormone release, and low levels usually have effects that increase hormone release.

Regulation by Nonhormonal Chemicals Circulating chemicals other than hormones can play a role in regulating hormone levels. Glucose, calcium, and sodium levels in the blood all influence the release of particular hormones. For example, you learned in Chapter 12 that increases in blood glucose increase the release of *insulin* from the *pancreas*, and insulin, in turn, reduces blood glucose levels.

FIGURE 13.5 A summary model of the regulation of gonadal hormones.

Pulsatile Hormone Release

Hormones tend to be released in pulses (Karsch, 1987); they are discharged several times per day in large surges, which typically last no more than a few minutes. Hormone levels in the blood are regulated by changes in the frequency and duration of the hormone pulses (Reame et al., 1984). One consequence of **pulsatile hormone release** is that there are often large minute-to-minute fluctuations in the levels of circulating hormones (e.g., Koolhaas, Schuurman, & Wierpkema, 1980). Accordingly, when the pattern of human male gonadal hormone release is referred to as "steady," it means that there are no major systematic changes in circulating gonadal hormone levels from day to day, not that the levels never vary.

A Summary Model of Gonadal Endocrine Regulation

Figure 13.5 is a summary model of the regulation of gonadal hormones. According to this model, the brain con-

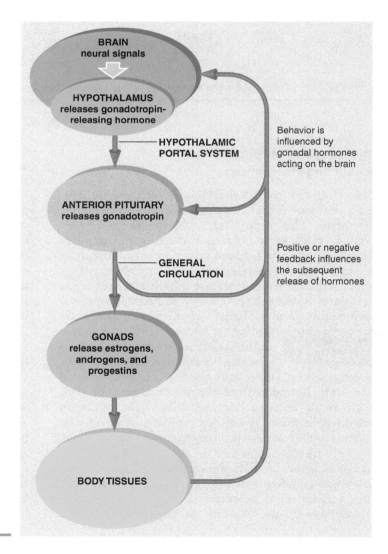

trols the release of gonadotropin-releasing hormone from the hypothalamus into the hypothalamopituitary portal system, which carries it to the anterior pituitary. In the anterior pituitary, the gonadotropin-releasing hormone stimulates the release of gonadotropin, which is carried by the circulatory system to the gonads. In response to the gonadotropin, the gonads release androgens, estrogens, and progestins, which feed back into the pituitary and hypothalamus to regulate subsequent gonadal hormone release.

Armed with this general perspective of neuroendocrine function, you are ready to consider how gonadal hormones direct sexual development and activate adult sexual behavior.

13.2
Hormones and Sexual Development

You have undoubtedly noticed that humans are *dimorphic*—that is, they come in two standard models: female and male. This section describes how the development of female and male characteristics is directed by hormones.

The next section discusses three cases of exceptional sexual development. I am sure you will be intrigued by these three cases, but that is not the only *Thinking Clearly* reason why I have chosen to include them. My main reason is expressed by a proverb: The exception proves the rule. Most people think this proverb means that the exception "proves" the rule in the sense that it establishes its truth, but this is clearly wrong: The truth of a rule is challenged by, not confirmed by, exceptions to it. The word *proof* comes from the Latin *probare*, which means "to test"—as in *proving ground* or printer's *proof*—and this is the sense in which it is used in the proverb. Hence, the proverb means that the explanation of exceptional cases is a major challenge for any theory. Accordingly, the primary purpose of discussing the three cases of exceptional sexual development in the next section is to test the theories presented in this section.

Sexual differentiation in mammals begins at fertilization with the production of one of two different kinds of zygotes: either one with an XX (female) pair of sex chromosomes or one with an XY (male) *Thinking Clearly* pair. It is the genetic information on the sex chromosomes that normally determines whether development will occur along female or male lines. But be cautious here: Do not fall into the seductive embrace of the men-are-men-and-women-are-women assumption. Do not begin by assuming that there are two parallel but opposite genetic programs for sexual development, one for female development and one for male development. As you are about to learn, sexual development unfolds according to an entirely different

principle, one that males who still stubbornly cling to notions of male preeminence find unsettling. This principle is that we are all genetically programmed to develop female bodies; genetic males develop male bodies only because their fundamentally female program of development is overruled.

Fetal Hormones and the Development of Reproductive Organs

Gonads   Figure 13.6 illustrates the structure of the gonads as they appear 6 weeks after fertilization. Notice that at this stage of development, each fetus, regardless of its genetic sex, has the same pair of gonadal structures, called *primordial gonads* (*primordial* means "existing at the beginning"). Each primordial gonad has an outer covering, or *cortex*, which has the potential to develop into an ovary; and each has an internal core, or *medulla*, which has the potential to develop into a testis.

Six weeks after conception, the **Sry gene** on the Y chromosome of the male triggers the synthesis of **Sry protein** (see Arnold, 2004), and this protein causes the medulla of each primordial gonad to grow and to develop into a testis. There is no female counterpart of Sry protein; in

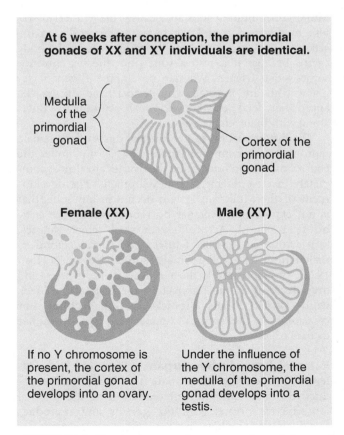

At 6 weeks after conception, the primordial gonads of XX and XY individuals are identical.

Medulla of the primordial gonad

Cortex of the primordial gonad

Female (XX)

If no Y chromosome is present, the cortex of the primordial gonad develops into an ovary.

Male (XY)

Under the influence of the Y chromosome, the medulla of the primordial gonad develops into a testis.

FIGURE 13.6   The development of an ovary and a testis from the cortex and the medulla, respectively, of the primordial gonadal structure that is present 6 weeks after conception.

the absence of Sry protein, the cortical cells of the primordial gonads automatically develop into ovaries. Accordingly, if Sry protein is injected into a genetic female fetus 6 weeks after conception, the result is a genetic female with testes; or if drugs that block the effects of Sry protein are injected into a male fetus, the result is a genetic male with ovaries. Such "mixed-gender" individuals expose in a dramatic fashion the weakness of the mamawawa.

Internal Reproductive Ducts Six weeks after fertilization, both males and females have two complete sets of reproductive ducts. They have a male **Wolffian system**, which has the capacity to develop into the male reproductive ducts (e.g., the *seminal vesicles*, which hold the fluid in which sperm cells are ejaculated; and the *vas deferens*, through which the sperm cells travel to the seminal vesicles). And they have a female **Müllerian system**, which has the capacity to develop into the female ducts (e.g., the *uterus;* the upper part of the *vagina;* and the *fallopian tubes*, through which ova travel from the ovaries to the uterus, where they can be fertilized).

In the third month of male fetal development, the testes secrete testosterone and **Müllerian-inhibiting substance**. As Figure 13.7 illustrates, the testosterone stimulates the development of the Wolffian system, and the Müllerian-inhibiting substance causes the Müllerian system to degenerate and the testes to descend into the **scrotum**—the sac that holds the testes outside the body cavity. Because it is testosterone—not the sex chromosomes—that triggers Wolffian development, genetic females who are injected with testosterone during the appropriate fetal period develop male reproductive ducts along with their female ones.

The differentiation of the internal ducts of the female reproductive system (see Figure 13.7) is not under the control of ovarian hormones; the ovaries are almost completely inactive during fetal development. The development of the Müllerian system occurs in any fetus that is not exposed to testicular hormones during the critical fetal period. Accordingly, normal female fetuses, ovariectomized female fetuses, and orchidectomized male fetuses all develop female reproductive ducts (Jost, 1972). **Ovariectomy** is the removal of the ovaries, and **orchidectomy** is the removal of the testes (the Greek word *orchis* means "testicle"). **Gonadectomy**, or *castration*, is the surgical removal of gonads—either ovaries or testes.

External Reproductive Organs There is a basic difference between the differentiation of the external reproductive organs and the differentiation of the internal reproductive organs (i.e., the gonads and reproductive ducts). As you have just read, every normal fetus develops separate precursors for the male (medulla) and female (cortex) gonads and for the male (Wolffian sys-

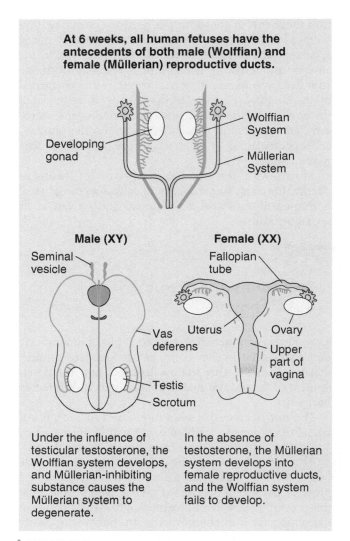

At 6 weeks, all human fetuses have the antecedents of both male (Wolffian) and female (Müllerian) reproductive ducts.

Developing gonad

Wolffian System

Müllerian System

Male (XY)

Seminal vesicle

Vas deferens

Testis

Scrotum

Female (XX)

Fallopian tube

Uterus

Ovary

Upper part of vagina

Under the influence of testicular testosterone, the Wolffian system develops, and Müllerian-inhibiting substance causes the Müllerian system to degenerate.

In the absence of testosterone, the Müllerian system develops into female reproductive ducts, and the Wolffian system fails to develop.

FIGURE 13.7 The development of the internal ducts of the male and female reproductive systems from the Wolffian and Müllerian systems, respectively.

tem) and female (Müllerian system) reproductive ducts; then, only one set, male or female, develops. In contrast, both male and female **genitals**—external reproductive organs—develop from the same precursor. This *bipotential precursor* and its subsequent differentiation are illustrated in Figure 13.8.

In the second month of pregnancy, the bipotential precursor of the external reproductive organs consists of four parts: the glans, the urethral folds, the lateral bodies, and the labioscrotal swellings. Then it begins to differentiate. The *glans* grows into the head of the *penis* in the male or the *clitoris* in the female, the *urethral folds*

mypsychkit

The *Differentiation of the External Genitals* module will help you visualize this process.

fuse in the male or enlarge to become the *labia minora* in the female, the *lateral bodies* form the shaft of the penis in

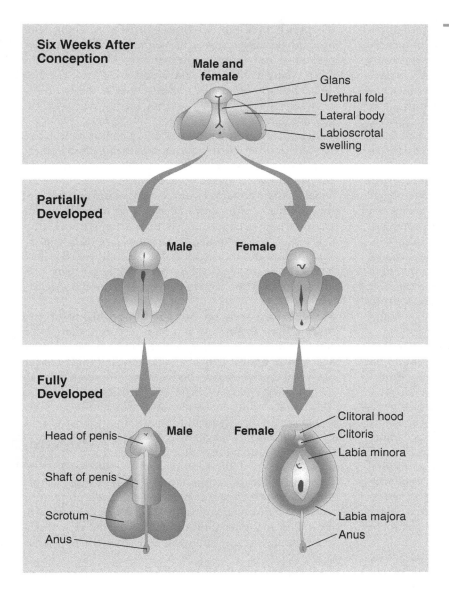

Six Weeks After Conception

Male and female

- Glans
- Urethral fold
- Lateral body
- Labioscrotal swelling

Partially Developed

Male   Female

Fully Developed

Male   Female

- Head of penis
- Shaft of penis
- Scrotum
- Anus

- Clitoral hood
- Clitoris
- Labia minora
- Labia majora
- Anus

FIGURE 13.8 The development of male and female external reproductive organs from the same bipotential precursor.

other anatomical differences exist. There are major sex differences in the volumes of various nuclei and fiber tracts, in the numbers and types of neural and glial cells that compose various structures, and in the numbers and types of synapses that connect the cells in various structures. *Sexual dimorphisms* (male–female structural differences) of the brain are typically studied in nonhuman mammals, but many have also been documented in humans (see Arnold, 2003; Cahill, 2005, 2006).

Research on sexual dimorphisms of mammalian brains is in transition. Initially, neuroscientists focused on identifying and describing examples, but now that so many have been documented, they are trying to understand the causes and functions of the differences. Before I can describe this important area of current research, I need to tell you how the first example of sexual dimorphism in the brain was identified and studied. It set the stage for everything that followed.

Discovery of the First Mammalian Sexual Dimorphism of the Brain   The first attempts to discover sex differences in the mammalian brain focused on the factors that control the development of the steady and cyclic patterns of gonadotropin release in males and females, respec-

The Evolutionary Perspective

the male or the hood of the clitoris in the female, and the *labioscrotal swellings* form the *scrotum* in the male or the *labia majora* in the female.

Like the development of the internal reproductive ducts, the development of the external genitals is controlled by the presence or absence of testosterone. If testosterone is present at the appropriate stage of fetal development, male external genitals develop from the bipotential precursor; if testosterone is not present, the development of the external genitals proceeds along female lines.

Sex Differences in the Brain

The brains of men and women may look the same on casual inspection, and it may be politically correct to believe that they are—but they are not. The brains of men tend to be about 15% larger than those of women, and numerous

tively. The seminal experiments were conducted by Pfeiffer in 1936. In his experiments, some neonatal rats (males and females) were gonadectomized and some were not, and some received gonad transplants (ovaries or testes) and some did not.

Remarkably, Pfeiffer found that gonadectomizing neonatal rats of either genetic sex caused them to develop into adults with the female cyclic pattern of gonadotropin release. In contrast, transplantation of testes into gonadectomized or intact female neonatal rats caused them to develop into adults with the steady male pattern of gonadotropin release. Transplantation of ovaries had no effect on the pattern of hormone release. Pfeiffer concluded that the female cyclic pattern of gonadotropin release develops unless the preprogrammed female cyclicity is overridden by testosterone during perinatal development (see Harris & Levine, 1965).

Pfeiffer incorrectly concluded that the presence or absence of testicular hormones in neonatal rats influenced the development of the pituitary because he was not aware of something we know today: The release of gonadotropins from the anterior pituitary is controlled by the hypothalamus. Once this was discovered, it became apparent that Pfeiffer's experiments had provided the first evidence of the role of *perinatal* (around the time of birth) androgens in the sexual differentiation of the hypothalamus.

> *Neuroplasticity*

Soon a complication to the simple androgen theory of hypothalamic differentiation was discovered. You see, all gonadal and adrenal sex hormones are steroid hormones, and because all steroid hormones are derived from cholesterol, they have similar structures and are readily converted from one to the other. For example, a slight change to the testosterone molecule that occurs under the influence of the *enzyme* (a chemical that influences a chemical reaction without participating in it) **aromatase** converts testosterone to estradiol. This process is called **aromatization** (see Balthazart & Ball, 1998).

According to the **aromatization hypothesis**, perinatal testosterone does not directly masculinize the brain; the brain is masculinized by estradiol that has been aromatized from perinatal testosterone. Although the idea that estradiol—the alleged female hormone—masculinizes the brain is counterintuitive, there is strong evidence for it. This evidence is of two types: (1) findings demonstrating the masculinizing effects on the brain of early estradiol injections, and (2) findings showing that masculinization of the brain does not occur in response to testosterone that is administered with agents that block aromatization or in response to androgens that cannot be aromatized (e.g., dihydrotestosterone).

> *The Evolutionary Perspective*

Although support for the aromatization hypothesis is substantial, there is a major species difference. The conversion of testosterone to estradiol is critical for the masculinizing effects of testosterone on mouse, rat, and guinea pig brains; however, its role appears to be much less critical in primates (see Baum, 2006; Swaab, 2004; Wallen, 2005). Moreover, even in rodents the role of aromatization on brain masculinization is specific rather than global: Aromatase is found in only a few neural structures (e.g., the hypothalamus), and aromatization is critical for testosterone's masculinization of only these structures (see Ball & Balthazart, 2006; Balthazart & Ball, 2006).

> *The Evolutionary Perspective*

How do genetic females of species whose brains are masculinized by estradiol keep from being masculinized by their mothers' estradiol, which circulates through the fetal blood supply? In the rat, alpha fetoprotein is the answer. **Alpha fetoprotein** is present in the blood of rats during the perinatal period, and it deactivates circulating estradiol by binding to it (Bakker et al., 2006). How, then, does estradiol masculinize the brain of the male fetus in the presence of the deactivating effects of alpha fetoprotein? Because testosterone is immune to alpha fetoprotein, it can travel unaffected from the testes to the brain, where it enters cells and is converted there to estradiol. The estradiol is not broken down in the brain because alpha fetoprotein does not readily penetrate the blood–brain barrier.

In humans, aromatization does not appear to be necessary for testosterone to have masculinizing effects on the brain; nevertheless, estradiol is capable of masculinizing effects similar to those of testosterone. How then are female fetuses protected from the masculinizing effects of the mother's estrogens? They are protected by the *placental barrier*. Unfortunately, this barrier is not as effective against some synthetic estrogens (e.g., *diethylstilbestrol*). As a result, the female babies of mothers who have been exposed to synthetic estrogens while pregnant may display some male characteristics (see McEwen, 1983).

Modern Research on Sexual Dimorphisms of the Mammalian Brain As you have just read, there is no support for two common misconceptions about male and female brains: that male and female brains are the same and that differences between them develop through the opposite effects of male and female sex hormones (that is, according to mamawawa principles). Early research on the development of sexual dimorphisms in the mammalian brain suggested that the same general mechanism that guides the differentiation of the reproductive organs guides the differentiation of the brain—that is, that the default program is female and the male program is activated by early exposure to testosterone. However, in the 1980s, many niggling exceptions to this view began to accumulate (e.g., Guillamón & Segovia, 1996; Segovia et al., 1999).

> *Neuroplasticity*

The view that there is a default female program of brain development that is converted to a male program by testosterone has been attacked on three fronts. First, there is now substantial evidence that the sex chromosomes contribute directly to brain dimorphism: XX and XY cells differ from one another even before they have been exposed to testosterone or estradiol, and differences between XX and XY cells persist even after the cells have been exposed to the same controlled doses of these hormones (Arnold, 2003; Arnold et al., 2004). Second, recent evidence suggests that the female program of brain development may not unfold automatically in the absence of estrogens: Various methods (e.g., gene knockouts) have been used to interfere with estradiol receptors, and this interference has disrupted normal female patterns of brain development (Bakker et al., 2003). The third challenge to the conventional view of the development of brain sexual dimorphisms focuses on the premise that there is a single mechanism that accounts for the development of all differences between male and female brains.

There is now overwhelming evidence that various sexual dimorphisms of the brain emerge at different stages of development under different influences (see McCarthy, Auger, & Perrot-Sinal, 2002; Woodson & Gorski, 2000; Wagner, 2006). Thus, although the conventional view of the development of sexual dimorphisms does an excellent job of explaining differentiation of the reproductive organs, it falters when it comes to the brain.

In studying the many sexual dimorphisms of the mammalian brain, it is easy to lose sight of the main point: We still do not understand the functional significance of any of the anatomical differences that have been identified.

Perinatal Hormones and Behavioral Development

In view of the fact that perinatal hormones influence the development of the brain, it should come as no surprise that they also influence the development of behavior. Much of the research on hormones and behavioral development has focused on the role of perinatal hormones in the development of sexually dimorphic copulatory behaviors in laboratory animals.

Phoenix and colleagues (1959) were among the first to demonstrate that the perinatal injection of testosterone **masculinizes** and **defeminizes** a genetic female's adult copulatory behavior. First, they injected pregnant guinea pigs with testosterone. Then, when the litters were born, the researchers ovariectomized the female offspring. Finally, when these ovariectomized female guinea pigs reached maturity, the researchers injected them with testosterone and assessed their copulatory behavior. Phoenix and his colleagues found that the females that had been exposed to perinatal testosterone displayed more male-like mounting behavior in response to testosterone injections in adulthood than did adult females that had not been exposed to perinatal testosterone. And when as adults the female guinea pigs were injected with progesterone and estradiol and mounted by males, they displayed less **lordosis**—the intromission-facilitating arched-back posture that signals female rodent receptivity.

In a study complementary to that of Phoenix and colleagues, Grady, Phoenix, and Young (1965) found that the lack of early exposure of male rats to testosterone both **feminizes** and **demasculinizes** their copulatory behavior as adults. Male rats castrated shortly after birth failed to display the normal male copulatory pattern of mounting, **intromission** (penis insertion), and **ejaculation** (ejection of sperm) when they were treated with testosterone and given access to a sexually receptive female; and when they were injected with estrogen and progesterone as adults, they exhibited more lordosis than did uncastrated controls.

The Evolutionary Perspective

The aromatization of perinatal testosterone to estradiol seems to be important for both the defeminization and the masculinization of rodent copulatory behavior (Goy & McEwen, 1980; Shapiro, Levine, & Adler, 1980). In contrast, that aromatization does not seem to be critical for these effects in monkeys (Wallen, 2005).

Because much of the research on hormones and behavioral development has focused on the copulatory act itself, we know less about the role of hormones in the development of **proceptive behaviors** (solicitation behaviors) and in the development of gender-related behaviors that are not directly related to reproduction. However, perinatal testosterone has been reported to disrupt the proceptive hopping, darting, and ear wiggling of receptive female rats; to increase the aggressiveness of female mice; to disrupt the maternal behavior of female rats; and to increase rough social play in female monkeys and rats.

In thinking about hormones and behavioral development, it is important to remember two things. First, feminizing and demasculinizing effects do not always go together; nor do defeminizing and masculinizing effects. Hormone treatments can enhance or disrupt female behavior without affecting male behavior, and vice versa (Bloch, Mills, & Gale, 1995). Second, timing is important. The ability of single injections of testosterone to masculinize and defeminize the rat brain seems to be restricted to the first 11 days after birth. However, large multiple doses of testosterone can have masculinizing effects outside this *sensitive period* (Bloch & Mills, 1995); the masculinizing effects of testosterone injections occur much earlier in fetal development.

Thinking Clearly

There have been many efforts to study the role of prenatal androgen exposure in the development of behavioral differences between men and women. The studies are of two types: (1) studies of clinical populations that have atypical exposure to early androgens, and (2) studies relating the level of early exposure of healthy subjects to androgens, often estimated from levels found in the mother. Cohen-Bendahan, van de Beek, and Berenbaum (2005) reviewed this extensive and complicated research literature. They concluded that, despite much inconsistency, the weight of evidence indicated that prenatal androgen exposure contributes to the differences in interests, spatial ability, and aggressiveness typically observed between men and women. However, there is no convincing evidence that differences in prenatal androgen exposure contribute to behavioral differences observed *among* women or *among* men.

Puberty: Hormones and the Development of Secondary Sex Characteristics

During childhood, levels of circulating gonadal hormones are low, reproductive organs are immature, and males and females differ little in general appearance. This period of developmental quiescence ends abruptly with the onset of *puberty*—the transitional period between childhood and adulthood during which fertility is achieved, the adolescent growth spurt occurs, and the secondary sex characteristics develop. **Secondary sex characteristics** are those features other than the reproductive organs that distinguish sexually mature men and women. The body changes that occur during puberty are illustrated in Figure 13.9; you are undoubtedly familiar with at least half of them.

Puberty is associated with an increase in the release of hormones by the anterior pituitary (see Grumbach, 2002). The increase in the release of **growth hormone**—the only anterior pituitary hormone that does not have a gland as its primary target—acts directly on bone and muscle tissue to produce the pubertal growth spurt. Increases in the release of gonadotropic hormone and **adrenocorticotropic hormone** cause the gonads and adrenal cortex to increase their release of gonadal and adrenal hormones, which in turn initiate the maturation of the genitals and the development of secondary sex characteristics.

The general principle guiding normal pubertal sexual maturation is a simple one: In pubertal males, androgen levels are higher than estrogen levels, and masculinization is the result; in pubertal females, the estrogens predominate, and the result is feminization. Individuals castrated prior to puberty do not become sexually mature unless they receive replacement injections of androgens or estrogens.

But even during puberty, its only major time of relevance, the men-are-men-and-women-are-women assumption stumbles badly. You see, **androstenedione**, an androgen that is released primarily by the adrenal cortex, is normally responsible for the growth of pubic hair and *axillary hair* (underarm hair) in females. It is hard to take seriously the practice of referring to androgens as "male hormones" when one of them is responsible for the development of the female pattern of pubic hair growth. The male pattern is a pyramid, and the female pattern is an inverted pyramid (see Figure 13.9).

Do you remember how old you were when you started to go through puberty? In most North American and

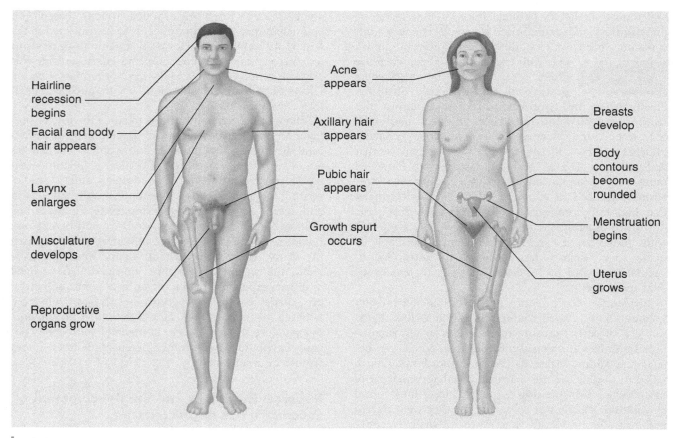

FIGURE 13.9   The changes that normally occur in males and females during puberty.

European countries, puberty begins at about 10.5 years of age for girls and 11.5 years for boys. I am sure that you would have been unhappy if you had not started puberty until you were 15 or 16, but this was the norm in North America and Europe just a century and a half ago. Presumably, this acceleration of puberty has resulted from an improvement in dietary, medical, and socioeconomic conditions.

Scan Your Brain

Before you proceed to a consideration of three cases of exceptional human sexual development, scan your brain to see whether you understand the basics of normal sexual development. Fill in the blanks in the following sentences. The correct answers are provided below. Review material related to your errors and omissions before proceeding.

1. Six weeks after conception, the Sry gene on the Y chromosome of the human male triggers the production of _____.
2. In the absence of the Sry protein, the cortical cells of the primordial gonads develop into _____.
3. In the third month of male fetal development, the testes secrete testosterone and _____ substance.
4. The hormonal factor that triggers the development of the human Müllerian system is the lack of _____ around the third month of fetal development.
5. The scrotum and the _____ develop from the same bipotential precursor.
6. The female pattern of cyclic _____ release from the anterior pituitary develops in adulthood unless androgens are present in the body during the perinatal period.
7. It has been hypothesized that perinatal testosterone must first be changed to estradiol before it can masculinize the male rat brain. This is called the _____ hypothesis.
8. _____ is normally responsible for pubic and axillary hair growth in human females during puberty.
9. Girls usually begin puberty _____ boys do.
10. The simplistic, seductive, but incorrect assumption that sexual differentiation occurs because male and female sex hormones trigger programs of development that are parallel but opposite to one another has been termed the _____.

Scan Your Brain answers: (1) Sry protein, (2) ovaries, (3) Müllerian-inhibiting, (4) androgens (or testosterone), (5) labia majora, (6) gonadotropin, (7) aromatization, (8) Androstenedione, (9) before, (10) mamawawa.

13.3
Three Cases of Exceptional Human Sexual Development

So far in this chapter, you have learned the "rules" according to which hormones seem to influence normal sexual development. Now, three exceptional cases are offered to prove (to test) these rules.

The Case of Anne S., the Woman Who Wasn't

Anne S., an attractive 26-year-old female, sought treatment for two sex-related disorders: lack of menstruation and pain during sexual intercourse (Jones & Park, 1971). She sought help because she and her husband of 4 years had been trying without success to have children, and she correctly surmised that her lack of a menstrual cycle was part of the problem. A physical examination revealed that Anne was a healthy young woman. Her only readily apparent peculiarity was the sparseness and fineness of her pubic and axillary hair. Examination of her external genitals revealed no abnormalities; however, there were some problems with her internal genitals. Her vagina was only 4 centimeters long, and her uterus was underdeveloped.

Clinical Implications

At the start of this chapter, I said that you would encounter some remarkable things, and the diagnosis of Anne's case certainly qualifies as one of them. Anne's doctors concluded that her sex chromosomes were those of a man. No, this is not a misprint; they concluded that Anne, the attractive young housewife, had the genes of a genetic male. Three lines of evidence supported their diagnosis. First, analysis of cells scraped from the inside of Anne's mouth revealed that they were of the male XY type. Second, a tiny incision in Anne's abdomen, which enabled Anne's physicians to look inside, revealed a pair of internalized testes but no ovaries. Finally, hormone tests revealed that Anne's hormone levels were those of a male.

Anne suffers from complete **androgenic insensitivity syndrome**; all her symptoms stem from a mutation to the androgen receptor gene that rendered her androgen receptors totally unresponsive (see Fink et al., 1999; Goldstein, 2000). Complete androgen insensitivity is rare, occurring in about 5 of 100,000 male births.

During development, Anne's testes released normal amounts of androgens for a male, but her body could not respond to them because of the mutation to her androgen receptor gene; and thus, her development proceeded as if no androgens had been released. Her external genitals, her brain, and her behavior developed along female lines, without the effects of androgens to override the female program, and her testes could not descend from her body cavity with no scrotum for them to descend into. Furthermore, Anne did not develop normal internal female reproductive ducts because, like other genetic males, her testes released Müllerian-inhibiting substance; that is why her vagina was short and her uterus undeveloped. At puberty, Anne's testes released enough estrogens to feminize her body in the absence of the counteracting effects of androgens; however, adrenal androstenedione was not able to stimulate the growth of pubic and axillary hair.

Although the samples are small, patients with complete androgen insensitivity have been found to be comparable to genetic females. All aspects of their behavior that have been studied—including gender identity, sexual orientation, interests, and cognitive abilities—have been found to be typically female (see Cohen-Bendahan, van de Beek, & Berenbaum, 2005).

An interesting issue of medical ethics is raised by the androgenic insensitivity syndrome. Many people believe that physicians should always disclose all relevant findings to their patients. If you were Anne's physician, would you tell her that she is a genetic male? Would you tell her husband? Her doctor did not. Anne's vagina was surgically enlarged, she was counseled to consider adoption, and, as far as I know, she is still happily married and unaware of her genetic sex. On the other hand, I have heard from several women who suffer from partial androgenic insensitivity, and they recommended full disclosure. They had faced a variety of sexual ambiguities throughout their lives and learning the cause helped them.

The Case of the Little Girl Who Grew into a Boy

The patient—let's call her Elaine—sought treatment in 1972. Elaine was born with somewhat ambiguous external genitals, but she was raised by her parents as a girl without incident, until the onset of puberty, when she suddenly began to develop male secondary sex characteristics. This was extremely distressing. Her treatment had two aspects: surgical and hormonal. Surgical treatment was used to increase the size of her vagina and decrease the size of her clitoris; hormonal treatment was used to suppress androgen release so that her own estrogen could feminize her body. Following treatment, Elaine developed into an attractive young woman—narrow hips and a husky voice being the only signs of her brush with masculinity. Fifteen years later, she was married and enjoying a normal sex life (Money & Ehrhardt, 1972).

Clinical Implications

Elaine suffered from adrenogenital syndrome, which is the most common disorder of sexual development, affecting about 1 in 10,000. **Adrenogenital syndrome** is caused by **congenital adrenal hyperplasia**—a congenital deficiency in the release of the hormone *cortisol* from the adrenal cortex, which results in compensatory adrenal hyperactivity and the excessive release of adrenal androgens. This has little effect on the development of males, other than accelerating the onset of puberty, but it has major effects on the development of genetic females. Females who suffer from the adrenogenital syndrome are usually born with an enlarged clitoris and partially fused labia. Their gonads and internal ducts are usually normal because the adrenal androgens are released too late to stimulate the development of the Wolffian system.

Most female cases of adrenogenital syndrome are diagnosed at birth. In such cases, the abnormalities of the external genitals are immediately corrected, and cortisol is administered to reduce the levels of circulating adrenal androgens. Following early treatment, adrenogenital females grow up to be physically normal except that the onset of menstruation is likely to be later than normal. This makes them good subjects for studies of the effects of fetal androgen exposure on psychosexual development.

Adrenogenital teenage girls who have received early treatment typically display a high degree of tomboyishness and little interest in maternity (e.g., Hines, 2003). They prefer boys' clothes and toys, play mainly with boys, show little interest in handling babies, and tend to daydream about future careers rather than motherhood. It is important not to lose sight of the fact that many teenage girls display similar characteristics—and why not? Accordingly, the behavior of treated adrenogenital females, although tending toward the masculine, is usually within the range considered normal by the current standards of our culture.

The most interesting questions about the development of females with adrenogenital syndrome concern their romantic and sexual preferences as adults. They seem to lag behind normal females in dating and marriage—perhaps because of the delayed onset of their menstrual cycle. Most are heterosexual, although some studies have found an increased tendency for these women to express interest in bisexuality or homosexuality and a tendency to be less involved in heterosexual relationships (see Gooren, 2006). Complicating the situation further is the fact that these slight differences may not be direct consequences of early androgen exposure but arise from the fact that some adrenogenital girls have ambiguous genitalia and other male characteristics (e.g., body hair), which may result in different experiential influences.

Thinking Clearly

The results of a study by Meyer-Bahlburg and colleagues (2006) can account for some of the inconsistencies of previous studies of adrenogenital syndrome. These researchers determined that there are three different forms of adrenogenital syndrome, which have different molecular causes associated with different degrees of early exposure to androgen. The researchers found no shifts in sexual orientation of the females with the mildest form of the syndrome, slight shifts in some of those with the intermediate form, and clear shifts in some of those with the most severe form. However, most of the women, even those with the most severe form of adrenogenital syndrome, were well within the normal range for sexual orientation, and what distinguished those in the normal range from those who showed shifts was not apparent.

Prior to the development of cortisol therapy in 1950, genetic females with adrenogenital syndrome were left untreated. Some were raised as boys and some as girls, but the direction of their pubertal development was unpredictable. In some cases, adrenal androgens predominated and masculinized their bodies; in others, ovarian estrogens predominated and feminized their bodies. Thus, some who were raised as boys were transformed at puberty into women, and some who were raised as girls were transformed into men, with devastating emotional consequences.

The Case of the Twin Who Lost His Penis

One of the most famous cases in the literature on sexual development is that of a male identical twin whose penis was accidentally destroyed during circumcision at the age of 7 months. Because there was no satisfactory way of surgically replacing the lost penis, a respected expert in such matters, John Money, recommended that the boy be castrated, that an artificial vagina be created, that the boy be raised as a girl, and that estrogen be administered at puberty to feminize the body. After a great deal of consideration and anguish, the parents followed Money's advice.

Money's (1975) report of this case of **ablatio penis** has been influential. It has been seen by some as the ultimate test of the *nature–nurture controversy* (see Chapter 2) with respect to the development of sexual identity and

Clinical Implications

behavior. It seemed to pit the masculinizing effects of male genes and male prenatal hormones against the effects of being reared as a female. And the availability of a genetically identical control subject, the twin brother, made the case all the more interesting.

According to Money, the outcome of this case strongly supports the *social-learning theory* of sexual identity. Money reported in 1975, when the patient was 12, that "she" had developed as a normal female, thus confirming his prediction that being gonadectomized, having the genitals surgically altered, and being raised as a girl would override the masculinizing effects of male genes and early androgens. Because it is such an interesting case, Money's description of it continues to be featured in some textbooks, each time carrying with it the message that the sexual identity and sexual behavior of men and women are largely a matter of upbringing.

However, a long-term follow-up study published by experts other than those who initially prescribed the treatment tells an entirely different story (Diamond & Sigmundson, 1997). Despite having female genitalia and being treated as a female, John/Joan developed along male lines. Apparently, the organ that determines the course of psychosocial development is the brain, not the genitals (Reiner, 1997). The following paraphrases from Diamond and Sigmundson's report give you a glimpse of John/Joan's life:

> From a very early age, Joan tended to act in a masculine way. She preferred boys' activities and games and displayed little interest in dolls, sewing, or other conventional female activities. When she was four, she was watching her father shave and her mother put on lipstick, and she began to put shaving cream on her face. When she was told to put makeup on like her mother, she said, "No, I don't want no makeup, I want to shave."
>
> "Things happened very early. As a child, I began to see that I felt different about a lot of things than I was supposed to. I suspected I was a boy from the second grade on."
>
> Despite the absence of a penis, Joan often tried to urinate while standing, and she would sometimes go to the boys' lavatory.
>
> Joan was attractive as a girl, but as soon as she moved or talked her masculinity became apparent. She was teased incessantly by the other girls, and she often retaliated violently, which resulted in her expulsion from school.
>
> Joan was put on an estrogen regimen at the age of 12 but rebelled against it. She did not want to feminize; she hated her developing breasts and refused to wear a bra.
>
> At 14, Joan decided to live as a male and switched to John. At that time, John's father tearfully revealed John's entire early history to him. "All of a sudden everything clicked. For the first time I understood who and what I was."
>
> John requested androgen treatment, a *mastectomy* (surgical removal of breasts), and *phaloplasty* (surgical creation of a penis). He became a handsome and popular young man. He married at the age of 25 and adopted his wife's children. He is strictly heterosexual.
>
> John's ability to ejaculate and experience orgasm returned following his androgen treatments. However, his early castration permanently eliminated his reproductive capacity.

John remained bitter about his early treatment and his inability to produce offspring. To save others from his experience, he cooperated in writing his biography, *As Nature Made Him* (Colapinto, 2000). His real name was David Reimer (see Figure 13.10 on page 336). David never recovered from his emotional scars. On May 4, 2004, he committed suicide.

David Reimer's case suggests that the clinical practice of surgically modifying a person's sex at birth should be curtailed. Any such irrevocable treatments should await

FIGURE 13.10   David Reimer, the twin whose penis was accidentally destroyed.

early puberty and the emergence of the patient's sexual identity and sexual attraction. Then, a compatible course of treatment can be selected.

Do the Exceptional Cases Prove the Rule?

Do current theories of hormones and sexual development pass the test imposed by the three preceding cases of exceptional sexual development? In my view, the answer is an emphatic yes. Although current theories do not supply all of the answers, especially when it comes to brain dimorphisms and behavior, they have contributed greatly to the understanding of exceptional sexual development.

Thinking Clearly

For centuries, cases of abnormal sexual development have befuddled scholars, but now, armed with a basic understanding of the role of hormones in sexual development, they have been able to make sense of even the most puzzling of such cases. Moreover, the study of sexual development has pointed the way to effective treatments. Judge these contributions for yourself by comparing your current understanding of these three cases with the understanding that you would have had if you had encountered them before beginning this chapter.

Notice one more thing about the three cases: Each of the three subjects was male in some respects and female in others. Accordingly, each case is a serious challenge to the men-are-men-and-women-are-women assumption: Male and female are not opposite, mutually exclusive categories.

13.4
Effects of Gonadal Hormones on Adults

Once an individual reaches sexual maturity, gonadal hormones begin to play a role in activating reproductive behavior. These activational effects are the focus of the first two parts of this section, which has four parts. The first deals with the role of hormones in activating the reproduction-related behavior of men, and the second deals with the role of hormones in activating the reproduction-related behavior of women. The third and fourth parts of this section deal with the clinical effects of gonadal hormone administration in adults. The third discusses the epidemic of anabolic steroid use, and the fourth describes the neuroprotective effects of estradiol.

Male Reproduction–Related Behavior and Testosterone

The important role played by gonadal hormones in the activation of male sexual behavior is clearly demonstrated by the asexualizing effects of orchidectomy. Bremer (1959) reviewed the cases of 157 orchidectomized Norwegians. Many had committed sex-related offenses and had agreed to castration to reduce the length of their prison terms.

Two important generalizations can be drawn from Bremer's study. The first is that orchidectomy leads to a reduction in sexual interest and behavior; the second is that the rate and the degree of the loss are variable. About half the men became completely asexual within a few weeks of the operation; others quickly lost their ability to achieve an erection but continued to experience some sexual interest and pleasure; and a few continued to copulate successfully, although somewhat less enthusiastically, for the duration of the study. There were also body changes: a reduction of hair on the trunk, extremities, and face; the deposition of fat on the hips and chest; a softening of the skin; and a reduction in strength.

Of the 102 sex offenders in Bremer's study, only 3 were reconvicted of sex offenses. Accordingly, he recommended castration as an effective treatment of last resort for male sex offenders.

Why do some men remain sexually active for months after orchidectomy, despite the fact that testicular hormones are cleared from their bodies within days? It has been suggested that adrenal androgens may play some role in the maintenance of sexual activity in some castrated men, but there is no direct evidence for this hypothesis.

Orchidectomy removes, in one fell swoop—or, to put it more precisely, in two fell swoops—a pair of glands that release many hormones. Because testosterone is the major testicular hormone, the major symptoms of orchidectomy have been generally attributed to the loss of testosterone, rather than to the loss of some other testicular hormone or to some nonhormonal consequence of the surgery. The therapeutic effects of **replacement injections** of testosterone have confirmed this assumption.

The Case of the Man Who Lost and Regained His Manhood

The very first case report of the effects of testosterone replacement therapy concerned an unfortunate 38-year-old World War I veteran, who was castrated in 1918 at the age of 19 by a shell fragment that removed his testes but left his penis undamaged.

Clinical Implications

His body was soft; it was as if he had almost no muscles at all; his hips had grown wider and his shoulders seemed narrower than when he was a soldier. He had very little drive. . . .

Just the same this veteran had married, in 1924, and you'd wonder why, because the doctors had told him he would surely be **impotent** [unable to achieve an erection]. . . . he made some attempts at sexual intercourse "for his wife's satisfaction" but he confessed that he had been unable to satisfy her at all. . . .

Dr. Foss began injecting it [testosterone] into the feeble muscles of the castrated man. . . .

After the fifth injection, erections were rapid and prolonged. . . . But that wasn't all. During twelve weeks of treatment he had gained eighteen pounds, and all his clothes had become too small. Originally, he wore fourteen-and-a-half inch collars. Now fifteen-and-a-half were too tight. . . . testosterone had resurrected a broken man to a manhood he had lost forever. (de Kruif, 1945, pp. 97–100)

Since this first clinical trial, testosterone has breathed sexuality into the lives of many men. Testosterone does not, however, eliminate the *sterility* (inability to reproduce) of males who lack functional testes.

The fact that testosterone is necessary for male sexual behavior has led to two widespread assumptions: (1) that the level of a man's sexuality is a function of the amount of testosterone he has in his blood, and (2) that a man's sex drive can be increased by increasing his testosterone levels. Both assumptions are incorrect. Sex drive and testosterone levels are uncorrelated in healthy men, and testosterone injections do not increase their sex drive.

It seems that each healthy male has far more testosterone than is required to activate the neural circuits that produce his sexual behavior and that having more than the minimum is of no advantage in this respect (Sherwin, 1988). A classic experiment by Grunt and Young (1952) clearly illustrates this point.

The Evolutionary Perspective

First, Grunt and Young rated the sexual behavior of each of the male guinea pigs in their experiment. Then, on the basis of the ratings, the researchers divided the male

guinea pigs into three experimental groups: low, medium, and high sex drive. Following castration, the sexual behavior of all of the guinea pigs fell to negligible levels within a few weeks (see Figure 13.11 on page 338), but it recovered after the initiation of a series of testosterone replacement injections. The important point is that although each subject received the same, very large replacement injections of testosterone, the injections simply returned each to its previous level of copulatory activity. The conclusion is clear: With respect to the effects of testosterone on sexual behavior, more is not necessarily better.

Dihydrotestosterone, a nonaromatizable androgen, restores the copulatory behavior of castrated male primates (e.g., Davidson, Kwan, & Greenleaf, 1982); however, it fails to restore the copulatory behavior of castrated male rodents (see MacLusky & Naftolin, 1981). These findings indicate that the restoration of copulatory behavior by testosterone occurs by different mechanisms in rodents and primates. It appears to be a direct effect of testosterone in primates, whereas in rodents restoration appears to be produced by estradiol aromatized from testosterone (see Ball & Balthazart, 2006).

Female Reproduction–Related Behavior and Gonadal Hormones

Sexually mature female rats and guinea pigs display 4-day cycles of gonadal hormone release. There is a gradual increase in the secretion of estrogens by the developing *follicle* (ovarian structure in which eggs nature) in the 2 days 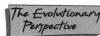 prior to ovulation, followed by a sudden surge in progesterone as the egg is released. These surges of estrogens and progesterone initiate **estrus**— a period of 12 to 18 hours during which the female is *fertile, receptive* (likely to assume the lordosis posture when mounted), *proceptive* (likely to engage in behaviors that serve to attract the male), and *sexually attractive* (smelling of chemicals that attract males).

The close relation between the cycle of hormone release and the **estrous cycle**—the cycle of sexual receptivity—in female rats and guinea pigs and in many other mammalian species suggests that female sexual behavior in these species is under hormonal control. The effects of ovariectomy confirm this conclusion; ovariectomy of female rats and guinea pigs produces a rapid decline of both proceptive and receptive behaviors. Furthermore, estrus can be induced in ovariectomized rats and guinea pigs by an injection of estradiol followed about a day and a half later by an injection of progesterone.

Women are different from female rats, guinea pigs, and other mammals when it comes to the hormonal control of their sexual behavior. Neither the sexual motivation nor the sexual behavior of women is linked to their menstrual cycles (see Sanders & Bancroft, 1982)—indeed, women are the only female mammals that are motivated

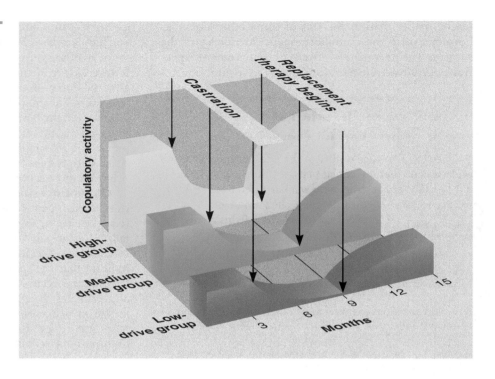

FIGURE 13.11 The sexual behavior of male guinea pigs with low, medium, and high sex drive. Sexual behavior was disrupted by castration and returned to its original level by very large replacement injections of testosterone. (Adapted from Grunt & Young, 1952.)

to copulate during periods of nonfertility (Zeigler, 2007). Moreover, ovariectomy has surprisingly little direct effect on either their sexual motivation or their sexual behavior (e.g., Martin, Roberts, & Clayton, 1980). Other than sterility, the major consequence of ovariectomy in women is a decrease in vaginal lubrication.

Paradoxically, there is evidence that the sex drive of women is under the control of androgens, not estrogens (see Davis & Tran, 2001; Sherwin, 1988). Apparently, enough androgens are released from the human adrenal glands to maintain the sexual motivation of women even after their ovaries have been removed. Support for the theory that androgens control human female sexuality has come from three sources:

- Experiments in nonhuman female primates: Replacement injections of testosterone, but not estradiol, increase the proceptivity of ovariectomized and adrenalectomized rhesus monkeys (see Everitt & Herbert, 1972; Everitt, Herbert, & Hamer, 1971).
- Correlational studies in healthy women: Various measures of sexual motivation are correlated with testosterone levels but not with estradiol levels (see Bancroft et al., 1983; Morris et al., 1987).
- Clinical studies of women following ovariectomy and adrenalectomy: Replacement injections of testosterone, but not of estradiol, rekindle their sexual motivation (see Sherwin, 1985; Sherwin, Gelfand, & Brender, 1985).

This research has led to the recent development of a testosterone skin patch for the treatment of low sex drive in women. The patch has been shown to be effective for women who have lost their sex drive following radical hysterectomy (Buster et al., 2005), Although a few studies have reported positive correlations between blood testosterone levels and the strength of sex drive in women (e.g., Turna et al., 2004), most women with low sex drive do not have low blood levels of testosterone (Davis et

Clinical Implications

Thinking Clearly

al., 2005; Gerber et al., 2005). Thus, the testosterone skin patch is unlikely to help most women with libido problems.

Although neither the sexual motivation nor the sexual activity of women is linked to their menstrual cycles, the type of men they prefer is. Several studies have shown that women prefer masculine faces more on their fertile days than on their nonfertile days (e.g., Gangestad, Thornhill, & Garver-Apgar, 2005; Penton-Voak & Perrett, 2000).

Anabolic Steroid Abuse

Anabolic steroids are steroids, such as testosterone, that have *anabolic* (growth-promoting) effects. Testosterone itself is not very useful as an anabolic drug because it is broken down soon after injection and because it has undesirable side effects. Chemists have managed to synthesize a number of potent anabolic steroids that are long-acting, but they have not managed to synthesize one that does not have side effects.

We are currently in the midst of an epidemic of anabolic steroid abuse. Many competitive athletes and bodybuilders are self-administering appallingly large doses to increase their muscularity and strength, but the problem is even more extensive than this. In recent years, the cosmetic use of steroids has reached troubling proportions.

Clinical Implications

Because steroids are illegal in most parts of the world, it has been difficult to determine the incidence of their use. However, a 2005 survey by the U.S. Centers for Disease Control and Prevention found that almost 5% of high school students had used illicit steroids.

Effects of Anabolic Steroids on Athletic Performance

Do anabolic steroids really increase the muscularity and strength of the athletes who use them? Surprisingly, the early scientific evidence was inconsistent (see Yesalis & Bahrke, 1995), even though many athletes and coaches believe that it is impossible to compete successfully at the highest levels of their sports without an anabolic steroid boost. The failure of experiments to confirm the benefits that have been experienced by many athletes likely results from two shortcomings of the experimental research. First, the experimental studies have tended to use doses of steroids smaller than those used by athletes and for shorter periods of time. Second, the experimental studies have often been conducted on subjects who are not involved in intense training. However, despite the lack of firm experimental evidence, the results achieved by numerous individual steroid users, such as the man pictured in Figure 13.12, are convincing.

Physiological Effects of Anabolic Steroids There is general agreement (see Maravelias et al., 2005; Yesalis & Bahrke, 1995) that people who take high doses of anabolic steroids risk side effects. In men, the negative feedback from high levels of anabolic steroids reduces gonadotropin release; this leads to a reduction in testicular activity, which can result in *testicular atrophy* (wasting

FIGURE 13.12 An athlete who used anabolic steroids to augment his training program.

away of the testes) and sterility. *Gynecomastia* (breast growth in men) can also occur, presumably as the result of the aromatization of anabolic steroids to estrogens. In women, anabolic steroids can produce *amenorrhea* (cessation of menstruation), sterility, *hirsutism* (excessive growth of body hair), growth of the clitoris, development of a masculine body shape, baldness, shrinking of the breasts, and deepening and coarsening of the voice. Unfortunately, some of the masculinizing effects of anabolic steroids on women appear to be irreversible.

Both men and women who use anabolic steroids can suffer muscle spasms, muscle pains, blood in the urine, acne, general swelling from the retention of water, bleeding of the tongue, nausea, vomiting, and a variety of psychotic behaviors, including fits of depression and anger (Maravelias et al., 2005). Oral anabolic steroids produce cancerous liver tumors.

A controlled evaluation of the effects of exposure to anabolic steroids was conducted in adult male mice. Adult male mice were exposed for 6 months to a cocktail of four anabolic steroids at relative levels comparable to those used by human athletes (Bronson & Matherne, 1997). None of the mice died during the period of steroid exposure; however, by 20 months of age (6 months after termination of the steroid exposure), 52% of the steroid-exposed mice had died, whereas only 12% of the controls had died.

The Evolutionary Perspective

Behavioral Effects of Anabolic Steroids Most of the research on the behavioral effects of anabolic steroids, aside from that focusing on athletic performance, has focused on aggression. There have been numerous anecdotal reports that steroid use increases aggression. However, these reports must be treated with caution for at least three reasons. First, because many people believe that testosterone is linked to aggression, reports of aggressive behavior in male steroid users might be a consequence of expectation. Second, many individuals (e.g., professional fighters or football players) who use steroids are likely to have been aggressive before they started treatment. And third, aggressive behavior might be an indirect consequence of increased size and muscularity.

Thinking Clearly

Despite the need for experimental assessment of the effects of anabolic steroids on aggression, few such experiments have been conducted. Pope, Kouri, and Hudson (2000) administered either testosterone or placebo injections in a double-blind study of 53 men. The subjects completed tests of aggression and kept daily aggression-related diaries; a similar diary was also kept by a "significant other" of each subject. Pope and colleagues found increases in aggression in only a few of the subjects.

There is no indication that the chronic use of high doses of steroids increases, improves, or redirects sexual motivation or sexual behavior. However, there are a few reports of disruptive effects in human steroid users, and some anabolic steroids have been shown to disrupt the copulatory behavior of both male and female rodents (see Clark & Henderson, 2003).

Here are two important points about the adverse effects of anabolic steroids: First, the use of anabolic steroids in puberty, before developmental programs of sexual differentiation are complete, is particularly risky (see Farrell & McGinnis, 2003). Second, many of the adverse effects of anabolic steroids may take years to be manifested—steroid users who experience few immediate adverse effects may pay the price later.

The Neuroprotective Effects of Estradiol

Although estradiol is best known for its sex-related organizational and activational effects, this hormone also can reduce the brain damage associated with stroke and various neurodegenerative disorders. For example, Yang and colleagues (2003) showed that estradiol administered just before, during, or just after the induction of *cerebral hypoxia* (reduction of oxygen to the brain) substantially reduces subsequent brain damage (see Chapter 10).

Estradiol has been shown to have several neurotrophic effects that might account for its neuroprotective properties (see Chapter 10). It has been shown to reduce inflammation, encourage axonal regeneration, promote synaptogenesis (see Stein & Hoffman, 2003; Zhang et al., 2004), and increase adult neurogenesis *Neuroplasticity* (see Chapter 10). Injection of estradiol initially increases the number of new neurons created in the dentate gyri of the hippocampi of adult female rats and then, about 48 hours later, there is a period of reduced neurogenesis (see Galea et al., 2006; Ormerod, Falconer, & Galea, 2003). As well as increasing adult neurogenesis, estradiol increases the survival rate of the new neurons (see Galea et al., 2006; Ormerod & Galea, 2001b).

The discovery of estradiol's neuroprotective properties is creating a lot of excitement among neuroscientists. These properties may account for women's greater longevity and their lower incidence of several common neuropsychological disorders, such as Parkinson's disease. *Clinical Implications* They may also explain the decline in memory and some other cognitive deficits experienced by postmenopausal women (see Bisagno, Bowman, & Luine, 2003; Gandy, 2003).

Several studies have assessed the ability of estradiol treatments to reduce the cognitive deficits experienced by postmenopausal women. The results of some studies have been encouraging, but others have observed no benefit. Two suggestions have been made for improving the effectiveness of estradiol therapy. First, Sherwin (2005) pointed out that in both humans and nonhumans such therapy appears to be effective only if the estradiol treatment is commenced at menopause or shortly thereafter. Second, Marriott and Wenk (2004) argued that the chron-

ically high doses that have been administered to postmenopausal women are unnatural and potentially toxic. They recommend instead that estradiol therapy should mimic the natural cycle of estradiol levels in premenopausal women.

Thinking Clearly

Scan Your Brain

You encountered many clinical problems in the preceding two sections of the chapter. Do you remember them? Write the name of the appropriate condition or syndrome in each blank, based on the clues provided. The answers appear below. Before proceeding, review material related to your errors and omissions.

Name of the disorder	Clues
1. _____	Genetic male, sparse pubic hair, short vagina
2. _____	Congenital adrenal hyperplasia, little effect on males, elevated androgen levels
3. _____	David Reimer, John Money, destruction of penis
4. _____	Castrated males, gonadectomized males
5. _____	Castrated females, gonadectomized females
6. _____	Can't achieve erection, castrated
7. _____	Anabolic steroids, breasts on men
8. _____	Anabolic steroids, cessation of menstruation
9. _____	Anabolic steroids, excessive body hair
10. _____	Reduction of oxygen to brain, causes brain damage that is reduced by estradiol

Scan Your Brain answers: (1) androgenic insensitivity syndrome, (2) adrenogenital syndrome, (3) ablatio penis, (4) orchidectomized, (5) ovariectomized, (6) impotent, (7) gynecomastia, (8) amenorrhea, (9) hirsutism, (10) cerebral hypoxia.

13.5
Neural Mechanisms of Sexual Behavior

Major differences among cultures in sexual practices and preferences indicate that the control of human sexual behavior involves the highest levels of the nervous system (e.g., association cortex), and this point is reinforced by controlled demonstrations of the major role played by experience in the sexual behaviors of nonhuman animals (see Woodson, 2002; Woodson & Balleine, 2002; Woodson, Balleine, & Gorski, 2002). Nevertheless, research on the neural mechanisms of sexual behavior has focused almost exclusively on hypothalamic circuits. Consequently, I am forced to do the same here: When it comes to the study of the neural regulation of sexual behavior, the hypothalamus is virtually the only game in town.

Why has research on the neural mechanisms of sexual behavior focused almost exclusively on hypothalamic circuits? There are three obvious reasons. First, because of the difficulty of studying the neural mechanisms of complex human sexual behaviors, researchers have focused on the relatively simple, controllable copulatory behaviors (e.g., ejaculation, mounting, and lordosis) of laboratory animals (see Agmo & Ellingsen, 2003), which tend to be controlled by the hypothalamus. Second, because the hy-

pothalamus controls gonadotropin release, it was the obvious place to look for sexually dimorphic structures and circuits that might control copulation. And third, early studies confirmed that the hypothalamus does play a major role in sexual behavior, and this finding led subsequent neuroscientific research on sexual behavior to focus on that brain structure.

Structural Differences between the Male Hypothalamus and the Female Hypothalamus

You have already learned that the male hypothalamus and the female hypothalamus are functionally different in their control of anterior pituitary hormones (steady versus cyclic release, respectively). In the 1970s, structural differences between the male and female hypothalamus were discovered in rats (Raisman & Field, 1971). Most notably, *The Evolutionary Perspective*

Gorski and his colleagues (1978) discovered a nucleus in the **medial preoptic area** of the rat hypothalamus that was several times larger in males (see Figure 13.13). They called this nucleus the **sexually dimorphic nucleus**.

At birth, the sexually dimorphic nuclei of male and female rats are the same size. In the first few days after birth, the male sexually dimorphic nuclei grow at a high rate and the female sexually dimorphic nuclei do not. The growth of the male sexually dimorphic nuclei is normally triggered by estradiol, which has been aromatized from testosterone (see McEwen, 1987). Accordingly, castrating day-old (but not 4-day-old) male rats significantly reduces the size of their sexually dimorphic nuclei as adults, whereas injecting neonatal (newborn) female rats with testosterone significantly increases the size of theirs (Gorski, 1980)—see Figure 13.14 on page 342. Although the overall size of the sexually dimorphic nucleus diminishes only slightly in male rats that are castrated in adulthood, specific areas of the nucleus do display significant degeneration (Bloch & Gorski, 1988).

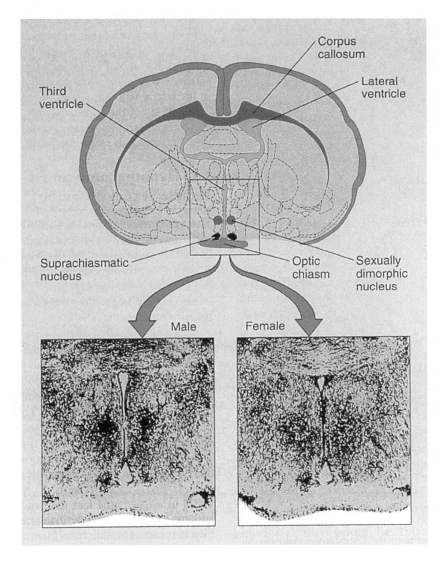

FIGURE 13.13 Nissl-stained coronal sections through the preoptic area of male and female rats. The sexually dimorphic nuclei are larger in male rats than in female rats. (Adapted from Gorski et al., 1978.)

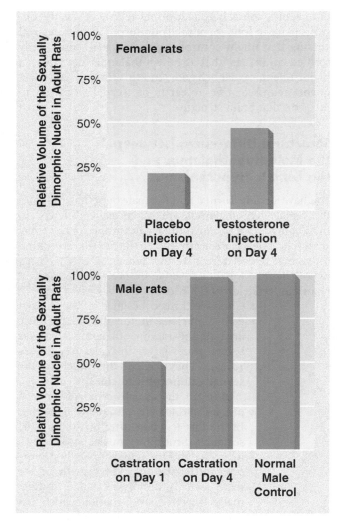

FIGURE 13.14 The effects of neonatal testosterone exposure on the size of the sexually dimorphic nuclei in male and female adult rats. (Adapted from Gorski, 1980.)

The size of a male rat's sexually dimorphic nucleus is correlated with the rat's testosterone levels and aspects of its sexual activity (Anderson et al., 1986). However, bilateral lesions of the sexually dimorphic nucleus have only slight disruptive effects on male rat sexual behavior (e.g., De Jonge et al., 1989; Turkenburg et al., 1988), and the specific function of this nucleus is unclear.

Since the discovery of the sexually dimorphic nuclei in rats, other sex differences in hypothalamic anatomy have been identified in rats and in other species (see Swaab & Hofman, 1995; Witelson, 1991). In humans, for example, there are nuclei in the preoptic (Swaab & Fliers, 1985), suprachiasmatic (Swaab et al., 1994), and anterior (Allen

The Hypothalamus and Male Sexual Behavior

The medial preoptic area (which includes the sexually dimorphic nucleus) is one area of the hypothalamus that plays a key role in male sexual behavior. Destruction of the entire area abolishes sexual behavior in the males of all mammalian species that have been studied (see Hull et al., 1999). In contrast, medial preoptic area lesions do not eliminate the female sexual behaviors of females, but they do eliminate the male sexual behaviors (e.g., mounting) that are often observed in females (Singer, 1968). Thus, bilateral medial preoptic lesions appear to abolish male copulatory behavior in both sexes. Conversely, electrical stimulation of the medial preoptic area elicits copulatory behavior in male rats (Malsbury, 1971; Rodriguez-Manzo et al., 2000), and copulatory behavior can be reinstated in castrated male rats by medial preoptic implants of testosterone (Davidson, 1980).

It is not clear why males with medial preoptic lesions stop copulating. One possibility is that the lesions disrupt the ability of males to copulate; another is that the lesions reduce the motivation of the males to engage in sexual behavior. The evidence is mixed, but it strongly favors the hypothesis that the medial preoptic area is involved in the motivational aspects of male sexual behavior (Paredes, 2003).

The medial preoptic area appears to control male sexual behavior via a tract that projects to an area of the midbrain called the *lateral tegmental field*. Destruction of this tract disrupts the sexual behavior of male rats (Brackett & Edwards, 1984). Moreover, the activity of individual neurons in the lateral tegmental field of male rats is often correlated with aspects of the copulatory act (Shimura & Shimokochi, 1990); for example, some neurons in the lateral tegmental field fire at a high rate only during intromission.

The Hypothalamus and Female Sexual Behavior

The **ventromedial nucleus (VMN)** of the rat hypothalamus contains circuits  that appear to be critical for female sexual behavior. Female rats with bilateral lesions of the VMN do not display lordosis, and they are likely to attack suitors who become too ardent.

You have already learned that an injection of progesterone brings into estrus an ovariectomized female rat that received an injection of estradiol about 36 hours before. Because the progesterone by itself does not induce estrus, the estradiol must in some way prime the nervous system so that the progesterone can exert its effect. This priming effect appears to be mediated by the large increase in the number of *progesterone receptors* that occurs in the VMN and surrounding area following an estradiol injection (Blaustein et al., 1988); the estradiol exerts this effect by entering VMN cells and influencing gene expression. Confirming the role of the VMN in estrus is the fact that microinjections of estradiol and progesterone directly into the VMN induce estrus in ovariectomized female rats (Pleim & Barfield, 1988).

The influence of the VMN on the sexual behavior of female rats appears to be mediated by a tract that descends to the *periaqueductal gray (PAG)* of the tegmentum. Destruction of this tract eliminates female sexual behavior (Hennessey et al., 1990), as do lesions of the PAG itself (Sakuma & Pfaff, 1979).

In conclusion, although many parts of the brain play a role in sexual behavior, much of the research has focused on the role of the hypothalamus in the copulatory behavior of rats. Several areas of the hypothalamus influence this copulatory behavior, and several hypothalamic nuclei are sexually dimorphic in rats, but the medial preoptic area and the ventromedial nucleus are two of the most widely studied. Male rat sexual behavior is influenced by a tract that runs from the medial preoptic area to the lateral tegmental field, and female rat sexual behavior is influenced by a tract that runs from the ventromedial nucleus to the periaqueductal gray (see Figure 13.15).

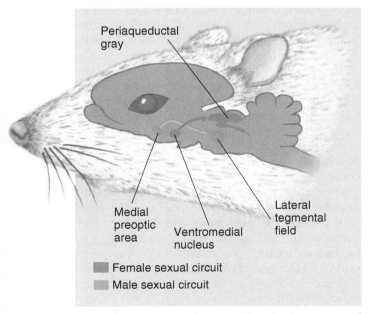

FIGURE 13.15 The hypothalamus-tegmentum circuits that play a role in female and male sexual behavior in rats.

13.6
Sexual Orientation, Hormones, and the Brain

So far, this chapter has not addressed the topic of sexual orientation. As you know, some people are **heterosexual** (sexually attracted to members of the other sex), some are **homosexual** (sexually attracted to members of the same sex), and some are **bisexual** (sexually attracted to members of both sexes). A discussion of research on sexual orientation is a fitting conclusion to this chapter because it brings together the exception-proves-the-rule and anti-mamawawa messages.

Sexual Orientation and Genes

Research has shown that differences in sexual orientation have a genetic basis. For example, Bailey and Pillard (1991) studied a group of male homosexuals who had twin brothers, and they found that 52% of the monozygotic twin brothers and 22% of the dizygotic twin brothers were homosexual. In a comparable study of female twins by the same group of researchers (Bailey et al., 1993), the concordance rates for homosexuality were 48% for monozygotic twins and 16% for dizygotic twins.

Considerable excitement was created by the claim that a gene for male homosexuality had been localized on one end of the X chromosome (Hamer et al., 1993). However, subsequent research has not confirmed this claim (see Mustanski, Chivers, & Bailey, 2002; Rahman, 2005).

Sexual Orientation and Early Hormones

Many people mistakenly assume that homosexuals have lower levels of sex hormones. They don't: Heterosexuals and homosexuals do not differ in their levels of circulating hormones. Moreover, orchidectomy reduces the sexual behavior of both heterosexual and homosexual males, but it does not redirect it; and replacement injections simply reactivate the preferences that existed prior to surgery.

Many people also assume that sexual preference is a matter of choice. It isn't: People discover their sexual preferences; they don't choose them. Sexual preferences seem to develop very early, and a child's first indication of the direction of sexual attraction usually does not change as he or she matures. Could perinatal hormone exposure be the early event that shapes sexual orientation?

Efforts to determine whether perinatal hormone levels influence the development of sexual orientation have focused on nonhuman species. A consistent pattern of findings has emerged from this research (see Ellis & Ames, 1987). In rats, hamsters, ferrets, pigs, zebra finches, and dogs, perinatal castration of males and testosterone

The Evolutionary Perspective

treatment of females have been shown to induce same-sex preferences (see Adkins-Regan, 1988; Baum et al., 1990; Hrabovszky & Hutson, 2002).

On the one hand, we need to exercise prudence in drawing conclusions about the development of sexual preferences in humans based on the results of experiments on laboratory species; it would be a mistake to ignore the profound cognitive and emotional components of human sexuality, which have no counterpart in laboratory animals. On the other hand, it would also be a mistake to think that a pattern of results that runs so consistently through so many mammalian species has no relevance to humans (Swaab, 2004).

Although directly relevant evidence is sparse, there are some indications that the answer to the earlier question is yes—perinatal hormones do influence sexual orientation in humans. Support comes from the quasiexperimental study of Ehrhardt and her colleagues (1985). They interviewed adult women whose mothers had been exposed to *diethylstilbestrol* (a synthetic estrogen) during pregnancy. The subjects' responses indicated that they were significantly more sexually attracted to women than was a group of matched control subjects. Ehrhardt and her colleagues concluded that perinatal estrogen exposure does encourage homosexuality and bisexuality in women but that its effect is relatively weak: The sexual behavior of all but 1 of the 30 subjects was still primarily heterosexual.

One promising line of research on sexual orientation focuses on the **fraternal birth order effect**, the finding that the probability of a man's being homosexual increases as a function of the number of older brothers he has (Blanchard, 2004; Blanchard & Lippa, 2007). A recent study of blended families (families in which biologically related siblings were raised with adopted siblings or stepsiblings) found that the effect is related to the number of boys previously born to the mother, not the number of boys one is reared with (Bogaert, 2007). The effect is quite large: The probability of a male's being homosexual increases by 33.3% for every older brother he has (see Puts, Jordan, & Breedlove, 2006), and an estimated 15% of gay men can attribute their homosexuality to the fraternal birth order effect (Cantor et al., 2002). The **maternal immune hypothesis** has been proposed to explain the fraternal birth order effect; this hypothesis is that some mothers become progressively more immune to some masculinizing hormone in male fetuses (see Blanchard, 2004), and the mother's immune system might deactivate the masculinizing hormone in younger brothers.

What Triggers the Development of Sexual Attraction?

The evidence indicates that most girls and boys living in Western countries experience their first feelings of sexual attraction at about 10 years of age, whether they are heterosexual or homosexual (see Quinsey, 2003). This finding is at odds with the usual assumption that sexual interest is triggered by puberty, which, as you have learned, currently tends to occur at 10.5 years of age in girls and at 11.5 years in boys.

McClintock and Herdt (1996) have suggested that the emergence of sexual attraction may be stimulated by adrenal cortex steroids. Unlike gonadal maturation, adrenal maturation occurs at about the age of 10.

Is There a Difference in the Brains of Homosexuals and Heterosexuals?

The brains of homosexuals and heterosexuals must differ in some way, but how? There have been several reports of neuroanatomical, neuropsychological, and hormonal response differences between homosexuals and heterosexuals (see Gladue, 1994). Most studies have compared male heterosexuals and homosexuals; studies of lesbians are scarce.

In a highly publicized study, LeVay (1991) found that the structure of one hypothalamic nucleus in male homosexuals was intermediate between that in female heterosexuals and that in male heterosexuals. This study has not been consistently replicated, however. Indeed, no difference between the brains of heterosexuals and homosexuals has yet been discovered (see Rahman, 2005).

Transsexualism

Transsexualism is a disorder of sexual identity that causes an individual to believe that he or she is trapped in a body of the other sex. To put it mildly, the transsexual faces a bizarre conflict: "I am a woman (or man) trapped in the body of a man (or woman). Help!" It is important to appreciate the desperation of these individuals; they do not merely think that life might be better if their gender were different. Although many transsexuals do seek *surgical sexual reassignment* (surgery to change their sex), their desperation is better revealed by the ways in which some of them dealt with their problem before surgical sexual reassignment was an option: Some biological males (psychological females) attempted self-castration, and others consumed copious quantities of estrogen-containing face creams in order to feminize their bodies.

How does surgical sexual reassignment work? I will describe the male-to-female procedure. The female-to-male procedure is much more complex *Clinical Implications* (because a penis must be created) and far less satisfactory (for example, because a surgically created penis has no erectile potential), and male-to-female sexual reassignment is three times more prevalent.

The first step in male-to-female reassignment is thorough psychiatric assessment and counseling to establish that the individual is a true transsexual and to prepare "her" for what will follow. Second, a lifelong regimen of estrogen is initiated to feminize the body and maintain the changes. Third, the penis and testes are removed, and female external genitalia and a vagina are constructed. The vagina is lined with skin from the penis so that it will have sensory nerve endings that will respond to sexual stimulation. Finally, some patients have cosmetic surgery to feminize the face (e.g., to reduce the size of the Adam's apple). Generally, the adjustment of transsexuals after surgical sexual reassignment is good.

The causes of transsexualism are unknown. Transsexualism was once thought to be a product of social learning, that is, of inappropriate child-rearing practices (e.g., mothers dressing their little boys in dresses). The occasional case that is consistent with this view can be found, but in most cases, there is no obvious cause (see Swaab, 2004). One of the major difficulties in identifying the causes and mechanisms of transsexualism is that there is no comparable syndrome in nonhumans (Baum, 2006).

The Independence of Sexual Orientation and Sexual Identity

To complete this chapter, I would like to remind you of two of its main themes and show you how useful they are in thinking about one of the puzzles of human sexuality. One of the two themes is that the exception proves the rule: that a powerful test of any theory is its ability to explain exceptional cases. The second is that the mamawawa is seriously flawed: We have seen that men and women are similar in some ways (Hyde, 2005) and different in others (Cahill, 2006) but they are certainly not opposites, and their programs of development are neither parallel nor opposite.

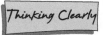

Here, I want to focus on the puzzling fact that sexual attraction, sexual identity, and body type are sometimes unrelated. For example, consider transsexuals: They, by definition, have the body type of one sex and the sexual identity of the other sex, but the orientation of their sexual attraction is an independent matter. Some transsexuals with a male body type are sexually attracted to

females, others are sexually attracted to males, and others are sexually attracted to neither—and this is not changed by sexual reassignment (see Van Goozen et al., 2002). Also, it is important to realize that a particular sex-related trait in an individual can lie at midpoint between the female and male norms.

Obviously, the mere existence of homosexuality and transsexualism is a challenge to the mamawawa, the assumption that males and females belong to distinct and opposite categories. Many people tend to think of "femaleness" and "maleness" as being at opposite ends of a continuum, with a few abnormal cases somewhere between the 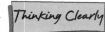 two. Perhaps this is how you tend to think. However, the fact that body type, sexual orientation, and sexual identity are often independent constitutes a serious attack on any assumption that femaleness and maleness lie at opposite ends of a single scale. Clearly, femaleness and maleness each combine several different attributes (e.g., body type, sexual orientation, and sexual identity), each of which can develop quite independently. This is a real puzzle for many people, including scientists, but what you have learned in this chapter suggests a solution.

Think back to the section on brain differentiation. Until recently, it was assumed that the differentiation of the human brain into its usual female and male forms occurred through a single testosterone-based mechanism. However, a different notion has developed from recent evidence. Now, it is clear that male and female brains usually differ in many ways and that the differences develop at different times and by different mechanisms. If you keep this developmental principle in mind, you will have no difficulty understanding how it is possible for some individuals to be female in some ways and male in others, and to lie between the two norms in still others.

This analysis exemplifies a point I make many times in this book. The study of biopsychology often has important personal and social implications: The search for the neural basis of a behavior frequently provides us with a greater understanding of that behavior. I hope that you now have a greater understanding of, and acceptance of, differences in human sexuality.

Themes Revisited

Three of the book's four major themes were repeatedly emphasized in this chapter: the evolutionary perspective, clinical implications, and thinking clearly themes.

The evolutionary perspective theme was pervasive. It received frequent attention because most experimental studies of hormones and sex have been conducted in nonhuman species. The other major source of information about

hormones and sex has been the study of human clinical cases, which is why the clinical implications theme was prominent in the cases of the woman who wasn't, the little girl who grew into a boy, the twin who lost his penis, and the man who lost and regained his manhood.

The thinking clearly theme was emphasized throughout the chapter because conventional ways of thinking about hormones and sex have often been at odds with the results of biopsychological research. If you are now better able to resist the seductive appeal of the men-are-men-and-women-are-women assumption, you are leaving this chapter a more broadminded and understanding person than when you began it. I hope you have gained an abiding appreciation of the fact that maleness and femaleness are multidimensional and, at times, ambiguous variations of each other.

Thinking Clearly

The fourth major theme of the book, neuroplasticity, arose during the discussions of the effects of hormones on the development of sex differences in the brain and of the neurotrophic effects of estradiol.

Neuroplasticity

mypsychkit

See Hard Copy for additional readings for Chapter 13.

Think about It

1. Over the last century and a half, the onset of puberty has changed from age 15 or 16 to age 10 or 11, but there has been no corresponding acceleration in psychological and intellectual development. Precocious puberty is like a loaded gun in the hand of a child. Discuss.
2. Do you think adult sex-change operations should be permitted? Explain.
3. What should be done about the current epidemic of anabolic steroid abuse? Would you make the same recommendation if a safe anabolic steroid were developed? If a safe drug that would dramatically improve your memory were developed, would you take it?
4. Heterosexuality cannot be understood without studying homosexuality. Discuss.
5. What treatment should be given to infants born with ambiguous external genitals? Why?
6. Sexual orientation, sexual identity, and body type are not always related. Discuss.

mypsychkit

Studying for an exam? Try the Practice Tests for Chapter 13.

Key Terms

13.1 The Neuroendocrine System

Exocrine glands
Endocrine glands
Hormones
Amino acid derivative hormones
Peptide hormones
Protein hormones
Steroid hormones
Gonads
Testes
Ovaries
Copulation
Zygote
Sex chromosomes
Androgens
Estrogens
Testosterone
Estradiol
Progestins
Progesterone
Adrenal cortex
Gonadotropin
Posterior pituitary
Pituitary stalk
Anterior pituitary
Menstrual cycle
Vasopressin
Oxytocin
Paraventricular nuclei
Supraoptic nuclei

Hypothalamopituitary portal system
Releasing hormones
Release-inhibiting factors
Thyrotropin-releasing hormone
Thyrotropin
Gonadotropin-releasing hormone
Follicle-stimulating hormone (FSH)
Luteinizing hormone (LH)
Pulsatile hormone release

13.2 Hormones and Sexual Development

Sry gene
Sry protein
Wolffian system
Müllerian system
Müllerian-inhibiting substance
Scrotum
Ovariectomy
Orchidectomy
Gonadectomy
Genitals
Aromatase
Aromatization

Aromatization hypothesis
Alpha fetoprotein
Masculinizes
Defeminizes
Lordosis
Feminizes
Demasculinizes
Intromission
Ejaculation
Proceptive behaviors
Secondary sex characteristics
Growth hormone
Adrenocorticotropic hormone
Androstenedione

13.3 Three Cases of Exceptional Human Sexual Development

Androgenic insensitivity syndrome
Adrenogenital syndrome
Congenital adrenal hyperplasia
Ablatio penis

13.4 Effects of Gonadal Hormones on Adults

Replacement injections
Impotent

Estrus
Estrous cycle
Anabolic steroids

13.5 Neural Mechanisms of Sexual Behavior

Medial preoptic area
Sexually dimorphic nucleus
Ventromedial nucleus (VMN)

13.6 Sexual Orientation, Hormones, and the Brain

Heterosexual
Homosexual
Bisexual
Fraternal birth order effect
Maternal immune hypothesis
Transsexualism

mypsychkit

Need some help studying the key terms for this chapter? Check out the electronic flash cards for Chapter 13.

13 Cognition and Emotion

Affect is the least investigated aspect of human problem solving, yet it is probably the aspect most often mentioned as deserving future investigation. . . . If cognitive psychology aspires to an understanding of human thought and action, it can ill afford to leave out their emotional aspects.

(MANDLER, 1989, PP. 3–4)

Although the computer metaphor has been a dominant guide for years in cognitive psychology, people are much more than computational machines. One of the big differences between us and our silicon-based creations is in the realm of emotions. We've got them, and they don't. Although much of the research in cognitive psychology might be described by some as "cold cognition," because it does not take people's emotions into account, there is more and more new research doing just that (see Mather & Sutherland, 2011, for a nice overview of major issues). What has been found is that emotion can influence cognition in a variety of complex but systematic ways.

This chapter presents an overview of various ways that cognition is affected by emotion. In a sense, this chapter serves to recapitulate many of the topics already covered in the book. We start with a consideration of how emotion can influence seemingly basic perceptual and attention processes. We then consider how emotion influences memory, making it better in some cases and worse in others. After this we consider roles of emotion in language, followed by some coverage of how emotion can influence our ability to make decisions and solve problems.

WHAT IS EMOTION?

Although we all have an intuitive sense about what emotions are, we need to go beyond that here and offer a formal definition to work with. Consider **emotion** to be *both the state of mind a person is in at a particular moment, as well as the physiological response a person is experiencing at that time* (in terms of heart rate, pupillary dilation, neurotransmitter release, and so on). There are other, similar, related terms that mean somewhat different things, such as affect, mood, and arousal, but we leave these aside for now. Our purpose here is to look at some basic ideas about how emotion can influence and interact with other aspects of cognition, such as perception, attention, and memory.

Types of Emotion

There are a number of ways of dividing up and classifying different types of emotion. Also, it certainly is the case that we all have a lot of variety and subtlety in the different types of emotions that we experience. However, for our purposes, we use a simple approach of looking at two dimensions of emotion and use these to guide our coverage of how emotion influences cognition. The first of these dimensions is the **valence** of an emotion. This is simply *whether an emotion is positive, like happiness, joy, and ecstasy, or negative, such as sadness, anger, or disgust*. The second dimension is the **intensity** of the emotion. This is basically *how strongly an emotion is experienced*. For example, dislike would be less emotionally intense than hatred. We use these two dimensions because many of the cognitive phenomena that we discuss can be understood in terms of where an emotion is along the two dimensions—that is, closer to the positive or negative end of the valence dimension, or closer to the low or high end of the intensity dimension.

Neurological Underpinnings

Emotion has both physical and mental components. It is certainly a visceral experience. We feel it in our bodies—our hearts race, our breathing speeds up. It also triggers a different kind of mental experience than basic kinds of thought. As a mental experience, it has the power to influence brain and cognition in meaningful ways. In the brain, emotional experience is associated with a number of structures and areas, but we focus on two here that are most relevant for understanding how cognition and emotion interact. These structures are the amygdala and the prefrontal cortex.

Explore
Do You Fly or Flight? in
MyPsychLab

Watch *Brain Stem and the Limbic System* in **MyPsychLab**

As noted in Chapter 2, the **amygdala** is an almond-shaped structure located next to the hippocampus. The amygdala is critically involved in more instinctual emotions that are important for survival, such as the experience of fear (e.g., Davis, 1997; LeDoux, 2000) and is more active when a person is in an emotional state. The amygdala receives sensory information from various parts of the brain, allowing for a fast emotional response to environmental conditions. This is particularly true for biologically related emotions related to fear (e.g., seeing a snake), as compared with socially related emotions (e.g., seeing a happy family) (Sakaki, Niki, & Mather, 2012).

One interesting aspect of the amygdala is that there are very few neural synapses in the chain between the olfactory receptors of your sense of smell and the amygdala, which is why odors can be strongly associated with emotions (Herz & Engen, 1996). The amygdala in turn sends its signals to the hypothalamus and brainstem, which helps regulate the body's arousal state, as well as to areas tied to cognitive processes, such as the prefrontal cortex (attention) and the hippocampus (memory). Thus, emotional responses have the potential to directly influence the context and processing of thoughts in ways that differ from when we are not in an emotionally aroused state.

In addition to the amygdala, another region of the brain that is important in emotional processing is the **ventro-medial prefrontal cortex** (B.A. 10). This part of the brain is involved in the identification and interpretation of emotional stimuli and responses, and the integration of that emotional interpretation with the surrounding context (Roy, Shohamy, & Wager, 2012), as well as the regulation and control of those experiences.

The famous case of Phineas Gage illustrates the important role of the prefrontal cortex in emotion regulation. Specifically, Gage suffered a massive trauma that destroyed a large portion of his frontal lobe. This occurred in 1848 Vermont when Gage was working on a blasting crew for a railroad. He was using a tamping rod to press some blasting power into a hole that had been drilled into a rock formation. The powder accidentally ignited, shooting the rod through Gage's skull, destroying part of his brain. Miraculously, Gage survived. After the accident, however, people claimed that Gage was no longer Gage. One of the biggest changes was that he was less able to control his emotions and would impulsively act and express himself in ways that were inconsistent with who he was before the accident. This was because the part of his brain in the frontal lobe that was responsible for controlling and regulating emotional responses and behaviors was seriously damaged in the accident.

Section Summary

- Emotion is a characteristic of human thought that varies in valence and intensity. Emotional experiences have meaningful influences on cognition.
- Two important neurological structures important for emotion processing are the amygdala and the prefrontal cortex. The amygdala is important for the experience of emotion, and the prefrontal lobes are important for the control of emotional responses.

EMOTION, PERCEPTION, AND ATTENTION

We turn now to the question of how emotion can influence cognition. We start with perception and attention, just as we started out this text. After this, we move on to topics in memory, language, and decision making and problem solving.

Perception

Our first question seems very simple—Can emotion influence even basic perceptual processes? There is some evidence to suggest that the answer is "yes," emotions *can* meaningfully influence perception, making some things easier to perceive than others. For instance, people generally recognize things faster if they are emotionally meaningful (such as identifying briefly flashed words like "death" and "love") than if they are not (Zeelenberg, Wagenmakers, & Rotteveel, 2006). This can be seen in Figure 13-1. Thus, the emotional content of an item can influence the accuracy with which it is processed. Looking more deeply, we can see that emotion appears to actually increase the amount of neural activity in perceptual brain areas, such as the occipital and occipital-parietal cortex areas (Taylor, Liberzon, & Koeppe, 2000).

However, it is not the case that there is a uniform boost in the ability to perceive emotional items. Instead, what appears to be happening is that there is an increase in the ability to process broad, global, or general characteristics of the threating item, but a decline in the ability to perceive details (Bocanegra & Zeelenberg, 2011). That is,

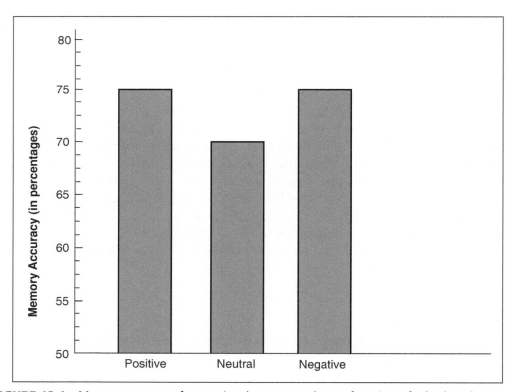

FIGURE 13-1   Memory accuracy for previously seen words as a function of whether they were emotionally positive, neutral, or emotionally negative. Memory is better for emotionally charged items.

Data from Zeelenberg, Wagenmakers, & Rotteveel (2006).

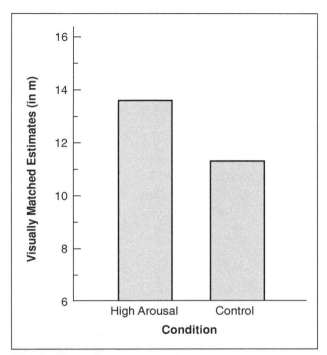

FIGURE 13-2   Estimated height of a balcony as a function of whether a person was emotionally aroused (by viewing pictures) or not. Emotional arousal results in greater height estimations.

Data from Stefanucci & Storbeck (2009).

when are emotions are aroused by a threating stimulus, the perceptual processes in our cognitive system direct processing efforts to knowing generally what and where that emotional something is, so that we can be safe from it. In doing so, the cognition system is, in some sense, making sure that it does not waste its limited energies and resources on details that are probably trivial, thereby increasing the probability of survival.

In addition to influencing the ease with which different objects and entities in the world are recognized, emotion can alter the subjective perception of the world when the situation has characteristics that are emotionally arousing in a person. Take the example of the height of a balcony on a building. When you are standing on the balcony looking down, how high off the ground do you perceive yourself to be? A study by Stefanucci and Storbeck (2009) found that people who were more emotionally aroused (by viewing a series of emotionally arousing pictures), either positively or negatively, experienced the height of the balcony as greater (see Figure 13-2). What may have been happening here is that the emotional arousal a person was experiencing, although it was different from any emotions elicited by the height itself, was interpreted cognitively as being part of the experience of looking down from the balcony. In a sense, the perceptual processes were saying, "Hmmm . . . if I am feeling aroused, then the balcony must be pretty high." And so, people who were already emotionally aroused rated the balcony as being higher than those people who were not so aroused.

Emotional stimuli have a way of capturing our attention.

Emotional Guidance of Attention

In addition to these effects on perceptual processes, there is some evidence that emotion can influence attention as well. A moment's reflection will reveal that this basic idea is not all that surprising. If there is something that elicits our emotions, we are more likely to pay attention to it, whatever that thing is. What the work on emotion and attention has shown is that this influence can be more extensive and unconscious than a casual moment's reflection might reveal. Let's start by looking at a very basic form of attention, namely the orienting reflex that was discussed in Chapter 4.

Cowan (1995) noted that the kinds of stimuli that can trigger the orienting reflex boil down to two basic categories: (a) stimuli that are significant for the organism (the rock thrown toward your head) and (b) stimuli that are novel or unexpected. The important point here is that what is significant to you often has some relation to emotions, either positive or negative. What is important to keep in mind is that emotion and attention use some of the same neural components. These include structures such as the amygdala, portions of the frontal lobes, and the anterior cingulate cortex (B. A.s 24, 32, & 33). Thus, emotion can affect the direction of attention (Vuilleumeir, 2005). For example, people are more likely to direct their attention to emotionally arousing stimuli, such as a seeing a snake in the grass. Attention can also influence how you feel about things. For example, people can develop a negative emotional response toward things that they try to ignore (Fenske & Raymond, 2006).

Visual Search

One of the tasks in cognitive psychology that has been used extensively for the study of the operation of attention is visual search—trying to find an object in a display of irrelevant distractors. Research using this task has found that emotions, particularly negative emotions such as fear, can influence the visual search processes (e.g., Öhman, Flykt, & Esteves, 2001). The inclusion of emotion-eliciting stimuli in a display, such as spiders or fearful faces, facilitates the direction of attention to such objects during visual search. In some sense this seems like a form of attention capture, with attention being preferentially moved to more fearful stimuli. This shifting of attention to emotional items seems to be directed more by the amygdala than by emotional control processes in the frontal lobe (Vuilleumeir & Huang, 2009). Also, it may have more to do with an increase in attentional resources because even the processing of non-emotional targets in a visual search task is facilitated when emotions are triggered (Becker, 2009).

During visual search, it is easier to direct our attention to emotionally charged items, such as a spider.

Looking more deeply at emotion and the processing of visual stimuli, several investigators have tested the effects of emotional stimuli on the attentional blink phenomenon you read about earlier; as a reminder, if two stimuli are presented very rapidly in sequence, we sometimes miss the second one, as if our attentional mechanism had "blinked" for a brief moment while the second one was present. Researchers have now found that the length of this attentional blink is attenuated if the stimulus that occurs during that critical "moment" is emotionally loaded. As an example, there is a reduced or absent attentional blink for an emotion-eliciting word, such as "whore," compared to emotionally neutral words, such as "veiled" (Anderson, 2005). Thus, emotional relevance and intensity can override other, standard operating features of the cognitive system, such as the normal attentional blink phenomenon.

Emotional Stroop

Emotional processing can even influence attention and cognition in ways where it might at first seem irrelevant. An example of this is the **emotional Stroop task** (see Williams, Matthews, & MacLeod, 1996, for a review). As a reminder, in the standard form of the Stroop task, people are given a series of color words printed in a color that may be inconsistent with the word names; you see the word "red" printed in blue ink, but you need to name the ink color, that is, need to say "blue." The standard Stroop effect is that people are slower to name the color a word is printed in if the word and ink color are inconsistent (see Chapter 4).

In the emotional Stroop task, words are still presented in different colors, and the people are asked to name those colors. However, rather than having color words on the list, the critical comparison has to do with words that elicit an emotional response in a person, such as "spider," as compared to more neutral words, such as "spade." What is typically found with this task is that people name the color of the word more slowly if the word is emotional for them. For example, a person who has a deathly fear of spiders would be slower to say "green" if "spider" were printed in green ink, whereas a person without this fear would not show this effect. The explanation is actually very straightforward. Even though the person is supposed to focus on the color of ink, reading the word and accessing its meaning happens automatically. If the word is related to an emotional stressor for the person, it intrudes on the person's cognitive processing, and thus takes away resources from the other cognitive processes necessary for focusing on and naming the ink color. Thus color naming is slowed down for the emotional word condition, but not for the neutral word condition. This emotional Stroop task has been used to study a number of psychopathologies, including depression (e.g., Mitterschiffthaler et al., 2008), anxiety (e.g., Dresler, Mériau, Heekeren, & van der Meer, 2009), and post-traumatic stress disorder (e.g., Cisler et al., 2011).

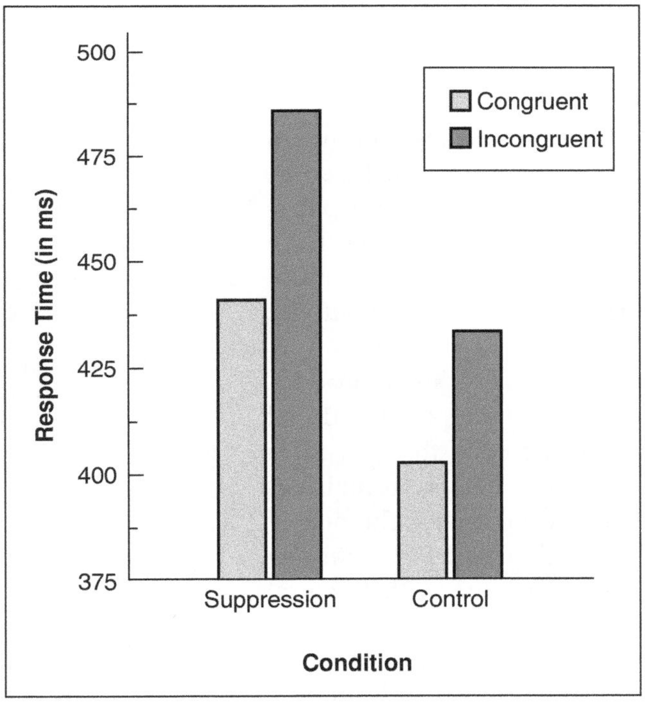

Emotion and Self-Control

An important function for attention is to guide thoughts and behavior. To some degree this is automatic, but to some degree it is under conscious control. What role does emotion play in this self-control? One would intuitively think that expressing emotions would lead to less self-control; however, there is some evidence that *suppression* of your emotions can lead to attentional control problems. An example of this is a study by Inzlicht and Gutsell (2007) in which people watched an emotional movie and were either asked to simply watch the movie (the control condition) or were asked to suppress their emotions while viewing the film (experimental suppression condition). After this they were asked to do a traditional color-word Stroop task. What was found, as can be seen in Figure 13-3, was that people who had suppressed their emotions had a harder time doing the Stroop task.

The explanation was that suppressing one's emotions drained resources from the error monitoring aspect of attentional control, which is

FIGURE 13-3 Response times to Stroop color words (when both the word and printed color were either congruent or incongruent) when people had either just spent time suppressing their emotions while watching an emotional movie or not. As can be clearly seen, previously suppressing one's emotions made the task harder.

Data from Inzlicht & Gutsell (2007).

guided by the anterior cingulate cortex (B.A.s 24, 25, & 32). When these attentional resources were drained by the effort to control one's emotions over a long period of time, there were fewer resources available for doing other tasks.

So, overall, there is clear evidence that emotional content and responses can influence even basic perceptual and attention processes. This suggests that emotion serves as a primary and fundamental force in guiding and influencing cognition.

Section Summary

- Emotion can influence perceptual processing by channeling cognitive processing resources toward those stimuli in the environment that are more emotional.
- The estimation of some perceptual qualities, such as size or height, can be influenced by whether an emotional state is aroused.
- Emotional responses can guide where attention is directed, even to the extent of sending attention to nominally irrelevant information in the environment, which can produce a processing cost, as in the emotional Stroop effect.
- The experience of intense emotions can consume cognitive resources, such as attention, to the point that that there is less available for other tasks and performance shows a deficit.

EMOTION AND MEMORY

One of the aspects of cognition where emotion has its largest effects is with memory. The influence of emotion on memory is somewhat complicated. In some ways and under certain circumstances, emotion can make memories more pleasant, but in other ways or under different circumstances, emotion can make have the opposite effect on memory. Let's take a systematic look at these different influences and try to make clear to you when your emotions help and hinder what you remember from an event.

The influence of emotion on memory is not a simple and direct process. Again, as a reminder, two primary brain areas for the processing of emotional information are the amygdala and the prefrontal cortex. In general, the amygdala is more involved in more implicit aspects of memory, whereas the prefrontal cortex is more involved in explicit memory processes. This differential influence of these areas on memory can be seen in patients with brain damage. For example, Bechera et al. (1995) reported three case studies of patients, one with bilateral damage to the amygdala, one with bilateral damage to the hippocampus, and one with bilateral damage to both. These patients were exposed to stimuli, either a tone or a visual image, that were paired with an aversive stimulus (i.e., a loud boat horn), a standard classical conditioning study. The results were fascinating. For the patients with damage to the amygdala, there was no evidence of classical conditioning when the tone or image were shown again; they had not learned the pairing with the loud boat horn. The results were very different when the damage was to the hippocampus, a structure that the prefrontal lobe relies on for conscious memories. In this case, the patients showed normal classical conditioning of the

PROVE IT
Emotional Memory

The influence of emotion on memory is a powerful one. This can easily be demonstrated by giving people lists of words and asking them to remember them later. Below is a sample list of words. This list is 20 words long to make sure that it exceeds your participants' working memory capacity and that they are using long-term memory to retrieve the items. What you should do is read the list of words, in a random order to your participants. Read these words aloud at a rate of about 1 per second, using a metronome or a watch to help your pacing. After you have read all of the words, give people a distractor task, such as solving three-digit math problems (e.g., $284 + 923 = ?$) for two minutes. This will displace any memory for the words in the list that still may be in working memory. After the two minutes are up, give your participants a sheet of paper and have them recall as many words from the original list of 20 as they can remember. What you should find is that people will remember more of the emotional words than the non-emotional words. If you want, try mixing things up by creating word lists of your own that compare emotionality to other things that can influence memory, such as word frequency, generation effects, or von Restorff effects.

Emotional words: hate, happy, joy, anger, disgust, fear, thrill, love, sad, pleased
Non-emotional words: date, caddy, boy, ranger, digest, near, drill, live, had, pleated

tone (image)-to-horn pairing—but they had no conscious memory for either the tone or the visual image. In other words, with damage to the amygdala, there was no implicit learning, and with damage to the hippocampus, there was no explicit learning. Thus, the different aspects of emotion processing in the brain directly influence different types of learning and memory.

In terms of the role of emotion in memory, a study by Kissler, Herbert, Peyk, and Junghofer (2007) asked people to read a series of words while event-related potential (ERP) recordings were made (they were given a free recall test at the end to make sure they were actually reading). The results showed a difference in cortical processing as a function of the emotional intensity of the words that were read. Specifically, in the occipito-temporal area (around where there occipital and temporal lobes meet), about 250 ms after the presentation of the word, there was an increase in cortical activity for more emotionally intense words relative to emotionally neutral words. Thus, when people access information in semantic memory, any emotional content becomes available as well. Emotion is part of semantic memory.

Making Memory Better

If you think about your own life, and the things you remember, one of the things you quickly notice is that your emotional experiences are often the most memorable. This can include negative memories such as losing a close family member or friend, an emotional breakup, or being in a serious car accident, as well as positive memories, such as a new birth in the family, a marriage, or landing a greatly desired job. Thus, emotion can have clear benefits for memory. Emotional information is generally remembered better than more neutral information (see Kensinger, 2009, for a review), even when the emotional words, such as "happy," "disgust," or "sad," are compared to more neutral words, such as "hammer," "digest," or "fad." The quality of emotion that seems to be influencing memory the most is not the *valence* of the emotion (such as whether it is positive or negative), but how intense the emotional experience is (Talarico, LaBar, & Rubin, 2004). In other words, what is important about the influence of emotion on memory is how strong the emotion is, not whether you feel good or bad about the event.

The idea that people remember emotional information better than neutral information has also been demonstrated in laboratory work. For example, people remember emotionally arousing pictures better than neutral ones (Bradley, Greenwald, Petry, & Lang, 1992), particularly the details of negative images (Kensinger, Garoff-Eaton, & Schacter, 2006). People also remember emotional utterances better than neutral ones (Armony, Chochol, Fecteau, & Belin, 2007). Work using functional magnetic resonance imaging (fMRI) scanning, such as that by Dolcos, Labar, and Cabeza (2005) and Kensinger and Corkin (2004; see also Kensinger, 2007), has shown that the superior memory for emotional memories appears to reflect the involvement of the amygdala and medial temporal-lobe structures, such as the hippocampus, with the amygdala-hippocampus network being more important for emotional intensity, and a hippocampal–frontal lobe network being more important for emotional valence (whether the emotion is positive or negative, happy or sad).

It is important to note that the emotional benefit of memory does not need to be present at the time the event is originally learned. In a fascinating study that exploits the phenomenon of reconsolidation (see Chapter 8), Finn and Roediger (2011) had people learn a set of English–Swahili vocabulary pairs (essentially the English translations of Swahili words). What was so interesting about this study is that after the initial learning phase was over, people were asked to recall the word pairs. As they recalled each pair, they were shown either a blank screen, or a neutral or an emotional picture. Then, after another period of time, they were asked to recall the word pairs again. On this final test, memory was better for words that had been followed by the emotional pictures, as can be seen in Figure 13-4. It seemed that when the word pairs were retrieved the first time, they were in a labile and fluid state, not yet firmly in memory. If an emotional picture was shown with the pairs, the person's emotional

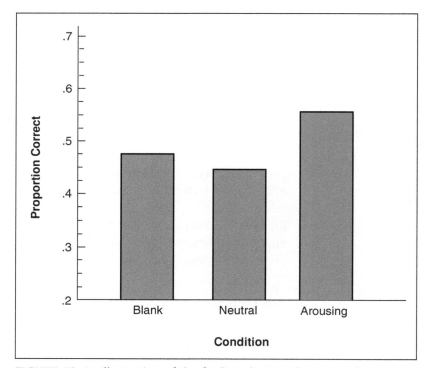

FIGURE 13-4 Illustration of the finding that recall memory for English–Swahili word pairs was better when people were looking at an emotional picture compared to looking at either a blank screen or a neutral picture.

Data from Finn & Roediger (2011).

response to the picture was incorporated into the memory trace and stored with it during the reconsolidation process. Thus, emotional responses can be incorporated into memory traces after the event has occurred if we experience an emotion when we are remembering the event. Note that Finn and Roediger did not find this benefit when people merely restudied the information, but only when they actively retrieved, as would be expected in a reconsolidation process.

So, why does emotion help memory so much? There are probably a number of reasons that, together, help make emotional memories easier to remember. First, emotional events are likely to be things that are important to us. As a consequence, people are likely to devote more attention to processing that information relative to something that is more emotionally neutral. Part of this is driven by the recruitment of the amygdala, which is a critical brain structure for processing emotions. There is also some evidence that emotionally charged memories appear to benefit more from the process of memory consolidation offered by sleep compared to emotionally neutral memories (Hu, Stylos-Allan, & Walker, 2006).

Another reason why emotion may help memory is that emotional information is more distinctive. Much of what we encounter in our day-to-day lives does not elicit much in the way of a strong emotional reaction. Thus truly emotional information is more likely to be distinctive, resulting in a kind of a von Restorff effect, which orients an increase in attention toward the emotion-eliciting stimulus (e.g., Talmi & Garry, 2012; Talmi, Schimmack, Paterson, & Moscovitch, 2007).

EMOTIONAL CONTEXT Emotions influence memory beyond just the fact than emotional memories are better. Another way that your emotions influence memory involves the kind of information that becomes activated or primed in long-term memory. With **mood-congruent memories**, your emotional state at the time makes knowledge in long-term memory that is more consistent with that mood more available. So, when you are in a happy mood, you tend to think more about things that make you happy, such as rainbows, butterflies, and home, but when you are sad, you are more likely to think of things that make you sad, such as death, taxes, and arguments. Most of what is going on with mood-congruent memories happens below consciousness, where you are not aware of it. It is a kind of priming. This can be seen in the fact that mood-congruent priming can be observed when people are doing a lexical decision task and are unaware that the influence of their emotional state on their performance is being tested (Olafson & Ferraro, 2001).

As noted earlier, emotions are visceral experiences. They reflect and influence the internal physiological state of your body. If you remember from Chapter 6, the internal state of your body can be a kind of contextual information that is stored in memory. In other words, emotions can be contexts as well. As a consequence, we should see encoding specificity effects for emotions, just as we do for external environments and physiological states. As it turns out, that is exactly what happens. People have **mood-dependent memories**, in which they find it easier to remember things when they are in the same mood at retrieval as they were during encoding (Bower, 1981). Thus, it is easier to remember happy times when you are happy than when you are sad, depressed, angry, or in some other emotional state.

Distinctiveness or rated memorability is an important determinant of how accurately we remember an event, such as the attack on the World Trade Center.

FLASHBULB MEMORIES   We often seem to have—or believe we have—extremely accurate and very detailed memories of particular events, especially when the events were surprising and highly emotional. These are often called **flashbulb memories**. For example, Brown and Kulik (1977) examined the flashbulb memories of college students for the assassination of President Kennedy in 1963. People were asked to recall their own particular circumstances when they heard news of the event, not whether they remembered the event itself. The data showed an increase in the amount of recallable detailed information (see also Mahmood, Manier, & Hirst, 2004; and Winograd & Killinger, 1983; for flashbulb memories of emotional but not surprising events, such as good friends dying of AIDS, President Nixon's resignation, and the Apollo moon landings). Emotional experience is critical to the formation of flashbulb memories. Although no one has been able to measure brain activity when a person learns of news that would produce a false memory, fMRI scans of people remembering a flashbulb memory event, such as the terrorist attacks of September 11, 2001, show increased amygdala activity during retrieval (Sharot, Martorella, Delgado, & Phelps, 2007), highlighting the involvement of emotional experience in these memories.

Although distinctiveness of the event is important (Dodson & Schacter, 2002; Hunt & Lamb, 2001; Schmidt, 1985), reminiscent of the von Restorff effect you encountered earlier, as well as surprise (Hirshman, Whelley, & Palij, 1989), it's also important for a person to be emotionally involved in the event. Kensinger and Schacter (2006) reported people's memories of the 2004 Red Sox–Yankees World Series games. Not surprisingly, it made a difference if they were Red Sox fans (winners, positive affect), Yankees fans (losers, negative affect), or not a fan of either team (neutral). People who had either positive or negative emotions about the outcome had more detailed memories. People who had positive memories, however, showed less consistency (their memory reports changed over time) and more over-confidence (they were more inappropriately confident than the Yankees fans), but remembered more about the game overall (see also work by Breslin & Safer, 2011).

Several studies suggest that flashbulb memories share many qualities with ordinary types of memories (McCloskey, Wible, & Cohen, 1988). For instance, Christianson (1989) tested Swedes' memories for the assassination of their prime minister in 1986, once barely six weeks after the assassination and again a year later. He found that only general information about the assassination was recalled with accuracy. Details that were recalled, in contrast, seemed to be a creative mixture of a few specifics plus more general knowledge, exactly the kind of memory first identified by Bartlett (1932; see also Neisser, 1982; Weaver, 1993). In a similar vein, Talarico and Rubin (2003) tested undergraduates the day after the 9/11 terrorist attacks and then again either 1, 6, or 32 weeks afterward, asking them to record both their memory of when they first heard of the attack and also a recent "everyday" memory. They found that both flashbulb and everyday memories declined across time in their consistency, but that the people *believed* that their flashbulb memories remained highly accurate (see also Schmolck, Buffalo, & Squire, 2000, who tested people's recollections of the O. J. Simpson trial).

Conway et al. (1994) did a similar, extensive study and found evidence of special memory qualities. They tested people on their personal recollections at the time of British Prime Minister Margaret Thatcher's surprise resignation, first just two weeks after the event, then again nearly a year later. More than 86% of their sample from the United Kingdom had accurate, detailed recollections of the event, including specific personal details (e.g., what they had eaten for breakfast that day). Because fewer than 30% of the non-U.K. participants had such memories, the authors conclude that vivid, accurate flashbulb memories can be formed. Furthermore, you are more likely to form a flashbulb memory if you view the event as especially important to you and if it has an emotional effect on you (see also Libkuman, Nichols-Whitehead, Griffith, & Thomas, 1999, on the role of emotional arousal in remembering). Interestingly, visual imagery and emotions seem to be important in the recollection of autobiographical memories (Rubin, Schrauf, & Greenberg, 2003). And in addition to the visual images, Schmidt (2004) found that the participants' emotionality also influenced the errors made in recalling personal memories of the 9/11 attack (for a list of criteria needed to form a flashbulb memory, see Finkenhauer et al., 1998).

But here's the irony again: Is memory good, even flashbulb-quality good, or is it widely subject to the sins of misattribution, suggestibility, bias, and the rest? The circumstances Conway et al. (1994) isolated as important for forming flashbulb memories—high level of importance, high affective response to the event—should also characterize memories of traumatic events, exactly those that are in dispute in cases of repressed and recovered memories.

Making Memory Worse

When you are in an excited emotional state, there are certainly some things that you remember, really, really well. So, it is clear that there are ways in which emotions make memories better. However, when your emotions are running high, there also happen to be a lot of things that get missed, and so there are ways that emotions make memories less complete. In this section we cover some ideas about how the accuracy of memory is tied to how intense your memories are, and then discuss some ways in which memory is harmed by emotions.

INTENSITY AND MEMORY   Emotions can be described in terms of how intense they are, how much you are emotionally aroused. This level of arousal is systematically related to how much is remembered. In general sense, memory follows what is known as the **Yerkes-Dodson law**, which is shown in Figure 13-5. According to the Yerkes-Dodson law, when you are in a low arousal state, such as when you are tired and bored, your memory for information is not that good. However, as your arousal level goes up, so does your memory performance—but only up to a point. That point is an optimal level of arousal that allows the most learning to occur. Beyond that, things change. At even higher levels of arousal your memory starts to decline. You are too agitated and excited, and the amount of information you can adequately remember goes down. As you can see, at high levels of arousal, emotions can make memory worse.

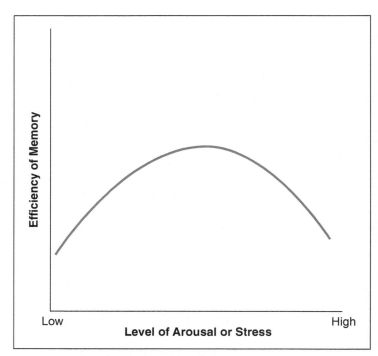

FIGURE 13-5   Illustration of the Yerkes-Dodson law, in which performance is poor at low levels of intensity, then increases as intensity grows larger, and then decreases for high levels of intensity.

Although the Yerkes-Dodson law accurately captures what is going on with emotional arousal in a general sense, the actual situation is a bit more complex. At higher levels of arousal, memory does not decline for everything—there are some things for which memory actually continues to improve. This is captured by the **Easterbrook hypothesis**, which says that at higher levels of emotional arousal there is a narrowing of attention onto whatever is eliciting the emotions in a person. *That* information can be thought of as being at the center of the event. The more irrelevant details of the event are less emotionally arousing, however, and can be thought of as the peripheral information. According to the Easterbrook hypothesis, when people are in more highly emotion arousing situations, their attention narrows in on the central information and away from the peripheral information. As a consequence, with high levels of emotional intensity, memory for the central details continues to get better, but memory for peripheral details declines. Because there are more peripheral than central details, overall memory is getting worse at high levels of emotional arousal, but things that are most important might be remembered really well.

This idea is supported by several memory studies. For example, in a study by Safer, Christiansen, Autry, and Österlund (1998), people were shown a series of pictures. Some of these depicted emotionally arousing scenes, such as a bloody body on the hood of a car, and others showed more emotionally neutral scenes, such as a picture of a woman in a park. On the later memory test, as can be seen in Figure 13-5, performance was better for central aspects of the scene in the emotionally arousing pictures compared to the more emotionally neutral pictures. Safer et al. called these **tunnel memories**—it was as if people were narrowing or tunneling their vision in on the emotional central details, causing them to be remembered better. There was no tunneling on the neutral scenes, however: Memory performance was more expansive and inclusive for the peripheral details in the emotionally neutral than the arousing scenes.

A related result is called the **weapon focus effect** (Maass & Köhnken, 1989; Steblay, 1992). This is the finding that when there are emotionally arousing elements in a scene, such as a gun or a knife, people's attention will go to the weapon. This presumably occurs because, at some level, people want to know where that weapon is directed and whether it could harm them. Note that this occurs not only in scenes depicting violence, but even when a weapon is present in nonviolent scenes (Kramer, Buckout, & Eugenio, 1990). As with other tunnel memories, when a weapon is present, memory for that weapon is better, but memory for the other details in the scene get worse.

So, as you can see, emotional information can both make memories better and make memories worse, depending on which aspect of an event is focused on. Memory for central information from an event is heightened by emotion, but memory for peripheral information is harmed by emotion. This differential influence of emotion on memory is exaggerated as time goes on during the consolidation process, particularly the consolidation that occurs during sleep (e.g., Payne & Kensinger, 2010). The neural processing that occurs during rapid–eye-movement (REM) sleep seems to be particularly important for the consolidation of emotional information in memory because of the increase in cortisol levels during this time, which reinstates the emotional experience.

Section Summary

- There is a general benefit for remembering emotional over neutral information. However, people who have suffered brain damage to areas critical for emotion processing, such as the amygdala, do not exhibit such a benefit.
- The memory benefit for emotional information comes from a number of sources, including its importance, its distinctiveness, the amount of attention and rehearsal it is given, and the superior benefit it seems to derive from neural consolidation processes.
- Emotion can serve as a form of contextual information that can facilitate some memory processes, as with mood-congruent and mood-dependent memories.
- The highly detailed memories we have for very emotional events, and for the contexts in which we learn about such events, are called flashbulb memories. Flashbulb memories, although not perfect and prone to some forgetting, appear to be more durable than normal everyday memories.
- Although emotion can improve some types of memories, it can also impose a cost on later memory. Specifically, at high levels of emotional intensity, attention is captured by central information at the cost of processing of

peripheral information. As a consequence, memory for more peripheral information is worse under conditions of higher emotional intensity. The weapon focus effect is an example of the kind of memory impairment that can occur with high levels of emotion.

EMOTION AND LANGUAGE

Emotion can also influence language processes in cognition and is a quality that is communicated by language. In this section we cover the transmission and impact of emotional information. This includes emotional tone that is carried by the speech signal, as well as the tracking of emotional information in a situation model and how that influences the cognitive processing of other event dimensions.

Prosody

Language is typically not delivered in a monotone, but involves *a moving up and down in pitch, somewhat like a melody;* this is called **prosody**. Prosody conveys meaning in language, although a different kind of meaning than the semantic meanings of the words themselves. For example, the sentences "Those are my shoes." and "Those are my shoes?" contain exactly the same words but are spoken with different prosodies. One conveys a statement and the other a question, often with a rise in pitch at the end of the sentence. One other aspect of meaning that prosody can convey is the emotional tone of the speaker. For example, imagine the sentence "Those are my shoes." spoken in happy, sad, and angry tones of voice, and notice the different prosodies that are used to convey this emotional meaning.

As you should recall from our earlier discussions of language, in most people, most language-processing components are lateralized in the left hemisphere. For example, this is the location of Broca's and Wernicke's areas. However, not all language processing is strongly left lateralized, and the processing of emotional prosody is one example of this. A number of studies, including research involving fMRI imaging, have found that the brain is right lateralized for the processing of emotional prosody (e.g., Buchanan et al., 2000). This is further supported by evidence from people with damage to the right hemispheres. Patients with right hemisphere damage often have difficulty deriving emotional information from linguistic prosody (e.g., Pell, 1999).

Note that although damage to the right hemisphere can impede the processing of linguistic prosody, damage to other brain structures involved in emotion processing, such as the amygdala, does not (Adolphs & Tranel, 1999). In other words, the processing of emotional prosody by the right hemisphere does not depend of emotional input from the amygdala, but involves a determination of emotional content from the pitch information in speech that is heard. Overall, although prosody is a deeply linguistic characteristic, this meaning is processed more by the right hemisphere than the left.

Hearing language that conveys characteristics of emotion does not mean that a listener will be convinced that the person speaking is experiencing that particular emotion. Sometimes, we know that people are only play-acting and that the emotion expressed is not one that he person is actually feeling. What people need to do is take the emotional information conveyed by the prosody, along with other characteristics of the language, to determine whether the emotion is genuinely being experienced or not. There is some evidence that people have some success at doing this and that different regions of the brain are involved in such detection (e.g., Drolet, Schubotz, & Fischer, 2012). For example, if vocal expressions of emotion are taken from the radio and played to people, the detection of genuine emotion is above chance, particularly for emotions such as anger and sadness. Moreover, as measured by fMRI recordings, there is greater activity in the medial prefrontal cortex and the temporal-parietal junction. The latter is often found to be important in perspective taking. Thus people are able to use information in the language signal to determine not only the emotion that is being expressed by the prosody of the spoken words, but also the genuineness of that emotion.

Words and Situations

Let's shift our focus at this point away from *how* language is said to *what* is said, and how language is influenced by emotional processing. First, and most obviously, some words are about emotion, such as "happy," "sad," and "angry." We have specific words that aim to capture and communicate the experience of emotion, and the fact that such words are common in the language attests to the fact that such ideas are readily transmitted and received.

However, are these words the only ones that communicate emotional information? Probably not. There is some suggestion that many words in the language communicate some emotional character, even if they are abstract words. If you remember from Chapter 6, words can vary along a number of dimensions, which can then influence cognition in meaningful ways. For example, words can be classified along the concrete-abstract dimension. Concrete words—words that refer to some physical entity, such as "ball"—are often remembered better than abstract words, such as "truth," because people can generate mental images of concrete words. Because of this, people can exploit dual encoding and form mental images of the concrete words, boosting their memory performance.

The temptation at that point is to say that abstract words are more poorly remembered because they do not have any perceptual/embodied/grounded qualities. However, a closer look reveals that this is not the case. Abstract words do convey embodied information, but more in terms of emotional connotations than the more perceptual qualities of concrete words (e.g., Altarriba, Bauer, & Benvenuto, 1999). For example, words such as "courage" and "revenge" are abstract words that convey emotional qualities. If people are asked to process abstract words, those with higher emotional content are processed faster than neutral words (Kousta, Vigliocco, Vinson, Andrews, & Campo, 2010). Thus, emotional but abstract words can show an advantage in cognition, and this advantage is due to the fact that people can take advantage of the embodied nature of emotion to facilitate their processing of these words.

Emotional information is also processed and tracked at the situation model level. As was described in Chapter 10, during language comprehension people track a number of aspects of a described situation, such as spatial location, time frame, and people's goals. There is some evidence to suggest that people are actively tracking emotional reactions of story characters as they experience various events in the narrative world (de Vega, León, & Díaz, 1996; Gernsbacher, Hallada, & Robertson, 1998; Gernsbacher & Robertson, 1992; Gygax, Garnham, & Oakhill, 2004). Moreover, when there is a change in a story character's emotional state, there is an increase in cognitive effort expended, as revealed by reading time, as a reader updates the emotional information in a story (Komeda & Kusumi, 2006). Thus, emotion is important enough to people for them to want to know what even fictional characters are experiencing.

Thinking further about emotion, and how it factors into our understanding of events, there can be two ways that emotion can be experienced. One way is by the person who is feeling the emotion. This is the mental and physiological state of the person depending on the emotion they are experiencing. The second is by people other than the person experiencing the emotion. For example, some external person might see the emotion-experiencer smiling, scowling, blushing, and so on. These are external manifestations of emotion that are available to viewers. When comprehending language that involves emotion, how emotion is represented in the situation model may reflect, in part, whose perspective is emphasized by the language, the person experiencing or observing the emotion. These different ways of thinking about and processing emotional information may require different kinds of cognitive processes.

In a study by Oosterwijk et al. (2012), people read individual sentences that conveyed emotional information. A given sentence conveyed emotion either from an internal perspective of the experiencer, such as "Hot embarrassment came over her," or the external perspective that some other person would see "His nose wrinkled in disgust." People were simply asked to judge the sensibility of the sentences as fast and as accurately as possible (some non-sensible sentences were included as well). The researchers found that people showed a processing cost when they had to switch from an internal emotional focus to an external one (or vice versa) from one sentence to the next, but not when the nature of the emotional focus stayed the same across the sentences. This shows that we mentally represent emotional information in our understanding of situations and events depending on the perspective we take, and the kind of experience that needs to be captured in the situation model.

Why would it be important to track emotional information in a story, other than the additional experience one gets from reading about a story character's emotional state? It is important to keep in mind that emotions do not exist in a vacuum, but are human reactions to events that are experienced. More specifically, emotions can be seen as being strongly tied to people's goals. For example, negative emotions come from having one's goals impeded or blocked, such as not being able to buy a bicycle or not having one's parents continue to be healthy. Likewise, positive emotions come from having one's goals achieved, such as getting to go on a hot date or winning the lottery. Goals are important for language comprehension because they help provide an understanding of the motivations and causes of narrative events as the circumstances unfold.

Section Summary

- A great deal of emotional meaning is conveyed by the prosody of spoken utterances. Brain-damaged people, particularly those with damage to the right hemisphere, may be able to understand the words spoken to them but often lack the ability to process the prosody of what is being said, and so miss out on emotional cues in the speech stream.
- Emotion is infused in a lot of language processing, even beyond auditory cues such as prosody. Some words, even abstract words, carry emotional meaning in their lexical entries, thereby influencing how people process that information.
- People actively track and simulate emotional experiences in the situation models that are created during comprehension. There is evidence that people show processing costs of changes in emotional quality of a character, and in changes in the internal or external experience of an emotion.

EMOTION AND DECISION MAKING

Decision making is another area of cognition that is affected by emotion. The effectiveness and quality of the decisions a person makes in a heightened emotional state differ from those made in a more relaxed and neutral state. Note that the terms *emotion*, *stress*, and *pressure* have different meanings, but for our current purposes, we gloss over some of these.

Stress Impairs Performance

It is clear to anyone who has ever been under emotional stress, such as being anxious, that decision-making and problem-solving performance can decline under these conditions. Essentially, when people experience anxiety, they tend to crowd their working memory with irrelevant thoughts about whatever it is they are anxious about. For example, people who are math anxious (i.e., they avoid doing math problems, taking math classes, exploring careers that use a lot of math) do more poorly on math problems because their working memory capacity is consumed by off-topic irrelevant thoughts that stem from their anxiety about doing math (Ashcraft & Krause, 2007). These thoughts take away from the limited capacity they have to devote to the problem, and their performance suffers. This may also disrupt the mental representations people hold in memory, making them less precise, thereby decreasing performance (Maloney, Ansari, & Fugelsang, 2011).

People who are threatened also experience physiological changes due to the stress they are placed under (e.g., Kassam, Koslov, & Mendes, 2009). Specifically, there is a decrease in cardiovascular efficiency, reducing blood flow to the body and brain, causing the body to slow down. This makes thinking, including decision making, less effective. Part of the reason for this is that when a person is in a threatened state, it may be adaptive (under certain circumstances) to be more immobile, and for the body to be prepared for some damage. Although this may have some survival advantages in the wild, in the circumstances we are faced with

Sometimes we choke under pressure as when our performance deviates from what normally do, such as missing a shot at a critical time in a game.

in our everyday lives, this is a maladaptive response because we cannot make decisions that would be to our advantage.

CHOKING UNDER PRESSURE   We've all been there. The pressure is on. We've done well in this situation before. It comes time to step up and do it again. And we choke *(rats!)*. When people become anxious because of external pressures, their performance can decline.

If you recall from Chapter 4, as a process becomes increasingly practiced, it becomes more and more automatized, allowing people to do it better and more quickly. Thus, as people gain expertise, they become more fluid in the task as its components become more and more unconscious. For the most part, this is a good thing. However, it can also cause problems, especially when the pressure is on. In a pressure situation, what skilled people should do is allow their unconscious cognitive processes to play themselves out. However, what can sometimes happen is that these people start to consciously think about what they are doing and how they are doing it. This is the classic case of when a person, such as a basketball player, chokes under pressure. What can happen under these circumstances is that the athlete's conscious thought processes about what he or she is doing begins to intrude on and compete with more unconscious and automatic cognitive processes.

In a classic demonstration of this, Beilock and Carr (2001) tested people in a golf-putting situation. There were two groups of people in this study—people who were expert golf players, and golf novices. At first Beilock and Carr had people just putt to gain a sense of how well they did normally. Then they placed these people under pressure, asking them to consciously focus on their putting. What happened, not surprisingly, was that novices did better when they focused on accuracy. Surprisingly, however, the golf experts did worse when they focused on their putting. This is because the conscious thoughts disrupted their normally automatic performance on this task. In fact, people who are experts actually did better if they focused on speed (Beilock, Bertenthal, McCoy, & Carr, 2004).

There are two different types of pressure that can influence performance (DeCaro, Thomas, Albert, & Beilock, 2011). One type is **outcome-based pressure** in which *a person is distracted from focusing on what he or she supposed to be doing, but instead focuses on the outcome of the task.* For example, if a person is worried about passing an exam, attention is directed toward thoughts about the outcome, depleting resources from doing the task itself. The consequence is that performance declines and the grade suffers. This type of pressure results in a decline in attentional control for the person. That is, their attention is more likely to wander away from what it is that they are supposed to be processing toward task-irrelevant thoughts.

An example of outcome-based pressure, and the cognitive distraction that can accompany it, is when people are solving math problems (e.g., Beilock, 2008; Beilock, Kulp, Holt, & Carr, 2004). People in the low-pressure groups were simply instructed to do their best. In comparison, the high-pressure groups were told that if they did well, then they could earn some money (some pressure). However, they could only earn the money if both they and a person they were partnered with did well, and the partner had already finished and had done well (increasing the pressure on the participant). Finally, people were told that their performance on the test was being video-recorded to be used as examples for other teachers and students (even more pressure). What was found was that people under high pressure did worse than those under low pressure, particularly for the more challenging problems. The explanation is that people under high pressure generate more off-task thoughts about things generating the pressure. These off-task thoughts use up working memory capacity that would otherwise be used by the primary task, solving math problems.

Interestingly, one recommendation that has been made to help keep thoughts focused on the task at hand, rather than being distracted by pressure-related irrelevant thoughts, is to talk aloud when solving a problem (DeCaro, Rotar, Kendra, & Beilock, 2010). Talking aloud is thought to keep mental resources dedicated to doing the task at hand and keep working memory from being co-opted by irrelevant thoughts. Performance can then be more like normal.

The other type of pressure situation is **monitoring pressure** in which *a person focuses too much attention on the task and how they are doing it.* For example, if a person is trying to make a free throw to win the game, he may start focusing on how he is standing, how he is holding the ball, how his arm is moving through the shot, and so on. This type of pressure is a result of conscious working memory processes disrupting more automatic processes, where any conflicts between the two disrupt performance. That is, a more automatic process that works well with largely unconscious control is disrupted when conscious thoughts in working memory jostle and conflict with those automatic processes.

STEREOTYPE THREAT The influence of emotion and stress on cognition can come from any number of different sources. Some sources that people often do not think about are the social and ethnic groups we belong to and identify with, along with the cultural stereotypes of these groups that we carry around with us. When these stereotypes convey a negative view of our abilities in a typical domain, there can be an (unconscious) mental activation of this knowledge. This activation may happen even when doing something as simple as indicating gender or ethnic group when beginning to fill out a questionnaire. **Stereotype threat** occurs when this *unconscious activation of negative stereotypes leads a person to perform worse on a task than they would otherwise.* This can come about in any way that orients a person to identify with the stereotyped group, such as indicating membership in that group on a form, or being placed in a situation in which the person feels like a minority (e.g., Murphy, Steele, & Gross, 2007). For example, asking people to indicate their gender before taking tests in science or engineering can lead women to do more poorly on such tests because of a (mistaken) cultural stereotype that women are not as good at these tasks (or lead Whites to do more poorly when exposed to the stereotype that Asians do better).

Stereotype threat can influence the types of choices and decisions a person makes (Carr & Steele, 2010). For example, people do worse at solving math problems, as a consequence of stereotype threat, if they belong to a group for which the stereotype claims that they should not be good at math (e.g., Beilock, Rydell, & McConnell, 2007). As with the research on choking under pressure, stereotype threat lowers performance because a person's thoughts, and consequently working memory capacity, are consumed to some degree by counterproductive thoughts related to the stereotype. This is the case even if that effort is oriented toward suppressing the stereotype-related thoughts (Schmader, 2010). As a result, less mental capacity is available for doing the task at hand, and performance suffers.

Note that priming can also lead to an increase in performance. For example, in a study by Lang and Lang (2010), students were asked to do a series of verbal analogy problems. Before actually doing the task, one group of students was asked to imagine a person who is successful at solving problems and write down a number of abilities such a person would have, the personality traits of such a person, and how such a person would feel just before starting to solve a problem. Compared to a control group that did not do this, people who spent time imagining what it was like to be such a successful person did better on the analogy test. Thus, it is possible to attenuate test anxiety as well as magnify it.

Stress Improves Performance

Emotion, stress, and pressure can decrease performance, but it should also be noted that there are times when they can increase performance. There is bad stress and good stress. Performance can improve when the stress being experienced is viewed as challenging rather than threatening (e.g., Kassam et al., 2009). Under these circumstances there is an increase in cardiovascular efficiency, and more blood and oxygen is delivered to the body and brain, allowing it to perform at a heightened level. So, people perform better under these conditions.

As an example, consider a study by LePine, LePine, and Jackson (2004). In this study, people were assessed for their stress level at school, along with other factors such as exhaustion and academic aptitude, and their performance as measured by their grade point average. Importantly, stress was identified as being either negative stress, where school work was viewed as negative stressor and a threat, or as positive stress, where school work was viewed as a positive stressor and a challenge. Their results showed that when there was negative stress, performance was negatively affected—grades were lower. However, when it was viewed as a challenge, performance was positively affected—students had higher grades.

In addition to physiological changes that can facilitate performance, there are also more cognitive changes where pressure can improve performance. For example, if people learned a skill in a way that involved more implicit unconscious processes, such as learning to putt under dual-task conditions where attention is divided (Masters, 1992), then most of the cognitive processes involved in the task were unconscious. People trained under more explicit conscious conditions did worse under pressure. However, placing people under pressure after divided-attention training, and more implicit learning, actually improved performance. To be sure, the implicit learning people had slower learning and had worse overall accuracy—but they experienced less disruption, compared to their baseline, when they were put under pressure. Thus, the overall effect of making a task more unconscious is to insulate it more from the disruption that can occur when a person is put in stressful situations. This is why it is valuable for some professions to constantly drill and practice their skills, in a variety of settings, to the point that they are automatic and unconscious. This way, when people need these skills for real, say in a genuine emergency, they can execute the skills without succumbing to the detrimental effects of pressure.

Section Summary

- When the source of stress is viewed as a threat, there can be declines in performance, causing people to choke under pressure.
- Choking under pressure can occur when the pressure is outcome based and the focus is on the outcome of the task, or monitoring-based and the focus is on how the task is done. These different types of pressure arise under different kinds of situations.
- Some forms of pressure may be more subtle and unconscious, such as when a person experiences stereotype threat. This occurs when people are reminded of their membership in a group that cultural stereotypes suggest will not do well, and so their performance goes down.
- Stress can also improve performance when it involves activities that are highly overpracticed, or when the stress is viewed as a challenge rather than a threat.

Key Terms

amygdala
Easterbrook hypothesis
emotion
emotional Stroop task
flashbulb memories
intensity

mood-congruent
  memories
mood-dependent
  memories
outcome-based
  pressure

monitoring pressure
prosody
stereotype threat
tunnel memories
valence

ventro-medial
  prefrontal cortex
weapon focus effect
Yerkes-Dodson law

4 Attention

Everyone knows what attention is. It is the taking possession by the mind, in clear and vivid form, of one out of what seem several simultaneously possible objects or trains of thought. Focalization, concentration of consciousness are of its essence. It implies withdrawal from some things in order to deal effectively with others.

(JAMES, 1890, PP. 381–382)

As he did every morning after waking, Bill went into the bathroom to begin his morning ritual. After squeezing toothpaste onto his toothbrush, he looked into the mirror and began to brush his teeth. Although he brushed the teeth on the right side of his mouth quite vigorously, for the most part he ignored those on the left side. . . . He shaved all the stubble from the right side of his face impeccably but did a spotty job on the left side. . . . [After eating at a diner,] when Bill asked for the check, the waitress placed it on the left side of the table. After a few minutes, he waved the waitress over and complained, saying "I asked for my tab 5 minutes ago. What is taking so long?"

(Banich, 1997, p. 235)

Attention—one of cognitive psychology's most important topics and one of our oldest puzzles. What does it mean to pay attention to something? To direct your attention to something? To be unable to pay attention because of boredom, lack of interest, or fatigue? What sorts of things grab or capture our attention? How much control do we have over our attention? (Cognitive science says "attend to," meaning "pay attention," even though some dictionaries say that is an archaic usage.) We have to work at paying attention to some things (most topics in a faculty meeting, for example). But for other topics, it seems effortless: A good spy novel can rivet your attention.

MULTIPLE MEANINGS OF ATTENTION

Attention is one of the thorniest topics in cognitive psychology, possibly because we mean so many different things by the term. We use the term *attention* to describe a wide range of phenomena, from the basic idea of arousal and alertness all the way up to consciousness and awareness. Some attention processes are extremely rapid, so that we are aware only of their outcomes, if that, and others are slow enough that we seem to be aware of them—and able to control them—throughout. In some cases, attention is reflexive. Even when we deliberately concentrate on something, that concentration can be disrupted and redirected by an unexpected, attention-grabbing event, such as the sudden loud noise in the otherwise quiet library. In other cases, we are frustrated that our deliberate attempts to focus on some task are so easily disrupted by another train of thought; you try very hard to pay attention to a lecture, only to find yourself daydreaming about last weekend's party.

Table 4-1 presents six different connotations of the term *attention*. For organizational purposes, this chapter is structured around that list to impose some coherence on the field, to help you see the forest and prevent your getting lost in the trees (the final type of attention in the table is nearly synonymous with short-term or working memory, so it is not discussed until the next chapter). Although other organizational schemes are possible, this approach should help you develop an understanding of attention and see how some topics flow into others. The list

TABLE 4-1   Six Meanings of Attention

Input Attention	Controlled Attention
Alertness or arousal	Selective attention
Orienting reflex or response	Mental resources and conscious processing
Spotlight attention and search	Supervisory attentional system

will also help avoid some confusion that arises when the term *attention* is used for processes or mechanisms more precisely described by another term, such as *arousal*.

Moreover, this list tends to map on to different parts of the brain that are involved in different kinds of attention (Posner & Rothbart, 2007). For example, *alertness* is associated with the neurotransmitter norepinephrine, and with activity in the brain stem, the right frontal lobe, and portions of the parietal cortex. *Orienting* is associated with the neurotransmitter acetylcholine, and with activity in the tectum (in the midbrain), the superior parietal lobe (B.A. 7), and the temporal parietal junction (B.A. 19). Finally, *executive attention*, which encompasses spotlight, selective, and resource attention, is associated with the neurotransmitter dopamine, and with activity in the anterior cingulate (B.A. 24), the prefrontal cortex (B.A. 10), and the basal ganglia.

At every turn in considering attention, we confront four interrelated ideas. *First,* we are constantly presented with more information than we can attend to. *Second,* there are serious limits in how much we can attend to at once. *Third,* we can respond to some information and perform some tasks with little if any attention. And *fourth,* with sufficient practice and knowledge, some tasks become less and less demanding of our attention.

BASICS OF ATTENTION

Let's start by giving two general metaphors for *attention*, both of which apply throughout the list in Table 4-1.

ATTENTION AS A MENTAL PROCESS   **Attention** can be thought of as *the mental process of concentrating effort on a stimulus or a mental event*. By this, we mean that attention is an activity that occurs within cognition. This activity focuses a mental resource—effort—on either an external stimulus or an internal thought. When it refers to an external stimulus, attention is the mental mechanism by which we actively process information in the sensory registers pertaining to that entity. When you examine a picture like that in Figure 4-1, you focus your mental energies on an external stimulus, the splotches and patches of black and white in a photograph. If you have never seen this before, you struggle to identify it, to recognize the pattern in it. Your focus in the attempt to identify the pattern was attention. Sustained attention then led, after some time, to identify the Dalmatian. In fact, iconic memory and spatial visual attention use the same neural substrates, such as a shared frontal-parietal network (Ruff, Kristkjánsson, & Driver, 2007). Moreover, although much of this chapter discusses the use of attention in perceptual processes, such as vision and hearing, this neural network of attention is involved in other cognitive processes, such as memory retrieval, that require attention (Nee & Jonides, 2008).

In principle, the focusing of your attention on a visual stimulus is no different than when you focus attention on a word, idea, or concept. For example, your professor says something unexpected (e.g., describing an idea as "green"), and you puzzle over the remark, trying to find a way to interpret it that makes sense. (Can an idea that promotes conservation and ecology be described as "green"? See also Chapter 9.) It is this concentration of attention we are illustrating

FIGURE 4-1 First identification of the pattern relies almost exclusively on data-driven processing, whereas later identification relies heavily on conceptually driven processing.

here: attention focused on and driving the mental event of remembering, searching for information stored in memory, and attempting to comprehend.

ATTENTION AS A LIMITED MENTAL RESOURCE   Now consider attention as a mental resource, a kind of mental fuel. In this sense, attention is *the limited mental energy or resource that powers cognition*. It is a mental commodity, the stuff that gets used when we pay attention. According to this metaphor, attention is the all-important mental resource needed to run cognition.

A fundamentally important idea here is that of limitations: Attention is limited, finite. We usually state this by talking about the limited capacity of attention. Countless experiments, to say nothing of everyday experiences, reveal the limits of our attention, the capacity to attend to stimuli, to remember events that just happened, to remember things we are supposed to do. In short, there is a limit to how many different things we can attend to and do at once.

It does not take long to think of everyday situations that reveal these limitations. You can easily drive down an uncrowded highway in daylight while carrying on a conversation. You can easily listen to the news on the radio under normal driving conditions. In the middle of a heavy rainstorm, however, you can't talk to the person sitting in the passenger seat; in rush hour traffic, you can't (and shouldn't try to) do business on the cell phone. Under such demanding circumstances, the radio or the conversation are annoyances or irritating—and dangerous—distractions, and you have to turn down the volume, or turn off the phone.

Watch *IT Video: Cell Phones* in **MyPsychLab**

BASIC INPUT ATTENTIONAL PROCESSES

We'll start with a section on the more basic types of attention listed in Table 4-1, those occurring early in the stream of processing. These are the processes that seem either reflexive or automatic, are low-level in terms of informational content, and occur rapidly. They are especially involved in *getting sensory information into the cognitive system,* so they can generally be called forms of **input attention**.

Alertness and Arousal

It almost seems axiomatic to say that part of what we mean by *attention* involves the basic capacity to respond to the environment. This most basic sense refers to alertness and arousal as a necessary state of the nervous system: The nervous system must be awake, responsive, and able to interact with the environment. It seems intuitive that the nervous system must be aroused in order to pay attention. You cannot attend to something while you are unconscious, although certain things can impinge on us and rouse us to a conscious state (e.g., alarm clocks, smoke detectors, or other loud noises).

Although consciousness is important, to some degree there also needs to be an element of alertness. That is, we need to monitor the environment for new, interesting, and/or important events. Sometimes this can be difficult, especially when this alertness needs to be strung out over a long period of time during which nothing much happens. The *maintenance of attention for infrequent events over long periods of time* is known as **vigilance** or **sustained attention**. The study of vigilance began during World War II with British radar operators (Mackworth, 1948). However, vigilance is important in many other domains, including air traffic control, sonar detection, and nuclear power plant operations (Warm, 1984). Even quality inspections in a factory involve some degree of vigilance as workers constantly monitor for important but relatively infrequent flaws in products (Wiener, 1984).

There are a number of fundamental vigilance phenomena that have been observed over the years (see See, Howe, Warm, & Dember, 1995, for a review). For instance, there is a decline in performance as time on the task wears on, showing that people have difficulty maintaining attention on a single task over long periods of time. This decline takes place in about 20 to 35 minutes. Interestingly, the problems that occur with a decline in vigilance do not appear to involve people failing to notice the signal in the task they are doing. Instead, people have difficulty making the decision to respond that they have detected something, a shift in response bias. Vigilance is also affected by the neurological and physiological state of the person, such as a whether people are too hot or cold, their level of arousal, or if they have been taking drugs (Warm, 1984). Finally, there are also a number of aspects of the task that can influence how effective people are, such as how long the signal is (longer is better), how often there is a signal (more frequent is better), and how busy the background is (less busy is better) (Warm & Jerison, 1984). Interestingly, there is also some evidence that meditation training can improve vigilance performance (MacLean et al., 2010).

Although nobody disputes that arousal and alertness are a necessary precondition for most cognitive processes, this may overemphasize a kind of thinking known as **explicit processing**. That is, explicit processes are those *involving conscious awareness that a task is being performed, and usually conscious awareness of the outcome.* The opposite is known as **implicit processing**, *processing with no necessary involvement of conscious awareness* (Schacter, 1989, 1996). As you will see, the distinction between implicit and explicit is often in terms of memory performance, especially long-term memory. When you are asked to learn a list of words and then name them back, that's an explicit memory task: You are consciously aware of being tested and aware that you are remembering words you just studied. By contrast, you can also demonstrate memory for information *without* awareness, which is implicit memory. For example, you can reread a text more rapidly than you read it the first time, even if you have no recollection of ever reading it before (Masson, 1984).

There is some evidence showing that some mental processing can be done with only minimal attention. Much of this is discussed later. For now, consider a study by Bonebakker et al. (1996; see Andrade, 1995, for a review of learning under anesthesia) in which they played recorded lists of words to surgery patients, one list just before and another during surgery, and then tested memory up to 24 hours later. Despite the fact that all the patients were given general anesthesia, and so were unconscious during the surgery itself, they nonetheless showed memory for words they heard. Keep in mind, however, that they were only remembering 6% to 9% more words compared to a control condition of new words. They certainly did not learn any complex ideas. So, you do need to pay attention to learn well. It's just that small amounts of learning can sometimes occur unconsciously.

A powerful part of the study was that performance was based on an implicit memory task, the *word stem completion task*. Patients were given word stems and told to complete them with the first word they thought of. To ensure that the task was measuring implicit memory, patients were further asked to exclude any words they explicitly remembered hearing, such as the words they remembered hearing before receiving anesthesia. For example, say that they heard *BOARD* before surgery and *LIGHT* during surgery. When tested 24 hours after surgery, the patients completed the word stems (e.g., *LI_ _ _*) with words they had heard during surgery *(LIGHT)* more frequently than they did with presurgery words *(BO_ _ _)* or with control words that had never been presented. In other words, they remembered hearing *BOARD* and excluded it on the word stem task. Because they did not explicitly remember *LIGHT,* they finished *LI_ _ _* with *GHT,* presumably because their memory of *LIGHT* was implicit. The results demonstrated that the patients had implicit memory of the words they had heard while under the anesthesia.

So that you understand this procedure, and because it occurs in later chapters, here is a more focused version of the task. Imagine that you saw a list of words including *SCHOOL* and *SHELF.* Relying on explicit memory, you would probably complete the stem *SCH_ _ _* with *SCHOOL.* But if I asked you to exclude words you explicitly remembered, you would find another way of completing that stem, say *SCHEME;* likewise, you might exclude *SHELF* and write *SHELL.* By chance, you might complete the stem *CRA_ _ _* with *CRADLE* or *CRAYON,* neither of which you saw before. Here is the implicit part. Try it yourself. Complete the following word stems with the first word that comes to your mind: *PAP_ _*; *GRE_ _.* *PAPER* is a pretty common completion for the first one, probably because paper is a fairly common word (it has not appeared in this chapter yet). But if you completed the second word stem as *GREEN* without explicitly remembering that you read about "green ideas" earlier, then that probably was an implicit memory effect.

Orienting Reflex and Attention Capture

Now consider another kind of attention, the kind caused by a reflexive response in the nervous system. In a quiet room, an unexpected noise grabs your attention away from what you were doing and may involve a reflexive turning of your head toward the source of the sound. In vision, of course, you move your eyes and head toward the unexpected stimulus, the flash of light or sudden movement in your peripheral vision. This is the **orienting reflex**, *the reflexive redirection of attention toward the unexpected stimulus.* This response is found at all levels of the animal kingdom and is present very early in life. Although a host of physiological changes accompany the orienting reflex, including changes in heart rate and respiration (Bridgeman, 1988), we focus on its more mental aspects. The cognitive manifestation of all of this is a redirection of attention toward something, even if the eyes and body do not actually move toward the source. As such, we refer to this process as **attention capture**, which is *the spontaneous redirection of attention to stimuli in the world based on physical characteristics.*

The orienting reflex is a location-finding response of the nervous system. That is, an unexpected stimulus, a noise or a flash of light, triggers the reflex so that you can locate the stimulus—find where it is in space. This allows you to protect yourself against danger, in the reflexive, survival sense; after all, what if the unexpected movement is from a rock thrown at you or some other threat (e.g., Öhman, Flykt, & Esteves, 2001)? Note that this system also allows you to monitor for more positive survival stimuli, such as noticing a baby's face (Brosch, Sander, Pourtois, & Scherer, 2008). Given that the response helps you locate the stimulus, it is not surprising that some of the neural pathways involved correspond to the *"where" pathway* (as compared to the "what" pathway). As noted in Chapter 2, the "where" pathway projects from the visual cortex to upper (superior) rearward (dorsal) regions of the parietal lobe (and the "what" pathway is also called the ventral pathway).

Note also that attention is not only directed by objects and entities in the environment, but it can also be directed by social cues. Perhaps the biggest cue is noticing where other people are looking (Birmingham, Bischof, & Kingstone, 2008; Kingstone, Smilek, Ristic, Friesen, & Eastwood, 2003). In fact, it has been suggested that our face and eyes have evolved in such a way to communicate this sort of attention-directing information (Emery, 2000). Even our language can influence how we direct attention. For example, a study by Estes, Verges, and Barsalou (2008) showed that attention can be directed based on the meanings of words activated in long-term memory. In this study, people saw a cue word in the middle of the screen, which was soon followed by either an X or an O at either the top or the bottom of the screen. The task was to indicate which of these two letters was seen, by pressing one of two buttons. They found that people were faster to respond to a letter probe if the meaning of the cue word signified a direction consistent with the location of the letter. So, if the cue word was *hat*, people would respond to the letters faster if they were on the top of the screen rather than the bottom. Similarly, if the word was *boot*, the opposite was true.

We also orient toward things when something *unexpected* occurs: the unexpected sound in the quiet library, sudden and unexpected movement (Abrams &

A clearer picture of the image in Figure 4-1 in case you had trouble identifying the object.

Christ, 2003; Franconeri & Simons, 2003), the abrupt onset of a new object (Davoli, Suszko, & Abrams, 2007; Yantis & Jonides, 1984), a change in the color of an object (Lu & Zhou, 2005), an animate object moving (Pratt, Radulescu, Guo, & Abrams, 2010), the change in pitch in a professor's voice during a lecture, maybe the word *different* in italics in a textbook paragraph. Notice that what seems to capture attention is the occurrence of something *unexpected*, not just something *new* (Vachon, Hughes, & Jones, 2012). Thus, not all visual changes capture attention equally. Moreover, visual offsets, when something suddenly disappears from a scene, are much less likely to capture attention than a visual onset, something suddenly appearing (e.g., Cole & Kuhn, 2010).

Orienting focuses us so that we can devote deliberate attention to the stimulus if warranted; Cowan (1995) called these *voluntary attentive processes*. In this sense, orienting is a preparatory response, one that prepares the system for further voluntary processing. In visual attention, fMRI (functional magnetic resonance imaging) neurological scanning has shown that the attention capture process itself seems to involve retinotopic (specific places on the retina in your eye) portions of the occipital lobe, the part of the brain dedicated to vision. This is in contrast to more controlled aspects of attention that involve portions of the dorsal parietal and frontal cortex, further down the stream of neural activity in the brain (Serences et al., 2005; Yantis, 2008).

If the stimulus that triggers an orienting reflex occurs over and over again, however, it is no longer novel or different; now it has become part of the normal, unchanging background. The process of **habituation** begins to take over, *a gradual reduction of the orienting response back to baseline.* For example, if the unexpected noise in the quiet library is the ventilation fan coming on, you first notice it but then grow accustomed to it. You have oriented to it, and then that response habituates, to the point that you will probably orient again when the fan *stops* running. When the constant noise stops, *that* is a change that triggers the orienting response.

Spotlight Attention and Visual Search

The last sense of *attention* to be considered among the input attentional processes is a kind of visual attention. It is related to perceptual space, that is, the spatial arrangement of stimuli in your visual field and the way you search that space. It is different from the orienting response in that there is no necessary movement of the eyes or head, although there is a strong correlation with eye movements (researchers often exploit this relationship to have a general idea of where attention is directed, using eye-tracking devices). Instead, there is a mental shift of attentional focus, as if a spotlight beam were focused on a region of visual space, enabling you to pick up information in that space more easily (think of a "Superman beam").

A large amount of work on this kind of visual attention has been reported, including some work that has found regions of the brain that seem to be involved in focused, visual attention.

THE SPOTLIGHT OF VISUAL ATTENTION   Consider Figure 4-2, which depicts three kinds of displays in Posner's spatial cuing task (Posner, Nissen, & Ogden, 1978; Posner, Snyder, & Davidson, 1980). People in this task are first asked to fixate the

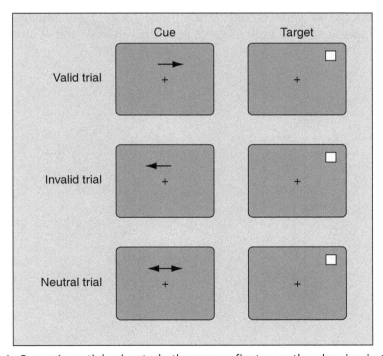

FIGURE 4-2   In Posner's spatial cuing task, the person fixates on the plus sign in the center of the screen, then sees an arrow pointing left or right or a two-headed arrow. For the targets shown in the figure, with a target appearing on the right, the right-pointing arrow is a valid cue, the left-pointing arrow an invalid cue, and the two-headed arrow a neutral cue. In this experiment, one-headed arrow cues were valid on 80% of the trials.

centered plus sign on the display, are then shown a directional cue, and finally see a simple target (the thing they are supposed to respond to). The task had people press a button when they detected the target. For 80% of the cued trials, the arrow pointed to the direction where the target actually did appear 1 second later. On the remaining 20% of the cued trials, however, the cue was invalid: It pointed to the wrong side. Neutral trials provided an uninformative cue, a two-headed arrow indicating that the target would appear equally often on the left or right. Throughout the task, people were required to maintain fixation on the plus sign. That is, they could shift only their *mental* attention to the space where they thought the target might appear, but were not allowed to move their eyes.

The results, shown in Figure 4-3, were very clear. When people shifted their visual attention to the correct area (the Valid 80% point in the figure), response time (RT) to detect the target was significantly faster than the neutral, uncued condition. This speedup is known as a **benefit or facilitation**, *a faster-than-baseline response resulting from useful advance information.* When the target appeared in the unexpected location, however, there was a significant **cost**, *a response slower than baseline because of a misleading cue.* Interestingly, further analysis suggested that the cost of having directed their attention to the wrong place resulted from a three-part process: (a) disengaging attention from its current focus, (b) moving the attentional spotlight to the target's true location, then (c) engaging attention at that new location.

Posner et al. (1980) concluded from this and related experiments that the attentional focus being switched was a cognitive phenomenon; it was not tied to eye movements but to an internal, mental mechanism. They suggested that attention is like a spotlight that highlights objects and events that it shines on. Thus,

FIGURE 4-3
Consider the response time (RT) points in the neutral condition to be baseline performance on detecting targets. When a valid cue was presented, there was a reduction in RT for targets in both the left and right visual fields ("Valid 80%"). When the cue was invalid, there was a slow-down in detecting the target in both visual fields ("Invalid 20%").

Source: From Posner, Snyder, & Davidson (1980).

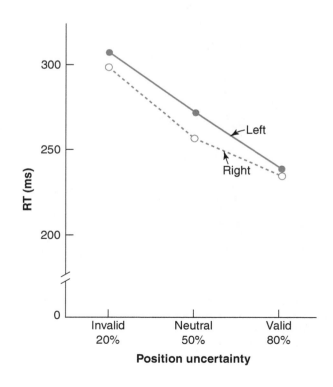

spotlight attention is *the mental attention-focusing mechanism that prepares you to encode stimulus information.* Furthermore, Posner et al. suggested that this shift in attention is essentially the same as the redirection of attention in the orienting reflex, with one big difference: It is voluntary. Therefore, it can happen before a stimulus occurs and can be triggered by cognitive factors such as expectations.

As Cave and Bichot (1999) pointed out, countless studies of visual attention, many of them inspired by Posner's work, have adopted the spotlight metaphor. Much of that work has explored the characteristics and limits of visual attention, attempting to evaluate how useful the metaphor is. The evidence suggests that the mental spotlight does not sweep, enhancing the intermediate locations along the way, but instead it jumps (much as the saccade does). On the other hand, there is also supportive evidence for the similarity between a real spotlight and spotlight attention. For example, it appears that the size of the spotlight beam can be altered, depending on circumstances (see Cave & Bichot, 1999, for an extensive review).

VISUAL SEARCH   Look at Figure 4-4, and do these quick demonstrations. In the first panel, search for *either* a letter *T* or a boldface letter; in the other two panels, search for a boldface *T*. As you did these visual searches, you surely noticed that searching for *T* in the first panel was stunningly simple; it hardly seemed like a search, did it? Instead, didn't the *T* just "pop out" at you? In contrast, searching for *T* in the middle panel probably was a slow process, and finding it in the last panel probably took even longer. A classic, everyday example of difficult visual search can be found in the *Where's Waldo?* children's books.

A series of studies by Treisman and her associates (Treisman, 1982, 1988, 1991; Treisman & Gelade, 1980) examined visual search. Typically, people were told to search a visual display for either of two simple features (e.g., letter *S* or a blue letter) or a conjunction of two features (e.g., a green *T*). The search for a simple feature was called a **feature search**: People responded "yes" when they detected the presence of either of the specified features, either a letter *S* or a blue letter. In the **conjunction search** condition, they had to search for the combination of two features, *T* and the color green. In the searches you did, the first were feature searches, and the last panel illustrated a conjunction search (the target had to be both boldfaced and a *T*).

In the typical result (Treisman & Gelade, 1980, Experiment 1), people could search rapidly for an item identified by the presence of a unique feature. It made little or no difference whether they searched through a small or a large display; for

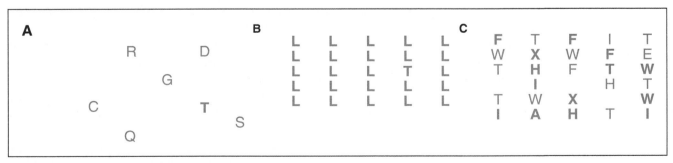

FIGURE 4-4   In panel **A**, search either for a capital *T* or a boldface letter. In panels **B** and **C**, search for a boldface capital *T*.

FIGURE 4-5 Search times when targets were of a specified color or shape. The dashed lines are for the disjunction search conditions (e.g., search for either a capital *T* or a boldface letter). The solid lines show search times for the conjunction condition (e.g., search for a boldface *T*). The important result is that disjunctive search times did not increase as the display size grew larger, but the conjunction search times did.

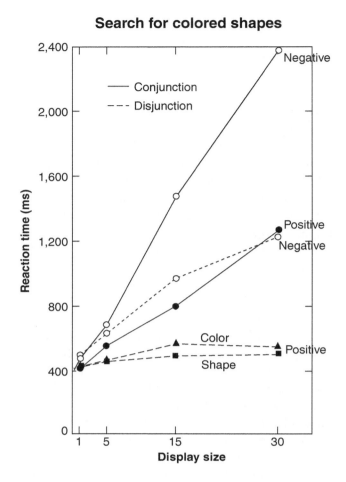

instance, people were able to search through as few as 5 items or as many as 30 in about the same amount of time, approximately 500 ms. The target object just seemed to "pop out" of the display, and so this is called a **pop-out effect**. Because there was no increase in RT across the display sizes, Treisman and Gelade concluded that visual search for a dimension such as shape or color occurs in parallel across the entire region of visual attention. Such a search must be largely automatic and must represent very early visual processing. In the results, shown in Figure 4-5, this is the flat, low function of the graph.

But when people had to do a conjunction search, such as a green *T*, they took more time, up to 2,400 ms, as more and more distractors filled the display (distractors for both conditions were brown *T*s and green *X*s). Such conjunction search seems a more serial, one-by-one process and a far more conscious, deliberate act. This is the steeply increasing function in Figure 4-5.

Because a visual search can be complex, people need a way to keep track of what they have already checked and what they have not. A big problem would occur if a person kept checking the same, useless items over and over again, and never checking others. To help people from returning to inappropriate locations, there is a special attention process. This is called **inhibition of return** (Klein, 2000; Posner & Cohen, 1984), in which *recently checked locations are mentally*

PROVE IT
The Visual Search Task

Here we have a fairly simple task to do with your friends and a stopwatch that illustrates the difference between feature and conjunction searches in visual attention. Using two different colors of marker pens, make up a few sheets of paper, or some 4 × 6 index cards, on which you draw letters in two distinct colors, say red and green. For simplicity's sake, let's restrict ourselves to Xs and Ts. In all cases, we'll have your participants search for a *green T.*

For the *feature* search trials, you will have a number of red Xs and Ts all over the paper. On the "yes" sheets, you'll put a green T in one spot on the paper; on the "no" sheets, you'll just have red Xs and Ts. Make a separate sheet, one for "yes" trials and one for "no" trials, with 4 Xs and Ts, then do the same for 6 Xs and Ts, then 8, 10, and 12 (don't forget to go back and put the green T in for your "yes" trials). For the *conjunction* trials, in addition to the green T for the "yes" sheets, you'll put green Xs and red Ts on the sheets; as before, you'll also have "no" sheets that only have green Xs and red Ts.

Tell your participants that the task is to find the green T as fast as possible. When they find the green T, have them raise their right hand. However, if they don't think the green T is there, have them raise their left hand. Time people (the second hand/display on your watch is fine) each time. The standard result is that the feature search items should show a fairly constant retrieval rate regardless of the number of distractors. This is because the target letter should pop out under these circumstances. In comparison, for the conjunction search items should be an average increase in response time as the number of distractors increases.

---

marked by attention as places that the search would not return to. This process appears to be guided by the operations of the superior colliculus (a.k.a. the tectum) and the parietal lobe (Klein, 2000; Vivas, Humphreys, & Fuentes, 2006), consistent with the idea that inhibition of return is an important visual process (involving the superior colliculus) as well as knowledge of where things are in space, the "where" neural pathway (involving the parietal lobe). Note that when people are not searching for something, but are simply scanning or memorizing a picture, the opposite is shown, with people being *more* likely to return to a previously fixated location—a facilitation of return (Dodd, Van der Stigchel, & Hollingworth, 2009).

In some sense, the locations are inhibited from or kept out of the search pattern. These items were highly activated in cognition because they were attended to, and what inhibition of return does is turn this activation down. So, you only continue to search through those locations that are likely to still have the item you're looking for. A consequence of this is that people are slower to respond to events (such as a change in brightness) in locations that have recently been searched, and inhibited, relative to other locations. It's similar to searching for a friend at the airport when many people are arriving from many different flights. You search visually through the faces as they come out of security, but you don't keep scanning those same faces over and over again. What inhibition of return does is keep you from returning to those already scanned faces, having your visual search move on to other faces, ideally allowing you to find your friend faster.

Although this description of visual search places a heavy emphasis on the influence of visual features, and the bottom-up processes that can use such features, most of our real-world, everyday searching is not this difficult. For example, when you walk into a new kitchen and are looking for the sink, not only do you scan the room for objects with sinklike features, but you also draw on your prior knowledge of how things are organized in space (Huang & Grossberg, 2010). The sink is more likely to be on an outside wall, perhaps by a window, than somewhere else. Thus, this is a top-down influence of *what* an object is on the *where* tracking system involved in visual search. Note, also, that attention can be influenced by embodied characteristics. For example, people find it easier to spot a target during visual search when their hands are placed near the display as compared to when they are further away (Davoli, Brockmole, & Goujon, 2012). The idea is that where our hands are correspond to locations in space that can be easily manipulated, as so is a more likely place for attention to be directed to, facilitating even tasks that do not require manipulating the environment, such as visual search.

Contrasting Input and Controlled Attention

Treisman's two conditions provide clear evidence of both a very quick, automatic attentional process—essentially the capture of attention due to "pop-out"—and a much slower, more deliberate attention, the type used for the conjunction search. In line with Johnston, McCann, and Remington's (1995) suggestion, we use the term *input attention* for the fast, automatic process of attention, the type of process we have been talking about in this section. The slower one, in Johnston et al.'s terms, is *controlled attention,* to which we turn in a moment. It is important to note that research has suggested that these two forms of attention operate with some degree of independence (Berger, Henik, & Rafal, 2005).

Consider the early, rapid stages of feature detection as relying on spotlight attention (Posner & Cohen, 1984). The spotlight is directed toward a visual display and enhances the detection of objects and events within it (Kanwisher & Driver, 1992). It provides the encoding route into the visual system. It is this attentional focus mechanism that provides early, extremely rapid feature detection for the ensuing process of pattern recognition. It is especially visual; for instance, it has been called posterior attention because the earliest stages of visual perception occur in the posterior region of the brain, in the occipital lobe, as illustrated in Figure 4-6 (see also the inside front cover illustration of neural activity in the occipital lobe when a visual stimulus is presented), as well as involving the superior colliculus, a midbrain structure (Berger et al., 2005).

The spotlight attention we are talking about—and we presume there is an equivalent mechanism for other senses—appears to be rapid, automatic, and perceptual. It is distinguished from the slower, controlled or conscious attention process that matches the more ordinary connotation of the term *attention.* The "regular" kind is the conscious attention that we have loosely equated with awareness. Based on some neurophysiological evidence, we might even call this frontal or anterior attention because activity in the frontal regions of the brain seems to accompany elements of conscious awareness, such as awareness of the meaning of a word (Posner et al., 1992).

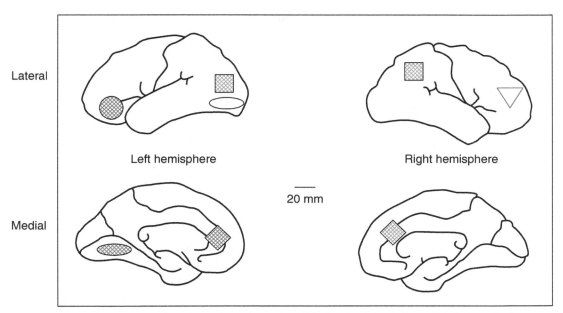

FIGURE 4-6 The top two drawings show lateral (side) views of the left and right hemispheres of the brain, and the bottom two show medial views, as if the hemispheres had been split down the center from front to back, showing inner portions of the cortex. The geometric shapes refer to different regions of the brain that are involved in attention; squares denote regions involved in the attentional network, the triangle denotes a region related to vigilance, and the diamond denotes a part of the anterior attentional network; the circle and oval denote word processing regions for semantic associates and visual word forms, respectively.

Source: From Solso (1998).

Conscious or controlled attention prepares us to respond in a deliberate way to the environment. It is slower, operates in a more serial fashion, and is especially influenced by conceptually driven processes. Spotlight attention, however, is a basic, rapid attentional mechanism that seems to operate in parallel across the visual field, in a highly automatic fashion. It is especially data driven, funneling aspects of the environment into the cognitive system. Conscious attention then enables us to respond to that environment.

Hemineglect: An Attention Deficit

In many cases, cognitive science has gained insight into a process when there has been some disruption to the system, as can happen with brain damage. The study of attention is no exception. Go back to the beginning of the chapter and reread the quotation from Banich (1997) about Bill. Bill suffers from *hemineglect,* a syndrome that leads to such behavior as brushing only the teeth on his right, washing only his right arm, and shaving only the right side of his face. To many people, this phenomenon is almost too bizarre to believe, maybe because the processes of mental attention have always been so closely tied to perception and voluntary movement and so automatic that we think they are indivisible parts of the same process. Look at yourself in a mirror, then look at the left side of your face—no problem, you merely move your eyes, shift your direction of gaze, and look at it. If I ask you to stare straight ahead and then attend to something in your left field of vision, say the letter X on a computer screen, your normal response is to shift your eyes toward the left and focus on the target. You simply look at the X and pay attention to it. You can even shift your mental attention to the left without moving your eyes.

The syndrome known as **hemineglect** (or hemi-inattention) is a disruption in the ability to refocus your attention to one side of your face or the other, to the X on the left of the computer screen. It is a *disruption or decreased ability to attend to something in the (often) left field of vision. Hemi* means "half," and *neglect* mean "to ignore" or "to fail to perceive." Thus, hemineglect is a disorder of attention in which one half of the perceptual world is neglected to some degree and cannot be attended to as completely or accurately as normal. Some form of hemineglect is often observed in stroke victims, even if it is in a more limited and temporary form. Very often, the neglect is of the left visual field, for stimuli to the left of the current fixation, the current focus of attention. And because of the principle of contralaterality, it is not surprising that the brain damage leading to hemineglect is often in the right hemisphere, in particular, certain regions of the right parietal lobe (see Intriligator & Cavanagh, 2001, for evidence that localizes selective attention in the parietal lobe).

Here are the facts (see Banich, 1997, or Rafal, 1997, for complete treatments). A patient with hemineglect cannot voluntarily direct attention to half of the perceptual world, whether the to-be-perceived stimulus is visual, auditory, or any other type of sensation. In some cases, the neglect is nearly total, as if half of the perceptual world has simply vanished, is simply not there in any normal sense of the word. In other cases, the neglect is partial, so for such people it is more accurate to say that they are *less able* to redirect their attention than are normal people. In either case, there is a disruption in the ability to control attention. Note that this is not a case of sensory damage like blindness or deafness. The patient with hemineglect receives input from both sides of the body and can make voluntary muscle movements on both sides. And in careful testing situations, such patients can also respond to stimuli in the neglected field. But somehow, the deliberate devotion of controlled attention to one side is deficient.

Bisiach and Luzatti (1978) present a compelling description of hemineglect. The afflicted individuals were from Milan, Italy, which they were quite familiar with before their brain damage. This study focused on the main piazza in town, a broad open square with buildings and shops along the sides and a large cathedral at one end. These patients were asked to imagine themselves standing at one end of the piazza, facing the cathedral, and to describe what they could see. They uniformly described only the buildings and shops on the right side of the piazza. When asked to imagine themselves standing on the steps of the cathedral, facing back the opposite way, they once again described what was on their right side. From this second view, of course, what they described was exactly what they had omitted from their earlier descriptions. Likewise, they now omitted what they had described earlier.

Critically important here is the observation that these reports, based on memory, were exactly the kind of reports patients with hemineglect give when actually viewing a scene; if these patients had been taken to the piazza, they probably would have seen and described it the same way as they did from memory. (For a

Model   Patient's copy

FIGURE 4-7
Drawings copied by a patient with contralateral neglect.

Source: From F. E. Bloom & A. Lazerson. *Brain, Mind, and Behavior,* 2nd ed. New York: W. H. Freeman and Co., p. 300. Copyright © 1988. Reprinted with permission of W. H. Freeman and Co.

similar account, see "Eyes Right!" in Sacks, 1970; the patient there eats the right half of everything on her dinner plate, then complains about not getting enough food.) Figure 4-7 shows some drawings made by patients with hemineglect. Here, patients were asked to copy drawings or to draw from memory, but the nature of their drawings was no different in either case. These drawings show a dramatic neglect for the left-hand sides of objects: a flower with no petals on the left, a clock face with no numbers on the left. In the standard line bisection task ("draw a slash through the middle of a horizontal line"), hemineglect patients position the slash too far to the right, as if bisecting only the right half of the entire horizontal line.

A careful analysis of the disruptions seen in patients with hemineglect has been provided by Duncan et al. (1999) in the context of the Theory of Visual Attention (Bundesen, 1990). Duncan et al. noted that several important advances in understanding hemineglect have been made, especially when the patients are tested with some standardized cognitive tasks such as Posner's spatial cuing task, which you read about earlier. For example, it turns out that patients with hemineglect often can attend to stimuli in the neglected field, but only if nothing else is displayed that might attract their attention. That is, they can detect a simple stimulus in the left visual field (the field contralateral to their brain damage), even if that is the portion of the world they normally neglect. The ability to detect the same stimulus is dramatically reduced if a stimulus in the right visual field (ipsilateral to their brain damage) is presented at the same time (see Danziger, Kingstone, & Rafal, 1998, for evidence of an orienting response in the neglected field).

This tendency to ignore the contralateral field when a competing stimulus is presented in the ipsilateral field is called *extinction*. It appears to be caused by something like attention capture. When a right-side (ipsilateral) stimulus is presented, it captures the person's attention and prevents attention from being devoted to the left (contralateral). In a sense, then, hemineglect patients may neglect one side only because there is usually something on the other side that captures their attention. In a very real sense, Bill might have been able to focus on shaving the left side of his face if he had not been able to see his right side.

In a way, hemineglect seems to disrupt both input and controlled attention. First, input attention is devoted largely or exclusively to a stimulus in the "good" or preserved field, the ipsilateral field (the term *ipsilesional* is also used, meaning "same side as the brain lesion"). The stimulus in this field captures the patient's input attention. But then it appears that hemineglect patients cannot disengage attention from that ipsilateral stimulus. Because attention toward the right cannot be disengaged, they cannot shift their attention voluntarily to the left. Thus, capture of attention on one side has disrupted a shift of controlled attention toward the other side.

In their analysis, Duncan et al. (1999) noted that their patients with hemineglect showed standard deficits in attention to the contralateral side but also some rather strong bilateral deficits related to attentional capacity; in other words, there were accuracy deficits on the neglected side but capacity difficulties on both sides. Interestingly, there was little evidence that the conceptually driven aspects of their attention were affected. It may be some time before such results and their implications for the normal processes of attention are fully understood. But even now, it is clear that such fractionation of performance—some abilities preserved, some disrupted—will be important in our further understanding of attention (for a neural net modeling approach to hemineglect, see Monaghan & Shillcock, 2004).

Section Summary

- Attention is a pervasive and complex topic, with meanings and connotations ranging from alertness and arousal up through the notions of automatic and conscious processing. Attention can be thought of as a mental process or mechanism or as a limited mental resource.
- Three basic senses of the term *attention* refer to alertness and arousal, the orienting reflex, and the spotlight of attention. These correspond to input attention, a fast process involved in encoding environmental stimuli into the mental system. Interestingly, in vision, the mental spotlight of attention can be shifted without any movement of the eyes, confirming the mental rather than perceptual nature of attention.
- A disorder known as hemineglect shows how attention can be affected by brain damage, thus informing us about normal attention. In hemineglect, a

patient is unable to direct attention voluntarily to one side of space, so he or she neglects stimuli presented in that side. The evidence suggests that this arises from an inability to disengage attention from a stimulus on the non-neglected side, hence disrupting the process of shifting attention to the opposite side.

CONTROLLED, VOLUNTARY ATTENTION

We turn now to several senses of the term *attention* that point to the controlled, voluntary nature of attention. **Controlled attention**, in contrast to what you've just been studying, refers to *a deliberate, voluntary allocation of mental effort or concentration. You* decide to pay attention to this stimulus and ignore others, and paying attention this way involves effort.

Cognitive psychology has always been intrigued by the fact that at any moment, scores of different sensory messages are impinging on us. We can't attend to all of them (we would be overwhelmed instantly), nor can we afford for our attention to be captured by one, then another, then another of the multiple sensory inputs (we would lose all coherence, all continuity). Therefore, it makes sense to ask questions about **selective attention**, *the ability to attend to one source of information while ignoring other ongoing stimuli around us.* How do we do this? How do you screen out the surrounding noises to focus on just one? How can you listen covertly to the person on your right, who is gossiping about someone you know, while overtly pretending to listen to a conversational partner on your left? (And how did you notice in the first place that the person on your right was gossiping?) Somewhat the converse of selective attention is the topic of divided attention: How do we divide or share our attentional capacity across more than one source of information at a time, and how much information are we picking up from the several sources?

Dangerously divided attention.

In a classroom situation, students must constantly filter out the unimportant from the important details. This is an example of selective attention in auditory perception.

Simulate
Selective Attention in
MyPsychLab

A modern example of how these questions involve real-world problems is the issue of whether we can really talk (or text message) on a cell phone and drive at the same time, dividing our attention between two demanding tasks (Kunar, Carter, Cohen, & Horowitz, 2008; Spence & Read, 2003; Strayer & Johnston, 2001). In short, the general answer is, "No, we really can't." Talking on the cell phone can lead to *inattention blindness*, in which people fail to attend to or process information about traffic, even if they are looking directly at it. This is equally true for both handheld and hands-free cell phone conversations, but not for listening to the radio or music (Strayer & Drews, 2007). This is because you are actively involved in cell phone conversations, but not in what is going on over the radio. In these studies, people drive a simulator while having their eye movements monitored (so the experimenter knows what they are looking at and for how long). Under these circumstances, people who are having phone conversations are less likely to recognize road signs or other important traffic events, even when they look directly at them. This is even revealed in electroencephalographic (EEG) recordings of drivers' brains, not just what they consciously report. What is happening is that when you are actively involved and interacting in a conversation, your limited-capacity attention is drawn away from your immediate environment. You have less attention to devote to driving, so as a consequence, your driving suffers and becomes more dangerous. At a more general level, the question is, when do we start reaching the limits of our attentional capacity?

Selective Attention and the Cocktail Party Effect

When there are many stimuli or events around you, you may try to focus on just one. The ones you are trying to ignore are distractions that must be excluded. *The mental process of eliminating those distractions* is called **filtering** or **selecting**.

Some aspect of attention seems to filter out unwanted, extraneous sources of information so we can select the one source we want to attend.

The process of selective attention seems straightforward in vision: You move your eyes, thereby selecting what you attend to. As you just saw, however, attention is separate from eye movements: You can shift your attention even without eye movements. But in hearing, attention has no outward, behavioral component analogous to eye movements, so cognitive psychology has always realized that selective attention in hearing was thoroughly cognitive. This accounts for the heavy investment in filter theories of auditory perception. If we cannot avoid hearing something, we then must select among the stimuli by some mental process, filtering out the unimportant and attending to the important.

DUAL TASK OR DUAL MESSAGE PROCEDURES A general characteristic of many attention experiments involves the procedure of *overload*. Briefly, we can overload a sensory system by presenting more information than it can handle at once and then test accuracy for some part of the information. This has usually involved a **dual task procedure**. *Two tasks are presented such that one task captures attention as completely as possible.* Because attentional resources are consumed by the primary task, there are few if any resources left over for attention to the other tasks. By varying the characteristics or content of the messages, we can make the listener's job easier or harder. For instance, paying attention to a message spoken in one ear while trying to ignore the other ear's message is more difficult when both messages are spoken by the same person.

Going a step further, when we examine performance to the attended task, we can ask about the accuracy with which a message is perceived and about the degree of interference caused by a second message. We can also look at accuracy for information that was not in the primary message, the unattended message in the other ear. If there is any evidence of remembering the unattended message, or even some of its features, we can discuss how unattended information is processed and registered in memory.

SHADOWING EXPERIMENTS Some of the earliest cognitive research on auditory selective attention was done by E. Colin Cherry (1953; Cherry & Taylor, 1954). Cherry was interested in speech recognition and attention. Cherry characterized his research procedures, and for that matter the question he was asking, as the cocktail party problem (although you can think of it as a dorm party problem): How do we pay attention to and recognize what one person is saying when we are surrounded by other spoken messages? To simulate this real-world situation in the laboratory, Cherry (see also Broadbent, 1952) devised the workhorse task of auditory perception research, the **shadowing task**. In this task, Cherry recorded spoken messages of different sorts, then played them to a person who was wearing headphones. The task was to "shadow" the message coming into the right ear, that is, *to repeat the message out loud as soon as it was heard.* In most of the experiments, people were also told to ignore the other message, the one coming to the left ear. (It makes no difference which ear is shadowed or ignored. For simplicity, assume that the right ear gets the to-be-shadowed attended message and the left ear gets the unattended message.)

Although this sounds simple, it takes a surprising amount of attention and concentration to shadow a message accurately. People were quite accurate in producing "shadows," although they spoke in a monotone, with little intonational stress, and lagged behind the message by a second or so. Interestingly, people seem unaware of the strangeness of their spoken shadows and usually cannot remember much of the content of the shadowed message once the task is over.

This task consumed enough attention to leave little, if any, for other purposes. In a typical session, the recording began with a continuous coherent message presented to the right (attended) ear and another coherent message to the left (unattended ear). Once the person began to shadow, the message in the left ear was changed. After some amount of time, people were interrupted and asked what, if anything, they could report about the unattended message. They could report accurately on a variety of physical characteristics, such as if it changed from human speech to a tone. They also usually detected a change from a male to a female voice. However, when the unattended message was changed to reversed speech, only a few people noticed "something queer about it." Changes from English to a different language generally went unnoticed, and, overall, people were unable to identify words or phrases in the unattended message. In a dramatic confirmation of this last result, Moray (1959) found that even a word presented 35 times in the unattended message was never recalled (see also Wood & Cowan, 1995b).

Selection Models

It appears that a physical difference between the messages permits people to distinguish between them and eases the job of selectively attending to the target task (Johnston & Heinz, 1978). Investigators routinely call this early selection. This refers to the some of the earliest phases of perception, an acoustic analysis based on physical features of the message. The evidence is that people can select a message based on sensory information, such as loudness, location of the sound source, or pitch (Egan, Carterette, & Thwing, 1954; Spieth, Curtis, & Webster, 1954; Wood & Cowan, 1995a).

EARLY SELECTION THEORY   This evidence, indicating that people could somehow tune their attention to one message over the other, prompted Donald Broadbent (1958) to propose an **early selection theory** of attention. In this view, attention acts as a selective filter, as shown in Figure 4-8. Regardless of how many competing channels or messages are coming in, the filter can be tuned, or switched, to any one of them, based on characteristics such as loudness or pitch. Note that only one message can pass through the filter at a time. In other words, despite the many incoming signals, only one message can be sent through the filter into the "limited-capacity decision channel" (essentially short-term memory). Only the information on the attended, "passed along" message affects performance, in Broadbent's view, because only it gets past the filtering mechanism.

It was soon realized that the filter idea had serious problems. For one, intuition tells us that we often notice information from a message we are not attending, as when you hear your name in a crowded, noisy place. Moray (1959) found evidence for this: Although people did not recall a word presented 35 times to the

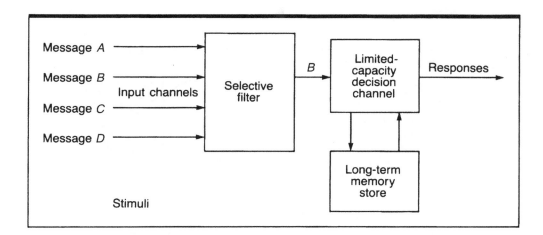

FIGURE 4-8
Broadbent's filter theory of selective attention. Four messages are presented, yet only one is selected and passed to the limited-capacity decision mechanism.

Source: Adapted from Broadbent (1958).

unattended ear, a third of the people heard their own name (see Wood & Cowan, 1995b, for a recent replication of this effect). Not everyone detects their name easily. Conway, Cowan, and Bunting (2001) found that people with less cognitive capacity (a.k.a. working memory; see Chapter 5) were more likely to detect their name. In other words, people who were less able to focus on a task, such as remembering a list of letters, appear to be more prone to distraction and are more likely to process and detect information that they are supposed to ignore, such as information on an unattended channel in this task.

More generally, these findings have implications about the nature of attention. If Broadbent's early filter theory were correct, then only the attended and passed-along information should be available, where attention is directed by physical cues. Yet clear evidence is available that unattended information can somehow slip past the filter (but see Lachter, Forster, & Ruthruff, 2004, who argue that some small amount of attention had been devoted to the "unattended" stimuli).

LATE SELECTION THEORY Treisman (1960, 1964) did a series of studies to explore this slippage more closely. She used the standard shadowing task but varied the nature of the unattended message across a more subtle range of differences. She first replicated Cherry's findings that selective attention was easy when physical differences existed. Then she turned to the situation in which physical differences were absent—both messages were recorded by the same speaker. Because the same pitch, intonation, stress, and so on were in both messages, early selection should not be possible. Yet she found that people could shadow accurately. The basis for the selection was *message content,* what the message was *about* rather than what it sounded like. In this situation, the grammatical and semantic features are the basis for selection (*semantic* refers to meaning). Because attentional selection occurs after all the initial processing of the message is done, this is called *late selection*. It is later in the stream of processing than early selection based on sensory features, yet before the moment of having to respond aloud with the shadowed speech.

To show the power of late selection, Treisman did a study now considered a classic (1960); the setup is depicted in Figure 4-9. Treisman arranged the recording

FIGURE 4-9 The
shadowing task.
Two messages
are played
simultaneously
into different ears;
then, at the slash,
the ear-of-arrival is
switched for the
two messages.

Source: Adapted from
Lindsay & Norman
(1977).

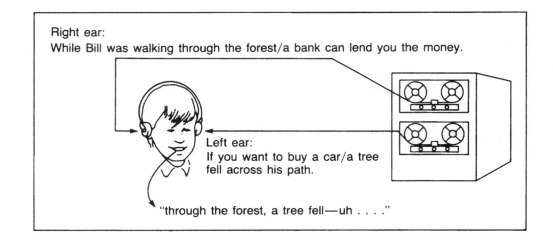

Right ear:
While Bill was walking through the forest/a bank can lend you the money.

Left ear:
If you want to buy a car/a tree fell across his path.

"through the forest, a tree fell—uh . . . ."

so that the coherent message being shadowed was unexpectedly shifted to the unattended channel. That is, the sentence that was being said switched from the right to the left ear. Despite the high degree of practice and concentration needed, people routinely switched to the unattended message, although they did not continue to shadow the "wrong" ear for long. Clearly, there must be some processing of the unattended message. Semantic elements of the unattended channel must be receiving some analysis or there would be no basis for preferring it when the sentences switched ears.

Based on such results, Treisman claimed that all incoming messages receive some amount of low-level analysis. When the unattended messages yield no useful or important information, they are attenuated; they are reduced not in their volume or physical characteristics but in their informational importance to ongoing processing. In the process of shadowing, we arrive at an identification of the words and phrases on the attended message.

Treisman (1965) felt that it was during this process of semantic analysis that we make our selection among messages, selection at a "late" stage. This permits attention to be affected by the semantic aspects of the message—that is, a top-down effect. A more extreme view, by Deutsch and Deutsch (1963), claimed that selection takes place only after *all* messages have received full acoustic and semantic analysis (i.e., just before the response stage).

So the evidence is that quite a bit of information is getting into cognition: the meaning of the words on the unattended channel, for example, in Treisman's study (1960; see also Lewis, 1970; Carr, McCauley, Sperber, & Parmalee, 1982, found comparable results for visual stimuli). Intrusion of the word *tree* into the shadow, as shown in Figure 4-9, makes sense only if *tree* has been recognized as related to the forest theme of the shadowed message, an effect that implies some rapid process of accessing the meanings of words. More recent work has shown that information that is not actively attended, and subject to inattention blindness, is processed if it is consistent with our goals and intentions (Koivisto & Revonsuo, 2007; Marsh, Cook, Meeks, Clark-Foos, & Hicks, 2007; Most, Scholl, Clifford, & Simons, 2005). In all of the cases in which unattended information was processed, it was consistent with some enduring or temporal goal a person had, such as hearing their own name, completing the idea conveyed by a sentence, or whatever may be satisfying a person's goals at the time. This is why when you are hungry, images of food are so hard to ignore, even if you are trying to concentrate on something else.

So, on the one hand, it seems that people use attention by means of an early filter based on physical qualities, such as spatial location or loudness. On the other hand, it also seems that people use attention by means of a later filter that relies on semantic meaning. Which of these is correct? There seems to be evidence for both. Some researchers, such as Lavie (2010), have suggested that an early attention filter is more likely to be used when there is a lot of perceptual information that needs to be sorted through, as in most shadowing situations, leading attention to select information based on physical features and qualities, if possible. However, a later filter is more likely to be used when attention is not being overly taxed, leading it to select information based on meaning.

INHIBITION AND NEGATIVE PRIMING   Most of the discussion of attention to this point has focused on what gets attended to and activated in cognition, as well as some filter to keep irrelevant information from entering the stream of processing. At this point, we would like to discuss a cognitive mechanism that has been proposed that goes beyond the idea of a filter that keeps out irrelevant information and only allows selected information to be processed further. This is the cognitive attention mechanism of **inhibition**. Inhibition is thought to *actively suppress mental representations of salient but irrelevant information so that the information's activation level is reduced, perhaps below the resting baseline level.* You encountered an example of this already, when we discussed inhibition of return. In this section we look further at how inhibition may be operating to help people select relevant information and filter out irrelevant information.

In order for inhibition to operate, there needs to be a salient source of interfering and irrelevant information. That is, the irrelevant information needs to be strong and wrong. Under those circumstances, inhibition will be involved. A classic demonstration of this was provided in a study by Tipper (1985). In this study, people were presented with a series of pairs of line drawings of objects, with one object presented in green and the other in red. The task was to name the red object as quickly as possible. The important condition here involved target trials on which the red object had appeared in green on the previous trial (called the *prime* trial). What was observed was that people were slower to respond to the target trials (red object) when they had been preceded by the to-be-ignored distractor primes (same object in green) compared to control trials where the ignored object on the prime trial was some other object. This response time slow-down is called **negative priming** (Neill, 1977; Tipper, 1985).

The explanation for this is that when people are looking at the display, in addition to their processing of the red object, there is some activation and processing of the green object as well, because people are looking directly at it. That is, the mental representation of the object becomes activated. However, because the identity of this object is irrelevant to the task—it was green, so it didn't need to be named—attention actively inhibited and suppressed the object's representation. Then, when the person needed this information on the next trial (because it was not the red object), it took longer to activate and use because it had been inhibited.

So the inhibition process slowed down the person's response time (however, see Mayr & Buchner, 2006; and Neill, Valdes, & Terry, 1995; for alternative accounts of negative priming that do not involve an active inhibitory mechanism).

The idea that inhibition is an important part of attention has been extended to many other areas of psychology, particularly those dealing with individual differences. For example, in developmental psychology, attentional inhibition is thought to develop slowly with age (Diamond & Gilbert, 1989), meaning that it is difficult, especially for young children, to maintain focus. In contrast, in older adults there is increased difficulty suppressing irrelevant information (Hasher & Zacks, 1988). Inhibitory problems are also thought be present in schizophrenia (Beech, Powell, McWilliams, & Claridge, 1989), with schizophrenics having trouble keeping unwanted thoughts out of consciousness. In less extreme cases, people who are depressed also have trouble inhibiting irrelevant information (MacQueen, Tipper, Young, Joffe, & Levitt, 2000), leading them to have trouble with focusing on the task at hand.

Section Summary

- Controlled or conscious attention is slower and more voluntary. Selective attention, the ability to focus on one incoming message while ignoring other incoming stimuli, is a complex ability, one investigated since the beginnings of modern cognitive science. The evidence shows that we can select one message, and reject others, based on physical characteristics or on more semantic characteristics. The later the process of selection acts, the more demanding it is of the limited capacity of the attention mechanism.
- We are able to use the attention process of inhibition to keep information that would otherwise be highly active, but is irrelevant, out of the current stream of processing. Keeping inappropriate information out helps us focus on whatever it is that we want to be processing.

ATTENTION AS A MENTAL RESOURCE

An important and far-reaching meaning of the term *attention*—this one may be closer to our everyday meaning—treats attention as mental effort, as a mental resource that fuels cognitive activity. If we selectively attend to one particular message, we are deliberately focusing mental energy on that message, concentrating on it to the exclusion of other messages (clearly what James had in mind in the quotation at the beginning of the chapter). This sense involves the idea that attention is a limited resource, that there is only so much mental fuel to be devoted here or there at any one time (Kahneman, 1973, also suggested that capacity might be elastic, in that increasing the task load might also increase a person's arousal, thus making additional resources available). Approaches that emphasize this meaning of attention are called resource theories.

A corollary to this idea of limited capacity is that attention, loosely speaking, is the same as consciousness or awareness. After all, if you can be consciously aware of only one thing at a time, doesn't that illustrate the limited capacity of attention? Even on a smaller scale, when we process very simple stimuli, there is evidence of this limit to attention. If you are asked to respond to a stimulus and then immediately to a second one, your second response is delayed a bit. This is the **psychological refractory period** or **attentional blink**, which is *a brief slow-down in processing due to having processed another very recent event* (e.g., Barnard, Scott, Taylor, May, & Knightley, 2004; Pashler & Johnson, 1998). The implication is that allocating attention to a first stimulus momentarily deprives you of the attention needed for a second stimulus. However, this blink can be overcome if the target item that occurs during the period of the blink is particularly important, such as predicting what to do on the next trial (Livesey, Harris, & Harris, 2009). Also, the strain on attention can be reduced when people view nature scenes (which only subtly demand attention) as compared to urban scenes (which have many elements that grab our attention), thereby freeing up attention for other tasks (Berman, Jonides, & Kaplan, 2008).

A related idea, which you encountered in the previous section, is that this kind of attention is deliberate, willful, intended—*controlled attention*. *You* decide to pay attention to a signal, or you decide *not* to attend to it. *You* decide to pay attention to the lecture instead of your memory of last night's date, and when you realize your attention has wandered, you redirect it to the lecture, determined *not* to daydream about last night until class is over.

The James quotation at the beginning of this chapter is also interesting because of another insight he had about attention: the idea that we may do more than one thing at a time if the other processes are habitual. When processes are less automatic, however, then attention must oscillate among them if they are done simultaneously, with no consequent gain of time. The key point is the idea of automatic processes—that some mental events can happen without draining the pool of resources: attention. Putting it simply, the germ of James's idea, automaticity, has become central to cognitive psychology's views on attention, pattern recognition, and a host of other topics. Cognitive science has devoted a huge effort to recasting James's ideas about automaticity and attention into more formal, quantifiable concepts.

Automatic and Conscious Processing

In place of the former approach, the limited-capacity attentional mechanism and the need for filtering in selective attention, the current view is that a variety of cognitive processes can be done automatically, *with little or no necessary conscious involvement*. Two such theories of **automaticity** have been proposed, one by Posner and Snyder (1975) and one by Shiffrin and Schneider (1977; Schneider & Shiffrin, 1977). These theories differ in some of their details but are similar in their overall message (see also Logan & Etherton, 1994; for discussions that oppose the idea of mental resources, see Navon, 1984, and Pashler, 1994).

AUTOMATIC PROCESSING Posner and Snyder described three diagnostic criteria for an automatic process, listed in Table 4-2. First, an automatic process occurs without intention; in other words, you can't prevent it from happening, and once it does start, you can't stop it. A compelling example of this is the **Stroop effect** (named after the task described in Stroop, 1935). Words such as *RED GREEN BLUE*

TABLE 4-2   Diagnostic Criteria for Automatic and Conscious Processing

Automatic	Conscious
The process occurs without intention, without a conscious decision.	The process occurs only with intention, with a deliberate decision.
The mental process is not open to conscious awareness or introspection.	The process is open to awareness and introspection.
The process consumes few if any conscious resources; that is, it consumes little if any conscious attention.	The process uses conscious resources; that is, it drains the pool of conscious attentional capacity.
(Informal) The process operates very rapidly, usually within 1 second.	(Informal) The process is slow, taking more than a second or two for completion.

YELLOW were presented visually, written in mismatching colors of ink (e.g., *RED* printed in green ink). When people have to name the ink color, they must ignore the printed words themselves. This leads to tremendous interference, a slowing of the ink color naming, caused by the mismatching information and the contradictory impulses to name the word and the ink color (this is an extremely easy demonstration to do, by the way). This is another case where inhibition is operating during attention, as the highly salient, but irrelevant, semantic meaning of the word must be suppressed. Note that this requires that a person be able to automatically read. People who are illiterate would not show a Stroop effect. That said, it is also the case that poor readers tend to show larger Stroop effects than good readers (Protopapas, Archonti, & Skaloumbakas, 2007), perhaps because better readers have greater executive control over their attentional resources.

In Posner and Snyder's terms, accessing the meaning of the written symbol *RED* is automatic: It requires no intention, it happens whether you want it to or not. In the research that demonstrates automatic access to word meaning, the term we use is **priming**. A word *activates* or primes its meaning in memory and, as a consequence, primes or activates meanings closely associated with it. This priming makes related meanings easier to access: Because of priming, they are boosted up, or given an extra advantage or head start (just as well water is pumped more easily when you prime the pump; see Dunbar & MacLeod, 1984, and MacLeod, 1991, for an explanation of Stroop interference based on priming).

Second, an automatic process does not reveal itself to conscious awareness. You cannot describe the mental processes of looking up the word *RED* in memory. Contrast this with the awareness you had when you answered the Aristotle or division questions in Chapter 1.

The third criterion of automaticity is that an automatic process consumes few if any resources. Such a process should not interfere with other tasks, certainly not those that rely on conscious resources.[1] As an example, walking is so automatic

---

[1]Interference in the Stroop task occurs because the two automatic processes, reading the word and detecting the ink color, compete with one another when it is time to make a response. That is, both processes are trying to output their results to the same speech mechanism, but the responses are incompatible ("red," "green"). When we say that an automatic process generally does not interfere with other processes, it is assumed that we are referring to situations in which the two processes are not competing for the same response mechanism.

PROVE IT
The Stroop Task

An almost fail-safe demonstration of automaticity, in particular the automatic nature of accessing word meaning, involves the Stroop task. With several different colors of marker pens, write a dozen or so color names on a sheet of paper, making sure to use a *different* color of ink than the word signifies (e.g., write *red* in green ink); alternatively, create a deck of 3 × 5 cards, with one word per card. Make a control list of noncolor words (e.g., *hammer, card, wall*), again in colored inks. (And try it yourself right now—name the color of the ink for the words at the top of the color plate, inside the back cover of the book.)

Explain to your participant that the task is to name the *ink color* as rapidly as possible. Time the person (the second hand/display on your watch is more than sufficient; or keep track of naming errors, another way to measure the Stroop interference) on each kind of list. The standard result is that the color word list will require substantially longer for ink color naming than the control list. Other useful control lists are simple blotches of color, to check on the speed of naming the colors, and pseudowords ("manty," "zoople," and the like) written in different ink colors.

According to several studies (e.g., Besner & Stolz, 1999; Manwell, Roberts, & Besner, 2004; Vecera, Behrmann, & McGoldrick, 2000), you should be able to eliminate the Stroop effect by getting people to focus on just *part* of the word or to say the first letter position (this might be easier if you used the 3 × 5 card method) or by printing only one letter in color. This work suggests that reading the whole word is a kind of "default" setting for visual attention, which might be changed depending on the task and instructions, and that our selective attention mechanism can select either whole objects (words) or their parts (letters) as the focus.

Simulate *Stroop Test* in **MyPsychLab**

for adults that it does not interfere with other processes; you can walk and talk at the same time.

A fourth criterion is that automatic processes tend to be fast; as a rule, a response taking no more than 1 second is heavily automatic. (For evidence of slow automatic processing, in a person with brain damage, see Wingfield, Goodglass, & Lindfield, 1997.)

CONTROLLED PROCESSING Let's contrast these diagnostic criteria for automaticity with those for conscious or controlled processing (see Table 4-2). First, controlled processes occur only with intention. They are optional and can be deliberately performed or not. Second, conscious processes are open to awareness; we know they are going on, and, within limits, we know what they consist of. Finally, and of greatest importance, conscious processes use *attention*. They consume some of the limited attentional resources we have.

A demanding controlled process should leave few resources available for a second task that also uses controlled processing. Driving during a hard rainstorm consumes too many resources for you to listen simultaneously to the news on the radio. Alternatively, you may stop walking if you are thinking about something that requires intense thought. Of course, if the second task can be done fairly automatically, then both tasks may proceed without interference; for example, you can easily walk and carry on a casual conversation at the same time.

INTEGRATION WITH CONCEPTUALLY DRIVEN PROCESSES   We can go one step further, integrating this explanation into the idea of conceptually driven processing. Think back to the shadowing research you read about. Attending to one of two incoming messages, and shadowing that message aloud, demands controlled attention. Such a process is under direct control, the person is aware of doing the process, and it consumes most of a person's available mental resources. Presumably, no other conscious process can be done simultaneously with the shadowing task without affecting performance in one or the other task (or both). When the messages are acoustically similar, then people must use differences of content to keep them separate. But by tracking the meaning of a passage, the person's conceptually driven processes come into play in an obvious way. Just as people "restored" the missing sound in "the *eel was on the axle" (Warren & Warren, 1970), the person in the shadowing task "supplies" information about the message from long-term memory. Once you have begun to understand the content of the shadowed message, then your conceptually driven processes assist you by narrowing down the possible alternatives, by suggesting what might come next.

Saying that conceptually driven processes "suggest what might come next" is an informal way of referring to priming. You shadow, "While Bill was walking through the forest." Your semantic analysis primes related information and thereby suggests the likely content of the next clause in the sentence; it is likely to be about trees, and it is unlikely to be about banks and cars. At this instant in time, your "forest" knowledge is primed or activated in memory. It is ready (indeed, almost *eager*) to be perceived because it is so likely to be contained in the rest of the sentence. Then *tree* occurs on the unattended channel. Because we access the meanings of words in an automatic fashion, the extra boost given to *tree* by the priming process pushes it over into the conscious attention mechanism. Suddenly, you're saying "a tree fell across" rather than sticking with the right-ear message. Automatic priming of long-term memory has exerted a top-down influence on the earliest of your cognitive processes, auditory pattern recognition and attention.

THE ROLE OF PRACTICE AND MEMORY   If accessing word meaning is automatic, then you might wonder about some of the shadowing research described earlier in which people failed to detect a word presented 35 times, the reversed speech, and so on. If word meaning access is automatic, why didn't these people recognize the words on the unattended channel? A plausible explanation is practice. It seems likely that the inability to be influenced by the unattended message was caused by a lack of practice on the shadowing task. With greater degrees of practice, even a seemingly complex and attention-consuming task becomes easy, or less demanding of attention's full resources. In fact, Logan and Klapp (1991; see also Zbrodoff & Logan, 1986) suggested that the effect of practice is to store the relevant information in memory; that is, that the necessary precondition for automatic processing is memory. Interestingly, once a process or procedure has become automatic, devoting explicit attention to it can even lead to worse performance (e.g., Beilock & Carr, 2001; Logan & Crump, 2009).

One way that you can sometimes help yourself and avoid the automatic processing of irrelevant material is to close your eyes (Perfect, Andrade, & Eagan, 2011). When you close your eyes, your brain stops automatically processing much of the information in the environment, even if that information is not even visual, such as noises, and your thinking becomes better.

One of the compelling strengths of the Shiffrin and Schneider (1977) theory of automatic and controlled processing is the role they award to old-fashioned, repetitive practice. They asked people to detect one or more targets in successively presented displays (e.g., hold targets *2* and *7* in memory, then search for either of them in successively presented displays). For some people, the targets were consistent across hundreds of trials, always digits, for instance. This was called Consistent Mapping. For people in the Varied Mapping groups, the targets were varied across trials (e.g., *2* and *7* might be targets on one trial, *3* and *B* on another, *M* and *Z* on yet another).

The essential ingredient here is practice. Unlike the Varied Mapping groups, people in the Consistent Mapping groups had enormous amounts of practice with the same targets. People in the Consistent Mapping conditions developed quick automatic detection processes for their unchanging targets. People in the Varied Mapping conditions, however, needed longer search times (Schneider & Shiffrin, 1977). They had not developed automatic detection processes because the stimuli they had to detect kept changing. In short, their search used controlled processing.

The role of practice in automaticity.

A Synthesis for Attention and Automaticity

Attention, in its usual, everyday sense, is equivalent to conscious mental capacity. We can devote attention to only one demanding task at a time or to two somewhat less demanding tasks simultaneously, as long as they do not exceed the total capacity available. This devotion of resources means that few, if any, additional resources are available for other demanding tasks. Alternatively, if a second task is performed largely at the automatic level, then it can occur simultaneously with the first because it does not draw from the conscious resource pool (or, to change the metaphor, the automatic process has achieved a high level of skill; see Hirst & Kalmar, 1987). The more automatically a task can be done, the more resources are available for other tasks.

The route to automaticity, it appears, is practice and memory. With repetition and overlearning comes the ability to perform automatically what formerly needed conscious processing. A particularly dramatic illustration of the power of practice was done by Spelke, Hirst, and Neisser (1976). With extensive practice, two people were able to read stories at normal rates and with high comprehension, while

The demands on attention and memory in flying a jet airplane are enormous. The pilot must simultaneously pay conscious attention to multiple sources of information while relying on highly practiced, automatic processes and overlearned actions to respond to others.

they simultaneously copied words at dictation or even categorized the dictated words according to meaning. Significantly, once practice has yielded automatic performance, it seems especially difficult to undo the practice, to overcome what has now become an automatic and, in a sense, autonomous process (Zbrodoff & Logan, 1986).

Disadvantages of Automaticity

We have been talking as if automaticity is always a positive, desirable characteristic, as if anything that reduces the drain on the limited available mental capacity is a good thing. This is not entirely true, however. There are several situations in which achieving automaticity can lead to difficulties (Reason, 1990). You may experience **action slips**, which are *unintended, often automatic, actions that are inappropriate for the current situation* (Norman, 1981).

Action slips can occur for a number of reasons, each involving a lapse of attention; the action seems foolish, and you wouldn't have done it if you had been paying more attention. In some cases, the environment has been altered from the way it would normally be, such as pressing a button to open a door that is already (unusually) propped open. Sometimes action slips are brought about by a change that requires people to relearn something they have become accustomed to doing another way. For example, your new car may have some of its controls in a different location from where they were on the older one, so you have to overcome the habit of reaching to the left dashboard to turn on the lights (this is why some controls, e.g., accelerator and brake pedals, do not change position). Often action slips occur when people have started something, but are distracted (Botvinick & Bylsma, 2006). They then lapse into a more automatic pattern of behavior of doing the wrong thing, or forgetting a needed step, such as turning on the coffee machine.

In other cases, people start doing something that they frequently do, but at an inappropriate time. A classic example involves the man whose wife told him to go back to the bedroom and change his tie one evening. When he did not return after a suitable amount of time, she went to the bedroom to find out what was keeping him. When she got there, she found that he had undressed and was in bed. What had happened was that there were a number of stimuli in the environment that triggered a more automatic pattern of action. Specifically, when he normally went to his room at night and took off his tie, this was the beginning of his routine that ended in his going to bed. This automatic pattern of behavior was triggered by these stimuli (it may sound like brain damage, but it's not—we all do things like this at one time or another). Another, more common example is when you find yourself driving to work or school when you meant to go someplace you go less often.

Sometimes we *should* be consciously aware of information or processes that have become too routine and automatic. Barshi and Healy (1993) provided an excellent example, using a proofreading procedure that mimics how we use checklists. People in their study scanned pages of simple multiplication problems. Five mistakes such as "7 × 8 = 63" were embedded in the pages of problems. People saw the same sets of 10 problems over and over. But in the fixed order condition, the problems were in the same order each time; in the varied order condition, the problems were in a different order each time. Those tested in the fixed order condition missed more of the embedded mistakes than those in the varied order condition; an average of 23% missed in fixed order, but only 9% missed with varied orders. Figure 4-10 shows this result across the five embedded errors. Performance did improve in the fixed order condition, as more and more of the mistakes were encountered. But the first multiplication error was detected only 55% of the time, compared with the 90% detection rate for the varied order group.

The fixed order of problems encouraged automatic proofreading, which disrupted accuracy at detecting errors. In fact, it took either an earlier error that *was* detected or a specific alerting signal (Experiment 3) to overcome the effects of routine, automatic proofreading.

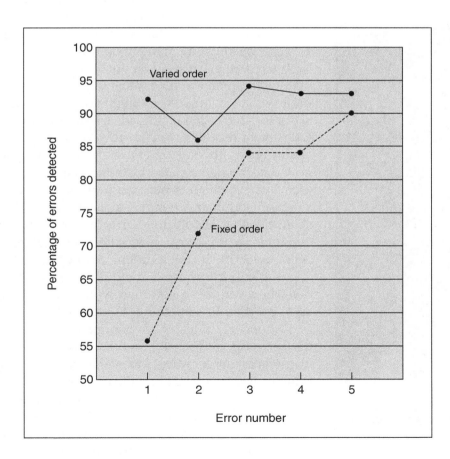

FIGURE 4-10
Results of Barshi and Healy's experiment, showing the percentage of participants detecting the five embedded errors in proofreading multiplication problems. Problems were presented in fixed or varied order.

Data from Barshi & Healy (1993).

The implications of this kind of result should be clear. Pilots are required to go through checklist procedures, say for landing an airplane, to ensure safety. Yet because the items on the checklist are in a fixed order, repeated use of the list probably leads to a degree of automaticity and probably a tendency to miss errors. This is exactly what happened in March 1983: A plane landed in Casper, Wyoming, without its landing gear down, even though the flight crew had gone through its standard checklist procedure and had "verified" that the wheels were down. In Barshi and Healy's words, this incident "reminded the crew and the rest of the aviation community that the countless repetition of the same procedure can lead to a dangerous automatization" (1993, P. 496). It's interesting to wonder which is worse, too much automatization of procedures, as exemplified by the Barshi and Healy study, or too much attention paid to the procedures, as in the Haines (1991) study you read about in Chapter 3 (hint: experienced pilots in flight simulators).

MIND WANDERING   Perhaps one of the most obvious and ubiquitous examples of not being able to use our attention the way that we want to is when our minds drift from the task that we are supposed to be focusing on to some other, irrelevant idea. **Mind wandering** is *the situation in which a person's attention and thoughts wander from the current task to some other, inappropriate line of thought.* We all regularly experience mind wandering, such as when we start to daydream during a boring lecture, start thinking about a significant other when sitting at a

Sometimes when we are trying to do one task, attention disengages and our minds wander.

traffic light, or get to the bottom of a page and realize that we have no idea what we just read. In these cases, we have decoupled our attention from the environment to focus more exclusively on our own internal thoughts, often without an awareness that our mind is wandering until we catch ourselves (Smallwood, McSpadden, & Schooler, 2007, 2008); this idea is now supported by ERP (event-related potential) recordings (Barron, Riby, Greer, & Smallwood, 2011). During reading, we can now detect when a person is mind wandering because their eye movements become more erratic, eyeblinks increase, and their eye movements are less tied to characteristics that should influence their reading patterns (such as word frequency) (Reichle, Reineberg, & Schooler, 2010; Smilek, Carriere, & Cheyne, 2010).

As you know, your mind is more likely to wander when you are bored than when you are engaged and absorbed in something. Essentially, when you are really concentrating, all of your attention is engaged in the task you are focused on, and it is difficult for distractions to lure it away. However, when your intended primary task is not taking all of your attention, other ideas can break through and take attention away (Smallwood & Schooler, 2006). Under these circumstances, attention will drift from what you are supposed to be thinking about to something else, leaving your memory for what you are supposed to be doing much poorer. The surprising prediction here is that people with *more* working memory capacity are more likely to mind wander. This is because they will be more likely to have capacity available over and above what is required by the current task. These people get distracted by things that are in the environment, but are not part of what they are supposed to be attending. Such a proneness to mind wander impedes cognition, such as the ability to learn things in school (Smallwood, Fishman, & Schooler, 2007). Because mind wandering involves a loss of attentional control, in some sense, it is not surprising that mind wandering is more likely when a person is under the influence of alcohol (Sayette, Reichle, & Schooler, 2009) or craving a cigarette (Sayette, Schooler, & Reichle, 2010).

An important point to note is that your mind does not wander randomly. Instead, you are more likely to disengage from the current task and mind wander by thinking about things that are current concerns for you, or are relevant to your long-term goals. If you think about those cases where your mind wanders, you'll find that you are often daydreaming about things that are important to you in one way or another. Often, there may be something in the environment, such as a person you see, a word that you hear or read, or a smell of perfume, that directs your attention away from what you need to be doing and toward something else.

Section Summary

- When attention is viewed as a limited mental resource, issues of task complexity become concerned with how automatic or controlled different mental processes are. Automatic processes are rapid, are not dependent on intent, are unavailable to conscious awareness, and place few if any demands on limited attentional resources. Conscious or controlled processes are the opposite: rather slow, requiring intention, open to conscious awareness, and heavily demanding of attentional resources.
- Mental processes become more automatic as a function of practice and over-learning. A disadvantage of automaticity is that it is difficult to reverse the effects of practice in an automated task, and automaticity can lead to errors of inattention, including action slips.
- When our attention is not fully engaged, our minds can wander off topic. Mind wandering is more likely to occur when there is mental capacity left over and available. Moreover, when we mind wander, the things that we allow our attention to drift to are typically things that we have enduring concerns about, such as things we are anxious or excited about.

Key Terms

action slips
attention
attention capture

attentional blink
automaticity

benefit or facilitation
conjunction search

controlled attention
cost

dual task procedure
early selection theory
explicit processing
feature search
filtering
habituation
hemineglect

implicit processing
inhibition
inhibition of return
input attention
late selection theory
mind wandering

negative priming
orienting reflex
pop-out effect
priming
psychological
    refractory period
selecting

selective attention
shadowing task
spotlight attention
Stroop effect
sustained attention
vigilance

Short-Term Working Memory

Elementary memory makes us aware of . . . the just past. The objects we feel in this directly intuited past differ from properly recollected objects. An object which is recollected, in the proper sense of that term, is one which has been absent from consciousness altogether, and . . . is brought back . . . from a reservoir in which, with countless other objects, it lay buried and lost from view. But an object of primary memory is not thus brought back; it never was lost; its date was never cut off in consciousness from that of the immediately present moment. In fact it comes to us as belonging to the rearward portion of the present space of time, and not to the genuine past.

(JAMES, 1890, PP. 643–647)

Primary memory, elementary memory, immediate memory, short-term memory (STM), short-term store (STS), temporary memory, supervisory attention system (SAS), working memory (WM)—all these terms refer to the same general type of memory where the "immediately present moment," in James's explanation, is held in consciousness. It is the seat of conscious attention discussed in Chapter 4. This is where comprehension occurs: short-term, working memory. What it is, what it does, and how it does it are the topics of this chapter.

A short-term working memory is the memory we are conscious of. Many of our intuitions and introspections about it match what has been discovered empirically. However, some mental processes of short-term working memory are not open to consciousness: They are automatic. These processes yield no useful introspections; indeed, people often feel that they do not exist. (This is why short-term working memory is only *roughly* the same as consciousness. We are aware of its contents, but not necessarily the *processes* that occur in it.)

Modern research on short-term working memory came hard on the heels of selective attention studies of the mid-1950s.[1] George Miller's (1956) classic article, which we discuss shortly, is an excellent example of this upsurge in interest. A common observation, that we can remember only a small number of isolated items presented rapidly, began to take on new significance as psychology groped toward a new approach to human memory. Miller's insightful remarks were followed shortly by the Brown (1958) and Peterson and Peterson (1959) reports. Amazingly, simple three-letter stimuli, such as *MHA*, *GPR*, or *JMW*, were forgotten almost completely within 15 seconds if the person's attention was diverted by a distractor task of counting backward by threes. Such reports were convincing evidence that the limited capacity of memory was finally being pinned down and given an appropriate name: short-term memory.

As we proceed, we will shift from the term *short-term memory* to *working memory*. Why the two terms? Basically, they have different connotations. *Short-term memory* conveys a simpler idea. It is the label we use to focus on the input and storage of new information. For example, when a rapidly presented series of digits is tested for immediate recall, we generally refer to short-term memory. Likewise, when we focus on the role of rehearsal, we are examining the short-term memory maintenance of new information. Short-term memory is observed whenever short retention is tested—no more than 15 or 20 seconds—and when little, if any, transfer of new information to long-term memory is involved.

Working memory, in comparison, is the newer term and has the connotation of a mental workbench, a place where mental effort is applied (Baddeley, 1992a, b; Baddeley & Hitch, 1974). Thus, when word meanings are retrieved from long-term memory and put together to understand a sentence, working memory is where this happens. Traditional immediate memory tasks are a subset of working

---

[1]There was also some research on short-term memory before the behaviorist period. For instance, Mary W. Calkins, the first woman to serve as president of the American Psychological Association, conducted work in the 1890s and reported several important effects that were "discovered" in the 1950s and 1960s. See Madigan and O'Hara (1992) for an account of the "truly remarkable legacy" (p. 174) of this pioneering woman.

memory research but usually are only secondary to reasoning, comprehension, or retrieval processes. For example, the short-term memory responsible for digit span performance is but a single component of the more elaborate working memory system.

SHORT-TERM MEMORY: A LIMITED-CAPACITY BOTTLENECK

If you hear a string of 10 digits, read at a rapid rate, and are asked to reproduce them in order, generally you cannot recall more than about 7. The same result is found with unrelated words (see the "Prove It" projects on page 147 for sample lists and try testing a few volunteers). This is roughly the amount you can say aloud in about 2 seconds (Baddeley, Thomson, & Buchanan, 1975) or the amount you can recall in 4 to 6 seconds (Dosher & Ma, 1998; see also Cowan et al., 1998). This limit has been recognized for so long, it was included in the earliest intelligence tests (e.g., Binet's 1905 test; see Sattler, 1982). Young children and people of subnormal intelligence generally have a shorter span of apprehension, or memory-span. In the field of intelligence testing, it is almost unthinkable to devise a test *without* a memory-span component. Note that this is a general aspect of short-term memory, not something special about spoken words or digits. For example, a similar finding is observed with letters in American Sign Language (ASL) (Wilson & Emmorey, 2006; Wilson & Fox, 2007), which clearly is more visual/motor relative to spoken English.

Short-Term Memory Capacity

Simulate
Digit Span in
MyPsychLab

For our purposes, the importance of this limitation is that it reveals something fundamental about human memory. Our immediate memory cannot encode vast quantities of new information and hold it accurately. It has a severe limit. Miller stated this limit aptly in the title of his 1956 paper: "The Magical Number Seven, Plus or Minus Two: Some Limits on Our Capacity for Processing Information." However, more recent work suggests that the situation is worse than this—that people can maintain only four plus or minus one units of information (e.g., Cowan, 2010), and that seven plus or minus two is actually a result of some chunking. We process large amounts of information in the sensory memories, and we can hold vast quantities of knowledge in permanent long-term memory. Yet, short-term memory is the narrow end of a funnel, the four-lane bridge with only one open tollgate; it is the bottleneck in our information-processing system.

OVERCOMING THE BOTTLENECK And so this limitation remains unless what we are trying to remember is made richer and more complex by grouping it in some way, as in the 3–3–4 grouping of a telephone number or the 3–2–4 grouping of a Social Security number. In Miller's terms, a *richer, more complex item* is called a **chunk** of information. By chunking items together into groups, we can overcome this limitation.

Toll booths force a bottleneck in a highway's traffic flow.

The following is a simple example of the power of chunking:

BYGROUPINGITEMSINTOUNITSWEREMEMBERBETTER

No one can easily remember 40 letters correctly if they are treated as 40 separate, unrelated items. But by chunking the letters into groups, we can retain more information. You can more easily remember the eight words because they are familiar ones that combine grammatically to form a coherent thought. You can remember a Social Security number more easily by grouping the digits into the 3–2–4 pattern. And you can remember a telephone number more easily if you group the last four digits into two two-digit numbers (of course the point generalizes beyond U.S. Social Security and phone numbers).

The term for this *process of grouping items together, then remembering the newly formed groups* is **recoding**. By recoding, people hear not the isolated dots and dashes of Morse code but whole letters, words, and so on. The principle behind recoding is straightforward: Recoding reduces the number of units held in short-term memory by increasing the richness, the information content, of each unit. Try recoding the longest digit list in the "Prove It" lists, at the end of the chapter, into two-digit numbers (28, 43, and so on). This illustrates the mental effort needed for recoding (in fact, Brooks & Watkins, 1990, suggested that there is already a subgrouping effect in the memory span, with the first half enjoying an advantage over the second).

Two conditions are important for recoding. First, we can recode if there is sufficient time or resources to use a recoding scheme. Second, we can recode if the scheme is well learned, as Morse code becomes with practice. In a dramatic demonstration of this, over the period of a few months, one person in a study by Chase and Ericsson (1982) could recall 82 digits in order by applying a highly practiced recoding scheme he invented for himself. But what about situations when an automatic recoding scheme is not available? What is the fate of items in short-term memory? Can we merely hold the usual small number of items?

Explore *Delay Interference* in **MyPsychLab**

Forgetting from Short-Term Memory

In addition to having a limited capacity, information in short-term memory, as the name says, is only around for a short period of time. Research by Brown (1958) and Peterson and Peterson (1959) provided a compelling demonstration of this. The central idea was that *forgetting might be caused simply by the passage of time before testing*—in other words, forgetting caused by **decay**. In their experiments, a simple three-letter trigram (e.g., *MHA*) was presented to people, followed by a three-digit number (e.g., *728*). People were told to attend to the letters, then to begin counting backward by threes from the number they were given. The counting was done aloud, in rhythm with a metronome clicking twice per second. The essential ingredient here is the distractor task of backward counting. This requires a great deal of attention (if you doubt this, try it yourself, making sure to count twice per second). Furthermore, it prevents rehearsal of the three letters because rehearsal uses the same cognitive mechanism as the backward counting. At the end of a variable period of time, the people reported the trigram. The results were so unexpected, and the number of researchers eager to replicate them so large, that the task acquired a name it is still known by—the **Brown–Peterson task**.

The surprising result was that memory of the three-letter trigram was only slightly better than 50% after 3 seconds of counting; accuracy dwindled to about 5% after 18 seconds (Figure 5-1). The letters were forgotten so quickly even though short-term memory was not overloaded—a 50% loss after only 3 seconds (assuming perfect recall with a zero-second delay). On the face of it, this seems evidence of a simple decay function: With an increasing period of time, less and less information remains in short-term memory.

Later research, especially by Waugh and Norman (1965), questioned some of the assumptions made. Waugh and Norman thought that the distractor task itself might be a source of interference. If the numbers spoken during backward counting interfered with the short-term memory trace, then longer counting intervals would have created more interference. Waugh and Norman's reanalysis of several studies confirmed their suspicion. Especially convincing were the results of their own probe digit task. People heard a list of 16 digits, read at a rate of either 1 or 4 per second. The final item in each list was a repeat of an earlier item, and it was the probe or cue to recall the digit that had *followed* the probe in the original list.

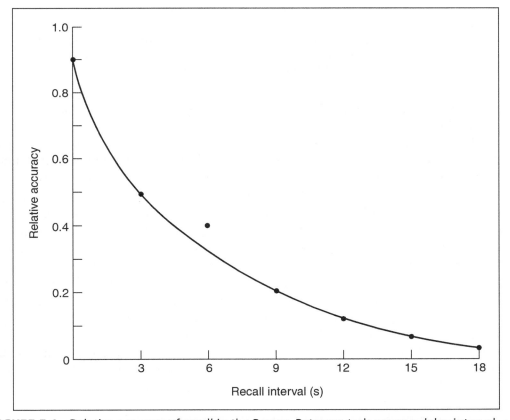

FIGURE 5-1 Relative accuracy of recall in the Brown–Peterson task across a delay interval from 0 to 18 seconds. People had to perform backward counting by threes during the interval.

Source: From Peterson & Peterson (1959).

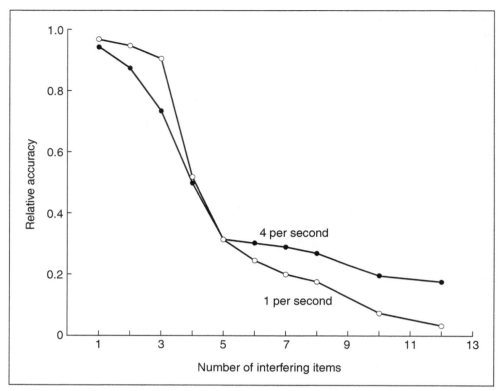

FIGURE 5-2   Relative accuracy in the Waugh and Norman (1965) probe digit experiment as a function of the number of interfering items spoken between the target item and the cue to recall; rate of presentation was either 1 or 4 digits per second.

For instance, if the sequence *7 4 6 9* had been presented, then the probe *4* would have cued recall of the *6*.

The important part of their study was the time it took to present the 16 digits. This took 16 seconds for one group (a long time) but only 4 seconds (a short time) for the other group. If forgetting were caused by decay (a time-based process), then the groups should have differed markedly in their recall because so much more time had elapsed in the 16 seconds group. Yet, as Figure 5-2 shows, the two groups differed little. This suggests that forgetting was influenced by the number of intervening items, not simply the passage of time. In other words, forgetting in short-term memory was caused by interference, not decay (for cross-species evidence of interference, see Wright & Roediger, 2003). Although it has been decades since the original work, the issue of decay versus interference explanations for forgetting in short-term memory continues to be of interest to cognitive psychologists (e.g., Unsworth, Heitz, & Parks, 2008). Some interesting recent work suggests that while the bulk of the forgetting is due to interference, there is still a small amount that can be attributed to a decay process as well (Altmann & Gray, 2002; Altmann & Schunn, in press; Berman, Jonides, & Lewis, 2009).

PROACTIVE AND RETROACTIVE INTERFERENCE (PI AND RI)   Shortly after the Peterson and Peterson report, Keppel and Underwood (1962) challenged the decay explanation for forgetting in short-term memory. They found that people forgot at a dramatic rate only after several trials. On the first trial, memory for the trigram was almost perfect. Keppel and Underwood's explanation was that as you experience more and more trials in the Brown–Peterson task, recalling the trigram becomes more difficult because the *previous* trials generate interference. This is called **proactive interference (PI)**, *when older material interferes forward in time with your recollection of the current stimulus.* This is the opposite of **retroactive interference (RI)**, in which *newer material interferes backward in time with your recollection of older items.* The loss of information in the Brown–Peterson task was caused by proactive interference.

RELEASE FROM PI   An important adaptation of the interference task was done by Wickens (1972; Wickens, Born, & Allen, 1963). He gave people three Brown–Peterson trials, using three words or numbers rather than trigrams. On the first trial, accuracy was near 90%, but it fell to about 40% on Trial 3. At this point Wickens changed to a different kind of item for Trial 4. People who had heard three words per trial were given three numbers, and vice versa. The results were dramatic. When the nature of the items was changed, performance on Trial 4 returned to the 90% level of accuracy (Wickens also included a control group who got the same kind of stimulus on Trial 4 as they had gotten on the first three trials, to make sure performance continued to fall, which it did). Figure 5-3 shows this result.

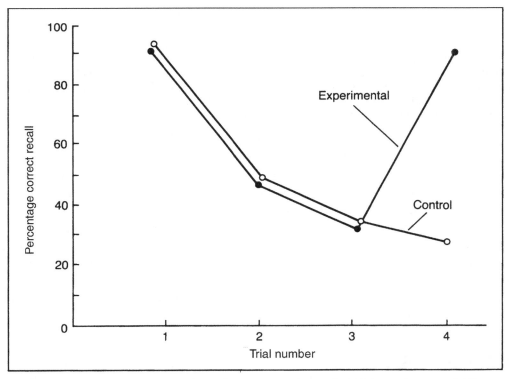

FIGURE 5-3   Recall accuracy in a release from PI experiment by Wickens, Born, and Allen (1963). Triads of letters are presented on the first three trials, and proactive interference begins to depress recall accuracy. On Trial 4, the control group gets another triad of letters; the experimental group gets a triad of digits and shows an increase in accuracy, known as release from PI.

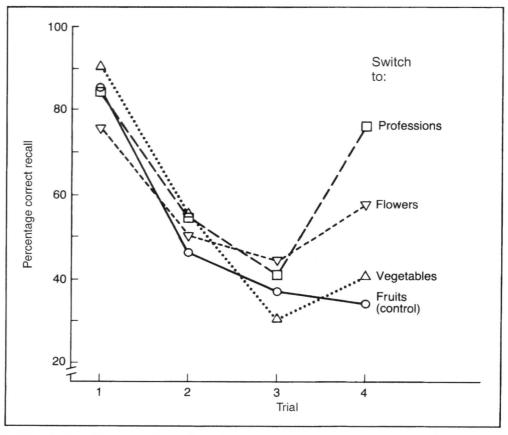

FIGURE 5-4   Recall accuracy in a release-from-PI experiment by Wickens and Morisano (reported in Wickens, 1972). All participants received word triads from the fruit category on Trial 4. On Trials 1 through 3, different groups received triads from the categories *fruits* (control condition), *vegetables, flowers,* and *professions*.

The interference interpretation is clear. Performance deteriorates because of the buildup of proactive interference. If the to-be-remembered information changes, then you are released from the interference. Thus, **release from PI** occurs *when the decline in performance caused by proactive interference is reversed because of a switch in the to-be-remembered stimuli.* Release from PI also occurs when the change is semantic, or meaning-based, as when the lists switched from one semantic category to another (see Figure 5-4). However, note that the more related the items on the fourth list were to the original category, the less release from PI was experienced. Thus, short-term memory, to some degree, uses semantic information.

Section Summary

- Short-term or working memory is an intermediate system between the sensory and long-term memories. Its capacity for holding information is limited, by some accounts, to only 7 ± 2 units of information, although other accounts suggest that it may only be able to hold 4 ± 1 chunks of information. The processes of chunking and recoding, grouping more information into a single unit, are ways of overcoming this limit or bottleneck.

• Whereas a decay explanation of forgetting from short-term memory is possible, most research implicates interference as the primary reason for forgetting. The research suggests two kinds of interference: retroactive and proactive interference.

SHORT-TERM MEMORY RETRIEVAL

In this section we consider retrieval from short-term memory. This refers to the act of bringing knowledge to the foreground of thinking, and perhaps reporting it. Our focus is on two aspects of retrieval. These are the serial position curve and studies of the retrieval process itself.

Serial Position Effects

Simulate *Serial Position Effect* in **MyPsychLab**

To start with, a **serial position curve** is a *graph of item-by-item accuracy on a recall task. Serial position* simply refers to the original position an item had in a study list. Figure 5-5 shows several serial position curves (which you encountered briefly in Chapter 1).

Before considering serial position curves per se, we'll cover the two tasks used to test people: **free recall** and **serial recall**. In free recall, people are free to *recall the list items in any order,* whereas in serial recall, people *recall the list items in their original order of presentation.* Not surprisingly, serial recall is the more difficult. Recalling items in order requires people to rehearse them as they are shown, trying to hold on to not only the information itself but also its position in the list. The more items there are, the harder the task becomes. In comparison, with free recall, people can recall the items in any order.

The early list positions are called the *primacy portion* of a serial position curve. *Primacy* here has its usual connotation of "first": It is the first part of the list that was studied. **Primacy effect**, then, refers to the *accuracy of recall for the early list positions.* A strong primacy effect means good, accurate recall of the early list items, usually because of rehearsal. The final portion of the serial position curve is the *recency portion.* **Recency effect** refers to *the level of correct recall on the final items of the originally presented list. High recency* means "high accuracy," and *low recency* means that this portion of the list was hardly recallable at all.

As Figure 5-5A shows, a strong recency effect is found across a range of list lengths; Murdock (1962) presented 20-, 30-, and 40-item lists at a rate of one item per second. Note that there is a slight primacy effect for each list length, but that the middle part had low recall accuracy. Apparently, the first few items were rehearsed enough to transfer them to long-term memory, but not enough time was available for rehearsing items in the middle of the list. For all lists, though, the strong recency effect can be attributed to recall from short-term memory.

The way to eliminate the recency effect should be no surprise. Glanzer and Cunitz (1966) showed people 15-item lists. For some people, after a list they needed to do an attention-consuming counting task for either 10 or 30 seconds

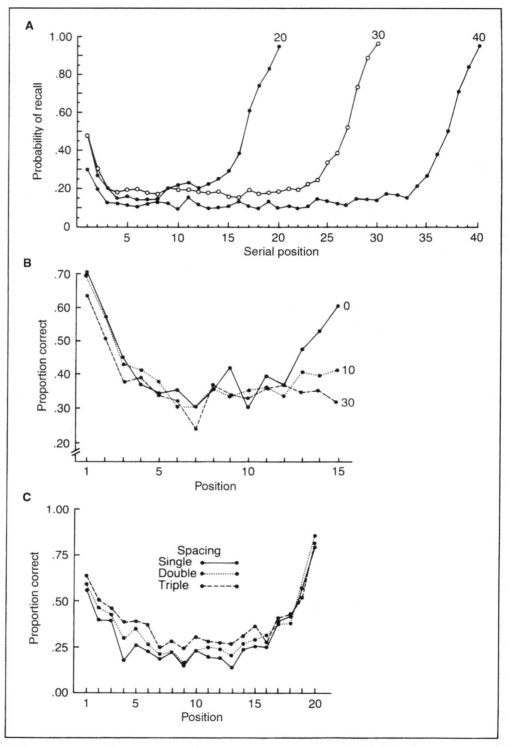

FIGURE 5-5 **A.** Serial position curves showing recall accuracy across the original positions in the learned list. Rate of presentation was one item per second. **B.** Serial position curves showing the decrease in recency when 10 or 30 seconds of backward counting is interpolated between study and recall. **C.** Three different rates of presentation: single (3 seconds), double (6 seconds), and triple (9 seconds).

before recalling the items. In contrast to people who gave immediate recall (0 seconds delay), the people who had to do a counting task showed very low recency (Figure 5-5B). However, the primacy portion of the list was unaffected. In other words, the early list items were more permanently stored in long-term memory to endure 30 seconds of counting. The most recent items in short-term memory were susceptible to interference.

Other manipulations, summarized by Glanzer (1972), showed how the two parts of the serial position curve are influenced by different factors. Note that providing more time per item during study (spacing of 3 versus 6 versus 9 seconds, in the figure) had almost no influence on recency but did alter the primacy effect (Figure 5-5C; from Glanzer & Cunitz, 1966). Additional time for rehearsal allowed people to store the early items more strongly in long-term memory. Moreover, additional time did not help the immediate recall of the most recent items. These items were held in short-term memory and recalled before interference could take place.

Short-Term Memory Scanning: The Sternberg Task

We turn now to a different question: How do we access or retrieve the information from short-term memory? To answer this question, we turn to another memory task: recognition.

PROVE IT
Tests of Short-Term, Working Memory

Several tests of short-term, working memory can be given with little difficulty, to confirm the various effects you are reading about in this chapter. Here are some suggestions.

Simple Memory Span

Make several lists, being sure that the items do not form unintended patterns; use digits, letters, or unrelated words. Read the items at a fairly constant and rapid rate (no slower than one item per second) and have the participant name them back in order. Your main dependent variable will be the number or percentage correct. See sample lists at the end of the chapter.

Try a few of these variations:

- To illustrate the importance of interference, have people do an interference task on half of the trials. On an interference trial, give them a number like 437 and have them count backward by threes, aloud, for 15 seconds, before recalling the list items.
- Keeping list length constant, give different retention intervals before asking for recall (e.g., 5 seconds, 10 seconds, 20 seconds), either with or without backward counting.
- Vary the presentation rate (e.g., one word per second versus one word per 3 seconds) to see how the additional time for rehearsal influences recall.

Working Memory Span

Follow the examples given in the text to construct a working memory span test—for example, from one to six unrelated sentences, each followed by an unrelated word, where the participant must process the sentence and then, at the end of the set, recall the unrelated words that appeared. Span size will be the number of words recalled correctly, assuming that the sentences were comprehended.

Essentially, a recognition test is one in which a person is presented with items and is asked to indicate whether or not the items were part of what had been studied before. A person would select "Yes" to indicate "Yes, I recognize that as being studied." Similarly, a person would select "No" to indicate "No, I didn't study that item." Making these decisions requires you to access stored knowledge, then compare the items to that knowledge. The important angle is that we can time people as they make their "yes/no" recognition decisions, and infer the underlying mental processes used on the basis of how long they took. It was this procedure Saul Sternberg used in addressing the question of how we access information in short-term memory.

Sternberg (1966, 1969, 1975) began by noting that the use of response time (RT) to infer mental processes had a venerable history, dating back at least to Donders in the 1800s. Donders proposed a subtractive method for determining the time for simple mental events. For example, if your primary task involves processes A, B, and C, you devise a comparison task that has only processes A and C in it. After giving both tasks, you subtract the A + C time from the A + B + C time. The difference should be a measure of the duration of process B because it is the process that was subtracted from the primary task.

Sternberg pointed out a major difficulty with Donders's subtractive method. It is virtually impossible to make sure that the comparison task, the A + C task, contains *exactly* the same A and C processes as in the primary task. There is always the possibility that the A and C components were altered when you remove process B. If so, then subtracting one from the other can't be justified. Sternberg's solution was to arrange it so that the critical process would have to *repeat* some number of times during a single trial. Across an entire study there would be many trials on which process B had occurred only once, many on which it occurred two times, three times, and so forth. He then examined the RTs for these conditions, and inferred the nature of process B by determining how much time was *added* to response times for each repetition of process B. This is referred to as the *additive factors* method.

THE STERNBERG TASK   The task Sternberg devised was a short-term memory scanning task, now simply called a Sternberg task. People were given a short list of letters, one at a time, at the rate of one per second, called the memory set. People then saw a single letter, the probe item, and responded "yes" or "no" depending on whether the probe was in the memory set. So, for example, if you stored the set *l r d c* in short-term memory and then saw the letter *d*, you would respond "yes." However, if the probe were *m* you would respond "no."

In a typical experiment, people saw several hundred trials, each consisting of these two parts, memory set then probe, as shown in Table 5-1. Memory sets were from one to six letters or digits long, within the span of short-term memory, and were changed on every trial. Probes changed on every trial, too, and were selected so that the correct response was "yes" on half the trials and "no" on the other half. This is illustrated by Trials 2 and 3 in Table 5-1. Take a moment to try several of these trials, covering the probe until you have the memory set in short-term memory, then covering the memory set and uncovering the probe, then make your "yes/no" judgment. (For a better demonstration, have someone read the memory sets and probe to you aloud.)

TABLE 5-1 Sample Sternberg Task

Trial	Memory Set Items	Probe Items	Correct Response
1	R	R	Yes
2	LG	L	Yes
3	SN	N	Yes
4	BKVJ	M	No
5	LSCY	C	Yes

Figure 5-6 illustrates the **process model** that Sternberg (1969) proposed, simply *a flowchart of the four separate mental processes that occurred during the timed portion of every trial.* At the point marked "Timer starts running here," the person encodes the probe. Then, the search or scan through short-term memory begins and the mentally encoded probe is compared with items in memory to see whether there was a match. A simple "yes" or "no" decision could then be made by pressing one of two buttons.

In Sternberg's task, it was the search process of the contents of short-term memory that was of interest. Notice—this is critical—that it was *this* process that was repeated different numbers of times, depending on how many items were in the memory set. Thus, by manipulating memory set size, Sternberg influenced the number of cycles through the search process. And by examining the slope of the RT results, he could determine how much time was needed for each cycle.

STERNBERG'S RESULTS Figure 5-7 shows Sternberg's (1969) results. There was a linear increase in RT as the memory set got larger, and this increase was nearly the same for both "yes" and "no" trials. The equation at the top of the figure shows that the *y*-intercept of this RT function was 397.2 ms. Hypothetically, if there had been zero items in short-term memory, the *y*-intercept would be the combined time for the encoding, decision, and response stages (refer back to Figure 5-6). More importantly, the slope of the equation was 37.9 ms; for each additional item in the memory set, the mental scanning process took 37.9 ms. Putting it slightly differently, the search through short-term memory is approximately 38 ms per item—*very* fast.

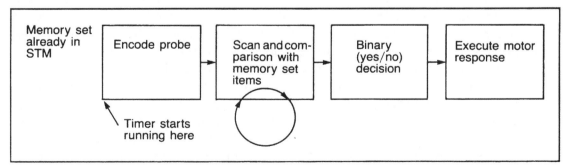

FIGURE 5-6 The four-stage process model for short-term memory scanning. Adapted from Sternberg (1969).

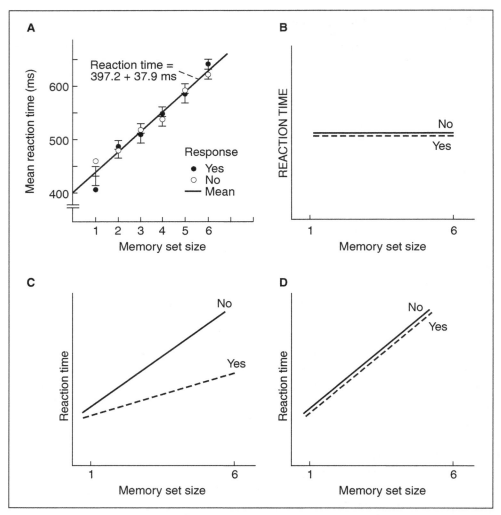

FIGURE 5-7 Reaction time in the short-term memory scanning task, for "yes" (shaded circles) and "no" (unshaded circles) responses. Reaction time increases linearly at a rate of 37.9 ms per additional item in the memory set.

What kind of mental search would produce these results? Sternberg considered three possibilities. The most intuitively appealing was a *serial self-terminating search* in which the positions in short-term memory are scanned one by one, and the scan stops when a match is found; this is how you search for a lost object, say your car keys. The idea is that, on the average, the slope of the RT trials for "yes" responses should be smaller than the slope for "no" responses. On the "no" trials, all positions have to be searched before you can decide that the probe was not in the set. But on "yes" trials, people would encounter matches at all positions in the memory set, sometimes early, sometimes late, with equal frequencies at all positions. This would yield a pattern similar to that of the visual search task you read about in Chapter 4; in Figure 4-5, the slopes of the positive curves ("yes, I found the target") were always smaller than those of the negative curves ("no, the target was not in the display"). However reasonable such a search seems, Sternberg's data did not match the prediction—he found the same slope for both kinds of trials.

The second possibility was a *parallel search*, in which each position in the memory set is scanned simultaneously. If short-term memory is scanned in parallel, then there should be no increase in RT—if all the positions are scanned simultaneously, it should not take longer to scan six items than three, for example. But again, the data did not match this prediction.

Instead, Sternberg inferred that short-term memory is searched in a fashion called **serial exhaustive search**. That is, *the memory set is scanned one item at a time (serial), and the entire set is scanned on every trial, whether or not a match is found (exhaustive)*. Notice that exhaustive search has to be correct for "no" trials because the positions have to be scanned exhaustively before you can confidently and accurately make a "no" decision. Because of the similarity of the "yes" and "no" curves in Figure 5-7, Sternberg argued strongly that both reflect the same mental process, serial exhaustive search (Sternberg, 1969, 1975).

LIMITATIONS TO STERNBERG'S CONCLUSIONS   Across the years, it has been suggested that increasing RTs could be the product of a parallel search in which each additional item slows down the rate of scanning for all items (much as a battery can run several motors at once, but each runs more slowly when more motors are connected; see Baddeley, 1976, for a review). Others have objected to the assumption that the several stages or processes are sequential and that one must be completed before the next one begins. For instance, McClelland (1979) proposed that the mental stages might overlap partially, in cascade fashion. Still, Sternberg's work pushed the field toward more useful ways of studying cognition. Most research based on RT tasks (e.g., visual search tasks and many long-term memory tasks) owes credit, even if only indirectly, to Sternberg's ground-breaking and insightful work.

Section Summary

- Serial position curves reveal two kinds of memory. Early positions in a list are sensitive to deliberate rehearsal that transfers information into long-term memory, whereas later positions tend to be recalled with high accuracy in the free recall task; this latter effect is called the recency effect and is due to the strategy of recalling the most recent items first. Asking people to do a distractor task before recall usually eliminates the recency effect because the distractor task prevents them from maintaining the most recent items in short-term memory.
- Sternberg's paradigm, short-term memory scanning, provided a way to investigate how we search through short-term memory. Sternberg's results indicated that this search is a serial exhaustive process occurring at a rate of about 38 ms per item to be searched.

WORKING MEMORY

Working memory can be viewed as an augmentation of short-term memory. By the mid-1970s, all sorts of functions were being attributed to short-term memory in tasks of problem solving, comprehension, reasoning, and the like. Yet, as Baddeley pointed out, remarkably little work had actually demonstrated those functions in STM (Baddeley, 1976; Baddeley & Hitch, 1974; Baddeley & Lieberman, 1980). For example, pay attention to how you solve the following problem:

$$\frac{(4 + 5) \times 2}{3 + (12/4)}$$

How can a simple limited-capacity system capture the problem-solving processes here? Didn't you compute part of the expression, hold that intermediate answer in memory while computing the next part, then hold the updated intermediate value, and so on? Likewise, sentence comprehension can sometimes tax short-term memory almost palpably; for instance:

> *I know that you are not unaware of my inability to speak German.*

Can you feel the burden on your controlled processing when you have to figure out—almost translate—the meaning of a sentence piece by piece, then put the pieces together? ("not unaware" equals "aware," "inability to speak German" means "cannot speak German," and so on). But ideas such as the burden or load on short-term memory, or switching between processing and remembering, are not addressed by simple approaches that emphasize a small number of "slots" or "chunks."

Going beyond intuitive examples, Baddeley and Hitch (1974) documented their position by describing a dramatic case study, originally reported by Warrington and Shallice (1969; also Shallice & Warrington, 1970; Warrington & Weiskrantz, 1970) of a patient "who by all normal standards, has a grossly defective STS. He has a digit span of *only two items,* and shows grossly impaired performance on the Peterson short-term forgetting task. If STS does indeed function as a central working memory, then one would expect this patient to exhibit grossly defective learning, memory, and comprehension. No such evidence of general impairment is found either in this case or in subsequent cases of a similar type" (Baddeley & Hitch, 1974, pp. 48–49, emphasis added; also Baddeley & Wilson, 1988; Vallar & Baddeley, 1984). In a similar vein, McCarthy and Warrington (1984) reported on a patient who had a memory span of only one word, but could nonetheless report back six- and seven-word sentences with about 85% accuracy. Despite the fact that both types of lists relied on short-term memory, performance on one type was seriously affected by the brain damage, and the other only minimally.

Baddeley and Hitch reasoned that the problem lies with a simple maintenance theory of STM. STM is but one component of a larger, more elaborate system, **working memory**.

The Components of Working Memory

A description of Baddeley's working memory model provides a useful context for the studies described later; (see Baddeley & Hitch, 1974; Salame & Baddeley, 1982; Baddeley, 2000a). Baddeley's model, shown in Figure 5-8, has four major components. The main part is the *central executive* (or sometimes *executive control*), assisted by two auxiliary systems: the *phonological loop* and the *visuo-spatial sketch pad.* Both of these had specific sets of responsibilities, assisting the central executive by doing some of the lower-level processing. Thus, in the arithmetic problem mentioned earlier, the central executive would be responsible for retrieving values from memory $(4 + 5, 9 \times 2)$ and applying the rules of arithmetic; a subsystem, the phonological loop, would then hold the intermediate value 18 in a rehearsal-like buffer until it was needed again. More recently, a third auxiliary system, the *episodic buffer*, was added (Baddeley, 2000a). This part is used to integrate information already in working memory with information retrieved from long-term memory. It is where different types of information are bound together to form a complete memory, such as storing together the sound of someone's voice with an image of his/her face.

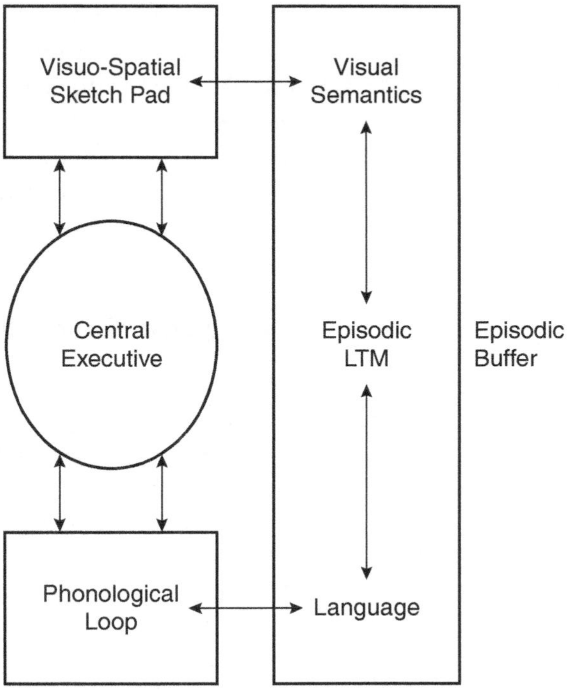

The idea of working memory being divided into components is supported by neurological evidence. Smith and Jonides (1999; also Smith, 2000) reviewed a number of brain imaging studies to identify regions of heightened activity in various working memory tasks. In general, the thinking is that those brain regions involved in perception are also recruited by working memory for the storage of information, regions toward the posterior (back) of the brain, and that the rehearsal and processing of information is controlled by those aspects of the

FIGURE 5-8 An overview of Baddeley's working memory model, including the central executive, the phonological loop, the visuo-spatial sketchpad, and the episodic buffer. Based on Baddeley (2000a).

brain involved in motor control and attention (Jonides, Lacey, & Nee, 2005). For the Sternberg task, the scanning evidence showed strong activations in a left hemisphere parietal region, noted at the numbered area 40 in the figure, and three frontal sites, Broca's area (B.A. 44), and the left supplementary motor area (SMA) and premotor area (B.A. 6).

As you will read in Chapter 9, Broca's area is important in the production of language, so finding increased activity here was not surprising. Alternatively, tasks that emphasize executive control, such as switching from one task to another, tend to show strong activity in the dorsolateral prefrontal cortex (DLPFC) (B.A. 46) (for an argument that task switching does not involve executive control, see Logan, 2003). This area is central to understanding executive attention (Kane & Engle, 2002). The neurological basis for executive control is also supported by work showing that executive functions in cognition may have a significant genetic basis (Friedman et al., 2008).

Other studies have shown specific brain regions involved in visuo-spatial working memory. In one (Jonides et al., 1993), people saw a pattern of three random dots; the dots were then removed for 3 seconds, and a circle outline appeared; the task was to decide whether the circle surrounded a position where one of the dots had appeared earlier. In a control condition, the dots remained visible while the circle was shown, thus eliminating the need to remember the locations. Positron emission tomography (PET) scans revealed that three right hemisphere regions showed heightened activity and so were involved in spatial working memory. They were a portion of the occipital cortex, a posterior parietal lobe region, and the premotor and DLPFC region of the frontal lobe (see also Courtney, Petit, Maisog, Ungerleider, & Haxby, 1998). In related work, when the task required spatial information for responding, it was the premotor region that was more active; when the task required object rather than spatial location information, the DLPFC was more active (Jonides et al., 1993; see also Miyake et al., 2000, for a review of various executive functions attributed to working memory).[2]

The Central Executive

The *central executive* is the heart of working memory. It's like a large corporation, in which the chief executive is in charge of the tasks of planning, initiating activities, and making decisions. Likewise in working memory, the **central executive** is in charge of *planning future actions, initiating retrieval and decision processes as necessary,* and *integrating information coming into the system.* Let's take an example to illustrate some of this. To continue with the arithmetic example, the central executive triggers the retrieval of facts such as "4 + 5 = 9" and invokes the problem-solving rules such as "how to multiply and divide." Furthermore, the central executive also "realizes" that the intermediate value 18 must be held momentarily while further processing occurs. Accordingly, it activates the phonological loop, sending it the value 18 to rehearse for a few moments until that value is needed again.

Each of the subsystems has its own pool of attentional resources, but the pools are limited. Give any of the subsystems an undemanding task, and it can proceed without disrupting activities occurring elsewhere in working memory. However, if a subsystem is given a particularly difficult task, then either it falters or it must drain additional resources from the central executive. To some degree, working memory resources are shared across processing domains, such as verbal or visual (Vergauwe, Barrouillet, & Camos, 2010). This is why closing your eyes can help you think by reducing distractions from the external environment (Vredeveldt, Hitch, & Baddeley, 2011).

The central executive has its own pool of resources that can be depleted if overtaxed. For example, people who do something that places a strain on the central executive, such as ignoring distracting information as it scrolls across the bottom of a television screen or exaggerating their emotional expressions, have greater difficulty with central executive processing immediately thereafter (Schmeichel, 2007). Moreover, damage to portions of the frontal lobes, such as the medial frontal lobes (B.A. 32) and the polar regions (B.A. 10) can disrupt working memory executive function (Banich, 2009). This produces dysexecutive syndrome, in which patients continue to pursue goals that are no longer relevant, and experience heighted distractibility when they do not have clear goals (Gevins, Smith, McEvoy, & Yu, 1997).

---

[2]The procedure of subtracting patterns in the control condition from those obtained in the experimental condition is straightforward conceptually, although the computations are mind boggling. But notice that conceptually it rests on the same type of logic that Donders used (and Sternberg rejected): finding a control task that contains all of the experimental tasks' components except the one of interest. It will be surprising if this method does not come under attack again, in its newer application to brain imaging.

The Phonological Loop

The **phonological loop** is *the speech- and sound-related component responsible for rehearsal of verbal information and phonological processing.* This component recycles information for immediate recall, including articulating the information in auditory rehearsal (see Baddeley, 2000b; Jones, Macken, & Nicholls, 2004; and Mueller, Seymour, Kieras, & Meyer, 2003, for a debate on the articulatory versus phonological basis of this subsystem).

There are two components of the phonological loop, the phonological store and the articulatory loop. The **phonological store** is essentially *a passive store component of the phonological loop.* This is the part that holds on to verbal information. However, information in the phonological store is forgotten unless it is actively rehearsed and refreshed. Thus, rehearsal is the role of the **articulatory loop**, *the part of the phonological loop involved in the active refreshing of information in the phonological store.* One way of thinking about these two components of the phonological loop is that the phonological store is like your inner ear—you can hear yourself talk to yourself, or imagine hearing music. Similarly, the articulatory loop is like your inner voice, when you mentally say things to yourself.

Researchers have found a number of effects that provide insight into how the phonological loop works. We cover two of them here: the articulatory suppression and phonological similarity effects. The **articulatory suppression effect** is *the finding that people have poorer memory for a set of words if they are asked to say something while trying to remember the words* (Murray, 1967). This effect is not complicated; it occurs even when you say something simple, like repeating the word "the" over and over again. What happens here is that the act of speaking consumes resources in the articulatory loop. As a result, words in the phonological store cannot be refreshed and are lost. A related phenomenon is the irrelevant speech effect (Colle & Welsh, 1976). It is hard to keep information in the phonological loop when there is irrelevant speech in the environment. This irrelevant speech intrudes on the phonological loop, consuming resources and causing you to forget verbal information. This is why it is so difficult to read (and then remember what you read) when you are in a room with other people talking. (So, try to study somewhere quiet.)

The **phonological similarity effect** is *the finding that memory is poorer when people need to remember a set of words that are phonologically similar, compared to a set of words that are phonologically dissimilar* (Baddeley, 1966; Conrad & Hull, 1964). For example, it is harder to remember the set "boat," "bowl," "bone," and "bore," compared to the set "stick," "pear," "friend," and "cake." This is because words that sound similar can become confused in the phonological store. One thing that happens is that, because the words sound similar, it is hard to keep track of what was rehearsed and what wasn't. As a consequence, some words may not get rehearsed and so are forgotten (Li, Schweickert, & Gandour, 2000). In addition, as bits and pieces of them become forgotten or lost, people need to reconstruct them. As a result, people are more likely to make a mistake by misremembering a word that sounded like it should have been in the set, but wasn't—for example, recalling the word "bold" in the first set of words. In general, when people misremember words in working memory, they tend to be words that sound similar, rather than having a similar meaning. This suggests that this aspect of working memory relies primarily on phonological rather than semantic information.

Although we have spent a great deal of time covering phonological aspects of the phonological loop, there is some evidence that there are broader aspects of this part of working memory. For example, it has been found that memory for musical pitches shows similar characteristics to language, in that working memory has a limited capacity for what can be remembered, and people become confused by similar pitches, much like the phonological similarity effect (Williamson, Baddeley, & Hitch, 2010). Also, in a very clever study, Shand (1982) tested people who were congenitally deaf and skilled at American Sign Language (ASL). They were given five-item lists for serial recall, presented as either written English words or ASL signs. One list contained English words that were phonologically similar *(SHOE, THROUGH, NEW)* though not similar in terms of the ASL signs. Another list contained words that were cherologically similar in ASL—that is, similar in the hand movements necessary for forming the sign (e.g., wrist rotation in the vicinity of the signer's face), although they did not rhyme in English. Recall memory showed confusions based on the cherological relatedness. In other words, the deaf people were recoding the written words into an ASL-based code and holding *that* in working memory. Their errors naturally reflected the physical movements of that code rather than verbal or auditory features of the words.

The Visuo-Spatial Sketch Pad

The **visuo-spatial sketch pad** is *a system for visual and spatial information*, maintaining that kind of information in a short-duration buffer. If you must generate and hold a visual image for further processing, the visuo-spatial sketch pad is at work. In general, there is some support for the idea that the visuo-spatial sketchpad shares some of the same neural processes when manipulating mental images as are used during active perception (Broggin, Savazzi, & Marzi, 2012; Kosslyn et al., 1993).

The operation of the visuo-spatial sketch pad can be illustrated by a study by Brooks (1968). People were asked to hold a visual image in working memory, a large block capital *F*, then scan that image clockwise, beginning at the lower left corner. In one condition, people said "yes" aloud if the corner they reached while scanning was at the extreme top or bottom of the figure and "no" otherwise; this was the "image plus verbal" condition. The other condition was an "image plus visual" search condition: While people scanned the mental image, they also had to search through a printed page, locating the column that listed the "yes" or "no" decisions in the correct order. Thus, two different secondary tasks were combined with the primary task of image scanning; all the tasks used the visuo-spatial sketch pad of working memory. The result was that making verbal responses—saying "yes" or "no"—was easy and yielded few errors. However, visual scanning of printed columns was more difficult and yielded substantial errors. This is because scanning the response columns forced the visuo-spatial sketch pad to divide its resources between two tasks, and performance suffered.

A number of effects have been observed that illustrate basic qualities of the visuo-spatial sketch pad. One of the overarching principles of this aspect of working memory is the influence of embodied cognition. As you will see, processing in the visuo-spatial sketch pad acts as if a person were actively interacting with objects in the world. It is not an abstract code, but a dynamic system that allows a person to predict what would happen next if he or she were actually involved in a situation.

The most dramatic evidence for the visuo-spatial sketch pad comes from work on mental rotation (Cooper & Shepard, 1973; Shepard & Metzler, 1971). **Mental rotation** involves people *mentally turning, spinning, or rotating objects in the visuo-spatial sketch pad of working memory.* In one study, people were shown drawings of pairs of three-dimensional objects and they had to judge whether they were the same shape. The critical factor was the degree to which the second drawing was "rotated" from the orientation of the first. To make accurate judgments, people had to mentally transform one of the objects, mentally rotating it into the same orientation as the other so they could judge it "same" or "different." Figure 5-9 displays several such pairs of drawings and the basic findings of the study.

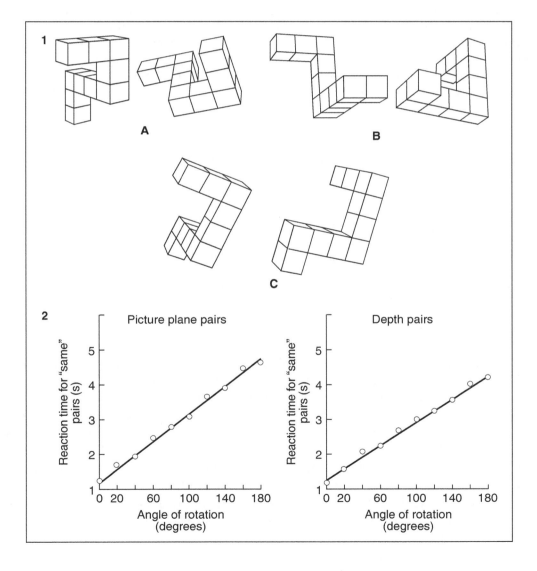

FIGURE 5-9
1. Three pairs of drawings are shown. For each, rotate the second drawing and decide whether it is the same figure as the first drawing. The *A* pair differs by an 80-degree rotation in the picture plane, and the *B* pair differs by 80 degrees in depth; the patterns in *C* do not match. **2.** The RTs to judge "same" are shown as a function of the degrees of rotation necessary to bring the second pattern into the same orientation as the first. Reaction time is a linear function of the degree of rotation.

PROVE IT
Articulatory Suppression

One of the mainstays of research on the phonological loop is the articulatory suppression task. For this task people are asked to repeat words aloud over and over again while trying to remember another set of verbal/linguistic information. The basic idea is that the repeated talking consumes the resources of the articulatory loop, making it difficult to maintain other information. On the face of it, the articulatory suppression task sounds very easy, and that it should not be too difficult. However, actually doing it is a humbling experience that shows how limited our working memory capacity is, and how poor our ability is to do more than one thing at a time when the same part of working memory needs to be used.

To illustrate the powerful influence of articulatory suppression, following are two lists of 10 words each. Copy them down onto a set of note cards. These are just examples, and you can make more lists if you want. Then find a few people to be your participants. Have them read each list of cards by allowing them to see each one for 1 second before moving on to the next. When the end of the list is reached, the person should write down as many words as can be remembered. For one list, have the people simply read the words. However, for the other list, the articulatory suppression list, have them say the word "the" over and over again (the, the, the, . . .) while reading the words; have them keep saying "the the the" until the end of the list is reached. What you should find is that performance is worse under articulatory suppression than when they can read in peace and quiet.

Across	Figure
Result	Action
Center	Mother
Reason	Became
Effect	Making
Period	Really
Behind	Either
Having	Office
Cannot	Common
Future	Moment

The overall result was that people took longer to make their judgments as the angular rotation increased. In other words, a figure that needed to be rotated 120 degrees took longer to judge than one needing only 60 degrees of rotation, much as what would be found if a person were to manually turn the objects. In fact, performance can be enhanced if people are given tactile feedback (by holding an object in their hands) when the object is the same shape and moves in the same way (Wraga, Swaby, & Flynn, 2008), consistent with an embodied interpretation. Moreover, also consistent with an embodied influence, people find it harder to mentally rotate pictures of easily manipulated objects compared to ones that are hard to physically manipulate (Flusberg & Boroditsky, 2011).

In the Cooper and Shepard (1973) report, people were shown the first figure and were told how much rotation to expect in the second figure. This advance information on the degree of rotation permitted people to do the mental rotation ahead of time. Interestingly, the mental processes seem much the same if you ask people to retrieve an image from long-term memory, then hold it in working memory while performing mental rotation on that image. That is, researchers have found regular time-based effects of rotation, and activation in the visual (parietal) lobes, when people are asked to retrieve an image from long-term memory and rotate it mentally in working memory (Just, Carpenter, Maguire, Diwadkar, & McMains, 2001).

Another illustration of properties of the visuo-spatial sketch pad is **boundary extension**, in which *people tend to misremember more of a scene than was actually viewed, as if the boundaries of an image were extended further out* (Intraub & Richardson, 1989; for a review, see Hubbard, Hutchison, & Courtney, 2010). In boundary extension studies, people see a series of pictures. Later, memory is tested for what was seen in the pictures. This can be done by having people either draw what they remember, or identify the image they saw earlier. What is typically found is that people tend to misremember having viewed the picture from further back than was the case. That is, people misremember information from beyond the bounds of the actual picture (for example, if a person saw a picture of a stuffed animal on a set of steps, he or she will misremember more steps than were actually seen). What is going on here is that visuo-spatial working memory adds knowledge of what is beyond the picture boundary, based on previous world knowledge of what is likely to be there. This is then stored in long-term memory. So, when you think back to a show you've seen on television or at the movies, you tend to remember the events as if you were actually there, with no edge to the world. You don't typically remember the image as it appeared on the screen (or even remember sitting there watching the show).

The last of the visuo-spatial phenomena considered here (and there are many more) is **representational momentum**, which is *the phenomenon of misremembering the movement of an object further along its path of travel than where it actually was when it was last seen* (Hubbard, 1995, 2005). In a typical representational momentum study, people see an object moving along a computer screen. At some point the object disappears. The task is to indicate the point on the screen where the object was last seen. The typical results show a bias to misremember the object as being further along its path of travel than it actually was (Freyd & Finke, 1984; Hubbard, 1990). It is as if visuo-spatial working memory is simulating the movement as if it were happening in the world, predicting where that object will be next. This prediction then enters into the decision process, and people place the object further along its path.

Representational momentum can be influenced by other embodied aspects of the situation as well. For example, there is also a bias to remember objects as being farther down than they actually were, as if they were being drawn down by gravity (Hubbard, 1990). There is also evidence that visuo-spatial working memory takes into account friction (Hubbard, 1990), centripetal, and impetus forces (Hubbard, 1996), even if physics has shown these ideas to be wrong, as in the case of impetus. Finally, if an object is moving in an oscillating motion, back and forth like a pendulum, and it disappears just before it is about to swing back, people will mis-remember it as having started its backswing (Verfaille & Y'dewalle, 1991).

Overall, it should be clear that there is a lot of active cognition in the visuo-spatial sketch pad. This part of working memory is doing a lot of work, even if you are not consciously aware of much of it. Moreover, this work is oriented around capturing physical aspects of the world (accurately or not) to help predict what objects will do next, so that you can better interact with them, such as inter-cepting or avoiding them, with a minimum of conscious cognitive mental effort.

The Episodic Buffer

As mentioned earlier, the **episodic buffer** is *the portion of working memory where information from different modalities and sources is bound together to form new episodic memories* (Baddeley, 2000a). In other words, this is the part of working memory where the all-important chunking process occurs, but it also includes per-ceptual processes, such as the integration of color with shape in visual memory (Allen, Baddeley, & Hitch, 2006).

One study that may clarify the workings of the episodic buffer was done by Copeland and Radvansky (2001). In this study, people were given a working memory span test (these sorts of tests are described in detail later). People read a series of sentences and had to remember the last word of the sentences in a given set. What was manipulated was the phonetic similarity of the words in a set. Some-times, the words were phonologically similar, and other times not. The phono-logical similarity effect described earlier in the phonological loop section predicts that working memory performance would be worse for the phonologically similar items. However, because the words were presented at the end of meaningful sen-tences, rather than alone, people could use their semantic understanding of the sentences and bind this with their memory for the words. The result was that, under these circumstances, memory for the phonologically similar words was bet-ter than for the dissimilar words, much as you would find with poetry or song lyrics. Thus, the episodic buffer's use of the meanings of the words trumped the normal loss of information that happens in the phonological loop.

Another study, by Jefferies, Lambdon Ralph, and Baddeley (2004), illustrates the capacity needed for integrating information in the episodic buffer. In their study, people were given lists of words, lists of unrelated sentences, and lists of sentences that formed a coherent story. People were asked to learn these lists either alone or under a more demanding dual task situation (see later) that involved pressing buttons on a keyboard when an asterisk appeared on the computer screen. They found that working memory resources were important for remember-ing the lists of words and the lists of unrelated sentences; when working memory resources were consumed by the dual task, memory for the words and unrelated sentences was compromised. In other words, the working memory capacity needed to chunk the information for words and unrelated sentences was being consumed by the secondary task. But for the related sentences, because the mean-ingful interrelations among them were easily derived, memory performance was relatively unaffected by the dual task. The ease of integrating the sentences into a coherent story reduced the demand for working memory resources.

Section Summary

- Working memory consists of a central executive and three major subsystems: the phonological loop for verbal and auditory information, the visuo-spatial sketch pad for visual and spatial information, and the episodic buffer for integrating or binding information from different parts of working memory and/or long-term memory.
- The various components of working memory are thought to operate relatively independently of one another, perhaps by using different neural substrates, although there can be some overlap for demanding tasks.
- There are capacity limits in the system. Dual task methods can be used to study strains on individual components, or on the overall capacity of working memory. For example, the subsystems may drain extra needed capacity from the central executive in situations of high working memory demands.

ASSESSING WORKING MEMORY

In general, there are two ways of assessing working memory: the dual task method and measures of working memory span. In the first case, performance is examined by having a person do a secondary task, one that consumes working memory resources at the same time as some primary task. This is the dual task method, often used to see how disruptive the secondary task is. In comparison, for working memory span tests, we get a measure of a person's working memory capacity. Across a range of people and abilities, we compare the span scores to performance on other tasks, to see what relationships emerge. Let's go over each of these methods in turn.

Dual Task Method

For the **dual task method**, one of the tasks done by a person is identified as the primary task we are most interested in. The other is a secondary task that is done simultaneously with the first. Both tasks must rely to some significant degree on working memory. In general, we are interested in how the two tasks can be done together and whether there is any competition or interference between them. Any two tasks that are done simultaneously may show complete independence, complete dependence, or some intermediate level of dependency. If neither task influences the other, then we infer that they rely on separate mental mechanisms or resources. If one task always disrupts the other, then they presumably use the same mental resources.

Finally, if the two tasks interfere with each other in some circumstances but not others, then there is evidence

One man band.

for a partial sharing of mental resources. Usually such interference is found when the difficulty of the tasks reaches some critical point at which the combination of the two becomes too demanding. Researchers manipulate the difficulty of the two tasks just as you would adjust the volume controls on a stereo, changing the left and right knobs independently until the combination hits some ideal setting. In research, we vary the difficulty of each task separately—we crank up the "difficulty knobs" on the two tasks, so to speak—and observe the critical point at which performance starts to suffer.

An important aspect of working memory that the dual task method highlights is that information processed in one component may not interfere with processing in another. For example, thinking that uses central executive resources will be relatively unaffected by processing that consumes resources in one of the subsystems.

Here's an example. In one experiment (Baddeley & Hitch, 1974, Experiment 3), people were asked to do a reasoning task. They were shown an item such as *AB* and were timed as they read and responded "yes" or "no" to sentences about it. A simple sentence here would be "*A* precedes *B*," an active affirmative sentence. An equivalent meaning is expressed by "*B* is preceded by *A*," but it's more difficult to verify because of the passive construction. There were also negative sentences, such as "*B* does not precede *A*," and "*A* is not preceded by *B*" (as well as false sentences, e.g., "*B* precedes *A*"). The sentence difficulty was a way of manipulating how much the central executive was needed. While doing the reasoning task, people also had to do one of three secondary tasks: (a) articulatory suppression, (b) repeating the numbers 1 through 6, or (c) repeating a random sequence of digits (the sequence was changed on every trial). Note how the amount of articulation in the three tasks was about the same (a speaking rate of four to five words per second was enforced), but the demands on the central executive steadily increased. There was also a control condition in which there was no concurrent articulation.

Figure 5-10 shows the reasoning times for these four conditions. The control condition showed that even when reasoning was done alone, it took more time to respond to the difficult sentences. Adding articulatory suppression or repeated counting added more time to reasoning but did not change the pattern of times to any great degree; the curves for "the the the" and "one two three . . ." in the figure have roughly the same slope as the control group. This is because these tasks do not strongly consume working memory resources. However, the random digit condition yielded a different pattern. As the sentences grew more difficult, the added burden of reciting a random sequence of digits took its toll. In fact, for the hardest sentences in the reasoning task, correct judgments took nearly 6 seconds in the random digit condition, compared with only 3 seconds in the control condition. When the secondary task is difficult, the articulatory loop must drain or borrow some of the central executive's resources, thereby slowing down or sacrificing accuracy.

This dual task interference has been shown in a variety of tasks, including showing that dividing attention during driving, such as talking on a cell phone, disrupts the ability to make important judgments, such as when to brake. In general, dual task processing leads to much slower braking (Levy, Pashler, & Boer, 2006). In

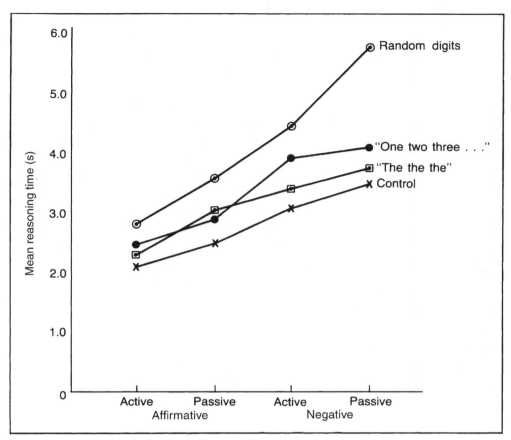

FIGURE 5-10 Average reasoning time is shown as a function of two variables: the grammatical form of the reasoning problem and the type of articulatory suppression task that was performed simultaneously with reasoning. In the random digits condition, a randomly ordered set of six digits had to be repeated out loud during reasoning; in the other two suppression tasks, either "the the the" or "one two three four five six" had to be repeated out loud during reasoning.

other words, when you tax working memory resources, the ability of the central executive to effectively process information is compromised.

Similar research has also been reported comparing the visuo-spatial sketch pad and the phonological loop. As one example, Logie, Zucco, and Baddeley (1990; but see Morey & Cowan, 2004, for a contrasting view) selected two different primary tasks: a visual memory span task and a letter span task. These were paired with two secondary tasks, one involving mental addition and the other visual imagery. In the visual memory span task, people saw a grid of squares on the computer screen, with a random half filled in. After a moment, the grid disappeared and was followed by an altered grid where one of the previously filled squares was now empty. People had to point to the square that was changed, using their visuo-spatial memory of the earlier pattern. In contrast, the letter memory span task, the other primary task, should use the phonological loop.

For the secondary tasks, Logie et al. used a mental addition task thought to be irrelevant to the visuo-spatial processing and an imaging task thought to be

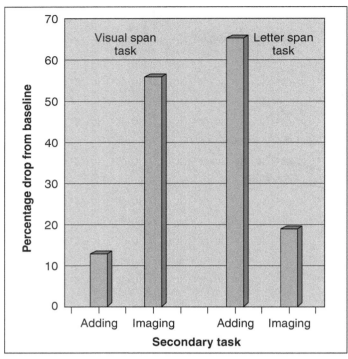

FIGURE 5-11   Results from Logie, Zucco, and Baddeley's (1990) experiment on the visuo-spatial sketch pad. Two secondary tasks, adding and imaging, were combined with two primary tasks, a visual span or a letter span task. The results are shown in terms of the percentage drop in performance measured from baseline; the larger the drop, the more disruption there was from the secondary task.

irrelevant to the phonological loop. The results are shown in Figure 5-11. First, look at the left half of the graph, which reports the results of the visual span (grid pattern) task. Each person did the span task alone, to determine baseline, then along with the secondary tasks. The graph shows the percentage *drop* in dual task performance as compared to baseline. For instance, visual span performance dropped about 15% when the addition task was paired with it; so, dual task performance was at 85% of the single-task baseline. In other words, mental addition disrupted visual memory only modestly. But when the secondary task was visual imagery, as shown by the second bar in the graph, visual memory span dropped about 55%. This is a large interference effect, suggesting that the visuo-spatial sketch pad was stretched beyond its limits.

The right half of the figure shows performance on the letter span task. Here, the outcome was reversed; mental addition was very disruptive to the letter span task, leading to a 65% decline, whereas the imaging task depressed letter span scores only a modest 20%. Thus, only minor declines were observed when the secondary task used a different part of working memory. But substantial declines occurred when the two tasks used the same pool of resources (see Baddeley & Lieberman, 1980, for some of the original research on the visuo-spatial sketch pad). Other work suggests that the impact dual tasks such as these are having is on the encoding aspect of a task, rather than the retention of information in working memory per se (Cowan & Morey, 2007).

Working Memory Span

A different way to study working memory is an individual differences approach. As in any area of psychology, when we speak of individual differences, we're talking about characteristics of individuals—anything from height to intelligence—that differ from one person to the next and can be measured and related to other factors.

Individual differences in working memory are related to various cognitive processes. In this research, people are first given a test to assess their working memory spans. They are then given standard cognitive tasks. Consider a program of research by Engle and his coworkers (Engle, 2001; Rosen & Engle, 1997; see Engle, 2002, for an excellent introduction). First, people are given a **working memory span** task: The task requires simultaneous mental processing and storage of information in working memory. For example, a person might see arithmetic statements along with a word, one at a time (from Turner & Engle, 1989):

$$(6 \times 2) - 2 = 10? \; SPOT$$
$$(5 \times 3) - 2 = 12? \; TRAIL$$
$$(6 \times 2) - 2 = 10? \; BAND$$

People first read the problem aloud, indicated whether the answer was correct, and then said the capitalized word, followed by the second problem and word, then the third. At that point, people tried to recall the three capitalized words, showing that they had stored them in working memory. Scores on this span task are based on the number of capitalized words recalled. Thus, someone who recalled "*SPOT TRAIL BAND*" and answered the arithmetic questions correctly would have a memory span of 3. In another version of the working memory span task, we use sentences instead of arithmetic problems. But both involve *processing* and *storage:* processing the problem or sentence for meaning, and storing the word for recall.

Many investigators have used span tasks to measure working memory capacity. The original work that used this method (Daneman & Carpenter, 1980) examined reading comprehension as a function of span. There were significant correlations between span scores and performance on the comprehension tasks. One of the most striking correlations was between span and verbal Scholastic Aptitude Test (SAT) scores; it was .59, whereas simple span scores seldom correlated significantly with SATs. (As a reminder, simple span tasks, such as remembering a string of digits, test only the storage of items, whereas working memory span tasks involve both storage and processing.) This strong correlation means that there is an important underlying relationship between one's working memory span and the verbal processing measured by the SAT.

The strongest correlation in Daneman and Carpenter's work was a .90 correlation between memory span and performance on a pronoun reference test. Here, people read sentences one by one and at some point confronted a pronoun that referred back to a previous noun. In the hardest condition, the noun had occurred up to six or seven sentences earlier. The results are shown in Figure 5-12. Here, people with the highest working memory span of 5 scored 100% correct on the pronoun test, even in the "seven sentences ago" condition. People with the lowest spans (of 2) got 0% correct. Thus, people with

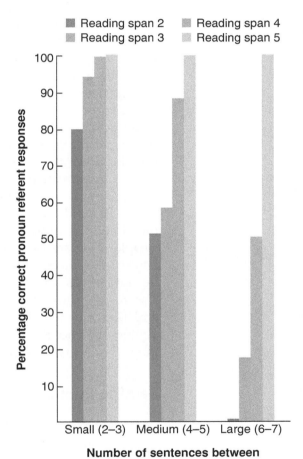

FIGURE 5-12 The percentage of correct responses to the pronoun reference task when the antecedent noun occurred a small, medium, or large number of sentences before the pronoun, as a function of participants' working memory (reading) span.

Source: From Daneman & Carpenter (1980).

higher working memory spans were able to keep more relevant information active in working memory as they comprehended the sentences.

Research since this has extended these findings. Basically, if a task relies on a need to control attention, scores on the task correlate strongly with working memory span. In fact, Engle (e.g., 2002) argued that working memory capacity *is* executive attention and offers the equation "WM = STM + controlled attention"—that is, working memory is the combination of traditional short-term memory plus our controlled attention mechanism (Kane & Engle, 2003; see also Daneman & Merikle, 1996; Engle, 2002; Miyake & Shah, 1999; Unsworth & Spillers, 2010). This involves both the maintenance of information in the short term as well as the ability to access needed information in long-term memory (Unsworth & Engle, 2007).

There is also some evidence that working memory abilities can change with practice. For example, women tend to perform less well than males on visuo-spatial tasks. However, with some training, such as 10 hours experience playing action-based video games, the performance of females can reach the levels of males (Feng, Spence, & Pratt, 2007). Such experience can also boost performance on visuo-spatially based scientific thinking, such as understanding plate tectonics (Sanchez, 2012). Also, it has been suggested that musical training can boost verbal intelligence (Moreno et al., 2011). Finally, there is some evidence that certain kinds of Buddhist meditation can also improve mental imagery abilities (Kozhevnikov, Louchakova, Josipovic, & Motes, 2009). Overall, this work, along with the research by Chase and Ericsson (1982) described earlier (as well as others, e.g., Verhaeghen, Cerella, & Basak, 2004), suggests that people can develop strategies to more efficiently and effectively use their working memories over and above any base level of capacity they may have.

That said, memory span scores do not provide insight into all aspects of cognitive abilities. For example, a study by Copeland and Radvansky (2004b) gave people a variety of memory span tasks, and also assessed performance at more complex levels of comprehension, such as remembering event descriptions, drawing inferences about causes and effects, and detecting inconsistencies in a text. The results showed little evidence of a relation between working memory span and performance. Thus, although memory span highlights important cognitive abilities, it is not the complete story. There is individual variation that can be attributed to other factors as well.

Section Summary

- One common method for assessing working memory is to use dual task methodologies. In these tasks, people are asked to simultaneously do at least two tasks. Researchers then assess how performance on the primary task is affected by the addition of the secondary task, and the theoretical relationship between the two.
- An alternative research strategy is to test working memory span, then examine differences in performance as a function of span scores. This has revealed a number of tasks that show a relationship between span and performance. The implication is that working memory span assesses controlled attentional processes, which are significant aspects of performance.

WORKING MEMORY AND COGNITION

As noted earlier, working memory does not exist or operate independently of other aspects of cognition. It is the vital nerve center of a great deal of activity. In the next few sections, we discuss ways in which working memory influences processing in a variety of domains, including attention, long-term memory, and reasoning.

Working Memory and Attention

Conway, Cowan, and Bunting (2001) examined working memory span and its relation to the classic cocktail party effect of hearing one's own name while paying attention to some other message. About 65% of the people with low memory spans detected their name in a dichotic listening task, versus only 20% of people with high spans. The idea was that high-span people were selectively attending to the shadowed message more effectively than the low-span people, so weren't as likely to detect their names on the unshadowed message. In contrast, the low-span people had difficulty blocking out or inhibiting attention to the distracting information in the unattended message—so they were more likely to hear their own names (see Kane et al., 2007, for evidence that high-span people are better at concentrating more generally and are less likely to engage in mind wandering).

In a similar demonstration, Kane and Engle (2003) used the classic Stroop task (see the "Prove It" box in Chapter 4)—you remember, name the ink color a word like RED is printed in, when the ink color mismatches. There was a strong Stroop effect, of course—approximately a 100-ms slowdown on mismatching items. More to the point, there was no difference in the Stroop effect for high- and low-span groups when the words were always in a mismatching color (*GREEN* printed in red ink) or when half of the words were presented that way; everyone remembered the task goal—ignore the word—in these conditions. But when only 20% of the words were in mismatching colors, low-span people made nearly twice as many errors as high-span people. Because mismatching trials were rarer, the low-span people seemed less able to maintain the task goal in working memory. High-span individuals had less difficulty maintaining that goal.

In a more everyday example, Sanchez and Wiley (2006) tested people with different memory spans, giving them texts to read that included illustrations. These illustrations were often irrelevant to the main points of the text, such as having a picture of snow in a passage about ice ages—the snow is related to the topic, but does not provide or support any new information. As such, performance is better if working memory capacity were to focus on the relevant details in the text. What was found was that people with lower memory spans were more likely to be "seduced" by the irrelevant details in the pictures. That is, they had more difficulty controlling the contents of their current stream of thought, and were more likely to be led astray by attractive, but unhelpful, sources of knowledge that served as a distraction.

Working Memory and Long-Term Memory

Long-term memory function can also depend on working memory. Rosen and Engle (1997), for instance, had high- and low-span people do a verbal fluency task: Generate members of the animal category as rapidly as possible for up to 15 minutes. High-span people outperformed their low-span counterparts, a difference noticeable

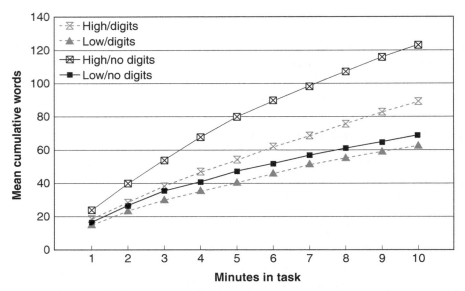

FIGURE 5-13   The cumulative number of animal names generated by participants of high (open points) or low (filled points) working memory span. Dashed lines indicate performance when participants performed the secondary task of monitoring a stream of digits while generating animal names.

Source: From Rosen & Engle (1997).

even 1 minute into the task. Intriguingly, in a second experiment, both groups were tested in the fluency task alone and in a dual-task setting. While naming animals, people had to simultaneously monitor the digits that showed up, one by one, on the computer monitor and press a key whenever three odd digits appeared in the sequence. This task reduced performance on the animal naming task, but only for the high-span people, as shown in Figure 5-13. Low-span people showed no decrease in performance.

Rosen and Engle suggested that the normal, automatic long-term memory search for animal names was equivalent in both groups. But high-span people were able to augment this with a conscious, controlled strategic search; in other words, along with regular retrieval, the high-span people could deliberately ferret out additional, hard-to-find animal names using a controlled attentional process. This additional "ferreting" process used working memory. As a consequence, the added digit monitoring task used up the working memory resources that had been devoted to the strategic search. This made the high-span group perform more like the low-span group when they had to perform the dual task.

Other studies have also shown the importance of working memory. For instance, Kane and Engle (2000) found that low-span people experience more proactive interference (PI) in the Brown–Peterson task than do high-span people. High-span people used their controlled attentional processes to combat PI, so they showed an increase in PI when they had to do a simultaneous secondary task (see Bunting, Conway, & Heitz, 2004; Cantor & Engle, 1993; and Radvansky & Copeland, 2006a; for an exploration of the role of working memory span in managing associative interference during retrieval). More generally, low-span people appear to search a wider range of knowledge, making them more prone to having irrelevant information intrude on retrieval (Unsworth, 2007). In Hambrick and Engle (2002; see also Hambrick & Meinz, 2011), high-span people had better performance than low-span people on a long-term memory retrieval task, even when both groups were equated for the rather specialized domain knowledge being tested (what a nice experiment to participate in—people listened to simulated radio broadcasts of baseball games).

Working Memory and Reasoning

The idea that working memory involves controlled attention can also be tied to general issues of cognitive and behavioral control, such as those needed in problem solving. People with lower memory span scores may be less effective at controlling their thought processes. One example of this is a study by Moore, Clark, and Kane (2008) that looked at working memory span and choices on moral reasoning problems. For example, suppose that there is a runaway trolley car. If you let it go, it will kill four unaware people a bit down the track. Alternatively, you could push a very large person next to you in front of the trolley; it will kill him, but derail the trolley and save the other four people. So, how morally acceptable is each of these choices? Moore et al. found that moral reasoning of this type was mediated by a person's working memory capacity, with high working memory capacity people making choices on a more consistent (i.e., principled) basis.

The influence of memory span is also seen on more traditional sorts of mental reasoning, such as solving logic problems like categorical syllogisms (see Chapter 11). In a study by Copeland and Radvansky (2004a; see also Markovits & Doyon, 2004), people with various working memory spans were asked to solve a set of logic problems. There were two primary findings. First, people with greater memory spans solved more syllogisms than people with smaller memory spans. Moreover, working memory span was also related to the strategies people used to reason; people with smaller memory spans used simpler strategies. It may be that having more working memory capacity allows one to keep more information active in memory, allowing a person to explore different alternatives when trying to reason and draw conclusions.

Sometimes Small Working Memory Spans Are Better

Intuitively, it would seem that people with more working memory capacity, or those who engage working memory resources more effectively, are more likely to succeed, and generally this is true. However, there are some interesting exceptions. One of these is illustrated in a study by Beilock and DeCaro (2007). In this study, high- and low-span people were given math problems to solve. Under normal conditions, high-span people tended to do better. However, people were then placed in a high-pressure situation; they were told that they were being timed, that their performance would be videotaped so math experts could evaluate them, that they would be paid for improving their performance, and so forth. In this high-pressure condition, working memory capacity was consumed with task-irrelevant anxiety-induced thoughts, and performance in both the high- and low-span groups was equivalent (and lower). Thus, when people have their working memory capacity consumed by irrelevant thoughts, they are more likely to use simpler, less effective strategies. This shift to simpler strategies equated people by causing the high-span people to solve the problems more like the low-span people, who were using simpler strategies in the first place.

Of particular interest, in a second experiment, people were asked to do a series of word problems that required a complex series of steps (i.e., B − A − 2 × C). Then under low- or high-pressure conditions, people were given a series of new problems, some of which required a simpler solution (i.e., A − C). Beilock and DeCaro (2007) found that the low-span people were actually more likely to use the simpler, correct solution than the high-span people. The explanation was that low-span people are less likely to derive rule-based strategies for solving problems (because they have less capacity to do so) and are more likely to draw from previous similar experiences. Thus, when given problems with the simpler solutions, the low-span people were less dependent on a complex, rule-based strategy they derived earlier, and so were more likely to use the more appropriate, simpler strategy (for other examples of better performance by people with smaller memory spans, see Colflesh & Conway, 2007; Cokely, Kelley, & Gilchrist, 2006).

Overview

The general conclusion from all these studies is that *working memory* is a more suitable name for the attention-limited workbench system. Working memory is responsible for the active mental effort of regulating attention, for transferring information into and from long-term memory.

Importantly, there is a limit to the mental resources available to working memory; when extra resources are drained by the subsystems, the central executive suffers along with insufficient resources for its own work. Naturally, as processes become more automatic, fewer resources are tied down (e.g., working memory is unrelated to counting when there are only two or three things to count but is influenced for larger quantities; Tuholski, Engle, & Baylis, 2001).

The "Engle tradition" emphasizes the general nature of working memory capacity as a measure of executive attention and de-emphasizes the multicomponent working memory approach advocated by Baddeley. Part of the reason for this is the generality of the working memory effects. Working memory span predicts performance on a variety of tasks. Of particular importance, working memory span routinely correlates with measures of intelligence, especially so-called fluid intelligence (Fukuda, Vogel, Mayr, & Awh, 2010; Kane et al., 2004; Salthouse & Pink, 2008; Shelton, Elliot, Matthews, Hill, & Gouvier, 2010), and more so if metacognitive control is taken into account (McCabe, 2010). The relationship between working memory and intelligence is that people who have greater cognitive control, and can manage sources of interference better, score better on intelligence tests. This is even supported by neuroimaging data in which people with higher working memory span and intelligence scores show better interference control in cortical areas tied to these processes, such as the dorsolateral prefrontal cortex (B.A. 9) and portions of the parietal cortex (B.A.s 7 and 40) (Burgess, Gray, Conway, & Braver, 2011).

Common to both the Baddeley and the Engle approaches, however, is a central set of principles. Working memory is intimately related to executive control, to the deliberate allocation of attention to a task, and to the maintenance of efficient, effective cognitive processing and behavior. There is a limitation, however, in the amount of attention available at any one time. Furthermore, the ability to deliberately focus and allocate attention, and to suppress or inhibit attention to extraneous factors, is key to higher-order cognitive processing.

Section Summary

- Working memory abilities and performance are critical to many tasks assessed by cognitive psychologists. For example, working memory capacity is strongly related to the ability to engage attention. It has also been shown to be strongly related to the efficiency with which simple facts can be retrieved from long-term memory.
- Although larger working memory capacity is associated with superior cognitive performance, there are cases where circumstances favor smaller working memory capacity. These are typically circumstances where it is better not to devote too much attention to a task.
- Although there is no clear view on exactly what working memory is, as evidenced by the Baddeley multicomponent model and the Engle attentional control view, there are a number of agreed-on characteristics of what working memory is able to do. These include its limited capacity, the ability to simultaneously handle certain types of noninterfering forms of information, the fact that people differ in their working memory capacities and abilities, and that these individual differences are related to performance on a variety of tasks.

Key Terms

articulatory loop
articulatory
    suppression effect
boundary extension
Brown–Peterson task
central executive
chunk
decay
dual task method

episodic buffer
free recall
mental rotation
phonological loop
phonological similarity
    effect
phonological store
primacy effect

proactive interference
    (PI)
process model
recency effect
recoding
release from PI
representational
    momentum
retroactive interference
    (RI)

serial exhaustive
    search
serial position curve
serial recall
visuo-spatial sketch
    pad
working memory
working memory span

Sample Lists for Simple Memory Span Tests

Digits
8 7 0 3 1 4
7 1 5 0 5 4 3 6
2 8 4 3 6 1 2 9 7 5
Words
leaf gift car fish rock
paper seat tire horse film beach forest brush
bag key book wire box wheel banana floor bar pad block radio boy

Learning and Remembering

Memory is the most important function of the brain; without it life would be a blank. Our knowledge is all based on memory. Every thought, every action, our very conception of personal identity, is based on memory. . . . Without memory, all experience would be useless.

(EDRIDGE-GREEN, 1900)

This is the first of three chapters devoted to long-term memory, the storage vault for a lifetime's worth of knowledge and experience. Why three chapters? First, as indicated in the quotation above: Long-term memory is fundamental to nearly every mental process, to almost every act of cognition. You cannot understand cognition unless you understand long-term memory. Second, long-term memory is an enormous research area—there's a lot to know

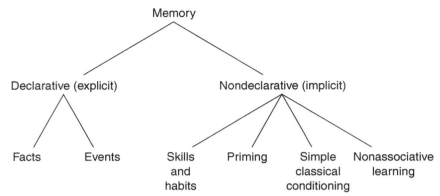

FIGURE 6-1   A taxonomy of long-term memories. Adapted from Squire (1993).

about. Third, people are curious about their own memories. Who has not complained, at some time, about forgetfulness or the unreliability of memory?

Long-term memory is divided and subdivided in various ways. Look at Figure 6-1, a taxonomy suggested by Squire (1986, 1993). As the figure shows, a distinction can be made between **declarative memory** (or **explicit memory**) and **nondeclarative memory** (or **implicit memory**). Here, declarative or explicit memory is *long-term memory knowledge that is retrieved and reflected on consciously.* The two types of declarative knowledge, episodic and semantic memory, are the topics of this chapter and the next. In contrast, nondeclarative or implicit memory is *knowledge that influences thought and behavior without any necessary involvement of consciousness.* The key to this distinction is conscious awareness—one has it, one doesn't.

Here's a brief example to help clarify the distinction between episodic and semantic memory. If you were asked what happened when you took your driver's license test, you retrieve knowledge from **episodic memory**, that is, *memory of the personally experienced events.* When you retrieve that information, you are conscious of it, you can talk about it, and so on. Episodic memory enables you to record your personal history. Alternatively, if you were asked what a driver's license is, you retrieve from **semantic memory**, your *general world knowledge.* You retrieve the concept of a driver's license, and it is now in your conscious awareness. Notice that whereas episodic memory is your mental slide show, semantic memory is your mental encyclopedia, and both involve knowledge that you can be consciously aware of (Tulving, 1972, 1983, 1993).

But there is more going on than what rises to the level of conscious awareness. As you read this sentence, you encounter the term *license* again. Although you are not conscious of it, you are faster at reading that term than you were the first time; the rereading speedup is called repetition priming. This happens at the nondeclarative, implicit level. Likewise, if we gave you some word stems an hour from now and asked you to fill in the blanks with the first word that comes to mind, you would be more likely than chance to complete "LIC___ " as "LICENSE" because you encountered it recently. Importantly, this happens even if you do not consciously recall having seen the word *license* (but teasing apart conscious and unconscious influences is no simple matter; see Buchner & Wippich, 2000; Jacoby, 1991; Jacoby, Toth, & Yonelinas, 1993).

An important aspect of episodic memories is that they are integrated mental representations. Different bits and pieces of information from different parts of our conscious and unconscious mental worlds are woven together. In Chapter 5 we introduced the episodic buffer, the part of working memory that integrates different types of knowledge together to form episodic memories. Although many of the examples given here use linguistic materials, such as word lists, episodic memories integrate various types of information, including sensory, motor, spatial, language, emotional, and narrative information, as well as other various encoding and retrieval processes (Rubin, 2007). Even this is not an exhaustive list. So, as you can see, episodic memory uses a rich variety of information about a broad range of human experience.

The main focus of this chapter is on episodic memory, although we also cover some issues about implicit memory as well. We progress, covering what is known about how storage and retrieval influence how we learn and remember. In the final section we discuss implicit memory along with a discussion of evidence about memory and amnesia.

PRELIMINARY ISSUES

Let's start by considering three preliminary issues. First, we talk about a classic, ancient approach to memory, mnemonic devices. We then spend time on the first systematic research on human memory, by Ebbinghaus, published in 1885. These topics suggest that people have always been aware of some of the workings—and failings—of memory. Such awareness is called **metamemory**, a type of **metacognition**. Here's a warning: As you read the chapters on long-term memory, keep in mind that just as your frustrations over your own memory problems probably are exaggerated, so is your certainty about remembering. It's a paradox; our memories are better than we often give ourselves credit for, and worse than we are often willing to believe or admit.

Mnemonics

The term *mnemonic* (pronounced *"ne-MAHN-ick"*) means "to help the memory"; it comes from the same Indo-European base word as *remember, mind,* and *think.* A **mnemonic** is an *active, strategic learning device or method.* Formal mnemonics use preestablished sets of aids and considerable practice. The strengths of mnemonics include: (1) The material to be remembered is practiced repeatedly, (2) the material is integrated into an existing memory framework, and (3) the mnemonic provides a way to retrieve the material. Let's consider two traditional mnemonics.

CLASSIC MNEMONICS The first historical mention of mnemonics is in Cicero's *De oratore,* a treatise on rhetoric (the art of public speaking, which in those days meant speaking from memory). The power of mnemonics is tremendous; among other things, mnemonics enabled Greek orators to memorize and recite epics such as *The Iliad* and *The Odyssey.* Cicero describes a technique, based on visual imagery and memorized locations, called the **method of loci** (*loci* is the plural of *locus,* meaning "a place"; pronounced *"LOW-sigh"*). There are two steps to this method.

TABLE 6-1   The Method of Loci

Set of Loci	Word to Be Remembered	Grocery List and Images
Driveway	Grapefruit	Grapefruit instead of rocks along side of driveway
Garage door	Tomatoes	Tomatoes splattered on garage door
Front door of house	Lettuce	Lettuce leaves hanging over door instead of awning
Coat closet	Oatmeal	Oatmeal oozing out the door when I hang up my coat
Fireplace	Milk	Fire got out of control, so spray milk instead of water
Easy chair	Sugar	Throw pillow is a 5-7lb bag of sugar
Television	Coffee	Mrs. Olson advertising coffee
Dining-room table	Carrots	Legs of table are made of carrots

First, choose a known set of locations that can be recalled easily and in order, such as locations you encounter in a walk across campus, or as you arrive home. Now form a mental image of the first thing you want to remember and mentally place it into the first location, the second item in the second location, and so on (see Table 6-1) for examples. When it's time to recall the items, you mentally stroll through your set of locations, "looking" at the places and "seeing" the items you have placed there.

Another mnemonic is the **peg word mnemonic** (Miller, Galanter, & Pribram, 1960), in which *a prememorized set of words serves as a sequence of mental "pegs" onto which the to-be-remembered material can be "hung."* The peg words rely on rhymes with the numbers one through ten, such as "One is a bun, two is a shoe," and so on (Table 6-2). The to-be-learned material is then hung on the pegs, making sure that the rhyming word and the to-be-remembered item form a mental image. For the list "cup, flag, horse, dollar, . . ." create a visual image of a flattened tin cup, dripping with ketchup, inside your hamburger bun; for flag, conjure up a

TABLE 6-2   The Peg Word Mnemonic Device

Numbered Pegs	Word to Be Learned	Image
One is a bun	Cup	Hamburger bun with smashed cup
Two is a shoe	Flag	Running shoes with flag
Three is a tree	Horse	Horse stranded in top of tree
Four is a door	Dollar	Dollar bill tacked to front door
Five is a hive	Brush	Queen bee brushing her hair
Six is sticks	Pan	Boiling a pan full of cinnamon sticks
Seven is Heaven	Clock	St. Peter checking the clock at the gates of Heaven
Eight is a gate	Pen	A picket fence gate with ballpoint pens as pickets
Nine is a vine	Paper	Honeysuckle vine with newspapers instead of blossoms
Ten is a hen	Shirt	A baked hen on the platter wearing a flannel shirt

visual image of your running shoes with little American flags fluttering in the breeze as you run; and so on. Now at recall, all you have to do is first remember what peg word rhymes with one, then retrieve the bun image you created, looking inside to see a cup. Similarly, what peg word rhymes with *two,* and what image do you find along with *shoe?*

Mnemonic effectiveness involves three principles. First, it provides a structure for acquiring the information. The structure may be elaborate, like a set of 40 loci, or simple, like rhyming peg words. It can even be arbitrary if the material is not extensive. (The mnemonic *HOMES* for the names of the five Great Lakes—Huron, Ontario, Michigan, Erie, and Superior—isn't related to the to-be-remembered material, but it is simple.) Second, using visual images, rhymes, or other kinds of associations and the effort and rehearsal to form them, this helps create a durable and distinctive memories (what's sticking out of your running shoes?). So, a mnemonic helps safeguard against forgetting (but see Thomas & Wang, 1996, for less optimistic long-term benefits of mnemonics). Finally, the mnemonic guides you through retrieval by providing cues for recalling information. This function is important because much of forgetting is often a case of retrieval difficulty. In fact, it can't be stressed enough how the active use of retrieval cues—and practicing retrieval—are important for successful remembering (extended practice was the key in Chaffin & Imreh's [2002] study of how a pianist learned, remembered, and performed a challenging piece).

This three-step sequence may sound familiar. It is the sequence we talk about every time we consider learning and memory: the *encoding* of new information, its *retention* over time, and *retrieval* of the information (Melton, 1963). Performance in any situation that involves memory depends on all three steps. A fault along any one of the three might account for poor performance. A good mnemonic, including those you invent for yourself (e.g., Wenger & Payne, 1995), ensures success at each of the three stages. (Incidentally, don't count on a magic bullet to enhance your memory. Research has found little if any evidence that ginkgo biloba, or any other "memory enhancer," has any real effect; Gold, Cahill, & Wenk, 2002, 2003; Greenwald, Spangenberg, Pratkanis, & Eskenazi, 1991; McDaniel, Maier, & Einstein, 2002).

The Ebbinghaus Tradition

We turn now to the first systematic research on human memory, done by the German psychologist Hermann von Ebbinghaus. As noted in Chapter 1, the Ebbinghaus tradition began with the publication of *Über das Gedächtnis* (1885; the 1964 English translation is titled *Memory: A Contribution to Experimental Psychology*). Ebbinghaus used himself as the only subject in his studies. He also had to invent his own memory task, his own stimuli, and his own procedures for testing and data analysis. Few could do as well today. In devising how to analyze his results, he even came close to inventing a within-groups *t* test (Ebbinghaus, 1885/1913, footnote 1, p. 67).

It is helpful to consider *why* Ebbinghaus felt compelled to invent and use nonsense syllables. His rationale was that he wanted to study the properties of memory and forgetting apart from the influence of prior knowledge. As such, words would complicate his results. If he had used words it would be less clear whether performance reflected the simple use of memory, or the influence of prior knowledge. Putting it simply, *learning* implies acquiring *new* information. Yet, words are not new. And a control factor he adopted, to reduce the possible intrusion of mnemonic factors, was the rapid presentation rate of 2.5 items per second.

The task Ebbinghaus devised was the **relearning task**, in which *a list is originally learned, set aside for a period of time, then later relearned to the same criterion of accuracy.* In most cases, this was one perfect recitation of the list, without hesitations. After relearning the list, Ebbinghaus computed a **savings score** as the measure of learning; the savings score was *the reduction in the number of trials (or the time) necessary for relearning, compared to original learning.* Thus, if it took 10 trials to originally learn a list but only 6 for relearning, there was a 40% savings (4 fewer trials on relearning divided by the 10 original trials). By this method, *any* information that was left over in memory from original learning could have an influence, conscious or not (see Nelson, 1978, 1985; Schacter, 1987). Work by MacLeod (1988) indicates that relearning seems to help retrieve information that was stored in memory yet is not recallable.

Figure 6-2 presents Ebbinghaus's forgetting curve (actually a retention curve), showing the reduction in savings as a function of time until relearning (as Slamecka, 1985, points out, for the data in Figure 6-2, Ebbinghaus used more than 1,200 lists of nonsense syllables). Ebbinghaus relearned the lists after one of seven intervals: 20 minutes, 1 hour, 9 hours, 1 day, 2 days, 6 days, or 31 days. As is clear

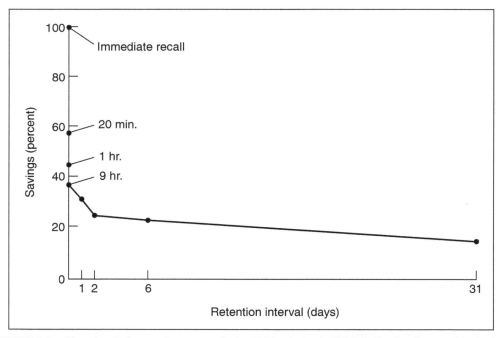

FIGURE 6-2 The classic forgetting curve from Ebbinghaus (1885/1913). The figure shows the reduction in savings across increasing retention intervals (time between original learning and relearning).

from the figure, the most dramatic forgetting occurs early after original learning. This is followed by a decrease in the rate of forgetting (technically, a negatively accelerating power function; Wixted & Ebbesen, 1991) and is found for a variety of other memory tests. That said, as outlined in a nice review by Erdelyi (2010), note that although generally and overall there is a loss of memories over time, it is possible for items that were previously forgotten to be remembered later (*reminiscence*). There are even cases when the rate of reminiscence may be greater than the rate of forgetting, and a person remembers more over time, a phenomenon called *hypermnesia*.

Other fundamentals Ebbinghaus found were impressive not because they were surprising, but because he first demonstrated them. For example, he studied the effects of repetitions, studying one list 32 times and another 64 times. Upon relearning, the more frequently repeated list showed about twice the savings of the less frequently repeated list; in other words, *overlearning* yields a stronger record in memory. Longer lists took more trials to learn than shorter lists but showed higher savings upon relearning. So, although it is harder to learn a long list originally, the longer list is remembered better, because there was more opportunity to overlearn it (there were more trials in learning before mastery of the whole list). The connection between learning difficulty and memory has been confirmed repeatedly (e.g., Schneider, Healy, & Bourne, 2002).

Finally, in one study, Ebbinghaus continued to relearn the same set of lists across a five-day period. The savings scores showed no forgetting at all. Ebbinghaus also reported his results on relearning passages of poetry (kept at 80 syllables). After the fourth day, the savings was 100%.

Beyond the idea of overlearning, there are issues involved with how people repeatedly study to learn something. Specifically, how quickly and effectively something is learned varies as a function of whether study sessions are grouped together, or spread out over time. If *study time is grouped together into one long session*, this is called **massed practice**, although many students know this better as *cramming*. In comparison, if *study time is spread out over many, shorter sessions*, this is called **distributed practice**. This distinction between these two types of studying is important because memory is much better with distributed practice than with massed practice (Glenberg & Lehmann, 1980), although many students incorrectly believe the opposite (Zechmeister & Shaughnessy, 1980). Students often report that they feel like they are working harder when they cram than when they study consistently throughout the term. And in general, that is true—people are working harder with massed practice. The problem is that a person is not learning much. So, you can save yourself a lot of time, and do better in your course work, if you spread your studying out across the term than if you cram (note that cramming also denies you of the beneficial effects of sleep on memory improvement). These benefits can even be seen a year later (Pashler, Rohrer, Cepeda, & Carpenter, 2007).

Metamemory

Think about these two issues, mnemonics and Ebbinghaus's work, from a larger perspective: They both involve intuitions about memory, what makes remembering easier or harder. This self-awareness about memory is **metamemory**, *knowledge about (meta) one's own memory, how it works or fails to work.* Research on this topic has raised at least two important issues. First is the importance of metacognitive awareness. A number of studies have focused on metamemory, such as people's "judgments-of-learning" and "feeling-of-knowing" estimates (Leonesio & Nelson, 1990; Nelson, 1988). Part of a person's behavior in a learning task involves self-monitoring, assessing how well one is doing and adjusting study strategies (e.g., Son, 2004). For example, these metacognitions guide people to know when to change their answers on multiple-choice exams (Higham & Garrard, 2005). However, metamemory can occasionally mislead us, leading to either over- or underconfidence that we've learned something (e.g., Koriat, Sheffer, & Ma'ayan, 2002).

The second issue involves self-regulation. If you realize you are not doing some task particularly well, what do you do to improve? Some of the research on metacognition gives some insight into some difficulties people have. For example, Mazzoni and Cornoldi (1993) report that people often "labor in vain," that is, devote more study time to difficult items, and yet do not improve much at all (see also Metcalfe, 2002; Nelson, 1993). Alternatively, Thiede (1999; see also Metcalfe & Kornell, 2003) argues that when study time is used appropriately, a positive, sensible relationship between monitoring and self-regulation emerges. This is what Son and Metcalfe (2000) call the *region of proximal learning*, studying information that is just beyond one's current knowledge and saving the more difficult material for later. The problem is that people are often poor judges of what they have and have not learned and make choices about what to study based on this inaccurate information (Metcalfe & Finn, 2008).

Section Summary

- Long-term memory is a divided between declarative memories and nondeclarative memories. Declarative memory consists of episodic and semantic memories; nondeclarative memory includes priming and procedural or motor learning. Declarative memories can be verbalized, but nondeclarative memories cannot; conscious awareness of the memory is unnecessary for implicit memory tasks but does accompany explicit memory tasks.
- A classic method for improving memory involves mnemonics. Mnemonics, such as the method of loci, use a variety of techniques, especially visual imagery, to improve performance.
- Ebbinghaus was the first person to extensively study memory and forgetting. Working on his own, he invented methods for doing so. The relearning task revealed a sensitivity to the demands of simple recall tasks—that they measure consciously retrievable information but underestimate the amount of information learned and remembered. The classic forgetting curve he obtained, along with his results on practice effects, inspired the tradition of verbal learning and, later, cognitive psychology.

STORING INFORMATION IN EPISODIC MEMORY

How do people store information in episodic memory? And how can we measure this storage? Ebbinghaus investigated one storage variable, repetition, and one memory task, relearning. He found that increasing the number of repetitions led to a stronger memory, a *trace* of the information in memory that could be relearned faster. Thus, frequency is a fundamental influence on memory: Information that is presented more frequently is stored more strongly.

A corollary of this is that people are good at remembering how frequently something has occurred (e.g., how many movies you've seen in the past month). Hasher and Zacks (1984) summarize a large body of research on how sensitive people are to event frequency. Because people's estimates of frequency generally are good, they proposed that frequency information is automatically encoded into memory, with no deliberate effort or intent. Although just how automatic this has been disputed (Greene, 1986; Hanson & Hirst, 1988; Jonides & Jones, 1992), there is no doubt that event frequency has an impact on long-term memory.

The flip side of frequency is distinctiveness. It is easier to remember unusual, unexpected, or distinctive events. This is technically called the **isolation effect**, but is more commonly known as the **von Restorff effect**, named after the woman who did the first study (von Restorff, 1933). The effect is simply *better memory for information that is distinct from the information around it,* such as printing one word in a list in red ink or changing its size (Cooper & Pantle, 1967; Kelley & Nairne, 2001). The isolation effect relies on memory for the distinctive item to be noticed as distinctive. Generally, the occurrence of unexpected and distinctive items can produce increased processing in the hippocampus (e.g., Axmacher et al., 2010). Thus, damage to the hippocampus should reduce or eliminate the von Restorff effect. In a study by Kishiyama, Yonelinas, and Lazzara (2004), people who were amnesic (as a result of damage to their medial temporal lobes and hippocampus) did not show a von Restorff effect (see Figure 6-3). That is because they could not remember the other items in the list very well, they could not identify the isolated item as unique, and so it did not stand out in memory. Thus, distinctiveness was not effective for this group of people.

But what about more typical situations, when the world doesn't highlight material to make it more frequent or more distinctive? How do you learn and remember something new? There are three important steps here: rehearsal, organization, and imagery. A summary of these will then lead us to the topic of retrieval and a discussion of forgetting.

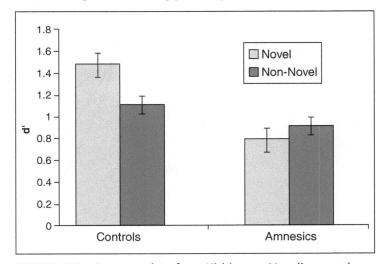

FIGURE 6-3 Accuracy data from Kishiyama, Yonelinas, and Lazzara (2004) (using the signal detection measure of d′) showing memory for a novel distinctive item (the von Restorff effect) for normal controls on the left and amnesics on the right. Notice that performance is better for the novel information for the normal controls, but not for the amnesics.

Why do we rehearse?

Rehearsal

In Atkinson and Shiffrin's (1968) important model of human memory, information in short-term memory was subject to **rehearsal**, *a deliberate recycling or practicing of information in the short-term store.* They proposed two effects of rehearsal. First, rehearsal maintains information in the short-term store. Second, the longer an item is held in short-term memory, the more likely it will be stored in long-term memory, with the strength of the item's long-term memory trace depending on the amount of rehearsal it received. In short, rehearsal transfers information into long-term memory (see also Waugh & Norman, 1965).

Frequency of Rehearsal

What evidence is there of this? Aside from Ebbinghaus, many experiments have shown that rehearsal leads to better long-term retention. For example, Hellyer (1962) used the Brown–Peterson task, with CVC trigrams, and with an arithmetic task between study and recall. On some trials the trigram had to be spoken aloud one, two, four, or eight times. Figure 6-4 shows the results. The more frequently an item was rehearsed, the better it was retained. However, although rehearsal does improve memory, other work suggests that it is not repeated study that produces the primary memory benefit, but the repeated attempts at trying to remember (Karpicke & Roediger, 2007).

FIGURE 6-4
Hellyer's (1962) recall accuracy results as a function of the number of rehearsals afforded the three-letter nonsense syllable and the retention interval.

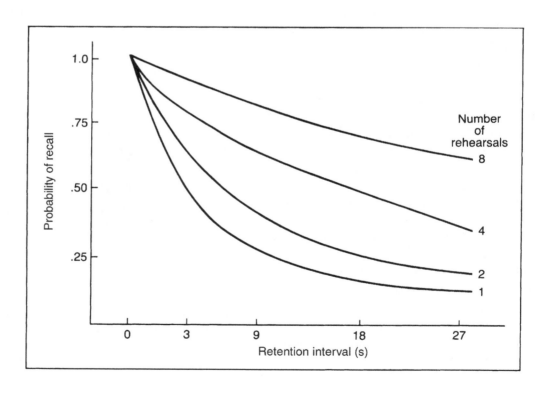

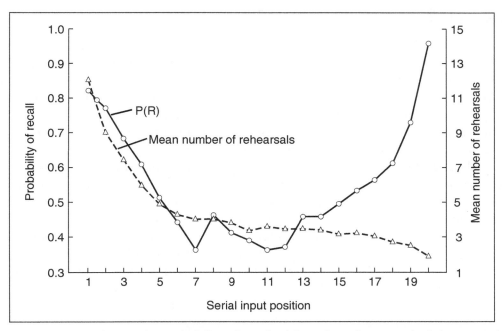

FIGURE 6-5   In the figure, the probability of recall, P(R), is plotted against the left axis, and the number of rehearsals afforded an item during storage is plotted against the right axis. The similar pattern of these two functions across the primacy portion of the list indicates that rehearsal is the factor responsible for primacy effects.

REHEARSAL AND SERIAL POSITION   More evidence on the effects of rehearsal was provided in a series of studies by Rundus (1971; Rundus & Atkinson, 1970). In these experiments, Rundus had people learn 20-item lists of words, presenting them at a rate of 5 seconds per word. People were told to rehearse aloud as they studied the lists, repeating whatever words they cared to during each 5-second presentation. Rundus then tabulated the number of times each word was rehearsed and compared this to the likelihood of later recalling the word. Figure 6-5 shows his most telling results. In the early primacy portion of the serial position effect, there was a positive relationship between the frequency of rehearsal and the rate of recall. In other words, the primacy effect depended on rehearsal. The early items are rehearsed more frequently and so are recalled better. High recall of the late positions, the recency effect, was viewed as recall from short-term memory, which is why they were recalled so well despite being rehearsed so little.

Although we discussed serial position curves in Chapter 5, similar curves are observed in long-term memory. That is, given an event of a certain type, such as going to the movies, people are likely to remember their first and last experiences better, and not so much those in the middle (e.g., Sehulster, 1989). This even applies to semantic information, such as knowledge of the presidents of the United States (Roediger & Crowder, 1976). Although some people have argued that the cognitive processes involved in long-term memory are different from those involved in short-term memory (Davelaar, Goshen-Gottstein, Ashkenazi, Haarman, & Usher, 2005), there has also been some suggestion that the same principles are driving the serial position curves in both the short- and long-term memory (e.g., Brown, Neath, & Chater, 2007).

Depth of Processing

A more refined idea is that there are two kinds of rehearsal (Craik & Lockhart, 1972). **Maintenance rehearsal** is *a low-level, repetitive information recycling.* This is the rehearsal you use to recycle a phone number to yourself until you dial it. Once you stop rehearsing, the information is lost. In Craik and Lockhart's view, maintenance rehearsal holds information at a particular level in memory, without storing it permanently. As long as information is maintained, it can be retrieved. Once rehearsal stops, however, it will likely vanish.

Elaborative rehearsal is *a more complex rehearsal that uses the meaning of the information to store and remember it.* Information that is elaboratively rehearsed is stored more deeply in memory and is remembered better. You might include imagery or mnemonic elaboration in your elaborative rehearsal, you might try to construct sentences from the words in a list, you might impose an organization on the list, or you might even convert nonsense syllables like BEF into more meaningful items like BEEF. Stating it differently, maintenance rehearsal maintains an item at its current level of storage, whereas elaborative rehearsal moves the item more deeply, and more permanently, into memory.

Simulate
Depth of Processing in
MyPsychLab

Craik and Lockhart (1972) proposed a theory of memory different from the stage approach of sensory, short-, and long-term memory. They embedded their two kinds of rehearsal into what they called the **levels of processing**, or **depth of processing**, framework. The essence of this is as follows. Information receives some amount of mental processing. Some items that get only incidental attention are processed at a shallow level (as in hearing the sounds of the words without attending to their meaning, as a daydreamer might do during a lecture). Other items get more intentional and meaningful processing that elaborates the memory of that item—for example, by drawing relationships between already-known information and what is being processed.

Several predictions from the depth of processing framework were tested with a fair degree of initial success. For example, if information is shallowly processed, using only maintenance rehearsal, then the information should not be well remembered later; if it is only maintained, then it should not be stored at a deep, meaningful level in long-term memory. This was the kind of result that was obtained. As an example, Craik and Watkins (1973) devised a monitoring task; people heard a long list of words but only had to keep track of the most recent word beginning with, say, a *G*. In a surprise recall test, people showed no recall differences for "*G*-words" held a long time versus those maintained only briefly (see also Craik & Tulving, 1975).

Challenges to Depth of Processing

As research continued on the depth of processing framework, some difficulties cropped up. One example was Baddeley's (1978) review paper "The Trouble with Levels." A major point in this review was the problem of defining levels independently of retention scores (see Glenberg & Adams, 1978; Glenberg, Smith, & Green, 1977). In essence, there is no method for deciding ahead of time whether a particular kind of rehearsal would lead to shallow or deep processing. Instead, we had to wait and see whether it improved recall. If it did, it must have been elaborative rehearsal; if it did not, it must have been maintenance rehearsal. The circularity of this reasoning should be obvious and was a serious problem for depth of processing ideas of memory retention.

TASK EFFECTS   A second point in Baddeley's (1978) review concerned task effects. That is, a difficulty arose with the levels of processing approach when different memory tasks were used. The reason was simply that very different results were obtained using one or another task.

We have known since Ebbinghaus that different memory tasks reveal different things about the variables that affect performance. Ebbinghaus used a relearning task, so that even material that was hard to retrieve might still influence memory performance. In a similar vein, a substantial difference is found between performance on recall and **recognition** tasks. In recognition, people are shown items that were originally studied, known as "old" or target items, as well as items that were not studied, known as "new," lure, or distractor items. They must then decide which are targets and which are distractors (multiple-choice tests are recognition tests, by the way). Recognition accuracy usually is higher than recall accuracy (see Table 6-3 for a description of these tasks). Furthermore, recognition is influenced by two different factors, recollection—the actual remembering of the information—and familiarity—the general sense that you've experienced the information before (e.g., Curran, 2000; Yonelinas, 2002). Indeed, studies on false memory that you'll read about in Chapter 8 often ask people whether they actually "remember" experiencing an event or whether they just "know" that it happened.

Recognition is easier than recall, in part because the answer is presented to a person, who then only has to make a new versus old decision. Because more information is stored in memory than can be retrieved easily, recognition shows greater sensitivity to the influence of stored information (the issue of *how much* easier recognition is than recall is difficult to resolve; see research by Craik, Govoni, Naveh-Benjamin, & Anderson, 1996, and by Hicks & Marsh, 2000).

The relevance of this to the depth of processing framework is that most of the early research that supported it used recall tasks. When recognition was used, however, maintenance rehearsal had clear effects on long-term memory. A clever set of studies by Glenberg et al. (1977) confirmed this. They used a Brown–Peterson task, asking people to remember a four-digit number as the (supposedly) primary task. During retention intervals that varied in duration, people had to repeat either one or three words aloud as a distractor task (don't confuse the distractor task here with distractor items, items in a recognition test that were not shown originally). Because people believed that digit recall was the important task, they devoted only minimal effort to the word repetitions, and so probably used only maintenance rehearsal. After the supposedly "main" part of the task was done, people were given a surprise recall task; the results showed the standard effect. But when they were given a surprise recognition task, the amount of time spent rehearsing *did* influence performance; words rehearsed for 18 seconds were recognized better than those rehearsed for shorter intervals. Thus, the generalization that maintenance rehearsal does not lead to improved memory performance was disconfirmed—it did not apply when memory was tested with a recognition task.

TABLE 6-3   Standard Memory Tasks and Terminology

Relearning Task

1. Original learning: Learn list items (e.g., list of unrelated words) to some accuracy criterion.
2. Delay after learning the list.
3. Learn the list a second time.

Dependent variables: The main dependent variable is the savings score: how many fewer trials are needed during relearning relative to number of trials for the original learning. If the original learning took 10 trials and relearning took 6, then relearning took 4 fewer trials. Savings score = 4/10; expressed as a percentage, savings was 40%.

Independent or control variables: Presentation rate, list item types, list length, accuracy criterion.

Paired-Associate Learning Task

1. A list of pairs is shown, one pair at a time. The first member of the pair is the stimulus, and the second member is the response (e.g., for the pair "ice–brush," "ice" is the stimulus term and "brush" is the correct response).
2. After one study trial, the stimulus terms are shown, one at a time, and the person tries to name the correct response term for that stimulus.
3. Typically, the task involves several successive attempts at learning, each including first a study trial, then a test trial; the order of the pairs is changed each time. In the anticipation method, there is one continuous stream of trials, each consisting of two parts, presenting the stimulus alone, then presenting the stimulus and response together. Across repetitions, people begin to learn the correct pairings.

Dependent variables: Typically the number of study test trials to achieve correct responding to all stimulus terms ("trials to criterion") is the dependent variable.

Independent and control variables: Presentation rate, length of list, the types of items in the stimulus and response terms, and the types of connections between them. Commonly, once a list had been mastered, then either the stimulus or response terms are changed, or the item pairings rearranged (e.g., "ice–brush" and "card–floor" in the first list, then "ice–floor" and "card–brush" on the second list).

Recall Task

Serial Recall Task: Learn a list of items, and then recall them in the original order of presentation.
Free Recall Task: Learn the list information, and then recall the items in any order.

1. Learn list items.
2. Optional delay or distractor task during delay.
3. Recall list items.

Dependent variables: The main dependent variable is the number (or proportion) of items recalled correctly. For serial recall, accuracy is scored as a function of the original position of the items in the list. Occasionally, other dependent variables involve speed, or organization of recall (e.g., items recalled by category—"apple, pear, banana, orange"—before items from a different category are recalled).

Independent or control variables: Rate of presentation (usually experimenter paced), type of list items, length of list.

Recognition Task (Episodic)

1. Learn list items.
2. Optional delay or distractor task during delay.
3. Make yes/no decisions to the items in a test list: "Yes," the item was on the list, or "no," it was not. This is often refers to deciding whether an item is "old"—that is, on the original list—or is "new" and not on the original list. Old items are also called targets, and new items are also called distractors or lures.

Dependent variables: The dependent variable usually is accuracy, such as the proportion correct. Correct "yes" responses to old items are called *hits*, and incorrect "yes" responses to new items are called *false alarms*.

Independent or control variables: Same as with recall tasks.

Generation and Enactment

An overarching idea in the depth of processing framework is that the more you do with information, the better it is remembered. There are numerous examples of this "hard work has its rewards" principle. In this section we look at four examples of this—four ways in which how information is processed, and the amount of effort a person puts into encoding it, affects performance. These are the self-reference effect, the generation effect, the impact of enactment on memory, and the consequences of taking a survival-based perspective.

The **self-reference effect** is the finding that *memory is better for information that you relate to yourself in some way* (e.g., Bellezza, 1992; Gillihan & Farah, 2005; Rogers, Kuiper, & Kirker, 1977; Symons & Johnson, 1997). If you think about it, you know a lot about yourself, and you tend to be motivated by such information. When you relate something to yourself, say a detail you're trying to remember, you link the new knowledge up with the old, yielding a more complex structure, an elaborative encoding (for example, the locations given earlier for the method of loci—driveway, garage door, etc.—were the memorized locations one of this book's authors used for his own mnemonic device for years, based on his own house). Thus, the elaborated structure becomes more memorable.

The **generation effect** is the finding that *information you generate or create yourself is better remembered compared to information you only heard or read.* This was first reported by Slamecka and Graf (1978). In their study, for the *read* condition, people simply read words printed on cards. However, for the *generate* condition, people needed to generate the word on their own. This was done by giving a word and the first letter of the word that was to be recalled, with the instruction that the to-be-generated word had to be related to the first word. For example a person might see Long-S_____ where the word "short" needed to be generated. The results showed that people remembered words better when they were generated as compared to when they were just read.

In their review of work on the generation effect, Bertsch, Peta, Wiscott, and McDaniel (2007) reported that this robust finding was more likely to occur with free recall, and that the effect grew larger over longer delays. Importantly, the generation effect not only applies to lists of words, but also to textbook material (e.g., de Winstanley & Bjork, 2004). In short, the generation effect is another example that the more effort you put into mentally processing information, the more likely you will remember it later, and for a longer time.

Another way to engage in deep encoding is to take advantage of the **enactment effect**, in which there is *improved memory for participant-performed tasks, relative to those that are not.* In such studies, actually doing some activity is compared with just watching someone else doing it. For example, a person might be told to "break the match," "point at the door," or "knock on the table," or to watch someone else do those actions. In general, people remember things better if they do them themselves (e.g., Engelkamp & Dehn, 2000; Saltz & Donnenwerth-Nolan, 1981). In essence, the additional mental effort needed to do the task is another form of deep processing. Even saying something aloud (the production effect) can improve memory (MacLeod, 2011; MacLeod, Gopie, Hourihan, Neary, & Ozubko, 2010).

The value of enactment can be seen in the practical application of learning lines of dialogue. There is evidence that even untrained nonactors (i.e., novice actors) learn dialogue, as in the script of a play, better when the dialogue and stage movements are rehearsed together (Noice & Noice, 2001; see also Freeman & Ellis, 2003, and Shelton & McNamara, 2001, for other multimodality effects on learning). Physical movement, in other words, can be part of an enhanced mnemonic. Enactment improves memory by helping people better organize and structure information about the actions that they do (Koriat & Pearlman-Avnion, 2003).

Finally, for memory to be of value to us, and be better remembered, it needs to give us something useful. It should help us survive in the world. The survival motivation is strong, and knowledge of what can either increase or decrease our survival is important. Thus, if a person can bring a survival perspective to bear on what they are learning, it can improve performance. This was shown in a study by Nairne, Thompson, and Pandeirada (2007; see also Nairne, Pandeirada, & Thompson, 2008; Weinstein, Bugg, & Roediger, 2008). In this study, people were given lists of words. During the first part of the study, people rated the words for pleasantness, relevance to moving to a foreign land, personal relevance, or survival value (e.g., finding food and water or avoiding predators). Words that were rated high on survival value were more likely to be remembered later. The survival angle has such a strong impact that it can outperform the effects of other well-known memory-enhancing strategies such as imagery, self-reference, and generation (Nairne, Pandeirada, & Thompson, 2008). So, if we think about how information relates to our ability to survive, endure, or otherwise be useful, this takes advantage of our fundamental motivations, and we can leverage these to improve memory (Wurm, 2007; Wurm & Seaman, 2008).

Organization in Storage

Another important piece of the storage puzzle involves **organization**, *the structuring of information as it is stored in memory*. Well-organized material can be stored and retrieved with impressive levels of accuracy. The earliest work on organization (or clustering) was done by Bousfield. In his earliest study (Bousfield & Sedgewick, 1944), he asked people to name, for example, as many birds as they could. The result was that people tended to name the words in subgroups, such as "robin, bluejay, sparrow—chicken, duck, goose—eagle, hawk." To study this further, Bousfield (1953) gave people a 60-item list to be learned for **free recall**. Unlike other work at that time, Bousfield used related words for his lists, 15 words each from the categories *animals, personal names, vegetables,* and *professions*. Although the words were shown in a random order, people tended to recall them by category; for instance, "dog, cat, cow, pea, bean, John, Bob."

Where did this organizing come from? Obviously, people noticed that several words were drawn from the same categories. They used the strategy of grouping the items together on the basis of category (this has a nice metamemory effect as well). The consequence of this reorganization was straightforward: The way the material had been stored governed how it was recalled.

GOOD ADVICE
Improving Your Memory

Baddeley (1978) was one of the critics of the depth of processing framework, concluding that it was valuable only at a rough, intuitive level but not as a scientific theory. Although that may be true, it is hard to beat Craik and Lockhart's insights if you're looking for a way to improve your own memory. Think of maintenance versus elaborative rehearsal as simple recycling in short-term memory versus meaningful study and transfer into long-term memory.

Apply this to your own learning. When you are introduced to someone, do you merely recycle that name for a few seconds, or do you think about it, use it in conversation, and try to find mnemonic connections to help you remember it? When you read, do you merely process the words at a simple level of understanding, or do you actively elaborate when you are reading, searching for connections and relationships that make the material more memorable? In other words, use the depth of processing ideas in your own metacognition. Try inventing a mnemonic (this invokes the generation effect), applying elaborative rehearsal principles, or actively doing something with the information, such as drawing a diagram (this invokes the enactment effect) to something you may need for this course, such as the seven themes of cognition presented in Chapter 1.

The power of organization for improving storage in long-term memory was demonstrated by Bower, Clark, Lesgold, and Winzenz (1969). Four hierarchies of words were presented in the organized condition, arranged as lists with headers (one of the four hierarchies is shown in Figure 6-6); for instance, under *stones* was *precious,* and under that were *sapphire, emerald, diamond,* and *ruby.* The control group was shown words in the same physical arrangements, but the words were randomly assigned to their positions. People got four trials to learn all 112 words; their performance is shown in Table 6-4. Presenting the words in the organized fashion led to 100% accuracy on Trials 3 and 4, an amazing feat given the number of words. In contrast, the control group managed to recall only 70 words out of 112 by Trial 4, 62% accuracy.

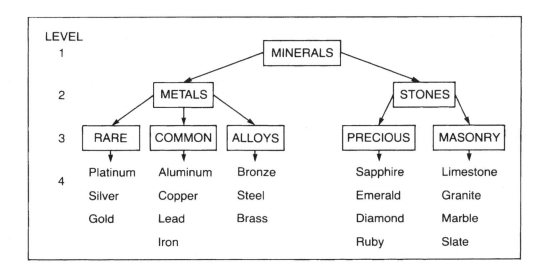

FIGURE 6-6 One of the hierarchies presented by Bower et al. (1969).

TABLE 6-4 Average Percentage of Words Recalled over Four Trials as a Function of Organization

Conditions	1	2	3	4
Organized	65%	94.7%	100%	100%
Random	18.3	34.7	47.1	62.5

Source: Adapted from Bower et al., 1969.

This organizational principle, if used effectively, can lead to astounding feats of memory. People with exceptional memories, such as those who memorize *pi* out to insane numbers of digits, are essentially using some organizational strategy (e.g., Ericsson, Delaney, Weaver, & Mahadevan, 2004), along with other basic memory skills, such as imagery (e.g., Takahashi, Shimizu, Saito, & Tomoyori, 2006). This not only applies to words and numbers, but to complex sets of information. As Anderson (1985) pointed out, a chapter outline can serve the same function as the Bower et al. hierarchies, with obvious implications for students' study strategies (*there's* a hint).

Another reason for clustering studies was that they demonstrated people's strategies for learning in an objective fashion. Many studies used a free recall task, then examined the effects of different degrees of list organization, different numbers of categories, different numbers of items within categories, and so on. Clustering and organization were then examined in terms of a creative array of dependent variables, such as order of recall, degree of clustering, speed and patterning of pauses during recall, and rehearsal (see reviews by Johnson, 1970; Mandler, 1967, 1972). As an example, Ashcraft, Kellas, and Needham (1975) had people rehearse aloud as they studied clustered or randomized lists. Their results suggested that recalling the words by category was due to reorganization during rehearsal. That is, people tended to rehearse by category; for instance, when "horse" was presented, this would trigger the rehearsal of "dog, cat, cow, horse" together. When sufficient time is provided, people can reorganize the words as they store them in memory. Furthermore, the number of times a word had been rehearsed during study is predictive of recall order; more frequently rehearsed categories, as well as words within those categories, are recalled earlier than categories and words that received less rehearsal.

SUBJECTIVE ORGANIZATION   Don't misunderstand the previous section: Organization is *not* limited to sets of items with obvious, known categories. A study by Tulving (1962) showed that people can and do use subjective organizations—literally, organization imposed by the participant (for an update, see Kahana & Wingfield, 2000). Tulving used a multitrial free recall task, in which the same list of words is presented repeatedly across several trials, where each trial had a new reordering of the words. His analysis looked at the regularities that developed in the recall orders. For example, a person might recall the words "dog, apple, lawyer, brush" together on several trials. This consistency suggested that the person had formed a cluster or chunk composed of those four items using some idiosyncratic basis. For example, a person might link the words together in a sentence or story: "The dog brought an apple to the lawyer, who brushed the dog's hair." Regardless of how they were formed, the clusters were used repeatedly during recall, serving as a kind of organized unit. Tulving called this **subjective organization**, that is, *organization developed by a person for structuring and remembering information*. In other words, even "unrelated" items become organized through the mental activity of a person imposing an organization.

Imagery

The last storage variable considered here is **visual imagery**, *the mental picturing of a stimulus that affects later recall or recognition*. Of course, we have discussed some imagery effects already, such as mental rotation, and the imagery-based mnemonic devices. What we focus on now is its effect on the storage of information in long-term memory, and the boost that it gives to material you are trying to learn.

An early contributor to understanding of how imagery impacts memory was Alan Paivio. Paivio (1971) reviewed scores of studies that showed the generally beneficial effects of imagery on memory. These effects are beyond those caused by other variables, such as word- or sentence-based rehearsal, or meaningfulness (Bower, 1970; Yuille & Paivio, 1967). One example is a **paired-associate learning** study by Schnorr and Atkinson (1969; see Table 6-5). The task is to *learn the list so that the correct response item can be reproduced whenever the stimulus item is presented*. Thus, if you saw "elephant–book" during study, you would be tested during recall by seeing the term "elephant" and your correct response would be "book" (the later section on interference describes this task in more detail). Schnorr and Atkinson had people study half of a list by forming a visual image of the two terms together. The other half of the list was studied by rote repetition. On immediate recall, the pairs learned by imagery were recalled at better than 80% accuracy, compared to about 40% for the rote repetition pairs. The superiority of imagery was found even one week later. It is also important to note that the creation of mental images is not automatic. It requires attention and effort, which is part of the reason for the benefit it provides.

Studies such as this led Paivio to propose the **dual coding hypothesis** (Paivio, 1971), which states that *words that denote concrete objects, as opposed to abstract words, can be encoded into memory twice*, once in terms of their verbal attributes and once in terms of their imaginal attributes. Thus a word like *book* enjoys an advantage in memory—because it can be recorded twice, once as a word and once as a visual image, there are two ways it can be retrieved from memory, one way for each code. A term such as *idea*, however, has only a verbal code because there is no obvious image that it evokes. (This is not to say that people cannot create an image for *idea*, such as a light bulb, but only that the image is much more available and natural for concrete words.)

Context and Encoding Specificity

We conclude this section on storage with a discussion that also previews several important ideas for the topic of retrieval. What generalizations can we draw from research on rehearsal, organization, and imagery? How are we to understand the

TABLE 6-5   Lists of Paired Associates

List 1 (*A–B*)	List 2 (*C–D*)	List 3 (*A–B$_r$*)
tall–bone	safe–fable	plan–bone
plan–leaf	bench–idea	mess–hand
nose–fight	pencil–owe	smoke–leaf
park–flea	wait–blouse	pear–kiss
grew–cook	student–duck	rabbit–fight
rabbit–few	window–cat	tall–crowd
pear–rain	house–news	nose–cook
mess–crowd	card–nest	park–few
print–kiss	color–just	grew–flea
smoke–hand	flower–jump	print–rain

List 4 (*A–B'*)	List 5 (*A–C*)	List 6 (*A–D*)
smoke–arm	tall–bench	smoke–fable
mess–people	plan–pencil	print–idea
rabbit–several	nose–wait	mess–owe
park–ant	park–student	pear–blouse
plan–tree	grew–window	rabbit–news
tall–skeleton	rabbit–house	grew–duck
nose–battle	pear–card	park–cat
grew–chef	mess–color	nose–nest
pear–storm	print–flower	plan–just
print–lips	smoke–safe	tall–jump

phenomenon of storage into episodic memory? The best way to understand storage is to consider it in light of retrieval.

In Tulving and Thompson's (1973; Unsworth Spillers, & Brewer, 2012) view, an important influence on memory is **encoding specificity**. This phrase means that information is encoded into memory *not* as a set of isolated, individual items. Instead, *each item is encoded into a richer memory representation that includes the context it was in during encoding*. So, when you read *cat* in a list of words, you are likely to store not only the word *cat* but also information about the context you read it in. In a classic study of encoding specificity, Godden and Baddeley (1975) had people learn a list of words. Half of these people learned the list on land, and the other learned the list under water (all of these people were scuba divers). They were then given a recall test for the list. The important twist is the context in which they tried to recall the information. Half of the people recalled the items in the same context they experienced during learning. However, the other half recalled the information in the other context. The interesting finding, as shown in Figure 6-7, was that memory was better when the encoding and retrieval contexts were the same, relative to when they were different.

A more everyday example of encoding specificity is the experience of going to a room in your home to do something, but when you arrive, you can't remember why you are there. However, when you go back to where you started, you remember. So, reinstating the original context helped you remember. This is also why witnesses may return to the scene of a crime. Being there again reinstates the context, helping them remember details that might otherwise be forgotten.

More generally, when your memory is tested, with free recall for instance, you attempt to retrieve the trace left by your original encoding. Encoding the context along with the item allows the context to serve as an excellent **retrieval cue**—*a useful prompt or reminder for the information*. The original context cues give you the best access to the information during retrieval, and these cues can be verbal, visual, or something else (Schab, 1990, for instance, has found that odors are effective contextual cues).

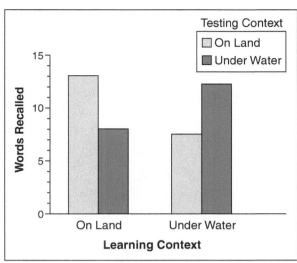

FIGURE 6-7 The classic encoding specificity result reported by Godden and Baddeley (1975), showing better performance when the encoding context matched the retrieval context. That is, memory for things learned on land was better when tested on land as opposed to underwater, whereas things learned underwater were better remembered when the people were tested underwater as opposed to on land.

The processing of content (what it is you are to remember), context, and their binding together is more complex than it initially may seem. As noted in Chapters 2, 3, and 4, the brain has separate processing streams for what something is and where it is. For context effects on memory, particularly spatial contexts, information about *what* something was is processed in the perirhinal cortex (B.A. 35), which part of the temporal lobe. In comparison, information about *where* something was, it's context, is processed in the parahippocampal cortex (B.A. 36), the part of the temporal lobe around the hippocampus. This information is then integrated, or bound, into a coherent memory in the hippocampus, thereby uniting content and context, along with contributions from controlled coordination on the part of the prefrontal cortex (Ranganath, 2010).

Another variant of the encoding specificity effect is *state-dependent learning*, which is the finding that people are more likely to remember things when their physiological state at retrieval matches that at encoding. For example, a study by Goodwin, Powell, Bremeer, Hoine, and Stern (1969) found that people made fewer errors on a memory test when they recalled information when they were drunk (a particular physiological state) if they had learned that information inebriated, than if they tried to recall it when they were sober!

In summary, the storage of information into episodic long-term memory is affected by a number of factors that can lead to better memory. Moreover, the congruence between study and test contexts can be vital. Relevant rehearsal, including organizational and imaginal elements, improves performance.

Section Summary

- Important variables in storage are rehearsal and organization, regardless of whether the information is verbal or perceptual. Maintenance and elaborative rehearsal have different functions, the former for mere recycling of information, the latter for more semantically based rehearsal, which was claimed to process the information more deeply into memory. Difficulties in this depth of processing framework involved specification of the idea of depth.
- Generally, the amount of rehearsal is positively related to recall accuracy for the primacy portion of a list. Organization, especially by category but also by subjectively defined chunks, improves memory because it stores the information securely and provides a useful structure for retrieval.
- According to encoding specificity, contextual information that was encoded along with the studied information can serve as an effective retrieval cue. The degree to which the context at learning can be reinstated at retrieval will improve performance.

RETRIEVING EPISODIC INFORMATION

We turn now to the other side of the coin, retrieving information from episodic memory. As we do, we reencounter the two theories of forgetting that have preoccupied cognitive psychology from the very beginning: decay and interference.

Decay

It's a bit unusual for the name of a theory to imply its content as clearly as does the term *decay*. Nonetheless, that is what decay theory was all about: The older a memory trace is, the more likely that it has been forgotten, just as the print on an old newspaper fades into illegibility. The principle dates back to Thorndike (1914), who called it the *law of disuse*: Habits, and by extension memories, are strengthened when they are used repeatedly, and those that are not are weakened through disuse. Thorndike's idea was a beautiful theory, easily understood and straightforward in its predictions. Unfortunately, it's wrong, at least as far as long-term memory is concerned.

The problem with the decay theory of forgetting is that it claims that the passage of time causes forgetting. The definitive attack on this claim was given by McGeoch (1932), who argued that it is the *activities* that occur during a period of time that cause forgetting, not time itself. In other words, time doesn't cause forgetting—it's what happens during that time that does. Although there are still some arguments for some, at least partial, influence of decay (Schacter, 1999), it is difficult to imagine a study that would provide a clean, uncontaminated demonstration of it. As time passes, there can be any number of opportunities for interference, even if by the momentary thoughts you have while your mind wanders. The time interval also gives opportunities for selective remembering and rehearsal, which would boost remembering old information.

Interference

Interference theory was a staple in the experimental diet of verbal learners. There were at least two reasons for this. First, the arguments against decay theory and for interference theory were convincing, on both theoretical and empirical grounds. Demonstrations such as the often-cited Jenkins and Dallenbach (1924) study made sense within an interference framework: After identical time delays, people who had remained awake after learning recalled less than those who slept (Figure 6-8). The everyday activities encountered by awake people interfered with memory. Fewer interfering activities occurred for sleeping people, so their memory was better.

This effect was replicated by Drosopoulos, Schulze, Fischer, and Born (2007), who further concluded that the memory benefit of sleep serves to mitigate the effects of interference. However, this was primarily for information that was not

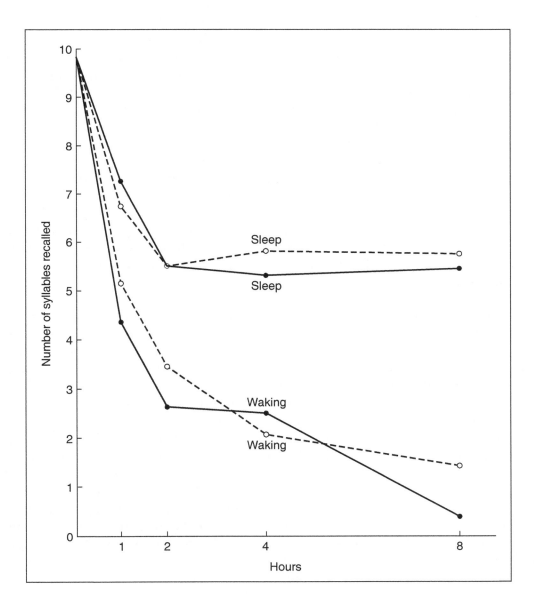

FIGURE 6-8 The classic Jenkins and Dallenbach (1924) result, showing higher recall of nonsense syllables for two people who slept after acquisition versus remaining awake after acquisition.

strongly encoded (that is, not well learned) to begin with. Although how much interference is experienced is linked to how related the material is (as seen in Chapter 5), there are other reasons for long-term memory forgetting that are influenced by whether you get some sleep.

Specifically, when you create and store new long-term memories, they don't instantly appear in your brain in a well-established form. Instead, there is a period of time during which memories go through a process of **consolidation**, *the more permanent establishment of memories in the neural architecture.* Later we see about the consequences of a dramatic disruption in consolidation that can result in amnesia. For now, it is important to note that the disruption when people are awake (and not asleep) is interference of the memory consolidation process (Wixted, 2005). New information is encoded into memory that uses the same neural parts (such as the hippocampus) that were used by the older information. This reuse of same neural networks interferes with memories for the older information, thereby disrupting consolidation and causing forgetting.

This interference is somewhat like writing messages in clay. Imagine writing a message in a bit of clay, then writing even more messages on the clay. Sometimes you'll write over messages that you had previously written, making the earlier ones harder to recover. This is the type of interference we are talking about. Still, sometimes a message doesn't get written over, and eventually the clay hardens. In this case, the message consolidates into the clay, making it harder to disrupt. Ultimately, these older memories are more robust, and less prone to the disruption.

A second reason for the popularity of interference studies is that these effects were easily obtained with a task already in wide use, the paired-associate learning task. This task was a natural for studying interference—and, it conformed to the behaviorist *Zeitgeist* or "spirit of the times" before the cognitive revolution. Unlike consolidation-disrupting interference, the interference explored using paired-associate tasks was due to *cue-overload*. In these cases, there are many memories that are related to a specific cue, and they compete with one another during retrieval.

PAIRED-ASSOCIATE LEARNING   A few moments studying the paired-associate learning task will help you understand interference theory. The basic paired-associate learning task is as follows (see also Table 6-3): *A list of stimulus terms is paired, item by item, with a list of response terms. After learning, the stimulus terms should prompt the recall of the proper response terms.*

Table 6-5 presents several paired-associate lists as a demonstration. Imagine learning List 1 to a criterion of one perfect trial (try it to get a good idea of what the task is like). After that, you switch to the second half of the study, which involves learning another list. The similarity of the first and second lists is critical. If you were switched to List 2, you would experience little or no interference because List 2 has terms that are dissimilar to List 1. In the lingo of interference theory, this was the *A–B, C–D* condition, where the letters *A* through *D* refer to different lists of stimulus or response terms. This condition represented a baseline condition because there is no similarity between the *A–B* and the *C–D* terms (however, you may need fewer trials on the second list because of "general transfer" effects from List 1, warmup or learning to learn).

TABLE 6-6   Designs to Study Two Different Kinds of Interference

Proactive Interference (PI)

	Learn	Learn	Test	Interference Effect
PI group	A–B	A–C	A–C	A–B list interferes with A–C; e.g., an A–B word intrudes into A–C
Control group	—	A–C	A–C	

Retroactive Interference (RI)

	Learn	Learn	Test	Interference Effect
RI group	A–B	A–C	A–B	A–C list interferes with A–B; e.g., an A–C word intrudes into A–B
Control group	A–B	—	A–B	

If you shifted to List 3, however, there would have been "massive" negative transfer; it would have taken you more trials to reach criterion on the second list. This is because the same stimulus and response terms were used again but in new pairings. Thus, your memory of List 1 interfered with the learning of List 3. The term for this was $A–B, A–B_r$, where the subscript r stood for "randomized" or "re-paired" items. Finally, if you switched to List 4 (the $A–B, A–B'$ condition), there would have been a great deal of positive transfer; you would need fewer trials to reach criterion on the second list because List 4 (designated B') is related to the earlier one (B). For instance, in List 1 you learned "plan–leaf"; in List 4, "plan" went with "tree."

These are all *proactive* interference effects, showing the effects a prior task has on current learning. We discussed proactive interference (PI) and release from PI in Chapter 5. Table 6-6 is the general experimental design for a proactive interference study as well as for a retroactive interference (RI) study. As a reminder, retroactive interference occurs when a learning experience interferes with recall of an *earlier* experience; the newer memory interferes backward in time ("retro").

Both proactive and retroactive interference have been examined extensively, with complex theories based on the results. Although the literature is extensive, no attempt is made to cover it in depth here (but see standard works, e.g., Postman & Underwood, 1973; Underwood, 1957; Underwood & Schultz, 1960; and Klatzky, 1980, Chapter 11, for a very readable summary).

Simulate
Forgetting in
MyPsychLab

Retrieval Failure

Beginning in the mid-1960s, a different theory came to dominate cognitive psychology's view of forgetting. Both the decay and interference theories suggest that information in long-term memory can be lost from memory. This definition of **forgetting**, *loss from memory,* was implicit in the mechanisms thought to account for it. Forgetting is now used without the idea of complete loss from memory, however, to refer to situations in which there is difficulty remembering.

For example, one line of research looks at "retrieval-induced forgetting," the temporary forgetting of information because of having recently retrieved related information (e.g., Anderson, Bjork, & Bjork, 2000; MacLeod & Macrae, 2001). Similarly, Anderson (2003; Storm, 2011) has suggested that forgetting is an active inhibition process, designed to override mistaken retrieval of related information ("activated competitors" in Anderson's terms). Note that even here, the unwanted information that is causing interference is still in memory—if it weren't, there'd be no need to override it. That said, it should be noted that the memories that are more likely to be inhibited are the ones that have recently been processed, whereas older memories are more likely to be facilitated by recently retrieved, related information (Bäuml & Samenieh, 2010).

So, there may be no *complete* forgetting from long-term memory, aside from loss due to organic or physical factors, such as stroke or diseases like Alzheimer's dementia. Instead, forgetting may be due to retrieval failure or a process of retrieval inhibition, a deliberate (though only partially successful) attempt to forget (e.g., when you try to forget an unpleasant memory or an incorrect fact; Bjork & Bjork, 2003).

AN EVERYDAY EXAMPLE   Everyone is familiar with retrieval failure. Students often claim that they knew the information but that they "blocked" on it during the exam; *sometimes* this is an example of retrieval failure. A straightforward experience of this is the classic **tip-of-the-tongue (TOT)** phenomenon.[1] People are in the TOT state when they are *momentarily unable to recall a word, often a person's name, that they know is in long-term memory*. Interestingly, although you may be unable to retrieve a word or name during a TOT state, you usually have access to partial information about it, such as the sound it starts with, its approximate length, and the stress or emphasis pattern in pronunciation. (See Brown & McNeill, 1966; Jones, 1989; Koriat, Levy-Sadot, Edry, & de Marcus, 2003; and Meyer & Bock, 1992; Burke, MacKay, Worthley, & Wade, 1991, provide a list of questions that can be used to trigger the TOT state, if you want to try it out.)

However, retrieval failure, like the TOT phenomenon, is not limited to lapses in remembering names or words. As Tulving and his associates found, it is a fundamental aspect of memory.

RESEARCH ON RETRIEVAL FAILURE   An early demonstration of retrieval failure is a study by Tulving and Pearlstone (1966) in which two groups of people studied the same list of 48 items, four words from each of 12 categories (e.g., animals, fruits, sports). The items were preceded by the appropriate category name, such as "crimes—treason, theft; professions—engineer, lawyer," and people were told that they had to remember only the items. At retrieval, one group was asked for standard free recall. The other group was given the names of the categories as retrieval cues, that is, a **cued recall** condition.

The results were both predictable and profound. The free recall group remembered 40% of the items, whereas the cued recall group named 62%. One

---

[1]TOT is pronounced "*tee-oh-tee*," not like the word *tot*. Furthermore, it is often used as a verb: "The subject TOTed ("*tee-oh-teed*") seven times on the list of 20 names." For another regrettable example of "cognitive verbs," see Chapters 9 and 10, on "garden pathing."

conclusion we can draw confirms intuitions dating back to Ebbinghaus: Recall often underestimates how much information was learned. Recognition scores, not to mention savings scores, usually show higher retention. More importantly, unsuccessful retrieval, say in the absence of cues, might be a critical, possibly major, cause of forgetting. On this view, *information stored in long-term memory remains there permanently,* and so is **available**, just as a book on the library shelf is available. Successful performance depends also on **accessibility**, *the degree to which information can be retrieved from memory.* Items that are not accessible are not immediately retrievable, just as the misshelved book in the library is difficult to locate or retrieve. This suggests that information is not lost *from* memory but is lost *in* memory, so to speak. This persists until an effective retrieval cue is presented that locates the memory that cannot be retrieved.

Retrieval Cues

We've already discussed how access can be increased by reinstating the original learning context. More generally, this can be thought of as providing effective retrieval cues. So, let's look at retrieval cues more generally. Any cue that was encoded along with the learned information should increase accessibility. This is why the category cues helped the people in Tulving and Pearlstone's study recall more than they otherwise would have. Similarly, this is why recognition usually reveals higher performance than recall. In a recognition test, you merely have to pick out which of several alternatives is the correct choice. What better retrieval cue could there be than the very information you are trying to retrieve? Subsequent research has shown the power of retrieval cues in dramatic fashion. (A convincing demonstration is presented in Tables 6-7 and 6-8, taken from Bransford & Stein, 1984; do that demonstration now, before reading further.)

Thomson and Tulving (1970) asked people to learn a list of words for later recall. Some of the words were accompanied by cue words printed in lowercase letters; people were told they need not recall the cue words but that the cues might be helpful in learning. Some of the cue words were high associates of the list items, such as "hot–COLD," and some were low associates, such as "wind–COLD." During recall, people were tested for their memory of the list in one of three conditions: low- or high-associate cues or no cues.

The results were that high associates used as retrieval cues benefited recall both when they had been presented during study and when no cue word had been given. When no cue word was given, people spontaneously retrieved the high associate during input and encoded it along with the list item. In contrast, when low associates had been given, only low associates functioned as effective retrieval cues. High-associate

You haven't really forgotten all seven names. If you need a big hint, try searching the Internet for "The Seven Dwarfs."

TABLE 6-7

This demonstration experiment illustrates the importance of retrieval cues. You need a blank sheet of paper and a pencil. Please follow the instructions exactly.

Instructions: Spend 3 to 5 seconds reading each of the following sentences, and read through the list only once. As soon as you are finished, cover the list and write down as many of the sentences as you can remember (you need not write "can be used" each time). Please begin now.

A brick can be used as a doorstop.
A ladder can be used as a bookshelf.
A wine bottle can be used as a candleholder.
A pan can be used as a drum.
A record can be used to serve potato chips.
A guitar can be used as a canoe paddle.
A leaf can be used as a bookmark.
An orange can be used to play catch.
A newspaper can be used to swat flies.
A TV antenna can be used as a clothes rack.
A sheet can be used as a sail.
A boat can be used as a shelter.
A bathtub can be used as a punch bowl.
A flashlight can be used to hold water.
A rock can be used as a paperweight.
A knife can be used to stir paint.
A pen can be used as an arrow.
A barrel can be used as a chair.
A rug can be used as a bedspread.
A telephone can be used as an alarm clock.
A scissors can be used to cut grass.
A board can be used as a ruler.
A balloon can be used as a pillow.
A shoe can be used to pound nails.
A dime can be used as a screwdriver.
A lampshade can be used as a hat.

Now that you have recalled as many sentences as you can, turn to Table 6-8.

---

retrieval cues were no better than no cues at all. In other words, if you had studied "wind–COLD," receiving "hot" as a cue for "COLD" was of no value. Retrieval cues thus can override existing associations during recall.

Demonstrations of the effectiveness of retrieval cues are common: For instance, you hear a "golden oldie" on the radio, and it reminds you of a particular episode (a special high school dance, with particular classmates, and so forth).

This even extends to general context effects: Marian and Neisser's (2000) bilingual participants remembered more experiences from the Russian-speaking period of their lives when they were interviewed in Russian, and more from the English-speaking period when interviewed in English (see also Schrauf & Rubin, 2000); actors remember their lines better when enacting their stage movements of a performance, even three months later (and with intervening acting roles; Noice & Noice, 1999).

TESTING IS LEARNING It is pretty clear that when you are listening to a lecture, reading a book, or studying in some other way, you are learning new information. Moreover, when you take a test, such as an essay exam, a fill-in-the-blank, or a multiple-choice test, the contents of your memory are being assessed. An interesting point is that you are learning even when you are being tested. Every time you encounter information, whether you are studying it or being tested on it, counts as a learning trial (e.g., Gates, 1917; Roediger & Karpicke, 2006). Essentially, the **testing effect** is the finding that the additional experience that you get from tests actually helps you remember the information better—better even than studying, especially if you take a recall test (McDaniel, Roediger, & McDermott, 2007). This testing benefit applies to recognition (multiple-choice)

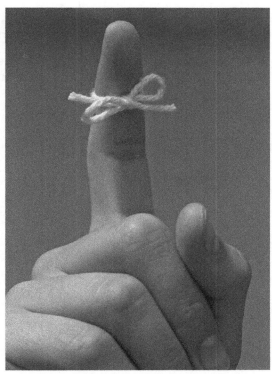

Even simple mnemonics, such as string around your finger, can serve as a memory cue to remind you of something important.

tests (Marsh, Roediger, Bjork, & Bjork, 2007) and to nonverbal material such as maps (Carpenter & Pashler, 2007), and it transfers to new items that were neither studied nor tested (Butler, 2010). So, an effective tool to help you study and learn the material for this or any other class you may take is for you to take practice tests if they are available. If they are not available, your study group could make up practice tests and give them to each other. It may sound like a lot of work, but your memory for the material will be much better than if you had just spent the same amount of time studying by yourself.

ALL THAT GLITTERS IS NOT GOLD There is no question that, for the most part, retrieval cues help memory. However, there are some notable exceptions. One is the **part-set cuing** effect (Slamecka, 1968), which is the finding that *if you cue people with a subset of a list, they will have more difficulty recalling the rest of the set than if they had not been cued at all.* In other words, cuing people with part of the information impairs memory compared to doing nothing. For example, if someone asked you to name the seven dwarves (from Disney's movie *Snow White*), you would have a harder time with the last three if you were told the names of four of them than if you were simply asked to name all seven of them by yourself. One cause of the part-set cuing effect is that when people are provided with part-set cues, these items disrupt the retrieval plan that a person would normally use by imposing a different organization of the material. Also, part-set cuing involves the

TABLE 6-8

Do *not* look back at the list of sentences in Table 6-7. Instead, use the following list as retrieval cues and write as many sentences as you can. Be sure to keep track of how many you can write down, so you can compare this with your earlier recall performance. Begin now.

flashlight	lampshade
sheet	shoe
rock	guitar
telephone	scissors
boat	leaf
dime	brick
wine bottle	knife
TV antenna	pen
bathtub	pan
record	board
orange	newspaper
ladder	barrel
rug	balloon

use of an active inhibitory mechanism (Aslan, Bäuml, & Grundgeiger, 2007), much like what would be occurring in retrieval practice. In short, when a person is given a part-set cue, this causes an implicit retrieval of those items. At that time, the related memory traces serve as competitors and are actively inhibited.

PROVE IT
Part-Set Cuing

It seems surprising that giving people part of a set of information makes their performance worse as compared to giving them nothing. And yet, this is exactly what the part-set cuing effect says will happen. Make several lists of words. Each list should be 48 words long from 4 categories (e.g., tools, birds, countries, etc.), with 12 words from each category. Then get two groups of your friends. For both groups, read the lists of words to them, with the words in a random order (not grouped by category). Do this at a pace of about 1 word per second. Then after reading the list, have one group try to recall the entire list of 48 words. For the other group, read to them a subset of 24 words (6 from each category), and then have them try to recall the remaining 24.

When scoring their recalls, for both groups, do not count the ones that were read to the second group (the part-set cue group), but only the other 24. This is because what you are trying to test is how well people do on those particular items as a function of whether they got the part-set cues or not. If everything goes well, you should find that the people to whom you read half of the list will have a harder time than the people who simply tried to recall the entire list.

Section Summary

- Decay and interference are proposed causes of forgetting from long-term memory. Retrieval failure is forgetting caused by information that is available in long-term memory, but which is, possibly temporarily, inaccessible. Effective retrieval cues provide access to otherwise irretrievable information. Part-set cuing is a rare exception to this rule.
- Tip-of-the-tongue states illustrate that even when information cannot be successfully retrieved, partial information may be available. This partial retrieval may be so strong that retrieval seems imminent.
- Taking a test on material not only serves to assess what is and is not known, it also provides an opportunity to reinforce what is learned.

AMNESIA AND IMPLICIT MEMORY

We study dysfunctions caused by brain damage, such as the agnosias you read about in Chapter 3, to understand cognition and its organization. Sometimes the patterns of disruptions and preserved abilities can tell us a great deal about how cognition works. This has been especially fruitful for understanding long-term memory in cases of amnesia.

Amnesia is *the catastrophic loss of memories or memory abilities caused by brain damage or disease.* Amnesia is one of the oldest and most thoroughly studied mental disruptions caused by brain disorders, as well as a common result of brain injury and damage. Although some amnesias are temporary, due to a blow to the head or even acute emotional or physical stress (e.g., transient global amnesia; Brown, 1998), the amnesias we are interested in here are relatively permanent, caused by enduring changes in the brain.

Many kinds of amnesias have been studied, and we have space to discuss only a few. A few bits of terminology will help you understand the material and alert you to the distinctions in memory that are particularly relevant. First, the loss of memory in amnesia is always considered in relation to the time of the injury. If a person suffers *loss of memory for events before the brain injury,* this is **retrograde amnesia**. Interestingly, retrograde amnesia commonly shows a temporal gradient—memories that are more distant in time from the injury are less impaired (e.g., Brown, 2002; Wixted, 2004). This temporal gradient is referred to as **Ribot's Law**. The other form of amnesia is **anterograde amnesia**, *disruption in acquiring new memories for events occurring after the brain injury.* A person can show both forms of amnesia, although the extent of the memory loss usually is different for events before and after the damage—for example, anterograde amnesia often seems more extensive, simply because it disrupts learning from the time of the brain damage on to the present. The cases we talk about here are extreme in that the memory disruption is so extensive. Most cases of amnesia are not as extensive.

Second, we are trying to understand the architecture of memory, how its components are interrelated, whether some are independent of others, and so on. This is an analysis of dissociations, where the term **dissociation** refers to *a disruption in one component of cognition, but no impairment of another.* If two mental

Watch
Memory in
MyPsychLab

processes—*A* and *B*—are dissociated, then *A* might be disrupted by brain damage while *B* remains normal; patient K. C., described later, displays this kind of pattern. Sometimes another patient is found who has the reverse pattern: *B* is disrupted by the brain damage, but *A* is intact. When two such complementary patients are found, with *reciprocal patterns of cognitive disruption*, then the abilities *A* and *B* are **doubly dissociated** (a simple example would be seeing and hearing, either of which can be damaged without affecting the other).

Importantly, a double dissociation implies not only that *A* and *B* are functionally independent, but also that *A* and *B* involve different regions of the brain. A simple dissociation is not as strong. If process *A* is damaged while *B* remains normal, it could be that research has not yet found a patient with the reciprocal pattern. Or it could be that process *A* can be selectively damaged without affecting *B* but that damage to *B* would always disrupt *A*. The opposite of a dissociation is an association, that is, a situation in which *A* and *B* are so completely connected that damage to one would always disrupt the other (e.g., recognizing objects and recognizing pictures of objects).

Finally, the most useful cases are those of focal brain lesions, in which the damage is to a small, restricted area of the brain. Cases such as that of patient K. C. illuminate the underlying mental processes more clearly because many of his mental processes are intact despite the dysfunction caused by the focal lesion. Unfortunately, the widespread damage and neural deterioration of some injuries or diseases, such as Alzheimer's disease, makes it difficult to pin down the neuro-generator of the cognitive functions that are disrupted: So many regions are damaged that no single one can be pinpointed as the region responsible for a particular ability.

Dissociation of Episodic and Semantic Memory

PATIENT K. C. We begin with a case history. Tulving (1989) described patient K. C. (you read a brief account of this in Chapter 2), who experienced serious brain injury, especially in the frontal regions, in a motorcycle accident. As a result of this injury, K. C. shows a seemingly complete loss of episodic memory: He is completely amnesic for his own autobiographical knowledge. K. C. has profound retrograde and anterograde amnesia. He shows great difficulty in both storing and retrieving personal experiences in long-term memory.

Interestingly, although K. C.'s episodic memory no longer works, his semantic memory does. He is adept at answering questions about his past by relying on general, semantic knowledge; when asked about his brother's funeral, he responded that the funeral was very sad, not because he remembers attending the funeral (he did not even remember that he had a brother) but because he knows that funerals are sad events.

K. C.'s memory disruption, intact semantic memory yet damaged episodic retrieval, is evidence of a dissociation between episodic and semantic memory. This suggests that episodic and semantic memories are separate systems, enough so that one can be damaged while the other stays intact. In Squire's (1987) taxonomy (look back to Figure 6-1), K. C. has lost one of the two major components of declarative knowledge, his episodic memory.

FUNCTIONAL IMAGING EVIDENCE   There are limitations on what can be learned about normal cognition from data from brain-damaged patients. Brain-damaged patients may be unique. Because we might worry about the generality of such results—K. C. could have been atypical before his accident—Tulving presented further support for his conclusions, studies of brain functioning among normal individuals (Nyberg, McIntosh, & Tulving, 1998).

Turn to the color illustration in the endpapers of this textbook, and you will see a set of photographs. In these pictures, the blood flow to the brain is being measured; you read about this technique in Chapter 2. The logic behind such a procedure is that mental activity—say, retrieving a memory—involves an increase in neural activity. This increase shows up as an increase in cerebral blood flow to those brain regions that are more activated. Thus, by injecting a small dose of radioactive material into the bloodstream, the apparatus detects regions of the brain that have higher concentrations of radioactivity on a short time scale (e.g., 12 separate intervals of 0.2 seconds each across an 80-second period).

The red areas in the pictures show regions where the blood flow was above the baseline level, and the green regions show where blood flow was lower than average.

Tulving and his colleagues took research such as this and other work to develop what they called the **Hemispheric Encoding/Retrieval Asymmetry (HERA) model** (Habib, Nyberg, & Tulving, 2003; Nyberg, Cabeza, & Tulving, 1996). Data from PET studies, such as the Nyberg et al. (1998) study discussed earlier, show that the left frontal lobe is more likely to be involved in the retrieval of semantic memories and the encoding of episodic memories. This makes sense, because when you encounter a new event, in order to create a new episodic memory you need to understand the event using your semantic knowledge. In comparison, the right frontal lobe is more likely to be involved in the retrieval of episodic memories. So, according to the HERA model, different parts of the brain are involved in different types of memory processing (see also Buckner, 1996; Shallice, Fletcher, & Dolan, 1998). Note that it is not the case that the HERA model is making the claim that episodic memories are stored in the right hemisphere and semantic memories in the left. Instead, it is just that those brain regions are more involved in those kinds of activities. Even researchers who do not agree with the HERA model do agree that the brain processes semantic and episodic memories differently (e.g., Ranganath & Pallar, 1999; Wiggs, Wiesberg, & Martin, 1999).

Anterograde Amnesia

The story of anterograde amnesia begins with a classic case history. A popular theoretical stance in 1950 was that memories are represented throughout the cortex, rather than concentrated in one place. This position was articulated by Karl Lashley in his famous 1950 paper "In Search of the Engram." Three years later, an accidental discovery was made by the neurosurgeon William Scoville. Scoville performed radical surgery on a patient, Henry Molaison, more commonly known as H. M., sectioning (lesioning) H. M.'s hippocampus in both the left and right hemispheres in an attempt to gain control over his severe epilepsy. To Scoville's surprise, the outcome of this surgery was pervasive anterograde amnesia; H. M. was unable to learn and recall anything new. Although his memory of events before the surgery remained intact, as did his overall IQ (118, well above average), he lost the ability to store new information in long-term memory.

Across the years, H. M. served as a participant in hundreds of tasks (e.g., Milner, Corkin, & Teuber, 1968), documenting the many facets of his anterograde amnesia. His memory of events prior to the surgery, including his childhood and school days, was quite good, with some gaps. His language comprehension was normal, and his vocabulary was above average. Yet any task that required him to retain information across a delay showed severe impairment, especially if the delay was filled with an interfering task. These impairments applied equally to nonverbal and verbal materials. For instance, after a 2-minute interference task of repeating digits, he was unable to recognize photographs of faces. He was unable to learn sequences of digits that went beyond the typical short-term memory span of seven. In a conversation reported by Cohen (in Banich, 1997), he told about some rifles he had (it was a childhood memory). This reminded him of some guns he had also had, so he told about them. Telling about the guns took long enough, however, that he forgot he had already talked about the rifles, so he launched into the rifle story again, which then reminded him of the guns—and so on until his attention was diverted to some other topic.

H. M.'S IMPLICIT MEMORY   Interestingly, the evidence also suggests that H. M.'s memory was normal when it involved implicit memory. That is, he was able to learn a motor skill, mirror-drawing; this task requires a person to trace between the lines of a pattern while looking at it and the pencil only in a mirror (Figure 6-9). H. M.'s performance (the bottom part of the figure) showed a normal learning curve, with very few errors on the third day of practice. Note, though, that on days 2 and 3 he did not remember having done the task before; he had no explicit memory of ever having done it, despite his normal performance based on implicit memory.

Likewise, H. M. showed systematic learning and improvement on the Tower of Hanoi problem (see Chapter 12). Although he did not remember the task itself, his performance nonetheless improved across repeated days of practice. Such empirical demonstrations confirm what clinicians working with amnesia patients have known or suspected for a long time: Despite profound difficulties in what we normally think of as memory, aspects of the patients' behavior do demonstrate a kind of memory—in other words, implicit memory (see Schacter, 1996). Referring back to Figure 6-1, all of the subtypes underneath "nondeclarative (implicit)" memory—skill learning, priming, and so forth—represent different aspects of implicit memory, that is, different forms and types of performance in which implicit memories can be displayed (Squire, 1993; see Gupta & Cohen, 2002, and Roediger, Marsh, & Lee, 2002, for reviews).

IMPLICATIONS FOR MEMORY   What do we know about human memory as a function of H. M.'s disrupted and preserved mental capacities? How much has this person's misfortune told us about memory and cognition?

The most apparent source of H. M.'s amnesia was a disruption in the transfer of information to long-term memory. That is, H. M.'s retrieval of information learned before surgery was intact, indicating that his long-term memory *per se*,

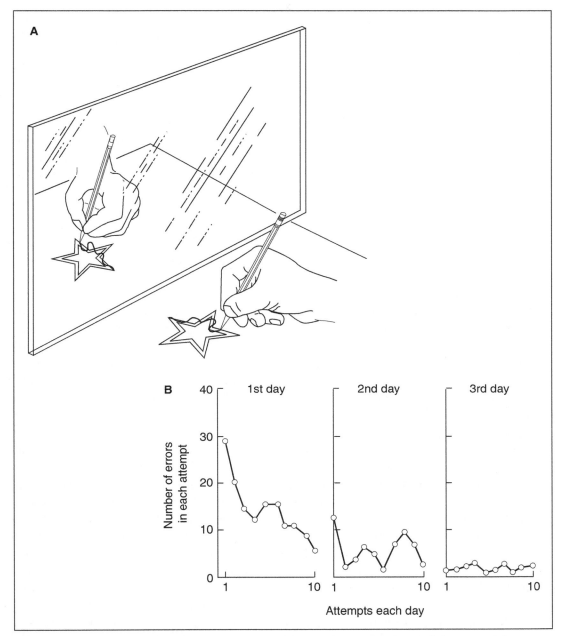

FIGURE 6-9 **A.** In this test the task is to trace between the two outlines of the star while viewing his or her hand in a mirror. The reversing effect of the mirror makes this a difficult task initially. Crossing a line constitutes an error. **B.** Patient H. M. shows clear improvement in the motor learning star task, an instance of implicit learning and memory. After Blakemore (1977).

including retrieval, was unaffected. Likewise, his ability to answer questions and do other simple short-term memory tasks indicates that his attention, awareness, and working memory functions also were largely intact. But he had a widespread disability in transferring new declarative information into long-term memory. This disability affected most or all of H. M.'s explicit storage of information in long-term memory (Milner, Corkin, & Teuber, 1968), including real-world episodic material.

It is a mistake to conclude from this that H. M.'s memory disruption—say, the process of explicit rehearsal—takes place in the hippocampus. Instead, it seems more likely that the hippocampus is on a critical *pathway* for successful transfer to long-term memory. Other research on patients with similar lesions (e.g., Penfield & Milner, 1958; Zola-Morgan, Squire, & Amalral, 1986) confirms the importance of the hippocampus to this process of storing new information in long-term, explicit memory. In some sense, then, the hippocampus is a gateway into long-term memory. Thus, the hippocampus is essential for declarative or explicit memory (see Eichenbaum & Fortin, 2003, for an introduction to the relationship between the hippocampus and episodic memory, and Barnier, 2002, for an extension of these effects to posthypnotic amnesia).

Implicit and Explicit Memory

To repeat a point made at the beginning of this chapter, the operative word in these definitions is *conscious*. Explicit memories, whether episodic or semantic, come to us with conscious awareness and therefore have an explicit effect on performance, an effect that could be verbalized. For example, name the third letter of the word meaning "unmarried man." The very fact that you can say *c* and name the word *bachelor* attests to the fact that this is an explicit memory. In contrast, fill in the following word stems: "gre__, lic__, fl__." Even without any involvement of conscious awareness, you may have filled these in with the words "green, license, flag" with greater likelihood than would have been expected by chance. The words *green, license,* and *flag* occurred in this chapter; we even made a point, early on, that you were reading *license* more rapidly after encountering it in an earlier paragraph, an effect called repetition priming. Importantly, we all demonstrate such implicit effects as repetition priming, amnesic or not (Graf & Schacter, 1987; Kolers & Roediger, 1984).

Repetition priming is a general form of implicit memory in which *a previous encounter with information facilitates later processing on the same information, even unconsciously.* Repetition priming has been established in a number of tasks, such as word identification and lexical decision (Morton, 1979), word and picture naming (Brown, Neblett, Jones, & Mitchell, 1991), and rereading fluency (Masson, 1984). In all these, a prior encounter with the stimulus yields faster performance on a later task, even though you may not consciously remember having seen it before (see Logan, 1990, for the connection of repetition priming to automaticity).

In a classic demonstration of repetition priming, Jacoby and Dallas (1981) had people study a list of familiar words, answering a question about each as they went through the list. Sometimes the question asked about the physical form of the word, as in, "Does it contain the letter *I*?" Sometimes it asked about the word's sound, as in, "Does it rhyme with *train*?" And sometimes, the question asked about a semantic characteristic, as in, "Is it the center of the nervous system?" This was a direct manipulation of *depth of processing*. Asking about the physical form of the word should induce shallow processing, leading to poor memory. Asking about rhymes demands somewhat deeper processing, and asking about semantic characteristics should demand full, elaborative processing on the list words.

At test, explicit memory was assessed by a yes/no recognition task ("Did this word occur in the study phase?"). Here, recognition accuracy was affected by the type of question answered during study. When a question related to the physical form, recognition was at chance, 51%. When it had asked about the sound of the word, performance improved. And when semantic processing had been elicited, recognition accuracy was high, 95%. This a test of explicit memory because people had to say "yes" or "no" based on whether they had seen the word earlier. As expected, more elaborative processing led to better explicit memory performance.

The other test given, the implicit memory test, was a perceptual test. Here, words were shown one at a time for only 35 ms, followed by a row of asterisks as a mask. People had to report the word they saw. In other words, the perceptual test did not require the people to remember which words they had seen earlier. They just had to identify the briefly presented words. For this test, word identification averaged about 80%, regardless of how they had been studied, in comparison to only 65% of control words that had not appeared earlier.

This is a typical implicit memory result. Even without conscious recollection of the original event, there is facilitation for a repeated stimulus. Explicit measures of memory, such as recall or recognition, show strong influences of how information was studied. However, implicit measures, such as a perceptual or word stem completion task, show clear priming regardless of how information was studied (see also Roediger, Stadler, Weldon, & Riegler, 1992; Thapar & Greene, 1994); for work on forgetting and interference in implicit memory, see Goshen-Gottstein & Kempinsky, 2001, and Lustig & Hasher, 2001, as well as Kinder & Shanks, 2003, for a counterargument).

Implicit memory is also involved in motor tasks, such as knowing how to ride a bicycle, play a musical instrument, play a sport, and so on. Here, implicit memory is often called *procedural memory*. Like other implicit memories, procedural memories are very durable, and, once acquired, show a very shallow forgetting curve. Remember the saying that once you learn to ride a bike, you never forget? This is also seen in cases of profound amnesia. These people may lose a great deal of declarative knowledge, but their procedural knowledge, or skills, remain largely intact. They can even acquire new skills, as shown by H. M.'s performance on the mirror drawing task.

Note that just because a memory is implicit does not mean it has no influence on conscious experience. For example, implicit memory may be involved in causing the *déjà vu* experience (Brown, 2004; Cleary, 2008). A new place may seem familiar to you, even though you've never been there before—not because of some psychic connection, but because the place is similar enough to other places you've been to. As a result, the new place elicits a feeling of familiarity. However, you are not consciously aware of being reminded of these other places. The end result is this eerie feeling of familiarity when you enter a place you know you've never been to before.

In addition, cognitive science learned an important lesson from patients such as H. M. and K. C. If we had stuck to laboratory-based experiments alone, and never paid attention to patients with amnesia, we would failed to realize the importance of that second, less obvious kind of long-term memory, the kind not dependent on conscious recollection. We would have missed implicit memory.

Section Summary

- Studies of people with amnesia caused by brain damage have taught us a great deal about long-term memory. Patient K. C. shows total amnesia for episodic information, although his semantic memory is unimpaired, suggesting a dissociation between episodic and semantic memories. Patients like H. M., a person with anterograde amnesia, typically are unable to acquire new explicit memories, but have intact implicit memory. The medial temporal area and especially the hippocampus are very important for the formation of new explicit memories, but different brain structures underlie implicit learning.

Key Terms

accessibility
amnesia
anterograde amnesia
available
consolidation
cued recall
declarative memory
depth of processing
dissociation
distributed practice
doubly dissociated
dual coding hypothesis
elaborative rehearsal
enactment effect

encoding specificity
episodic memory
explicit memory
forgetting
free recall
generation effect
Hemispheric Encoding/Retrieval Asymmetry (HERA) model
implicit memory
isolation effect
levels of processing
maintenance rehearsal

massed practice
metacognition
metamemory
method of loci
mnemonic
nondeclarative memory
organization
paired-associate learning
part-set cuing
peg word mnemonic
recognition
rehearsal
relearning task
repetition priming

retrieval cue
retrograde amnesia
Ribot's Law
savings score
self-reference effect
semantic memory
serial recall
subjective organization
testing effect
tip-of-the-tongue (TOT)
visual imagery
von Restorff effect

9 Language

*The beginning of wisdom is learning the names of things. (Confucius)
Language is a system of signs, different from the things signified, but
able to suggest them.*

(JAMES, 1890, P. 980)

Language, along with music, is one of the most common and universal features of human society. Language pervades every facet of our lives, from our most public behavior to our most private thoughts. We might imagine a society that has no interest in biology, or even one with no formal system of numbers and arithmetic. But a society without language is inconceivable. Every culture, no matter how primitive or isolated, has language; every person, unless deprived by nature or accident, develops skill in the use of language. The human use of language is astounding, with people typically being able to process around three words per second, drawing on a vocabulary of around 75,000 words.

This is a chapter on the basics of language, its characteristics, functions, structure, and form. **Linguistics** is *the discipline that takes language as its topic.* As you learned in Chapter 1, linguistics had a profound influence on cognitive psychology. It was a major turning point when Chomsky rejected behaviorism's explanation of language. Because approaches such as Chomsky's seemed likely to yield new insights and understanding, psychology renewed its interest in language in the late 1950s and early 1960s, borrowing heavily from linguistic theory.

And yet, as psychologists began to apply and test linguistic theory, they discovered an important limitation. Language is a purposeful activity. It's there to *do* something: to communicate, to express thoughts and ideas, to make things happen. Linguistics, however, focused on language itself as a formal, almost disembodied system. In such an approach, the *use* of language by humans was seen as less interesting, tangential, or even irrelevant. On reflection, this view denied a fundamental interest of psychology—behavior. Thus a branch of cognitive psychology evolved, called **psycholinguistics**, *the study of language as it is learned and used by people.*

We present only a brief survey of psycholinguistics here. This chapter and the next focus on the nature and structure of language and cover two of the three traditional concerns in psycholinguistics, language comprehension and production. The third concern, language acquisition, is covered in the chapter on development.

LINGUISTIC UNIVERSALS AND FUNCTIONS

Defining Language

One might define language as "the use of words and how they are spoken in various combinations so that the message can be understood by other people who also speak that language." That's not a bad start. For example, one critical idea in the definition is that meaning and understanding is *attributed* to the words and their pronunciation, rather than being part of those words. As an illustration, the difference in sound between the words *car* and *cars* is the *s* sound, denoting plural in English. But this meaning is not inherent in the *s* sound, any more than the word *chalk* necessarily refers to the white stuff used on blackboards. This is an important idea: Language is based on arbitrary connections between linguistic elements, such as sounds (pronunciations), and the meanings denoted by them.

The definition is a bit confining, however. For instance, it restricts language to human speech. By this rule, writing would not be language, nor would sign language for the deaf. It is true that writing is a recent development, dating back only about 5,000 years, compared to the development of articulate speech, thought to have occurred some 100,000 years ago (e.g., Corballis, 2004). It is equally true that the development of writing depends critically on a spoken language. Thus the spoken, auditory form of a language is more basic than the written version; is there any doubt that children would fail to acquire language if they were exposed only to books instead of to speech? Nonetheless, we include written language for the reason that reading and writing are major forms of communication.

Let's offer a definition that is more suitable here. **Language** is *a shared symbolic system for communication*. First, language is symbolic. It consists of units (e.g., sounds that form words) that symbolize or stand for the referent of the word; the referent, the thing referred to by the final *s,* is the meaning *plural*. Second, the symbol system is shared by all users of a language culture. Language users all learned the same set of arbitrary connections between symbols and meaning, and they also share a common rule system that translates the symbols-to-meaning connections. Third, the system enables communication. The user translates from the thought into a public message, according to the shared rule system. This enables the receiver to retranslate the message back into the underlying thought or meaning.

Language Universals

There are a large number of differences between languages. Take word order, for example. English is largely subject-verb-object (SVO) language in which the sentence subject comes first, followed by the verb and then the object of the sentence. Other languages

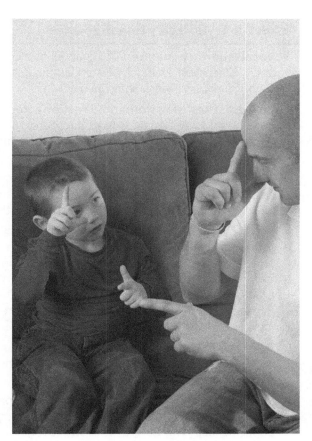

A language does not have to be spoken to be a true language, as sign language for the deaf and symbolic computer languages show.

have other structures. Japanese, for instance, is an SOV language in which the verb typically comes at the end. Despite the many differences among languages, there are some universal properties that they all share as human languages.

Hockett (1960a, b, 1966) proposed a list of 13 **linguistic universals**, *features or characteristics that are common to all languages*. To distinguish human language from animal communication, Hockett proposed that only human language contains all 13 features. Several of the universals he identified, such as the vocal–auditory requirement, are not essential characteristics of human language, although they were likely essential to its evolution. Other features are critically important to our analysis here. Hockett's full list is presented in Table 9-1, along with short explanations. We limit our discussion to four of these, plus two others implied, but absent from the list.

SEMANTICITY   As you already know, the term *semantic* means "meaning." It is an important point that language exhibits **semanticity**—that *language conveys meaning*. For example, the sounds of human language carry meaning, whereas other sounds that we make, say coughing or whistling, are not part of our language because they do not usually convey meaning in the normal sense. (I'm ignoring here the example of a roomful of students coughing in unison at, say, a professor's boastful

TABLE 9-1   Hockett's Linguistic Universals

- **Vocal–auditory channel.** The channel or means of transmission for all linguistic communication is vocal–auditory. Hockett excluded written language by this universal because it is a recent invention and because it is not found in all language cultures.

- **Broadcast transmission and directional reception.** Linguistic transmissions are broadcast, that is, transmitted in all directions from the source, and can be received by any hearer within range; therefore, the transmission is public. By virtue of binaural hearing, the direction or location of the transmission is conveyed by the transmission itself.

- **Transitoriness: rapid fading.** The linguistic transmission is of a transitory nature; it has to be received at exactly the right time, or it will fade (as contrasted with, say, a message transmitted to a recording device, which preserves the information). This implies that the hearer must perform the message preservation task by recording the message on paper or storing information in memory.

- **Interchangeability.** "Any speaker of a human language is capable, in theory, of saying anything he can understand when someone else says it. For language, humans are what engineers call 'transceivers': units freely usable for either transmission or reception" (Hockett, 1960a). In other words, because I can understand a sentence you say to me, I can therefore say that sentence back to you: I can both receive and transmit any message. Contrast this with certain animal systems in which males and females produce different calls or messages that cannot be interchanged.

- **Total feedback.** The human speaker has total auditory feedback for the transmitted message, simultaneous with the listener's reception of the message. This feedback is used for moment-to-moment adjustments to the production of sound.

- **Specialization.** The sounds of language are specialized to convey meaning, that is, linguistic intent, as opposed to nonlanguage sounds. Consider a jogger saying, "I'm exhausted," when the speech act conveys a specific meaning. Contrast this with a jogger panting loudly at the end of a run, when the sounds being produced have no necessary linguistic function (although a hearer might infer that the jogger is exhausted).

- **Semanticity.** Linguistic utterances, whether simple phrases or complete sentences, convey meaning by means of the symbols we use to form the utterance.

- **Arbitrariness.** There is no inherent connection between a symbol and the concept or object to which it refers; there is only an arbitrary connection between sound and meaning. Contrast this with iconic communication systems, such as the bee's waggle dance.

- **Discreteness.** Although sound patterns can vary continuously across several dimensions (e.g., duration of sound, loudness of sound), language uses only a small number of discrete ranges on those dimensions to convey meaning. Thus languages do not rely on continuous variation of vowel duration, for instance, to signal changes in meaning.

- **Displacement.** Linguistic messages are not tied in time or space to the topic of the communication; this implicates an elaborate memory system within the speaker or hearer to recall the past and anticipate the future.

- **Productivity.** Language is novel, consisting of utterances that have never been uttered or comprehended before; new messages, including words, can be coined freely by means of rules and agreement among the members of the language culture.

- **Duality of patterning (duality of structure).** A small set of sounds, or phonemes, can be combined and recombined into an infinitely large set of sentences, or meanings. The sounds have no inherent meaning; the combinations do have meaning.

- **Cultural or traditional transmission.** Language is acquired by exposure to the culture, to the language of the surrounding people. Contrast this with various courtship and mating communications of animals, in which the specific messages are genetically governed.

remark, to indicate a collective opinion. In this situation, the coughing sound is *paralinguistic* and functions much the way rising vocal pitch indicates anger. Then again, it could just be a roomful of coughing students.)

ARBITRARINESS   The feature of arbitrariness was encountered in the definition of language. **Arbitrariness** means that *there is no inherent connection between the units (sounds, words) used in a language and their meanings.* There are a few exceptions, such as onomatopoeias like *buzz, hum,* and *zoom* (but as Pinker, 1994, notes, some units we think of as onomatopoetic, such as a pig's oink, aren't; that sound is "boo-boo" in Japanese). But far more commonly, the language symbol bears no relationship to the thing itself. The word *dog* has no inherent correspondence to the four-legged furry creature, just as the spoken symbol *silence* does not resemble its referent, true silence. Hockett's example drives the point home; *whale* is a small symbol for a very big thing, and *microorganism* is a big symbol for an extremely small thing.

Because there are no built-in connections between symbols and their referents, knowledge of language must involve learning and remembering the arbitrary connections. It is in this sense that we speak of language as being a shared system. We all have learned essentially the same connections, the same set of word-to-referent associations, and stored them in memory as part of our knowledge of language. Thus, by convention—by agreement with the language culture—we all know that *dog* refers to one particular kind of physical object. Obviously, we have to know what word goes with what referent because there's no way to look at an object and decide what its name must be.

Two important consequences of the arbitrariness of language deserve special attention, partly because they help to distinguish human language from animal communication and partly because they tell us about the human language user. These two consequences concern flexibility and the principle of naming. Neither of these was listed by Hockett, although they are derived from his point about arbitrariness.

FLEXIBILITY OF SYMBOLS   Note that arbitrariness makes language symbolic. *Desk* and *pupitre* are the English and French symbols for a particular object. Were it not for the history of our language, we might call it a *zoople* or a *manty.* A consequence of this symbolic aspect of language is that the system demonstrates tremendous **flexibility**. That is, *because the connection between symbol and meaning is arbitrary, we can change those connections and invent new ones.* We routinely shift our terms for the things around us, however slowly such change takes place.

Although our names for things, such as "dog" seem so strongly tied to the object, the word is actually arbitrary and can vary from language to language. For example, instead of "dog," the same things would be called "chien," "gŏu," or "canis," in French, Chinese, and Latin.

Contrast this flexibility with the opposite of a symbolic system, called an iconic system. In an iconic system, each unit has a physical resemblance to its referent, just as a map is physically similar to the terrain it depicts. In such a system there is no flexibility because changing the symbol for a referent would make the connection arbitrary.

NAMING   A corollary to arbitrariness and flexibility involves **naming** (Glass & Holyoak, 1986). *We assign names to all the objects in our environment, to all the feelings and emotions we experience, to all the ideas and concepts we conceive of.* Obviously, wherever it is you are sitting right now as you read this text, each object in the room has a name. Of course, in an unfamiliar or unusual place (an airport control tower or a car repair shop) you may not know the name of something, but it never occurs to you that the thing might have no name.

Furthermore, we don't stop by naming just the physical objects around us. We have a vocabulary for referring to unseen characteristics, privately experienced feelings, and other intangibles and abstractions. Terms such as *perception, mental process, spreading activation,* and *knowledge* have no necessary physical referent, nor do words such as *justice, cause, truth, likewise,* and *however* refer to concrete objects. Indeed, we even have words such as *abstractions* and *intangibles* that refer to the *idea* of being abstract. Going one step further, we generate or invent names for new objects, ideas, activities, and so forth. Think of the new vocabulary that had to be invented and mastered to describe the various actions and operations for using the internet and modern technology, for instance. Because we need and want to talk about new things, new ideas, and new concepts, we invent new terms. (See Kaschak & Glenberg, 2000, on how we invent new verbs from already known words; e.g., "to crutch" or "to google.")

DISPLACEMENT   One of the most powerful tools of language is *the ability to talk about something other than the present moment,* a feature called **displacement**. By conjugating verbs to form past tense, future tense, and so on, we can communicate about objects, events, and ideas that are not present but are remembered or anticipated. When we use constructions such as "If I go to the library tomorrow, then I'll be able to . . .," we demonstrate a particularly powerful aspect of displacement: We can communicate about something that has never happened, and indeed might never happen, while anticipating future consequences of that never-performed action. To illustrate the power and importance of displacement, try speaking only in the present tense for about five minutes. You'll discover how incredibly limiting it would be if we were "stuck in the present."

PRODUCTIVITY   By most accounts, the principle of productivity (also called generativity) is important because it gives language a notable characteristic—novelty. Indeed, the novelty of language, and the productivity that novelty implies, formed the basis of Chomsky's (1959) critique of Skinner's book (see Chapter 1) and the foundation for Chomsky's own theory of language (1957, 1965). It is an absolute article of faith in both linguistics and psycholinguistics that the key to understanding language and language behavior lies in an understanding of novelty, an understanding of the productive nature of language.

Consider the following: Aside from trite phrases, customary greetings, and so on, hardly any of our routine language is standardized or repetitive. Instead, the bulk of what we say is novel. Our utterances are not memorized, are not repeated, but are new. This is the principle of **productivity**, that *language is a productive and inherently novel activity, that we generate utterances rather than repeat them.* We (your textbook authors) lecture on the principle of productivity every time we teach our memory and cognition classes, each time uttering a stream of sounds, a sequence of words and sentences, that is novel, new, literally invented on the spot—the ideas we talk about may be the same semester after semester, but the sentences are new each time. Even in somewhat stylized situations, as in telling a joke, the language is largely new. Only if the punchline requires a specific wording, do we try to remember the exact wording of a previously used sentence.

What does this mean? It means that language is *creative*, not just repetitive. We do not recycle sentences. Instead, we create them on the spur of the moment, now in the active voice, now in the passive, with a prepositional phrase sometimes at the beginning, sometimes at the end, and so on. In a very real sense then, applying our productive rules of language to the words in our vocabulary permits us to generate an infinite number of utterances.

How can we understand any and all of the infinite set of sentences? What does it mean for a theory of language that speakers and listeners can generate and comprehend any one of this numberless set? In brief, it means that language users must have some flexible basis for generating novel utterances, for coming up with the different sequences of symbols that can be comprehended. And, likewise, comprehenders must have the same flexible basis to hear the sequence of words and recover from them what the intended meaning is. By most accounts, the basis for such productivity is a set of rules. To anticipate later sections of the chapter, rules form the basis for each level of language we discuss, from our phonological system up through the highest level of analysis, the conceptual and belief systems we hold as we comprehend language.

Animal Communication

In contrast to flexible and productive human language, animal communication is neither. Animal communication is seen in a wide range of circumstances, from insects to primates. For example, bees communicate the location of honey through a waggle dance (Dyer, 2002; Sherman & Visscher, 2002; von Frisch, 1967). Essentially, they orient themselves within the hive to the relative position of the sun, and then act out a dance that conveys how the flight will progress to get to the source of the nectar. This is even more impressive given that it is fairly dark in a beehive, and the dance is performed on a vertical surface.

Closer to humans, consider the signaling system of vervet monkeys (Marler, 1967). This consists of several distress and warning calls, alerting an entire troupe to imminent danger. These monkeys produce a guttural "rraup" sound to warn of an eagle, one of the monkey's natural predators; they "chutter" to warn of snakes and "chirp" to warn of leopards. The system thus exhibits semanticity, an important characteristic of language. That is, each signal in the system has a different, specific referent (eagle, snake, and leopard). Furthermore, these seem to be arbitrary connections: "Rraup" doesn't resemble eagles in any physical way.

But as Glass and Holyoak (1986) note, the troupe of monkeys cannot get together and decide to change the meaning of "rraup" from *eagle* to *snake*. The arbitrary connections to meaning are completely inflexible. (This inflexibility results at least in part from genetic influence; compare this with Hockett's last universal, cultural transmission.) Furthermore, there is a vast difference between naming in human languages and in animal communication. There seem to be no words in the monkey system for other important objects and concepts in their environment, such as "tree." And as for displacement and productivity, consider the following quotation from Glass and Holyoak (1986, p. 448): "The monkey has no way of saying 'I don't see an eagle,' or 'Thank heavens that wasn't an eagle,' or 'That was some huge eagle I saw yesterday.'" Even human infants can use displacement by pointing to refer to things that are not immediately present, whereas chimpanzees do not (Liszkowski, Schäfer, Carpenter, & Tomasello, 2009), suggesting that nonhuman animals lack even the basic cognitive abilities required by language.

Although there are no true languages among the animal communication systems, this is not to say that nothing can be learned about language from studying animals. As one illustration, work by Hopkins, Russell, and Cantalupo (2007) used magnetic resonance imaging (MRI) with chimpanzees to show that there was a lateralization of function as a consequence of tool use. Moreover, those regions of the brain that were more affected corresponded to Broca's and Wernicke's areas in humans, which correspond to critical areas of human language production and comprehension (as you will see later in the chapter). This suggests that our development of language may be tied, to some extent, to the development of tool use by our ancestors.

In short, beyond a level of arbitrariness, animal communication does not exhibit the characteristics that appear to be universally true of human language. There are no genuine languages in animals, although there may be genuine precursors to human language among various apes. In human cultures, genuine language is the rule. (For a more up-to-date discussion of animal cognition, see Bekoff, Allen, & Burghardt, 2002.)

Levels of Analysis, a Critical Distinction, and the Sapir-Whorf Hypothesis

We conclude this introduction with three points. The first concerns the five levels of analysis for an exploration of language. The second is a traditional distinction between language performance and competence. And finally, we talk briefly about the relationship between language and cognition, specifically the question of how strongly our language influences our thinking, known as the Sapir-Whorf linguistic relativity hypothesis (Whorf, 1956).

LEVELS OF ANALYSIS   The traditional view of language from linguistics is that it is the set of all acceptable, well-formed utterances. In this scheme, the set of rules used to generate the utterances is called a **grammar**. In other words, the grammar of a language is *the complete set of rules that will generate all the acceptable utterances and will not generate any unacceptable, ill-formed ones.* According to most linguists (e.g., Chomsky, 1965), such a grammar operates at three levels: Phonology of language deals with the sounds of language; syntax deals with word order and grammaticality; and semantics deals with accessing and combining the separate word meanings into a sensible, meaningful whole.

TABLE 9-2   Miller's (1973) Five Levels of Language Analysis

Level	Explanation
1. Phonology	Analysis of the sounds of language as they are articulated and comprehended in speech
2. Syntax	Analysis of word order and grammaticality (e.g., rules for forming past tense and plurals, rules for determining word ordering in phrases and sentences)
3. Lexical or semantic	Analysis of word meaning and the integration of word meanings within phrases and sentences
4. Conceptual	Analysis of phrase and sentence meaning with reference to knowledge in semantic memory
5. Belief	Analysis of sentence and discourse meaning with reference to one's own beliefs and one's beliefs about a speaker's intent and motivations

Miller (1973) proposed that language is organized on five levels (Table 9-2). In addition to the three traditional levels of phonology, syntax, and lexical or semantic knowledge, Miller suggested two higher levels as well. He called these the conceptual knowledge and belief levels. For organizational purposes, we focus primarily on the first three of the levels in this chapter. The last two levels are addressed in Chapter 10.

A CRITICAL DISTINCTION   Chomsky (1957, 1965) insisted that there is an important distinction in any investigation of language, the distinction between **competence** and **performance**. Competence is *the internalized knowledge of language and its rules that fully fluent speakers of a language have*. It is an ideal knowledge, to an extent, in that it represents a person's complete knowledge of how to generate and comprehend language. Performance is *the actual language behavior a speaker generates, the string of sounds and words that the speaker utters*.

When we produce language, we are not only revealing our internalized knowledge of language, our competence, but we are also passing that knowledge through the cognitive system. So, it is not surprising that our performance sometimes reveals errors. Speakers may lose the train of thought as they proceed through a sentence, and so may be forced to stop and begin again. We pause, repeat ourselves, stall by saying "ummm," and so on. All these **dysfluencies**, these *irregularities or errors in otherwise fluent speech,* can be attributed to the language user. Lapses of memory, momentary distractions, intrusions of new thoughts, "hiccups" in the linguistic system—all of these are imperfections in the language user rather than in the user's basic competence or knowledge of the language. These were performance-related aspects that Chomsky was not particularly interested in, as a linguist. Psychology, on the other hand, views them as rich sources of evidence for understanding language and language users.

THE SAPIR-WHORF HYPOTHESIS   We tend to think of mental processes, including those related to language, as universal, as being equally true of all languages. Even

Dani tribe member from New Guinea.

slight familiarity with another language, however, reveals at least some of our beliefs to be misconceptions.

An organizing issue in studies of cultural influences on language and thought is how one's language affects one's thinking. This topic is called the Sapir-Whorf hypothesis, or more formally the **linguistic relativity hypothesis** by Whorf (1956). This idea comes out of work by Edward Sapir, a linguist and anthropologist, and his student Benjamin Whorf. The basic idea was that *the language you know shapes the way you think about events in the world around you.* In its strongest version, the hypothesis claims that language *controls* both thought and perception to a large degree; that is, you cannot think about ideas or concepts that your language does not name. In its weaker version, the hypothesis claims that your language *influences* and shapes your thought, for instance making it merely more difficult, rather than impossible, to think about ideas without having a name for them.

In a series of studies testing the Sapir-Whorf hypothesis, Eleanor Rosch tested members of the Dani tribe in New Guinea on a perceptual and memory test (Rosch-Heider, 1972). She administered both short- and long-term memory tasks, using chips of different colors as the stimuli. She found that the Dani learned and remembered more accurately when the chips were "focal" colors rather than "nonfocal" colors—for example, when the learning trial presented a "really red red" as opposed to a "sort-of-red red." In other words, the central, perceptually salient, "good" red was a better aid to accuracy than the nonfocal "off-red." The compelling aspect of the study that tested the Sapir-Whorf hypothesis involved the language of the Dani people; their language contains only two color terms, one for "dark" and one for "light." Nothing in their language expresses meanings such as "true red" or "off-red," and yet their performance was influenced by the centrality of focal versus nonfocal colors. Thus, this is an example where a person's language could have affected cognition (the language had very few color terms), and yet did not. There is other work showing that different ways of referring to objects, such as the distinction between count and mass nouns in English, which does not occur in Japanese and Chinese, does not influence object perception (Barner, Li, & Snedeker, 2010). Results such as these seem to disconfirm the strong Sapir-Whorf hypothesis.

Current research is finding more and more support for the weaker form of the Sapir-Whorf hypothesis, the hypothesis that language does influence our thoughts, sometimes to a surprising degree (e.g., Boroditsky, 2001, but see Chen, 2007; January & Kako, 2007). Here are two examples, the first involving number, the second involving intentionality. For the first, "English speakers have no difficulty expressing the idea that, if there are 49 men and 37 pairs of shoes, some men will have to go without shoes. There are non-literate societies where this would be a difficult situation to describe, because the language may have number terms only for 'one-two-many' (Greenberg, 1978)" (Hunt & Agnoli, 1991, p. 385; see also Roberson, Davies, & Davidoff, 2000; Malt, Sloman, & Gennari, 2003, discuss how one's linguistic and cultural history influence perception and naming). In other words, one person's language and culture would make it very difficult to think and talk about this situation—12 men going barefoot—whereas another person's language and culture supports that kind of thinking and expression.

Second, consider intentionality, whether someone did something on purpose or by accident. In English, we would say "Sue broke the vase" in both cases, both when she intended to break the vase and when she knocked the vase over by accident. But in Spanish and Japanese, the agent is less likely to be mentioned in the case of an accident; the appropriate sentence is much more like "the vase broke." In a test of this language effect, Fausey and Boroditsky (2011) showed English and Spanish speakers several videos of the two kinds of scenarios, intentional and accidental acts, and then gave them a surprise memory test. Both groups remembered the agent (Sue) well when the act was intentional, but the Spanish speakers tended not to remember the agent as well when the act was accidental; after all, their language-based way of thinking about the accident deemphasizes the agent and focuses on the breaking itself. Thus, there was a clear effect of the participants' language on their interpretation of the event, and their later memory for the event (see Boroditsky, 2011, for a highly readable summary of similar language effects).

Section Summary

- Language is our shared system of symbolic communication, unlike naturally occurring animal communication. True language involves a set of characteristics, linguistic universals, that emphasize the arbitrary connections between symbols and referents, the meaningfulness of the symbols, and our reliance on rules for generating and comprehending language.
- Three traditional levels of analysis—phonology, syntax, and semantics—are joined by two others in psycholinguistics, the levels of conceptual knowledge and beliefs. Linguists focus on an idealized language competence as they study language, but psycholinguists are also concerned with language performance. Therefore, the final two levels of analysis take on greater importance as we investigate language users and their behavior.
- To some degree, we can use people's linguistic intuitions, their linguistic competence, to discover what is known about language; language performance, on the other hand, is also affected by memory lapses and the like.
- The Sapir-Whorf linguistic relativity hypothesis made a claim that language controls or determines thought, making it impossible to think of an idea if there was no word for it in the language. The weak version of this hypothesis is generally accepted now; language exerts an influence on thought, by making it more difficult to think of an idea without having a word to name or express it.

PHONOLOGY: THE SOUNDS OF LANGUAGE

In any language interaction, the task of a speaker is to communicate an idea by translating that idea into spoken sounds. The hearer goes in the opposite direction, translating from sound to intended meaning. In essence, a person is transferring the contents of his or her mind to another person (a lot like ESP, only in a plausible—spoken!—way). Among the many sources of information available in the spoken message, the most obvious and concrete one is the sound of the language itself, the stream of speech signals that must be decoded. Other sources, say the gestures and facial expressions of the speaker, are also available, but we focus on the speech sounds here. Thus our study of the grammar of language begins at this basic level of **phonology**, *the sounds of language and the rule system for combining them.*

TABLE 9-3   English Consonants and Vowels

English Consonants

Manner of Articulation		Bilabial	Labio-dental	Dental	Alveolar	Palatal	Velar	Glottal
(oral) Stops	Voiceless	P (*p*ut)			t (*t*uck)		k (*c*ap)	
	Voiced	b (*b*ut)			d (*d*ug)		g (*g*ot)	
Nasal (stop)		m (*m*ap)			n (*n*ap)		η (so*ng*)	
Affricatives	Voiceless					č (*ch*urn)		
	Voiced					ǐ (*j*ump)		
Fricatives	Voiceless		f (*f*it)	Q(*th*ink)	s (*s*ad)	š (*f*ish)		h (*h*ad)
	Voiced		v (*v*ote)	∂ (*th*em)	z (*z*ip)	ž (a*z*ure)		
Glides		w (*w*on)				y (*y*es)		
Liquids					l (*l*ame)	r (*r*age)		

English Vowels

	Front	Center	Back
	i (b*ee*f)		u (b*oo*m)
High			U (b*oo*k)
	i (b*i*t)		
		l (b*i*rd)	o (b*ow*l)
Middle	e (b*a*be)	(sof*a*)	
	ε (b*e*d)		(b*ou*ght)
	æ (b*a*d)	(b*u*s)	
Low			
			a (p*a*lm)

Based on Glucksberg and Danks (1975).

Sounds in Isolation

To state an obvious point, different languages sound different: They are composed of different sets of sounds. *The basic sounds that compose a language* are called **phonemes**. If we were to conduct a survey, we would find around 200 different phonemes across all known spoken languages. No single language uses even half that many, however. English, for instance, uses about 46 phonemes (experts disagree on whether some sounds are separate phonemes or blends of two phonemes; the disagreement centers on diphthong vowel sounds, as in *few,* seemingly a combination of "ee" and "oo"). Hawaiian, however, uses only about 15 phonemes (Palermo, 1978). Note here that there is little significance to the total tally of phonemes in a language; no language is superior to another because it has more (or fewer) phonemes.

Table 9-3 shows the typology of the phonemes of English, based on the characteristics of their pronunciation. For consonants, three variables are relevant: place of articulation, manner of articulation, and voicing. *Place of articulation* is the place in the vocal tract where the disruption of airflow occurs; as shown in Figure 9-1, a bilabial consonant such as /b/ disrupts the airflow at the lips, whereas

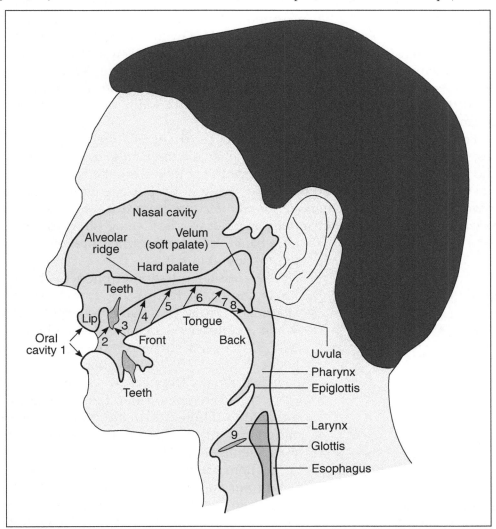

FIGURE 9-1 The vocal tract, illustrating places of articulation: 1, bilabial; 2, labiodental; 3, dental; 4, alveolar; 5, palatoalveolar; 7, velar; 8, uvular; 9, glottal.

Based on Fromkin & Rodman (1974).

/h/ disrupts the column of air at the rear of the vocal tract, at the glottis. Second, *manner of articulation* is how the airflow coming up from the lungs is disrupted. If the column of air is completely stopped and then released, it's called a stop consonant, such as the consonant sounds in *bat* and *tub*. A fricative consonant, such as the /f/ in *fine,* involves only a partial blockage of airflow. Finally, *voicing* refers to whether the vocal cords begin to vibrate immediately with the obstruction of airflow (for example, the /b/ in *bat*) or whether the vibration is delayed until after the release of air (the /p/ in *pat*).

Vowels, by contrast, involve no airflow disruption. Instead, they differ on two dimensions, placement in the mouth (front, center, or back) and tongue position in the mouth (high, middle, or low). Scan Table 9-3, pronouncing the sample words, and try to be aware of the characteristics that you (if you're a native or fluent English speaker) know so thoroughly at an unconscious, automatic level.

Let's develop a few more conscious intuitions about phonemes. Stop for a moment and put your hand in front of your mouth. Say the word *pot* and then *spot.* Did you notice a difference between the two /p/ sounds? Most speakers produce a puff of air with the /p/ sound as they say *pot;* we puff very little (if at all) for the /p/ in *spot* if it's spoken normally. Given this, you would have to agree that these two /p/ sounds are different at a purely physical level. And yet you hear them as the same sound in those two words. Figure 9-2 shows hypothetical spectrograph patterns for two families of syllables, the /b/ family on the left and the /d/ family on the right. Note how remarkably different "the same" phoneme can be.

For psycholinguistics, the two /p/ sounds, despite of their physical differences, are both instances of the same phoneme, the same basic sound group. That is, the fact that these two sounds are treated as if they were the same in English means that they represent one phoneme. So, let's redefine the term phoneme as *the category or group of language sounds that are treated as the same, despite physical differences among the sounds.* In other words, the English word *spot* does not change its meaning when pronounced with the /p/ sound in *pot.*

A classic illustration of phoneme boundaries is shown in Figure 9-3, from a study by Liberman, Harris, Hoffman, and Griffith (1957). When the presented sound crossed a boundary, that is, between stimulus values 3 and 5 and between 9 and 10, identifications of the sound switched rapidly from /b/ to /d/ and then from /d/ to /g/. Variations within the boundaries did not lead to different identifications; despite the variations, all the sounds from values 5 to 8 were identified as /d/.

There are two critical ideas here. First *all the sounds falling within a set of boundaries are perceived as the same, despite physical differences among them.* This is called **categorical**

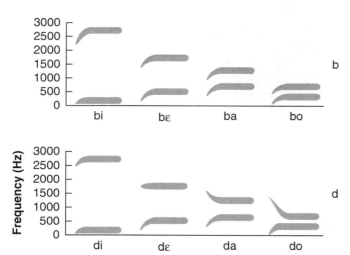

FIGURE 9-2 Illustrations of changes in vocal formant frequencies for different consonant-vowel pairings.

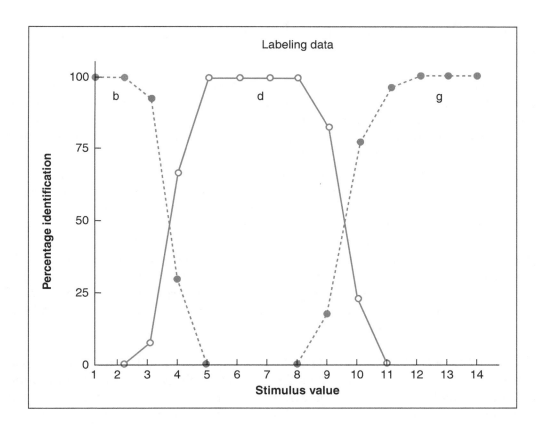

FIGURE 9-3 One person's labeling data for synthesized consonants ranging from /b/to /g/. Note that small changes in the stimulus value (e.g., from values 3 to 4) can result in a complete change in labeling, whereas larger changes (e.g., from values 4 to 8) that do not cross the phoneme boundary do not lead to a change in labeling.

From Liberman et al. (1957).

perception. Because English speakers discern no real difference between the hard /k/ sounds in *cool* and *keep,* they are perceived categorically, that is, perceived as belonging to the same category, the /k/ phoneme. Second, different phonemes are the sounds that are perceived as different by speakers of the language. The physical differences between /s/ and /z/ are important in English; changing from one to the other gives you different words, such as *ice* and *eyes.* Thus, the /s/ and /z/ sounds in English are different phonemes.

An interesting side effect of such phonemic differences is that you can be insensitive to differences of other languages if your own language doesn't make that distinction. Spanish does not use the /s/ versus /z/ contrast, so native speakers of Spanish have difficulty distinguishing or pronouncing *ice* and *eyes* in English. Conversely, the hard /k/ sounds at the beginning of *cool* and *keep* are interchangeable in English; they are the same phoneme. But, this difference is phonemic in Arabic; the Arabic words for *heart* and *dog* differ only in their initial sounds, exactly the two different hard /k/ sounds in *cool* and *keep.*

Combining Phonemes into Morphemes

From a stock of about 46 phonemes, English generates all its words, however many thousands that might be. This fact, that a small number of units can be combined so flexibly into so many words, is the linguistic universal of productivity at the level of phonology. So, from a small set of phonemes we can generate a functionally infinite number of words. Recall further that the essential ingredient of productivity is rules. We turn now to the rules of combining phonemes into words.

PHONEME COMBINATIONS   Let's work with a simple example here. There are three phonemes in the word *bat:* the voiced stop consonant /b/, the short vowel sound /ae/, and the final voiceless /t/. Substitute the voiceless /p/ for /b/, and you get *pat.* Now rearrange the phonemes in these words, and you'll discover that some of the arrangements don't yield English words, such as **abt, *tba,* and **atp.* Why? What makes **abt* or **atp* illegal strings in English?

Although it's tempting to say is that syllables like **abt* cannot be pronounced, a moment's reflection suggests that this is false. After all, many such "unpronounceable" strings are pronounced in other languages; for example, the initial *pn-* in the French word for *pneumonia* is pronounced, whereas English makes the *p* silent. Instead, the rule is more specific. English usually does not use a "voiced–voiceless" sequence of two consonants within the same syllable; in fact, it only seldom uses any two-consonant sequence when both are in the same "manner of articulation" category. (Of course, if the two consonants are in different syllables, then the rule doesn't apply.)

PHONEMIC COMPETENCE AND RULES   Why does this seem to be an unusual explanation? The reason is that our knowledge of English phonology and pronunciation is not particularly verbalizable. You can look at Table 9-3, try to think of words that combine consonants, and come up with tentative pronunciation rules. But this is different from knowing the rules in an easily accessed and expressible fashion. And yet you are a true expert at deciding what phoneme sequences can and cannot be used in English. Your implicit knowledge of how sounds are combined tells you that **abt* is illegal because it violates a rule of English pronunciation.

This *extensive knowledge of the rules of permissible English sound combinations* is your **phonemic competence**. These rules tell you what is and isn't permissible; *bat* is, but **abt* isn't. No one ever explicitly taught you these rules; you abstracted them from your experience as you acquired language. This competence tells you that a string of letters like "pnart" is legal only when the *p* is silent but that "snart" is a legal string—not a word, of course, but a legal combination of sounds. Speakers of the language have this phonemic competence as part of their knowledge of language, an implicit, largely unverbalizable part to be sure, but a part nonetheless.

Speech Perception and Context

We are now ready to approach the question of how people produce and perceive speech. Do we hear a word and segment it in some fashion into its separate phonemes? When we speak, do we string phonemes together, one after another, like stringing beads on a necklace?

CATEGORICAL PERCEPTION AND THE PROBLEM OF INVARIANCE   The answer to both questions is "No." Even when the "same" sound is being pronounced, it is not physically identical to other instances of that "same" sound. The sounds *change*—they change from speaker to speaker and from one time to the next

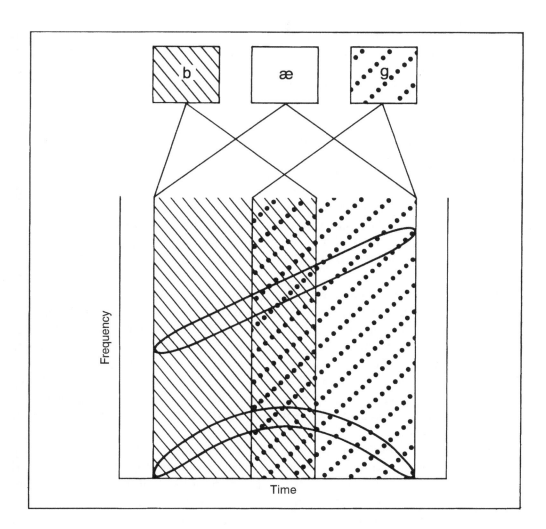

FIGURE 9-4
Coarticulation is illustrated for the three phonemes in the word *bag;* solid diagonals indicate the influence of the /b/ phoneme and dotted diagonals, the influence of /g/.

From Liberman (1957).

within the same speaker. Most prominently, they change or vary from one word to another, depending on what sounds precede and follow.

This *variability in sounds* is the **problem of invariance**. This term is somewhat peculiar because the problem in speech perception is that the sounds *are not* invariant; they change all the time. You saw an illustration of this in Figure 9-2, where the initial /b/ and /d/ sounds looked very different in the spectrographic patterns depending on the vowel that followed. A second illustration of the problem of invariance is in Figure 9-4, which shows the influence of each of the three phonemes in the word *bag*. To pronounce *bag*, do you simply articulate the /b/, then /ae/, then /g/? No! As the figure shows, the /ae/ sound influences both /b /and /g/, the /g/ phoneme (dotted lines) exerts an influence well back into the /b/ sound, and so on.

The term for this is **coarticulation**: *More than one sound is articulated at the same time.* As you type the word *the* on a keyboard, your right index finger starts moving toward *h* before your left index finger has struck the *t*. In like fashion, your vocal tract begins to move toward the /ae/ before you have articulated /b/ and toward /g/ before even finishing the /b/. This is another illustration of the problem of invariance: Each phoneme changes the articulation of each other phoneme and does so depending on what the other phonemes are. The problem of invariance is made clearer by considering what we do when we whisper. Whispering changes some of the vocal characteristics of the phonemes. For example, voiced phonemes become voiceless. Yet, we typically have little trouble understanding what is being whispered to us.

In short, the sounds of language, the phonemes, vary widely as we speak them. Yet we tolerate a fair degree of variability for the sounds within a phoneme category, both when listening and decoding from sound to meaning and also when speaking, converting meaning into spoken sound. This categorical perception of phonemes in spoken language is a decision-making process that requires some cognitive control to take into account a variety of factors to make this categorization decision. Studies using fMRI scans have found that the left inferior frontal sulcus (B.A. 44) is critically involved in this process (Myers, Blumstein, Walsh, & Eliassen, 2009), supporting the idea that some mental control is need to make these decisions.

THE EFFECT OF CONTEXT   But how do we do this? How do we tolerate the degree of variability—how do we make these decisions? The answer is *context and conceptually driven processing*. If we had to rely entirely on the spoken signal to figure out what was being said, then we would be processing speech in an entirely data-driven, bottom-up fashion. We would need some basis for figuring out what every sound in the word was and then retrieve it from memory. This is almost impossible, given the variability of phonemes. Instead, context—in this case the words, phrases, and ideas already identified—leads us to correct identification of new, incoming sounds.

A clever demonstration of this was done by Pollack and Pickett (1964). They recorded several spontaneous conversations, spliced out single words, then played them to people. When the words were isolated, people identified them correctly only 47% of the time. But performance improved when longer and longer segments of speech were played, because more and more supportive syntactic and semantic context was then available.

In a related study, Miller and Isard (1963) presented three kinds of sentences: fully grammatical sentences such as "Accidents kill motorists on the highways," semantically anomalous sentences such as "Accidents carry honey between the house," and ungrammatical strings such as "Around accidents country honey the shoot." They also varied the loudness of the background noise, from the difficult −5 ratio, when the noise was louder than speech, to the easy ratio of +15, when the speech was much louder than the noise. People shadowed the strings they heard, and correct performance was the percentage of their shadowing that was accurate. As shown in Figure 9-5, accuracy improved going from the difficult to easy levels of speech-to-noise ratios. More interestingly, the improvement was especially dramatic for grammatical sentences, as if grammaticality helped counteract the background noise. For instance, at the ratio labeled 0 in the figure, 63% of the grammatical sentences were shadowed accurately, compared with only 3% of the ungrammatical strings. Indeed, even at the easiest ratio of +15, fewer than 60% of the ungrammatical strings could be repeated correctly.

People use their linguistic knowledge even to the point of hearing things that are not there. In a study by Richard Warren (1970), people heard sentences in

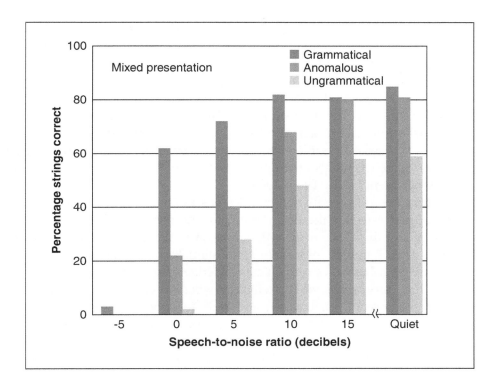

FIGURE 9-5
Percentage of strings shadowed correctly.

From Miller & Isard (1963).

which part of the sentence was removed from the recording and replaced with a cough. For example, in the sentence "The state governors met with their respective legislatures convening in the capital city," the "s" sound was replaced with a cough at the point indicated by the asterisk. The vast majority of people did not report that any speech sounds were missing and could not report the location of the cough when asked to do so on a printed version of the sentence later on. A similar finding has been reported with music (DeWitt & Samuel, 1990), with people reporting hearing music notes or tones that were obscured by noise. So, when people are listening, they are actively using their knowledge to interpret what they hear.

TOP-DOWN AND BOTTOM-UP PROCESSES More recent evidence is largely consistent with these early findings. That is, there is a combination of data-driven and conceptually driven processing in speech recognition, a position called the integrative or interactive approach (Rapp & Goldrick, 2000). At a general level, a variety of conceptually distinct language processes, from the perception of the sounds up through integration of word meanings, operate simultaneously, each having the possibility of influencing the ongoing activity of other processes. While features of the speech signal are analyzed perceptually, a listener's other linguistic knowledge is also called into play at the same time. These higher levels of knowledge and analysis operate in parallel with the phonemic analysis and help to identify the sounds and words (Dahan, 2010; Dell & Newman, 1980; Pitt & Samuel, 1995; Samuel, 2001). Moreover, to overcome the relative dearth of invariant information in the speech signal, it also appears that language perception relies heavily on characteristic knowledge of the speaker, such as whether the person speaks with a lisp (Kraljik, Samuel, & Brennan, 2008).

As a concrete example, imagine a sentence that begins "The grocery bag was. . . ." You are processing the *bag* segment of this speech signal. Having already processed the previous word to at least some level of semantic interpretation, you have developed a useful context for the sentence. To be simple about it, *grocery* limits the number of possibilities that can be mentioned in the sentence. Similar evidence of the role of context was reported by Marslen-Wilson and Welsh (1978) in a task that asked people to detect mispronunciations, and by Dell and Newman (1980) in a task that asked people to monitor spoken speech for the occurrence of a particular phoneme (recall also the demonstrations of context effects in Treisman's shadowing experiments, e.g., 1960, 1964).

Such results are so powerful that theories of speech recognition must account for both aspects of performance, the data driven and the conceptually driven. A specific connectionist model that does exactly that was proposed by McClelland and Elman (1986). In their TRACE model, information is continually being passed among the several levels of analysis. Lexical or semantic knowledge, if activated, can alter the ongoing analysis at the perceptual level by "telling" it what words are likely to appear next; the model's predictions of what words are likely to appear are based on semantic knowledge. At the same time, phonemic information is passed to higher levels, altering the patterns of activation there (see Dell, 1986, for a spreading activation network theory of sentence production, and Tyler, Voice, & Moss, 2000, for a useful review).

Embodiment in Speech Perception

The perception of speech is critical for language. Intuitively this may seem like an odd place for aspects of embodied cognition to show up. However, speech perception is actually where one of the first embodied theories of cognition came from (although it was not labeled as such at the time). This is the **motor theory of speech perception** (see, e.g., Liberman, Cooper, Shankwiler, & Studdert-Kennedy, 1967; Liberman & Mattingly, 1985).

According to the motor theory of speech perception, people perceive language, at least in part, by comparing the sounds that they are hearing with how they themselves would move their own vocal apparatus to make those sounds. That is, we create embodied representations of how those sounds might be spoken to help us perceive speech. There are several lines of evidence for this idea (for an excellent review, see Galantucci, Fowler, & Turvey, 2006). According to Galatucci et al., as some examples, people find it much easier to understand synthesized speech if it takes issues of coarticulation into account, rather than simply presenting a string of phonemes. Also, the parts of the cortex that are more active during speech perception overlap substantially with those involved in speech production. This is similar to the idea of mirror neurons that fire when primates observe actions of others. Finally, people find it easier to comprehend speech if they can see the person talking, which gives them more information about how the sounds are being made. It is also true that people can better understand song lyrics if they can see a person singing (Jesse & Massaro, 2010). This theory does not explain all aspects of speech perception, such as how people who could never speak can understand spoken language. However, it does illustrate how the structure of our bodies, and how we use them in the environment (in this case moving the air around with our vocal apparatus), influences cognition.

Related to the idea that motor programs are involved in speech perception, there is also some evidence that people activate mental motor programs just by thinking about words to themselves. Take the example of tongue twisters, which involve difficult movements of the vocal apparatus when they are spoken aloud. What is interesting is that people are likely to show evidence of articulation difficulty, such as reading times, when they are simply asked to read tongue twisters. That is, even when the people were only "saying" (inner speech) the twisters silently to themselves in their minds, the language processing system takes into account and simulates the muscle movements that would be involved if the person were actually speaking, and these simulated movements produce the normal tongue twister difficulty (Corley, Brocklehurst, & Moat, 2011; but see Oppenheim & Dell, 2010).

A Final Puzzle

As if the preceding sections weren't enough to convince you of the need for conceptually driven processing, consider one final feature of the stream of spoken speech. Despite coarticulation, categorical perception, and the problem of invariance, we naively believe that words are somehow separate from each other in the spoken signal—that there is a physical pause or gap between spoken words, just as there is a blank space between printed words.

This is not true. Our intuition is entirely wrong. Analysis of the speech signal shows that there is almost no consistent relationship between pauses and the ends of words. If anything, the pauses we produce while speaking are longer *within* words than between words. As evidence of this, see Figure 9-6, a spectrograph

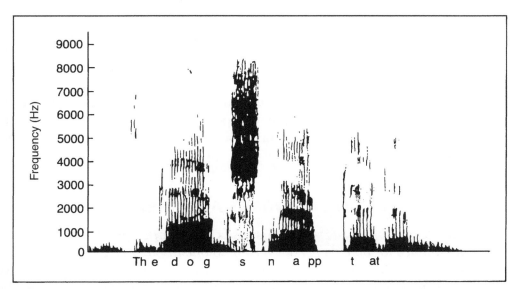

FIGURE 9-6   A spectrogram from the sentence "John said that the dog snapped at him," taken from fluent spoken speech. Note that the pauses or breaks do not occur regularly at the ends of words; if anything, they occur more frequently *within* the individual words (e.g., between the /s/ and /n/ sounds, between the /p/ and /t/ sounds; compare with the end of *the* and the beginning of *dog*).

From Foss & Hakes (1978).

recording of a spoken sentence. Inspection of the patterns in correspondence to the words listed at the bottom illustrates the point: The pauses in the spectrograph bear no particular relationship to the ends of words. There must be other kinds of information that human cognition uses to decode spoken language.

How can our intuitions about our own language, that words are articulated as separate units, be so wrong? (Note that our intuitions about foreign languages—they sound like a continuous stream of speech—are more accurate.) How do we segment the speech stream and come to know what the words and phrases are? Part of the answer is our knowledge of words in the language and the fact that some phoneme combinations simply cannot or do not form words (Norris, McQueen, Cutler, & Butterfield, 1997). Another part of the answer to these questions is syntax, the second level of language analysis and the topic we address next.

Section Summary

- Phonology is the study of the sounds of language. Spoken words consist of phonemes, the smallest units of sound that speakers of a language can distinguish. Surprisingly, a range of physically different sounds are classified as the same phoneme; we tolerate some variation in the sounds we categorize as "the same," called categorical perception.
- Categorical perception is particularly important in the study of speech recognition because the phonemes in a word exhibit coarticulation, overlapping effects among successive phonemes, such that an initial sound is influenced by the sounds that follow and the later sounds are influenced by what came before.
- Speech recognition relies heavily on conceptually driven processes. This includes our knowledge of the sentence and word context, our estimates of how we would produce the sounds ourselves, and our knowledge of what the words in our language are.
- As an illustration of embodied cognition, according to the motor theory of speech perception, part of the way that people go about understanding spoken language may be to try to mentally simulate those sounds as if they were actually being spoken.

SYNTAX: THE ORDERING OF WORDS AND PHRASES

At the second level of analysis we have **syntax**, *the arrangement of words as elements in a sentence to show their relationship to one another.* We've already studied how sounds combine to form meaningful words. At this level of analysis, we are interested in how the words are sequenced to form meaningful strings, the study of syntax. Just as with phonology, where the rules for combining sounds might be called a phonological grammar, our syntactic grammar is a set of rules for ordering words into acceptable, well-formed sentences.

If you have a connotation associated with the word *syntax,* it probably is not the psycholinguistic sense of *grammar* but the "school grammar" sense instead. In school, if you said "He ain't my friend no more," your teacher might have responded, "Watch your grammar." To an extent, this kind of school grammar is irrelevant to the psycholinguistic study of syntax. Your teacher was being *prescriptive* by teaching you what is proper or prestigious according to a set of cultural values. In another way, though, school grammar does relate to the psycholinguistic study of language; language is for expressing ideas, and anything that clarifies this expression, even arbitrary rules about "ain't" and double negatives, improves communication. (And finally, your teacher was sensitive to another level of language: People do judge others on the quality of their speech.)

WORD ORDER   Unlike the school grammar idea, the psycholinguistic study of syntax is *descriptive*; that is, it takes as its goal a description of the rules of how words are arranged to form sentences. Let's take a simple example, one that taps into your syntactic competence. Which is better, sentence 3 or 4?

(3) Beth asked the man about his headaches.

(4) *About the Beth headaches man asked his.

Your "school grammar" taught you that every sentence must have a subject and a verb. According to that rule, sentence 4 is just as much a sentence as 3. Your syntactic competence, on the other hand, tells you that sentence 4 is ill-formed, unacceptable. You can even specify some of the rules that are being violated; for example, definite articles such as *the* do not usually precede a person's name, and two nouns usually don't follow one another in the same phrase or clause.

The point here is that the meaning of a sentence is far more than the meanings of the words. The "far more" here is the arrangement or sequencing of the words. We're speaking of syntactic word order rules for English (Gershkoff-Stowe & Goldin-Medow, 2002, argue that word order is more than just syntax, and that it reflects a more general property of human thought). More than some languages (e.g., Latin), English relies heavily on word order. Consider "red fire engine" versus "fire engine red" (or even "red engine fire"). Despite the fact that *red* and *fire engine* can be nouns, our word-order knowledge tells us that the first word in these phrases is to be treated as an adjective, modifying the following noun. Thus by varying word order alone, "red fire engine" is a fire engine of the usual color, and "fire engine red" is a particular shade of red.

PHRASE ORDER   There's more to it than just word order, however. We also rely on the ordering of larger units such as phrases or clauses to convey meaning. Consider the following sentences:

(5) Bill told the men to deliver the piano on Monday.

(6) Bill told the men on Monday to deliver the piano.

In these examples, the positioning of the phrase "on Monday" helps us determine the intended meaning, whether the piano was to be delivered on Monday or whether Bill had told the men something on Monday. Thus, the sequence of words and phrases contains clues to meaning, clues that speakers use to express meaning and clues that listeners use to decipher meaning.

NUMBER AGREEMENT Yet another part of syntax involves the adjustments we make depending on other words in the sentence. In particular, a part of every sentence is a subject and a verb. It's required, furthermore, that the subject and verb agree in number—if the subject of the sentence is singular, you must use a singular verb, as in "The car has a flat tire" (obviously, pronouns have to be coordinated in terms of number, too). As Bock (1995, p. 56) noted, agreement helps listeners know what the topic of a sentence is going to be about. For example, consider "The mother of the girls who was . . ." versus "The mother of the girls who were. . . ." You're pretty sure that the first sentence is going to be about the mother, and the second one about the girls just because of the number agreement of "was" versus "were." So number agreement, like word and phrase order, is a clue to meaning, part of the spoken and written language that we rely on when we comprehend. (See Bock & Miller, 1991, and Hartsuiker, Anton-Mendez, & van Zee, 2001, for experimental work on number agreement errors, e.g., when you make the verb agree in number with the nearest noun rather than the subject noun, as in "*The difficulty with all of these issues are that. . . .")

In general, we need to understand what these syntactic clues are and how they are used. We need to explore the syntactic rules that influence comprehension. We begin by looking at the underlying syntactic structure of sentences, taking a piece-by-piece approach to Chomsky's important work.

Chomsky's Transformational Grammar

At a general level, Chomsky intended to "describe the universal aspects of syntactic knowledge" (Whitney, 1998), that is, to capture the syntactic structures of language. He noted that language has a hierarchical phrase structure: The words do not simply occur one after the other. Instead, they come in groupings, such as "on Monday," "the men," and "deliver the piano." Furthermore, these groupings can be altered, either by moving them from one spot to another in the structure or by modifying them to express different meanings (e.g., by changing the statement into a question). These two ideas—words come in phrase structure groupings, and the groupings can be modified or transformed—correspond to the two major syntactic rule systems in Chomsky's theory.

PHRASE STRUCTURE GRAMMAR Let's start with the phrase structure grammar that generates the overall structure of sentences. An important point in Chomsky's system is that the **phrase structure** grammar accounts for *the constituents of the sentence, the word groupings and phrases that make up the whole utterance, and the relationships among those constituents.* To illustrate this consider an example from Lachman, Lachman, and Butterfield (1979):

(7) The patio resembles a junkyard.

In a phrase structure grammar, the entire sentence is symbolized by an *S.* In this grammar, the sentence *S* can be broken down into two major components, a noun phrase *(NP)* and a verb phrase *(VP).* Thus the first line of the grammar illustrated in Figure 9-7A shows $S \rightarrow NP + VP$, to be read, "The sentence can be rewritten as a noun phrase plus a verb phrase." In the second rule, the *NP* can be

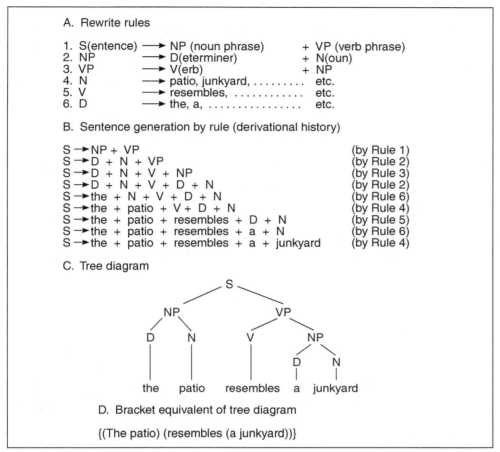

FIGURE 9-7   A depiction of a phrase structure grammar: **A.** The rewrite rules of the grammar; **B.** Sentence generation by the rules; **C.** A tree diagram or hierarchical representation; **D.** A "bracket equivalent" diagram of the sentence.

From Lachman, Lachman, & Butterfield (1979).

rewritten as a determiner *(D)*, an article such as *the* or *a*, plus a noun *(N)*: *NP → D + N*; in other words, a noun phrase can be rewritten as a determiner and a noun. In rule 3 we see the structure of a verb phrase; a *VP* is rewritten as a verb *(V)* plus an *NP: VP → V + NP*.

As Figure 9-7B shows, six rewrite rules are necessary for generating the sentence. A different but equivalent depiction of the grammar is shown in Figure 9-7C, in which a tree diagram shows the most general components at the top and the specific words at the bottom. An advantage of the tree diagram is that it reveals the hierarchical structure of the sentence as well as the internal structure and interrelations. Finally, a bracket equivalent is shown in Figure 9-7D.

THE INADEQUACY OF PHRASE STRUCTURE GRAMMAR ALONE   Chomsky's theory relied heavily on a phrase structure approach because it captures an important aspect of language—its productivity. That is, this kind of grammar is generative; by means of such phrase structure rules, an entire family of sentences can be generated.

Furthermore, the phrase structure grammar is joined with two other components, the lexical entries (the words of a sentence) and the lexical insertion rules (the rules for putting the words into their slots). These components, as shown in Figure 9-7, generated the first representation of the sentence, the **deep structure** representation. In Chomsky's view the deep structure is *an abstract syntactic representation of the sentence* being constructed, with only bare-bones lexical entries (words).

The deep structure is critical for two reasons. First, it is the representation passed to the transformational "fix-it" rules to yield the surface structure of the sentence; we deal with those in a moment. Second, the deep structure is also submitted to a semantic component that "computes" meaning. This takes the deep structure and produces a semantic representation that reflects the underlying meaning. Notice that, because of the separate treatment of the semantic component, a sentence's true meaning might not be reflected accurately in the **surface structure**; a surface structure might be **ambiguous**, or *have more than one meaning*. For instance, consider two classic examples of ambiguous sentences:

(8) Visiting relatives can be a nuisance.

(9) The shooting of the hunters was terrible.

A moment's reflection reveals the ambiguities. These alternative meanings are revealed when we **parse** the sentences, when we *divide the sentence into phrases and groupings,* much the way the phrase structure grammar does. The two meanings of sentence 8—that is, the two deep structures—correspond to two different phrase structures. For sentence 8, the ambiguity boils down to the grammatical function of *visiting,* whether it is used as an adjective or a verb. These two grammatical functions translate into two different phrase structures (*verb+noun* versus *adjective+noun*).

Sentence 9, however, has only one phrase structure; there is only one way to parse it: {[*the shooting of the hunters*] [*was terrible*]}. Thus sentence 9 is ambiguous at the level of surface structure. Because phrase structure rules can generate such ambiguous sentences, Chomsky felt that this illustrated a limitation of the pure phrase structure approach: There must be something missing in the grammar. If it were complete, it wouldn't generate ambiguous sentences.

A second difficulty Chomsky pointed out involves examples such as the following:

(10a) Pierre bought a fine French wine.

(10b) A fine French wine was bought by Pierre.

According to phrase structure rules, there is almost no structural similarity between these two sentences. And yet they mean nearly the same thing. People's intuitions, that active and passive paraphrases are more or less identical at the level of meaning, are not captured by the phrase structure approach.

TRANSFORMATIONAL RULES Chomsky's solution to such problems was to postulate a second component to the grammar, a set of **transformational rules** that handle the many specific surface forms that can express an underlying idea. These transformational rules *convert the deep structure into a surface structure, a sentence* *ready to be spoken.* By applying different transformations, we can form an active declarative sentence, a passive voice sentence, a question, a negative, a future or past tense, and so on. With still other transformations, phrases can exchange places, and words can be inserted and deleted. In this view, sentences 10a and 10b differ only in their surface structures; one deep structure (the core meaning) is transformed in two different fashions. Likewise, for a simple deep structure idea such as {(boy kisses girl)}, the **transformational grammar** could generate any of the following, depending on which particular grammatical transformations were selected:

(11a) The boy kissed the girl.

(11b) The girl was kissed by the boy.

(11c) Was the girl kissed by the boy?

More elaborate rules are also applied by this transformational component, including rules that allow us to combine ideas, such as the idea that {(boy kisses girl)} and the idea that {(girl is pretty)}:

(12a) The boy kissed the pretty girl.

(12b) The boy kissed the girl who was pretty.

(12c) The girl whom the boy kissed was pretty.

(12d) Will the girl who is pretty be kissed by the boy?

Thus one surface structure for the {(girl) (is) (pretty)} idea is merely "the pretty girl"; an equivalent structure, in terms of meaning, is "the girl who is pretty." On the other hand, sentences 12c and 12d are the most difficult to comprehend, largely because of the passive voice and the embedded relative "who" clauses.

Limitations of Transformational Grammar

A great deal of early psycholinguistic research was devoted to structural aspects of language. For example, there was a lot of focus on testing the derivational complexity hypothesis. This hypothesis suggests that the difficulty of comprehending a sentence is directly related to the number of grammatical transformations applied. So, if a deep structure has two transformations applied to it, it is more difficult to comprehend than if only one transformation is applied. Early results tended to support the theory (e.g., Palermo, 1978). However, over time, psychology became dissatisfied with this approach. Work by Fodor and Garrett (1966) was especially instrumental in dimming the enthusiasm. They noted that much of the support for the derivational complexity hypothesis failed to control potentially important factors. For instance, a derivationally more complex sentence generally has more words in it than a simpler one (contrast sentences 12a and 12c).

Moreover, there was a metatheoretical point of view. To oversimplify a bit, the major components were said to be the syntactic rules for generating first a deep then a surface structure.

Noam Chomsky, developer of Transformational Grammar Theory.

Meaning was literally off to the side. This depicts the difficulty psychology had with linguistic theory: It seemed that meaning was secondary to syntax. It's almost as if the theory, as it was applied to language *use,* suggested that we first make up our minds what phrase constituents we're going to use and only then decide what we're going to talk about. To psychologists concerned with how we use language to express meaning, this seemed wrong.

Note that this is an oversimplification, making it seem as if Chomsky encouraged linguists to avoid meaning. It was not that extreme. In fact, Chomsky repeatedly emphasized the importance of both syntax and semantics. He pointed out that even a perfectly grammatical, syntactically acceptable sentence may be semantically anomalous. His most famous example is "Colorless green ideas sleep furiously." The sentence is grammatically acceptable—consider a sentence with completely parallel syntax, such as "Tired young children sleep soundly." But, Chomsky's sentence has no meaning in any ordinary sense.

Still, Chomsky's work never dealt satisfactorily with meaning, in the view of psychologists. Furthermore, trying to apply his theory to the actual use of language—that is, turning his competence-based theory into a performance theory of language production and comprehension—only made it more apparent that a different approach was needed.

We turn to the major focus of this research, the semantic level of analysis, in a moment. But first, we must conclude this section on syntax with a psycholinguistic view of syntax.

The Cognitive Role of Syntax

From a psychological perspective, what is the purpose of syntax? Why follow syntactic rules? Essentially, we use syntax to help figure out meaning. If an infinite number of sentences are possible, then the one sentence being said to us right now could be about *anything.* Syntax helps listeners extract meaning and helps speakers convey it.

Bock's (1982) article on a cognitive psychology of syntax discusses several important issues that psycholinguistics must explain. She notes that the syntactic burden falls more heavily on the speaker than the listener. That is, when you have to produce a sentence rather than comprehend it, you must create a surface structure, a string of words and phrases to communicate your idea as well as possible. Thus, syntax is a feature of language that is related to the speaker's mental effort.

AUTOMATIC PROCESSING   Two points Bock raises should illustrate some issues in the psycholinguistic study of syntax. First, consider the issues of automatic and conscious processes as they apply to language production. As we know, automatic processes are the product of a high degree of practice or overlearning. Bock noted that several aspects of syntactic structure are consistent with the idea of automaticity. For instance, children rely heavily on regular word orders, even if the native language they are learning has irregular word order. The purpose is that by relying over and over on the same syntactic frames, they can be generated and used more automatically. Similarly, adults tend to use only a few syntactic structures with regularity, suggesting that they can be called into service rapidly and automatically.

Interestingly, the syntax you use can be influenced by a previous sentence, quite literally syntactic priming (Bock, 1986; West & Stanovich, 1986). Bock's later work (Bock & Griffin, 2000) found evidence that a particular syntactic construction can prime later ones up to lag 10 (i.e., with 10 intervening sentences), even in written language (Branigan, Pickering, & Cleland, 1999; Branigan, Pickering, Stewart, & McLean, 2000).

PLANNING   In Bock's second point, she reviewed evidence of an important interaction between syntax and meaning. In general, we tailor the syntax of our sentences to the accessibility of the lexical or semantic information being conveyed. This is known as the **given-new strategy** (Clark & Clark, 1977). Phrases that contain more accessible information, or given information, tend to occur earlier in sentences. This is information that is either well known or recently discussed in a discourse (and so more available). In comparison, less accessible, newer concepts tend to come later, possibly to give ourselves extra time for retrieval (but see Clifton & Frazier, 2004, for an alternative account). Ferreira and Swets (2002) demonstrated this in a clever experiment, by asking people to state the answer to easy and hard addition problems, in sentence frames like "The answer is __." They found that people delayed nearly a half a second more before they started talking when the problem was hard (e.g., 23 + 68) than when it was easy (e.g., 21 + 22). Clearly speech production is sensitive to the ease of memory retrieval.

Our planning and execution of speech is also sensitive to grammatical complexity and presumably to the possibility that a listener (or a speaker, for that matter) might lose track of information if too much time passes. As an example, Stallings, MacDonald, and O'Seaghdha (1998) showed a particular kind of syntactic adjustment used for complex noun phrases, "heavy NPs" in their words ("heavy" because they're long). Specifically, we tend to shift heavy NPs to the end of a sentence, and insert other material in between the subject and NP, but not when the noun phrase is short. Consider the simple sentence "The boy found the textbook in his car." The noun phrase (the textbook) is short, so doesn't need to be shifted. But, if there's more to say about the textbook, you might say "The boy found in his car the textbook that had been lost for so long," shifting the textbook phrase to the end and putting "in his car" in the middle. But you probably wouldn't shift the short noun phrase to the end, as in "The boy found in his car the textbook." Moving "the textbook" to the end isn't needed here because the listener's working memory isn't being over-taxed. But the heavy NP "the textbook that had been lost for so long" is sufficiently long that working memory might lose essential information, the connections between the boy, the car, and finding the book, if the phrase separated those ideas by too many intervening ideas. More generally, as syntactic complexity increases, this increasingly taxes working memory (e.g., Fedorenko, Gibson, & Rohde, 2006).

These effects tell us something interesting about the cognitive mechanisms that create sentences. Earlier theories of sentence planning, such as Fromkin's (1971; see Table 9-4), described planning as sequential: First you identify the meaning to be conveyed, then you select the syntactic frame, and so on. Recent research, however, shows how interactive and flexible the planning process is (Ferreira, 1996; Griffin & Bock, 2000). Difficulties in one component, for instance

Stage	Process
TABLE 9-4	**Fromkin's (1971) Model for the Planning and Production of Speech**
1	Identify meaning; generate the meaning to be expressed.
2	Select syntactic structure; construct a syntactic outline of the sentence, specifying word slots.
3	Generate intonation contour; assign stress values to different word slots.
4	Insert content words; retrieve appropriate nouns, verbs, adjectives, and so on from the lexicon and insert into word slots.
5	Add function words and affixes; fill out the syntax with function words (articles, prepositions, etc.), prefixes, suffixes.
6	Specify phonetic segments; express the sentence in terms of phonetic segments according to phonological (pronunciation) rules.

word retrieval, can prompt a return to an earlier planning component, say to rework the syntax (Ferreira & Firato, 2002), or can prompt you to delay the sentence. By selecting an alternative syntax, the speaker buys more time for retrieving the intended word (see also Kempen & Hoehkamp, 1987). Needless to say, such a highly interactive system runs counter to strictly hierarchical or sequential approaches, such as Chomsky's.

In general, we begin our utterances when the first part of the sentence has been planned but before the syntax and semantics of the final portion have been worked out (see Bachoud-Levi, Dupoux, Cohen, & Mehler, 1998, and Griffin, 2003, for comparable effects). The time it takes to begin speaking (e.g., Bock, Irwin, Davidseon, & Levelt, 2003) and hesitations in our spoken speech are clues to the nature of planning and memory retrieval, as are the effects of momentary changes in priming, lexical access, and working memory load (Bock & Miller, 1991; Lindsley, 1975). In fact, several reports detail how the false starts, hesitations, and restarts in speaking often reflect both the complexity of the intended sentence and a genuine online planning process that unfolds as the sentence is developed (Clark & Wasow, 1998; Ferreira, 1996; Ferreira & Dell, 2000; see Bock, 1996, for a review of methods of studying language production).

More recent work has taken Chomsky to task even further. In a connectionist model of language processing, Chang, Dell, and Bock (2006) have challenged Chomsky's idea that language has a strong genetic component, as compared to the strong learning stance taken by the behaviorists. That is, Chomsky suggested that although you may need to learn your own language, all humans have a strong genetic bias to learn some language, and that aspects of transformational grammar were somehow part of that genetic process. The Chang et al. model assumes, in contrast, that language processing has a strongly learned component, similar to other memory processes. Part of how the model learns a language is by comparing its predictions for what will be said next to what is actually said, and then adjusting the connection weights based on any discrepancy (see also Griffiths, Steyvers, & Tenebaum, 2007, for a predictive model of word meaning in the context of sentences).

Another interesting aspect of the Chang et al. connectionist model is the idea that language may operate in a parallel fashion to vision. That is, there are two routes in visual processing, one for processing *what* something is, and one for processing *where* it is (Ungerleider & Haxby, 1994), with the *what* system taking the ventral visual pathway toward the temporal lobe, and the *where* system taking the dorsal pathway toward the parietal lobe. An idea in the Chang et al. model is that there is a network for processing the meaning aspect of language, and a separate system for the sequencing of the words. Together, these two systems converge to predict what type of word will come next, allowing the system to learn and adjust to new input, such as new words, or new ways of using words (e.g., I *googled* you the other day and was surprised by how many hits there were).

Section Summary

- Syntax involves the ordering of words and phrases in sentence structure and features such as active versus passive voice. Chomsky's theory of language was a heavily syntactic scheme with two sets of syntactic rules. Phrase structure rules were used to generate a deep structure representation of a sentence, and then transformational rules converted the deep structure into the surface structure, the string of words that makes up the sentence.

- There are a variety of syntactic clues to the meaning of a sentence, so an understanding of syntax is necessary to psycholinguists. On the other hand, psycholinguistics has developed its own theories of language, at least in part because of linguists' relative neglect of semantic and performance characteristics.

- Studies of how we plan and execute sentences reveal a highly interactive set of processes, rather than a strictly sequential sequence. We pause, delay, and rearrange sentences as a function of planning and memory-related factors like accessibility and working memory load.

LEXICAL AND SEMANTIC FACTORS: THE MEANING IN LANGUAGE

We now turn to lexical and semantic factors. This is the level of meaning in language. In particular, we refer to retrieval from the **mental lexicon**, *the mental dictionary of words and their meanings.* After rapid perceptual and pattern recognition processes, the encoded word provides access to the word's entry in the lexicon and also to the semantic representation of the concept. The evidence you've read about throughout this book, such as results from the Stroop and the lexical decision tasks, attests to the close relationship between a word and its meaning and the seemingly automatic accessing of one from the other. Recall in the Stroop task that seeing the word *red* printed in green ink triggers an interference process with naming the ink color, clear evidence that *red* is processed to the level of meaning (MacLeod, 1992). Likewise, the lexical decision task does not

Simulate
*Lexical Bias
in Slips of the
Tongue* in
MyPsychLab

PROVE IT
Speech Errors

Work by Fromkin (1971), Garrett (1975), and others (e.g., Ferreira & Humphreys, 2001; for work on error monitoring, see Hartsuiker & Kolk, 2001) has tabulated and made sense of speech errors that occur when we substitute or change sounds, syllables, words, and so on. Speech errors are not random but are quite lawful. For instance, when we make an exchange error, the exchange is between elements at the same linguistic level; initial sounds exchange places with other initial sounds, syllables with syllables, words with words (e.g., "to cake a bake"). If a prefix switches places, its new location will be in front of another word, not at the end.

Collect a sample of speech errors, say, from radio news broadcasters or your professors' lectures, then analyze them in terms of the linguistic level of the elements involved and the types of errors such as (intended phrase in parentheses):

Shift	She decide to hits it. (decides to hit it)
Exchange	Your model renosed. (your nose remodeled)
Perseveration	He pulled a pantrum. (tantrum)
Blend	To explain clarefully. (clearly/carefully)

require that you access the word's meaning but only that you identify a letter string as a genuine word. Nonetheless, identifying *doctor* as a word primes your decision to *nurse* (e.g., Table 7-3).

Morphemes

A **morpheme** is *the smallest unit of language that has meaning.* To return to the example early in the chapter, the word *cars* is composed of two morphemes: *Car* refers to a concept and a physical object, and *-s* is a meaningful suffix, denoting "more than one of." Likewise, the word *unhappiness* is composed of three morphemes: *happy* as the base concept, the prefix *un-* meaning "not," and the suffix *-ness* meaning "state or quality of being." In general, morphemes that can stand on their own and serve as words are called *free morphemes,* such as *happy, car,* and *legal,* whereas morphemes that need to be linked onto a free morpheme are called *bound morphemes,* such as *un-, -ness,* and *-s.* Although the concept of a morpheme is important, note that there is some debate as to whether the meaning of more common words such as *unhappiness* may be stored directly in memory or "computed" from the three morphemes (see Carroll, 1986; Whitney, 1998).

Lexical Representation

Think about the word *chase* as an example of how free morphemes might be represented in the mental lexicon. The representation of *chase* must specify its meaning—indicate that it means "to run after or pursue, in hopes of catching." Like other semantic concepts, *chase* can be represented in reference to related information, like *run, pursue,* the idea of *speed.* Given this, along with what you know about events in the real world from schemas and scripts, you can easily understand a sentence like

(13) The policeman chased the burglar through the park.

From a more psycholinguistic perspective, however, you know more about *chase* than just its basic meaning. For one thing, you know it's a verb, specifying a kind of physical action. Related to that, you have a clear idea of how *chase* can be used in sentences, the kinds of things that can do the chasing, and the kinds of things that can be chased (e.g., McKoon & Macfarland, 2002). Imagine, then, that your lexical representation of *chase* also includes this knowledge; *chase* requires some animate thing to do the chasing, some other kind of thing to be chased, and a location where the chasing takes place.

Lexical knowledge can include information that can capture embodied characteristics of cognition. For example, in a study by Willems, Hagoort, and Casasanto (2010), people did a lexical decision task while in a functional MRI (fMRI) scanner. What they observed was that when people responded to action verbs, the appropriate motor areas of the cortex became more active. Moreover, for right-handers, this was more on the left hemisphere motor areas (which control the right side of the body), whereas for the left-handers, the opposite was true. So, when a word strongly implied using a specific part of the body, the lexical information associated with that word involved information about how to move that part of the body. In another study, Willems, Labruna, D'Espisito, Ivry, and Casasanto (2011) again had people do a lexical decision task, but this time in conjunction with TMS treatment in which the hand portion of the brain was stimulated. What they found was that when people are given verbs that involved using the hand, such as *throw* or *write*, people responded faster under stimulation, compared to verbs that did not involve using the hands, such as *earn* or *wander*. Thus, activating the part of the brain that controls that part of the body made it easier to identify and respond to words that also strongly involve that part of the body. This suggests that our mental lexicon contains motor information about how we do things.

POLYSEMY: ONE WORD, MULTIPLE MEANINGS   Whereas our understanding of words like *chase* is very clear, it's not too long before you run into cases of **polysemy**, the fact that *many words in a language may have multiple meanings*. The task of the language processing system is to figure out which meaning is the intended one. While a word may be polysemous, not all meanings are equal. Generally, there is one primary meaning that people typically would think of first when they hear the word, or would likely be listed first in a dictionary. This is the *dominant* meaning of a word. Other meanings then would be the *subordinate* meanings. So, take a simple word like *run*. The dominant meaning has something to do with using your legs to move fast. However, there are many subordinate meanings, too, such as having a run in your stockings, a movie having a run at the theater, having your nose run, to cut and run (retreat), to run your engine, watching paint colors run, and so on. The way you distinguish which specific meaning to use from the mental lexicon would depend on the context a word is in.

POLYSEMY AND PRIMING   Let's consider two examples of how context can resolve polysemy to determine the intended meaning. As one example, the word *count* is ambiguous by itself. Putting the word in a sentence may not help: "We had trouble keeping track of the count." You still can't tell the intended meaning. What's missing is context, some conceptual framework to guide the interpretation of the polysemous word. With an adequate context, you can determine which sense of the word *count* is intended in these two contexts:

My dog wasn't included in the final count.

The vampire was disguised as a handsome count.

These sentences, taken from Simpson's (1981, 1984) work on polysemy, point out the importance of context: Context can help determine the intended meaning. With neutral contexts, such as the "We had trouble" sentence, word meanings are activated as a function of their dominance: The number sense of *count* is dominant, so that meaning is more activated. But a context that biases the interpretation one way or the other results in a stronger activation for the biased meaning: With *vampire* you activated the meaning of *count* related to nobility and Count Dracula (see also Balota & Paul, 1996; Klein & Murphy, 2002; Piercey & Joordens, 2000; but cf. Binder, 2003; Binder & Rayner, 1998).

The resolution of lexical ambiguity with polysemous words is important for successful comprehension. If you don't get the intended meaning of a word, then you won't get the intended message. It appears that ambiguity resolution works, in part, in a two-stage process. When people encounter an ambiguous word, what they do is activate all of the meanings, at least to some degree. Then in the second stage, they deactivate the inappropriate ones, based on the information from the rest of the discourse context. However, not everyone does this equally well. Work by Gernsbacher and Faust (1991) shows that good readers suppress inappropriate meanings faster. In comparison, poor readers maintained multiple meanings for a much longer period of time, which may be contributing to the problems they are having.

Watch the video *Bilingual Education* in **MyPsychLab**

BILINGUALISM   What happens if you know more than one language? How does cognition deal with that? Generally, when people are multilingual, cognition needs to keep the words, syntax, idioms, and such for languages separate enough that they do not intrude on one another and end up intermixing in the person's speech. At the same time, the words and phrases in one language need to map onto the same underlying ideas in the other languages. In general, human cognition is able to handle this task quite well. People who learn a second language early on even show semantic priming effects across languages (Perea, Duñabeitia, & Carreiras, 2008), suggesting that the different words tap into the same underlying semantic knowledge base.

The need to keep two or more languages separate, but still be fluent in both of them, requires increased attention and cognitive control to mentally keep the languages from interfering with one another. This need for bilinguals to engage in such cognitive control spills over to other cognitive abilities that require cognitive control, such as showing larger negative priming effects (see Chapter 4), because bilinguals are more effective at suppressing salient but incorrect information (Treccani, Argyri, Sorace, & Della Salla, 2009). Thus, there seems to be an overall cognitive benefit to knowing more than one language; bilinguals show superior performance on intelligence tests compared to otherwise similar monolinguals (Lambert, 1990) and even do better on tests of their primary language (Bialystok, 1988; van Hell & Dijkstra, 2002).

Although bilingualism has advantages for cognition, learning a second language as an adult is more difficult and requires more cognitive attention and effort. For example, there is some evidence to suggest that when people are immersed in a second language that was learned as a adult, the person's first language is actively suppressed (Linek, Kroll, & Sunderman, 2010), which is not what is observed with people who grew up speaking more than one language.

CONTEXT AND ERPS   Let's consider a second example, an offshoot of the Kounios and Holcomb work with event-related potentials (ERPs) that you read about earlier. In one study, Holcomb, Kounios, Anderson, and West (1999; see also Laszlo & Federmeier, 2009; Lee & Federmeier, 2009; Sereno, Brewer, & O'Donnell, 2003) recorded ERPs in a simple sentence comprehension task. People saw sentences one word at a time and were asked to respond after seeing the last word, with "yes" if the sentence made sense and "no" if it did not. The experimental sentences varied along two dimensions, whether the last word was concrete or abstract and whether it was congruent with the sentence meaning or anomalous (i.e., made no sense). As an example, "Armed robbery implies that the thief used a weapon" was a concrete–congruent sentence; substituting *rose* for *weapon* made it concrete but anomalous. Likewise, "Lisa argued that this had not been the case in one single instance" was abstract–congruent sentence, and substituting *fun* for *instance* made it abstract–anomalous.

Figure 9-8 shows some of the ERP patterns obtained. In the left panel, you see the "normal" ERP patterns for the congruent, sensible sentences; the three profiles, from top to bottom, came from the three midline electrode sites shown in the schematic drawing (frontal, central, and parietal). In the right panel are the ERP patterns when the sentences ended in an anomalous word. Notice first in the left panel that the solid and dotted functions, for concrete and abstract sentences, tracked each other very closely: Whatever neural mechanisms operated during comprehension, they generated similar ERP patterns. But now make a left-to-right comparison of the patterns, seeing the differences in the right panel when the sentences ended in a nonsensical, anomalous word (*rose* in the armed robbery sentence, for example). Here, there were marked changes in the ERP profiles. At the central location, for example, there was a steadily downward trend (in the positive direction, in terms of electrical potentials) for sensible sentences but a dramatic reversal of direction for anomalous words.

In short, the neural mechanisms involved in comprehension generated dramatically different patterns when an anomalous word was encountered. The mismatch between the context, the already-processed meaning of the sentence, and the final word yielded not only an overt response (the response indicating "no, that sentence makes no sense"), but also a neural response, signifying the brain-related activity that detected the anomalous ending of the sentence. (Don't get confused about directions here. The functions underneath the gridline are electrically positive, so deflection upward in these graphs is a deflection toward the

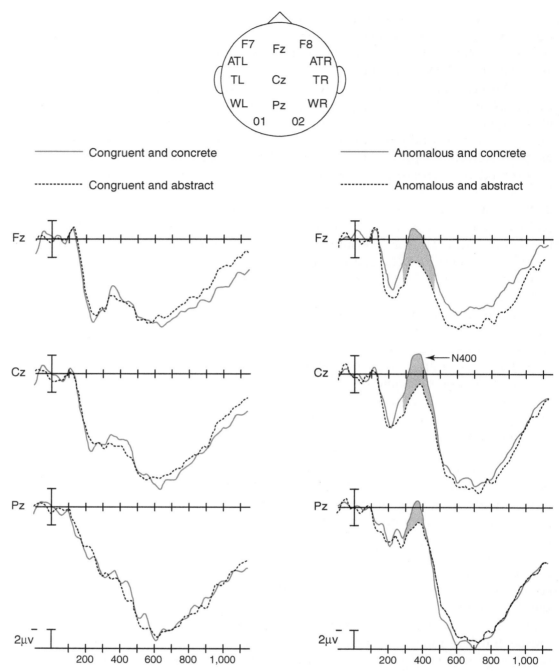

FIGURE 9-8 ERP profiles at three midline sites (frontal [F_z], central [C_z], parietal [P_z]) for sentences ending with a congruent (left panel) or contextually anomalous (right panel) word.

Adapted from Figures 3 and 4 in Holcomb et al. (1999).

negative, a deflection going in a negative direction; this is what the *N* in *N400* signifies, a "negative going" pattern.) Even at the level of neural functioning then, there is a rapid response to nonsensical ideas that follow sensible context, a kind of "something's wrong here" response that the brain makes some 400 ms after the nonsensical event.

Case Grammar

In this section we consider issues of how the language processing system knows what role a word or concept is playing in a sentence. This approach is called **case grammar**. The ideas came originally from Fillmore (1968). The basic idea is that *the semantic analysis of sentences involves figuring out what semantic role is being played by each word or concept in the sentence and computing sentence meaning based on those semantic roles.* Two sample sentences illustrate this:

(14) *The key will open the door.*

(15) *The janitor will open the door with the key.*

Fillmore pointed out that syntactic aspects of sentences—which words serve as the subject, direct object, and so on—often are irrelevant to sentence meaning. For example, in sentences 14 and 15 the word *key* plays different grammatical roles; subject of the sentence in 14 but object of the preposition in 15. For Fillmore, focusing on this difference misses a critical point for language. Regardless of its different grammatical roles, the key is doing exactly the same thing in both cases, playing the same semantic role of *instrument*. A purely syntactic analysis misses this, but a semantic analysis captures it perfectly.

Fillmore's theory was called case grammar. Fillmore proposed that sentence processing involves a semantic parsing that focuses on the semantic *roles played by the content words in the sentences.* These semantic roles are called **semantic cases**, or simply **case roles**. Thus, *door* is the recipient or patient of the action of *open* in sentences 14 and 15; *janitor* is the agent of *open; key* is the instrument; and so on. Stated simply, each content word plays a semantic role in the meaning of the sentence. That role is the word's *semantic case.* The significant—indeed, critical—point about such a semantic parsing is that it relies on people's existing semantic and lexical knowledge, their knowledge of what kinds of things will open, who can perform the opening, and so on.

Reconsider the *chase* sentence 13, "The policeman chased the burglar through the park," and three variations, thinking of the content words in terms of their semantic roles:

(16) *The mouse chased the cat through the house.*

(17) *His insecurities chased him even in his sleep.*

(18) **The book chased the flower.*

Your lexical and semantic knowledge of *chase* is that some animate being does the chasing, the agent case. Some other thing is the recipient of the chasing, the patient, but that thing need not be animate, just capable of moving rapidly (e.g., you can chase a piece of paper being blown by the wind). On this analysis, it is clear that sentence 13 conforms to the normal situation stored in memory, so it is easy to comprehend. Sentence 16, however, mismatches the typical state of affairs between mice and cats. Nonetheless, either of these creatures can serve as the required animate agent of the relation *chase,* so sentence 16 is sensible. Because of other semantic knowledge, you know that sentence 17 violates the literal meaning of *chase* but could still have a nonliteral, metaphorical meaning. But your semantic case analysis provides the reason sentence 18 is unacceptable. A book is inanimate, so it mismatches the required animate agent role for *chase;* *book* cannot play the role of agent for *chase.* Likewise, *flower* seems to violate the movable restriction on the patient case for *chase.*

Work by Bresnan (1978; Bresnan & Kaplan, 1982) and Jackendoff (1992) has amplified and extended work on case grammars. For example, in Jackendoff's theory of a cognitive grammar (1992; see Figure 9-9), the goal is to build a conceptual structure, an understanding of the sentence. We use language and language rules to get from the spoken or written sentence to a meaningful mental structure or understanding. Each lexical entry includes the meaning of the word and, for verbs, a list of the arguments or semantic cases that go along with it. Thus, the lexical entry *chase* would state that *chase* requires an animate agent, some recipient or patient, and so on. Likewise, for *give,* the case arguments would state that an animate agent and recipient are needed for the *give* relation, and some *object* is the thing being given (for an excellent summary of these positions, see Whitney, 1998).

Accordingly, when we perceive words, we look up the concepts in the lexicon. This look-up process accesses not only the word's meaning, but also its syntactic and semantic case roles and any other restrictions. Each word in the sentence is processed as it is encountered, with content words being assigned to their

FIGURE 9-9 In Jackendoff's (1992) conceptual semantics approach, comprehension of meaning is the process of arriving at a conceptual structure for the sentence. To accomplish this, we use both the syntactic structure of the sentence and a set of correspondence rules; the correspondence rules translate from syntactic roles (e.g., noun and verb) into semantic roles (agent, patient, and so forth).

Adapted from Whitney (1998).

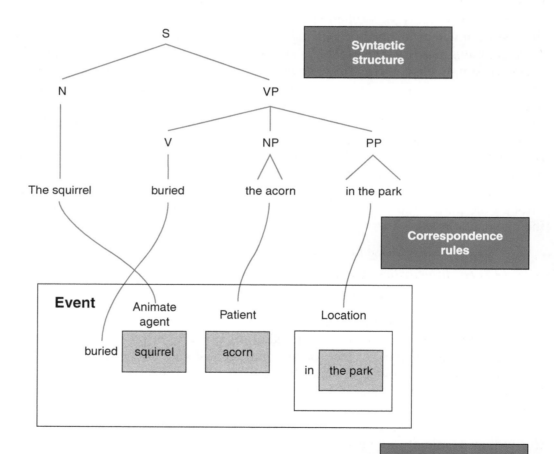

semantic roles. If all goes well, the sentence conveys an exact, specified meaning that is captured accurately by the analysis of the cognitive grammar.

Interaction of Syntax and Semantics

Note that semantic factors do not stand alone in language, just as syntactic factors are not independent of semantics. Syntax is more than just word and phrase order rules; it's a clue to how to understand sentences. For example, O'Seaghdha's (1997) evidence shows separable effects of syntactic assignment and semantic integration of word meanings, with syntactic processes occurring before semantic integration. His results, based on RTs, are largely consistent with those in other studies (e.g., Peterson, Burgess, Dell, & Eberhard, 2001, on how we process idioms), including ERP studies of syntactic and semantic processing (Ainsworth-Darnell, Shulman, & Boland, 1998; Friederici, Hahne, & Mecklinger, 1996; Osterhout, Allen, McLaughlin, & Inoue, 2002). And, as you just read, syntax in speech production is sensitive to a word's accessibility; words that can be easily retrieved right now tend to appear earlier in a sentence.

SEMANTIC FOCUS   Likewise, semantic factors refer to more than just word and phrase meanings, because different syntactic devices can be clues to meaning. To anticipate just a bit, note how syntactic differences in the following sentences influence the semantic interpretation:

> *(19a) I'm going downtown with my sister at four o'clock.*
>
> *(19b) It's at four o'clock that I'm going downtown with my sister.*
>
> *(19c) It's my sister I'm going downtown with at four o'clock.*

Sentences 19b and 19c differ subtly from 19a in the focus of the utterance. The focus of each sentence is different, so each means something slightly different. Imagine how inappropriate sentence 19c would be, for instance, as a response to the question "Did you say you're going downtown with your sister at three o'clock?" Our judgments about appropriateness make an important point: Our theories of language performance must be as sophisticated as our own knowledge of language is. We are sensitive to the focus or highlighted aspects of sentences and subtleties of the ordering of clauses, so a theory of language must reflect this in a psychologically relevant way.

SEMANTICS CAN OVERPOWER SYNTAX   Semantic features can do more than alter the syntax of sentences. Occasionally semantics can overpower syntax. Let's focus on a classic study by Fillenbaum (1974). As you read, note how current terminology would label this an effect of top-down processing.

Fillenbaum presented several kinds of sentences and asked people to write paraphrases that preserved the original meaning. Ordinary "threat" sentences such as "Don't print that or I'll sue you" were then reordered into "perverse" threats, such as "Don't print that or I won't sue you." Regular "conjunctive" sentences such as "John got off the bus and went into the store" were then changed into "disordered" sentences, such as "John went into the store and got off the bus." When Fillenbaum scored paraphrases of reordered sentences, he found remarkably high

FIGURE 9-10
Fillenbaum's (1974)
results. Two kinds
of normal sentences
were shown, threats
and conjunctives
(labeled C) such as
"John got off the
bus and went into
the store." Threats
were then altered
to be "perverse,"
and conjunctives
were disordered
(e.g., threat C,
"John dressed and
had a bath").

From Fillenbaum
(1974).

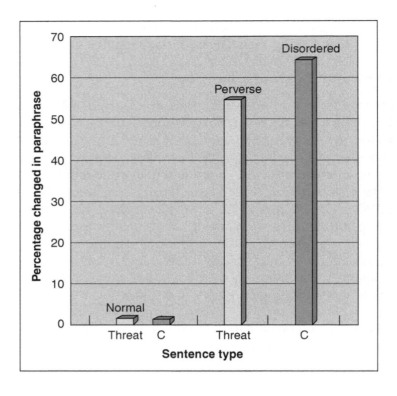

percentages of changes, as shown in Figure 9-10. More than 50% of people "normalized" the perverse threatening sentences, making them conform to the more typical state of affairs, and more than 60% normalized the "disordered" conjunctive sentences. He then asked people to reread their paraphrases to see whether there was even a "shred of difference" from the originals. More than half the time, people saw no discrepancies. Apparently, their general knowledge was influential enough that it overpowered the syntactic and lexical aspects of the sentences. (Try these examples: "Nice we're having weather, isn't it?" and "Ignorance is no excuse for the law.")

Sometimes, the information that guides language processing can also come from the context and the environment as well as what a person already knows. Essentially, according to such *interactionist* views of language processing, people are simultaneously, in parallel, deriving alternative interpretations of language they hear or read. Over (a very short period of) time, cognition uses the constraints derived from the preceding context and the environment to help determine which interpretation is preferred, and which to let go (Altmann, 1998; Altmann & Steedman, 1988).

This is most clearly illustrated in studies of eye movements as people listen to spoken instructions. Imagine a person is faced with the arrangement of objects in Figure 9-11. If people hear the sentence "Put the apple on the towel in the box" after hearing "put the apple" there is an equal probability that a person will look at either apple, but as soon as "on the towel" is heard, eye fixations converge on the apple on the bottom. This happens online during the comprehension of the sentence even though this sentence is technically ambiguous because the sentence could refer to a box that has a towel in it. However, because there is no such box

FIGURE 9-11
Picture of two apples and a box. Participants would have their eye movements tracked as they heard a sentence such as "Put the apple on the towel in the box."

in the environment, people don't experience any ambiguity and are unlikely to notice it. In short, the psycholinguistic approach to lexical and semantic factors in language relies on conceptually driven processing.

Evidence for the Semantic Grammar Approaches

A major prediction of semantic grammar theory can be stated in two parts. First, comprehenders begin to analyze a sentence immediately, as soon as the words are encountered. Second, this analysis assigns each word to a particular semantic case role, with each assignment contributing its part to overall sentence comprehension. As an example, read sentence 20:

> *(20) After the musician had bowed the piano was quickly taken off the stage.*

Your analysis of this sentence proceeds easily and without disruption; it's a fairly straightforward sentence. Now read sentence 21:

> *(21) After the musician had played the piano was quickly taken off the stage.*

What's different about sentence 21? The verb *played* suggests that the *piano* is the semantic recipient of *play*. When you read *played,* your semantic role assignment for piano was *recipient*. But then you read *was quickly* and realized you had made a mistake in interpretation. Sentences such as 21 are called **garden path sentences**: *the early part of the sentence sets you up so that the later phrases in the sentence don't make sense given the way you assigned case roles in the first part.* Figuratively speaking, the sentence leads you down the garden path; when you realize your mistake, you have to retrace your steps back up the path to reassign earlier words to different cases. Additional examples (from Singer, 1990) of this effect are shown in sentences 22 and 23:

> *(22) The groundsman chased the girl waving a stick in her hand.*

> *(23) The old train the young.*

Many research reports have studied how people comprehend garden path sentences as a way of evaluating case grammar theory (Frazier & Rayner, 1982; Mitchell & Holmes, 1985; but see McKoon & Ratcliff, 2007, for an account based on semantic plausibility). For the most part, the results have been supportive. For example, when people read such sentences, their eyes tend to fixate longer on the later phrases, signaling their error in comprehension (e.g., on "was quickly taken off" in sentence 21). As shown in Figure 9-12, people spent 40 to 50 ms longer when they encountered their error (at point D in the figure; D stands for the disambiguating part of the sentence that reveals the earlier misinterpretation). This is a recovery time effect; it takes additional time to recover from the initial role assignment when that turns out to be incorrect (see Christianson, Hollingworth, Halliwell, & Ferreira, 2001; and Ferreira, Henderson, Anes, Weeks, & McFarlane, 1996, for comparable results with spoken language). Interestingly, the more committed you are to an initial interpretation, that is, the more you "dig in," the harder it becomes to change your interpretation (Tabor & Hutchins, 2004).

There is also important work, also using the eye fixations and fMRI, on how we *parse*—figure out—the syntax of a sentence and the degree to which parsing can be overridden or at least affected by semantic context and other factors (see Clifton et al., 2003; Mason, Just, Keller, & Carpenter, 2003; Rayner & Clifton, 2002; Tannenhaus & Trueswell, 1995).

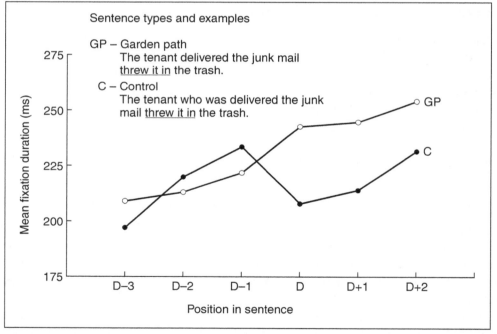

FIGURE 9-12 A depiction of the effect of garden path sentences on reading time. The curves show eye fixations on phrases before and after D, the point in the sentence where the ambiguity is noticed and disambiguated. The top curve shows the data from garden path sentences; eye fixation time grows noticeably longer for these curves at D, when the ambiguity is noticed (the D phrase is underlined in the sample sentences). The bottom curve shows data from the control sentences and no increase in reading time at point D.

Data from Rayner, Carlson, & Frazier (1983).

A final point to note is that the case restrictions sometimes can be violated intentionally, although there are still constraints on that violation. For instance, consider sentence 17 again: "His insecurities chased him even in his sleep." Such a sentence is understood as a technical but permissible violation of the animate restriction for the agent role of *chase*. In a metaphorical sense, we can "compute" how insecurities might behave like an animate agent; thoughts can behave as if they were animate and can take on the properties of pursuing relentlessly, catching, and so on. A particularly fascinating aspect of language involves such figurative uses of words and how case grammar accommodates such usage (see Glucksberg & Keysar, 1990; Keysar, Shen, Glucksberg, & Horton, 2000; Tourangeau & Rips, 1991).

Section Summary

- Semantic factors in language can sometimes override syntactic and phonological effects. The study of semantics breaks words down into morphemes, the smallest meaningful units in language; *cars* contains the free morpheme *car* and the bound morpheme *-s* signifying a "plural."
- Speech errors that people make can be used to help reveal the processes by which language is produced. These speech errors follow regularities that are likely to be produced by otherwise consistent and stable cognitive processes.
- As the study of language comprehension has matured, the dominant approach to semantics claims that we perform a semantic parsing of sentences, assigning words to their appropriate semantic case roles as we hear or read.
- Garden path sentences, where later phrases indicate an error in interpretation, have provided rich information about how syntax and semantics are processed online during comprehension and how we recover from comprehension errors.

BRAIN AND LANGUAGE

Although we have covered a number of ways that cognition is related to underlying cortical structure and function, perhaps one of the most fruitful areas of research on the brain-cognition relation is work on language processing. In this section we discuss aspects of language processing that have strong neural components. This includes a consideration of people with intact brains, as well as how language processing has been disrupted in people who have had the misfortune to suffer some sort of brain damage.

Language in the Intact Brain

With the advent of modern imaging methods, we have begun to learn an extraordinary amount about how the brain processes language from neurologically intact people. Consider a representative study, looking at people's sensitivity to the syntactic structure of sentences. Osterhout and Holcomb (1992) presented sentences to people and recorded the changes in their brain wave patterns (ERPs) as they comprehended. In particular, they examined ERP patterns for sentences that violated syntactic or semantic expectations, comparing these with the patterns obtained with control sentences. When sentences ended in a semantically anomalous fashion ("The woman buttered her bread with socks"), a significant N400 ERP pattern was observed, much as reported in Kounios and Holcomb's (1992) study of semantic relatedness (see Figure 9-8). But when the sentence ended in a syntactically anomalous fashion ("The woman persuaded to catch up"), a strong P600 pattern occurred (a positive electrical potential) 600 ms after the anomalous word "to" was seen; see Figure 9-13. This is confirms the important and seemingly separate role of syntactic processing during language comprehension.

A wealth of evidence illustrates the importance to cognitive science of such imaging and neuropsychological techniques and strongly suggests that the research on language processing will increasingly feature techniques such as imaging and ERP methods. Here are four examples.

LEARNING LANGUAGE McCandliss, Posner, and Givon (1997) taught people a new, miniature artificial language and recorded ERPs during learning. Early in training, words in the new language showed ERP patterns typical of nonsense material. But, after five weeks of training, the ERP patterns looked like those obtained with English words. Furthermore, left hemisphere frontal areas reacted to semantic aspects of the language, whereas posterior areas were sensitive to the visual characteristics of the words, the orthography.

SYNTACTIC PROCESSING Rosler, Pechmann, Streb, Roder, and Hennighausen (1998) did an ambitious study on syntactic processing, using ERPs. Sentences were

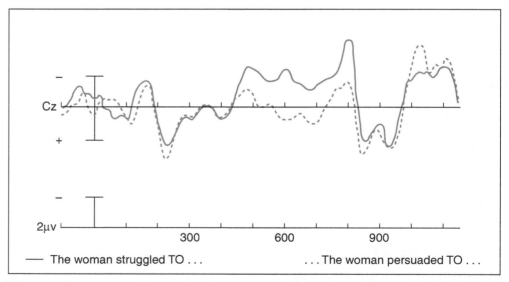

FIGURE 9-13 Mean ERPs to syntactically acceptable sentences (solid curve) and syntactically anomalous sentences (dotted curve). The P600 component, illustrated as a downward dip in the dotted curve, shows the effect of detecting the syntactic anomaly. Note that, in this figure, positive changes go in the downward direction.

presented word by word; to make sure people were comprehending, they had to answer a question about the sentence five seconds after they saw the last word. The sentences were all grammatical, but some of them differed from normal, canonical word order. The ERP patterns demonstrated a variety of effects; for example, the patterns differed appreciably when the sentences violated canonical word order and when elements in the sentence cued people that an unusual word order would follow. The especially compelling aspect of these results is that the ERP patterns tapped into purely mental processes that are not revealed by outward, behavioral measures such as RT or accuracy.

RIGHT HEMISPHERE LANGUAGE   Although the left hemisphere is typically credited with being the primary source of language processing, the right hemisphere has important work to do as well. A general characterization of the role of the right hemisphere in the cortex is that it serves to process information in a more wholistic way, rather than in the more analytic manner characteristic of the left hemisphere. In other words, the right hemisphere is more adept at processing information in a coarse-grained fashion, whereas the left hemisphere is more adept at processing information at a fine-grained level (Beeman, 1998). One role of the right hemisphere is in making more distant, remote semantic connections between words. For example, the connection between *tiger* and *stripe* is relatively direct and close, but the connection between *tiger* and *beach* is more remote and requires some creativity to see a connection. An illustration of this differential operation of the left and right hemispheres was shown in a study by Coulson, Federmeier, Van Petten, and Kutas (2005). In this study, ERP patterns were recorded in the left and right hemispheres as people read sentences. What Coulson et al. found was that the left hemisphere was more involved in integrating lexical information with sentence-level information, such as whether a word is sensible in the context of a given sentence (e.g., responses to the word *tire* after reading the sentence "They were truly stuck, since she didn't have a spare"), but not so much the lexical relations of the words to each other. In comparison, the right hemisphere was more involved in this sort of word-to-word associative processing (e.g., the fact that *spare* and *tire* are more associated than *spare* and *pencil*).

INDIVIDUAL DIFFERENCES   Reichle, Carpenter, and Just (2000) used fMRI to look at brain activity while people verified sentence–picture stimuli (e.g., "The star is above the plus," followed by a picture that did or did not match the sentence). When people used a verbal strategy to make their decisions, brain regions associated with language processing (especially Broca's area) were active; when people used a visual imagery strategy, regions in the parietal lobe were active, the same regions that are active when visual–spatial reasoning tasks are given. Interestingly, the language area activity was lower when high-verbal people were tested and likewise for visual areas in people high in visual–spatial abilities, as if high verbal or spatial ability reduced the amount of brain work needed to do the task.

Aphasia

A large literature exists on brain-related disorders of language, based on people who through the misfortune of illness or brain injury have lost the ability to use

TABLE 9-5   Brain-Related Disruptions of Language and Cognition

Disorder	Disruption of
Language Related	
Broca's aphasia	Speech production, syntactic features
Wernicke's aphasia	Comprehension, semantic features
Conduction aphasia	Repetition of words and sentences
Anomia (anomic aphasia)	Word finding, either lexical or semantic
Pure word deafness	Perceptual or semantic processing of auditory word comprehension
Alexia	Reading, recognition of printed letters or words
Agraphia	Writing
Other Symbolic Related	
Acalculia	Mathematical abilities, retrieval or rule-based procedures
Perception, Movement Related	
Agnosia	Visual object recognition
Prosopagnosia	(Visual) face recognition
Apraxia	Voluntary action or skilled motor movement

language. Formal studies of such disorders date back to the mid-1800s, although records dating back to 3500 BC mention language loss caused by brain injury (see McCarthy & Warrington, 1990). Table 9-5 provides a list and short explanation of these disruptions and some others you've already encountered.

The disruption of language caused by a brain-related disorder is called **aphasia**. Aphasia is always the product of some physical injury to the brain sustained either in an accident or a blow to the head or in diseases and medical syndromes such as stroke. A major goal in neurology is to understand the aphasic syndromes more completely so that people who suffer from aphasia may be helped more effectively. From the standpoint of cognitive neuroscience, the language disruptions of aphasic patients can also help us understand language and its neurological basis.

Although there are many different kinds of aphasias, with great variety in their effects and severity, three basic forms are the most common: *Broca's aphasia, Wernicke's aphasia,* and *conduction aphasia.*

Simulate
Broca's Area and Wernicke's Area in **MyPsychLab**

BROCA'S APHASIA   As described by Kertesz (1982), **Broca's aphasia** is characterized by *severe difficulties in producing speech;* it is also called expressive or production aphasia. Patients with Broca's aphasia show speech that is hesitant, effortful, and phonemically distorted. Aside from stock phrases such as "I don't know," such patients generally respond to questions with one-word answers. If words are strung together, there are few if any grammatical markers, such as bound morphemes like *-ing, -ed,* and *-ly.* In less severe cases, the aphasia may be limited to more complex aspects of language production, such as the production of verb inflections (Faroqi-Shah & Thompson, 2007). Interestingly, such patients typically show less (or even no) impairment of comprehension for both spoken and written language.

This syndrome was first described in the 1860s by French neurosurgeon Pierre Broca, who also identified the damaged area responsible for the disorder. The site of the brain damage, an area toward the rear of the left frontal lobe, is therefore called Broca's area. Broca's area lies adjacent to a major motor control center in the brain.

WERNICKE'S APHASIA   Loosely speaking, the impairments in **Wernicke's aphasia** are the opposite of those in Broca's aphasia; see Table 9-6 for a listing of the typical impairments in both aphasias, including speech samples. In patients affected by Wernicke's aphasia, *comprehension is impaired, as are repetition, naming, reading, and writing, but the syntactic aspects of speech are preserved;* it is sometimes called receptive or comprehension aphasia. In this syndrome there may be unrecognizable content words; recognizable but often inappropriate semantic substitutions; or neologisms, invented nonsense words. What is striking is that victims of this disorder are sometimes unaware of the aphasia.

German investigator Carl Wernicke identified this disorder, and the left-hemisphere region that is damaged, in 1874. This region is thus known as Wernicke's area. Note that the area, toward the rear of the left temporal lobe, is adjacent to the

TABLE 9-6   Classic Impairments in Broca's and Wernicke's Aphasias

Broca's Aphasia	Wernicke's Aphasia
Quality of Speech	
Severely impaired; marked by extreme effort to generate speech, hesitant utterances, short (one-word) responses.	Little if any impairment; fluent speech productions, clear articulation, no hesitations.
Nature of Speech	
Agrammatical; marked by loss of syntactic markers and inflections and use of simple noun and verb categories.	Neologistic; marked by invented words (neologisms) or semantically inappropriate substitutions; long strings of neologistic jargon.
Comprehension	
Unimpaired compared with speech production. Word-finding difficulty caused by production difficulties.	Severely impaired; marked by lack of awareness that speech is incomprehensible; comprehension impaired also in nonverbal tasks (e.g., pointing).

Speech Samples

Broca's aphasia. Experimenter asks the patient's address.

"Oh dear. Um. Aah. O! O dear. Very-there-were-ave. avedeversher avenyer." (Correct address was Devonshire.)

Wernicke's aphasia. Experimenter asks about the patient's work before hospitalization. "I wanna tell you this happened when happened when he rent. His-his kell come down here and is—he got ren something. It happened. In these ropliers were with him for hi-is friend—like was. And he roden all of these arranjen from the pedis on from iss pescid."

auditory cortex, in the left temporal lobe, a very different area with very different abilities than Broca's area in the frontal lobe. Note also that this demonstrates a double dissociation, a basic distinction at the level of brain organization between syntax and semantics (see Breedin & Saffran, 1999, for a case study showing loss of semantic knowledge but preserved syntactic performance).

CONDUCTION APHASIA   Much less common than Broca's and Wernicke's aphasias, **conduction aphasia** is a more narrow disruption of language ability. Both Broca's and Wernicke's areas seem to be intact in conduction aphasia, and people with conduction aphasia can understand and produce speech quite well. Their language impairment is that they are *unable to repeat what they have just heard*. In intuitive terms, the intact comprehension and production systems seem to have lost their normal connection or linkage. Indeed, the site of the brain lesion in conduction aphasia appears to be the primary pathway between Broca's and Wernicke's areas, called the *arcuate fasciculus* (Geschwind, 1970). Quite literally, the pathway between the comprehension and production areas is no longer able to conduct the linguistic message.

ANOMIA   Another type of aphasia deserves brief mention here because it relates to the separation of the semantic and lexical systems discussed earlier. **Anomia** or **anomic aphasia** is a disruption of word finding, an *impairment in the normal ability to retrieve a semantic concept and say its name;* you encountered this briefly back in Chapter 7. In anomia, some aspect of the normally automatic semantic or lexical components of retrieval has been damaged. Although moderate word-finding difficulty can result from damage almost anywhere in the left hemisphere, full-fledged anomia seems to involve damage especially in the left temporal lobe (Coughlan & Warrington, 1978; see McCarthy & Warrington, 1990, for details). Although there is a similarity between anomia and the tip-of-the-tongue (TOT) phenomenon, the similarity is superficial. Several researchers (e.g., Geschwind, 1967; Goodglass, Kaplan, Weintraub, & Ackerman, 1976) have found no evidence among anomic patients of the partial knowledge that characterizes a TOT state. Evidence also indicates that anomia can involve retrieval blockage only for the lexical component of retrieval, leaving semantic retrieval of the concept intact (e.g., the patient described in Chapter 7; Kay & Ellis, 1987). This, along with other cases (e.g., Ashcraft, 1993), suggests preserved semantic retrieval but a blockage in finding the lexical representation that corresponds to the already retrieved semantic concept.

OTHER APHASIAS   As Table 9-5 shows, a variety of highly specific aphasias are also possible. Although most of these are quite rare, they nonetheless give evidence of the separability of several aspects of language performance. For instance, in *alexia* (or dyslexia), there is a disruption of reading without any necessary disruption of spoken language or aural comprehension. In *agraphia,* conversely, the patient is unable to write. Amazingly, a few reports describe patients with alexia but without agraphia—in other words, patients who can write but cannot read what they have just written (Benson & Geschwind, 1969). In *pure word deafness,* a patient cannot comprehend spoken language, although he or she is still able to read and produce written and spoken language.

There is documentation for even more specific forms of aphasia than those—for instance, difficulties in retrieval of verbs in written but not spoken language (Berndt & Haendiges, 2000) and difficulties in naming just visual stimuli, without either generalized visual agnosia or generalized anomia (Sitton, Mozer, & Farah, 2000).

RIGHT HEMISPHERE DAMAGE   Despite the fact that most of the aphasias discussed here involve processing in the left hemisphere of the cortex, there is also evidence of the right hemisphere's contribution to language comprehension and production (see Beeman & Chiarello, 1998, for a useful overview of the complementary right- and left-hemisphere language processes).

Work by Beeman (1993, 1998) suggests that a problem right-hemisphere–damaged people have is an inability to activate an appropriately diverse set of information from long-term memory from which inferences can be derived. In one study, after reading a text, people were given a lexical decision task. Some of the words in the task were related to inferences that needed to be drawn for comprehension. For example, read the following short text: "Then he went into the bathroom and discovered that he had left the bathtub water running. He had forgotten about it while watching the news. The mess took him a long time to mop up." After reading, you are then given a lexical decision probe word like "overflow." Because the tub overflowing was not mentioned in the text, responding to "overflow" faster than baseline would be evidence of having inferred it based on reading the text itself. The results showed that normal controls responded 49 ms faster relative to neutral control words—they drew the appropriate inference. However, the right-hemisphere–damaged patients responded 148 ms more *slowly* to these words.

Generalizing from Cases of Brain Damage

Although it is a mistake to believe that our eventual understanding of language will be reducible to a catalog of biological and neurological processes (e.g., Mehler, Morton, & Jusczyk, 1984), knowledge of the neurological aspects of language is useful for something beyond the rehabilitation and treatment of aphasia. What do studies of such abnormal brain processes tell us about normal cerebral functioning and language?

Well, for one, the different patterns of behavioral impairments in Broca's and Wernicke's aphasias, stemming from different physical structures in the brain, implies that these two physical structures are responsible for different aspects of linguistic skill. Furthermore, these selective impairments reinforce the notion that syntax and semantics are two separable but interactive aspects of normal language (e.g., O'Seaghdha, 1997; Osterhout & Holcomb, 1992). That is, the double dissociations indicate that different, independent modules govern comprehension and speech production. Other dissociations indicate yet more independent modules of processing, such as separate modules corresponding to reading and writing.

An intriguing inference from such studies is that the specialized regions signal an innate, biological basis for language; that is, the human nervous system is specifically adapted to learn and use language, as opposed to simply being able to do so. Several theorists have gone so far as to discuss possible evolutionary mechanisms responsible for lateralization, hemispheric specialization, the dissociation of syntax and semantics revealed by Broca's and Wernicke's aphasias, and even cognition in general (Corballis, 1989; Geary, 1992; Lewontin, 1990). These are fascinating lines of reasoning on the nature of language and cognition as represented in the brain.

Section Summary

- Extensive evidence from studies with brain-damaged people and more modern work using imaging and ERP methods reveals several functional and anatomical dissociations in language ability.
- The syntactic and articulatory aspects of language seem centered in Broca's area, in the left frontal lobe, whereas comprehension aspects are focused more on Wernicke's area, in the posterior left hemisphere junction of the temporal and parietal lobes.
- The study of these and other deficits, such as anomia and right hemispheric damage, converges with evidence from imaging and ERP studies to illustrate how various aspects of language performance act as separable, distinct components within the overall broad ability to produce and comprehend language.

Key Terms

ambiguous
anomia
anomic aphasia
aphasia
arbitrariness
Broca's aphasia
case grammar
case roles
categorical perception
coarticulation
competence
conduction aphasia
deep structure

displacement
dysfluencies
flexibility
garden path sentences
given-new strategy
grammar
language
linguistic relativity
    hypothesis
linguistic universals
linguistics
mental lexicon

morpheme
motor theory of speech
    perception
naming
parse
performance
phonemes
phonemic competence
phonology
phrase structure
polysemy
problem of invariance

productivity
psycholinguistics
semantic cases
semanticity
surface structure
syntax
transformational
    grammar
transformational rules
Wernicke's aphasia

10 Comprehension: Written and Spoken Language

*Language simply does not work in isolation. . . . Understanding
what one has heard is a complex process that . . . cannot be
reasonably isolated into [separate] linguistic and memory
components but must be a combined effort of both.*

(SCHANK, 1972, PP. 626–628)

Comprehension—even the title of this chapter must be explained a bit, if only because much of Chapter 9 dealt with language, too. What does the word *comprehension* mean here? Basically, the expanded meaning here includes not only the fundamental language processes we studied in Chapter 9, but also the additional processes we use when comprehending realistic samples of language, say a passage in a book or a connected, coherent conversation, or even a perceived event. How do we comprehend? What do we *do* when we read, understand,

and remember connected sentences? By taking a larger unit of analysis than isolated sentences, we confront a host of issues that are central to communication and to cognitive psychology. And by confronting Miller's (1973) highest two levels of analysis, conceptual knowledge and beliefs, we address the important issues Miller (1977) described as the "distant bridge that may someday need to be crossed." In short, it's time to cross the bridge.

GETTING STARTED: AN OVERVIEW

Conceptual and Rule Knowledge

You read about the first three levels of language analysis—the phonological, syntactic, and lexical and semantic levels—in Chapter 9. Let's start digging into Miller's (1977) fourth and fifth levels, the conceptual and belief levels. Here's the sentence Miller uses to illustrate these:

(1) Mary and John saw the mountains while they were flying to California.

If this sentence were spoken aloud, your comprehension would begin with phonological processes, translating the stream of sounds into words. Your syntactic knowledge would parse the sentence into phrases and would assist the semantic level of analysis as you determined the case roles for each important word: Mary and John are the agents of *see*, the word *mountains* is assigned the patient or recipient role, *they* is the agent of *fly* in the second main clause, and so on.

So far so good. But this sentence is more challenging than that. It's ambiguous, has more than one meaning. There's the obvious one, that Mary and John looked out the plane window and saw mountains during a flight to California. But there's also the possibility that *they* refers to the mountains. *They* merely denotes something plural, after all, so syntactically, the *they* could refer to the mountains.

Those of you who noticed this ambiguity probably rejected it immediately for the obvious reason: Mountains don't fly. We're getting close to the Miller's point. Knowing that mountains don't fly is part of your semantic, **conceptual knowledge**. Look in as many dictionaries as you'd like, and you won't find "mountains don't fly" in any of them. Accordingly, your comprehension of sentence 1 must also have included a conceptual level of analysis, in which you compared your interpretation with semantic knowledge.

Miller also argues that **beliefs** are important for comprehension. I could tell you "No, I'm not saying that Mary and John were flying to California. I'm saying that it was the *mountains* that were flying." Although you can understand that I might think mountains can fly, you wouldn't change your mind about the issue; your belief in your own knowledge and your feeling that I'm lying or playing some kind

Language comprehension involves a complex set of processes that need to occur in real time.

of trick (or just plain crazy) are an important for comprehension. A purely linguistic analysis of language misses this critical aspect of comprehension as well: Think how prominent your beliefs are, and how important they are to comprehension and memory, when you hear advertisements or speeches in political campaigns.

Rules are yet another part of the knowledge that must be taken into account. In Chapter 9 we discussed tacit knowledge at the phonological and syntactic levels, and the semantic knowledge of case rules. But additional rules are operating when we deal with more complex passages of text or with connected conversation. Some rules have the flavor of strategies; for example, we tend to interpret sentence 2 as focusing on Tina, largely because she is mentioned first in the sentence (Gernsbacher, 1990):

(2) Tina gathered the kindling as Lisa set up the tent.

Several lines of evidence speak to this idea, that we provide a focus to our sentences by using mechanisms such as first mention and certain kinds of reference (e.g., "There was this guy who . . ." instead of "A guy . . .").

Other rules have to do with reference, building bridges between words referring to the same thing. For example, after reading sentence 2, how do you know that the phrase "After she got the fire started" refers to Tina? Still more rules parade under the name **pragmatics** and refer to a variety of extralinguistic factors. As an example, indirect speech acts such as "Do you have the time?" or "Can you open the window?" mean something different from what a literal reading would suggest. And finally, high-level rules operate in conversational interactions, rules that specify how people in a conversation structure their remarks and how they understand the remarks of others. As always, simply because you can't state the rule or were never explicitly taught it doesn't mean that it isn't there. It simply means that the rules are part of your implicit, tacit knowledge.

Comprehension Research

Much of the traditional evidence about comprehension relied on people's linguistic intuitions, their (leisurely) judgments about the acceptability of sentences, or simple measures of recall and accuracy. The Sachs (1967) study you read about in Chapter 8 was a classic example of early comprehension research, with a straightforward conclusion. Recall that as people were reading a passage, they were interrupted and tested on a target sentence, either 0, 80, or 160 syllables after the end of the target. Their recognition of the sentence was very accurate at the immediate interval. But beyond that, they were accurate only at rejecting the choice that changed the sentence meaning. That is,

The difficulty of language comprehension when working memory is overloaded.

people could not accurately discriminate between a verbatim target sentence and a paraphrase: If the choice preserved the original meaning, then people mistakenly "recognized" it. Clearly, these results showed that memory for meaningful passages does not retain verbatim sentences for long but does retain meaning quite well.

Online Comprehension Tasks

As work on comprehension developed, researchers needed *a task that measures comprehension as it happens*, or an **online comprehension** task. Such tasks involve the same approach you've been reading about throughout this book: Find a dynamic, time- or action-based task that yields measurements of the underlying mental processes as they occur. Contrast performance in a variety of conditions, pitting factors against each other to see how they affect comprehension speed or difficulty. Then draw conclusions about the underlying mental processes, based on the performance measures.

WRITTEN LANGUAGE   A common assessment of cognition during comprehension involves reading times. These can be gathered by using eye movement data, or having people control the presentation of text by pressing a button to advance to the next word, clause, or sentence. Reading times for these individual components can then be analyzed, and inferences about online comprehension can be drawn. In general, language that a person is prepared for is read faster, whereas those aspects that require a large involvement of mental resources result in longer reading times.

In one commonly used method to assess what a person is thinking about while reading, a text appears on a computer screen and is immediately followed by a probe word. Sometimes a person must make a "yes" or "no" response, indicating whether the word was in the just-read sentence. Sometimes the person must simply name the word or perform a lexical decision task on it. Look at Table 10-1 to see some sample stimuli and test words for these tasks. Response times would lead us to inferences about the nature and operation of cognition. For example, if the ambiguous word *boxer* activates both the dog and the fighter meanings, then we might expect RT to dog and fight to be about the same, but faster than to the neutral word *plate*. But if *boxer* is interpreted only in one of its two senses, then dog would be faster than fight (or the other way around, depending on which meaning is dominant).

TABLE 10-1   Sample Stimuli and Test Words for Online Comprehension Tasks

Task	Sentence	Yes	Related	Unrelated	No
Was this word in the sentence?	Ken really liked the boxer.	Ken			Bill
Naming	Ken really liked the boxer.		Dog/fight	Plate	
Lexical decision	Ken really liked the boxer.		Dog/fight	Plate	Lamt

Another way to assess online comprehension is the think-aloud verbal protocol method (e.g., Magliano, Trabasso, & Graesser, 1999). In this method, people are asked to verbalize their thoughts as they read a passage of text. The verbal protocols can then be analyzed later to assess what conscious thoughts people were having as they read. For example, how do they link up a current portion of text with events that occurred earlier, were they making predictions about what would happen next, did they notice an inconsistency in the text, and so on? The data generated from think-aloud protocols can provide insight into what aspects of a text might be fruitful candidates for further research. For example, this information can be used to focus investigation of which aspects of a text will yield interesting reading time data, or what kind of information to test using a probe task.

Finally, as in many other areas of cognitive psychology, there has been an increase in the use of neural imaging to aid our investigations. For online comprehension, these measures often require the temporal resolution necessary to capture understanding across relatively brief periods of time, as would be done with event-related potential (ERP) and functional magnetic resonance imaging (fMRI) recordings. Using these methods, we can reveal aspects of comprehension that might be difficult to uncover otherwise.

Metacomprehension

Explore
What Learning Techniques Do You Use? in **MyPsychLab**

Reading a passage, and having some understanding of what you've read, doesn't mean you've actually learned something or will remember it later. Yet, we need to use our **metacomprehension** abilities (e.g., Dunlosky & Lipko, 2007) to *monitor how well we are understanding and will remember information later.* Metacomprehension is important because it can influence how much we may study information later, and just what information we devote our time to.

A popular measure of metacomprehension is **judgments of learning (JOLs)** (Arbuckle & Cuddy, 1969). These are *estimates people are asked to make of how well they feel they have learned some material they have just read* (recall that we talked about judgments of learning in Chapter 9, too). Research on JOLs typically compares people's estimates of how well they have learned information with how they actually do. Unfortunately, in many cases, the relationship between JOLs and actual performance is quite low—in other words, people are typically not very good at estimating whether they've learned something or not. As a consequence, when you plan your studying, say for an upcoming exam, you may not spend the time you need on some material because you think you know it better than you really do. Your test performance would be better if you could better monitor what you have and have not learned.

In addition to difficulty in judging whether something was learned, people also have metacomprehension problems when it comes to choosing how to plan or distribute their study time. Here's an example: Although you learned in Chapter 8 that memory is worse when people study using massed practice (cramming), rather than distributed practice, many people are unaware that massed practice is a poor learning strategy. Another metacomprehension error that people make is to spend their study time focusing on very difficult material. The problem with this is that it is an inefficient strategy (Nelson & Leonesio, 1988). This **labor-in-vain effect** occurs when *people spend large amounts of time trying to learn information that is too far beyond their current level of knowledge, but end up with little to no new learning.*

A better strategy is to spend time learning information that falls within the **region of proximal learning** (e.g., Metcalfe, 2002). This is *information that is just beyond a person's current level of understanding.* So, what we have here a bit like the Goldilocks and the Three Bears story. Obviously it is a waste of time to study information that one knows well (this material is too soft). Also, as the labor-in-vain effect shows, trying to study information that is far too difficult will not help either (this material is too hard). However, learning that occurs in the region of proximal learning is just beyond what a person currently knows, so they can draw on their existing knowledge as a scaffolding to integrate new information (this material is just right).

Some classroom settings are set up to take advantage of the region of proximal learning, provided you've had the prerequisites, and you keep up with the material in the class. In addition to this, what are some other ways to improve your metacomprehension? Here are three (cf. Dunlosky & Lipko, 2007; Griffin, Wiley, & Thiede, 2008). First, before making a judgment about whether you've learned something, wait a few minutes (Dunlosky & Nelson, 1991). Often, when people are making judgments of learning, they are assessing whether they can retrieve the information from long-term memory into working memory. But when you make these judgments right after reading material, there is still a lot of information *in* working memory, and so you are overconfident in your ability to remember the information. Second, rereading the material can also be very helpful. Reading the material before lecture, then going to lecture can give you the same benefit and will save you time and effort later. Finally, generating summaries, or even lists of key words, can boost the accuracy of your JOLs. In this way, you help reveal to yourself what you do and do not yet know.

Comprehension as Mental Structure Building

A convenient way to organize thinking about comprehension is to use Gernsbacher's (1990) **structure-building** framework. The theory is summarized in Table 10-2. The basic theme is that comprehension is a process of building mental structures.

TABLE 10-2   Summary of Gernsbacher's Structure-Building Framework

Process	Explanation
1. Laying a foundation	Initiate a structure for representing clause or sentence meaning.
2. Mapping information	Map or store congruent information into the current structure.
3. Shifting	Initiate a new structure to represent a new or different idea.

Control Mechanisms	Function
1. Enhancement	Increase the activation of coherent, related information.
2. Suppression	Dampen the activation of information no longer relevant to current structure.

Laying a foundation, mapping information onto the structure, and shifting to new structures are the three principal components.

LAYING A FOUNDATION   As we read we begin to build a mental structure that captures the meaning of a sentence. A foundation is initiated as the sentence begins and typically is built around the first mentioned character or idea. This is equivalent to saying that sentence 6 is about Dave and studying:

> *(6) Dave was studying hard for his statistics midterm.*

MAPPING INFORMATION   As more elements appear, they are added to the structure, by the process called **mapping**. Mapping here simply means that additional word and concept meanings are added to the "DAVE" structure by specifying Dave's activities. For instance, the prepositional phrase "for his statistics midterm" is processed. Because the concept "MIDTERM" is coherent in the context of studying, these concepts are added to the structure. Also, any inferences that you draw would be added to the structure. For instance, when your knowledge about "MIDTERM" was activated, you drew the inference that Dave probably was enrolled in a statistics course.

SHIFTING TO A NEW STRUCTURE   We continue trying to map incoming words to the current structure on the assumption that those words belong to the structure under construction right now. But at some point, a different idea is encountered that signals a change in focus or topic shift. As an example, consider this continuation of the Dave story:

> *(7) Because the professor had a reputation for giving difficult exams, the students knew they'd have to be well prepared.*

When you read "Because the professor," a coherence process detects the change in topic or focus. One clue is the word *because* or other connectives (e.g., *later, although, meanwhile*). Another clue involves the introduction of a new character and the inferences you need to draw to figure out who the professor is; you inferred that Dave must be enrolled in a statistics class, and because midterms are exams given in college classes that are taught by professors, the professor must be the one who teaches that statistics class. At such moments, you close off or finish the "Dave structure" and begin a new one, one about the professor. Although the "Dave structure" still retains its prominence in memory, you are now working on a new current structure, mapping the incoming ideas (e.g., reputation, difficult exams) onto it. And at the end of that phrase, you will have constructed two related structures, one for each meaning (the phrase beginning "the students" will trigger yet another structure to be built, yielding three substructures).

ENHANCEMENT AND SUPPRESSION   Finally, let's consider the two control mechanisms. Let's add one more sentence to the Dave story:

> *(6) Dave was studying hard for his statistics midterm.*
>
> *(7) Because the professor had a reputation for giving difficult exams, the students knew they'd have to be well prepared.*
>
> *(8) Dave wanted an A on that test.*

As noted earlier, reading sentence 7 results in a new substructure and a change in focus. Still, the new substructure is related to the first one. That is, two ideas in sentence 7 map onto those from sentence 6: *Exams* refers to the same concept as *midterms*, and the *professor* maps onto the statistics course implied by sentence 6. Such mappings reflect the activation of related concepts, especially those mapped into the foundation of the first structure (Millis & Just, 1994). This activation combines with the activation from *midterm* and *statistics course* because of their semantic relatedness. This is the process of **enhancement**, that the many related *concepts are now boosted or enhanced in their level of activation*. This enhancement process is the priming process in semantic memory. It is the degree of enhancement and activation among concepts that predicts which ones will be remembered better or responded to more rapidly. The more frequently the same set of concepts is enhanced across a sentence, the more coherent the passage is.

Note, however, that the enhancement of some concepts implies that others lose activation. That is, while sentence 7 enhances the activation of concepts related to "PROFESSOR," "EXAM," and so on, there is also **suppression** of concepts that are now out of the main discourse focus. In other words, *activated concepts that become unrelated to the focus decrease in activation* by the process of suppression. Figure 10-1 is an illustration of these competing tendencies. Note that as the professor clause is processed (ideas 3 and 4), the activation level for "DAVE" is suppressed because it's no longer the main discourse focus. Then, as the story unfolds further (ideas 5 to 7), the concept "DAVE" regains its enhancement, and

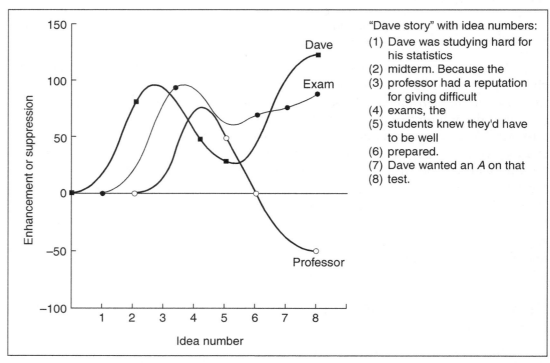

FIGURE 10-1 Hypothetical activation curves for the concepts *Dave, exam,* and *professor* from the "Dave story" in the text. As concepts are introduced or mentioned again (*Dave, exam*), their activation becomes enhanced. When the focus shifts, old concepts (*professor*) become suppressed; that is, their activation dwindles.

the "PROFESSOR" dwindles. Thus the original Dave structure from sentence 6 receives renewed enhancement when you read in sentence 8 that Dave wanted an *A* on the test (O'Brien et al., 1995; for an extension of enhancement and suppression to the topic of metaphor comprehension, see Gernsbacher, Keysar, Robertson, & Werner, 2001, and Kintsch, 2000). And, in the meantime, less important concepts are suppressed (e.g., McNamara & McDaniel, 2004).

Levels of Comprehension

As you read earlier, comprehension is a complex process, involving a number of different levels. One of the ways of characterizing these different levels was already discussed in Chapter 8, namely van Dijk and Kintsch's (1983) levels of representation theory. As a reminder, at one level is the **surface form**. This is our verbatim mental representation of the exact words and syntax used. At an intermediate level is the **propositional textbase**, which captures the basic idea units present in a text. Finally, there is the level of the **situation model** (Johnson-Laird, 1983; Van Dijk & Kintsch, 1983; Zwaan & Radvansky, 1998), which is *a mental representation that serves as a simulation of a real or possible world as described by a text*. These different levels of comprehension involve different cognitive processes that operate at different time scales, with surface-level cognitive processing occurring more rapidly than situation-model–level processing (Huang & Gordon, 2011).

As you read, try to keep in mind and understand how comprehension may depend on these different levels. For example, research on order of mention in establishing discourse reference will depend on the surface form. Work on bridging inferences requires processing at the textbase level. And finally, work showing how people monitor various aspects of experience involves the situation model.

Section Summary

- A variety of online tasks have been devised to investigate comprehension, such as tasks involving reading times, the use of probes, think-aloud protocols, and neuroimaging evidence.
- Successful comprehension is best achieved when people can self-monitor what they are and are not learning, though judgments of learning. However, these judgments are often poor estimates of how much has actually been learned. Estimates can be improved by delaying these judgments, rereading, and providing summaries of the material.
- Comprehension involves processing at many levels, including the surface form, textbase, and situation model levels. Evidence of processing at each of these levels can be derived across many different aspects of understanding.

READING

For years, the standard way to study reading was to have people read a passage of text, then take a memory test, such as a multiple choice or recall test. Such tasks certainly have face validity; they test memory for the text, because much of our reading is for the purpose of learning and remembering what we read.

But this approach suffers from the fact that it doesn't gather online measures of comprehension, only what people remember after reading (not that this isn't important, there's just more to what's going on). In Figure 10-1, you saw a graph of the hypothetical activation levels for concepts in a set of sentences. We would like to know *directly* how concepts vary in their activation levels across a passage because that tells us a great deal about online reading comprehension. A multiple-choice test is too blunt to give us such answers.

Gaze Duration

At the end of Chapter 9, you saw a figure of eye gaze fixation times, where those times went up when the ambiguity of a sentence became apparent (see Figure 9-12). This methodology reveals mental processing at the level of eye gazes, levels of activation, and so on. You'll read about it in this section.

In reading research that assesses gaze duration, the equipment used is an **eye tracker**, a camera- and computer-based apparatus that records eye movements and the exact words that are fixated on during reading; one is depicted in Figure 10-2. In this system, continuous recording of at least one eye, while keeping track of head position, enables the system to determine exactly what you're looking at on the computer screen. As such, the machine records the duration of the eyes' gaze as they scan across lines of text (this system has other purposes in addition to reading, such as evaluating the usefulness of web pages). Typically, people simply see a passage of text on the screen, and the eye tracker records the eye movements and durations as the words in the passage are read. In this task, the researcher knows which word is being processed on a moment-by-moment basis and *how long the eyes dwell*

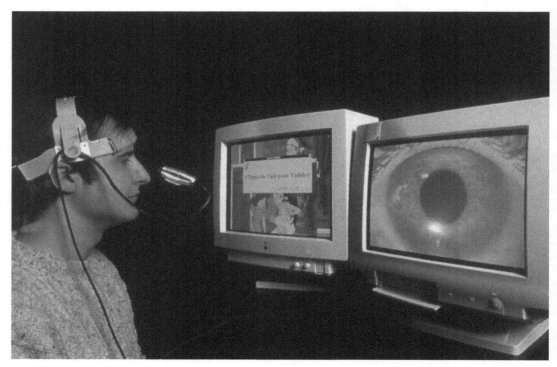

FIGURE 10-2   Researcher uses eye access interactive computer.

on each word, so **gaze duration** is a prime measure of what's going on when people read (see Kambe, Duffy, Clifton, & Rayner, 2003, and Rayner, 1998, for thorough discussions of alternatives). Time-based eye movement data provide a window on the process of comprehension and reading.

Recall from Chapter 3 that the eyes move in rapid sweeps—*saccades*—and then stop to focus on a word—**fixations**. Fixations in reading (English) last about 200 to 250 ms, and the average saccade size is from seven to nine letter spaces, although as Figure 10-3 shows, there is considerable variability in these measures (Rayner, 1998). Eye tracking gives us gaze durations on a word-by-word basis, as shown in Figure 10-4. Notice in the left panel of the figure, a good reader moves fairly rapidly through the text (fixation durations in milliseconds are in the circles above the words) and in a forward direction, at least on this passage. In contrast, the poor reader shown in the right panel moves more slowly through the text and makes many regressive eye movements—that is, returns to an already fixated word. Even at this level of detail, we can draw two conclusions. First, poor readers spend more time going back to reread what they've already processed and can spend considerably more time on some words than good readers do (e.g., 2,065 ms versus 267 ms on "topography"). Second, even good readers spend variable amounts of time on different words, for example as little as 100 ms on "such" but 566 ms on "a knowledge." This second point is important because characteristics of the words and passages exert a tremendous influence on how we read.

Two assumptions that have guided much of the work using eye movements were the immediacy and the eye-mind assumptions (Just & Carpenter, 1980, 1987, 1992). The **immediacy assumption** states that *readers try to interpret each content word of a text as that word is encountered.* In other words, we do not wait until we take in a group of words, say in a phrase, before we start to process them. Instead, we begin interpreting and comprehending immediately, as soon as we encounter a word. The **eye–mind assumption** is the idea that *the pattern of eye movements directly reflects the complexity of the underlying cognitive processes.*

Although these assumptions are fairly robust, they do have some limitations. For example, eye gazes often take in more than one word, depending on the length of the words, the size of the text fonts, and the span of the perceptual beam. So, there is not always a direct one-to-one relationship between an eye fixation and the words being

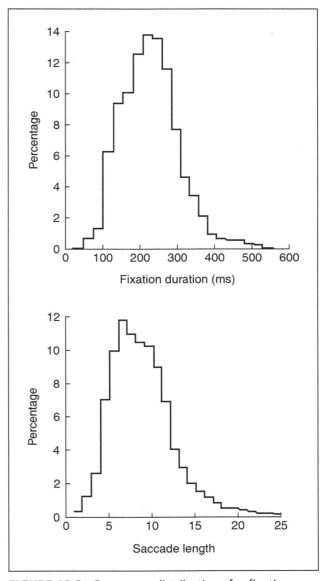

FIGURE 10-3 Frequency distributions for fixation durations (top) in ms, and saccade length (bottom) in number of character spaces.
From Rayner (1998).

Good Reader

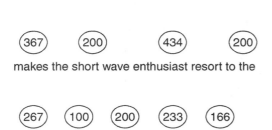

makes the short wave enthusiast resort to the

study of such seemingly unrelated subjects as

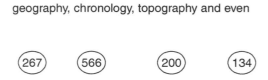

geography, chronology, topography and even

meteorology. A knowledge of these factors is

(233) (200) (300) (367) (200)

decidedly helpful in logging foreign stations.

Poor Reader

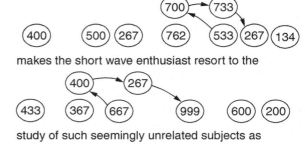

makes the short wave enthusiast resort to the

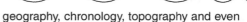

study of such seemingly unrelated subjects as

geography, chronology, topography and even

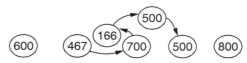

meteorology. A knowledge of these factors is

(600) (467) (166) (700) (500) (800)

decidedly helpful in logging foreign stations.

FIGURE 10-4 The pattern of fixations of a good (left panel) and poor (right panel) reader, showing where the fixations occurred in the sentences and the duration of the fixations (in the circles above the fixation points, measured in milliseconds). Arrows indicate regressive eye movements to earlier words; otherwise the fixations went from left to right.

From Just, M. A., & Carpenter, P. A. (1987), *The psychology of reading and language comprehension.* Boston: Allyn & Bacon. Figure 2.1 (p. 27). Credited source: Buswell, G. T. (1937). *How adults read.* Chicago: Chicago University Press, Plates II and IV, pp. 6–7.

processed. Moreover, eye gazes do not reflect only the processing of the current word; they can also reflect some spillover processing of previous words and some anticipatory processing of upcoming words (Kliegl, Nuthmann, & Engbert, 2006). Despite these limits, eye tracking is still a powerful tool for the reading researcher.

Also, keep in mind that outside of reading, eye gaze can be used to understand other aspects of comprehension, such as the understanding of spoken language. For example, if you listen to and follow a set of directions, say to pick up and move an object from one place to another, your eye movements track the spoken instructions very closely—as you hear, "Put the apple in the box," your eyes fixate immediately on those objects in the visual scene (Spivey, Tanenhaus, Eberhard, & Sedivy, 2002; see Crosby, Monin, & Richardson, 2008, for an application of eye tracking to social cognition).

Basic Online Reading Effects

An example of online reading research examined regressive eye movements back to a portion of text that had been read earlier. Just (1976) was interested in such eye movements when the referents in the sentence could not be immediately determined: If an initial assignment of a character to a case role was wrong, then what happened? Was there a regressive eye movement back to the correct referent? People read sentences such as 17 and 18, and eye movements were monitored:

(17) *The tenant complained to his landlord about the leaky roof. The next day, he went to the attic to get his luggage.*

(18) *The tenant complained to his landlord about the leaky roof. The next day, he went to the attic to repair the damage.*

In sentence 17, when *luggage* was encountered, eye movements bounced up immediately to the word *tenant*. In sentence 18, they bounced up to *landlord*. These eye movements provided evidence of the underlying mental processes of finding antecedents and determining case roles.

Another study provides a demonstration of the detail afforded by eye trackers. Look at Figure 10-5, taken from Just and Carpenter (1987; see also Just & Carpenter, 1980). You see two sentences taken from a larger passage. Above the words are two numbers. The top number indicates the order in which people fixated on the elements in the sentence; 1 to 9 in the first sentence and 1 to 21 in the second. The number below is the gaze duration (in milliseconds). So, for example, the initial word in sentence 1, *Flywheels*, was fixated for 1,566 ms. The next word, *are*, was fixated only 267 ms. The fourth word, *of*, wasn't fixated at all by this person, so neither a gaze number nor time is presented there. In fact, you can raerragne the lteters in wodrs, usch as is odne in this snetence, and people have little trouble extracting the meaning. There is some disruption to reading, but not as much as if different letters are substituted for correct letters (Rayner, White, Johnson, & Liversedge, 2006). So, reading does not *require* a strict adherence to the printed form.

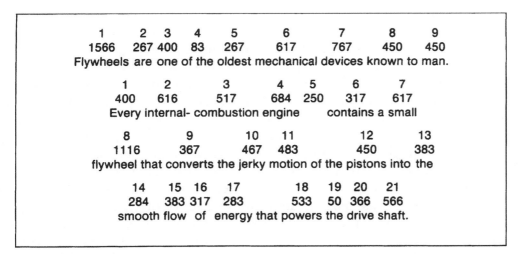

FIGURE 10-5 Eye fixations of a college student reading a scientific passage. Gazes within each sentence are sequentially numbered above the fixated words with the durations (in milliseconds) indicated below the sequence number.

From Just & Carpenter (1980).

In the Just and Carpenter study, these passages were technical writing, in which a new concept, such as a flywheel, is introduced, defined, and explained. The average reading rate was about 225 words per minute, slower than for simpler material, such as newspaper stories or novels. At a general level, note that every content word was fixated. According to Just and Carpenter, this is the norm for all kinds of text. In fact, about 85% of the content words are fixated. Short function words, however, like *the* or *of* often tend not to be fixated; Rayner and Duffy (1988) estimate that function words are fixated only about 35% of the time. Readers also tend to skip some content words if the passage is very simple for them (say, a children's story given to an adult), if they are skimming or speed reading, or if a word is very predictable (Rayner & Well, 1996).

As noted already, gaze durations are quite variable, and the duration of a saccade is about 100 ms, followed by a fixation of 200 to 250 ms. These estimates come from situations in which the viewer is merely gazing out on a scene. In reading studies, however, people don't move their eyes as far, averaging 2 degrees of angle versus 5 degrees in scene perception. Hence, saccades during reading are shorter—they take about 30 ms. Although word fixations may be brief, readers often make repeated fixations on the *same* word. In some studies, successive fixation times are summed together; alternatively, investigators report both the first-pass fixations and total fixation duration.

A Model of Reading

A strength of online reading measures is that they provide evidence at *two* levels of comprehension. First, there are word-level processes operating at the surface form level. These are crucial to an understanding of reading. For instance, several studies attest to the early use of syntactic features of a sentence when we comprehend not just major syntactic characteristics such as phrase boundaries but even characteristics such as subject–verb agreement (Pearlmutter, Garnsey, & Bock, 1999) and pronoun gender (McDonald & MacWhinney, 1995). Reichle, Pollatsek, Fisher, and Rayner (1998) provide an account of such word-level processes with their E-Z Reader models of eye movement control in reading.

Second, reading time measures can also be used to examine larger, macroscopic processes, such as at the textbase and situation model levels. We'll hold off a discussion of situation model processing until the next section. At the textbase level, Table 10-3 presents Just and Carpenter's (1980) analysis of the "flywheel" passage. To the left of each line is a category label; each sector was categorized as to its role in the overall paragraph structure. To the right are two columns of numbers— observed gaze durations for a group of people and estimated durations—based on the "READER" model's predictions. For example, the 1,921 ms observed for sector 1 is the sum of the separate gaze durations for that sector (averaged across people). Note that different kinds of sectors take different amounts of time; for instance, definition sectors have more difficult words and are longer than other sector types, so they show longer gaze durations. Even a casual examination of the observed and predicted scores shows that the model does a good job of predicting reading times.

So, in general, an analysis of reading times needs to take into account a number of surface form and textbase factors that are tied to the text itself. Reading time is

TABLE 10-3   Sector-by-Sector Analysis of "Flywheel" Passage

| Category | Sector | Gaze Duration (ms) | |
		Observed	Estimated
Topic	Flywheels are one of the oldest mechanical devices	1,921	1,999
Topic	known to man.	478	680
Expansion	Every internal-combustion engine contains a small flywheel	2,316	2,398
Expansion	that converts the jerky motion of the pistons into the smooth flow of energy	2,477	2,807
Expansion	that powers the drive shaft.	1,056	1,264
Cause	The greater the mass of a flywheel and the faster it spins,	2,143	2,304
Consequence	the more energy can be stored in it.	1,270	1,536
Subtopic	But its maximum spinning speed is limited by the strength of the material	2,400	2,553
Subtopic	it is made from.	615	780
Expansion	If it spins too fast for its mass,	1,414	1,502
Expansion	any flywheel will fly apart.	1,200	1,304
Definition	One type of flywheel consists of round sandwiches of fiberglass and rubber	2,746	3,064
Expansion	providing the maximum possible storage of energy	1,799	1,870
Expansion	when the wheel is confined in a small space	1,522	1,448
Detail	as in an automobile.	769	718
Definition	Another type, the "superflywheel," consists of a series of rimless spokes.	2,938	2,830
Expansion	This flywheel stores the maximum energy	1,416	1,596
Detail	when space is unlimited.	1,289	1,252

From Just & Carpenter (1980).

strongly influenced by word length, with words that are composed of more letters or syllables taking longer to read than shorter words. Also, word frequency plays a vital role, with infrequent words resulting in longer reading times as the reader needs to engage in extra mental effort to retrieve this lexical information from memory. Serial position is also an important factor. The further along a person is in a passage, the more of a foundation there is from which to build mental structures, thereby making comprehension easier and faster. A more complete listing of factors is shown in Table 10-4.

TABLE 10-4   Variables that Affect Reading Times

Variables That Increase Reading Times:

Surface form effects: sweep of the eyes to start a new line, sentence wrap-up, number of syllables, low frequency or new word, unusual spelling patterns

Textbase effects: integration of information (after clauses, sentences, sectors, etc.), topic word, new argument, other error recovery, reference and inference processes, difficulty of passage/topic

Variables That Decrease Reading Times:

Surface form effects: familiar word, higher word frequency, repetition of infrequent word

Textbase effects: appropriate title, supportive context, semantic-based expectation (if confirmed)

MODEL ARCHITECTURE AND PROCESSES   Figure 10-6 illustrates the architecture and processes of the Just and Carpenter (1980, 1987, 1992) model. Note that several elements are already familiar. For instance, working memory is where different types of knowledge—visual, lexical, syntactic, semantic, and so on—are combined. Not surprisingly, working memory capacity is important in reading comprehension (e.g., Kaakinen, Hyona, & Keenan, 2003). Long-term memory contains a wide variety of knowledge used during reading. Each of these types of knowledge can match the

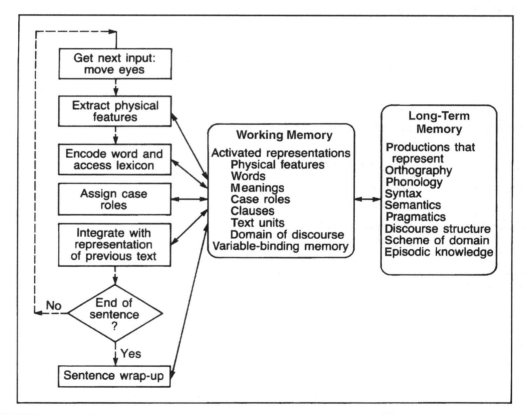

FIGURE 10-6   The Just & Carpenter (1980) model, showing the major structures and processes that operate during reading. Solid lines represent the pathways of information flow; the dashed line shows the typical sequence of processing.

current contents of working memory and update or alter those contents. In simple terms, what you know combines with what you've already read and understood, and together these permit comprehension of what you are reading. Finally, wrap-up is an integrative process that occurs at the end of a sentence or clause. During wrap-up, readers tie up any loose ends; for instance, any remaining inconsistencies or uncertainties about reference are resolved here.

Summary

An in-depth description of all of the variables that influence reading is not possible here—there are simply too many. Here is just a brief list of some of the important factors listed in Table 10-4:

- The effects of word frequency, syntactic structure, and context (Altmann, Garnham, & Dennis, 1992; Inhoff, 1984; Juhasz & Rayner, 2003; Schilling, Rayner, & Chumbley, 1998)
- The effects of sentence context on word identification (Paul, Kellas, Martin, & Clark, 1992; Schustack, Ehrlich, & Rayner, 1987; Simpson, Casteel, Peterson, & Burgess, 1989), including ERP work showing how rapidly we resolve anaphoric references (van Berkum, Brown, & Hagoort, 1999)
- The effects of ambiguity (Frazier & Rayner, 1990; Rayner & Frazier, 1989) and figurative language (Frisson & Pickering, 1999)
- The effects of topic, plausibility, and thematic structure on reading (O'Brien & Myers, 1987; Pickering & Traxler, 1998; Rayner, Warren, Juhasz, & Liversedge, 2004; Speer & Clifton, 1998; Taraban & McClelland, 1988), especially the relatedness of successive paragraphs and the presence of an informative introductory paragraph (Lorch, Lorch, & Matthews, 1985) or title (Wiley & Rayner, 2000)
- The effects of scripted knowledge on word recognition and comprehension (Sharkey & Mitchell, 1985)
- The effects of discourse structure on the understanding of reference (Malt, 1985; Murphy, 1985) and the resolution of ambiguity (Vu, Kellas, Metcalf, & Herman, 2000)

In addition, even phonology plays an important role in reading comprehension, such as research showing that phonological information is activated as rapidly as semantic knowledge in silent reading (Lee, Rayner, & Pollatsek, 1999; Rayner, Pollatsek, & Binder, 1998), especially for readers of lower skill levels who rely more on print-to-sound-to-meaning processes than a direct print-to-meaning route (Jared, Levy, & Rayner, 1999).

Section Summary

- Tremendous progress has been made in understanding the mental processes of reading, largely by using the online measures of comprehension, such as reading times and gaze durations.
- Modern models of reading make predictions about comprehension based on a variety of factors; for instance, word frequency and recency in the passage influence surface form and textbase processing, respectively.

- Online measures of language comprehension provide a unique window into human cognition. Using these sorts of measures, we can gain moment-to-moment insights into the effectiveness of processing, but also into the very contents of people's minds.

REFERENCE, SITUATION MODELS, AND EVENTS

Although the cognitive mechanisms and processes involved in comprehension at the surface form and textbase levels are critically important, they are not the goal of comprehension. A person who has successfully comprehended something that's been read has not only derived an adequate representation of the text itself. This person also has an understanding of the circumstances being described—the reference of the text. In this section, we address this process of reference, the creation of the mental representations of a described state of affairs, the situation model, and explore how research on comprehension has moved on beyond language to capture event comprehension more generally.

Reference

Reference involves finding the connections between elements in a passage of text, finding the words that refer to other concepts in the sentence. In sentence 6 from earlier, "Dave was studying hard for his statistics midterm," the word *his* refers back to *Dave*. In this situation *Dave* is the **antecedent** of *his*, because *Dave* comes before the pronoun. And *the act of using a pronoun or possessive later on* is **anaphoric reference**. So, **reference** is the *linguistic process of alluding to a concept by using another name*. Commonly we use pronouns or synonyms to refer to the antecedent, although there are other types of reference. For example, using a person's name would be a form of identity reference in that it refers back to a previous instance of using their name.

Reference is as common in language as any other feature we can identify. Part of reference is that it reduces redundancy and repetition. Contrast a normal passage such as 9a with 9b to see how boring and repetitive language would be without synonyms, pronouns, and so on.

> (9a) *Mike went to the pool to swim some laps. After his workout, he went to his psychology class. The professor asked him to summarize the chapter that he'd assigned the class to read.*

> (9b) *Mike went to the pool to swim some laps. After Mike swam some laps, Mike went to Mike's psychology class. The professor of Mike's psychology class asked Mike to summarize the chapter that Mike's psychology professor had assigned Mike's psychology class to read.*

This repetition of identity reference can actually be detrimental to comprehension. Research has shown a **repeated name penalty**, *an increase in reading times when a direct reference is used again (e.g., the person's name) compared to when a pronoun is used* (e.g., Almor, 1999; Gordon & Chan, 1995; Gordon & Scearce, 1995). That said, when we produce language, if there is more than one character being discussed or present in a situation, people are less likely to use indirect references, such as pronouns, and are more likely to use a direct reference, such as a person's name (Arnold & Griffin, 2007). This may be more acceptable under these circumstances because there may be some ambiguity as to who is being referenced.

SIMPLE REFERENCE In natural discourse, different kinds of reference can occur; Clark's (1977) useful list is shown in Table 10-5. Consider three simple forms of reference:

(10) I saw a convertible yesterday. The convertible was red.

(11) I saw a convertible yesterday. The car was red.

(12) I saw a convertible yesterday. It was red.

In sentence 10 the reference is so direct that it requires no inference on the part of the listener; this is identity reference, using the definite article *the* to refer back to a previously introduced concept, *a convertible*. Synonym reference requires that you consider whether the second word is an adequate synonym for the first, as in sentence 11; can a convertible also be referred to as "the car"? Pronoun reference requires similar reference and inference steps. In sentence 12 *it* can refer only to the *convertible*, because it is the only concept in the earlier phrase that can be equated with "it." That is, in English, the word *it* must refer to an ungendered

---

TABLE 10-5 Types of Reference and Implication

Direct Reference

Identity. Michelle bought a computer. The computer was on sale.

Synonym. Michelle bought a computer. The machine was on sale.

Pronoun. Michelle bought a computer. It was on sale for 20% off.

Set membership. I talked to two people today. Michelle said she had just bought a computer.

Epithet. Michelle bought a computer. The stupid thing doesn't work.

Indirect Reference by Association

Necessary parts. Eric bought a used car. The tires were badly worn.

Probable parts. Eric bought a used car. The radio doesn't work.

Inducible parts. Eric bought a used car. The salesperson gave him a good price.

Indirect Reference by Characterization

Necessary roles. I taught my class yesterday. The time I started was 1:30.

Optional roles. I taught my class yesterday. The chalk tray was empty.

Other

Reasons. Rick asked a question in class. He hoped to impress the professor.

Causes. Rick answered a question in class. The professor had called on him.

Consequences. Rick asked a question in class. The professor was impressed.

Concurrences. Rick asked a question in class. Vicki tried to impress the professor too.

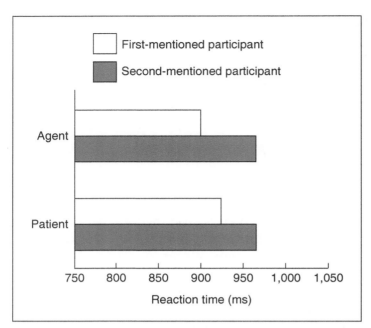

FIGURE 10-7 Mean response time to names that had appeared in the studied sentences when the name was the first- or second-mentioned participant and when the name played the agent or patient case role in the sentence.

Data from Gernsbacher & Hargreaves (1988).

concept, just as *he* must refer to a male, and so on. In some languages the nouns have gender and pronouns must agree with the gender of the noun; translated literally from French, we get, "Here is the Eiffel Tower. She is beautiful."

Another important idea is that there is some evidence that the order in which antecedents are encountered influences the likelihood that they will be linked to later reference. Two effects of this type are the **advantage of first mention** and the **advantage of clause recency**. In the advantage of first mention, *characters and ideas that were mentioned first have a special significance.* For example, in a study by Gernsbacher and Hargreaves (1988), after reading a sentence such as "Tina gathered the kindling as Lisa set up the tent," people responded faster to *Tina* than *Lisa* (see Figure 10-7).

Conversely, there is also a period of time, at the end of the sentence, when the most recent character has an advantage—this is the *advantage of clause recency.* Again, for the sentence "Tina gathered the kindling as Lisa set up the tent," if you are probed immediately after it, Lisa has a slight advantage due to recency, but this advantage is short-lived, showing an advantage at about 50 to 60 ms, but disappearing by 150 ms (Gernsbacher, Hargreaves, & Beeman, 1989).

In other work, it has been found that even the article (e.g., *a* or *the*) used can influence reference. Definite articles, such as *the*, convey given information and make sentences seem more coherent and sensible as compared to when indefinite articles (e.g., *a*, *an*, and *some*) are used (Robertson et al., 2000; see Table 10-6 for sample sentences), and sentences with definite articles are remembered better later (Haviland & Clark, 1974). For Gernsbacher (1997), *the* is a cue for discourse coherence, enabling us to map information more efficiently and accurately. In one study (Robertson et al., 2000), people read sentences, followed by a recognition test (to make sure people actually tried to comprehend the sentences). Overall, sentences using *the* showed

TABLE 10-6 Sample Sentences with Indefinite and Definite Articles

Indefinite	Definite
A grandmother sat at a table.	The grandmother sat at the table.
A child played in a backyard.	The child played in the backyard.
Some rain began to pour down.	The rain began to pour down.
An elderly woman led some others outside.	The elderly woman led the others outside.

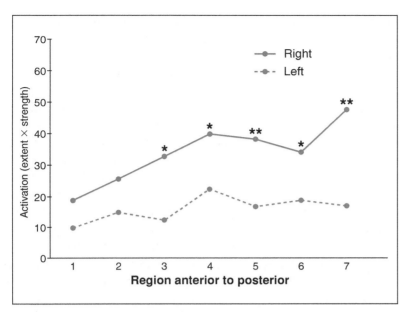

FIGURE 10-8 Activation levels for sentences presented with definite versus indefinite articles (levels in the figure are difference scores, showing how much greater the activations for definite than indefinite article sentences were), for seven left and right hemisphere locations in the brain.

From Robertson et al. (2000).

greater evidence of coherence than those with the indefinite *a*, *an*, and *some*. Importantly, people in this study were tested using fMRI, and the levels of activity of different brain regions were measured. As Figure 10-8 shows, sentences that used the definite article showed greater activation than those with indefinite articles. Moreover, these activations were greater in the right hemisphere than the left, whereas more commonly it's the left hemisphere that's implicated in language processing (e.g., Polk & Farah, 2002), as you recall from Chapter 9. Thus, the right hemisphere is particularly involved in establishing coherence in language comprehension.

Situation Models

In constructing and using a situation model (Johnson-Laird, 1983; Van Dijk & Kintsch, 1983; Zwaan & Radvansky, 1998), a person combines information that is available from the text, along with prior semantic and episodic knowledge, to create a mental simulation of the events being described. This mental representation is a **situation model**, *a mental representation that serves as a simulation of a real or possible world as described by a text.* The important idea is that comprehension is a search after meaning (Graesser, Singer, & Trabasso, 1994). Although comprehension does use some passive activation of semantic and episodic memories (e.g., McKoon & Ratcliff, 1992), we also actively build situation models that elaborate on the causal structure of the event a person is trying to understand. In this section we cover two basic processes in the use of situation models in comprehension. The first is the use of inferences to elaborate on the information provided by a text, and the second is the updating of the situation model as shifts in the described events are encountered.

Instead of specifying everything, we rely on people to know the meanings of words, to know about syntactic devices that structure our discourse, and to share our general conceptual knowledge of the world (e.g., to know that swimming laps can be a workout, or that professors assign chapters for their students to read; you remember a similar point from the earlier chapter, in discussing scripts). In fact, as you'll read later, if you *do* specify everything exactly, you're breaking an important conversational rule, and people will be unhappy with you. Let's turn to how comprehenders flesh out some missing information: implication and inference.

In **implication** there is *an intended reference in a sentence or utterance, but it is not mentioned explicitly.* The intention here is on the part of the speaker (or writer), who implies but does not state some conclusion or connection; in a sense, implication is in the mind of the speaker. If the listener (reader) draws the appropriate conclusion or connection during comprehension, then we say that the listener has drawn an inference. Thus, **inference** is *the process by which the comprehender draws connections between concepts, determines the referents of words and ideas, and derives conclusions from a message.* Implication is something that language producers do, and drawing inferences is something comprehenders do. If your professor says in class, "The next exam is on Wednesday, and it covers a lot of material," he or she is implying something about the difficulty of the exam, but is leaving it up to the students to draw that inference.

PROVE IT

People spontaneously draw inferences as they comprehend language. These inferences are then incorporated into the situation models of what was being heard or read. As a result, people frequently misremember information as having been heard or read, when in fact it was not. For this prove it section, a list of sentences follows. Along with each sentence is an inference that people are likely to make (in parentheses). What you should do is read these sentences to a group of volunteers. Then, after all of the sentences have been read, give your volunteers some distractor task, such as having them solve math problems for 3 to 5 minutes. When the distractor period is over, have your volunteers try to recall the sentences. What you should find is that people will likely report the inferences that they made while they were comprehending. That is, they will "recall" more information that you actually read to them. These inferences—false memories, in a sense—are now part of their memory.

1. The housewife spoke to the manager about the increased meat prices (complained)
2. The paratrooper leaped out of the door (jump out of a plane/helicopter)
3. The cute girl told her mother she wanted a drink (asked)
4. The weatherman told the people of the approaching tornado (warned)
5. The karate champion hit the cement block (broke)
6. The absent-minded professor didn't have his car keys (lost or forgot)
7. The safecracker put the match to the fuse (lit)
8. The hungry python caught the mouse (ate)
9. The man dropped the delicate glass pitcher (broke)
10. The clumsy chemist had acid on his coat (spilled)
11. The barnacle clung to the sides (ship)
12. Dennis sat in Santa's chair and asked for an elephant (lap)

Source: Adapted from Harris & Monaco (1978).

INFERENCE MAKING AND SITUATION MODEL CREATION   A simple type of inference making is what Clark (1977) termed a **bridging inference**, which is *a process of constructing a connection between concepts*. A bridging inference binds two units of language together. For example, determining that a reference like the epithet *the stupid thing* refers to the same entity as *a computer* is a bridging inference—it builds a connection between these two forms of reference, indicating that they refer to the same discourse entity. In bridging inference, the language producer uses reference to indicate the intended kinds of implications. For their part, comprehenders interpret the statement in the same fashion, computing the references and drawing the inferences needed. When the implication and inferences are intended, we call it **authorized**. Alternatively, unintended implications and inferences are called **unauthorized**, as when I say, "Your hair looks pretty today," and you respond, "So you think it was ugly yesterday?" (see also McKoon & Ratcliff, 1986).

The examples in Table 10-6 make it clear that the bridges we need to build for comprehension vary in their complexity, from simple and direct to difficult and remote. Even on intuitive grounds, consider how the following sentences differ in the ease of comprehension:

(13) Marge went into her office. It was very dirty.

(14) Marge went into her office. The floor was very dirty.

(15) Marge went into her office. The African violet had bloomed.

Whereas sentence 13 is a simple case of pronoun reference, sentence 14 refers back to *office* with the word *floor*. Because an office necessarily has a floor, it is clear that the implication in sentence 14 is that it was Marge's office floor that was dirty. One property you retrieve from semantic memory is that an office has a floor. Thus, if you comprehend that the office floor was dirty, you draw this inference. But it's an even longer chain of inference to draw the inference in sentence 15 that Marge has an African violet in her office; a floor is necessary, but an African violet isn't. Overall, the integration of this semantic knowledge with the information in the text is part and parcel of creating a situation model.

Think back to the discussion of semantic memory and the typicality of category instances and properties. It seems likely that the structure of concepts in semantic memory activation influences the ease with which information is inferred during situation model construction (e.g., Cook & Myers, 2004). So, more predictable pieces of information are processed faster (McKoon & Ratcliff, 1989; O'Brien, Plewes, & Albrecht, 1990). Marge's office necessarily has a floor as well as a desk, a chair, some shelves, and so on. It's conceivable that it has some plants, but that is optional enough that sentence 15 would take more time to comprehend.

Further evidence that people are drawing on their semantic knowledge, and that this knowledge has an embodied character, was given in a study by Zwaan, Stanfield, and Yaxley (2002). People read short descriptions of situations and then were shown pictures of objects. The task was to indicate whether the pictured object had been in the description they read. The critical manipulation was whether the picture either matched or mismatched the perceptual characteristics of the object in the description. For example, the critical sentence could be either *The ranger saw the eagle in the sky* or *The ranger saw the eagle in its nest* followed by a picture of either an eagle with its wings outstretched or perched (see Figure 10-9). Zwaan et al. found that people responded faster when the picture matched the described state. That is, even though they saw an eagle in both pictures, the eagle with its wings outstretched "matched" the "eagle in the sky" description better, so people responded faster (see also Connell & Lynott, 2009, for the activation of perceptual color information). Thus, people seemed to be activating perceptual qualities of objects during comprehension. Conversely, if people view a picture before reading, they are faster if the sentence matches the picture than if it doesn't (Wassenburg & Zwaan, 2010).

People are also aware of the intended consequence of someone saying something, called a **speech act** (Searle, 1969). For example, if you ask your roommate to turn down the stereo, the *speech* itself is the set of words you say, but the *speech act* is your intention, getting your roommate to let you study for an upcoming exam. Not only do people spontaneously derive the implied speech acts of what other people say, but they may misremember what was said in terms of the speech act itself. For instance, in a study by Holtgraves (2008b), people read a series of short vignettes, some of which conveyed speech acts. For example, suppose people read the following story: "Gloria showed up at the office wearing a new coat. When her coworker Heather saw it she said to her, 'Gloria, I like your new coat.'" The last sentence conveys the speech act of complimenting Gloria. What Holtgraves found was that people were more likely to mistakenly remember that they had read "I'd like to compliment you on your new coat," an utterance

FIGURE 10-9
Examples of pictures of an eagle in flight or on a perch.

that actually describes the speech act. However, a different group of people read a different version of the story, in which the last two sentences were: "When her coworker Heather saw it, she said to *her friend Stacy*: 'I like *her* new coat.'" In this condition, people were less likely to misremember having read "I'd like to compliment her on her new coat." Because there was no actual complimenting speech act to Gloria, people did not store this information in memory and so did not make the memory error.

It should be noted that we do not automatically and spontaneously draw all possible inferences while we read. Although some inferences are directly and typically drawn, such as simple and straightforward references, others are more complex and may not be drawn, and possibly shouldn't be drawn. If we did, our cognitive resources would be quickly overwhelmed (Singer, Graesser, & Trabasso, 1994). For example, when you read a sentence like 13 or 14, you are likely not to draw an inference that Marge decided to clean her office, although if the next sentence in the story said that, you'd certainly understand it. Most of the inferences people make are *backward* inferences. That is people are trying to understand what has already been described, and how it all goes together. *Forward* inferences—that is, trying to predict what will happen next—are made under much rarer circumstances (Millis & Graesser, 1994).

Moreover, the creation of the situation model needs to take into account constraints of embodiment. For example, in a study by de Vega, Robertson, Glenberg, Kaschak, and Rinck (2004; see also Radvansky, Zwaan, Federico, & Franklin, 1998), people were asked to read a series of passages. Embedded in those passages were critical sentences that described two actions that a character was doing, either at the same time or in sequence. If a person is described as doing two things that require the same parts of the body, such as *While chopping wood with his large axe, he painted the fence white*, reading times were slower, as if readers were trying to figure out how this could be done. However, reading times were faster when either different parts of the body were being used, such as *While whistling a lively folk melody, he painted the fence white*, or were done in sequence, such as *After chopping wood with his large axe, he painted the fence white*. Thus, people take into account the limits of our human bodies, and the way actions happen in time, to help them comprehend what they are reading.

INDIVIDUAL DIFFERENCES Interestingly, reference and inference processes depend significantly on individual characteristics of the reader, particularly on the reader's skill. For instance, Long and De Ley (2000) found that less skilled readers resolve ambiguous pronouns just as well as more skilled readers, but they do so only when they are integrating meanings together; the more skilled readers resolve the pronouns earlier, probably when they first encounter a pronoun.

Several studies have also examined inferences as a function of working memory capacity (e.g., Fletcher & Bloom, 1988). One study by Singer, Andrusiak, Reisdorf, and Black (1992) explored individual differences in bridging as a function of working memory capacity and vocabulary knowledge. The gist of this work is that the greater your working memory capacity and vocabulary size, the greater the likelihood that information necessary for an inference will still be in working memory and can be used (see also Long, Oppy, & Seely, 1997; Miyake, Just, & Carpenter, 1994).

Evidence for individual differences in comprehension has also revealed itself in neurological measures. In a study by Virtue, van den Broek, and Linderholm (2006), people read sentences that had causal constraints that were either weak (e.g., *As he arrived at the bus stop, he saw his bus was already five blocks away.*) or strong (*As he arrived at the bus stop, he saw his bus was just pulling away.*). During reading, the researchers presented lexical decision probes that corresponded to likely inference that the readers might make (e.g., *run* in this case). Importantly, this presentation was done to the left and right hemispheres by presenting the words on either the right or left half (respectively) of the computer screen. The data showed that the right hemisphere was more involved in generating remote associations (that is, associated concepts that are not closely semantically related to the concepts in the sentences). Moreover, people with high working memory capacity activated fewer remote associations than low-span people. Essentially, people with a high working memory span were more focused in the amount of knowledge they activated during comprehension.

UPDATING   Situations that we experience or read about are often in a state of flux. Things are always changing, and the events may differ from one moment to the next. Thus, the cognitive processes involved in comprehension must be able to shift the current understanding to adapt to these ongoing changes. There are a number of **updating** processes that *alter a person's situation model in the face of information about how the situation has changed.* To provide a framework for understanding how these changes can occur, we'll use Rolf Zwaan's Event Indexing Model (Zwaan, Langston, & Graesser, 1995; Zwaan, Magliano, & Graesser, 1995; Zwaan & Radvansky, 1998). According to this theory, people actively monitor multiple event dimensions during reading to assess whether there has been a meaningful change along any of them.

In the original version of the theory, five dimensions were proposed: space, time, entity, intentionality (goals), and causality. When there is a disruption along any one of these dimensions, people update their situation models, and this updating process takes time. For example, a break along the space and time dimensions could happen if a story protagonist moves to a new location, or there is a jump in time (e.g., a week later . . .). Similarly if a new character is introduced into a story, the person would need to update the entity dimension, and so on. Further research has shown that people actually monitor more than just these five dimensions. For example, people also track emotional information (e.g., Komeda & Kusumi, 2006).

To give you a better idea of what goes on in situation model updating, let's look at a classic paradigm that explores updating along the spatial dimension. In a seminal paper by Morrow, Greenspan, and Bower (1987), people memorized a diagram of a research lab, where each room had four objects in it (see Figure 10-10). They then read narratives about people moving about in that space. During reading, people were occasionally probed with pairs of object names, such as *sink-furnace.* The task was to indicate whether the two

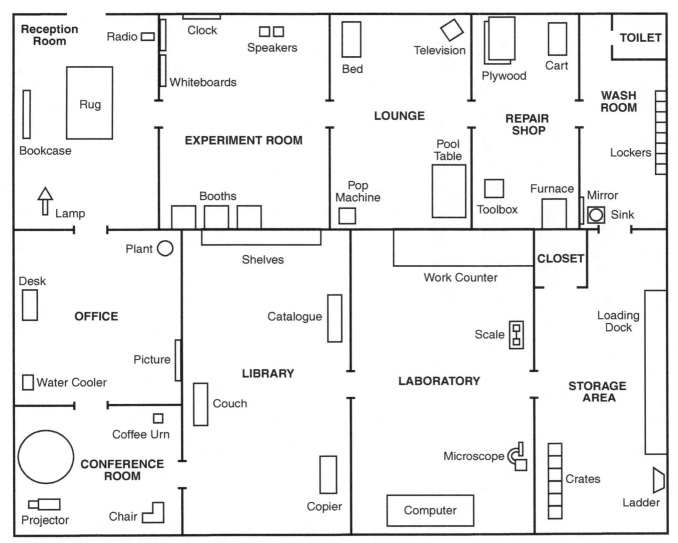

FIGURE 10-10 Example of the map of the research center memorized by people in Morrow, Greenspan, & Bower's (1987) study of spatial updating during language comprehension.

objects were in the same room or not (in this case, they were not). The critical factor was the distance on the map between the story protagonist's current location, and the location of the probe objects. Moreover, these memory probes came after motion sentences in which the person moved from one room to another, such as "He walked from the laboratory into the wash room." Based on this, four conditions were defined. The Location Room was the room that the person just moved to—the wash room in this case. The Path Room was the (unmentioned) room that the person walked through to get to the Location room—the storage room here. The Source Room was the room the person was in just before moving to the Location Room—the laboratory here. Finally, there was an Other Room condition, which corresponded to probes from any other room in the building.

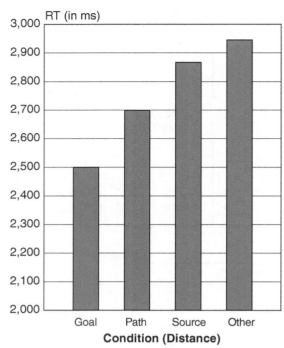

FIGURE 10-11 Response time data from a study by Morrow, Greenspan, & Bower (1987). While reading a passage about a character moving about the building in Figure 10-10, people were interrupted with memory probes. In this case, the probes were two objects, and the person's task was to indicate whether they were in the same room or not. In this task, the Goal room is the room the story character had just moved to (the goal of the movement), the Path room is a room along the character's path of travel, the Source room is the room that the movement started from (the source from which the movement began), and the Other room is just some other room in the building.

The results from one study, shown in Figure 10-11, reveal that response times to the memory probes increased with an increase in distance between the protagonist and the objects. It is as if people were mentally scanning their situation models from the protagonist's current place in the building to another room. The further away that other room was, the longer it took people to scan. People actively updated their situation models as there were changes in spatial locations in the texts. When a person reads that a story character has moved from one room to another, they update their situation model so that the spatial framework that is at the focus of comprehension is now different. What is particularly compelling here are the response times to the probes from the Path Room condition—this room was not even mentioned, yet people are scanning their situation model in a way that activates that information. If people were simply activating knowledge of the rooms that the protagonist was in, then this would not have occurred. But, because people are mentally simulating the environment as they read, this activation of an intermediate location emerges.

Similar influences of situation model updating can be seen for other situation model dimensions, including shifts in time (Gennari, 2004; Zwaan, 1996), monitoring characteristics of story characters (Albrecht & O'Brien, 1995), the processing of character goal information (Lutz & Radvansky, 1997; Suh & Trabasso, 1993), and so on.

Tracking these changes along various dimensions is part of an attempt to create an analog to the world. Work with fMRI recordings have shown that there are increases in brain activity when event shifts are encountered and people need to update their situation models (Speer, Zacks, & Reynolds, 2007). For example, looking at the dimension of time in a story, memory access to events earlier in a sequence is more difficult if the described intervening events are longer in duration (e.g., a year) than if they are shorter (e.g., a day), even if the event is presented as a flashback (that is later in the text than the intervening events) (Claus & Kelter, 2006).

Events

ON BEYOND LANGUAGE   Our discussion of comprehension up to now has largely focused on language comprehension of either written or spoken language, and this reflects the thrust of research in this area. However, this is not the only type of comprehension that people can engage in. We also comprehend events that we see or are involved in. As an example of the first type, work by Magliano (Magliano, Miller, & Zwaan, 2001; Magliano, Taylor, & Kim, 2005) and Zacks (Zacks et al., 2001; Zacks, Speer, Swallow, Braver, & Reynolds, 2007) show that people are actively comprehending events viewed on video or film. For example, in a study by Magliano et al. (2001), rather than having people read texts, people watched narrative films such as *Star Trek 2: The Wrath of Khan*. As people watched these movies, they indicated when they thought the situation depicted by the film changed. The results showed that people made these indications at the same points as situation model theory suggested they would update their understanding. For example, people indicated that there was a change in the film if a new character entered a scene, if there was a change in spatial location, if something unexpected happened, and so on, exactly as the theory predicts.

There have also been extensions of the study of comprehension to how people understand interactive events that they find themselves in. The development of virtual reality technologies has been helpful here because the experimenter has a great deal of control in creating environments that a person can interact with, which allows the experimenter to make precise, controlled measurements. An example of this is a study by Tamplin, Krawietz, Copeland, and Radvansky (in press) that was modeled after the Morrow et al. (1987) studies described earlier. In these experiments, people memorized the map of a research center, as was done in the earlier text comprehension work. Then, rather than reading a story, people navigated through a virtual representation of the environment. As they moved about, their primary task was to respond to memory probes that consisted of object names at critical points, similar to what had been done in the text comprehension work. However, the pattern of data that was obtained was very different, as shown in Figure 10-12.

As can be seen, rather than having information about objects become less available as one moves farther and farther away from them, this information is similarly available in memory, except for objects in the Path Room. Response times to probes in this condition were much slower, suggesting that people suppressed this information. So, there is something different about how people comprehend events that they are involved in compared to ones that they just read about. Now why would people want to suppress this knowledge? Why isn't it more available since the person had just been in that room? Well, when people passed through the Path Room, this information was salient because they were actually in that (virtual) context. However, because this was not their destination, this information was irrelevant. As such, knowledge about objects in the Path Room was interfering knowledge in memory. Similar to other examples of interference in cognition that you have studied, this interference can disrupt cognitive processing. So, this is a similar cognitive process (in this case, retrieval interference) that has been observed with simpler materials (e.g., lists of words) showing up in a more real-to-life situation, with similar consequences (i.e., interfering knowledge hinders memory).

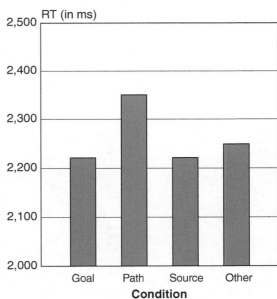

FIGURE 10-12 Response time data from a study by Tamplin, Krawietz, Copeland, & Radvansky (in press). Rather than reading a text, people navigated a virtual environment after memorizing the map of the research center in Figure 10-10. Note the different pattern of data compared to the reading comprehension task illustrated in Figure 10-11.

Section Summary

- Reference in language involves the idea of bridging together different elements of a statement. The source of knowledge that permits speakers to include reference in their messages and listeners to infer the basis for those bridges is not just our knowledge of syntax and word meanings, but the entirety of semantic memory and much top-down processing.
- Situation models are created by combining information from the language itself as well as inferences people draw based on their prior semantic and episodic knowledge.
- The capacity and operation of working memory are known to be important factors in understanding individual differences in reading comprehension.
- Situation model updating occurs when people detect a meaningful change in an event dimension. This updating process is cognitively effortful, resulting in increases in reading times and brain activity.
- Comprehension occurs not only for language that people hear or read, but also for other aspects of experience, including narrative films, videos, and interactive experiences.

CONVERSATION AND GESTURE

We turn now to the comprehension of conversation and gesture. We focus on conversation, normal, everyday language interactions, such as an ordinary talk among friends. The issues we consider, however, apply to all kinds of linguistic interactions: how professors lecture and students comprehend, how people converse on the telephone, how an interviewer and a job applicant talk, how we reason and argue with one another (Rips, 1998), and so on. Furthermore, we look at how we expand on what we say by moving our hands about, making gestures, and by examining the cognitive role of these gestures.

The Structure of Conversations

Let's examine two characteristics of conversations, the issues of turn taking and social roles, to get started and introduce some of the more cognitive effects we're interested in.

TAKING TURNS Conversations are structured by a variety of cognitive and social variables and rules governing the what and how of our contributions. To begin with, we take turns. Typically, there is little overlap between participants' utterances.

During a conversation, speakers develop a rhythm as each person takes successive turns speaking. Nonverbal interaction can occur during a turn, such as when a listener nods to indicate attention or agreement.

Generally, two people speak simultaneously only at the change of turns, when one speaker is finishing and the other is beginning. In fact, interchanges in conversation often come in an adjacency pair, a pair of turns that sets the stage for another part of the conversation. For instance, if Ann wants to ask Betty a question, there can be an adjacency pair of utterances in which Ann sets the stage for the actual question:

> Ann: Oh there's one thing I wanted to ask you.
>
> Betty: mhm
>
> Ann: in the village, they've got some of those . . . rings. . . . Would you like one? (From Svartvik & Quirk, 1980, cited in Clark, 1994.)

The neutral "mhm" is both an indication of attention and a signal that Ann can go ahead and ask the question (Duncan, 1972).

The rules we follow for turn taking are straightforward (Sacks, Schegloff, & Jefferson, 1974). First, the current speaker is in charge of selecting the next speaker. This is often done by directing a comment or question toward another participant ("What do you think about that, Fred?"). The second rule is that if the first rule isn't used, then anyone can become the current speaker. Third, if no one else takes the turn, the current speaker may continue but is not obliged to.

Speakers use a variety of signals to indicate whether they are finished with their turn. For example, a long pause at the end of a sentence is a turn-yielding signal, as are a comment directed at another participant, a drop in the pitch or loudness of the utterance, and establishing direct eye contact with another person; the last is often merely a nonverbal way of selecting the next speaker. If the current speaker is not relinquishing the conversational turn, however, these signals are withheld. Other "failure to yield" signals include trailing off in midsentence without completing the grammatical clause or the thought, withholding such endings as "you know," or even looking away from other participants during a pause (Cook, 1977).

In addition to overt signals of when turn taking may occur, there are neurological underpinnings. Margaret and Thomas Wilson (Wilson & Wilson, 2005) have suggested that conversational turn taking may be tied to neurological oscillators that help us keep track of time. The idea is that these oscillators become synchronized to one another on the basis of the rate at which people are producing syllables. These oscillators give us a neurologically based intuition about the pace of the conversation, and when it would be appropriate to step in and take our turn.

SOCIAL ROLES AND SETTINGS The social roles of conversational partners, along with conversational setting, influence the contributions made by participants (Kemper & Thissen, 1981). Formal settings among strangers or mere acquaintances lead to more structured, rule-governed conversations than informal settings among friends (Blom & Gumperz, 1972). Conversations with a "superior"—for instance, your boss or a police officer—are more formal and rule-governed than those with peers (e.g., Brown & Ford, 1961; Edwards & Potter, 1993, and Holtgraves, 1994, discuss the social and interpersonal aspects of such situations). More generally, when involved in conversation, people take into account a wide variety of information, not just the words and syntax, but the context and who is speaking (Van Berkum, 2008).

Cognitive Conversational Characteristics

Conversations are structured by cognitive factors. We focus on three: the conversational rules we follow, the issue of topic maintenance, and the online theories of conversational partners.

CONVERSATIONAL RULES   Grice (1975; see also Norman & Rumelhart, 1975) suggested four **conversational rules** or maxims, *rules that govern our conversational interactions with others*, all derived from the **cooperative principle**, *the idea that each participant in a conversation implicitly assumes that all speakers are following the rules and that each contribution to the conversation is a sincere, appropriate contribution.* In a sense, we enter into a pact with our conversational partner, pledging to abide by certain rules and adopting certain conventions to make our conversations manageable and understandable (Brennan & Clark, 1996; Wilkes-Gibbs & Clark, 1992). This includes issues of syntax, where we choose syntactic structures that mention important discourse focus information early in our sentences (Ferreira & Dell, 2000) and use syntactic structures that are less ambiguous (Haywood, Pickering, & Branigan, 2005); we use intonation and prosody that helps disambiguate an otherwise ambiguous syntactic form (Clifton, Carlson, & Frazier, 2006); we decide on word choice, as in situations when two conversational partners settle on a mutually acceptable term for referring to some object (Metzing & Brennan, 2003; Shintel & Keysar, 2007); and we often use gestures to amplify or disambiguate our speech (Goldin-Meadow, 1997; Kelly, Barr, Church, & Lynch, 1999; Özyürek, 2002). As Table 10-7 shows, the four maxims specify in detail how to follow the cooperative principle. (Two further rules have been added to the list for purposes that will become clear in a moment.)

TABLE 10-7   **Grice's (1975) Conversational Maxims, with Two Additional Rules**

The Cooperative Principle

Be honest, reasonable, and germane

- **Relevance:** Your utterances should be relevant to the discourse (e.g., stay on topic; don't make statements on things that others aren't interested in).

- **Quantity:** As needed, provide as much information as is necessary (e.g., don't give too much information; don't go beyond or give short shrift to what you know; don't give too much information).

- **Quality:** Have what you say be truthful (e.g., don't give misleading information; don't lie; don't exaggerate).

- **Manner and tone:** Aim for clarity (e.g., avoid saying things that are unnecessarily ambiguous or obscure); keep it brief, but polite, and don't interrupt someone else.

Two Additional Rules

- **Relations with conversational partner:** Infer and respond to partner's knowledge and beliefs (e.g., tailor contributions to partner's level; correct misunderstandings).

- **Rule violations:** Signal or mark intentional violations of rules (e.g., use linguistic or pragmatic markers [stress, gestures]; use blatant violations; signal the reason for the violation). From Grice (1975); see also Norman and Rumelhart (1975).

A simple example or two should help you understand the point of these maxims. When a speaker violates or seems to violate a maxim, the listener assumes there is a reason for this and may not detect a violation (Engelhardt, Bailey, & Ferreira, 2006). That is, the listener assumes that the speaker is following the overarching cooperative principle and so must have intended the remark as something else, maybe sarcasm, or maybe a nonliteral meaning (Kumon-Nakamura, Glucksberg, & Brown, 1995). As an example, imagine studying in the library when your friend asks:

(21) Can I borrow a pencil?

This is a straightforward speech act, a simple request you could respond to directly. But if you had just lent a pencil to your friend, and he said,

(22) Can I borrow a pencil with lead in it?

the question means something different. Assuming that your friend was being cooperative, you now have to figure out why he broke the quantity maxim about overspecifying; all pencils have lead in them, and mentioning the lead is a violation of a rule. You infer that it was a deliberate violation, where the friend's authorized implication can be expressed as "The pencil you lent me doesn't have any lead in it, so would you please lend me one I *can* use?" In general, people are fairly adept at decoding speech acts and knowing what a person is trying to achieve by what they say (Holtgraves, 2008a).

TOPIC MAINTENANCE   We also follow the conversational rules in terms of **topic maintenance**, *making our contributions relevant to the topic and sticking to it.* Topic maintenance depends on two processes, comprehension of the speaker's remark and expansion, contributing something new to the topic.

Schank (1977; see also Litman & Allen, 1987) provides an analysis of topic maintenance and topic shift, including a consideration of what is and is not a permissible response, called simply a move, after one speaker's turn is over. The basic idea is that the listener comprehends the speaker's comment and stores it in memory. As in reading, the listener must infer what the speaker's main point was or what the discourse focus was. If the speaker, Ben, says,

(23) I bought a new car in Baltimore yesterday,

then Ed, his conversational partner, needs to infer Ben's main point and expand on that in his reply. Thus, sentence (24) is legal because it apparently responds to the speaker's authorized implication, whereas sentence *(25#) is probably not a legal move (denoted by the # sign)*:

(24) Ed: Really? I thought you said you couldn't afford a car.

(25#) Ed: I bought a new shirt yesterday.

Sentence 24 intersects with two main elements for sentence 23, "BUY" and "CAR," so it is probably an acceptable expansion. Sentence 25# intersects with "BUY," but the other common concept seems to be the time case role "YESTER-DAY," an insufficient basis for most expansions. Thus, in general a participant's responsibility is to infer the speaker's focus and expand on it in an appropriate way. That's the relevance maxim: Sticking to the topic means you have to infer it correctly. Ed seems to have failed to draw the correct inference.

On the other hand, maybe Ed *did* comprehend Ben's statement correctly. If so, then he deliberately violated the relevance maxim in sentence 25#. But it's such a blatant violation that it suggests some other motive; Ed may be expressing disinterest in what Ben did or may be saying indirectly that he thinks Ben is bragging. And if Ed suspects Ben is telling a lie, then he makes his remark even more blatant, as in 26:

(26) *Yeah, and I had lunch with the Queen of England.*

ONLINE THEORIES DURING CONVERSATION   A final point involves the theories we develop of our conversational partners, something called **theory of mind**. The most obvious one is a **direct theory.** This is the mental model of *what the conversational partner knows and is interested in, what the partner is like.* We tailor our speech so that we're not being too complex or too simplistic, so we're not talking about something of no interest to the listener. Some clear examples of this involve adult–child speech, where a child's smaller vocabulary and knowledge prompt adults to modify and simplify their utterances in a number of ways (DePaulo & Bonvillian, 1978; Snow, 1972; Snow & Ferguson, 1977). But sensitivity to the partner's knowledge and interests is present to some degree in all conversations—although not perfectly, of course. We don't talk to our college classes the way we would to a group of second graders, nor do we launch into conversations with bank tellers about our research. Horton and Gerrig (2002) call this "audience design," that is, being aware of the need to design your speech to the characteristics of your audience (e.g., Lockridge & Brennan, 2002). Alternatively, if we don't know much about you, we may make an assumption that you know what we know (Nickerson, 2001) and then revise our direct theory as we observe how well you follow our remarks (Clark & Krych, 2004).

Audience design has implications beyond conversations. When we tell stories, we modify what we tell our listeners based on who they are and our social relationship to them. This retelling is not the same as recall. We modify the information we report to fit the social situation. In retelling stories, people often exaggerate some parts, minimize others, add information that was not there originally, and leave some bits out, all to suit our audience and the broader message we are trying to convey (Marsh, 2007).

There is another layer of theories during a conversation, an interpersonal level related to "face management," or public image (Holtgraves, 1994, 1998). Let's call this the **second-order theory**. This second-order theory is *an evaluation of the other participant's direct theory: what you think the other participant believes about you.* Let's develop an example of these two theories to illustrate their importance. Imagine that you're registering for classes next semester and say to your friend Frank that you've decided to take Psychology of Personality. What would your reaction be if Frank responded to you with these statements?

(27) *Why would you want to take that? It's just a bunch of experiments with rats, isn't it?*

(28) Yeah, I'm taking Wilson's class next term too. John told me he's going to assign some books he thinks I'll really like.

(29) Maybe you shouldn't take Wilson's class next term. Don't you have to be pretty smart to do all that reading?

In sentence 27, you assume that your friend has made the remark in sincerity, that it was intended to mean what it says. Because you know that research on laboratory animals had little to do with the field of personality, you conclude that your friend knows a lot less about personality theory than you do. This becomes part of your direct theory, as shown in Table 10-8. For sentence 28, you probably interpret Frank's remark as boastful, intended to show that he's on a first-name basis with the professor. Frank has authorized that inference by using a more familiar term of address. You update both your direct theory of Frank and your second-order theory. You update your direct and second-order theories after sentence 29, too, but the nature of the updates is different: You've been insulted by the implication in Frank's response, something like "He thinks I'm not smart enough to take the class."

Empirical Effects in Conversation

INDIRECT REQUESTS   Let's conclude with some evidence about the conversational effects we've been discussing. One of the most commonly investigated aspects of conversation involves **indirect requests**, such as when *we ask someone to do something* ("Close the window"; "Tell me what time it is") *by an indirect and presumably more polite statement* ("It's drafty in here"; "Excuse me, but do you have the correct time?").

TABLE 10-8   Examples of Direct and Second-Order Theories

Setting: For all three conversations, Chris's first sentence and direct theory are the same.

Chris: "I think I'll take Personality with Dr. Wilson next term."

Chris's direct theory: Frank is interested in the courses I'm taking.

Conversation 1

Frank replies: "Personality? Ah, that's just a bunch of experiments with rats, isn't it?"

Chris's updated direct theory: Frank doesn't know much about personality research.

Conversation 2

Frank replies: "Yeah, I am too. John told me he's going to assign some books he thinks I'll really like."

Chris's updated direct theory: Frank knows the professor on a first-name basis, and he's bragging about it by calling him John.

Chris's second-order theory: Frank thinks I'll be impressed that he calls the professor John.

Conversation 3

Frank replies: "Hmm, maybe you shouldn't take that class. Don't you have to be pretty smart to do all that reading?"

Chris's updated direct theory: Frank is a jerk, he just insulted me.

Chris's second-order theory: Frank thinks I'm not smart.

PROVE IT

One of the best student demonstration projects we've ever graded was a test of the politeness ethic in conversational requests. On five randomly selected days, the student sat next to a stranger on the bus, turned, and asked, "Excuse me, but do you have the correct time?" All five strangers answered her. On five other randomly selected days, she said to the stranger, "Tell me what time it is," not in an unpleasant tone, but merely in a direct fashion; none of the strangers answered. Devise other situations in which you violate the politeness ethic or other conversational rules and note people's reactions. If you do it properly, you'll learn about the rules of conversation; but be careful that it doesn't turn into a demonstration project on aggression. Do the same thing again, but this time with a close friend or family member. You'll see how necessary some polite forms are with strangers and how inappropriate they are with people you know well.

An impressive investigation of indirect requests was reported by Clark (1979). The study involved telephone calls to some 950 merchants in the San Francisco area in which the caller asked a question that the merchant normally would be expected to deal with on the phone (e.g., "What time do you close?" "Do you take credit cards?" "How much does something cost?"). The caller would immediately write down a verbatim record of the call immediately after hanging up. A typical conversational interaction was as follows:

(30) Merchant: "Hello, Scoma's Restaurant."

Caller: "Hello. Do you accept any credit cards?"

Merchant: "Yes we do; we even accept Carte Blanche."

Of course, the caller's question here was indirect: "Yes" isn't an acceptable answer to "Do you accept any credit cards?" because the authorized implication of the question was, "What credit cards do you take?" Merchants almost always responded to the authorized implication rather than merely to the literal question. Furthermore, they tailored their answers to be informative while not saying more than is necessary (obeying the second rule, on quantity), as in "We accept *only* Visa and MasterCard," or "We accept *all* major credit cards." Such responses are both informative and brief.

Such research has been extended to include not just indirect requests, but a variety of indirect statements and replies to questions. For instance, Holtgraves (1994) examined comprehension speed for indirect requests as a function of whether the speaker was of higher status than the listener (e.g., boss and employee) or whether they were of equal status (two employees). People read a short scenario (e.g., getting a conference room ready for a board of directors meeting), which concluded with one of two kinds of indirect statements. Conventional statements were normal indirect requests, such as, "Could you go fill the water glasses?" Negative state remarks were more indirect, merely stating a negative situation and only indirectly implying that the listener should do something (e.g., "The water glasses seem to be empty."). People showed no effects of status when comprehending regular indirect requests; it didn't matter whether it was a peer or the boss who said, "Could you go fill the water glasses?" But comprehension time increased significantly with negative state remarks made by peers. In other words, when the boss says, "The water glasses seem to be empty," we comprehend the conventional indirect request easily. But when a peer says it, we need additional time to comprehend.

INDIRECT REPLIES   Holtgraves (1998) also focused on indirect replies, especially the idea of making a "face saving" reply. His participants read a description of a situation, such as:

> *(31) Nick and Paul are taking the same history class. Students in this class have to give a 20-minute presentation to the class on some topic.*

They then read a sentence that gave positive (32) or negative (33) information about Nick's presentation or a sentence that was neutral (34):

> *(32) Nick gave his presentation and it was excellent. He decides to ask Paul what he thought of it: "What did you think of my presentation?"*

> *(33) Nick gave his presentation and it was truly terrible. He decides to ask Paul what he thought of it: "What did you think of my presentation?"*

> *(34) Nick gave his presentation and then decided to ask Paul what he thought of it: "What did you think of my presentation?"*

If you were Paul and faced the prospect of telling Nick that his presentation was awful, wouldn't you look for some face-saving response? This is exactly how people responded when they comprehended Paul's responses. In the excuse condition, Paul says,

> *(35) It's hard to give a good presentation,*

in effect giving Nick a face-saving excuse for his poor performance. Another possible move is to change the topic, to avoid embarrassing Nick, as in

> *(36) I hope I win the lottery tonight.*

Holtgraves (1998) collected several measures of comprehension, including overall comprehension time for the critical sentences 35 or 36. The comprehension times, shown in Figure 10-13 (from Experiment 2), were very clear. When people had heard positive information—the talk was excellent— it took them a long time to comprehend either the excuse (35) or topic change (36) responses. But having heard negative information—the talk was terrible—was nearly the same as having heard nothing about the

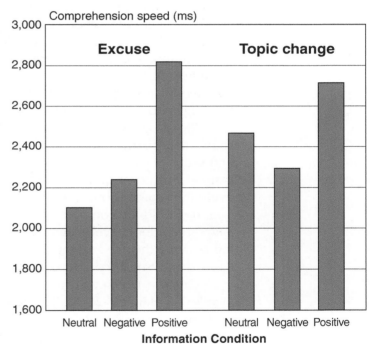

FIGURE 10-13   Comprehension times from Holtgraves's (1998) study. Participants read settings in which negative information, positive information, or neutral information was offered about a character, followed by a conversational move in which the speaker made an excuse for the character or changed the topic. In both cases it took longer to comprehend the remark when positive information about the character had just been encountered.

talk; people comprehended the excuse or topic change responses more rapidly, and there was no major difference between no information and negative information. People interpreted the violations of the relevance maxim as attempts to save face and avoid embarrassment.

Another role of indirect speech is to provide some element of *plausible deniability* (Lee & Pinker, 2010). Indirect requests and responses may carry implicit requests and replies that would be inappropriate otherwise. For example, suppose you are told by a not-so-savory relative of the defendant of a trial "I hear you're the foreman of the jury. It's an important responsibility. You have a wife and kids. We know you'll do the right thing." Thus, while the literal wording is acceptable, the implied meaning (a threat) is not. Thus, indirect speech can play many roles in human communication.

Watch *The Role of Gesture in Thinking: Susan Goldwin-Meadow* in **MyPsychLab**

Gesture

When we speak, we not only move our lips, tongues, throats and so on, we may also move our arms and hands. This movement, or **gesture**, is *done to facilitate communication to listeners, and excludes sign language and noncommunicative mannerisms, such as touching one's hands to one's face* (McNeill, 1992). That is, if they are not *beat gestures* that mark out important words or ideas, the movements we make with our hands communicates information to augment the words we are using. For example, when describing the route you took to get to school, you may make gestures to convey information about turns to made, obstructions you encountered, speeders that you saw, and so on. Although gesturing may serve a more holistic function when we use it while speaking, when people gesture in the absence of spoken speech, it takes on more linguistic characteristics, much as sign languages do (Goldin-Meadow, 2006).

Work by researchers such as Bavelas, Gerwing, Sutton, and Prevost (2008) shows that people even gesture when they are talking on the telephone, and they know the person on the other end cannot see them (although they gesture less than when they can see the other person). So, there must be something cognitively important about gesturing that facilitates language production in conversation. It should also be noted that people gesture less when they are speaking into a tape recorder (Bavelas et al., 2008) or when listeners do not appear to be attending to what they are saying (Jacobs & Garnham, 2007), so this impact of gesture has a strong social component and is not purely psycholinguistic.

Gesture may even help learning and thinking (for a review, see Goldin-Meadow & Beilock, 2010). The gestures a person produces when trying to solve a problem may reveal knowledge that the person has that is in a nascent, implicit stage. In some way, the gestures reveal to the person that knowledge is present, but not fully developed in a way that can be used consciously. So, if people are encouraged to gesture, they may make the knowledge conscious faster and facilitate learning. In a study by Broaders, Cook, Mitchell, and Goldin-Meadow (2007), third- and fourth-grade children were told to gesture while they solved math problems. They then showed an increased ability to develop new strategies and solve those types of math problems and were faster than children who did not gesture. Moreover, when two people are solving problems together, such as assembling a piece of furniture, they can solve the problems more effectively when the person communicating gestures, and the person assembling can use the gestures (Lozano & Tversky, 2006). In essence, gestures communicate embodied information that cognition is able to more directly process than linguistic information alone (Hostetter & Alibali, 2008; Kelly, Özyürek, & Maris, 2010).

Section Summary

- Conversations follow a largely implicit set of conversational rules. Some of these involve turn taking and social status and conventions, but many more govern the nature or topic of participants' contributions. Topic shifts involve selecting some part of a person's utterance to form the basis for a new contribution but then adding some new information. Schank's work on topic shift is a particularly important analysis of this process of topic shifting.
- Participants in a conversation develop theories of mind of the other speakers, called direct theories, as well as theories of what the other speakers think of them, called second-order theories. When we converse, we tailor our contributions to these theories and also follow a set of conversational rules, the unspoken contract between conversational partners. When a rule is violated intentionally, usually to make some other point (e.g., sarcasm), we mark our violation so that its apparent illegality as a conversational move is noticed and understood.
- Empirical work on conversational interaction often tests general notions about direct theories, the politeness rule, or indirect requests. Although we sometimes attempt to manipulate another person's direct theory of us, research also shows that the initially planned utterance usually is from a very egocentric perspective, whereas later adjustments may take the other person's perspective into account.
- Gestures made during conversation are a way that simulated spatial and action information can be communicated. Making gestures is part of the social act of conversation, although it may sometimes occur when our partner cannot see us, as when we are talking on the telephone. Gesture even has the ability to serve as a working memory aid and help people solve problems.

Key Terms

advantage of clause recency	beliefs	enhancement	implication
advantage of first mention	bridging inference	eye–mind assumption	indirect requests
anaphoric reference	conceptual knowledge	eye tracker	inference
antecedent	conversational rules	fixations	judgments of learning (JOLs)
authorized	cooperative principle	gaze duration	labor-in-vain effect
	direct theory	gesture	mapping
		immediacy assumption	

metacomprehension
online comprehension
pragmatics
propositional textbase

reference
region of proximal
    learning
repeated name penalty
second-order theory

situation model
speech act
structure-building
suppression
surface form

theory of mind
topic maintenance
unauthorized
updating

12 Problem Solving

The Newell and Simon approach to problem-solving did not produce a flurry of related experiments by other cognitive psychologists, and problem solving never became a central research area in information-processing cognition. . . . Newell and Simon's conceptual work, however, formed a cornerstone of the information-processing approach.

(LACHMAN, LACHMAN, AND BUTTERFIELD, 1979, P. 99)

Afavorite example of "problem solving in action" is the following true story. When I (M.H.A.) was a graduate student, I attended a departmental colloquium at which a candidate for a faculty position was to present his research. As he started his talk, he realized that his first slide was projected too low on the screen. A flurry of activity around the projector ensued, one professor asking out loud, "Does anyone have a book or something?" Someone volunteered a book, the professor tried it, but it was too thick; the slide image was now too high. "No, this one's too big. Anyone got a thinner one?" he continued. After several more seconds of hurried searching for something thinner, another professor finally exclaimed, "Well, for Pete's sake, I don't believe this!" He marched over to the projector, grabbed the book, opened it halfway, and put it under the projector. He looked around the lecture hall and shook his head, saying, "I can't believe it. A roomful of PhDs, and no one knows how to open a book!"

This chapter examines the slow and deliberate cognitive processing called problem solving. As with decision making and reasoning, problem solving studies a person who is confronted with a difficult, time-consuming task: A problem has been presented, the solution is not immediately obvious, and the person often is uncertain what to do next. We are interested in all aspects of the person's activities, from initial understanding of the problem to the steps that lead to a final solution, and, in some cases, how a person decides that a problem has been solved. Our interest needs no further justification than this: We confront countless problems in our daily lives, problems that are important for us to figure out and solve. We rely on our wits in these situations. We attempt to solve problems by mentally analyzing the situation, devising a plan of action, then carrying out that plan. Therefore, the mental processing involved in problem solving is, by definition, part of cognitive psychology.

Let's start with a simple "recreational" problem (Anderson, 1993). It will take you a minute or two at most to solve it, even if you lose patience with brain teasers very quickly; VanLehn's (1989) nine-year-old child seemed to understand it completely in about 20 seconds and solved it out loud in about two minutes:

Three men want to cross a river. They find a boat, but it is a very small boat. It will only hold 200 pounds. The men are named Large, Medium, and Small. Large weighs 200 pounds, Medium weighs 120 pounds, and Small weighs 80 pounds. How can they all get across? They might have to make several trips in the boat. (VanLehn, 1989, p. 532)

Why should we be interested in such recreational problems? The answer is straightforward. As is typical of all scientific disciplines, cognitive science studies the simple before the complex, searching simpler settings to find basic principles that generalize to more complex settings. After all, not all everyday problems are tremendously complex; figuring out how to prop up a slide projector is not of earthshaking significance (well, it probably was to the fellow interviewing for the job). In either case, the reasoning is that we often see large-scale issues and important processes more clearly when they are embedded in simple situations. Indeed, one aspect of problem solving you'll read about, functional fixedness, accounts for why a roomful of PhDs didn't think about opening the book to make it thinner. Functional fixedness was discovered with a simple, recreational problem.

STUDYING PROBLEM SOLVING

Unlike many areas of cognitive psychology, the study of significant problem solving requires us to examine a lengthy sample of behavior, often up to 20 or 30 minutes of activity. A major kind of data in problem solving is the **verbal protocol**, *the transcription and analysis of people's verbalizations as they solve the problem*. Without a doubt, the use of verbal protocols influenced many opinions about problem solving. In fact, the status of verbal reports as data is still a topic of some debate (see Dunlosky & Hertzog (2001); Ericsson & Simon (1980, 1993); Fleck & Weisberg (2004); and Russo, Johnson, & Stephens (1989) for a range of views).

Let's begin with a description of the classic problem-solving research of the Gestalt psychologists. As you read in Chapter 1, the Gestalt movement coexisted with behaviorism early in the 20th century but never achieved the central status that behaviorism did. In retrospect, however, it was an important influence on cognitive psychology.

By the way, possibly more than in any material you've read so far, it's important in this chapter for you to spend some time working through the examples and problems. Hints usually accompany the problems, and the solutions are presented in the text or, for numbered problems, at the end of the chapter. Many of the insights of the problem-solving literature pertain to conscious, strategic activities you'll discover on your own as you work through the sample problems. Furthermore, simply by working the examples, you'll probably improve your own problem-solving skills.

GESTALT PSYCHOLOGY AND PROBLEM SOLVING

Gestalt is a German word that translates poorly into English; the one-word translations "whole," "shape," or "field" fail to capture what the term means. Roughly speaking, a **Gestalt** is *a whole pattern, a form, or a configuration*. It is a cohesive grouping, a perspective from which the entire field can be seen. A variety of translations have been used, but none ever caught on, which prompted Boring (1950) to remark that Gestalt psychology "suffered from its name." So, we use the German term *Gestalt*, rather than an inadequate translation. Chapter 4 covered perceptual patterns that demonstrate various Gestalt principles (e.g., closure, good continuation). They show that humans tend to perceive and deal with integrated, cohesive wholes.

Early Gestalt Research

The connection between *Gestalt* psychologists and problem solving is best explained by anecdote (see Boring, 1950, pp. 595–597). In 1913, Wolfgang Köhler, a German psychologist, went to the Spanish island of Tenerife to study "the psychology of anthropoid apes" (p. 596). Trapped there by the outbreak of World War I, Köhler experimented with visual discrimination among several animal species. In the course of this research, he began to apply Gestalt principles to animal perception. His ultimate conclusion was that animals do not perceive individual elements in a stimulus, but that they perceive relations among stimuli. Furthermore, "Köhler also observed that the perception of relations is a mark of intelligence, and he called the sudden perception of useful or proper relations *insight*' (p. 596).

Still stranded on the island, Köhler continued to examine "insight learning." He presented problems to chimpanzees and searched for evidence of genuine problem solving in their behavior. By far, the most famous of his subjects was a chimpanzee named Sultan (Köhler, 1927). In a simple demonstration, Sultan was able to use a long pole to reach through the bars of his cage and get a bunch of bananas. Köhler made the situation more difficult by giving Sultan two shorter poles, neither of which was long enough to reach the bananas. After failing to get the bananas, and sulking in his cage for a while, Sultan (as the story goes) suddenly went over to the poles and put one inside the end of the other, thus creating one pole that was long enough to reach the bananas.

Köhler found this to be an apt demonstration of insight, a sudden solution to a problem by means of an insightful discovery. In another situation, Sultan discovered how to stand on a box to reach a banana that was otherwise too high to reach. In yet another, he discovered how to get a banana that was just out of reach through the cage bars: He walked *away* from the banana, out a distant door, and around the cage. All these problem solutions seemed to illustrate Sultan's perception of relations and the importance of insight in problem solving.

Grande builds a three-box structure to reach the bananas, while Sultan watches from the ground. *Insight*, sometimes referred to as an "Ah-ha" experience, was the term Kohler used for the sudden perception of useful relations among objects during problem solving.

Difficulties in Problem Solving

Other Gestalt psychologists, most notably Duncker and Luchins, pursued research with humans. Two major contributions of this work are essentially the two sides of the problem-solving coin. One involved a set of negative effects related to rigidity or difficulty in problem solving; the other, insight and creativity during problem solving.

FUNCTIONAL FIXEDNESS   Two articles on functional fixedness, one by Maier (1931) and one by Duncker (1945), identify and define this difficulty. **Functional fixedness** is *a tendency to use objects and concepts in the problem environment in only their customary and usual way.* Maier (1931), for instance, had people work on the two-string problem. Two strings are suspended from the ceiling, and the goal is to tie them together. The problem is that the strings are too far apart for a person to hold one, reach the other, then tie them together. Also available are several other objects, including a chair, some paper, and a pair of pliers. Even standing on the chair does not get the person close enough to the two strings.

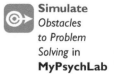

Simulate
Obstacles to Problem Solving in **MyPsychLab**

In Maier's results only 39% of the people came up with the correct solution during a 10-minute period. The solution (if you haven't tried solving the problem, do so now) involves using an object in the room in a novel way. A correct solution is to tie the pliers to one string, swing it like a pendulum, then catch it while holding the other string. Thus the functional fixedness in this situation was failing to think of the pliers in any but their customary function; people were fixed on the normal use for pliers and failed to appreciate how they could be used as a weight for a pendulum.

A similar demonstration is shown in Figure 12-1, the candle problem from Duncker (1945). The task is to find a way to mount the candle on a wall using just the objects illustrated. Can you solve the problem? If you haven't come up with a solution after a minute or two, here's a hint: Can you think of another use for a box besides using it as a container? In other words, the idea of functional fixedness is that we generally think only of the customary uses for objects, whereas successful problem solving may involve finding novel uses. By thinking of the box as a platform or means of support, you can then solve the problem (empty the box, thumbtack it to the door or wall, then mount the candle in it).

It's probably not surprising that problem solvers experience functional fixedness. After all, we comprehend the problem situation by means of our world knowledge, along with whatever procedural knowledge we have that might be relevant. When you find "PLIERS" in semantic memory, the most accessible properties involve the normal use for pliers. Far down on your list would be characteristics related to their weight or aspects of their shape that would enable you to tie a string to them. Likewise, "BOX" probably is stored in semantic memory in terms of "container" meanings—that a box can hold things, that you put things into a

FIGURE 12-1 The candle problem used by Duncker. Using only the pictured objects, figure out how to mount the candle to the wall.

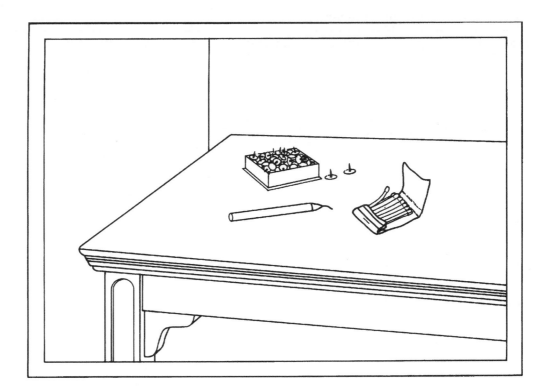

box—and not in terms of "platform or support" meanings (see Greenspan, 1986, for evidence on retrieval of central and peripheral properties). Simply from the standpoint of routine retrieval from memory, then, we can understand why people experience functional fixedness.

NEGATIVE SET   A related difficulty in problem solving is **negative set** (or simply *set effects*). This is *a bias or tendency to solve problems in a particular way, using a single specific approach, even when a different approach might be more productive*. The term *set* is a rough translation of the original German term **Einstellung**, which means something like "approach" or "orientation."

A classic demonstration of set effects comes from the water jug problem, studied by Luchins (1942). In this problem, you are given three jugs, each of a different capacity, and are to measure out a quantity of water using just the three jugs. As a simple illustration, consider the first problem in Table 12-1. You need to measure out 28 cups of water and can use containers that hold 5, 40, and 18 cups (jugs *A, B,* and *C*). The solution is to fill *A* twice, then fill *C* once, each time pouring the contents into a destination jug. This approach is an addition solution because you add the quantities together. For the second problem, a subtraction solution is appropriate: Fill *B* (127), subtract jug *C* from it twice (−3, −3), then subtract jug *A* (−21), yielding 100.

Luchins's (1942) demonstration of negative set involved sequencing the problems so that people developed a particular set or approach for measuring out the quantities. The second group of problems in Table 12-1 illustrates such a sequence. Go ahead and work the problems now before you read any further.

TABLE 12-1   Water-Jug Problems

Problem	Capacity of Jug A	Capacity of Jug B	Capacity of Jug C	Desired Quantity
1	5 cups	40 cups	18 cups	28 cups
2	21 cups	127 cups	3 cups	100 cups

Luchins's Water-Jug Problems				
Problem	Capacity of Jug A	Capacity of Jug B	Capacity of Jug C	Desired Quantity
1	21	127	3	100
2	14	163	25	99
3	18	43	10	5
4	9	42	6	21
5	20	59	4	31
6	23	49	3	20
7	15	39	3	18
8	28	76	3	25
9	18	48	4	22
10	14	36	8	6

Note. All volumes are in cups.

If you were like most people, your experience on Problems 1 through 7 led you to develop a particular approach or set: specifically, $B - 2C - A$: Fill jug B, subtract C from it twice, then subtract A from it to yield the necessary amount (subtracting A can be done before subtracting $2C$, of course). People with such a set or *Einstellung* generally failed to notice the simpler solution possible for Problems 6 and 10, simply $A - C$. That is, about 80% of the people who saw all 10 problems used the lengthy $B - 2C - A$ method for these problems. Compare this with the control participants, who saw only Problems 6 through 10: Only 1% of people used the longer method. Clearly, the control people had not developed a set for using the lengthy method, so they were better able to find the simpler solution.

Consider Problem 8 now. Only 5% of Luchins's control people failed to solve Problem 8. This was a remarkable because 64% of the "negative set" people, those who saw all 10 problems, failed to solve it correctly. These people had such a bias to use the method they had already developed that they were unable to generate a method that would solve Problem 8 ($B - 2C - A$ does not work on this problem). Greeno's (1978) description here is useful: By repeatedly solving the first seven problems with the same formula, people learned an integrated algorithm. This algorithm was strong enough to bias their later solution attempts and prevent them from seeing the simple solution, $28 - 3 = 25$. Consistent with this idea—that if people develop a routine way of solving problems then they are more likely to experience Einstellung— there is evidence that experts at a task are more prone to this than others (Bilalić, McLeod, & Gobet, 2008) because they are more likely to have developed a set of routines for solving certain kinds of problems. Also, people are less likely to show mental set effects if they are given actual water jugs as compared to just paper and pencil problems (Vallée-Tourangeau, Euden, & Hearn, 2011). Moreover, if more varied initial problems are given, then people can more easily generalize their solution to a variety of other problems (e.g., Chen & Mo, 2004).

Several problems that often yield such negative set effects are presented in Table 12-2; hints to help overcome negative set, if you experience it, are at the bottom of the table. These problems lack the precision of Luchins's demonstration, of course: We cannot point to the exact equation or method that is the negative set in these problems but only to the general approach or incorrect representation people often adopt. However, they are useful in that they resemble real-world problems more closely than the rather arbitrary water jugs do.

As the slide projector problem in the introduction suggests, functional fixedness and negative set are common occurrences. The occurrence of mental set in problem solving can result from people focusing their attention on information that is consistent with an initial solution attempt for a problem, at the expensive of other possible solutions. For example, eye tracking data reveal that people look more often at information consistent with their first solution attempt than at other information (Bilalić, McLeod, & Gobet, 2010). Possibly because we eventually find an adequate solution to our everyday problems despite the negative set or without overcoming our functional fixedness (e.g., eventually locating a thinner book), we are less aware of these difficulties in our problem-solving behavior. The classic demonstrations, however, illustrate dramatically how rigid such behavior can be and how barriers to successful problem solving can arise.

TABLE 12-2   Sample Negative Set Problems

Buddhist Monk

One morning, exactly at sunrise, a Buddhist monk began to climb a tall mountain. The narrow path, no more than a foot or two wide, spiraled around the mountain to a glittering temple at the summit. The monk ascended the path at varying rates of speed, stopping many times along the way to rest and to eat the dried fruit he carried with him. He reached the temple shortly before sunset. After several days of fasting and meditation, he began his journey back along the same path, starting at sunrise and again walking at variable speeds with many pauses along the way. His average descending speed was, of course, greater than his average climbing speed.

Show that there is a spot along the path that the monk will occupy on both trips at precisely the same time of day.

Drinking Glasses

Six drinking glasses are lined up in a row. The first three are full of water, the last three are empty. By handling and moving only one glass, change the arrangement so that no full glass is next to another full one, and no empty glass is next to another empty one.

Six Pennies

Show how to move only two pennies in the left diagram to yield the pattern at the right.

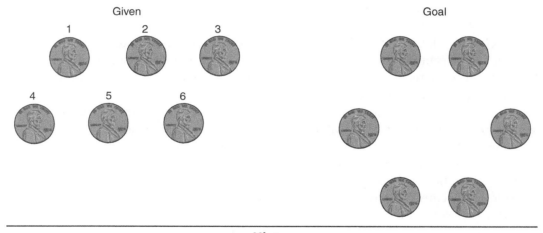

Hints

Buddhist Monk. Although the problem seems to ask for a quantitative solution, think of a way of representing the problem using visual imagery.

Drinking Glasses. How else can you handle a glass of water besides moving it to another location?

Six Pennies. From a different perspective, some of the pennies might already be in position.

Section Summary

• Cognitive psychology often studies how people solve "recreational" problems, simple brain teasers, as a way of understanding problem solving. A common kind of data collected is the verbal protocol, a transcription of the person's verbalizations as the problem is being solved.

- The early Gestalt psychologists studied problem solving and discovered two major barriers to successful performance: functional fixedness and negative set. Kohler also studied chimpanzees and found evidence for insight during problem solving.

INSIGHT AND ANALOGY

Insight

On a more positive side of problem solving are the topics of insight and problem solving by analogy. **Insight** is *a deep, useful understanding of the nature of something, especially a difficult problem.* We often include the idea that insight occurs suddenly—the "Aha!" reaction—possibly because a novel approach to the problem is taken, or a novel interpretation is made (Sternberg, 1996), or even just because you've overcome an impasse (for research on the various sources of difficulty in insight problems, see Chronicle, MacGregor, & Ormerod, 2004, and Kershaw & Ohlsson, 2004). Puzzle over the insight problems in Table 12-3 for a moment to see whether you have a sudden "Aha!" experience when you realize how to solve the problems.

Sometimes, the necessary insight for solving a problem comes from an analogy: An already-solved problem is similar to a current one, so the old solution can be adapted to the new situation. The historical example of this is the story of Archimedes, the Greek scientist who had to determine whether the king's crown was solid gold or whether some silver had been mixed with the gold. Archimedes knew the weights of both gold and silver per unit of volume but could not imagine how to measure the volume of the crown. As the anecdote goes, he stepped into his bath one day and noticed how the water level rose as he sank into the water. He then realized the solution to his problem. The volume of the crown could be determined by immersing it in water and measuring how much water it displaced. Excited by his insight, he then jumped from the bath and ran naked through the streets, shouting "Eureka! I have found it!"

Metcalfe and Wiebe (1987; also Metcalfe, 1986) studied how people solved such problems and compared that with how they solved algebra and other routine problems. They found two interesting results. First, people were rather accurate in predicting whether they'd be successful in solving routine problems but not in predicting success with insight problems. Second, solutions to the insight problems seemed to come suddenly, almost without warning. This result is shown in Figure 12-2. That is, as they worked through them, people were interrupted and asked to indicate how "warm" they were, that is, how close they felt they were to finding the solution. For routine algebra problems, "warmth" ratings grew steadily as people worked through the problems, reflecting their feeling of getting closer and closer to the solution. But there was little or no such increase for the insight problems even 15 seconds before the solution was found.

Although these results support the idea that insight arrives suddenly, insight problems can be thought of in simpler terms, say overcoming functional fixedness or negative set (as in prisoner's escape and nine-dot), taking a different perspective

TABLE 12-3 Insight Problems

Chain Links

A woman has four pieces of chain. Each piece is made up of three links. She wants to join the pieces into a single closed ring of chain. To open a link costs 2 cents and to close a link costs 3 cents. She has only 15 cents. How does she do it?

Four Trees

A landscape gardener is given instructions to plant four special trees so that each one is exactly the same distance from each of the others. How would you arrange the trees?

Prisoner's Escape

A prisoner was attempting to escape from a tower. He found in his cell a rope which was half long enough to permit him to reach the ground safely. He divided the rope in half and tied the two parts together and escaped. How could he have done this?

Bronze Coin

A stranger approached a museum curator and offered him an ancient bronze coin. The coin had an authentic appearance and was marked with the date 544 B.C. The curator had happily made acquisitions from suspicious sources before, but this time he promptly called the police and had the stranger arrested. Why?

Nine Dots

Connect the nine dots with four connected straight lines without lifting your pencil from the page as you draw.

Bowling Pins

The ten bowling pins below are pointing toward the top of the page. Move any three of them to make the arrangement point down toward the bottom of the page.

Hints

Chain links. You don't have to open a link on each piece of chain.
Four trees. We don't always plant trees on flat lawns.
Prisoner's escape. Is there only one way to divide a rope in half?
Bronze coin. Imagine that you lived in 544 B.C. What did it say on your coins?
Nine dots. How long a line does the problem permit you to draw?
Bowling pins. Pins 1, 2, 3, and 5 form a diamond at the top of the drawing. Consider where the diamond might be for the arrangement that points down.

Adapted from Metcalfe (1986) and Metcalfe & Wiebe (1987).

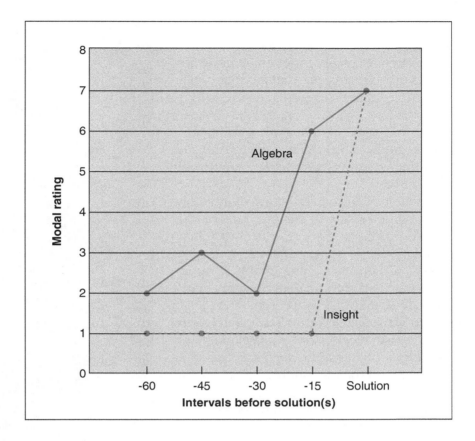

FIGURE 12-2
Modal (most frequent) warmth rating in the four time periods leading up to a problem solution.

Data from Metcalfe & Wiebe (1987).

(bronze coin), and the like (Smith, 1995). A neuroimaging study by Kounios et al. (2006) provides some support for this idea. Using both electroencephalographic and functional magnetic resonance imaging recordings, they found increased cortical activity centered on the frontal lobes (particularly the anterior cingulate cortex) when people produced insight solutions as compared to normal problem solving. Kounios et al.'s theory is that this part of the frontal lobe suppresses the irrelevant information (an attentional process; see Chapter 4) that tends to dominate a person's thinking up to that point. When these dominant thoughts become suppressed, this allows more weakly activated ideas, such as those remote associations drawn by the right hemisphere, to come to the fore, possibly providing the solution to a problem. In other words, part of a person's thought processes are working on the problem along with the steps that are being worked on at the forefront of consciousness (which are going nowhere). When these dead-end thoughts are moved aside, alternative solutions can then present themselves.

This release from irrelevant modes of thinking, seen in the neuroimaging data, can be extended to a process called *incubation*. With incubation, when people have difficulty solving a problem, they may stop working on it for a while. Then at some point, the solution or key to a solution may present itself to them. Although this can work at times, it appears that incubation is most useful when people have originally been provided with misleading information, either by others or themselves, that steers them away from the correct solution. What happens during incubation is that the representations for these misleading ideas lose strength, so that later on the more successful alternatives can then present themselves (Vul & Pashler, 2007).

In some circumstances, *insight* may mean that we've drawn a critical inference that leads to a solution; for example, there's more than one way to divide a rope in half (Wickelgren, 1974). Weisberg (1995) reports that some people solve insight problems like those in the table without any of the sudden restructuring or understanding that supposedly accompanies insight.

Other evidence, however, suggests that verbalization can interfere with insight, can disrupt "nonreportable processes that are critical to achieving insight solutions" (Schooler, Ohlsson, & Brooks, 1993, p. 166). Furthermore, being unable to report the restructuring that accompanies insight, or the actual insight itself, may be more common in insight situations than we realize. For instance, Siegler and Stern (1998; see also Siegler, 2000) reported a study of second-graders solving arithmetic problems, then reporting verbally on their solutions. There was the regular computational, noninsightful way to solve the problems, which the second-graders followed, but also a shortcut way that represented an insight (e.g., for a problem like $18 + 24 - 24$, simply state 18). Almost 90% of the sample discovered the insight for solving such problems, as shown by the dramatic decrease in their solution times from around 12 seconds for the computational method to a mean of 2.7 seconds with the shortcut. However, the children were unaware of their discovery when questioned about how they solved the problems. Within another five trials, however, 80% of the children's verbal reports indicated that they were aware of their discovery.

Sometimes we can take a long time to figure out a problem, but with effort, the passage of time, and insight, we can reach sometimes stunning and novel conclusions.

Analogy

In general, an **analogy** is *a relationship between two similar situations, problems, or concepts.* Understanding an analogy means putting the two situations into some kind of alignment so that the similarities and differences are made apparent (Gentner & Markman, 1997). Take a simple example, the analogy "MERCHANT : SELL :: CUSTOMER : _____." Here, you must figure out the structure for the first pair of terms and then project or *map* that structure onto the second part of the analogy. Because "SELL" is the critical activity of "MERCHANT," the critical activity relationship is then mapped onto "CUSTOMER," and retrieval from memory yields "BUY."

Researchers argue that analogies provide excellent, widely applicable methods for solving problems. That is, if you're confronted with a difficult problem, a useful heuristic is to find a similar or related situation and build an analogy from it to the current problem. Such reasoning and problem solving may help us understand a variety of situations, such as how students should be taught in school, how people adopt professional role models, and how we empathize with others (Holyoak & Thagard, 1997; Kolodner, 1997). Furthermore, it's long been held that important scientific ideas, breakthroughs, and explanations have often depended on finding analogies—for instance, that neurotransmitters fit into the receptor sites of a neuron much the way a key fits into a lock (see Gentner & Markman, 1997, for a description of reasoning by analogy in Kepler's discovery of the laws of planetary motion). Curiously, analogical problem solving is better when people receive the information by hearing about it rather than reading it (Markman, Taylor, & Gentner, 2007), perhaps reflecting the more natural use of spoken over written language.

ANALOGY PROBLEMS   To gain some feeling for analogies, read the parade story at the top of Table 12-4, a story used by Gick and Holyoak (1980). Try to solve the problem now, before reading the solution at the bottom of the table.

Gick and Holyoak had people read the parade problem, a somewhat different army fortress story, or no story at all. They then asked them to read and solve a second problem, the classic Duncker (1945) radiation problem, shown in Table 12-5 (which you should read and try to solve now).

The radiation problem is interesting for a variety of reasons, including the fact that it is rather ill defined and thus comparable to many problems in the real world. Duncker's participants produced two general approaches that led to dead

---

TABLE 12-4   The Parade Problem

A dictator ruled over a small country. He ruled from a strong fortress. The fortress was located in the center of the country, surrounded by numerous towns, villages, and farms. Like spokes on a wheel, many roads radiated out from the fortress. As part of a celebration of his glorious grab of power, this dictator demanded from one of his generals a large, over-the-top parade of his military might. The general's troops were assembled for the march in the morning, the day of the anniversary, at the end of one of these roads that led up to the dictator's fortress. At that time, the general was given a report by one of his captains that brought him up short. As commanded by the dictator, this parade needed to be far more spectacular and impressive than any other parade that had ever been seen in the land (or else). The dictator demanded that everyone in every region of the country see and hear his army at the same time. Given this demand, it seemed nearly impossible for the general to have the whole country see the parade as requested.

The Solution

The general, however, knew just what to do. He divided his army up into small groups and dispatched each group to the head of a different road. When all was ready he gave the signal, and each group marched down a different road. Each group continued down its road to the fortress, so that the entire army finally arrived together at the fortress at the same time. In this way, the general was able to have the parade seen and heard through the entire country at once, and thus please the dictator.

TABLE 12-5   Radiation and Attack Dispersion Problems

Radiation Problem

Suppose you are a doctor faced with a patient who has a malignant tumor in his stomach. It is impossible to operate on the patient, but unless the tumor is destroyed the patient will die. There is a kind of ray that can be used to destroy the tumor. If the rays reach the tumor all at once at a sufficiently high intensity, the tumor will be destroyed. Unfortunately, at this intensity the healthy tissue that the rays pass through on the way to the tumor will also be destroyed. At lower intensities the rays are harmless to healthy tissue, but they will not affect the tumor either. What type of procedure might be used to destroy the tumor with the rays without destroying the healthy tissue?

Attack Dispersion Story

A small country was controlled by a dictator. The dictator ruled the country from a strong fortress. The fortress was situated in the middle of the country, surrounded by farms and villages. Many roads radiated outward from the fortress like spokes on a wheel. A general arose who raised a large army and vowed to capture the fortress and free the country of the dictator. The general knew that if his entire army could attack the fortress at once, it could be captured. The general's troops were gathered at the head of one of the roads leading to the fortress, ready to attack. However, a spy brought the general a disturbing report. The ruthless dictator had planted mines on each of the roads. The mines were set so that small bodies of men could pass over them safely because the dictator needed to be able to move troops and workers to and from the fortress. However, any large force would detonate the mines. Not only would this blow up the road and render it impassable, but the dictator would then destroy many villages in retaliation. It therefore seemed impossible to mount a full-scale direct attack on the fortress.

Solution to the Radiation Problem

The ray can be divided into several low-intensity rays, no one of which will destroy the healthy tissue. If these several rays are positioned at different locations around the body and focused on the tumor, their effect will combine, thus being strong enough to destroy the tumor.

Solution to the Attack Dispersion Story

The general, however, knew just what to do. He divided his army up into small groups and dispatched each group to the head of a different road. When all was ready he gave the signal, and each group marched down a different road. Each group continued down its road to the fortress, so that the entire army finally arrived together at the fortress at the same time. In this way, the general was able to capture the fortress and thus overthrow the dictator.

ends: trying to avoid contact between the ray and nearby tissue, and trying to change the sensitivity of surrounding tissue to the effects of the ray. But the third approach, reducing the intensity of the rays, was more productive, especially if an analogy from some other, better understood situation was available.

Gick and Holyoak (1980) used this problem to study analogy. In fact, we've just simulated one of their experiments here by having you read the parade story first and then the radiation problem. In case you didn't notice, there are strong similarities between the problems, suggesting that the parade story can be used to develop an analogy for the radiation problem.

Gick and Holyoak found that 49% of people who first solved the parade problem realized it could be used as an analogy for the radiation problem. A different initial story, in which armies are attacking a fortress, provided a stronger hint about the radiation problem. Fully 76% of these participants used the attack analogy in solving the radiation problem. In contrast, only 8% of the control group, which merely attempted to solve the radiation problem, came up with the dispersion solution (i.e., multiple pathways) described at the bottom of Table 12-5.

When Gick and Holyoak provided a strong hint, telling people that the attack solution might be helpful as they worked on the radiation problem, 92% of them used the analogy, and most found it "very helpful." In contrast, only 20% of the people in the no-hint group produced the dispersion solution, even though they too had read the attack dispersion story. In short, only 20% spontaneously noticed and used the analogous relationship between the problems. Table 12-6 summarizes Gick and Holyoak's results.

MULTICONSTRAINT THEORY   Holyoak and Thagard (1997) proposed a theory of analogical reasoning and problem solving, based on such results. The theory, called the multiconstraint theory, predicts how people use analogies in problem solving and what factors govern the analogies people construct. In particular, the theory says that people are constrained by three factors when they try to use or develop analogies.

The first factor is problem similarity. There must be some degree of similarity between the already-understood situation, the *source* domain, and the current

TABLE 12-6   Summary of Gick and Holyoak's (1980) Results

Study 1 (Experiment II originally; after Gick & Holyoak, Table 10)

People in groups A and B are given a general hint that their solution to one of the earlier stories may be useful in solving the radiation problem.

Group	Order of Stories	Percentage of People Who Used the Analogy on the Radiation Problem
Group A	Parade, radiation	49%
Group B	Attack dispersion, radiation	76%
Group C	No story, radiation	8%

Study 2 (Experiment IV originally)

People in group A are given the general hint (as above). People in group B are given no hint whatsoever.

Group	Order of Stories	Percentage of People Who Used the Analogy on the Radiation Problem
Group A (hint)	Attack dispersion, radiation	92%
Group B (no hint)	Attack dispersion, radiation	20%

problem, the *target* domain. In the parade story, for example, the fortress and troops are similar to the tumor and the rays. Similarity between source and target has been shown to be important. Chen, Mo, and Honomichl (2004), for example, found that similarities from well-known folk tales to new problems were especially important for finding problem solutions, even if participants did not report remembering the folk tale. Alternatively, Novick (1988) found that novices focus especially on similarities, even when they are only superficial, which can interfere with performance.

The second factor is problem structure. People must find a parallel structure between the source and target problems to map elements from the source to elements in the target. Figuring out these correspondences or mappings is important because it corresponds to working out the relationships of the analogy. In the parade–radiation analogy, you have to map troops onto rays so that the important relationship of different converging roads can serve as the basis for the solution. The most prominent mappings from parade to radiation are shown in Figure 12-3. It turns out that mapping the relations is hard; for instance, in a dual-task setting, Waltz, Lau, Grewal, and Holyoak (2000) found that holding on to a working memory load seriously reduced the ability to find correct mappings between two problems. Also, Bassok, Pedigo, and Oskarsson (2008) found that the semantic memory can interfere with drawing analogies. For example, when people are doing addition-based word problems, making the analogy between the word problem and addition was easier when items are semantically similar, such as *tulips* and *daisies* (which are separate things that can easily be added together), but not when there is an inconsistency, such as *records* and *songs*. In this case, the knowledge that songs are parts of records implies a hierarchical, part-whole relationship, so it is more difficult to make the additional analogy where is it easier to think of things that can be treated on more equal footing.

The third factor that constrains people is the purpose of the analogy. The person's goals, and the goal stated in the problem, are important. This is deeper

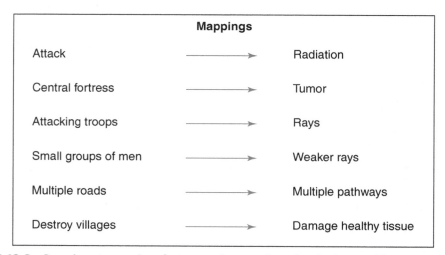

FIGURE 12-3 Prominent mappings between the attack and radiation problems.

than merely the general purpose of trying to solve the problem. Notice that the goals in the attack and radiation stories match, whereas the goals do not match for parade and radiation (parade involves sending troops *out* from the central fortress, for display purposes, but radiation involves sending rays *in* toward the tumor). This mismatch may have been responsible for the low use of parade as a source for the analogy to radiation. Likewise, Spellman and Holyoak (1996) report a study in which college students drew analogies between two soap opera plots. When different purposes or goals were given in the instructions, the students developed different analogies; that is, their problem solving by analogy was sensitive to purposes and overall goals. Kurtz and Loewenstein (2007) reported that people are more likely to draw on analogies from previous problems when they are comparing two other problems than if they are working on a single problem alone. This suggests that the processing goals and tactics, in this case direct comparison, in use can influence whether people actually use analogies or not.

A final point is that most of the work on analogy, like many studies of problem solving, has focused on the conscious, explicit use of analogies. However, there is some evidence to suggest that people may use analogies in a more unconscious, implicit manner as well. In a study by Day and Gentner (2007), people were given pairs of texts to read. When the events described by the second text were analogous to those described in the first (in terms of their relational structure), people read the second text faster. That is, people were able to use their unconscious knowledge of the event structure from the first text to help them understand the second text. When asked, people showed no awareness of this relationship between the two texts. So, in some sense, by having people read the first text, the relational structure of the event was primed, and this made the processing of the second text easier.

Neurocognition in Analogy and Insight

Some exciting work has been reported on the cognitive neuropsychology of analogical reasoning and insight. Wharton et al. (2000) identified brain regions that are associated with the mapping process in analogical reasoning. In their study, people saw a source picture of geometric shapes, followed by a target picture. They had to judge whether the target picture was an analog pattern—whether it had the same system of relations as the source picture. In the control condition, they judged whether the target was literally the same as the source. See Figure 12-4 for sample stimuli. In the top stimulus, the correct target preserves both the spatial relations in the source (a shape in all four quadrants) and the object relations (the patterned figures on the main diagonal are the same shape, and the shapes on the minor diagonal are different). Response times to analogy trials were in the 1,400 to 1,500 ms range and approximately 900 to 1,000 ms in the literal condition; accuracy was at or above 90% in both kinds of trials.

But the stunning result came from positron emission tomography (PET) scan images that were taken. Wharton et al. found significant activation in the medial frontal cortex, left prefrontal cortex, and left inferior parietal cortex.

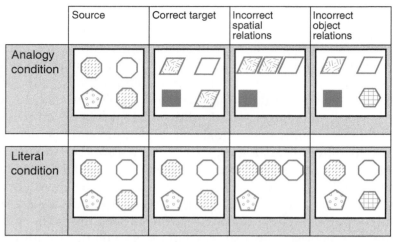

FIGURE 12-4 A depiction of analogy condition and literal condition trials. The first column shows the source stimuli, the second shows the correct choice, and the third and fourth show incorrect choices for the stated reasons.

From Wharton et al. (2000), Figure 2, p. 179.

Explore
Intuition and Discovery in Problem Solving in **MyPsychLab**

In contrast, Bowden and Beeman (1998; Beeman & Bowden, 2000) found a significant role for *right* hemisphere processing in solving insight problems. Before reading further, try this demonstration:

> *What one word can form a compound word or phrase with each of the following? Palm Shoe House*

> *What one word can form a compound word or phrase with each of the following? Pie Luck Belly?*

People were given such word triples—called "compound remote associates"—and had to think of a fourth word that combines with each of the three initial words to yield a familiar word pair. On many trials, people fail to find an immediate solution and end up spending considerable time working on the problem. They also report that when they finally solve the problems, the solution came to them as an insight—an "Aha!" type of solution.

In the Bowden and Beeman (1998) study, people saw the problems and then after 15 seconds were asked to name a new word that appeared on the screen (if they solved the problem before the 15-second period was up, they were given the word immediately). When the target word was unrelated to the three words seen before (e.g., "planet"), there was the typical effect—that targets presented to the right visual field, hence the left hemisphere of the brain, were named faster than those presented to the left visual field–right hemisphere. But when the target was the word that solved the insight problem (*tree* in the first problem, *pot* in the second one), there was a significant priming effect. As shown in Figure 12-5, naming time was shorter for the solution words than for the unrelated words. And the priming effect—the drop-off from "unrelated" to "solution"—was greater for targets presented to the right hemisphere than to the left (in other words, presented to the left visual field so going first to the right hemisphere).

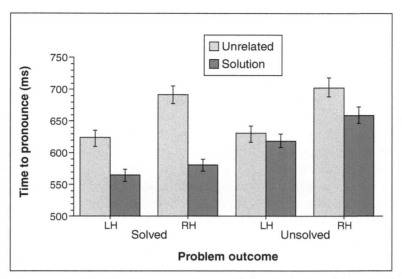

FIGURE 12-5   Mean naming time (time to pronounce) the target word for solved and unsolved trials. Bars labeled LH refer to target words presented to the right visual field, left hemisphere of the brain; RH means left visual field, right hemisphere. The figure shows priming effects for solution words, especially in the right hemisphere.

From Bowden & Beeman (1998).

Putting it differently, semantic priming in the right hemisphere was more prominent than in the left hemisphere for these problems: People were faster to name *pot* when it was presented to the right hemisphere, presumably because it had been primed by the initial three words. As the authors noted, these results fit nicely with other results concerning the role in language comprehension that the right hemisphere plays (you read about this in Chapter 10), especially the part having to do with drawing inferences (Bowden, Beeman, & Gernsbacher, 1995).

Section Summary

- Insight is a deep understanding of a situation or problem, often thought to occur suddenly and without warning. Although there is some debate on the nature of insight, insights may be discovered and used unconsciously and only later be available to consciousness.
- Reasoning by analogy is a complex kind of problem solving in which relationships in one situation are mapped onto another. People are better at developing analogies if given a useful source problem and an explicit hint that the problem might be used in solving a target problem. Holyoak and Thagard's multiconstraint theory of analogical problem solving claims that we work under three constraints as we develop analogies: constraints related to the similarity of the source and target domains, the structure of the problems, and our purposes or goals in developing the analogies.
- Some new evidence suggests a particularly important role for the left frontal and parietal lobes in solving problems by analogy and a right hemisphere role in insight problems involving semantic priming.

BASICS OF PROBLEM SOLVING

Compared to the Gestalt tradition, modern cognitive psychology has adopted a more reductionistic approach to the study of problem solving. For instance, Newell and Simon's analysis of a cryptarithmetic problem (1972, Chapter 6) is a microscopic analysis and interpretation of every statement made by one person as he solved a problem, all 2,186 words and 20 or so minutes of problem-solving activity. In Newell and Simon's (1972) description, "A person is confronted with a *problem* when he wants something and does not know immediately what series of actions he can perform to get it" (p. 72). The "something" can be renamed for more general use as a **goal**, *the desired end-point of the problem-solving activity.* Problem solving consists of goal-directed activity, moving from some initial configuration or state through a series of intermediate steps until finally the overall goal has been reached: an adequate or correct solution. The difficulty is determining which intermediate states are on a correct pathway ("Will step *A* get me to step *B* or not?") and in devising operations or moves that achieve those intermediate states ("How do I get to step *B* from here?").

Characteristics of Problem Solving

Let's start by listing several characteristics that define what is and is not a genuine instance of problem solving. Anderson (1980, 1985), for example, lists the following:

- *Goal directedness.* The overall activity we're examining is directed toward achieving some goal or purpose. As such, we exclude daydreaming, for instance; it's mental, but it's not goal directed. Alternatively, if you've locked your keys in your car, both physical and mental activity are going on. The goal-directed nature of those activities, your repeated attempts to get into the locked car, makes this an instance of true problem solving.
- *Sequence of operations.* An activity must have a sequence of operations or steps to be problem solving. A simple retrieval from memory, say, remembering that 2×3 is 6, is not problem solving because it is not a slow, discernible sequence of separate operations. Alternatively, doing a long-division problem or solving the locked-car problem definitely involves a sequence of mental operations, so these are instances of problem solving.
- *Cognitive operations.* Solving the problem involves the application of various cognitive operations. Various operators can be applied to different problems, where each operator is a distinct cognitive act, a permissible step or move in the problem space. For long division, retrieving an answer would be an operator, as would be subtracting or multiplying two numbers at some other stage in problem solution. Often, the cognitive operations have a behavioral counterpart, some physical act that completes the mental operation, such as writing down a number during long division.
- *Subgoal decomposition.* As implied by the third characteristic, each step in the sequence of operations is itself a kind of goal, a **subgoal**. A subgoal is *an intermediate goal along the route to eventual solution of the problem.* Subgoals represent the decomposition, or breaking apart, of the overall goal into separate components. In many instances, subgoals themselves must be

further decomposed into smaller subgoals. Thus solving a problem involves breaking the overall goal into subgoals, then pursuing the subgoals, and *their* subgoals, one after another until the final solution is achieved. This yields a hierarchical or nested structure to the problem-solving attempt.

An intuitive illustration of such a nested solution structure is presented in Figure 12-6, a possible solution route to the locked-car problem. Note that during the solution, the first two plans led to barriers or blocks, thus requiring that another plan be devised (much like the radiation problem). The problem solver finally decided on another plan, breaking a window to get into the locked car. This decision is followed by a sequence of related acts: the search for some heavy object that will break a window, the decision as to which window to break, and so forth. Each of these decisions is a subgoal nested within the larger subgoal of breaking into the car, itself a subgoal in the overall solution structure.

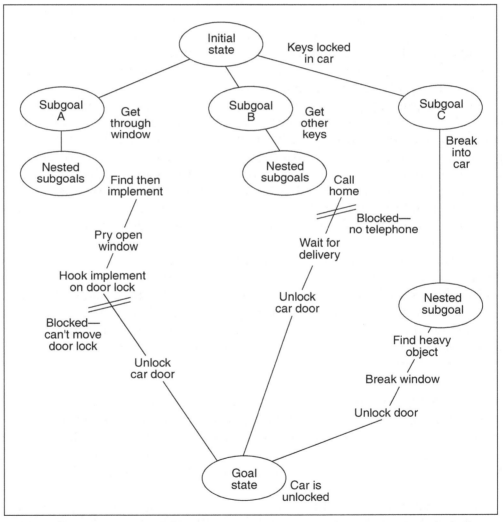

FIGURE 12-6 A representation of part of the problem space for getting into a locked car. Note the barriers encountered under plans *A* and *B*.

A Vocabulary of Problem Solving

These four characteristics define what qualifies as problem solving. Many important ideas are embedded in these four points, however. Let's reexamine some of these points, looking now toward an expanded vocabulary of problem solving, a set of terms we use to describe and understand how people solve problems.

THE PROBLEM SPACE   The term *problem space* is critical. Anderson (1985) defines it as the various states or conditions that are possible. More concretely, the **problem space** includes *the initial, intermediate, and goal states of the problem. It also includes the problem solver's knowledge at each of these steps,* both knowledge that is currently being applied and knowledge that could be retrieved from memory and applied. Any external devices, objects, or resources that are available can also be included in the description of the problem space. Thus, a difficult arithmetic problem that must be completed mentally has a different problem space than the same problem as completed with pencil and paper.

To illustrate, VanLehn (1989) describes one man's error in the "three men and a rowboat" problem. The man focused only on the arithmetic of the problem and said essentially "400 pounds of people, 200 pounds per trip, it'll take two trips of the boat." When he was reminded that the boat couldn't row itself back to the original side, he adopted a different problem space.

In some problem contexts, we can speak of problem solving as a search of the problem space or, metaphorically, a search of the solution tree, in which each branch and twig represents a possible pathway from the initial state of the problem. For problems that are "wide open," that is, those with many possibilities that must be checked, there may be no alternative but to start searching the problem space, node by node, until some barrier or block is reached. As often as not, however, there is information in the problem that permits us to restrict the search space to a manageable size. Metaphorically, this information permits us to *prune* the search tree.

A general depiction of this is in Figure 12-7. The initial state of the problem is the top node, and the goal state is some terminal node at the bottom. For "wide open" problems, each branch may need to be searched until a dead end is encountered. For other problems, information may be inferred that permits a restriction in the branches that are searched (the shaded area of the figure). Clearly, if the search space can be restricted by pruning off the dead-end branches, then problem-solving efficiency is increased.

THE OPERATORS   **Operators** are *the set of legal moves that can be done during problem solution.* The term *legal* means permissible in the rules of the problem. For example, an illegal operator in the six-penny problem of Table 12-2 would be to move more than two pennies. In "three men and a rowboat," an illegal operator is having the men swim across the river or loading the boat with too heavy a load.

For transformation problems (Greeno, 1978), applying an operator transforms the problem into a new or revised state from which further work can be done. In general, a legal operator moves you from one node to the next along

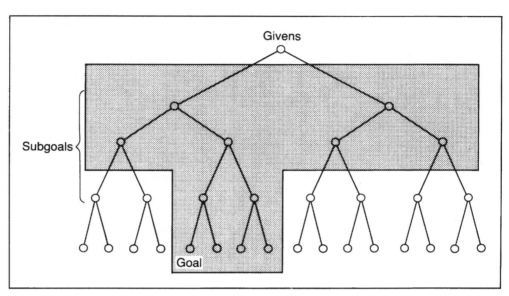

FIGURE 12-7 A general diagram of a problem space, with various branches of the space illustrated. Often a hint or an inference can prune the search tree, restricting the search to just one portion; this idea is represented by the shaded area of the figure. Note that, in most problems, the problem space tree is much larger, so the beneficial effect of pruning is far greater.

Adapted from Wickelgren (1974).

some connecting pathway in the search space. For instance, in solving algebraic equations, one transformation operator is "move the unknowns to the left." Thus for the equation $2X + 7 = X + 10$, applying the operator would move the single X to the left of the equal sign by subtracting X from both sides of the equation.

Often, constraints within the problem prevent us from applying certain operators. In a vague way, the destruction of healthy tissue was such a constraint in the radiation problem. That constraint prevented the simple solution of applying the ray directly, where direct application would be a simple operator. In algebra, by contrast, constraints are imposed by the rules of algebra; for example, you can't subtract X from one side of the equation without subtracting it from the other side, too.

THE GOAL The goal is the ultimate destination or solution to the problem. For recreational problems in particular, the goal is typically stated explicitly in the problem. Given that recreational problems usually present *an explicit and complete specification of the initial and goal states,* we call them as **well-defined problems**. Solutions involve progressing through the legal intermediate states, by means of known operators, until the goal is reached. In contrast, in **ill-defined problems,** *the states, operators, or both may be only vaguely specified.* For instance, the Buddhist monk problem in Table 12-2 states a vague goal ("Show that there is a spot . . ."). Likewise, problems with more real-world character often are distressingly vague in their specification of the goal ("write a term paper that will earn you an *A,*" "write a computer program that does X in as economical and elegant a fashion as possible," and so on).

AN EXAMPLE: DONALD + GERALD Let's consider one recreational problem, to pin down some of these terms and ideas. The problem is a cryptarithmetic problem, in which letters of the alphabet have been substituted for the digits in an addition problem. Your task is to reverse the substitutions—to figure out which digits go with which letters to yield a correct addition problem. The restriction is that the digits and letters must be in one-to-one correspondence (only one digit per letter and vice versa). Plan on spending 15 minutes or so, about the amount of time it takes people on their first attempt. Make notes on paper as you work so you can go back later to retrace and analyze your attempt to solve the problem. (Incidentally, this is the cryptarithmetic problem Newell and Simon's single person worked on.)

$$DONALD \qquad (Hint: D = 5)$$
$$+ \ GERALD$$
$$\overline{ROBERT}$$

Now that you've worked on the problem and have found (or come close to) the solution, we can use the insights you developed to fill in our definitions of terms. To begin with, the initial state consists of the statement of the problem, including the rules, restrictions, and hint you are given. These, along with your own knowledge of arithmetic (and pencil and paper), are your problem-solving tools. Each conceivable assignment of letters to digits makes up the problem space, and each substitution operator you might apply constitutes a branch or pathway on the search tree (a substitution operator here is an operator that substitutes a digit for a letter). Like the shaded area of Figure 12-7, the hint $D = 5$ prunes the search tree by a tremendous amount. Without the hint, you can only start working on the problem by trying arbitrary assignments, then working until an error shows up, then returning to an earlier node and reassigning the letters to different digits. (Even without the hint, however, there is only one solution.)

You no doubt started working on the problem by replacing the Ds in the 1s column with 5s, then immediately replacing the T with a 0. You also probably wrote a 1 above the 10s column, for the carry operation from $5 + 5$. A quick scan revealed one more D that could be rewritten. Note that the position you were in at this point, with three Ds and a T converted to digits, is a distinct step in the solution, an intermediate state in the problem, a node in the problem space. Furthermore, each substitution you made reflected the application of an operator, a cognitive operation that transforms the problem to a different intermediate state.

As you continued to work, you were forced to infer information as a way of making progress. For instance, in working on the 10s column, $L + L +$ the carried 1, you can infer that R is an odd number because any number added to itself and augmented by 1 yields an odd number. Likewise, you can infer from the $D + G$ column that R must be in the range 5 to 9 and that $5 + G$ can't produce a carried 1. Putting these together, R must be a large odd number, and G must be 4 or less. Each of these separate inferences, each mental conclusion you draw, is also an instance of a cognitive operation, a simple mental process or operator

TABLE 12-7   Intermediate

State	Known Values	Reasons and Statements from Protocol
1 5ONAL5 <u>GERAL5</u> ROBERØ	Ø123456789 T D R is odd	Because D is 5, then T = Ø, and carry a 1 to the next column. So the first column is 5 + something = odd because L + L + 1 = R will make R odd
	G is less than 5 R is odd and greater than 5	R must be bigger than 5 because less than 5 would yield a two-digit sum in the D + G column and there would be an extra column in the answer. G is less than 5.
1 1 5ONAL5 <u>G9RA15</u> ROB9RØ	Ø123456789 T D E G is less than 5 R is odd, greater than 5	O + E is next. If E were Ø, it would be fine, but T is already Ø So this column must have a carry brought to it. This means that E must be 9, so that the O + 9 + the carried 1 = O.
1 11 5ONAL5 <u>G9RAL5</u> ROB9RØ		If E = 9, then A + A must have a carry brought to it, so then the A + A + the carried 1 = 9. 4 would work for A and so would 9, but 9 is already taken
1 11 5ON4L5 <u>G9R4L5</u> ROB9RØ	Ø123456789 T AD E R is odd, greater than 5 G is less than 5 L is greater than 5	So A has to be 4. So L + L + the carried 1 has to produce a carry, so L is greater than 5. 5 and 9 are taken.
1 11 5ON4L5 <u>G974L5</u> 7OB97Ø	Ø123456789 T AD R E G is less than 5, L is greater than 5	So the odd R must be 7. Because L + L yields a carry, L isn't 3.
11 11 5ON485 <u>G97485</u> 7OB97Ø	Ø123456789 T AD RLE N is greater than or equal to 3 G is less than 5	L must be 8 because 8 + 8 + 1 = 17. That only leaves O, N, G, and B. Because O + 9 needs a carry, N + 7 has to yield a carry. So N has to be at least 3.
11 11 5ON485 <u>197485</u> 7OB97Ø	Ø123456789 TG AD RLE N is greater than or equal to 3	So G looks like 1. That leaves O, N, and B, for 2, 3, and 6. N can't be 3 because B can't be the Ø in 3 + 7 = 1Ø And it can't be 2 because 2 + 7 = 9 and the 9 is taken.
11 11 5O6485 <u>197485</u> 7O397Ø	Ø123456789 TGBADNRLE	That leaves N to be 6, so that makes B = 3.
11 11 526485 <u>197485</u> 723970	Ø123456789 TGOBADNRLE	So O has to be 2. Check the addition.

A sample solution of the DONALD problem, showing intermediate states, known values, and an edited protocol. (Zero is drawn with the slash, Ø, to distinguish it from the letter O.)

TABLE 12-8	Additional Cryptarithmetic Problems				
6.	CROSS	7.	LETS	8.	SEND
	+ ROADS		+ WAVE		+ MORE
	DANGER		LATER		MONEY
Hint: $R = 6$					

that composes a step in the problem-solving sequence. Each of these, furthermore, accomplishes progress toward the immediate subgoal, find out about *L*.

Greeno (1978) calls this process a constructive search. Rather than blindly assigning digits and trying them out, people usually draw inferences from the other columns and use those to limit the possible values the letters can take. This approach is typical in arrangement problems, the third of Greeno's categories, in which some combination of the given components must be found that satisfies the constraints in the problem. In other kinds of arrangement problems, say anagrams, a constructive search heuristic would be to look for spelling patterns and form candidate words from those familiar units. The opposite approach, sometimes known as generate and test, merely uses some scheme to generate all possible arrangements, then tests those one by one to determine whether the problem solution has been found.

A related aspect of problem solving here (it can be postponed, but your solution will be more organized if it's done now) is quite general and almost constitutes good advice rather than an essential feature of performance. Some mechanism or system for keeping track of the information you know about the letters is needed, if only to prevent you from forgetting inferences you've already drawn. Indeed, such an external memory aid can go a long way toward making your problem solving more efficient. In some instances it may even help you generalize from one problem variant to another (as in the next example, the Tower of Hanoi problem). Table 12-7 presents a compressed verbal protocol of the solution to the DONALD problem, which you might want to compare with your own solution pathway. The table also shows intermediate steps and a notational system for keeping track of known values. Table 12-8 presents more cryptarithmetic problems that you might want to solve.

Section Summary

- We are solving a problem when our behavior is goal directed and involves a sequence of cognitive steps or stages. The sequence involves separate cognitive operations, where each goal or subgoal can be decomposed into separate, smaller subgoals. The overall problem, including our knowledge, is called the problem space, within which we apply operators, draw inferences, and conduct a constructive search for moves that bring us closer to the goal.

MEANS–END ANALYSIS: A FUNDAMENTAL HEURISTIC

Several problem solving heuristics have been discovered and investigated. You've already read about analogy, and the final section of the chapter illustrates several others. But in terms of overall significance, no other heuristic comes close to means–end analysis. This formed the basis for Newell and Simon's groundbreaking work (1972), including their very first presentation of the information-processing framework in 1956 (on the "day cognitive psychology was born"; see footnote 2 in Chapter 1). Because it shaped the entire area and the theories devised to account for problem solving, it deserves special attention.

The Basics of Means–End Analysis

In this **means–end analysis** approach, *the problem is solved by repeatedly determining the difference between the current state and the goal or subgoal state, then finding and applying an operator that reduces this difference.* Means–end analysis nearly always implies the use of subgoals because achieving the goal state usually involves the intermediate steps of achieving several subgoals along the way.

The basic notions of a means–end analysis can be summarized in a sequence of five steps:

1. *Set up a goal or subgoal.*
2. *Look for a difference between the current state and the goal or subgoal state.*
3. *Look for an operator that will reduce or eliminate this difference. One such operator is the setting of a new subgoal.*
4. *Apply the operator.*
5. *Apply steps 2 through 4 repeatedly until all subgoals and the final goal are achieved.*

At an intuitive level, means–end analysis and subgoals are familiar and represent "normal" problem solving. If you have to write a term paper for class, you break the overall goal down into a series of subgoals: Select a topic, find relevant material, read and understand the material, and so on. Each of these may contain its own subgoals.

The Tower of Hanoi

The most thoroughly investigated problems are the missionary–cannibals problem in Table 12-9 (it's also known as the Hobbits–Orcs problem) and the Tower of

---

TABLE 12-9   The Missionary–Cannibal Problem

Three missionaries and three cannibals are on one side of a river and need to cross to the other side. The only means of crossing is a boat, and the boat can hold only two people at a time. Devise a set of moves that will transport all six people across the river, bearing in mind the following constraint: The number of cannibals can never exceed the number of missionaries in any location, for the obvious reason. Remember that someone will have to row the boat back across each time.

Hint: At one point in your solution, you will have to send more people back to the original side than you just sent over to the destination.

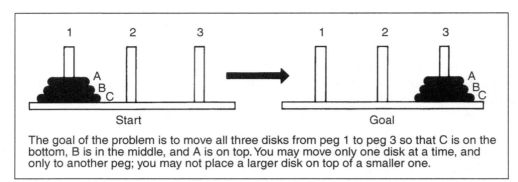

FIGURE 12-8   The Tower of Hanoi problem.

Hanoi problem in Figure 12-8. These problems show clearly the strengths and limitations of the means–end approach.

THE THREE-DISK VERSION   Work on the Tower of Hanoi problem carefully, using the three-disk version in the figure. Try to keep track of your solution so you'll understand how it demonstrates the usefulness of a means–end analysis. So that you'll be familiar with the problem and be able to reflect on your solution, do it several times again after you've solved it. See whether you can become skilled at solving the three-disk problem by remembering your solution and being able to generate it repeatedly. (By the way, an excellent heuristic for this problem is to solve it physically; draw the pegs on a piece of paper and move three coins of different sizes around to find the solution.)

Having done that, consider your solution in terms of subgoals and means–end analysis. Your goal, as stated in the problem, is to move the *ABC* stack of disks from peg 1 to peg 3. Applying the means–end analysis, your first step sets up this goal. The second step reveals a difficulty: There is a difference between your current state and the goal, simply the difference between the starting and ending configurations. You look for a method or operator that reduces this difference and then apply it. As you no doubt learned from your solution, your first major subgoal is "Clear off disk *C*." This entails getting *B* off *C,* which entails another subgoal, getting *A* off *B*.

The next step involves a simple operator that satisfies the most immediate subgoal, "Move *A* to 3," which permits satisfying the next subgoal, "getting *B* off *C*." So the next operator is "move *B* to 2"; it can't go on top of *A* (rule violation), and it can't stay on top of *C* because that prevents achieving a subgoal. Now peg 3 can be cleared by moving *A* to 2. This allows the major subgoal to be accomplished, putting *C* on 3.

From here, it's easy to see the final route to solution: "unpack" *A* from 2, putting it temporarily on 1, move *B* to 3, then move *A* to 3. The seven moves that solve the problem are shown in Figure 12-9.

THE FOUR-DISK VERSION   After you've done the problem several times, solving it becomes easy. You come to see how each disk must move to get *C* on 3, then *B*, and finally *A*. Spend some time now on the same problem but use four disks

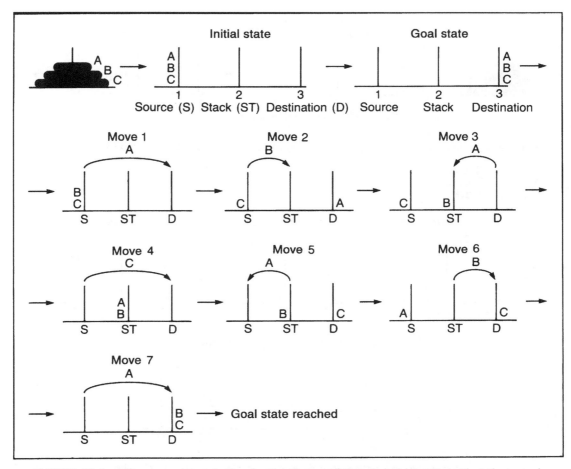

FIGURE 12-9 The seven-step solution for the Tower of Hanoi problem. Note that the pegs have been renamed as "Source," "Stack," and "Destination." Moving the three disks takes seven moves. Consider these seven moves as one unit, called "moving a pyramid of three disks."

instead of three. Don't work on this version blindly, however. Think of it as a variation on the three-disk problem, where parts of the new solution are "old." As a hint, try renaming the pegs as the source peg, the stack peg, and the destination peg. Furthermore, think of the seven moves not as seven discrete steps but as a single chunk, "moving a pyramid of three disks," which should help you see the relationships between the problems more clearly (Simon, 1975). According to Catrambone (1996), almost any label attached to a sequence of moves probably will help you remember the sequence better.

What did you discover as you solved the four-disk problem? Most people come to realize that the four-disk problem has two three-disk problems embedded in it, separated by the bridging move of *D* to 3. That is, to free *D* so it can move to peg 3 you must first move the top three disks out of the way, moving a "pyramid of three disks," getting *D* to peg 3 on the eighth move. Then the *ABC* pyramid has to move again to get them on top of *D*—another seven moves. Moving the disks entails the same order of moves as in the simpler problem, although the pegs take on different functions: For the four-disk problem, peg 2 serves as the destination for the first half of the solution, then as the source for the last half. The entire

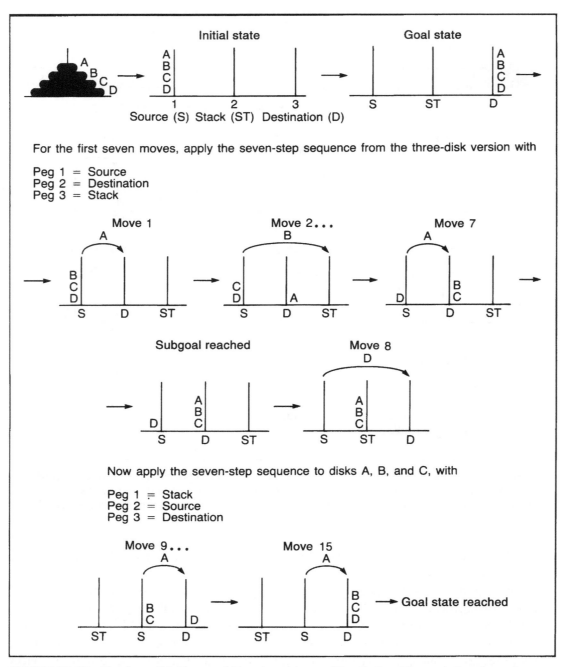

FIGURE 12-10 The four-disk Tower of Hanoi problem, with solution. The variation from the three-disk version is that the pegs must switch roles. In the beginning, the subgoal is to move a pyramid of three disks so that *D* can move to peg 3. After that, the subgoal again is to move a three-disk pyramid. In both the first and second halves, the pegs must switch roles for the problem to be solved.

scheme of 15 moves is illustrated in Figure 12-10. Because the three-disk solution is embedded in the four-disk problem—and, likewise, the four-disk solution is embedded in the five-disk problem—this is known as a recursive problem, where *recursive* simply means that simpler components are embedded in the more difficult versions.

General Problem Solver

Means–end analysis was an early focus of research on problem solving, largely because of early work by Newell, Shaw, and Simon (1958; Ernst & Newell, 1969; Newell & Simon, 1972). Their computer simulation was called **general problem solver (GPS)**. This program was *the first genuine computer simulation of problem-solving behavior.* It was a general-purpose, problem-solving program, not limited to just one kind of problem but widely applicable to a large class of problems in which means–end analysis was appropriate. Newell and Simon ran their simulation on various logical proofs, on the missionary–cannibal problem, on the Tower of Hanoi, and on many other problems to demonstrate its generality. (Notice the critical analogy here. Newell and Simon drew an analogy between the way computer programs solve problems and the way humans do: Human mental processes are of a symbolic nature, so the computer's manipulation of symbols is a fruitful analogy to those processes. This was a stunningly provocative and useful analogy for the science of cognition.)

PRODUCTION SYSTEMS   An important characteristic of GPS was its formulation as a production system model, essentially the first such model proposed in psychology. A **production** is a pair of statements, called either *a condition–action pair or an if–then pair.* In such a scheme, if the production's conditions are satisfied, the action part of the pair takes place. In the GPS application to the Tower of Hanoi, three sample productions might be

1. *If the destination peg is clear and the largest disk is free, then move the largest disk to the destination peg.*
2. *If the largest disk is not free, then set up a subgoal to free it.*
3. *If a subgoal to free the largest disk is set up and a smaller disk is on it, then move the smaller disk to the stack peg.*

Such an analysis suggests a very "planful" solution by GPS: Setting up a goal and subgoals that achieve the goal sounds exactly like what we call planning. And indeed, such planning characterizes both people's and GPS's solutions to problems, not just the Tower of Hanoi but all kinds of transformation problems. GPS had what amounted to a planning mechanism, a mechanism that abstracted the essential features of situations and goals then devised a plan that would produce a problem-solving sequence

PROVE IT

The problems you've been solving throughout the chapter can be used without change to demonstrate the principles of problem solving. Here are some interesting contrasts and effects you might want to test.

Compare either the time or number of moves people make in learning and mastering the Tower of Hanoi problem when the pegs are labeled *1*, *2*, and *3* and when they are labeled *source*, *stack*, and *destination*. Try drawing the pegs in a triangular pattern rather than in a left-to-right display to see whether that makes the "stack" peg idea more salient. Compare how long it takes to master the problem when your participants learn to do it by moving three coins around on paper and when they keep track of their moves mentally.

of moves. Provided with such a mechanism and the particular representational system necessary to encode the problem and the legal operators, GPS yielded an output that resembles the solution pathways taken by human problem solvers.

LIMITATIONS OF GPS   Later investigators working with the general principles of GPS found some cases when the model did not do a good job of characterizing human problem solving. Consider the missionary–cannibal problem in Table 12-9; the solution pathway is presented in Figure 12-11. The problem is difficult, most people find, at step 6, where the only legal move is to return one missionary and one cannibal back to the original side of the river. Having just brought two missionaries over, this return trip seems to be moving away from the overall goal. That is, returning one missionary and one cannibal seems to be incorrect because it appears to increase the distance to the goal: It's the only return trip that moves two characters back to the original side. Despite the fact that this is the only available move (other than returning the same two missionaries who just came over), people have difficulty in selecting this move (Thomas, 1974).

GPS did not have this difficulty because sending one missionary and one cannibal back was consistent with its immediate subgoal. On the other hand, at step 10, GPS is trying to fulfill its subgoal of getting the last cannibal to the destination side and seemingly can't let go of this subgoal. People, however, realize that this subgoal should be abandoned: Anyone can row back over to bring the last cannibal across and in the process finish the problem (Greeno, 1974). GPS was simply too rigid in its application of the means–end heuristic, however: It tried to bring the last cannibal across and then send the boat back again.

BEYOND GPS   Newell and Simon's GPS model, and models based on it, often provided a good description of human problem-solving performance (Atwood &

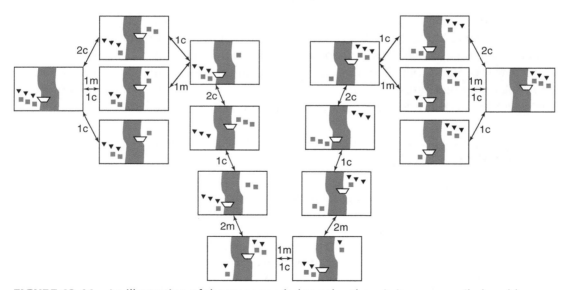

FIGURE 12-11   An illustration of the steps needed to solve the missionary–cannibal problem. The left half of each box is the "start side" of the river, and the right half is the "destination side." The numbers and letters next to the arrows represent who is traveling on the boat.

Based on Glass & Holyoak (1986).

Polson, 1976) and provided a set of predictions against which new experimental results could be compared (Greeno, 1974). Despite some limitations (Hayes & Simon, 1974), the model demonstrated the importance of means–end analysis for an understanding of human problem solving.

Section Summary

- The best-known heuristic for problem solving is means–end analysis, in which the problem solver cycles between determining the difference between the current and goal states and applying legal operators to reduce that difference. The importance of subgoals is revealed most clearly in problems such as the Tower of Hanoi.
- Newell and Simon's general problem solver (GPS) was the earliest cognitive theory of problem solving, implemented as a computer simulation. Studying GPS and comparing its performance with human problem solving showed the importance of means–end analysis.

IMPROVING YOUR PROBLEM SOLVING

Sprinkled through the chapter have been hints and suggestions about how to improve your problem solving. Some of these were based on empirical research and some on intuitions that people have had about problem solving. Let's close the chapter by pulling these hints and suggestions together and offering a few new ones. Table 12-10 provides a list of these suggestions.

Increase Your Domain Knowledge

In thinking about what makes problems difficult, Simon suggests that the likeliest factor is **domain knowledge,** what one knows about the topic. Not surprisingly,

TABLE 12-10   Suggestions for Improving Problem Solving
Increase your domain knowledge.
Automate some components of the problem-solving solution.
Follow a systematic plan.
Draw inferences.
Develop subgoals.
Work backward.
Search for contradictions.
Search for relations between problems.
Find a different problem representation.
Stay calm.
If all else fails, try practice.

a person who has only limited knowledge or familiarity with a topic is less able to solve problems efficiently in that domain (but see Wiley, 1998, on some disadvantages of too much domain knowledge). In contrast, extensive domain knowledge leads to expertise, a fascinating topic in its own right (see Ericsson & Charness, 1994, and Medin, Lynch, Coley, & Atran, 1997, for example).

Much of the research supporting this comes from Simon's work with chess (Chase & Simon, 1973; Gobet & Simon, 1996; see also Reeves & Weisberg, 1993). In several studies of chess masters, an important but not surprising result was obtained: Chess masters need only a glimpse of the arrangement of chess pieces to remember the arrangement, far beyond what novices or players of moderate skill can do. This advantage holds, however, only when the pieces are in legal locations (i.e., sensible within the context of a real game of chess). When the locations of the pieces are random, then there is no advantage for the skilled players. This advantage of expertise in remembering legal board positions is attributed to experts' more skilled perceptual encoding of the board, literally more efficient eye movements and fixations while looking at the board (Reingold, Charness, Pomplun, & Stampe, 2001).

Automate Some Components of the Problem-Solving Solution

A second connection also exists between the question, "What makes problems difficult?" and the topics you've already studied. Kotovsky, Hayes, and Simon (1985) tested adults on various forms of the Tower of Hanoi problem and also on problem isomorphs, problems with the same form but different details. Their results showed that a heavy working memory load was a serious impediment to successful problem solving: If the person had to hold three or four nested subgoals in working memory all at once, performance deteriorated.

Thus, a solution to this memory load problem was to automate the rules that govern moves, just as you were supposed to master and automate the seven-step sequence in the Tower of Hanoi. This frees working memory to be used for higher-level subgoals (Carlson, Khoo, Yaure, & Schneider, 1990). This is the same reasoning you encountered early in the book, where automatic processing uses few if any of the limited conscious resources of working memory.

Follow a Systematic Plan

Especially in long, multistep problems, it's important to follow a systematic plan (Bransford & Stein, 1993; Polya, 1957). Although this seems straight-forward, people do not always generate plans when solving problems, although doing so can dramatically improve performance (Delany, Ericsson, & Knowles, 2004). A plan helps you keep track of what you've done or tried and also keep you focused on the overall goal or subgoals you're working on. For example, on DONALD + GERALD, you need to devise a way to keep track of which digits you've used, which letters remain, and what you know about them. If nothing else, developing and following a plan helps you avoid redoing what you've already done. Keep in mind that people often make errors when planning how long a task will take, but can plan their time better if they break the task down into the problem subgoals, estimate the time needed for each of those, and then add those times together (Forsyth & Burt, 2008).

Draw Inferences

Wickelgren's (1974) advice is to draw inferences from the givens, the terms, and the expressions in a problem before working on the problem itself. If you do this appropriately, it can often save you from wasting time on blind alleys, as in the two trains problem in Table 12-11. It can also help you abandon a misleading representation of the problem and find one that's more suitable to solving the problem (Simon, 1995). Here's a hint: Don't think about how far the bird is flying; think of how far the trains will travel and how long that will take.

Beware of unwarranted inferences, the kinds of restrictions we place on ourselves that may lead to dead ends. For instance, for the nine-dot problem in Table 12-3, an unwarranted inference is that you must stay within the boundaries of the nine dots.

Develop Subgoals

Wickelgren also recommends a subgoal heuristic for problem solving, that is, breaking a large problem into separate subgoals. This is the heart of the means–end approach. There is a different slant to the subgoal approach, however, that bears mention. Sometimes in our real-world problem solving, there is only a vaguely specified goal and, as often as not, even more vaguely specified subgoals. How do you know when you've achieved a subgoal, say when the subgoal is "find enough articles on a particular topic to write a term paper that will earn an *A*"?

Simon's (1979) *satisficing* heuristic is important here; recall from Chapter 11 that satisficing is a heuristic in which we find a solution to a goal or subgoal that is satisfactory although not necessarily the best possible one. For some problems, the term paper problem included, an initial satisfactory solution to subgoals may

---

TABLE 12-11   Two Trains and Fifteen Pennies Problems

Two Trains

Two train stations are 50 miles apart. At 2 P.M. one Saturday afternoon, the trains start toward each other, one from each station. Just as the trains pull out of the stations, a bird springs into the air in front of the first train and flies ahead to the front of the second train. When the bird reaches the second train it turns back and flies toward the first train. The bird continues to do this until the trains meet.

If both trains travel at the rate of 25 miles per hour and the bird flies at 100 miles per hour, how many miles will the bird fly before the trains meet?

Fifteen Pennies

Fifteen pennies are placed on a table in front of two players. Players must remove at least one but not more than five pennies on their turns. The players alternate turns of removing pennies until the last penny is removed. The player who removes the last penny from the table is the winner. Is there a method of play that will guarantee victory?

Hints

Fifteen pennies. What do you want to force your opponent to do to leave you with the winning move? What will the table look like when your opponent makes that move?

give you additional insight for further refinement of your solution. For instance, as you begin to write your rough draft, you realize there are gaps in your information. What seems originally to be a satisfactory solution to the subgoal of finding references turns out to be insufficient, so you can recycle back to that subgoal to improve your solution. You might only discover this deficiency by going ahead and working on that next subgoal, the rough draft.

Work Backward

Another heuristic is working backward, in which a well-specified goal may permit a tracing of the solution pathway in reverse order, thus working back to the givens. The fifteen pennies problem in Table 12-11 is an illustration, a problem that is best solved by working backward. Many math and algebra proofs can also be worked backward or in a combination of forward and backward methods.

Search for Contradictions

In problems that ask "Is it possible to?" or "Is there a way that?" you should search for contradictions in the givens or goal state. Wickelgren uses the following illustration: Is there an integer x that satisfies the equation $x^2 + 1 = 0$? A simple algebraic operation, subtracting 1 from both sides, yields $x^2 = -1$, which contradicts the known property that any squared number is positive. This heuristic can also be

Drawing a diagram to represent a problem helps to improve problem-solving abilities.

helpful in multiple-choice exams. That is, maybe some of the alternatives contradict some idea or fact in the question or some fact you learned in the course. Either will enable you to rule those choices out immediately.

Search for Relations among Problems

In searching for relations among problems, you actively consider how the current problem may resemble one you've already solved or know about. The four- and more-disk Tower of Hanoi problems are examples of this, as are situations in which you search for an analogy (Bassok & Holyoak, 1989; Ross, 1987). Don't become impatient. Bowden (1985) found that people often found and used information from related problems, but only if sufficient time was allowed for them to do so. Try it on the problem in Figure 12-12.

Find a Different Problem Representation

Another heuristic involves the more general issue of the problem representation, or how you choose to represent and think about the problem you're working on. Often, when you get stuck on a problem, it is useful to go back to the beginning and reformulate or reconceptualize it. For instance, as you discovered in the Buddhist monk problem, a quantitative representation of the situation is unproductive. Return to the beginning and try to think of other ways to think about the situation, such as a visual imagery approach, especially a mental movie that includes action. In the Buddhist monk problem, superimposing two such mental movies permits you to see him walking up and down at the same time, thus yielding the solution. Likewise, animated diagrams, with arrows moving in toward a point of convergence, helped participants solve the radiation problem in Pedone, Hummel, and Holyoak's (2001) study, as compared to either static diagrams or a series of diagrams showing intermediate points in problem solution (see also Reed & Hoffman, 2004).

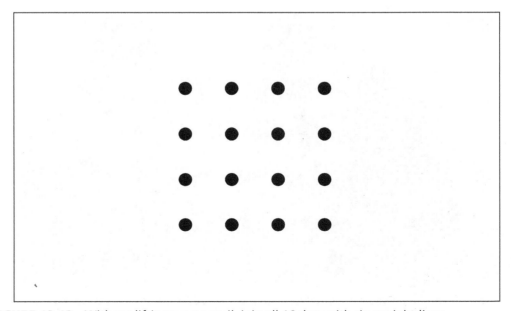

FIGURE 12-12 Without lifting your pencil, join all 16 dots with six straight lines.

For other kinds of problems, try a numerical representation, including working the problem out with some examples, or a physical representation, using objects, scratch paper, and so forth. Simon (1995) makes a compelling point that one representation of a problem may highlight a particular feature of a problem while masking or obscuring a different, possibly important feature. According to Ahlum-Heath and DiVesta (1986), verbalizing your thinking also helps in the initial stages of problem solving.

Earlier, it was suggested that you can master the Tower of Hanoi problem more easily if you used three coins of different sizes. This is more than just good advice. Recall from Chapter 6 where you read about patient H. M., who had profound anterograde amnesia. H. M. was unable to form new explicit long-term memories but was normal when implicit learning was tested. The major result you read about was the mirror tracing study: In a mirror tracing study, H. M. showed normal learning curves on this task, despite not remembering the task from day to day. Interestingly, H. M. was also tested on the Tower of Hanoi task, and he learned it as well as anyone (although he had no explicit memory of ever having done it before). The important ingredient here is the motor aspect of the tower problem: Learning a set of motor responses, even a complex sequence, relies on implicit memory. Thus, working the Tower of Hanoi manually by moving real disks or coins around should enable you to learn how to solve the problem from both an explicit and an implicit basis.

If All Else Fails, Try Practice

Finally, for problems we encounter in classroom settings, from algebra or physics problems up through such vague problems as writing a term paper and studying

Becoming an effective problem solver requires practice to strengthen certain knowledge, as these chess players exhibit.

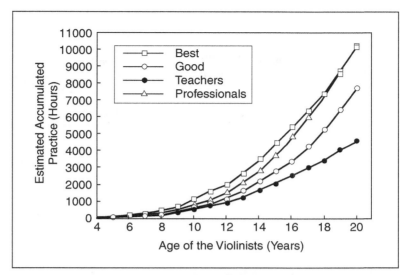

FIGURE 12-13 Illustration of the relationship between amount of practice over the course of years and the level of expertise.

From Ericsson, Krampe, & Tesch-Römer (1993).

effectively for an exam, a final heuristic should help. It's well known in psychology; even Ebbinghaus recommended it. If you want to be good at problem solving, *practice* problem solving. Practice within a particular knowledge domain strengthens that knowledge, pushes the problem-solving components closer to an automatic basis, and gives you a deeper understanding of the domain. Although it isn't flashy, practice is a major component of skilled problem solving and of gaining expertise in any area (Ericsson & Charness, 1994).

In Ericsson and Charness's (1994) review, people routinely believe that stunning talent and amazing accomplishments result from inherited, genetic, or "interior" explanations, when the explanation usually is dedicated, regular, long-term practice. This relationship between practice and performance level is seen in an analysis of practice and expertise data by Ericsson, Krampe, and Tesch-Römer (1993) shown in Figure 12-13. As can be seen, the people who had higher levels of expertise also were the ones who engaged in more practice. So, practice is important to becoming an expert. However, it is unclear whether there is also some innate characteristic such as motivation, interest, or talent that could also be driving those people to practice more. Regardless, if you want to become highly skilled at something, your elementary school clarinet teacher was right—you really do need to practice.

Section Summary

- The set of recommendations for improving your problem solving includes increasing your knowledge of the domain, automaticity of components in problem solving, developing and following a plan, and not becoming anxious. Several special-purpose heuristics are also listed, including the mundane yet important advice about practice.

Key Terms

analogy
domain knowledge
Einstellung
functional fixedness

general problem
   solver (GPS)
Gestalt
goal
ill-defined problems

insight
means–end analysis
negative set
operators
problem space

production
subgoal
verbal protocol
well-defined problems

Answers to Chapter 12 Problems

Three Men and a Rowboat   Medium and Small row themselves across the river, then either one of them rows back to the start side. Large rows himself across to the destination side. The man who stayed on the destination side now rows back to the start side, and both of the lighter men row to the destination.

Buddhist Monk   Rather than thinking in terms of one monk, let a different monk walk down from the top on the same day as the other walks up. Looking at it this way, isn't it obvious that the two will meet during their journey? Thus, his walking on separate days is irrelevant to the goal, "Show that there is a spot. . . ."

Six Glasses   Numbering the glasses from left to right, pour the contents of glass 2 into glass 5.

Six Pennies   Coins 1, 2, 4, and 6 are already in place, so move coins 3 and 5.

Chains and Links   Open all three links on one chain; that's 6 cents. Put one opened link at the end of each other piece, then join the pieces by looping a closed link into an opened one. Closing the three links costs 9 cents, for a total of 15 cents.

Four Trees   Dead-end approaches try to arrange the trees on a flat, two-dimensional lawn. Instead, think in three dimensions. Put three trees around the base of a hill and the fourth one at the top of the hill. The arrangement is that of an equilateral, three-sided pyramid.

Prisoner's Escape   Divide the rope in half by cutting with the length rather than across the length, similar to unbraiding the rope. Tie the two thinner pieces together and lower yourself to the ground.

Bronze Coin   In 544 B.C., no one knew what might happen 544 years later, so coins could not have had B.C. stamped on them. The dealer is a crook.

Nine Dots

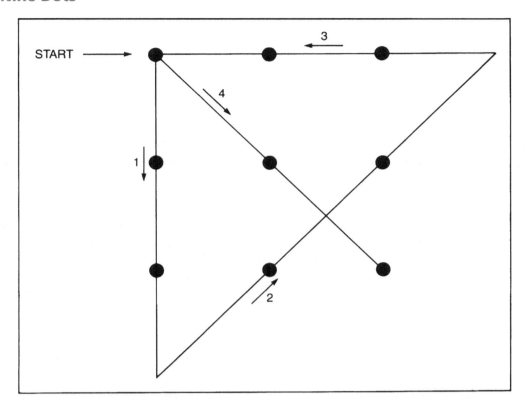

Ten Bowling Pins

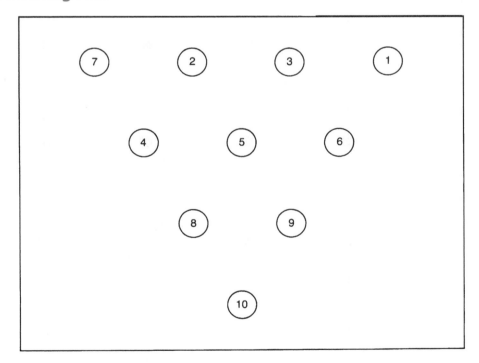

Cryptarithmetic

6. *Cross + Roads*   7. *Lets + Wave*   8. *Send + More*

96,233	1,567	9,567
+ 62,513	+ 9,085	+ 1,085
158,746	10,652	10,652

Two Trains   The trains are 50 miles apart and travel at 25 miles per hour. The trains will meet halfway between the cities in exactly 1 hour. The bird flies at 100 miles per hour, so it will fly 100 miles.

Fifteen Pennies   On your last move you must remove the final penny or pennies. There must be from one to five pennies on the table for you to be the winner. By working backward from this goal, on your next-to-last turn, you must force your opponent to leave you at least one penny on the table. So, leave your opponent six pennies when you finish your next-to-last turn. To guarantee victory, make sure that your opponent leaves you from one to five pennies, so remove only as many pennies as you must to leave your opponent with six pennies on the table.

Sixteen Dots

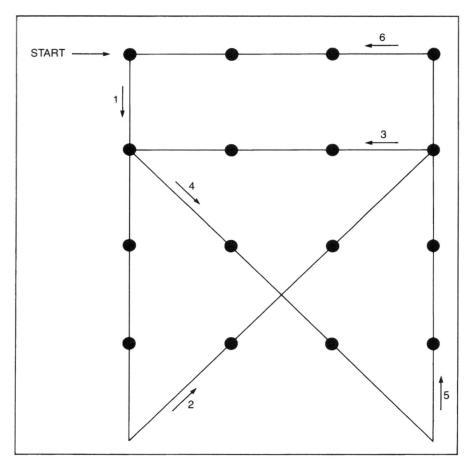

References

A

Adamec, R. (1997) Transmitter systems involved in neural plasticity underlying increased anxiety and defense – implications for understanding anxiety following traumatic stress. *Neuroscience and Biobehavioral Reviews,* **21**, 755–765.

Ader, R. and Cohen, N. (1985) CNS-immune system interactions: conditioning phenomena. *Behavioral and Brain Sciences,* **8**, 379–394.

Adkins-Regan, E. (2004) *Hormones and Animal Social Behavior,* Princeton University Press, Princeton.

Aghajanian, G.K. (1994) Serotonin and the action of LSD in the brain. *Psychiatric Annals,* **24**, 137–141.

Ainslie, G. (1975) Specious reward: a behavioral theory of impulsiveness and impulse control. *Psychological Bulletin,* **82**, 463–496.

Alexander, B. (2008) *The Globalization of Addiction: A Study in the Poverty of the Spirit,* Oxford University Press, Oxford.

Alexander, B.K. and Hadaway, P.F. (1982) Opiate addiction: the case for an adaptive orientation. *Psychological Bulletin,* **92**, 367–381.

Allan, R. and Scheidt, S. (1996b) Empirical basis for cardiac psychology. In *Heart and Mind. The Practice of Cardiac Psychology* (eds R. Allan and S. Scheidt), American Psychological Association, Washington, pp. 63–123.

Amaral, D.G. and Sinnamon, H.M. (1977) The locus coeruleus: neurobiology of a central noradrenergic nucleus. *Progress in Neurobiology,* **9**, 147–196.

Anisman, H., Zaharia, M.D., Meaney, M.J. and Merali, Z (1998) Do early-life events permanently alter behavioral and hormonal responses to stressors? *International Journal of Developmental Neuroscience,* **16**, 149–164.

Archer, J. (1979) *Animals under Stress,* Edward Arnold, London.

Aserinsky, E. and Kleitman, N. (1955) Two types of ocular motility occurring in sleep. *Journal of Applied Physiology,* **8**, 1–10.

Aydede, M. (2006) *Pain: New Essays on its Nature and the Methodology of its Study.* MIT Press, Cambridge.

B

Baddeley, A.D., Bressi, S., Della Sala, S., Logie, R. and Spinnler, H. (1991) The decline of working memory in Alzheimer's disease. *Brain,* **114**, 2521–2542.

Baker, D.A., Khroyan, T.V., O'Dell, L.E., Fuchs, R.A. and Neisewander, J.L. (1996) Differential effects of intra-accumbens sulpiride on cocaine-induced locomotion and conditioned place preference. *Journal of Pharmacology and Experimental Therapeutics,* **279**, 392–401.

Baker, T.B., Piper, M.E., McCarthy, D.E., Majeskie, M.R. and Fiore, M.C. (2004) Addiction motivation reformulated: an affective processing model of negative reinforcement. *Psychological Review,* **111**, 33–51.

Ballieux, R.E. and Heijnen, C.J. (1987) Brain and immune system: a one-way conversation or a genuine dialogue? In *Progress in Brain Research,* Vol. 72 (eds E.R. de Kloet, V.M. Wiegant and D. de Wied), Elsevier Science, Amsterdam, pp. 71–77.

Bandura, A., O'Leary, A., Taylor, C.B., Gauthier, J. and Gossard, D. (1987) Perceived self-efficacy and pain control: opioid and nonopioid mechanisms. *Journal of Personality and Social Psychology,* **53**, 563–571.

Bantick, S.J., Wise, R.G., Ploghaus, A., Clare, S., Smith, S.M. and Tracey, I. (2002) Imaging how attention modulates pain in humans using functional MRI. *Brain,* **125**, 310–319.

Bao, A.M., Meynen, G. and Swaab, D.F. (2008) The stress system in depression and neurodegeneration: focus on the human hypothalamus. *Brain Research Reviews,* **57**, 531–553.

Barden, N., Reul, J.M.H.M. and Holsboer, F. Do anti-depressants stabilize mood through actions on the hypothalamic–pituitary–adrenocortical system? *Trends in Neurosciences,* **18**, 6–11.

Bardo, M.T. (1998) Neuropharmacological mechanisms of drug reward: beyond dopamine in the nucleus accumbens. *Critical Reviews in Neurobiology,* **12**, 37–67.

Baxter, D.W. and Olszewski, J. (1960) Congenital universal insensitivity to pain. *Brain,* **83**, 381–393.

Baxter, J.D. and Rousseau, G.G. (1979) Glucocorticoid hormone action: an overview. In *Glucocorticoid Hormone Action* (eds J.D. Baxter and G.G. Rousseau), Springer-Verlag, Berlin, pp. 1–24.

Bechara, A. (2005) Decision making, impulse control and loss of willpower to resist drugs: a neurocognitive perspective. *Nature Neuroscience,* **8**, 1458–1463.

Bechara, A., Nader, K. and van der Kooy, D. (1998) A two-separate-motivational-systems hypothesis of opioid addiction. *Pharmacology, Biochemistry and Behavior,* **59**, 1–17.

Beecher, H.K. (1955) The powerful placebo. *Journal of the American Medical Association,* **159**, 1602–1606.

Benedetti, F. and Amanzio, M. (1997) The neurobiology of placebo analgesia: from endogenous opioids to cholecystokinin. *Progress in Neurobiology,* **51**, 109–125.

Benington, J.H. and Heller, H.C. (1995) Restoration of brain energy metabolism as the function of sleep. *Progress in Neurobiology,* **45**, 347–360.

Bennett, M. (2010) *Neuropathic Pain.* Oxford University Press, Oxford.

Bernstein, G.A., Carroll, M.E., Thuras, P.D., Cosgrove, K.P. and Roth, M.E. (2002) Caffeine dependence in teenagers. *Drug and Alcohol Dependence,* **66**, 1–6.

Berridge, C.W., Devilbiss, D.M., Andrzejewski, M.E., Arnsten, A.F.T., Kelley, A.E., Schmeichel, B., Hamilton, C. and Spencer, R.C. (2006) Methylphenidate preferentially increases catecholamine neurotransmission within the prefrontal cortex at low doses that enhance cognitive function. *Biological Psychiatry,* **60**, 1111–1120.

Berthoud, H-R. (2002) Multiple neural systems controlling food intake and body weight. *Neuroscience and Biobehavioral Reviews,* **26**, 393–428.

Billings, J.H., Scherwitz, L.W., Sullivan, R., Sparler, S. and Ornish, D.M. (1996) The life-style heart trial: comprehensive treatment and group support therapy. In *Heart and Mind. The Practice of Cardiac Psychology* (eds R. Allan and S. Scheidt), American Psychological Association, Washington, pp. 233–253.

Blundell, J.E. and Halford, J.C.G. (1998) Serotonin and appetite regulation: implications for the pharmacological treatment of obesity *CNS Drugs,* **9**, 473–195.

Bohus, B. and de Kloet, E.R. (1981) Adrenal steroids and extinction behaviour: antagonism by progesterone, deoxycorticosterone and dexamethesone of a specific effect of corticosterone. *Life Sciences,* **28**, 433–440.

Bohus, B. and Koolhaas, J.M. (1993) Stress and the cardiovascular system: central and peripheral physiological mechanisms. In *Stress – From Synapse to Syndrome* (eds S.C. Stanford and P. Salmon), Academic Press, London, pp. 75–117.

Bolles, R.C. (1980) Historical note on the term 'appetite'. *Appetite,* **1**, 3–6.

Bolles, R.C. and Fanselow, M S. (1980) A perceptual–defensive–recuperative model of fear and pain. *Behavioral and Brain Sciences,* **3**, 291–323.

Bostwick, J.M. and Bucci, J A (2008) Internet sex addiction treated with naltrexone. *Mayo Clinic Proceedings,* **83**, 226–230.

Bovard, E.W. (1985) Brain mechanisms in effects of social support on viability. In *Perspectives in Behavioral Medicine,* Vol. 2 (ed. R.B. Williams), Academic Press, Orlando, pp. 103–129.

Bozarth, M.A. (1987) *Methods of Assessing the Reinforcing Properties of Abused Drugs,* Springer-Verlag, New York.

Bracke, P.E. and Thoresen, C.E. (1996) Reducing Type A behavior patterns: a structured-group approach. In *Heart and Mind. The Practice of Cardiac Psychology* (eds R. Allan, and S. Scheidt), American Psychological Association, Washington, pp. 255–290.

Breier, A., Kelsoe, J.R., Kirwin, P.D., Beller, S.A., Wolkowitz, O.M. and Pickar, D. (1988) Early parental loss and development of adult

psychopathology. *Archives of General Psychiatry,* **45**, 987–993.

Bremner, J.D. (1999) Does stress damage the brain? *Biological Psychiatry,* **45**, 797–805.

Broadbent, D.E. (1958) *Perception and Communication,* Pergamon Press, Oxford.

Bromm, B. (1995) Consciousness, pain and cortical activity. In *Pain and the Brain: From Nociception to Cognition* (Advances in Pain Research and Therapy, Vol. 22) (eds B. Bromm and J.E. Desmedt), Raven Press, New York, pp. 35–59.

Brown, M., Keynes, R. and Lumsden, A. (2001) *The Developing Brain,* Oxford University Press, Oxford.

Bruer, J.T. (1998) Brain and child development: time for some critical thinking *Public Health Reports,* **113**, 388–397.

Burell, G. (1996) Group psychotherapy in project new life: treatment of coronary-prone behaviors for patients who have had coronary artery bypass graft surgery. In *Heart and Mind. The Practice of Cardiac Psychology* (eds R. Allan and S. Scheldt), American Psychological Association, Washington, pp. 291–310.

Burgdorf, J. and Panksepp, J. (2006) The neurobiology of positive emotions. *Neuroscience and Biobehavioral Reviews,* **30**, 173–187.

Buss, D.M., Haselton, M.G., Shackelford, T.K., Bleske, A.L. and Wakefield, J.C. (1998) Adaptations, exaptations, and spandrels. *American Psychologist,* **53**, 533–548.

C

Cabanac, M. (1971) Physiological role of pleasure. *Science,* **173**, 1103–1107.

Campbell, C.M. and Edwards, R.R. (2009) Mind-body interactions in pain: the neurophysiology of anxious and catastrophic pain-related thoughts. *Translational Research,* **153**, 97–101.

Castanon, N. and Mormede, P. (1994) Psychobiogenetics: adapted tools for the study of the coupling between behavioral and neuroendocrine traits of emotional reactivity. *Psychoneuroendocrinology,* **19**, 257–282.

Charney, D.S., Deutch, A.Y., Southwick, S.M. and Krystal, J.H. (1995) Neural circuits and mechanisms of post-traumatic stress disorder In *Neurobiological and Clinical Consequences of Stress. From Normal Adaptation to Posttraumatic Stress Disorder* (eds M.J. Friedman, D.S. Charney and A.Y. Deutch), Lippincott-Raven, Philadelphia, pp. 271–287.

Chaves, J.F. and Dworkin, S.F. (1997) Hypnotic control of pain: historical perspectives and future prospects. *International Journal of Clinical and Experimental Hypnosis,* **XLV**, 356–376.

Chiamulera, C. (2005) Cue reactivity in nicotine and tobacco dependence: a 'multiple-action' model of nicotine as a primary reinforcement and as an enhancer of the effects of smoking-associated stimuli. *Brain Research Reviews,* **48**, 74–97.

Chick, J. and Erickson, C.K. (1996) Conference summary: consensus conference on alcohol dependence and the role of pharmacotherapy in its treatment. *Alcoholism: Clinical and Experimental Research,* **20**, 391–402.

Childress, A.R., Mozley, P.D., McElgin, W., Fitzgerald, J., Reivich, M. and O'Brien, C.P. (1999) Limbic activation during cue-induced cocaine craving. *American Journal of Psychiatry,* **156**, 11–18.

Childress, A.R., Ehrman, R.N., Wang, Z., Li, Y., Sciortino, N., Hakun, J., Jens, W., Suh, J., Listerud, J., Marquez, K., Franklin, T., Langleben, D., Detre, J and O'Brien, C.P. (2008) Prelude to passion: limbic activation by 'unseen' drug and sexual cues. *PLoS One,* 3, e1506. doi: 10.1371/journal.pone.0001506.

Chomsky, N. (1959) Review of 'Verbal Behaviour' by B.F. Skinner. *Language,* **35**, 26–58.

Chorpita, B.F. and Barlow, D.H. (1998) The development of anxiety: the role of control in the early environment. *Psychological Bulletin,* **124**, 3–21.

Christie, M.J., Williams, J.T., Osborne, P.G. and Bellchambers, C.E. (1997) Where is the locus in opioid withdrawal? *Trends in Pharmacological Sciences,* **18**, 134–140.

Clark, R.W. (1980) *Freud – The Man and the Cause,* Random House, New York.

Clow, A. and Hucklebridge, F. (2002) *International Review of Neurobiology. 52. The Neurobiology of the Immune System.* Academic Press, New York.

Cobb, L.A., Thomas, G.I., Dillard, D.H., Merendino, K.A. and Bruce, R.A. (1959) An evaluation of internal-mammary-artery ligation by a double-blind technique. *New England Journal of Medicine,* **260**, 1115–1118.

Cohen, S. (1996) Psychological stress, immunity, and upper respiratory infections *Current Directions in Psychological Science,* **5**, 86–90.

Coleman, E. (2005) Neuroanatomical and neurotransmitter dysfunction and compulsive sexual behavior In *Biological Substrates of Human Sexuality* (ed. J.S. Hyde), American Psychological Association, Washington, pp. 147–169.

Contreras, M., Ceric, F. and Torrealba, F. (2007) Inactivation of the interoceptive insula disrupts drug craving and malaise induced by lithium. *Science,* **318**, 655–658.

Cooper, C.L. and Dewe, P. (2004) *Stress: A Brief History,* Blackwell Publishing, Oxford.

Coover, G.D., Ursin, H. and Levine, S. (1973) Plasma-corticosterone levels during active-avoidance learning in rats. *Journal of Comparative and Physiological Psychology,* **82**, 170–174.

Craig, A.D. (2003) Pain mechanisms: labelled lines versus convergence in central processing. *Annual Review of Neuroscience,* **26**, 1–30.

Craig, K.D. (1994) Emotional aspects of pain. In *Textbook of Pain* (eds P.D. Wall and R. Melzack), Churchill Livingstone, Edinburgh, pp. 261–274.

Craig, K.D. (1995) From nociception to pain: the role of emotion. In *Pain and the Brain: From Nociception to Cognition* (Advances in Pain Research and Therapy, Vol. 22) (eds B. Bromm and J.E. Desmedt), Raven Press, New York, pp. 303–317.

Cullinan, W.E., Flerman, J.P., Flelmreich, D.L. and Watson, S.J. (1995) A neuroanatomy of stress. In *Neurobiological and Clinical Consequences of Stress. From Normal Adaptation to Post-traumatic Stress Disorder* (eds M.J. Friedman, D.S. Charney and A.Y. Deutch), Lippincott-Raven, Philadelphia, pp. 3–26.

Cunningham-Williams, R.M., Gattis, M.N., Dore, P.M., Shi, P. and Spitznagel, E.L. (2009) Towards DSM-V: considering other withdrawal-like symptoms of pathological gambling disorder. *International Journal of Methods in Psychiatric Research,* **18**, 13–22 .

Curtis, A.L. and Valentino, R.J. (1994) Corticotropin-releasing factor neurotransmission in locus coeruleus: a possible site of antidepressant action. *Brain Research Bulletin,* **35**, 581–587.

D

Dampney, R. (1990) The subretrofacial nucleus: its pivotal role in cardiovascular regulation. *News in Physiological Sciences,* **5**, 63–67.

Dampney, R.A.L. (1994) Functional organization of central pathways regulating the cardiovascular system. *Physiological Reviews,* **74**, 323–364.

Dani, J.A. and Heinemann, S. (1996) Molecular and cellular aspects of nicotine abuse. *Neuron,* **16**, 905–908.

Davidson, D. and Amit, Z. (1997) Effect of ethanol drinking and naltrexone on subsequent drinking in rats. *Alcohol,* **14**, 581–584.

Davis, L.L., Suris, A., Lambert, M.T., Heimberg, C. and Petty, F. (1997) Post-traumatic stress disorder and serotonin: new directions for research and treatment. *Journal of Psychiatry and Neuroscience,* **22**, 318–326.

de Charms, R.C., Maeda, F., Glover, G.H., Ludlow, D., Pauly, J.M., Soneji, D., Gabrieli, J.D.E. and Mackey, S.C. (2005) Control over brain activation and pain learned by using real-time functional MRI. *Proceedings of the National Academy of Sciences,* **102**, 18626–18631.

Delgado, P.L. and Moreno, F.A. (1998) Hallucinogens, serotonin and obsessive-compulsive disorder. *Journal of Psychoactive Drugs,* **30**, 359–366.

Derbyshire, S.W.G., Whalley, M.G. and Oakley, D.A. (2009) Fibromyalgia pain and its modulation by hypnotic and non-hypnotic suggestion: an fMRI analysis. *European Journal of Pain,* **13**, 542–550.

Deroche-Gamonet, V., Belin, D. and Piazza, P.V. (2004) Evidence for addiction-like behavior in the rat. *Science,* **305**, 1014–1017.

Dickman, A. and Simpson, K.H. (2008) *Chronic Pain.* Oxford University Press, Oxford.

Dienstbier, R.A. (1989) Arousal and physiological toughness: implications for mental and physical health. *Psychological Review,* **96**, 84–100.

Donny, E.C., Caggiula, A.R., Mielke, M.M., Jacobs, K.S., Rose, C. and Sved, A.F. (1998) Acquisition of nicotine self-administration in rats: the effects of dose, feeding schedule and drug contingency. *Psychopharmacology,* **136**, 83–90.

Dunn, A.J. and Berridge, C.W. (1990) Physiological and behavioral responses to corticotropin-releasing factor administration: is CRF a mediator of anxiety or stress responses? *Brain Research Reviews,* **15**, 71–100.

E

Eccleston, C. and Crombez, G. (1999) Pain demands attention: a cognitive–affective model of the interruptive function of pain. *Psychological Bulletin,* **125**, 356–366.

Edelman, S. and Kidman, A.D. (1997) Mind and cancer: is there a relationship? – A review of evidence. *Australian Psychologist,* **32**, 1–7.

Eisenberger, N.I., Lieberman, M.D. and Williams, K.D. (2003) Does rejection hurt? An fMRI study of social exclusion. *Science,* **302**, 290–292.

Ellinwood, E.H. (1967) Amphetamine psychosis: I. Description of the individuals and process. *Journal of Nervous and Mental Disease,* **144**, 273–283.

Ellinwood, E.H. (1968) Amphetamine psychosis: II. Theoretical implications. *International Journal of Neuropsychiatry,* **4**, 45–54.

Ellinwood, E.H. and Escalante, O. (1970) Chronic amphetamine effect on the olfactory forebrain. *Biological Psychiatry,* **2**, 189–203.

Ellinwood, E.H. and Kilbey, M.M. (1975) Amphetamine stereotypy: the influence of environmental factors and prepotent behavioral patterns on its topography and development. *Biological Psychiatry,* **10**, 3–16.

Erikson, K., Drevets, W. and Schulkin, J. (2003) Glucocorticoid regulation of diverse cognitive functions in normal and pathological emotional states. *Neuroscience and Biobehavioral Reviews,* **27**, 233–246.

Evans, A.H., Pavese, N., Lawrence, A.D., Tai, Y.F., Appel, S., Doder, M., Brooks, D.J., Lees, A.J. and Piccini, P. (2006) Compulsive drug use linked to sensitized ventral striatal dopamine transmission. *Annals of Neurology,* **59**, 852–858.

Evans, P., Clow, A. and Hucklebridge, F. (1997) Stress and the immune system. *The Psychologist,* **10**, 303–307.

Evans, P., Hucklebridge, F. and Clow, A. (2000) *Mind, Immunity and Health: The Science of Psychoneuroimmunology,* Free Association Books, London.

Everitt, B.J., Dickinson, A. and Robbins, T.W. (2001) The neuropsychological basis of addictive behaviour. *Brain Research Reviews,* **36**, 129–138.

F

Falk, J.L. (1994) The discriminative stimulus and its reputation: role in the instigation of drug abuse. *Experimental and Clinical Psychopharmacology,* **2**, 43–52.

Fields, H.L. and Basbaum, A.I. (1994) Central nervous system mechanisms of pain modulation. In *Textbook of Pain* (eds P.D. Wall and R. Melzack), Churchill Livingstone, Edinburgh, pp. 243–275.

Filbey, F.M., Schacht, J.P., Myers, U.S., Chavez, R.S. and Hutchison, K.E. (2009) Marijuana craving in the brain. *Proceedings of the National Academy of Sciences USA*, **106**, 13016–13021.

Filshie, J. and Morrison, P.J. (1988) Acupuncture for chronic pain: a review. *Palliative Care*, **2**, 1–14.

Flint, J., Greenspan, R.J. and Kendler, K.S. (2010) *How Genes Influence Behavior.* Oxford University Press, New York.

Flor, H. and Diers, M. (2009) Sensorimotor training and cortical reorganization. *Neuro-Rehabilitation,* **25**, 19–27.

Flor, H., Denke, C., Schaefer, M. and Grüsser, S. (2001) Effect of sensory discrimination training on cortical reorganization and phantom limb pain. *The Lancet,* **357**, 1763–1764.

Flor, H., Knost, B. and Birbaumer, N. (2002) The role of operant conditioning in chronic pain: an experimental investigation. *Pain,* **95**, 111–118.

Flor, H., Nikolajsen, L. and Jensen, T.S. (2006) Phantom limb pain: a case of maladaptive CNS plasticity? *Nature Reviews Neuroscience,* **7**, 873–881.

Fowles, D.C. (1982) Heart rate as an index of anxiety: failure of a hypothesis In *Perspectives in Cardiovascular Psychophysiology* (eds J.T. Cacioppo and R.E. Petty), Guilford Press, New York, pp. 93–123.

Franken, I.H.A. (2003) Drug craving and addiction: integrating psychological and neuropsychopharmacological approaches. *Progress in Neuro-Psychopharmacology and Biological Psychiatry,* **27**, 563–579.

Friedlander, Y., Kark, J.D. and Stein, Y. (1987) Religious observance and plasma lipids and lipoproteins among 17-year-old Jewish residents of Jerusalem. *Preventive Medicine,* **16**, 70–79.

Friedman, M. and Rosenman, R.H. (1959) Association of specific overt behavior pattern with blood and cardiovascular findings *Journal of American Medical Association,* **169**, 1286–1296.

Fuchs, R.A., Tran-Nguyen, L.T.L., Specio, S.E., Groff, R.S. and Neisewander, J.L. (1998) Predictive validity of the extinction/reinstatement model of drug craving. *Psychopharmacology,* **135**, 151–160.

G

Gallo, L.C. and Matthews, K.A. (2003) Understanding the association between socioeconomic status and physical health. *Psychological Bulletin,* **129**, 10–51.

Ganzel, B.L., Morris, P.A. and Wetherington, (2010) Allostasis and the human brain: Integrating models of stress from the social and life sciences. *Psychological Review,* **117**, 134–174.

Gatchel, R.J., Peng, Y.B., Peters, M.L., Fuchs, P.N. and Turk, D.C. (2007) The biopsychosocial approach to chronic pain: scientific advances and future directions. *Psychological Bulletin,* **133**, 581–624.

Gay, P. (1988) *Freud – A Life for our Time,* J. M. Dent, London.

Gessa, G., Melis, M., Muntoni, A. and Diana, M. (1998) Cannabinoids activate mesolimbic dopamine neurons by an action on cannabinoid CB, receptors. *European Journal of Pharmacology,* **341**, 39–44.

Gianaros, P.J. and Sheu, L.K. (2009) A review of neuroimaging studies of stressor-evoked blood pressure reactivity: emerging evidence for a brain-body pathway to coronary heart disease risk. *Neuroimage,* **47**, 922–936.

Gilbert, D.G., McClerlon, F.J. and Gilbert, B.O. (1997) The psychology of the smoker. In *The Tobacco Epidemic* (eds C.T. Bollinger and K.O. Fagerstrom), Karger, Basle, pp. 132–150.

Gladue, B.A. (1994) The biopsychology of sexual orientation. *Current Directions in Psychological Science,* **3**, 150–154.

Glue, P., Nutt, D. and Coupland, N. (1993) Stress and psychiatric disorder: reconciling social and biological approaches. In *Stress – From Synapse to Syndrome* (eds S.C. Stanford and P. Salmon), Academic Press, London, pp. 53–73.

Goodman, A. (2008) Neurobiology of addiction: an integrative review. *Biochemical Pharmacology,* **75**, 266–322.

Gottlieb, G. (1973) *Behavioral Embryology: Studies on the Development of Behavior and the Nervous System,* Academic Press, New York.

Goudriaan, A.E., Oosterlaan, J., de Beurs, and van den Brink, W. (2004) Pathological gambling: a comprehensive review of biobehavioural findings. *Neuroscience and Biobehavioral Reviews,* **28**, 123–141.

Grace, A.A. (2001) Psychostimulant actions on dopamine and limbic system function: rel-

evance to the pathophysiology and treatment of ADHD. In *Stimulant Drugs and ADHD: Basic and Clinical Neuroscience* (eds M.V. Solanto, A.F.T. Arnsten and FX. Castellanos), Oxford University Press, Oxford, pp. 134–157.

Gracely, R.H., Geisser, M.E., Giesecke, T., Grant, M.A.B., Petzke, F., Williams, D.A. and Clauw, D.J. (2004) Pain catastrophising and neural responses to pain among persons with fibromyalgia. *Brain,* **127**, 835–843.

Grant, N., Hamer, M. and Steptoe, A. (2009) Social isolation and stress-related cardiovascular, lipid, and cortisol responses. *Annals of Behavioral Medicine,* **37**, 29–37.

Graven-Nielsen, T., Kendall, S.A., Henriksson, G., Bengtson, M., Sorenson, J., Johnson, A., Gerdle, B. and Arendt-Nielson, L. (2000) Ketamine reduces muscle pain, temporal summation, and referred pain in fibromyalgia patients. *Pain,* **85**, 483–491.

Greenough, W.T. (1976) Enduring brain effects of differential experience and training. In *Neural Mechanisms of Learning and Memory* (eds M.R. Rosenzweig and E.L. Bennett), MIT Press, Cambridge, pp 255–278.

Griffiths, M. (1999) Internet addiction: fact or fiction? *The Psychologist,* **12**, 246–250.

Griffiths, R.R. and Woodson, P.P. (1988) Caffeine physical dependence: a review of human and laboratory animal studies. *Psychopharmacology,* **94**, 437–451.

Griffiths, R.R., Brady, J.V. and Bradford, L.D. (1979) Predicting the abuse liability of drugs with animal drug self-administration procedures: psychomotor stimulants and hallucinogens. In *Advances in Behavioral Pharmacology,* Vol. 2 (eds T. Thompson and PB. Dews), Academic Press, New York, pp. 163–208.

Gunne, L.M., Änggård, E. and Jönsson, L.E. (1972) Clinical trials with amphetamine-blocking drugs. *Psychiatria, Neurologia and Neurochirurgia,* **75**, 225–226.

Guyton, A.C. (1991) *Textbook of Medical Physiology,* W.B. Saunders, Philadelphia.

H

Harris, A.J. (1999) Cortical origin of pathological pain *Lancet,* **354**, 1464–1466.

Harris, J.A. (1996) Descending antinociceptive mechanisms in the brainstem: their role in the animal's defensive system. *Journal of Physiology (Paris),* **90**, 15–25.

Harris, R.E., Sundgren, PC., Pang, Y., Hsu, M.,

Petrou, M., Kim, S-H., McLean, S.A., Gracely, R.H. and Clauw, D.J. (2008) Dynamic levels of glutamate within the insula are associated with improvements in multiple pain domains in fibromyalgia. *Arthritis and Rheumatology,* **58**, 903–907.

Harris, R.E., Sundgren, P.C., Craig, A.D., Kirshenbaum, E., Sen, A., Napadow, V. and Clauw, D.J. (2009) Elevated insular glutamate in fibromyalgia is associated with experimental pain. *Arthritis and Rheumatism,* **60**, 3146–3152.

Hart, B.L. (1988) Biological basis of the behavior of sick animals. *Neuroscience and Biobehavioral Reviews,* **12**, 123–137.

Haughey, H.M., Marshall, E., Schacht, J.P., Louis, A. and Hutchison, K.E. (2008) Marijuana withdrawal and craving: influence of the cannabinoid receptorl (CNR1) and fatty acid amide hydrolase (FAAH) genes. *Addiction,* **103**, 1676–1686.

Henningfield, J.E., Johnson, R.E. and Jasinski, D.l. (1987) Clinical procedures for the assessment of abuse potential. In *Methods of Assessing the Reinforcing Properties of Abused Drugs* (ed. M.A. Bozarth) Springer-Verlag, New York.

Henry, J.R. (1982) The relation of social to biological processes in disease. *Social Science and Medicine,* **16**, 369–380.

Hinkelmann, K., Moritz, S., Botzenhardt, J., Riedesel, K., Wiedemann, K., Kellner, M. and Otte, C. (2009) Cognitive impairment in major depression: association with salivary cortisol. *Biological Psychiatry,* **66**, 879–885.

Hogarth, L., Dickinson, A. and Duka, T. (2003) Discriminative stimuli that control instrumental tobacco-seeking by human smokers also command selective attention. *Psychopharmacology,* **168**, 435–145.

Holsboer, F. and Barden, N. (1996) Antidepressants and hypothalamic–pituitary–adrenocortical regulation. *Endocrine Reviews,* **17**, 187–205.

Huxley, A. (1972) *The Doors of Perception and Heaven and Hell,* Chatto and Windus, London.

Huxley, L.A. (1969) *This Timeless Moment: A Personal View of Aldous Huxley,* Chatto and Windus, London.

Hyde, J.S. (2005a) The genetics of sexual orientation. In *Biological Substrates of Human Sexuality* (ed. J.S. Hyde), American Psychological Association, Washington, pp. 9–20.

Hyde, J.S. (2005b) *Biological Substrates of Human Sexuality,* American Psychological Association, Washington.

I

Iacoboni, M. (2008) *Mirroring People,* Farrar, Straus and Giroux, New York.

J

Jessell, T.M. and Kelly, D.D. (1991) Pain and analgesia. In *Principles of Neural Science* (eds E.R. Kandel, J.H. Schwartz and T.M. Jessell), Appleton and Lange, East Norwalk, pp. 385–399.

Jönsson, L-E., Änggård, E. and Gunne, L.-M. (1971) Blockade of intravenous amphetamine euphoria in man. *Clinical Pharmacology and Therapeutics,* **12**, 889–896.

K

Kassel, J.D. and Shiftman, S. (1992) What can hunger teach us about drug craving? A comparative analysis of the two constructs. *Advances in Behaviour Research and Therapy,* **14**, 141–167.

Keefe, F.J., Abernethy, A.P. and Campbell, L.C. Psychological approaches to understanding and treating disease-related pain. *Annual Review of Psychology,* **56**, 601–630.

Keller, P.A., McCluskey, A., Morgan, J. and O'Connor, S.M. (2006) The role of the HPA axis in psychiatric disorders and CRF antagonists as potential treatments. *Archiv der Pharmazie,* **339**, 346–355.

Kenshalo, D.R. and Douglass, D.K. (1995) The role of cerebral cortex in the experience of pain. In *Pain and the Brain: From Nociception to Cognition* (Advances in Pain Research and Therapy, Vol. 22) (eds B. Bromm and J.E. Desmedt), Raven Press, New York, pp. 21–34.

Kiecolt-Glaser, J.K., Page, G.G., Marucha, P.T., MacCallum, R.C. and Glaser, R. (1998) Psychological influences on surgical recovery: perspectives from psychoneuroimmunology. *American Psychologist,* **53**, 1209–1218.

Kim, J.J. and Diamond, D.M. (2002) The stressed hippocampus, synaptic plasticity and lost memories. *Nature Reviews Neuroscience,* **3**, 453–462.

Klee, H. and Morris, J. (1997) Amphetamine misuse: the effects of social context on injection related risk behaviour. *Addiction Research,* **4**, 329–342.

Koepp, M.J., Gunn, R.N., Lawrence, A.D., Cunningham, V.J., Dagher, T., Jones, T., Brooks, D.J., Bench, C.J. and Grasby, P.M. (1998) Evidence for striatal dopamine release during a video game. *Nature,* **393**, 266–268.

Koob, G.F. (1999) Drug reward addiction. In *Fundamental Neuroscience* (eds M.J. Zigmond, F.E. Bloom, S.C. Landis, J.L. Roberts and L.R. Squire), Academic Press, San Diego, pp. 1261–1279.

Koob, G.F. and Le Moal, M. (*2006) Neurobiology of Addiction,* Elsevier, Amsterdam.

Kozlowski, L.T., Wilkinson, A., Skinner, W., Kent, C., Franklin, T. and Pope, M. (1989) Comparing tobacco cigarette dependence with other drug dependencies. *Journal of the American Medical Association,* **261**, 898–901.

L

Larson, S.J. (2002) Behavioral and motivational effects of immune-system activation. *Journal of General Psychology,* **129**, 401–414.

Laudenslager, M.L., Ryan, S.M., Drugan, R.C., Hyson, R.L. and Maier, S.F. (1983) Coping and immunosuppression: inescapable but not escapable shock suppresses lymphocyte proliferation. *Science,* **221**, 568–570.

Lawrence, A.D., Evans. A.H., Lees, A.J. (2003) Compulsive use of dopamine replacement therapy in Parkinson's disease: reward systems gone awry? *The Lancet Neurology,* **2**, 595–604.

Le Doux, J. (1998) *The Emotional Brain,* Weidenfeld and Nicolson, London.

Le Strat, Y., Ramoz, N., Horwood, J., Falissard, B., Hassler, C., Romo, L., Choquet, M., Fergusson, D. and Gorwood, P. (2009) First positive reactions to cannabis constitute a priority risk factor for cannabis dependence. *Addiction,* **104**, 1710–1717.

Leiblum, S.R. and Rosen, R.C. (2000) *Principles and Practice of Sex Therapy,* Guilford Press, New York.

LeVay, S. (1991) A difference in hypothalamic structure between heterosexual and homosexual men. *Science,* **253**, 1034–1037.

Levenstein, S. (1998) Stress and peptic ulcer: life beyond *helicobacter. British Medical Journal,* **316**, 538–541.

Levine, J.D., Gordon, N.C. and Fields, H.L. (1978) The mechanism of placebo analgesia. *The Lancet,* **2**, 654–657.

Leyton, M. (2010) The neurobiology of desire: dopamine and the regulation of mood and motivational states in humans. In *Pleasures of the Brain* (eds M.L. Kringelbach and K.C. Berridge), Oxford University Press, New York, pp. 222–243.

Lim, S-Y., Evans, A.H., and Miyasaki, J.M. (2008) Impulse control and related disorders in Parkinson's disease. *Annals of the New York Academy of Sciences*, **1142**, 85–107.

Liu, T. (2009) Acupuncture: what underlies needle administration? *Evidence-Based Complementary and Alternative Medicine*, **6**, 185–193.

M

MacRae, J.R. and Siegel, S. (1997) The role of self-administration in morphine withdrawal in rats. *Psychobiology*, **25**, 77–82.

Maier, S.F. and Watkins, L.R. (1998) Cytokines for psychologists: implications of bidirectional immune-to-brain communication for understanding behavior, mood, and cognition. *Psychological Review*, **105**, 83–107.

Maier, S.F., Watkins, L.R. and Fleshner, M. (1994) Psychoneuro-immunology. *American Psychologist*, **49**, 1004–1017.

Maldonado, R., Robledo, P., Chover, A.J., Caine, S.B. and Koob, G.F. (1993) D1 dopamine receptors in the nucleus accumbens modulate cocaine self-administration in the rat. *Pharmacology, Biochemistry and Behavior*, **45**, 239–242.

Marissen, M.A.E., Franken, I.H.A., Blanken, P., van den Brink, W. and Hendriks, V.M. (2005) Cue exposure therapy for opiate dependent clients. *Journal of Substance Use*, **10**, 97–105.

Markou, A., Weiss, F., Gold, L.H., Caine, B., Schulteis, G. and Koob, G.F. (1993) Animal models of drug craving. *Psychopharmacology*, **112**, 163–182.

Markou, A., Kosten, T.R. and Koob, G.F. (1998) Neurobiological similarities in depression and drug dependence: a self-medication hypothesis. *Neuropsychopharmacology*, **18**, 135–174.

Marmot, M.G. and Syme, S.L. (1976) Acculturation and coronary heart disease in Japanese-Americans. *American Journal of Epidemiology*, **104**, 225–247.

Marshall, B.J. (1995) *Helicobacter pylori* in peptic ulcer: have Koch's postulates been fulfilled? *Annals of Medicine*, **27**, 565–568.

Martin, J.H. (1996) *Neuroanatomy: Text and Atlas*, Prentice Hall, London.

Martini, F.H., Timmons, M.J. and McKinley, M.P. (2000) *Human Anatomy*, Prentice Hall, Upper Saddle River.

Mason, G.J. (1991) Stereotypies: a critical review. *Animal Behaviour*, **41**, 1015–1037.

Mason, P. (1999) Central mechanisms of pain modulation. *Current Opinion in Neurobiology*, **9**, 436–441.

McBride, W.J. and Li, T-K. (1998) Animal models of alcoholism: neurobiology of high alcohol-drinking behaviour in rodents. *Critical Reviews in Neurobiology*, **12**, 339–369.

McEwen, B.S. (2004) *The End of Stress as We Know It*, Joseph Henry Press, Washington.

McKee, D.P. and Quigley, E.M.M. (1993) Intestinal motility in irritable bowel syndrome: is IBS a motility disorder? Part 2. Motility of the small bowel, esophagus, stomach, and gall-bladder. *Digestive Diseases and Sciences*, **38**, 1773–1782.

McMurray, G.A. (1950) Experimental study of a case of insensitivity to pain *Archives of Neurology and Psychiatry*, **64**, 650–667.

Meddis, R. (1977) *The Sleep Instinct*, Routledge and Kegan Paul, London.

Meissner, W. (2009) The role of acupuncture and transcutaneous-electrical nerve stimulation for postoperative pain control. *Current Opinion in Anaesthesiology*, **22**, 623–626.

Melzack, R. (1988) The tragedy of needless pain: a call for social action. In *Proceedings of the Vth World Congress on Pain* (eds R. Dubner, G.F. Gubner and M.R. Bond), Elsevier Science Publishers, Amsterdam, pp. 1–11.

Melzack, R. (1989) Phantom limbs, the self and the brain (The D.O. Hebb Memorial Lecture). *Canadian Psychology*, **30**, 1–16.

Melzack, R. (1993) Pain: past, present and future. *Canadian Journal of Experimental Psychology*, **47**, 615–629.

Melzack, R. and Wall, P.D. (1965) Pain mechanisms: a new theory. *Science*, **150**, 971–979.

Melzack, R. and Wall, P. (2008) *The Challenge of Pain*, Penguin Books, Harmondsworth.

Mercer, M.E. and Holder, M.D. (1997) Food cravings, endogenous opioid peptides and food intake: a review. *Appetite*, **29**, 325–352.

Meyer, E.A. and Gebhart, G.F. (1994) Basic and clinical aspects of visceral hyperalgesia. *Gastroenterology*, **107**, 271–293.

Milner, B. (1964) Some effects of frontal lobectomy in man In *The Frontal Granular Cortex and Behavior* (eds J.M. Warren and K. Akert), McGraw-Hill, New York, pp. 313–334.

Milner, B. (1966) Amnesia following opera-

tion on the temporal lobes In *Amnesia* (eds C.W.M. Whitty and O.L. Zangwill), Butterworths, London, pp. 109–133.

Mistlberger, R.E. (2005) Circadian regulation of sleep in mammals: role of the suprachiasmatic nucleus. *Brain Research Reviews*, **49**, 429–454.

Mitchell, A.J. (1998) The role of corticotropin releasing factor in depressive illness: a critical review. *Neuroscience and Biobehavioral Reviews*, **22**, 635–651.

Moberg, G.P. (1985) Biological response to stress: key to assessment of animal wellbeing. In *Animal Stress* (ed. G.P. Moberg), American Physiological Society, Bethesda, pp. 27–49.

Moberg, G.P. and Mench, J.A. (2000) *The Biology of Animal Stress*, CAB International, Wallingford.

Moore, R.Y. (1999) Circadian timing. In *Fundamental Neuroscience* (eds M.J. Zigmond, F.E. Bloom, S.C. Landis, J.L. Roberts and L.R. Squire), Academic Press, San Diego, pp. 1189–1206.

Moruzzi, G. and Magoun, H.W. (1949) Brain stem reticular formation and activation of the EEG. *Electroencephalography and Clinical Neurophysiology*, **1**, 455–473.

Moscovitch, M. and Umiltà, C. (1990) Modularity and neuropsychology: modules and central processes in attention and memory. In *Modular Deficits in Alzheimer-type Dementia* (ed. M.F. Schwartz), MIT Press, Cambridge, pp. 1–60.

Moseley, G.L. (2003) A pain neuromatrix approach to patients with chronic pain. *Manual Therapy*, **8**, 130–140.

Murotani, T., Ishizuka, T., Nakazawa, H., Wang, X., Mori, K., Sasaki, K., Ishida, T. and Yamatodani, A. (2010) Possible involvement of histamine, dopamine, and noradrenalin in the periaqueductal gray in electroacupuncture pain relief. *Brain Research*, **1306**, 62–68.

Musselman, D.L., Evans, D.L. and Nemeroff, C.B. (1998) The relationship of depression to cardiovascular disease. *Archives of General Psychiatry*, **55**, 580–592.

Mutschler, N.H. and Miczek, K.A. (1998) Withdrawal from IV cocaine 'binges' in rats: ultrasonic distress calls and startle. *Psychopharmacology*, **135**, 161–168.

N

Naqvi, N.H. and Bechara, A. (2009) The hidden island of addiction: the insula. *Trends in Neurosciences*, **32**, 56–66.

Naqvi, N.H., Rudrauf, D., Damasio, H. and Bechara, A. (2007) Damage to the insula disrupts addiction to cigarette smoking. *Science,* **315**, 531–534.

Nesse, R.M. and Berridge, K.C. (1997) Psychoactive drug use in evolutionary perspective. *Science,* **278**, 63–66.

O

O'Leary, A. (1990) Stress, emotion and human immune function. *Psychological Bulletin,* **108**, 363–382.

Orford, J. (2001) *Excessive Appetites: A Psychological View of Addictions,* Wiley, Chichester.

Orr, S.P., Lasko, N.B., Shalev, A.Y. and Pitman, R.K. (1995) Physiological responses to loud tones in Vietnam veterans with posttraumatic stress disorder. *Journal of Abnormal Psychology,* **104**, 75–82.

Oshiro, Y., Quevedo, A.S., McHaffie, J.G., Kraft, R.A. and Coghill, R.C. (2009) Brain mechanisms supporting discrimination of sensory features of pain: a new model. *Journal of Neuroscience,* **29**, 14924–14931.

Overmier, J.B. and Murison, R (1997) Animal models reveal the psych' in the psychosomatics of peptic ulcers. *Current Directions in Psychological Science,* **6**, 180–184.

P

Pallmeyer, T.P., Blanchard, E.B. and Kolb, L.C. (1986) The psychophysiology of combat-induced post-traumatic stress disorder in Vietnam veterans. *Behaviour Research and Therapy,* **24**, 645–652.

Panksepp, J. (1982) Toward a general psychobiological theory of emotions. *Behavioral and Brain Sciences,* **5**, 407–467.

Peele, S. (1985) *The Meaning of Addiction,* Lexington Books, Lexington.

Peele, S. and Alexander, B.K. (1985) Theories of addiction. In *The Meaning of Addiction* (ed. S. Peele), Lexington Books, Lexington, pp. 47–72.

Peele, S. and Degrandpre, R.J. (1998) Cocaine and the concept of addiction: environmental factors in drug compulsions. *Addiction Research,* **6**, 235–263.

Peres, M.F.P., Zukerman, E., Senne Soares, C.A., Alonso, E.O., Santos, B.F.C. and Faulhaber, M.H. (2004) Cerebrospinal fluid glutamate levels in chronic migrane. *Cephalalgia,* **24**, 735–739.

Petrovic, P. (2010) Placebo analgesia and the brain. In *Pleasures of the Brain* (eds M.L. Kringelbach and K.C. Berridge), Oxford University Press, Oxford, pp. 287–301.

Petrovic, P., Kalso, E., Petersson, K.M. and Ingvar, M. (2002) Placebo and opioid analgesia – imaging a shared neuronal network. *Science,* **295**, 1737–1740.

Pfaff, D.W., Martin, E.M. and Ribeiro, A.C. (2007) Relations between mechanisms of CNS arousal and mechanisms of stress. *Stress,* **10**, 316–325.

Phillips-Bute, B.G. and Lane, J.D. (1998) Caffeine withdrawal symptoms following brief caffeine deprivation. *Physiology and Behavior,* **63**, 35–39.

Phoenix, C.H., Goy, R.W., Gerall, A.A. and Young, W.C. (1959) Organizing action of prenatally administered testosterone propionate on the tissues mediating mating behavior in the female guinea pig. *Endocrinology,* **65**, 369–382.

Pierce, R.C. and Kalivas, P.W. (1997) A circuitry model of the expression of behavioral sensitization to amphetamine-like psychostimulants. *Brain Research Reviews,* **25**, 192–216.

Pineda, J.O.A. and Oberman, L.M. (2006) What goads cigarette smokers to smoke? Neural adaptation and the mirror neuron system. *Brain Research,* **1121**, 128–135.

Pitman, R.K., Orr, S.P. and Shalev, A.Y. (1993) Once bitten, twice shy: beyond the conditioning model of PTSD. *Biological Psychiatry,* **33**, 145–146.

Pomeranz, B., Wall, P.D. and Weber, W.V. (1968) Cord cells responding to fine myelinated afferents from viscera, muscle and skin. *Journal of Physiology,* **199**, 511–532.

Pomerleau, O.F. and Pomerleau, C.S. (1984) Neuroregulators and the reinforcement of smoking: towards a biobehavioral explanation. *Neuroscience and Biobehavioral Reviews,* **8**, 503–513.

Post, S.G. (2007) *Altruism and Health: Perspectives from Empirical Research,* Oxford University Press, New York.

Povinelli, D.J. and Preuss, T.M. (1995) Theory of mind: evolutionary history of a cognitive specialization. *Trends in Neurosciences,* **18**, 418–424.

R

Råberg, L., Grahn, M., Hasselquist, D. and Svensson, E. (1998) On the adaptive significance of stress-induced immunosuppression. *Proceedings of the Royal Society of London B,* **265**, 1637–1641.

Rahn, E.J. and Hohmann, A.G. (2009) Cannabinoids as pharmacotherapies for neuropathic pain: from the bench to the bedside. *Neurotherapeutics,* **6**, 713–737.

Rainville, P., Duncan, G.H., Price, D.D., Carrier, B. and Bushnell, M.C. (1997) Pain affect encoded in human anterior cingulate but not somatosensory cortex. *Science,* **277**, 968–971.

Ramachandran, V.S. and Altschuler, E.L. (2009) The use of visual feedback, in particular mirror visual feedback, in restoring brain function. *Brain,* **132**, 1693–1710.

Ramachandran, V.S. and Blakeslee, S. (1998) *Phantoms in the Brain: Human Nature and the Architecture of the Mind.* Fourth Estate, London.

Ramachandran, V.S. and Brang, D. (2009) Sensations evoked in patients with amputation from watching an individual whose corresponding intact limb is being touched. *Archives of Neurology,* **66**, 1281–1284.

Rechtschaffen, A. (1998) Current perspectives on the function of sleep. *Perspectives in Biology and Medicine,* **41**, 359–390.

Reid, M.S., Mickalian, J.D., Delucchi, K.L., Hall, S.M. and Berger, S.P. (1998) An acute dose of nicotine enhances cue-induced cocaine craving. *Drug and Alcohol Dependence,* **49**, 95–104.

Ribot, T.H. (1885) *Diseases of Memory,* Kegan Paul, Trench and Co., London.

Richardson, L.K., Frueh, B.C. and Acierno, R. (2010) Prevalence estimates of combat-related post-traumatic stress disorder: critical review. *Australian and New Zealand Journal of Psychiatry,* **44**, 4–19.

Robbins, T.W., Everitt, B. and Nutt, D. (2010) *The Neurobiology of Addiction,* Oxford University Press, Oxford.

Roberts, G.M.P., Nestor, L. and Garavan, (2009) Learning and memory deficits in ecstasy users and their neural correlates during a face-learning task. *Brain Research,* **1292**, 71–81.

Robins, L.N., Helzer, J.E. and Davis, D.H. (1975) Narcotic use in Southeast Asia and afterward. *Archives of General Psychiatry,* **32**, 955–961.

Robinson, M.J., Edwards, S.E., Iyengar, S., Bymaster, F., Clark, M. and Katon, W. (2009) Depression and pain. *Frontiers in Bioscience,* **14**, 5031–5051.

Robinson, T.E. and Berridge, K.C. (1993) The neural basis of drug craving: an incentive-sensitization theory of addiction. *Brain Research Reviews,* **18**, 247–291.

Robinson, T.E. and Berridge, K.C. (2008) The incentive sensitization theory of addiction: some current issues. *Philosophical Transactions of the Royal Society B,* **363**, 3137–3146.

Rose, J.E. and Corrigal, W.A. (1997) Nicotine self-administration in animals and humans: similarities and differences. *Psychopharmacology,* **130**, 28–40.

Rosen, J.B. and Schulkin, J. (1998) From normal fear to pathological anxiety. *Psychological Review,* **105**, 325–350.

Rozin, P.N. and Schulkin, J. (1990) Food selection. In *Handbook of Behavioral Neurobiology,* Vol. 10, *Neurobiology of Food and Fluid Intake (ed.* E.M. Strieker), Plenum Press, New York, pp. 297–328.

S

Sakakibara, M., Takeuchi, S. and Hayano, J. (1994) Effect of relaxation training on cardiac parasympathetic tone. *Psychophysiology,* **31**, 223–228.

Salomons, T.V., Johnstone, T., Backonja, M-M., Shackman, A.J. and Davidson, R.J. (2007) Individual differences in the effects of perceived controllability on pain perception: critical role of the prefrontal cortex. *Journal of Cognitive Neuroscience,* **19**, 993–1003.

Sapolsky, R. (2005) Sick of poverty. *Scientific American,* **293**(6), 92–99.

Sapolsky, R., Rivier, C., Yamamoto, G., Plotsky, P. and Vale, W. (1987) Interleukin-1 stimulates the secretion of hypothalamic corticotropinreleasing factor. *Science,* **238**, 522–524.

Sapolsky, R.M. (1990a) Adrenocortical function, social rank, and personality among wild baboons. *Biological Psychiatry,* **28**, 862–878.

Sapolsky, R.M. (1990b) Stress in the wild. *Scientific American,* **262**, No. 1, 106–113.

Sapolsky, R.M. (1992) Neuroendocrinology of the stress response. In *Behavioral Endocrinology* (eds J.B. Becker, S.M. Breedlove and D. Crews), MIT Press, Cambridge, pp. 287–324.

Sapolsky, R.M. (2004) *Why Zebras don't get Ulcers,* St Martin's Press, New York.

Scheidt, S. (1996) A whirlwind tour of cardiology for the mental health professional. In *Heart and Mind. The Practice of Cardiac Psychology* (eds R. Allan and S. Scheidt), American Psychological Association, Washington, pp. 15–62.

Schenck, C.H., Bundlie, S.R., Ettinger, M.G. and Mahowald, M.W. (1986) Chronic behavioral disorders of human REM sleep: a new category of parasomnia. *Sleep,* **9**, 293–308.

Schneider, J. and Weiss, R. (2001) *Cybersex Exposed: Simple Fantasy or Obsession?,* Hazelden, Center City.

Schneider, W. and Shiffrin, R.M. (1977) Controlled and automatic human information processing: I. Detection, search and attention. *Psychological Review,* **84**, 1–66.

Schulkin, J. (1994) Melancholic depression and the hormones of adversity: a role for the amygdala. *Current Directions in Psychological Science,* 3, 41–44.

Scott, D.J., Stohler, C.S., Egnatuk, C.M., Wang, H., Koeppe, R.A. and Zubieta, J-K. (2008) Placebo and nocebo effects are defined by opposite opioid and dopaminergic responses. *Archives of General Psychiatry,* **65**, 220–231.

Scoville, W.B. and Milner, B. (1957) Loss of recent memory after bilateral hippocampal lesions. *Journal of Neurology, Neurosurgery and Psychiatry,* **20**, 11 –21.

Seeman, T.E. and Robbins, R.J. (1994) Aging and hypothalamic-pituitary-adrenal response to challenge in humans. *Endocrine Reviews,* **15**, 233–260.

Segerstrom, S.C. and Sephton, S.E. (2010) Optimistic expectancies and cell-mediated immunity: the role of positive affect *Psychological Science,* **21**, 448–455.

Seifert, F. and Maihofner, C. (2009) Central mechanisms of experimental and chronic neuropathic pain: findings from functional imaging studies. *Cellular and Molecular Life Sciences,* **66**, 375–390.

Seligman, M. (1975) *Helplessness,* W.H. Freeman, San Francisco.

Selye, H. (1973) The evolution of the stress concept. *American Scientist,* **61**, 692–699.

Seminowicz, D.A. and Davis, K.D. (2006) Cortical responses to pain in healthy individuals depends on pain catastrophising. *Pain,* **120**, 297–306.

Shaham, Y. and Stewart, J. (1995) Stress reinstates heroin-seeking in drug-free animals: an effect mimicking heroin, not withdrawal. *Psychopharmacology,* **119**, 334–341.

Shallice, T. and Jackson, M. (1988) Lissauer on agnosia. *Cognitive Neuropsychology,* **5**, 153–156.

Sherry, D.F. (1992) Memory, the hippocampus, and natural selection: studies of food-storing birds. In *Neuropsychology of Memory* (eds R. Squire and N. Butters), Guilford Press, New York, pp. 521–532.

Shoaib, M., Swanner, L.C., Yasar, S. and Goldberg, S.R. (1999) Chronic caffeine exposure potentiates nicotine self-administration in rats. *Psychopharmacology,* **142**, 327–333.

Siegel, A. (2005) *The Neurobiology of Aggression and Rage,* CRC Press, Boca Raton.

Siegel, J.M. (2004) Hypocretin (orexin): role in normal behavior and neuropathology. *Annual Review of Psychology,* **55**, 125–148.

Siegel, J.M. (2005) The incredible, shrinking sleep-learning connection. *Behavioral and Brain Sciences,* **28**, 82–83.

Siegel, R.K. and Jarvik, M E. (1980) DMT self-administration by monkeys in isolation. *Bulletin of the Psychonomic Society,* **16**, 117–120.

Siegel, S. (1984) Pavlovian conditioning and heroin overdose: reports by overdose victims. *Bulletin of the Psychonomic Society,* **22**, 428–430.

Singer, J.L. (1993) Experimental studies of ongoing conscious experience. In *Experimental and Theoretical Studies of Consciousness* (eds G.R. Bock and J. Marsh), Wiley, Chichester, pp. 100–122.

Singer, T., Seymour, B., O'Doherty, J., Kaube, H., Dolan, R.J. and Frith, C.D. (2004) Empathy for pain involves the affective but not sensory components of pain. *Science,* **303**, 1157–1162.

Skoubis, P.D., Lam, H.A., Shoblock, J., Narayanan, S. and Maidment, N.T. (2005) Endogenous enkephalins, not endorphins, modulate basal hedonic state in mice. *European Journal of Neuroscience,* **21**, 1379–1384.

Solomon, R.L. and Corbit, J.D. (1974) The opponent-process theory of motivation. I. *Psychological Review,* **81**, 119–145.

Sorg, B.A. and Kalivas, P.W. (1995) Stress and neuronal sensitization. In *Neurobiological and Clinical Consequences of Stress. From Normal Adaptation to Post-traumatic Stress Disorder* (eds M.J. Friedman, D.S. Charney and A.Y. Deutch), Lippincott-Raven, Philadelphia, pp. 83–102.

Stahl, S.M. (1996) *Essential Psychopharmacology*, Cambridge University Press, Cambridge.

Stahl, S.M. (1998) Getting stoned without inhaling: anandamide is the brain's natural marijuana. *Journal of Clinical Psychiatry*, **59**, 566–567.

Stam, R., Akkermans, L.M.A. and Wiegant, M. (1997) Trauma and the gut: interactions between stressful experience and intestinal function. *Gut*, **40**, 704–709.

Steele, T.D., McCann, U.D. and Ricaurte, G.A. 3,4-Methylenedioxymethamphetamine (MDMA, Ecstasy): pharmacology and toxicology in animals and humans. *Addiction*, **89**, 539–551.

Stein, M., Miller, A H and Trestman, R.L. Depression, the immune system, and health and illness. *Archives of General Psychiatry*, **48**, 171–177.

Steptoe, A. (1993) Stress and the cardiovascular system: a psychosocial perspective. In *Stress – From Synapse to Syndrome* (eds S.C. Stanford and P. Salmon), Academic Press, London, pp. 119–141.

Steptoe, A., Dockray, S. and Wardle, J. (2009) Positive affect and psychobiological processes relevant to health. *Journal of Personality*, **77**, 1747–1775.

Stewart, J., de Wit, H. and Eikelboom, R. (1984) Role of unconditioned and conditioned drug effects in the self-administration of opiates and stimulants. *Psychological Review*, **91**, 251–268.

Stewart-Williams, S. and Podd, J. (2004) The placebo effect: dissolving the expectancy versus conditioning debate. *Psychological Bulletin*, **130**, 324–340.

Stolerman, I.P. and Jarvis, M.J. (1995) The scientific case that nicotine is addictive. *Psychopharmacology*, **117**, 2–10.

Stroop, J.R. (1935) Studies of interference in serial verbal reactions. *Journal of Experimental Psychology*, **18**, 643–662.

Sufka, K. and Turner, D. (2005) An evolutionary account of chronic pain: integrating the natural method of evolutionary psychology. *Philosophical Psychology*, **18**, 243–257.

Sulloway, F.J. (1979) *Freud – Biologist of the Mind*, Burnett Books, London.

Szechtman, H. and Woody, E. (2004) Obsessive-compulsive disorder as a disturbance of security motivation. *Psychological Review*, **111**, 111–127.

Szuster, R.R., Pontius, E.B. and Campos, P.E. (1988) Marijuana sensitivity and panic attack. *Journal of Clinical Psychiatry*, **49**, 427–429.

T

Tache, Y. and Brunnhuber, S. (2008) From Hans Selye's discovery of biological stress to the identification of corticotrophin-releasing factor signaling pathways. *Annals of the New York Academy of Sciences*, **1148**, 29–41.

Takahashi, H., Takada, Y., Nagai, N., Urano, T. and Takada, A. (1998) Effects of nicotine and footshock stress on dopamine release in the striatum and nucleus accumbens. *Brain Research Bulletin*, **45**, 157–162.

Taylor, S.E., Kemeny, M.E., Reed, G.M., Bower, J.E. and Gruenewald, T.L. (2000) Psychological resources, positive illusions, and health. *American Psychologist*, **55**, 99–109.

Thewissen, R., van den Hout, M., Havermans, R.C. and Jansen, A. (2005) Context-dependency of cue-elicited urge to smoke. *Addiction*, **100**, 387–396.

Thorn, B.E. (2004) *Cognitive Therapy for Chronic Pain*, Guilford Press, New York.

Tiffany, S.L. (1990) A cognitive model of drug urges and drug-use behaviour: role of automatic and nonautomatic processes, *Psychological Review*, **97**, 147–168.

Toates, F. (1995) *Stress – Conceptual and Biological Aspects*, Wiley Chichester.

Toates, F. (1997c) Human sexuality. In *The Human Condition* (SK220, Book 4) (ed. F. Toates), The Open University, Milton Keynes, pp. 43–65.

Toates, F. (1998b) The biological bases of behaviour. In *Psychology – An Integrated Approach* (ed. M. Eysenck), Addison Wesley Longman, Harlow, pp. 23–67.

Toates, F. (2004) Introduction to brains, mind and consciousness In *From Cells to Consciousness*. Book 1 of Course SD226 *Biological Psychology: Exploring the Brain*, The Open University, Milton Keynes.

Tokar, J.T., Brunse, A.J., Stefflre, V.J., Sodergren, J.A. and Napior, D.A. (1975) Determining what heroin means to heroin addicts. *Diseases of the Nervous System*, **36**, 77–81.

Tracey, I., Ploghaus, A., Gati, J.S., Clare, S., Smith, S., Menon, R.S. and Matthews, P.M. (2002) Imaging attentional modulation of pain in the periaqueductal gray in humans. *The Journal of Neuroscience*, **22**, 2748–2752.

Tulving, E. (1972) Episodic and semantic memory. In *Organization of Memory* (ed. E. Tulving and W. Donaldson), Academic Press, New York, pp. 381–403.

U

Uno, H., Tarara, R., Else, J.G., Suleman, M.A. and Sapolsky, R.M. (1989) Hippocampal damage associated with prolonged and fatal stress in primates. *Journal of Neuroscience*, **9**, 1705–1711.

Ur, E., White, P.D. and Grossman, A. (1992) Hypothesis: cytokines may be activated to cause depressive illness and chronic fatigue syndrome. *European Archives of Psychiatry and Clinical Neuroscience*, **241**, 317–322.

Ursin, H. and Olff, M. (1993) The stress response. In *Stress – From Synapse to Syndrome* (eds S.C. Stanford and P. Salmon), Academic Press, London, pp. 3–22.

V

Vahle-Hinz, C. Brtiggemann, J. and Kniffki, K-D. (1995) Thalamic processing of visceral pain. In *Pain and the Brain: From Nociception to Cognition* (Advances in Pain Research and Therapy, Vol. 22) (eds B. Bromm and J.E. Desmedt), Raven Press, New York, pp. 125–141.

van Dijken, H.H., de Goeij, D.C.E., Sutanto, W., Mos, J., de Kloet, E.R. and Tilders, F.J.H. Short inescapable stress produces long-lasting changes in the brain-pituitary-adrenal axis of adult male rats. *Neuroendocrinology*, **58**, 57–64.

van Honk, J., Tuiten, A., van den Hout, M., Koppeschaar, H., Thijssen, J., de Haan, E. and Verbaten, R. (1998) Baseline salivary cortisol levels and preconscious selective attention for threat. A pilot study. *Psychoneuroendocrinology*, **23**, 741–747.

van Os, J. and Kapur, S. (2009) Schizophrenia. *The Lancet*, **374**, 635–645.

Vander, A.J., Sherman, J.H. and Luciano, D.S. (1994) *Human Physiology*, McGraw-Hill, New York.

Vanderschuren, L.J.M.J. and Everitt, B.J. (2004) Drug seeking becomes compulsive after prolonged cocaine self-administration. *Science*, **305**, 1017–1019.

Viamontes, C.T. (2009) The sickness response: an adaptive brain-body reaction to medical illness. *Psychiatric Annals*, **39**, 985–996.

Volkow, N.D., Wang, G.-J., Fowler, J.S., Logan, J., Gatley, S.J., Hitzemann, R., Chen, A.D., Dewey, S.L. and Pappas, N. (1997) Decreased striatal dopaminergic responsiveness in detoxified cocaine-dependent subjects. *Nature, 386,* 830–833.

Volkow, N.D., Fowler, J.S. and Wang, J-W. (2002) Role of dopamine in drug reinforcement and addiction in humans: results from imaging studies. *Behavioural Pharmacology,* **13,** 355–366.

von Holst, E. and Mittlestaedt, H. (1950) Das Reafferenzprinzip. *Naturwissenschaften,* **37,** 464–476. English translation in Gallistel, C.R. (1980) *The Organization of Action: A New Synthesis,* Lawrence Erlbaum, Hillsdale, pp. 176–209.

W

Wager, T.D., Rilling, J.K., Smith, E.E., Sokolik, A., Casey, K.L., Davidson, R.J., Kosslyn, S.M., Rose, R.M. and Cohen, J.D. (2004) Placebo-induced changes in fMRI in the anticipation and experience of pain. *Science,* **303,** 1162–1167.

Wall, P.D. (1993) Pain and the placebo response. In *Experimental and Theoretical Studies of Consciousness* (eds G.R. Bock and J. Marsh), Wiley, Chichester, pp. 187–216.

Wall, P.D. (2002) *Pain: The Science of Suffering,* Columbia University Press, New York.

Wand, G.S., Mangold, D., El Deiry, S., McCaul, M.E. and Hoover, D. (1998) Family history of alcoholism and hypothalamic opioidergic activity. *Archives of General Psychiatry,* **55,** 1114–1119.

Wang, J.Q. and McGinty, J.F. (1999) Glutamate-dopamine interactions mediate the effects of psychostimulant drugs. *Addiction Biology,* **4,** 141–150.

Wang, Z., Neylan, T.C., Mueller, S.G., Lenoci, M., Truran, D., Marmar, C.R., Weiner, M.W. and Shuff, N. (2010) Magnetic resonance imaging of hippocampal subfields in post-traumatic stress disorder. *Archives of General Psychiatry,* **67,** 296–303.

Warrington, E.K. and Weiskrantz, L. (1970) Amnesic syndrome: consolidation or retrieval? *Nature,* **228,** 628–630.

Waugh, C.E., Wager, T.D., Fredrickson, B.L., Noll, D.C., Taylor, S.F. (2008) The neural correlates of trait resilience when anticipating and recovering from threat. *Social Cognitive and Affective Neuroscience,* **8,** 322–332.

Weiner, H. (1996) Use of animal models in peptic ulcer disease. *Psychosomatic Medicine,* **58,** 524–545.

Weingarten, H.P. (1984) Meal initiation controlled by learned cues: basic behavioral properties. *Appetite,* **5,** 147–158.

Weisenberg, M. (1994) Cognitive aspects of pain. In *Textbook of Pain* (eds P.D. Wall and R. Melzack), Churchill Livingstone, Edinburgh, pp. 275–289.

Weiss, J.M. (1971) Effects of coping behaviour in different warning signal conditions on stress pathology in rats. *Journal of Comparative and Physiological Psychology,* **77,** 1–13.

Weiss, J.M. (1972) Psychological factors in stress and disease. *Scientific American,* **226,** No. 6, 104–113.

Weiss, J.M., Pohorecky, L.A., Salman, S. and Gruenthal, M. (1976) Attenuation of gastric lesions by psychological aspects of aggression in rats. *Journal of Comparative and Physiological Psychology,* **90,** 252–259.

Wernicke, C. (1874) *Der Aphasische Symptomenkomplex,* Cohn und Weigert, Breslau.

West, R. (2006) *Theory of Addiction,* Wiley-Blackwell, Hoboken.

Wikler, A. (1965) Conditioning factors in opiate addiction and relapse. In *Narcotics* (eds D.I. Wilner and G.G. Kassanbaum), McGraw-Hill, New York, pp. 399–114.

Williams, C.L., Villar, R.G., Peterson, J.M. and Burks, T.F. (1988) Stress-induced changes in intestinal transit in the rat: a model for irritable bowel syndrome. *Gastroenterology,* **94,** 611–621.

Williams, R. (1989) *The Trusting Heart,* Times Books, New York.

Willner, P. (1993) Animal models of stress: an overview. In *Stress – From Synapse to Syndrome* (eds S.C. Stanford and P. Salmon), Academic Press, London, pp. 145–165.

Willner, P., James, D. and Morgan, M. (2005) Excessive alcohol consumption and dependence are associated with parallel increases in subjective ratings of both 'wanting' and 'liking'. *Addiction,* **100,** 1487–1495.

Wise, R.A. (1987) Sensorimotor modulation and the variable action pattern (VAP): toward a noncircular definition of drive and motivation. *Psychobiology,* **15,** 7–20.

Wise, R.A. (1988) The neurobiology of craving: implications for the understanding and treatment of addiction. *Journal of Abnormal Psychology,* **97,** 118–132.

Wise, R.A. and Bozarth, M.A. (1987) A psychomotor stimulant theory of addiction. *Psychological Review,* **94,** 469–192.

Wolffgramm, J. and Heyne, A. (1991) Social behavior, dominance, and social deprivation of rats determine drug choice. *Pharmacology Biochemistry and Behavior,* **38,** 389–399.

Wurtz, R.H., Goldberg, M.E. and Robinson, D.L. (1982) Brain mechanisms of visual attention. *Scientific American,* **246,** No. 6, 100–107.

Y

Yehuda, R., Giller, E.L., Levengood, R.A., Southwick, S.M. and Siever, L.J. (1995) Hypothalamic-pituitary-adrenal functioning in post-traumatic stress disorder. In *Neurobiological and Clinical Consequences of Stress. From Normal Adaptation to Post-traumatic Stress Disorder* (eds M.J. Friedman, D.S. Charney and A.Y. Deutch), Lippincott-Raven, Philadelphia, pp. 351–365.

Z

Zhou, Q., Filllingim, R.B., Riley, J.L., Malarkey, W.B. and Verne, G.N. (2010) Central and peripheral hypersensitivity in the irritable bowel syndrome. *Pain,* **148,** 454–461.

Zigmond, M.J., Finlay, J.M. and Sved, A.F. (1995) Neurochemical studies of central noradrenergic responses to acute and chronic stress. In *Neurobioiogicai and Clinical Consequences of Stress. From Normal Adaptation to Post-traumatic Stress Disorder* (eds M.J. Friedman, D.S. Charney and A.Y. Deutch), Lippincott-Raven, Philadelphia, pp. 45–60.

Zubieta, J-K. and Stohler, C.S. (2009) Neurobioiogicai mechanisms of placebo responses. *Annals of the New York Academy of Sciences,* **1156,** 198–210.

REFERENCES

Abrams, R. A, & Christ, S. E. (2003). Motion onset captures attention. *Psychological Science, 14,* 427–432.

Adolphs, R. & Tranel, D. (1999). Intact recognition of emotional prosody following amygdala damage. *Neuropsychologia, 37,* 1285–1292.

Ahlum-Heath, M. E. & DiVesta, F. J. (1986). The effect of conscious controlled verbalization of a cognitive strategy on transfer in problem solving. *Memory & Cognition, 14,* 281–285.

Ainsworth-Damell, K., Shulman, H. G., & Boland, J. E. (1998). Dissociating brain responses to syntactic and semantic anomalies: Evidence from event-related potentials. *Journal of Memory and Language, 38,* 112–130.

Allen, R. J., Baddeley, A. D., & Hitch, G. J. (2006). Is the binding of visual features in working memory resource-demanding? *Journal of Experimental Psychology: General, 135,* 298–313.

Almor, A. (1999). Noun-phrase anaphora and focus: The informational load hypothesis. *Psychological Review, 106,* 748–765.

Altarriba, J., Bauer, L. M., & Benvenuto, C. (1999). Concreteness, context availability, and imageability ratings and word associations for abstract, concrete, and emotion words. *Behavior Research Methods, 31,* 578–602.

Attmann, E. M., & Gray, W. D. (2002). Forgetting to remember: The functional relationship of decay and interference. *Psychological Science, 13,* 27–33.

Altmann, G. T. M. (1998). Ambiguity in sentence processing. *Trends in Cognitive Sciences, 2,* 146–157.

Altmann, G. T. M., Gambam, A, & Dennis, Y. (1992). Avoiding the garden path: Eye movements in context. *Journal of Memory and Language, 31,* 685–712.

Altmann, G. T. M., & Steedman, M. (1988). Interaction with context during human sentence processing. *Cognition, 30,* 191–238.

Anderson, A. K. (2005). Affective influences on the attentional dynamics supporting awareness. *Journal of Experimental Psychology: General, 134,* 258–281.

Anderson, J. R. (1980). *Cognitive psychology and its implications.* San Francisco: Freeman.

Anderson, J. R. (1985). *Cognitive psychology and its implications* (2nd ed.). New York: Freeman.

Anderson, J. R. (1993). Problem solving and learning. *American Psychologist, 48,* 35–44.

Anderson, M. C. (2003). Rethinking interference theory: Executive control and mechanisms of forgetting. *Journal of Memory and Language, 49,* 415–445.

Anderson, M. C., Bjork, E. L., & Bjork, R. A. (2000). Retrieval-induced forgetting: Evidence for a recall-specific mechanism. *Psychonomic Bulletin & Review, 7,* 522–530.

Andrade, J. (1995). Learning during anaesthesia: A review. *British Journal of Psychology, 86,* 479–506.

Arbuckle, T. Y., & Cuddy, L. L. (1969). Discrimination of item strength at time of presentation. *Journal of Experimental Psychology, 81,* 126–131.

Armony, J. L., Chochol, C., Fecteau, S., & Belin, P. (2007). Laugh (or cry) and you will be remembered. *Psychological Science, 18,* 1027–1029.

Arnold, J. E., & Griffin, Z. M. (2007). The effect of additional characters on choice of referring expression: Everyone counts. *Journal of Memory and Language, 56,* 521–536.

Ashcraft, M. H. (1993). A personal case history of transient anomia. *Brain and Language, 44,* 47–57.

Ashcraft, M. H., Kellas, G., & Needham, S. (1975). Rehearsal and retrieval processes in free recall of categorized lists. *Memory & Cognition, 3,* 506–512.

Ashcraft, M. H., & Krause, J. A. (2007). Working memory, math performance, and math anxiety. *Psychonomic Bulletin & Review, 14,* 243–248.

Aslan, A., Baüml, K-H., & Grundgeiger, T. (2007). The role of inhibitory processes in part-list cuing. *Journal of Experimental Psychology: Learning, Memory, and Cognition, 33,* 335–341.

Atkinson, R. C., & Shiffrin, R. M. (1968). Human memory: A proposed system and its control processes. In W. K. Spence & J. T. Spence (Eds.), *The psychology of learning and motivation: Advances in research and theory* (Vol. 2, pp. 89–195). New York: Academic Press.

Atwood, M. E., & Poison, P. (1976). A process model for water jug problems. *Cognitive Psychology, 8,* 191–216.

Axmacher, N., Cohen, M. X., Fell, J., Haupt, S., Dümpelmann, M., Eiger, C. E., et al. (2010). Intracranial EEG correlates of expectancy and memory formation in the human hippocampus and nucleus accumbens. *Neuron, 65,* 541–549.

Bachoud-Levi, A. C., Dupoux, E, Cohen, L., & Mehler, J. (1998). Where is the length effect? A cross-linguistic study of speech production. *Journal of Memory and Language, 39,* 331–346.

Baddeley, A. D. (1966). Short-term memory for word sequences as a function of acoustic, semantic, and formal similarity. *Quarterly Journal of Experimental Psychology, 18,* 302–309.

Baddeley, A, D. (1976). *The psychology of memory.* New York: Basic Books.

Baddeley, A. D. (1978). The trouble with levels: A reexamination of Craik and Lockhart's framework for memory research. *Psychological Review, 85,* 139–152.

Baddeley, A. D. (1992a). Is working memory working? The Fifteenth Bartlett Lecture. *Quarterly Journal of Experimental Psychology, 44A,* 1–31.

Baddeley, A. D. (1992b). Working memory. *Science, 255,* 556–559.

Baddeley, A. D. (2000a). The episodic buffer: A new component of working memory? *Trends in Cognitive Sciences, 4,* 417–423.

Baddeley, A. D. (2000b). The phonological loop and the irrelevant speech effect: some comments on Neath (2000). *Psychonomic Bulletin & Review, 7,* 544–549.

Baddeley, A. D., & Hitch, G. (1974). Working memory. In G. H. Bower (Ed.), *The psychology of learning and motivation* (Vol. 8, pp. 47–89). New York: Academic Press.

Baddeley, A. D., & Lieberman, K. (1980). Spatial working memory. In R. Nickerson (Ed.), *Attention and performance VLLL.* Hillsdale, NJ: Erlbaum.

Baddeley, A. D., Thomson, N., & Buchanan, M. (1975). Word length and the structure of short-term memory. *Journal of Verbal Learning and Verbal Behavior, 14,* 575–589.

Baddeley, A. D., & Wilson, R. (1988). Comprehension and working memory: A single case neuropsychological study. *Journal of Memory and Language, 27,* 479–498.

Balota, D. A., & Paul, S. T. (1996). Summation of activation: Evidence from multiple primes that converge and diverge within semantic memory. *Journal of Experimental Psychology: Learning, Memory, and Cognition, 22,* 827–845.

Banich, M. T. (1997). *Neuropsychology: Tloe neural bases of mental function.* Boston: Houghton Mifflin.

Banich, M. T. (2009). Executive function: The search for an integrated account. *Current Directions in Psychological Science, 18,* 89–94.

Barnard, P. J., Scott, S., Taylor, J., May, J., & Knightley, W. (2004). Paying attention to meaning. *Psychological Science, 15,* 179–186.

Barner, D. Li. P., & Snedeker, J. (2010). Words as windows to thought: The case of object representation. *Current Directions in Psychological Science, 19,* 195–200.

Barnier, A. J. (2002). Posthypnotic amnesia for autobiographical episodes: A laboratory model for functional amnesia? *Psychological Science, 13,* 242–237.

Barron, E., Riby, L. M., Greer, J., & Smallivood, J. (2011). Absorbed in thought: The effect of mind wandering on the processing of relevant and irrelevant events. *Psychological Science, 22,* 596–601.

Barshi, I., & Healy, A. F. (1993). Checklist procedures and the cost of automaticity. *Memory & Cognition, 21,* 496–505.

Bartlett, F. C. (1932). *Remembering: A study in experimental and social psychology.* London: Cambridge University Press.

Bassok, M., & Holyoak, K. H. (1989). Interdomain transfer between isomorphic topics in algebra and physics. *Journal of Experimental Psychology: Learning, Memory, and Cognition, 15,* 153–166.

Bassok, M., Pedigo, S. F., & Oskarsson, A. T. (2008). Priming addition facts with semantic relations. *Journal of Experimental Psychology: Learning, Memory, and Cognition, 34,* 343–352.

Bäuml, K-H. T., & Samenieh, A. (2010). The two faces of memory retrieval. *Psychological Science, 21,* 793–795.

Bavelas, J., Gerwing, J., Sutton, C., & Prevost, D. (2008). Gesturing on the telephone: Independent effects of dialogue and visibility. *Journal of Memory and Language, 58,* 495–520.

Bechera, A., Tranel, D., Damasio, H., Adolphs, R, Rockland, C., & Damasio, A. R. (1995) Double dissociation of conditioning and declarative knowledge relative to the amygdala and hippocampus in humans. *Science, 269,* 1115–1118.

Becker, M. W. (2009). Panic search: Fear produces efficient visual search for nonthreatening objects. *Psychological Science, 20,* 435–437.

Beech, A., Powell, T., McWilliams, J., & Claridge, G. (1989) Evidence of reduced cognitive inhibition in schizophrenics. *British Journal of Psychology, 28,* 109–116.

Beeman, M. J. (1993). Semantic processing in the right hemisphere may contribute to drawing inferences from discourse. *Brain and Language, 44,* 80–120.

Beeman, M. J. (1998). Coarse semantic coding and discourse comprehension. In M. Beeman & C. Chiarello (Eds.), *Brain right hemisphere language comprehension: perspectives from cognitive neuroscience* (pp. 255–284). Malwah, NJ: Erlbaum.

Beeman, M. J., & Bowden, E. M. (2000). The right hemisphere maintains solution-related activation for yet-to-be-solved problems. *Memory & Cognition, 28,* 1231–1241.

Beeman, M. J., & Chiarello, C. (1998). Complementary right- and left-hemisphere language comprehension. *Current Directions in Psychological Science, 7,* 2–8.

Beilock, S. L. (2008). Math performance in stressful situations. *Current Directions in Psychological Science, 17,* 339–343.

Beilock, S. L., Bertenthal, B. I., McCoy, A. M., & Carr, T. H. (2004). Haste does not always make waste: Expertise, direction of attention, and speed versus accuracy in performing sensorimotor skills. *Psychonomic Bulletin & Review, 11,* 373–379.

Beilock, S. L., & Carr, T. H. (2001). On the fragility of skilled performance: What governs choking under pressure? *Journal of Experimental Psychology: Learning, Memory, and Cognition, 33,* 983–998.

Beilock, S. L., & DeCaro, M. S. (2007). From poor performance to success under stress: Working memory, strategy selection, and mathematical problem solving under pressure. *Journal of Experimental Psychology, 130,* 701–725.

Beilock, S. L., Kulp, C. A., Holt, L. E., & Carr, T. H. (2004). More on the fragility of performance: Choking under pressure in mathematical problem solving. *Journal of Experimental Psychology: General, 133,* 584–600.

Beilock, S. L., Rydell, R. J., & McConnell, A. R. (2007). Stereotype threat and working memory: Mechanisms, alleviation, and spillover. *Journal of Experimental Psychology: General, 136,* 256–276.

Bekoff, M., Allen, C., & Burghardt, G. (Eds.) (2002). *The cognitive animal: Empirical and theoretical perspectives on animal cognition.* Cambridge, MA: MIT Press.

Bellezza, F. S. (1992). Recall of congruent information in the self-reference task. *Bulletin of the Psychonomic Society, 30,* 275–278.

Benson, D. J., & Geschwind, N. (1969). The alexias. In P. Vincken & G. W. Bruyn (Eds.), *Handbook of clinical neurology* (Vol. 4, pp. 112–140). Amsterdam: North-Holland.

Berger, A., Henik, A., & Rafal, R. (2005). Competition between endogenous and exogenous orienting of visual attention. *Journal of Experimental Psychology: General, 134,* 207–221.

Berman, M. G., Jonides, J., & Kaplan, S. (2008). The cognitive benefits of interacting with nature. *Psychological Science, 19,* 1207–1212.

Berndt, R. S., & Haendiges, A. N. (2000). Grammatical class in word and sentence production: Evidence from an aphasic patient. *Journal of Memory and Language, 43,* 249–273.

Bertsch, S., Pesta, B. J., Wiscott, R., & McDaniel, M. A. (2007). The generation effect: A meta-analytic review. *Memory & Cognition, 35,* 201–210.

Besner, D., & Stolz, J. A. (1999). What kind of attention modulates the Stroop effect? *Psychonomic Bulletin & Review, 6,* 99–104.

Bialystok, E. (1988). Levels of bilingualism and levels of linguistic awareness. *Developmental Psychology, 24,* 560–567.

Biederman, I., Glass, A. L., & Stacy, E. W. (1973). Searching for objects in real world scenes. *Journal of Experimental Psychology, 97,* 22–27.

Bilalić, M., McLeod, P., & Gobet, F. (2008). Inflexibility of experts—Reality or myth? Quantifying the Einstellung effect in chess masters. *Cognitive Psychology, 56,* 73–102.

Bilalić, M., McLeod, P., & Gobet, F. (2010). The mechanism of the Einstellung (set) effect: A pervasive source of cognitive bias. *Psychological Science, 19,* 111–115.

Binder, K. S. (2003). Sentential and discourse topic effects on lexical ambiguity processing: An eye movement examination. *Memory & Cognition, 31,* 690–702.

Binder, K. S., & Rayner, K. (1998). Contextual strength does not modulate the subordinate bias effect: Evidence from eye fixations and self-paced reading. *Psychonomic Bulletin & Review, 5,* 271–276.

Birmingham, E., Bischof, W. F., & Kingstone, A. (2008). Social attention and real world scenes: The roles of action, competition and social content. *Quarterly Journal of Experimental Psychology, 61,* 986–998.

Bisiach, E., & Luzzatti, C. (1978). Unilateral neglect of representational space. *Cortex, 14,* 129–133.

Bjork, E. L., & Bjork, R. A. (2003). Intentional forgetting can increase, not decrease, residual influences of to-be-forgotten information. *Journal of Experimental Psychology: Learning, Memory, and Cognition, 29,* 524–531.

Blakemore, C. (1977). *Mechanics of the mind.* Cambridge, England: Cambridge University Press.

Blom, J. P., & Gumperz, J. J. (1972). Social meaning in linguistic structure: Code-switching in Norway. In J. J. Gumperz & D. Hymes (Eds.), *Directions in sociolinguistics: The ethnography of communication* (pp. 407–434). New York: Holt.

Bloom, F. E., & Lazerson, A. (1988). *Brain, mind, and behavior.* New York: W. H. Freeman.

Bocanegra, B. R., & Zeelenberg, R. (2011). Emotion-induced trade-offs in spatiotemporal vision. *Journal of Experimental Psychology: General, 140,* 272–282.

Bock, J. K. (1982). Toward a cognitive psychology of syntax: Information processing contributions to sentence formulation. *Psychological Review, 89,* 1–47.

Bock, J. K. (1986). Meaning, sound, and syntax: Lexical priming in sentence production. *Journal of Experimen-*

tal Psychology: Learning, Memory, and Cognition, 12, 575–586.

Bock, K. (1995). Producing agreement. *Current Directions in Psychological Science, 4*, 56–61.

Bock, K. (1996). Language production: Methods and methodologies. *Psychonomic Bulletin & Review, 3*, 395–421.

Bock, K., & Griffin, Z. M. (2000). The persistence of structural priming: Transient activation or implicit learning? *Journal of Experimental Psychology: General, 129*, 177–192.

Bock, K., Irwin, D. E., Davidson, D. J., & Levelt, W. J. M. (2003). Minding the clock. *Journal of Memory and Language, 48*, 653–685.

Bock, K., & Miller, C. A. (1991). Broken agreement. *Cognitive Psychology, 23*, 45–93.

Bonebakker, A. E., Bonke, B., Klein, J., Wolters, G., Stijnen, T., Passchier, J., et al. (1996). Information processing during general anesthesia: Evidence for unconscious memory. *Memory & Cognition, 24*, 766–776.

Boring, E. G. (1950). *A history of experimental psychology* (2nd ed.). New York: Appleton-Century-Crofts.

Boroditsky, L. (2001). Does language shape thought? Mandarin and English speakers' conceptions of time. *Cognitive Psychology, 43*, 1–22.

Boroditsky, L. (2011). How language shapes thought. *Scientific American*, 63–65.

Botvinick, M. M., & Bylsma, L. M. (2006). Distraction and action slips in an everyday task: Evidence for a dynamic representation of task context. *Psychonomic Bulletin & Review, 12*, 1011–1017.

Bousfield, W. A. (1953). The occurrence of clustering in the recall of randomly arranged associates. *Journal of General Psychology, 49*, 229–240.

Bousfield, W. A., & Sedgewick, C. H. W. (1944). An analysis of sequences of restricted associative responses. *Journal of General Psychology, 30*, 149–165.

Bowden, E. M. (1985). Accessing relevant information during problem solving: Time constraints on search in the problem space. *Memory & Cognition, 13*, 280–286.

Bowden, E. M., & Beeman, M. J. (1998). Getting the right idea: Semantic activation in the right hemisphere may help solve insight problems. *Psychological Science, 9*, 435–440.

Bowden, E. M., Beeman, M., & Gernsbacher, M. A. (1995, March). *Two hemispheres are better than one: Drawing coherence inferences during story comprehension.* Paper presented at the annual meeting of the Cognitive Neuroscience Society, San Francisco.

Bower, G. H. (1970). Analysis of a mnemonic device. *American Scientist, 58*, 496–510.

Bower, G. H. (1981). Mood and memory. *American Psychologist, 36*, 129–148.

Bower, G. H., Clark, M. C., Lesgold, A. M., & Winzenz, D. (1969). Hierarchical retrieval schemes in recall of categorical word lists. *Journal of Verbal Learning and Verbal Behavior, 8*, 323–343.

Bradley, M. M., Greenwald, M. K., Petry, M. C., & Lang, P. J. (1992). Remembering pictures: Pleasure and arousal in memory. *Journal of Experimental Psychology: Learning, Memory, and Cognition, 18*, 379–390.

Branigan, H. P., Pickering, M. J., & Cleland, A. A. (1999). Syntactic priming in written production: Evidence for rapid decay. *Psychonomic Bulletin & Review, 6*, 635–640.

Branigan, H. P., Pickering, M. J., Stewart, A. J., & McLean, J. F. (2000). Syntactic priming in spoken production: Linguistic and temporal interference. *Memory & Cognition, 28*, 1297–1302.

Bransford, J. D., & Stein, B. S. (1984). *The ideal problem solver.* New York: Freeman.

Bransford, J. D., & Stein, B. S. (1993). *The ideal problem solver* (2nd ed.). New York: Freeman.

Breedin, S. D., & Saffran, E. M. (1999). Sentence processing in the face of semantic loss: A case study. *Journal of Experimental Psychology: General, 128*, 547–562.

Brennan, S. E., & Clark, H. H. (1996). Conceptual pacts and lexical choice in conversation. *Journal of Experimental Psychology: Learning, Memory, and Cognition, 22*, 1482–1493.

Breslin, C. W., & Safer, M. A. (2011). Effects of event valence on long-term memory for two baseball championship games. *Psychological Science, 22*, 1408–1412.

Bresnan, J. (1978). A realistic transformational grammar. In J. Bresnan, M. Halle, & G. Miller (Eds.), *Linguistic theory and psychological reality* (pp. 1–59). Cambridge, MA: MIT Press.

Bresnan, J., & Kaplan, R. M. (1982). Introduction: Grammars as mental representations of language. In J. Bresnan (Ed.), *The mental representation of grammatical relations* (pp. xvii–iii). Cambridge, MA: MIT Press.

Bridgeman, B. (1988). *The biology of behavior and mind.* New York: Wiley.

Broadbent, D. E. (1952). Speaking and listening simultaneously. *Journal of Experimental Psychology, 43*, 267–273.

Broadbent, D. E. (1958). *Perception and communication.* London: Pergamon.

Broaders, S. C., Cook, S. W., Mitchell, Z., & Goldin-Meadow, S. (2007). Making children gesture brings out implicit knowledge and leads to learning. *Journal of Experimental Psychology: General, 136,* 539–550.

Broggin, E., Savazzi, S., & Marzi, C. A. (2012). Similar effects of visual perception and imagery on simple reaction time. *Quarterly Journal of Experimental Psychology, 65,* 151–164.

Brooks, J. O. III, & Watkins, M. J. (1990). Further evidence of the intricacy of memory span. *Journal of Experimental Psychology: Learning, Memory, and Cognition, 16,* 1134–1141.

Brooks, L. R. (1968). Spatial and verbal components of the act of recall. *Canadian Journal of Experimental Psychology, 22,* 349–368.

Brosch, T., Sander, D., Pourtois, G., & Scherer, K. R. (2008). Beyond fear: Rapid spatial orienting toward positive emotional stimuli. *Psychological Science, 19,* 362–370.

Brown, A. S. (1998). Transient global amnesia. *Psychonomic Bulletin & Review, 5,* 401–427.

Brown, A. S. (2002). Consolidation theory and retrograde amnesia in humans. *Psychonomic Bulletin & Review, 9,* 403–425.

Brown, A. S. (2004). The déjà vu illusion. *Current Directions in Psychological Science, 13,* 256–259.

Brown, A. S., Neblett, D. R., Jones, T. C., & Mitchell, D. B. (1991). Transfer of processing in repetition priming: Some inappropriate findings. *Journal of Experimental Psychology: Learning, Memory, and Cognition, 17,* 514–525.

Brown, G. D. A., Neath, I., & Chater, N. (2007). A temporal ratio model of memory. *Psychological Review, 114,* 539–576.

Brown, J. A. (1958). Some tests of the decay theory of immediate memory. *Quarterly Journal of Experimental Psychology, 10,* 12–21.

Brown, R., & Ford, M. (1961). Address in American English. *Journal of Abnormal and Social Psychology, 62,* 375–385.

Brown, R., & Kulik, J. (1977). Flashbulb memories. *Cognition, 5,* 73–99.

Brown, R., & McNeill, D. (1966). The "tip-of-the-tongue" phenomenon. *Journal of Verbal Learning and Verbal Behavior, 5,* 325–337.

Buchanan, T. W., Lutz, K., Mirzazade, S., Specht, K., Shab, N. J., Zilles, K., et al. (2000). Recognition of emotional prosody and verbal components of spoken language: An fMRI study. *Cognitive Brain Research, 9,* 227–238.

Buchner, A., & Wippich, W. (2000). On the reliability of implicit and explicit memory measures. *Cognitive Psychology, 40,* 227–259.

Buckner, R. L. (1996). Beyond HERA: Contributions of specific prefrontal brain areas to long-term memory retrieval. *Psychonomic Bulletin & Review, 3,* 149–158.

Bundesen, C. (1990). A theory of visual attention. *Psychological Review, 97,* 523–547.

Bunting, M. F., Conway, A. R. A., & Heitz, R. P. (2004). Individual differences in the fan effect and working memory capacity. *Journal of Memory and Language, 51,* 604–622.

Burgess, G. C., Gray, J. R., Conway, A. R. A., & Braver, T. S. (2011). Neural mechanisms of interference control underlie the relationship between fluid intelligence and working memory span. *Journal of Experimental Psychology: General, 140,* 674–692.

Burke, D. M., MacKay, D. G., Worthley, J. S., & Wade, E. (1991). On the tip of the tongue: What causes word finding failures in young and older adults? *Journal of Memory and Language, 30,* 542–579.

Buswell, G. T. (1937). *How adults read.* Chicago: Chicago University Press.

Butler, A. C. (2010). Repeated testing produces superior transfer of learning relative to repeated studying. *Journal of Experimental Psychology: Learning, Memory, and Cognition, 36,* 1118–1133.

Butler, C., Muhlert, N., & Zeman, A. (2010). Accelerated long-term forgetting. In S. Della Sala (Ed.) *Forgetting* (pp. 211–238). New York: Psychology Press.

Cantor, J., & Engle, R. W. (1993). Working-memory capacity as long-term memory activation: An individual differences approach. *Journal of Experimental Psychology: Learning, Memory, and Cognition, 19,* 1101–1114.

Carlson, R. A., Khoo, B. H., Yaure, R. G., & Schneider, W. (1990). Acquisition of a problem-solving skill: Levels of organization and use of working memory. *Journal of Experimental Psychology: General, 119,* 193–214.

Carpenter, S. K., & Pashler, H. (2007). Testing beyond words: Using tests to enhance visuospatial map learning. *Psychonomic Bulletin & Review, 14,* 474–478.

Carr, P. B., & Steele, C. M. (2010). Stereotype threat affects financial decision making. *Psychological Science, 21,* 1411–1416.

Carr, T. H., McCauley, C., Sperber, R. D., & Parmalee, C. M. (1982). Words, pictures, and priming: On semantic activation, conscious identification, and the automaticity of information processing. *Journal of Experimental Psychology: Human Perception and Performance, 8,* 757–777.

Carroll, D. W. (1986). *Psychology of language.* Pacific Grove, CA: Brooks/Cole.

Catrambone, R. (1996). Generalizing solution procedures learned from examples. *Journal of Experimental Psychology: Learning, Memory, and Cognition, 22,* 1020–1031.

Cave, K. R., & Bichot, N. P. (1999). Visuospatial attention: Beyond a spotlight model. *Psychonomic Bulletin & Review, 6,* 204–223.

Chaffin, R., & Imreh, G. (2002). Practicing perfection: Piano performance as expert memory. *Psychological Science, 13,* 342–349.

Chang, F., Dell, G. S., & Bock, J. K. (2006). Becoming syntactic. *Psychological Review, 113,* 234–272.

Chase, W. G., & Ericsson, K. A. (1982). Skill and working memory. In G. H. Bower (Ed.), *The psychology of learning and motivation* (Vol. 16, pp. 1–58). New York: Academic Press.

Chase, W. G., & Simon, H. A. (1973). Perception in chess. *Cognitive Psychology, 4,* 55–81.

Chen, Y. (2007). Chinese and English speakers think about time differently? Failure of replicating Boroditsky (2001). *Cognition, 104,* 427–436.

Chen, Z., & Mo, L. (2004). Schema induction in problem solving: A multidimensional analysis. *Journal of Experimental Psychology: Learning, Memory, and Cognition, 30,* 583–600.

Chen, Z., Mo, L., & Honomichl, R. (2004). Having the memory of an elephant: Long-term retrieval and the use of analogues in problem solving. *Journal of Experimental Psychology: General, 133,* 415–433.

Cherry, E. C. (1953). Some experiments on the recognition of speech, with one and with two ears. *Journal of the Acoustical Society of America, 25,* 975–979.

Cherry, E. C., & Taylor, W. K. (1954). Some further experiments on the recognition of speech with one and two ears. *Journal of the Acoustical Society of America, 26,* 554–559.

Chomsky, N. (1957). *Syntactic structures.* The Hague: Mouton.

Chomsky, N. (1959). A review of Skinner's *Verbal Behavior. Language, 35,* 26–58.

Chomsky, N. (1965). *Aspects of a theory of syntax.* Cambridge, MA: Harvard University Press.

Chomsky, N. (1968). *Language and mind.* New York: Harcourt Brace Jovanovich.

Christianson, K., Hollingworth, A., Halliwell, J. F., & Ferreira, F. (2001). Thematic roles assigned along the garden path linger. *Cognitive Psychology, 42,* 368–407.

Christianson, S. (1989). Flashbulb memories: Special, but not so special. *Memory & Cognition, 17,* 435–443.

Chronicle, E. P., MacGregor, J. N., & Ormerod, T. C. (2004). What makes an insight problem? The roles of heuristics, goal conception, and solution recoding in knowledge-lean problems. *Journal of Experimental Psychology: Learning, Memory, and Cognition, 30,* 14–27.

Cisler, J. M., Wolitzky-Taylor, K. B., Adams, T. G., Babson, K. A., Badou, C. L., & Willems, J. L. (2011). The emotional Stroop task and posttraumatic stress disorder: A meta-analysis. *Clinical Psychology Review, 31,* 817–828.

Clark, H. H. (1977). Bridging. In P. N. Johnson-Laird & P. C. Wason (Eds.), *Thinking: Readings in cognitive science* (pp. 411–420). Cambridge, England: Cambridge University Press.

Clark, H. H. (1979). Responding to indirect speech acts. *Cognitive Psychology, 11,* 430–477.

Clark, H. H. (1994). Discourse in production. In M. A. Gernsbacher (Ed.), *Handbook of psycholinguistics* (pp. 985–1021). San Diego, CA: Academic Press.

Clark, H. H., & Clark, E. V. (1977). *Psychology and language.* New York: Harcourt Brace Jovanovich.

Clark, H. H., & Krych, M. A. (2004). Speaking while monitoring addressees for understanding. *Journal of Memory and Language, 50,* 62–81.

Clark, H. H., & Wasow, T. (1998). Repeating words in spontaneous speech. *Cognitive Psychology, 37,* 201–242.

Claus, B., & Kelter, S. (2006). Comprehending narratives containing flashbacks: Evidence for temporally organized representations. *Journal of Experimental Psychology: Learning, Memory, and Cognition, 32,* 1031–1044.

Cleary, A. M. (2008). Recognition memory, familiarity, and déjà vu experiences. *Current Directions in Psychological Science, 17,* 353–357.

Clifton, C., Jr., Carlson, K., & Frazier, L. (2006). Tracking the what and why of speakers' choices: Prosodic boundaries and the length of constituents. *Psychonomic Bulletin & Review, 13,* 854–861.

Clifton, C., & Frazier, L. (2004). Should given information come before new? Yes and no. *Memory & Cognition, 32,* 886–895.

Clifton, C., Jr., Traxler, M. J., Mohamed, M. T., Williams, R. S., Morris, R. K., & Rayner, K. (2003). The use of thematic role information in parsing: Syntactic processing autonomy revisited. *Journal of Memory and Language, 49,* 317–334.

Cokely, E. T., Kelley, C. M., & Gilchrist, A. L. (2006). Sources of individual differences in working memory capacity: Contributions of strategy to capacity. *Psychonomic Bulletin & Review, 13,* 991–997.

Cole, G. G., & Kuhn, G. (2010). Attentional capture by object appearance and disappearance. *Quarterly Journal of Experimental Psychology, 63,* 147–159.

Colflesh, G. J. H., & Conway, A. R. A. (2007). Individual differences in working memory capacity and divided attention in dichotic listening. *Psychonomic Bulletin & Review, 14,* 699–703.

Colle, H. A., & Welsh, A. (1976). Acoustic masking in primary memory. *Journal of Verbal Learning and Verbal Behavior, 15,* 17–32.

Connell, L., & Lynott, D. (2009). Is a bear white in the woods? Parallel representation of implied object color during language comprehension. *Psychonomic Bulletin & Review, 16,* 573–577.

Conrad, R., & Hull, A. (1964). Information, acoustic confusion, and memory span. *British Journal of Psychology, 55,* 75–84.

Conway, A. R. A., Cowan, N., & Bunting, M. F. (2001). The cocktail party phenomenon revisited: The importance of working memory capacity. *Psychonomic Bulletin & Review, 8,* 331–335.

Conway, M. A., Anderson, S. J., Larsen, S. F., Donnelly, C. M., McDaniel, M. A., McClelland, A. G. R., et al. (1994). The formation of flashbulb memories. *Memory & Cognition, 22,* 326–343.

Cook, A. E., & Myers, J. L. (2004). Processing discourse roles in scripted narratives: The influences of context and world knowledge. *Journal of Memory and Language, 50,* 268–288.

Cook, M. (1977). Gaze and mutual gaze in social encounters. *American Scientist, 65,* 328–333.

Cooper, E. H., & Pantle, A. J. (1967). The total-time hypothesis in verbal learning. *Psychological Bulletin, 68,* 221–234.

Cooper, L. A., & Shepard, R. N. (1973). Chronometric studies of the rotation of mental images. In W. G. Chase (Ed.), *Visual information processing* (pp. 75–176). New York: Academic Press.

Copeland, D. E., & Radvansky, G. A. (2001). Phonological similarity in working memory. *Memory & Cognition, 29,* 774–776.

Copeland, D. E., & Radvansky, G. A. (2004a). Working memory and syllogistic reasoning. *Quarterly Journal of Experimental Psychology, 57A,* 1437–1457.

Copeland, D. E., & Radvansky, G. A. (2004b). Working memory span and situation model processing. *American Journal of Psychology, 117,* 191–213.

Corballis, M. C. (1989). Laterality and human evolution. *Psychological Review, 96,* 492–505.

Corballis, M. C. (2004). The origins of modernity: Was autonomous speech a critical factor? *Psychological Review, 111,* 543–552.

Corley, M., Brocklehurst, P. H., & Moat, H. S. (2011). Error biases in inner and overt speech: Evidence from tongue twisters. *Journal of Experimental Psychology: Learning, Memory, and Cognition, 37,* 162–175.

Coughlan, A. K., & Warrington, E. K. (1978). Word comprehension and word retrieval in patients with localised cerebral lesions. *Brain, 101,* 163–185.

Coulson, S., Federmeier, K. D., Van Petten, C., & Kutas, M. (2005). Right hemisphere sensitivity to word- and sentence-level context: Evidence from event-related brain potentials. *Journal of Experimental Psychology: Learning, Memory, and Cognition, 31,* 127–147.

Courtney, S. M., Petit, L. Maisog, C. M., Ungerleider, L. G., & Haxby, J. V. (1998). An area specialized for spatial working memory in human frontal cortex. Science, 279, 1347–1351.

Cowan, N. (1995). *Attention and memory: An integrated framework.* New York: Oxford University Press.

Cowan, N. (2010). The magical mystery four: How is working memory capacity limited, and why? *Current Directions in Psychological Science, 19,* 51–57.

Cowan, N., & Morey, C. C. (2007). How can dual-task working memory retention limits be investigated? *Psychological Science, 18,* 686–688.

Cowan, N., Wood, N. L., Wood, P. K., Keller, T. A., Nugent, L. D., & Keller, C. V. (1998). Two separate verbal processing rates contributing to short-term memory span. *Journal of Experimental Psychology: General, 127,* 141–160.

Craik, F. I. M., Govoni, R., Naveh-Benjamin, M., & Anderson, N. D. (1996). The effects of divided attention on encoding and retrieval processes in human memory. *Journal of Experimental Psychology: General, 125,* 181–194.

Craik, F. I. M., & Lockhart, R. S. (1972). Levels of processing: A framework for memory research. *Journal of Verbal Learning and Verbal Behavior, 11,* 671–684.

Craik, F. I., & Tulving, E. (1975). Depth of processing and the retention of words in episodic memory. *Journal of experimental Psychology: General, 104*(3), 268–294.

Craik, F. I., & Watkins, M. J. (1973). The role of rehearsal in short-term memory. *Journal of verbal learning and verbal behavior, 12*(6), 599–607.

Crosby, J. R., Monin, B., & Richardson, D. (2008). Where do we look during potentially offensive behavior? *Psychological Science, 19,* 226–228.

Curran, T. (2000). Brain potentials of recollection and familiarity. *Memory & Cognition, 28,* 923–938.

Dahan, D. (2010). The time course of interpretation in speech comprehension. *Current Directions in Psychological Science, 19,* 121–126.

Daneman, M., & Carpenter, P. A. (1980). Individual differences in working memory and reading. *Journal of Verbal Learning and Verbal Behavior, 19,* 450–466.

Daneman, M., & Merikle, P. M. (1996). Working memory and language comprehension: A meta-analysis. *Psychonomic Bulletin & Review, 3,* 422–433.

Danziger, S., Kingstone, A., & Rafal, R. D. (1998). Orienting to extinguished signals in hemispatial neglect. *Psychological Science, 9,* 119–123.

Davelaar, E. J., Goshen-Gottstein, Y., Ashkenazi, A., Haarmann, H. J., & Usher, M. (2005). The demise of short-term memory revisited: Empirical and computational investigations of recency effects. *Psychological Review, 112,* 3–42.

Davis, M. (1997). Neurobiology of fear responses: The role of the amygdala. *Journal of Neuropsychiatry and Clinical Neurosciences, 9,* 382–402.

Davoli, C. C., Brockmole, J. R., & Goujon, A. (2012). A bias to detail: how hand position modulates visual learning and visual memory. *Memory & Cognition, 40,* 352–359.

Davoli, C. C., Suszko, J. W., & Abrams, R. A. (2007). New objects can capture attention without a unique luminance transient. *Psychonomic Bulletin & Review, 14,* 338–343.

Day, S. B., & Gentner, D. (2007). Nonintentional analogical inference in text comprehension. *Memory & Cognition, 35,* 39–49.

DeCaro, M. S., Rotar, K. E., Kendra, M. S., & Beilock, S. L. (2010). Diagnosing and alleviating the impact of performance pressure on mathematical problem solving. *Quarterly Journal of Experimental Psychology, 63,* 1619–1630.

DeCaro, M. S., Thomas, R. D., Albert, N. B., & Beilock, S. L. (2011). Choking under pressure: Multiple routes to skill failure. *Journal of Experimental Psychology: General, 140,* 390–406.

Delany, P. F., Ericsson, K. A., & Knowles, M. E. (2004). Immediate and sustained effects of planning in a problem-solving task. *Journal of Experimental Psychology: Learning, Memory, and Cognition, 30,* 1219–1234.

Dell, G. S. (1986). A spreading-activation theory of retrieval in sentence production. *Psychological Review, 93,* 283–321.

Dell, G. S., & Newman, J. E. (1980). Detecting phonemes in fluent speech. *Journal of Verbal Learning and Verbal Behavior, 20,* 611–629.

DePaulo, B. M., & Bonvillian, J. D. (1978). The effect on language development of the special characteristics of speech addressed to children. *Journal of Psycholinguistic Research, 7,* 189–211.

Descartes, R. (1637). *Treatise on man* (T. S. Hall, Trans.). Cambridge, MA: Harvard University Press, 1972. (Original work published in 1637.)

Deutsch, J. A., & Deutsch, D. (1963). Attention: Some theoretical considerations. *Psychological Review, 70,* 80–90.

de Vega, M., León, I., & Díaz, J. M. (1996). The representation of changing emotions in reading comprehension. *Cognition and Emotion, 10,* 303–321.

de Vega, M., Robertson, D. A., Glenberg, A. M., Kaschak, M. P., & Rinck, M. (2004). On doing two things at once: Temporal constraints on action in language comprehension. *Memory & Cognition, 32,* 1033–1043.

Dewitt, L. A., & Samuel, A. G. (1990). The role of knowledge-based expectations in music perception: Evidence from musical restoration. *Journal of Experimental Psychology: General, 119,* 123–144.

Diamond, A., & Gilbert, J. (1989). Development as progressive inhibitory control of action: Retrieval of a contiguous object. *Cognitive Development, 4,* 223–249.

Dodd, M. D., Van der Stigchel, S., & Hollingworth, A. (2009). Inhibition of return and facilitation of return as a function of visual task. *Psychological Science, 20,* 333–339.

Dodson, C. S., & Schacter, D. L. (2002). When false recognition meets metacognition: The distinctiveness heuristic. *Journal of Memory and Language, 46,* 782–803.

Dolcos, F., Labar, K. S., & Cabeza, R. (2005). Remembering one year later: Role of the amygdala and the medial temporal lobe memory system in retrieving emotional memories. *Proceedings of the National Academy of Sciences, 102,* 2626–2631.

Donders, F. C. (1969). *Over de snelheid van psychische processen [Speed of mental processes].* Onderzoekingen gedann in het Psysiologish Laboratorium der Utrechtsche Hoogeschool (W. G. Koster, Trans.). In W. G. Koster (Ed.), Attention and performance II. *Acta Psychologica, 30,* 412–431. (Original work published 1868)

Dosher, B. A., & Ma, J-J. (1998). Output loss or rehearsal loop? Output-time versus pronunciation-time limits in immediate recall for forgetting-matched materials. *Journal of Experimental Psychology: Learning, Memory, and Cognition, 24,* 316–335.

Dresler, T., Mériau, K., Heekeren, H. R., & van der Meer, E. (2009). Emotional Stroop task: effect of word arousal and subject anxiety on emotional interference. *Psychological Research, 73,* 364–371.

Drolet, M., Schubotz, R. I., & Fischer, J. (2012). Authenticity affects the recognition of emotions in speech: Behavioral and fMRI evidence. *Cognitive, Affective & Behavioral Neuroscience, 12,* 140–150.

Drosopoulos, S., Schulze, C., Fischer, S., & Born, J. (2007). Sleep's function in the spontaneous recovery and consolidation of memories. *Journal of Experimental Psychology: General, 136,* 169–183.

Dunbar, K., & MacLeod, C. M. (1984). A horse race of a different color: Stroop interference patterns with transformed words. *Journal of Experimental Psychology: Human Perception and Performance, 10,* 622–639.

Duncan, J., Bundesen, C., Olson, A., Humphreys, G., Chavda, S., & Shibuya, H. (1999). Systematic analysis of deficits in visual attention. *Journal of Experimental Psychology: General, 128,* 450–478.

Duncan, S. (1972). Some signals and rules for taking speaking turns in conversations. *Journal of Personality and Social Psychology, 23,* 283–292.

Duncker, K. (1945). On problem solving. *Psychological Monographs, 58* (Whole no. 270).

Dunlosky, J., & Hertzog, C. (2001). Measuring strategy production during associative learning: The relative utility of concurrent versus retrospective reports. *Memory & Cognition, 29,* 247–253.

Dunlosky, J., & Lipko, C. (2007). Metacomprehension: A brief history and how to improve its accuracy. *Current Directions in Psychological Science, 16,* 228–232.

Dunlosky, J., & Nelson, T. O. (1994). Does the sensitivity of judgments of learning (JOLs) to the effects of various activities depend on when the JOLs occur? *Journal of Memory and Language, 33,* 545–565.

Dyer, F. C. (2002). When it pays to waggle. *Nature, 419,* 885–886.

Ebbinghaus, H. (1885/1913). *Memory: A contribution to experimental psychology* (H. A. Ruger & C. E. Bussenius, Trans.). New York: Columbia University, Teacher's College. (Reprinted 1964, New York: Dover).

Edridge-Green, F. W. (1900). *Memory and its cultivation.* New York: Appleton & Co.

Edwards, D., & Potter, J. (1993). Language and causation: A discursive action model of description and attribution. *Psychological Review, 100,* 23–41.

Egan, P., Carterette, E. C., & Thwing, E. J. (1954). Some factors affecting multichannel listening. *Journal of the Acoustic Society of America, 26,* 774–782.

Eichenbaum, H., & Fortin, N. (2003). Episodic memory and the hippocampus: It's about time. *Current Directions in Psychological Science, 12,* 53–57.

Emery, N. J. (2000). The eyes have it: The neuroethology, function and evolution of social gaze. *Neuroscience and Biobehavioral Review, 24,* 581–604.

Engelhardt, P. E., Bailey, K. G. D., & Ferreira, F. (2006). Do speakers and listeners observe the Gricean maxim of quantity? *Journal of Memory and Language, 54,* 554–573.

Engelkamp, J., & Dehn, D. M. (2000). Item and order information in subject-performed tasks and experimenter-performed tasks. *Journal of Experimental Psychology: Learning, Memory, and Cognition, 26,* 671–682.

Engle, R. W. (2001). What is working memory capacity? In H. L. Roediger, J. S. Nairne, I. Neath, & A. M. Suprenant (Eds.), *The nature of remembering: Essays in honor of Robert G. Crowder* (pp. 297–314). Washington, DC: American Psychological Association Press.

Engle, R. W. (2002). Working memory capacity as executive attention. *Current Directions in Psychological Science, 11,* 19–23.

Erdelyi, M. H. (2010). The ups and downs of memory. *American Psychologist, 65,* 623–633.

Ericsson, K. A., & Charness, N. (1994). Expert performance: Its structure and acquisition. *American Psychologist, 49,* 725–747.

Ericsson, K. A., Delaney, P. F., Weaver, G., & Mahadevan, R. (2004). Uncovering the structure of a memorist's superior "basic" memory capacity. *Cognitive Psychology, 49,* 191–237.

Ericsson, K. A., Krampe, R. T., & Tesch-Römer, C. (1993). The role of deliberate practice in the acquisition of expert performance. *Psychological Review, 100,* 363–406.

Ericsson, K. A., & Simon, H. A. (1980). Verbal reports as data. *Psychological Review, 87,* 215–251.

Ericsson, K. A., & Simon, H. A. (1993). *Protocol analysis: Verbal reports as data* (Rev. ed.). Cambridge, MA: MIT Press.

Ernst, G. W., & Newell, A. (1969). *GPS: A case study in generality and problem solving.* New York: Academic Press.

Estes, Z., Verges, M., & Barsalou, L. W. (2008). Head up, foot down: object words orient attention to the objects' typical location. *Psychological Science, 19,* 93–97.

Faroqi-Shah, Y., & Thompson, C. K. (2007). Verb inflections in agrammatic aphasia: Encoding of tense features. *Journal of Memory and Language, 56,* 129–151.

Fausey, C. M., & Boroditsky, L. (2011). Who dunnit? Cross-linguistic differences in eye-witness memory. *Psychonomic Bulletin & Review, 18,* 150–157.

Fedorenko, E., Gibson, E., & Rohde, D. (2006). The nature of working memory capacity in sentence comprehension: Evidence against domain-specific working memory resources. *Journal of Memory and Language, 54,* 541–553.

Feng, J., Spence, I., & Pratt, J. (2007). Playing an action video game reduces gender differences in spatial cognition. *Psychological Science, 18,* 850–855.

Fenske, M. J., & Raymond, J. E. (2006). Affective influences of selective attention. *Current Directions in Psychological Science, 15,* 312–316.

Ferreira, F., Henderson, J. M., Anes, M. D., Weeks, P. A., Jr., & McFarlane, D. K. (1996). Effects of lexical frequency and syntactic complexity in spoken-language comprehension: Evidence from the auditory moving-window technique. *Journal of Experimental Psychology: Learning, Memory, and Cognition, 22,* 324–335.

Ferreira, F., & Swets, B. (2002). How incremental is language production? Evidence from the production of utterances requiring the computation of arithmetic sums. *Journal of Memory and Language, 46,* 57–84.

Ferreira, V. S. (1996). Is it better to give than to donate? Syntactic flexibility in language production. *Journal of Memory and Language, 35,* 724–755.

Ferreira, V. S., & Dell, G. S. (2000). Effect of ambiguity and lexical availability on syntactic and lexical production. *Cognitive Psychology, 40,* 296–340.

Ferreira, V. S., & Firato, C. E. (2002). Proactive interference effects on sentence production. *Psychonomic Bulletin & Review, 9,* 795–800.

Ferreira, V. S., & Humphreys, K. R. (2001). Syntactic influences on lexical and morphological processing in language production. *Journal of Memory and Language, 44,* 52–80.

Fillenbaum, S. (1974). Pragmatic normalization: Further results for some conjunctive and disjunctive sentences. *Journal of Experimental Psychology, 102,* 574–578.

Fillmore, C. J. (1968). Toward a modern theory of case. In D. A. Reibel & S. A. Schane (Eds.), *Modern studies in English* (pp. 361–375). Englewood Cliffs, NJ: Prentice Hall.

Finkenhauer, C., Luminet, O., Gisle, L., El-ahmadi, A., van der Linden, M., & Philipott, P. (1998). Flashbulb memories and the underlying mechanisms of their formation: Toward an emotional-integrative model. *Memory & Cognition, 26,* 516–531.

Finn, B., & Roediger, H. L. (2011). Enhancing retention through reconsolidation: Negative emotional arousal following retrieval enhances later recall. *Psychological Science, 22,* 781–786.

Fleck, J. I., & Weisberg, R. W. (2004). The use of verbal pro-tocols as data: An analysis of insight in the candle problem. *Memory & Cognition, 32,* 990–1006.

Fletcher, C. R., & Bloom, C. P. (1988). Causal reasoning in the comprehension of simple narrative texts. *Journal of Memory and Language, 27,* 235–244.

Flusberg, S. J., & Boroditsky, L. (2011). Are things that are hard to physically move also hard to imagine moving? *Psychonomic Bulletin & Review, 18,* 158–164.

Fodor, J. A., & Garrett, M. (1966). Some reflections on competence and performance. In J. Lyons & R. J. Wales (Eds.), *Psycholinguistic papers* (pp. 135–154). Edinburgh, Scotland: Edinburgh University Press.

Forsyth, D. K., & Burt, C. D. B. (2008). Allocating time to future tasks: The effect of task segmentation on planning fallacy bias. *Memory & Cognition, 36,* 791–798.

Foss, D. J., & Hakes, D. T. (1978). *Psycholinguistics: An introduction to the psychology of language.* Englewood Cliffs, NJ: Prentice Hall.

Franconeri, S. L., & Simons, D. J. (2003). Moving and looming stimuli capture attention. *Perception & Psychophysics, 65,* 999–1010.

Frazier, L., & Rayner, K. (1982). Making and correcting errors during sentence comprehension: Eye movements in the analysis of structurally ambiguous sentences. *Cognitive Psychology, 14,* 178–210.

Frazier, L., & Rayner, K. (1990). Taking on semantic commitments: Processing multiple meanings vs. multiple senses. *Journal of Memory and Language, 29,* 181–200.

Freud, S. (1899/1938). Childhood and concealing memories. In A. A. Brill (Ed.), *The Basic Writings of Sigmund Freud.* New York: Modern Library.

Freud, S. (1953/1905). Three essays on the theory of sexuality. In J. Strachey (Ed.), *The standard edition of the complete psychological works of Sigmund Freud* (Vol. 7, pp. 135–423). London: Hogarth. (Original work published in 1905.)

Freyd, J. J., & Finke, R. A. (1984). Representational momentum. *Bulletin of the Psychonomic Society, 23,* 443–446.

Friederici, A. D., Hahne, A., & Mecklinger, A. (1996). Temporal structure of syntactic parsing: Early and late event-related brain potential effects. *Journal of Experimental Psychology: Learning, Memory, and Cognition, 22,* 1219–1248.

Friedman, N. P., Miyake, A., Young, S. E., DeFries, J. C., Corley, R. P., & Hewitt, J. K. (2008). Individual differences in executive functions are almost entirely genetic in origin. *Journal of Experimental Psychology: General, 137,* 201–225.

Frisson, S., & Pickering, M. J. (1999). The processing of

metonymy: Evidence from eye movements. *Journal of Experimental Psychology: Learning, Memory, and Cognition, 25,* 1366–1383.

Fromkin, V. A. (1971). The non-anomalous nature of anomalous utterances. *Language, 47,* 27–52.

Fromkin, V. A., & Rodman, R. (1974). *An introduction to language.* New York: Holt, Rinehart & Winston.

Fukuda, K., Vogel, E., Mayr, U., & Awh, E. (2010). Quality, not quantity: the relationship between fluid intelligence and working memory capacity. *Psychonomic Bulletin & Review, 17,* 673–679.

Galantucci, B., Fowler, C. A., & Turvey, M. T. (2006). The motor theory of speech perception reviewed. *Psychonomic Bulletin & Review, 13,* 361–377.

Garrett, M. F. (1975). The analysis of sentence production. In G. H. Bower (Ed.), *The psychology of learning and memory* (Vol. 9, pp. 133–177). New York: Academic Press.

Gates, A. I. (1917). Recitation as a factor in memorizing. *Archives of Psychology, 40,* 104.

Geary, D. C. (1992). Evolution of human cognition: Potential relationship to the ontogenetic development of behavior and cognition. *Evolution and Cognition, 1,* 93–100.

Gennari, S. P. (2004). Temporal references and temporal relations in sentence comprehension. *Journal of Experimental Psychology: Learning, Memory, and Cognition, 30,* 877–890.

Gentner, D., & Markman, A. B. (1997). Structure mapping in analogy and similarity. *American Psychologist, 52,* 45–56.

Gernsbacher, M. A. (1990). *Language comprehension as structure building.* Hillsdale, NJ: Erlbaum.

Gernsbacher, M. A. (1997). Two decades of structure building. *Discourse Processes, 23,* 265–304.

Gernsbacher, M. A., & Faust, M. E. (1991). The mechanism of suppression: A component of general comprehension skill. *Journal of Experimental Psychology: Learning, Memory, & Cognition, 17,* 245–262.

Gernsbacher, M. A., & Hargreaves, D. (1988). Accessing sentence participants: The advantage of first mention. *Journal of Memory and Language, 27,* 699–717.

Gernsbacher, M. A., Hallada, B. M., & Robertson, R. R. W. (1998). How automatically do readers infer fictional characters' emotional states? *Scientific Studies of Reading, 2,* 271–300.

Gernsbacher, M. A., Hargreaves, D., & Beeman, M. (1989). Building and accessing clausal representations: The advantage of first mention versus the advantage of clause recency. *Journal of Memory and Language, 28,* 735–755.

Gernsbacher, M. A., Keysar, B., Robertson, R. R. W., & Werner, N. K. (2001). The role of suppression and enhancement in understanding metaphors. *Journal of Memory and Language, 45,* 433–450.

Gernsbacher, M. A., & Robertson, R. R. W. (1992). Knowledge activation vs mapping when representing fictional characters' emotional states. *Language and Cognitive Processes, 7,* 337–353.

Gershkoff-Stowe, L., & Goldin-Meadow, S. (2002). Is there a natural order for expressing semantic relations? *Cognitive Psychology, 45,* 375–412.

Geschwind, N. (1967). The varieties of naming errors. *Cortex, 3,* 97–112.

Geschwind, N. (1970). The organisation of language and the brain. *Science, 170,* 940–944.

Gevins, A., Smith, M. E., McEvoy, L., & Yu, D. (1997). High resolution EEG mapping of cortical activation related to working memory: Effects of task difficulty, type of processing, and practice. *Cerebral Cortex, 7,* 374–385.

Gick, M. L., & Holyoak, K. J. (1980). Analogical problem solving. *Cognitive Psychology, 12,* 306–355.

Gillihan, S. J., & Farah, M. J. (2005). Is the self special? A critical review of evidence from experimental psychology and cognitive neuroscience. *Psychological Bulletin, 131,* 76–97.

Glanzer, M. (1972). Storage mechanisms in recall. In G. H. Bower & J. T. Spence (Eds.), *The psychology of learning and motivation* (Vol. 5, pp. 129–193). New York: Academic Press.

Glanzer, M., & Cunitz, A. R. (1966). Two storage mechanisms in free recall. *Journal of Verbal Learning and Verbal Behavior, 5,* 351–360.

Glass, A. L., & Holyoak, K. J. (1986). *Cognition* (2nd ed.). New York: Random House.

Glenberg, A., & Adams, F. (1978). Type I rehearsal and recognition. *Journal of Verbal Learning and Verbal Behavior, 17,* 455–464.

Glenberg, A. M., & Lehmann, T. S. (1980). Spacing repetitions over 1 week. *Memory & Cognition, 8,* 528–538.

Glenberg, A., Smith, S. M., & Green, C. (1977). Type I rehearsal: Maintenance and more. *Journal of Verbal Learning and Verbal Behavior, 11,* 403–416.

Glucksberg, S., & Danks, J. H. (1975). *Experimental psycholinguistics: An introduction.* Hillsdale, NJ: Erlbaum.

Glucksberg, S., & Keysar, B. (1990). Understanding metaphorical comparisons: Beyond similarity. *Psychological Review, 97,* 3–18.

Gobet, F., & Simon, H. A. (1996). Recall of random and distorted chess positions: Implications for the theory of expertise. *Memory & Cognition, 24,* 493–503.

Godden, D. B., & Baddeley, A. D. (1975). Context-dependent memory in two natural environments: On land and underwater. *British Journal of Psychology, 66,* 325–331.

Gold, P. E., Cahill, L., & Wenk, G. L. (2003). The lowdown on ginkgo biloba. *Scientific American, 288,* 86–92.

Goldin-Meadow, S. (1997). When gestures and words speak differently. *Psychological Science, 6,* 138–143.

Goldin-Meadow, S. (2006). Talking and thinking with our hands. *Current Directions in Psychological Science, 15,* 34–39.

Goldin-Meadow, S., & Beilock, S. L. (2010). Action's influence on thought: The case of gesture. Perspectives on *Psychological Science, 5,* 664–674.

Goodglass, H., Kaplan, E., Weintraub, S., & Ackerman, N. (1976). The "tip-of-the-tongue" phenomenon in aphasia. *Cortex, 12,* 145–153.

Goodwin, D. W., Powell, B., Bremeer, D., Hoine, H., & Stern, J. (1969). Alcohol and recall: State-dependent effects in man. *Science, 163,* 2358–2360.

Gordon, P. C., & Chan, D. (1995). Pronouns, passives, and discourse coherence. *Journal of Memory and Language, 34,* 216–231.

Gordon, P. C., & Scearce, K. A. (1995). Pronominalization and discourse coherence, discourse structure and pronoun interpretation. *Memory & Cognition, 23,* 313–323.

Goshen-Gottstein, Y., & Kempinski, H. (2001). Probing memory with conceptual cues at multiple retention intervals: A comparison of forgetting rates on implicit and explicit tests. *Psychonomic Bulletin & Review, 8,* 139–146.

Graesser, A. C., Singer, M., & Trabasso, T. (1994). Constructing inferences during narrative text comprehension. *Psychological Review, 101,* 371–395.

Graf, P., & Schacter, D. L. (1987). Selective effects of interference on implicit and explicit memory for new associations. *Journal of Experimental Psychology: Learning, Memory, and Cognition, 13,* 45–53.

Greenberg, J. H. (1978). Generalizations about numeral systems. In J. H. Greenberg (Ed.), *Universals of human language: Vol. 3. Word structure* (pp. 249–295). Stanford, CA: Stanford University Press.

Greene, R. L. (1986). Effects of intentionality and strategy on memory for frequency. *Journal of Experimental Psychology: Learning, Memory, and Cognition, 12,* 489–495.

Greeno, J. G. (1974). Hobbits and orcs: Acquisition of a sequential concept. *Cognitive Psychology, 6,* 270–292.

Greeno, J. G. (1978). Natures of problem-solving abilities. In W. K. Estes (Ed.), *Handbook of learning and cognitive processes: Vol. 5. Human information processing* (pp. 239–270). Hillsdale, NJ: Erlbaum.

Greenspan, S. L. (1986). Semantic flexibility and referential specificity of concrete nouns. *Journal of Memory and Language, 25,* 539–557.

Greenwald, A. G., Spangenberg, E. R., Pratkanis, A. R., & Eskenazi, J. (1991). Double-blind tests of subliminal self-help audiotapes. *Psychological Science, 2,* 119–122.

Grice, H. P. (1975). Logic and conversation. In P. Cole & J. L. Morgan (Eds.), *Syntax and semantics: Vol. 3. Speech acts* (pp. 41–58). New York: Seminar Press.

Griffin, T. D., Wiley, J., & Thiede, K. W. (2008). Individual differences, rereading, and self-explanation: Concurrent processing and cue validity as constraints on metacomprehension accuracy. *Memory & Cognition, 36,* 93–103.

Griffin, Z. M. (2003). A reversed word length effect in coordinating the preparation and articulation of words in speaking. *Psychonomic Bulletin & Review, 10,* 603–609.

Griffin, Z. M., & Bock, K. (2000). What the eyes say about speaking. *Psychological Science, 11,* 274–279.

Griffiths, T. L., Steyvers, M., & Tenebaum, J. B. (2007). Topics in semantic representation. *Psychological Review, 114,* 211–244.

Gupta, P., & Cohen, N. J. (2002). Theoretical and computational analysis of skill learning, repetition priming, and procedural memory. *Psychological Review, 109,* 401–448.

Gygax, P., Garnham, A., & Oakhill, J. (2004). Inferring characters' emotional states: Can readers infer specific emotions? *Language and Cognitive Processes, 19,* 613–639.

Habib, R., Nyberg, L., & Tulving, E. (2003). Hemispheric asymmetries of memory: The HERA model revisited. *Trends in Cognitive Science, 7,* 241–245.

Haines, R. F. (1991). A breakdown in simultaneous information processing. In G. Obrecht & L. W. Stark (Eds.), *Presbyopia research* (pp. 171–175). New York: Plenum Press.

Hambrick, D. Z., & Engle, R. W. (2002). Effects on domain knowledge, working memory capacity, and age on cognitive performance: An investigation of the knowledge-ispower hypothesis. *Cognitive Psychology, 44,* 339–387.

Hambrick, D. Z., & Meinz, E. J. (2011). Limits on the predictive power of domain-specific experience and knowledge in skilled performance. *Current Directions in Psychological Science, 20,* 275–279.

Hanson, C., & Hirst, W. (1988). Frequency encoding of

token and type information. *Journal of Experimental Psychology: Learning, Memory, and Cognition, 14,* 289–297.

Harris, R. J., & Monaco, G. E. (1978). Psychology of pragmatic implication: Information processing between the lines. *Journal of Experimental Psychology, 107,* 1–22.

Hartsuiker, R. J., Anton-Mendez, I., & van Zee, M. (2001). Object attraction in subject-verb agreement construction. *Journal of Memory and Language, 45,* 546–572.

Hartsuiker, R. J., & Kolk, H. H. J. (2001). Error monitoring in speech production: A computational test of the perceptual loop theory. *Cognitive Psychology, 42,* 113–157.

Hasher, L., & Zacks, R. T. (1984). Automatic processing of fundamental information: The case of frequency of occurrence. *American Psychologist, 39,* 1372–1388.

Hasher, L., & Zacks, R. T. (1988). Working memory, comprehension, and aging: A review and a new view. In G. H. Bower (Ed.), *The psychology of learning and motivation* (Vol. 22, pp. 193–225). New York: Academic Press.

Haviland, S. E., & Clark, H. H. (1974). What's new? Acquiring new information as a process in comprehension. *Journal of Verbal Learning and Verbal Behavior, 13,* 512–521.

Hayes, J. R., & Simon, H. A. (1974). Understanding written problem instructions. In L. W. Gregg (Ed.), *Knowledge and cognition* (pp. 167–200). Hillsdale, NJ: Erlbaum.

Haywood, S. L., Pickering, M. J., & Branigan, H. P. (2005). Do speakers avoid ambiguities during dialogue? *Psychological Science, 16,* 362–366.

Hellyer, S. (1962). Frequency of stimulus presentation and short-term decrement in recall. *Journal of Experimental Psychology, 64,* 650.

Herz, R. S., & Engen, T. (1996). Odor memory: Review and analysis. *Psychonomic Bulletin & Review, 3,* 300–313.

Hicks, J. L., & Marsh, R. L. (2000). Toward specifying the attentional demands of recognition memory. *Journal of Experimental Psychology: Learning, Memory, and Cognition, 26,* 1483–1498.

Higham, P. A., & Garrard, C. (2005). Not all errors are created equal: Metacognition and changing answers on multi-ple-choice tests. Canadian *Journal of Experimental Psychology, 59,* 28–34.

Hirshman, E., Whelley, M. M., & Palij, M. (1989). An investigation of paradoxical memory effects. *Journal of Memory and Language, 28,* 594–609.

Hirst, W., & Kalmar, D. (1987). Characterizing attentional resources. *Journal of Experimental Psychology: General, 116,* 68–81.

Hockett, C. F. (1960a). Logical considerations in the study of animal communication. In W. E. Lanyon & W. N. Tavolga (Eds.), *Animal sounds and communication* (pp. 392–430). Washington, DC: American Institute of Biological Sciences.

Hockett, C. F. (1960b). The origin of speech. *Scientific American, 203,* 89–96.

Hockett, C. F. (1966). The problem of universals in language. In J. H. Greenberg (Ed.), *Universals of language* (2nd ed., pp. 1–29). Cambridge, MA: MIT Press.

Holcomb, P. J., Kounios, J., Anderson, J. E., & West, W. C. (1999). Dual-coding, context availability, and concreteness effects in sentence comprehension: An electrophysiological investigation. *Journal of Experimental Psychology: Learning, Memory, and Cognition, 25,* 721–742.

Holtgraves, T. (1994). Communication in context: Effects of speaker status on the comprehension of indirect requests. *Journal of Experimental Psychology: Learning, Memory, and Cognition, 20,* 1205–1218.

Holtgraves, T. (1998). Interpreting indirect replies. *Cognitive Psychology, 37,* 1–27.

Holtgraves, T. (2008a). Automatic intention recognition in conversation processing. *Journal of Memory and Language, 58,* 627–645.

Holtgraves, T. (2008b). Conversation, speech acts, and memory. *Memory & Cognition, 36,* 361–374.

Holyoak, K. J., & Thagard, P. (1997). The analogical mind. *American Psychologist, 52,* 35–44.

Hopkins, W. D., Russell, J. L., & Cantalupo, C. (2007). Neuroanatomical correlates of handedness for tool use in chimpanzees (Pan troglodytes): Implication for theories on the evolution of language. *Psychological Science, 18,* 971–977.

Horton, W. S., & Gerrig, R. J. (2002). Speakers' experiences and audience design: Knowing when and knowing *how* to adjust utterances to addressees. *Journal of Memory and Language, 47,* 589–606.

Hostetter, A. B., & Alibali, M. (2008). Visible embodiment: Gestures as simulated action. *Psychonomic Bulletin & Review, 15,* 495–514.

Hu, P., Stylos-Allan, M., & Walker, M. P. (2006). Sleep facilitates consolidation of emotional declarative memory. *Psychological Science, 17,* 891–898.

Huang, T-R., & Grossberg, S. (2010). Cortical dynamics of contextually cued attentive visual learning and search: Spatial and object evidence accumulation. *Psychological Review, 117,* 1080–1112.

Huang, Y. T., & Gordon, P. C. (2011). Distinguishing the time course of lexical and discourse processes through context, coreference, and quantified expressions. *Journal of Experimental Psychology: Learning, Memory, and Cognition, 37,* 966–978.

Hubbard, T. L. (1990). Cognitive representation of linear motion: Possible direction and gravity effects in judged displacement. *Memory & Cognition, 18,* 299–309.

Hubbard, T. L. (1995). Environmental invariants in the representation of motion: Implied dynamics and representational momentum, gravity, friction, and centripetal force. *Psychonomic Bulletin & Review, 2,* 322–338.

Hubbard, T. L. (1996). Representational momentum, centripetal force, and curvilinear impetus. *Journal of Experimental Psychology: Learning, Memory, and Cognition, 22,* 1049–1060.

Hubbard, T. L. (2005). Representational momentum and related displacements in spatial memory: A review of the findings. *Psychonomic Bulletin & Review, 12,* 822–851.

Hubbard, T. L., Hutchinson, J. L., & Courtney, J. R. (2010). Boundary extension: Findings and theories. *Quarterly Journal of Experimental Psychology, 63,* 1467–1494.

Huang, Y. T., & Gordon, P. C. (2011). Distinguishing the time course of lexical and discourse processes through context, coreference, and quantified expressions. *Journal of Experimental Psychology: Learning, Memory, and Cognition, 37,* 966–978.

Hunt, E., & Agnoli, F. (1991). The Whorfian hypothesis: A cognitive psychology perspective. *Psychological Review, 98,* 377–389.

Hunt, R. R., & Lamb, C. A. (2001). What causes the isolation effect? *Journal of Experimental Psychology: Learning, Memory, and Cognition, 27,* 1359–1366.

Inhoff, A. W. (1984). Two stages of word processing during eye fixations in the reading of prose. *Journal of Verbal Learning and Verbal Behavior, 23,* 612–624.

Intraub, H., & Richardson, M. (1989). Wide-angle memories of close-up scenes. *Journal of Experimental Psychology: Learning, Memory, and Cognition, 15,* 179–187.

Intriligator, J., & Cavanagh, P. (2001). The spatial resolution of visual attention. *Cognitive Psychology, 43,* 171–216.

Inzlicht, M., & Gutsell, J. N. (2007). Running on empty: Neural signals for self-control failure. *Psychological Science, 18,* 933–937.

Jackendoff, R. S. (1992). *Languages of the mind: Essays on mental representation.* Cambridge, MA: MIT Press.

Jacobs, N., & Garnham, A. (2007). The role of conversational hand gestures in a narrative task. *Journal of Memory and Language, 56*(2), 291–303.

Jacoby, L. L. (1991). A process dissociation framework: Separating automatic from intentional uses of memory. *Journal of Memory and Language, 30,* 513–541.

Jacoby, L. L., & Dallas, M. (1981). On the relationship between autobiographical memory and perceptual learning. *Journal of Experimental Psychology: General, 110,* 306–340.

Jacoby, L. L., Toth, J. P., & Yonelinas, A. P. (1993). Separating conscious and unconscious influences of memory: Measuring recollection. *Journal of Experimental Psychology: General, 122,* 139–154.

James, W. (1890). *The principles of psychology.* New York: Dover.

January, D., & Kako, E. (2007). Re-evaluating evidence for linguistic relativity: Reply to Boroditsky (2001). *Cognition, 104,* 417–426.

Jared, D., Levy, B. A., & Rayner, K. (1999). The role of phonology in the activation of word meanings during readings: Evidence from proofreading and eye movements. *Journal of Experimental Psychology: General, 128,* 219–264.

Jefferies, E., Lambdon Ralph, M. A., & Baddeley, A. D. (2004). Automatic and controlled processing in sentence recall: The role of long-term and working memory. *Journal of Memory and Language, 51,* 623–643.

Jesse, A., & Massaro, D. W. (2010). Seeing a singer helps comprehension of the song's lyrics. *Psychonomic Bulletin & Review, 17,* 323–328.

Jenkins, J. G., & Dallenbach, K. M. (1924). Obliviscence during sleep and waking. *American Journal of Psychology, 35,* 605–612.

Johnson, N. F. (1970). The role of chunking and organization in the process of recall. In G. H. Bower (Ed.), *The psychology of learning and motivation* (Vol. 4, pp. 172–247). New York: Academic Press.

Johnson-Laird, P. N. (1983). *Mental models: Towards a cognitive science of language, inference and consciousness.* Cambridge, MA: Harvard University Press.

Johnston, J. C., McCann, R. S., & Remington, R. W. (1995). Chronometric evidence for two types of attention. *Psychological Science, 6,* 365–369.

Johnston, W. A., & Heinz, S. P. (1978). Flexibility and capacity demands of attention. *Journal of Experimental Psychology: General, 107,* 420–435.

Jones, D. M., Macken, W. J., & Nicholls, A. P. (2004). The phonological store of working memory: Is it phonological and is it a store? *Journal of Experimental Psychology: Learning, Memory, and Cognition, 30,* 656–674.

Jones, G. V. (1989). Back to Woodworth: Role of interlopers in the tip-of-the-tongue phenomenon. *Memory & Cognition, 17,* 69–76.

Jonides, J., & Jones, C. M. (1992). Direct coding for frequency of occurrence. *Journal of Experimental Psychology: Learning, Memory, and Cognition, 18,* 368–378.

Jonides, J., Lacey, S. C., & Nee, D. E. (2005). Processes of working memory in mind and brain. *Current Directions in Psychological Science, 14,* 2–5.

Jonides, J., Smith, E. E., Koeppe, R. A., Awh, E., Minoshima, S., & Mintun, M. A. (1993). Spatial working-memory in humans as revealed by PET. *Nature, 363,* 623–625.

Juhasz, B. J., & Rayner, K. (2003). Investigating the effects of a set of intercorrelated variables on eye fixation durations in reading. *Journal of Experimental Psychology: Learning, Memory, and Cognition, 29,* 1312–1318.

Just, M. A. (1976, May). *Research strategies in prose comprehension.* Paper presented at the meetings of the Midwestern Psychological Association, Chicago.

Just, M. A., & Carpenter, P. A. (1980). A theory of reading: From eye fixations to comprehension. *Psychological Review, 87,* 329–354.

Just, M. A., & Carpenter, P. A. (1987). *The psychology of reading and language comprehension.* Boston: Allyn & Bacon.

Just, M. A., & Carpenter, P. A. (1992). A capacity theory of comprehension. *Psychological Review, 99,* 122–149.

Just, M. A., Carpenter, P. A., Maguire, M., Diwadkar, V., & McMains, S. (2001). Mental rotation of objects retrieved from memory: A functional MRI study of spatial processing. *Journal of Experimental Psychology: General, 130,* 493–504.

Kaakinen, J. K., Hyona, J., & Keenan, J. M. (2003). How prior knowledge, WMC, and relevance of information affect eye fixations in expository text. *Journal of Experimental Psychology: Learning, Memory, and Cognition, 29,* 447–457.

Kahana, M. J., & Wingfield, A. (2000). A functional relation between learning and organization in free recall. *Psychonomic Bulletin & Review, 7,* 516–521.

Kahneman, D. (1973). *Attention and effort.* Englewood Cliffs, NJ: Prentice Hall.

Kambe, G., Duffy, S. A., Clifton, C. Jr., & Rayner, K. (2003). An eye-movement-contingent probe paradigm. *Psychonomic Bulletin & Review, 10,* 661–666.

Kane, M. J., Brown, L. H., McVay, J. C., Silvia, P. J., Myin-Germeys, I., & Kwapil, T. R. (2007). For whom the mind wanders, and when. *Psychological Science, 18,* 614–621.

Kane, M. J., & Engle, R. W. (2000). Working memory capacity, proactive interference, and divided attention: Limits on long-term memory retrieval. *Journal of Experimental Psychology: Learning, Memory, and Cognition, 26,* 336–358.

Kane, M. J., & Engle, R. W. (2002). The role of prefrontal cortex in working-memory capacity, executive attention, and general fluid intelligence: An individual-differences perspective. *Psychonomic Bulletin & Review, 9,* 637–671.

Kane, M. J., & Engle, R. W. (2003). Working-memory capacity and the control of attention: The contributions of goal neglect, response competition and task set to Stroop interference. *Journal of Experimental Psychology: General, 132,* 47–70.

Kane, M. J., Hambrick, D. Z., Tuholski, S. W., Wilhelm, O., Payne, T. W., & Engle, R. W. (2004). The generality of working memory capacity: A latent-variable approach to verbal and visuospatial memory span and reasoning. *Journal of Experimental Psychology: General, 133,* 189–217.

Kanwisher, N., & Driver, J. (1992). Objects, attributes, and visual attention: Which, what, and where. *Psychological Science, 1,* 26–31.

Karpicke, J. D., & Roediger, H. L. (2007). Repeated during retrieval is the key to long-term retention. *Journal of Memory and Language, 57,* 151–162.

Kaschak, M. P., & Glenberg, A. M. (2000). Constructing meaning: The role of affordances and grammatical constructions in sentence comprehension. *Journal of Memory and Language, 43,* 508–529.

Kassam, K. S., Gilbert, D. T., Swencionis, J. K., & Wilson, T. D. (2009). Misconceptions of memory: The Scooter Libby effect. *Psychological Science, 20,* 551–552.

Kassam, K. S., Koslov, K., & Mendes, W. B. (2009). Decisions under distress: Stress profiles influence anchoring and adjustment. *Psychological Science, 20,* 1394–1399.

Kay, J., & Ellis, A. (1987). A cognitive neuropsychological case study of anomia: Implications for psychological models of word retrieval. *Brain, 110,* 613–629.

Kelley, M. R., & Nairne, J. S. (2001). von Restorff revisited: Isolation, generation, and memory of order. *Journal of Experimental Psychology: Learning, Memory, and Cognition, 27,* 54–66.

Kelly, S. D., Barr, D. J., Church, R. B., & Lynch, K. (1999). Offering a hand to pragmatic understanding: The role of speech and gesture in comprehension and memory. *Journal of Memory and Language, 40,* 577–592.

Kelly, S. D., Özyürek, A., & Maris, E. (2010). Two sides of the same coin: Speech and gesture mutually interact to enhance comprehension. *Psychological Science, 21,* 260–267.

Kempen, G., & Hoehkamp, E. (1987). An incremental procedural grammar for sentence formulation. *Cognitive Science, 11,* 201–258.

Kemper, S., & Thissen, D. (1981). Memory for the dimensions of requests. *Journal of Verbal Learning and Verbal Behavior, 20,* 552–563.

Kensinger, E. A. (2007). Negative emotion enhances memory accuracy: Behavioral and neuroimaging evidence. *Current Directions in Psychological Science, 16,* 213–218.

Kensinger, E. A. (2009). *Emotional memory across the adult lifespan.* New York: Psychology Press.

Kensinger, E. A., & Corkin, S. (2004). Two routes to emotional memory: Distinct neural processes for valence and arousal. *Proceedings of the National Academy of Sciences, 101,* 3310–3315.

Kensinger, E. A., Garoff-Eaton, R. J., & Schacter, D. L. (2006). Memory for specific visual details can be enhanced by negative arousing content. *Journal of Memory and Language, 54,* 99–112.

Kensinger, E. A., & Schacter, D. L. (2006). When the Red Socks shocked the Yankees: Comparing negative and positive memories. *Psychonomic Bulletin & Review, 13,* 757–763.

Keppel, G., & Underwood, B. J. (1962). Proactive inhibition in short-term retention of single items. *Journal of Verbal Learning and Verbal Behavior, 1,* 153–161.

Kershaw, T. C., & Ohlsson, S. (2004). Multiple causes of difficulty in insight: The case of the nine-dot problem. *Journal of Experimental Psychology: Learning, Memory, and Cognition, 30,* 3–13.

Kertesz, A. (1982). Two case studies: Broca's and Wernicke's aphasia. In M. A. Arbib, D. Caplan, & J. C. Marshall (Eds.), *Neural models of language processes* (pp. 25–44). New York: Academic Press.

Keysar, B., Shen, Y., Glucksberg, S., & Horton, W. S. (2000). Conventional language: How metaphorical is it? *Journal of Memory and Language, 43,* 576–593.

Kinder, A., & Shanks, D. R. (2003). Neuropsychological dissociations between priming and recognition: A single-system connectionist account. *Psychological Review, 110,* 728–744.

Kingstone, A., Smilek, D., Ristic, J., Friesen, C. K., & Eastwood, J. D. (2003). Attention, researchers! It is time to take a look at the real world. *Current Directions in Psychological Science, 12,* 176–180.

Kintsch, W. (2000). Metaphor comprehension: A computational theory. *Psychonomic Bulletin & Review, 7,* 257–266.

Kishiyama, M. M., Yonelinas, A. P., & Lazzara, M. M. (2004). The von Restorff effect in amnesia: The contribution of the hippocampal system to novelty-related memory enhancements. *Journal of Cognitive Neuroscience, 16,* 15–23.

Kissler, J., Herbert, C., Peyk, P., & Junghofer, M. (2007). Buzzwords: Early cortical response to emotional words during reading. *Psychological Science, 18,* 475–480.

Klatzky, R. L. (1980). *Human memory: Structures and processes* (2nd ed.). San Francisco: Freeman.

Klein, D. V., & Murphy, G. L. (2002). Paper has been my ruin: conceptual relations of polysemous senses. *Journal of Memory and Language, 47,* 548–570.

Klein, R. (2000). Inhibition of return. Trends in Cognitive Sciences, 4, 138–147.

Kliegl, R., Nuthmann, A., & Engbert, R. (2006). Tracking the mind during reading: The influence of past, present, and future words on fixation durations. *Journal of Experimental Psychology: General, 135,* 12–35.

Köhler, W. (1927). The mentality of apes. New York: Harcourt, Brace.

Koivisto, M., & Revonsuo, A. (2007). How meaning shapes seeing. *Psychological Science, 18,* 845–849.

Kolers, P. A., & Roediger, H. L. III (1984). Procedures of mind. *Journal of Verbal Learning and Verbal Behavior, 23,* 425–449.

Kolodner, J. L. (1997). Educational implications of analogy: A view from case-based reasoning. *American Psychologist, 52,* 57–66.

Komeda, H., & Kusumi, T. (2006). The effect of a protagonist's emotional shift on situation model construction. *Memory & Cognition, 34,* 1548–1556.

Koriat, A., Levy-Sadot, R., Edry, E., & de Marcus, S. (2003). What do we know about what we cannot remember? Accessing the semantic attributes of words that cannot be recalled. *Journal of Experimental Psychology: Learning, Memory, and Cognition, 29,* 1095–1105.

Koriat, A., & Pearlman-Avnion, S. (2003). Memory organization of action events and its relationship to memory performance. *Journal of Experimental Psychology: General, 132,* 435–454.

Koriat, A., Sheffer, L., & Ma'ayan, H. (2002). Comparing objective and subjective learning curves: Judgments of learning exhibit increased underconfidence with practice. *Journal of Experimental Psychology: General, 131,* 147–162.

Kosslyn, S. M., Alpert, N. M., Thompson, W. L., Maljkovic, V., Weise, S. B., Chabris, C. F., et al. (1993). Visual mental imagery activates topographically organized visual cortex: PET investigations. Journal of Cognitive Neuroscience, 5, 263–287.

Kotovsky, K., Hayes, J. R., & Simon, H. A. (1985). Why are some problems hard? Evidence from Tower of Hanoi. *Cognitive Psychology, 17,* 248–294.

Kounios, J., Frymiare, J. L., Bowden, E. M., Fleck, J. I., Subramaniam, K., Parrish, T. B., et al. (2006). The prepared mind: Neural activity prior to problem presentation predicts subsequent solution by sudden insight. *Psychological Science, 17,* 882–890.

Kounios, J., & Holcomb, P. J. (1992). Structure and process in semantic memory: Evidence from event-related brain potentials and reaction times. *Journal of Experimental Psychology: General, 121,* 459–479.

Kousta, S-T., Vigliocco, G., Vinson, D. P., Andrews, M., & Campo, E. D. (2010). The representation of abstract words: Why emotion matters. *Journal of Experimental Psychology: General, 140,* 14–34.

Kozhevnikov, M., Louchakova, O., Josipovic, Z., & Motes, M. A. (2009). The enhancement of visuospatial processing efficiency through Buddhist Deity Meditation. *Psychological Science, 20,* 645–653.

Kraljik, T., Samuel, A. G., & Brennan, S. E. (2008). First impressions and last resorts: How listeners adjust to speaker variability. *Psychological Science, 19,* 332–338.

Kramer, T. H., Buckout, R., & Eugenio, P. (1990). Weapon focus, arousal, and eyewitness memory. *Law and Human Behavior, 14,* 167–184.

Krawietz, S. A., Tamplin, A. K., & Radvansky, G. A. (2012). Aging and mind wandering during text comprehension. *Psychology and Aging, 27,* 951–958

Kumon-Nakamura, S., Glucksberg, S., & Brown, M. (1995). How about another piece of pie? The allusional pretense theory of discourse irony. *Journal of Experimental Psychology: General, 124,* 3–21.

Kunar, M. A., Carter, R., Cohen, M., & Horowitz, T. S. (2008). Telephone conversation impairs sustained visual attention via a central bottleneck. *Psychonomic Bulletin & Review, 15,* 1135–1140.

Kurtz, K. J., & Loewenstein, J. (2007). Converging on a new role for analogy in problem solving and retrieval: When two problems are better than one. *Memory & Cognition, 35,* 334–341.

Lachman, R., Lachman, J. L., & Butterfield, E. C. (1979). *Cognitive psychology and information processing: An introduction.* Hillsdale, NJ: Erlbaum.

Lachter, J., Forster, K. I., & Ruthruff, E. (2004). Forty-five

years after Broadbent (1958): Still no identification without attention. *Psychological Review, 111,* 880–913.

Lakens, D., Schneider, I. K., Jostmann, N. B., & Schubert, T. W. (2011). Telling things apart: The distance between response keys influences categorization times. *Psychological Science, 22,* 887–890.

Lambert, W. E. (1990). Issues in foreign language and second language education. *Proceedings of the Research Symposium on Limited English Proficient Students' Issues* (1st, Washington, DC, September 10–12, 1990).

Lang, J. W. B., & Lang, J. (2010). Priming competence diminishes the link between cognitive test anxiety and test performance: Implications for the interpretation of test scores. *Psychological Science, 21,* 811–819.

Lashley, K. D. (1950). In search of the engram. *Symposia for the Society for Experimental Biology, 4,* 454–482.

Laszlo, S., & Federmeier, K. D. (2009). A beautiful day in the neighborhood: An event-related potential study of lexical relationships and prediction in context. *Journal of Memory and Language, 61,* 326–338.

Lavie, N. (2010). Attention, distraction, and cognitive control under load. *Current Directions in Psychological Science, 19,* 143–148.

LeDoux, J. E. (2000). Emotion circuits in the brain. *Annual Review of Neuroscience, 23,* 155–184.

Lee, C-L., & Federmeier, K. D. (2009). Wave-ering: An ERP study of syntactic and semantic context effects on ambiguity resolution for noun/verb homographs. *Journal of Memory and Language, 61,* 538–555.

Lee, H-W., Rayner, K., & Pollatsek, A. (1999). The time course of phonological, semantic, and orthographic coding in reading: Evidence from the fast-priming technique. *Psychonomic Bulletin & Review, 6,* 624–634.

Lee, J. J., & Pinker, S. (2010). Rationales for indirect speech: The theory of the strategic speaker. *Psychological Review, 117,* 785–807.

Leonesio, R. J., & Nelson, T. O. (1990). Do different metamemory judgments tap the same underlying aspects of memory? *Journal of Experimental Psychology: Learning, Memory, and Cognition, 16,* 464–470.

LePine, J. A., LePine, M. A., & Jackson, C. L. (2004). Challenge and hindrance stress: Relationships with exhaustion, motivation to learn, and learning performance. *Journal of Applied Psychology, 89,* 883–891.

Levy, J., Pashler, H., & Boer, E. (2006). Central interference in driving: Is there any stopping the psychological refractory period? *Psychological Science, 17,* 228–235.

Lewis, J. L. (1970). Semantic processing of unattended messages using dichotic listening. *Journal of Experimental Psychology, 85,* 225–228.

Lewontin, R. C. (1990). The evolution of cognition. In D. N. Osherson & E. E. Smith (Eds.), *Thinking: An invitation to cognitive science* (Vol. 3, pp. 229–246). Cambridge, MA: MIT Press.

Li, X., Schweickert, R., & Gandour, J. (2000). The phonological similarity effect in immediate recall: Positions of shared phonemes. *Memory & Cognition, 28,* 1116–1125.

Liberman, A. M. (1957). Some results of research on speech perception. *Journal of the Acoustical Society of America, 29,* 117–123.

Liberman, A. M., Cooper, F. S., Shankweiler, D. P., & Studdert-Kennedy, M. (1967). Perception of speech code. *Psychological Review, 74,* 431–461.

Liberman, A. M., Harris, K. S., Hoffman, H. S., & Griffith, B. C. (1957). The discrimination of speech sounds within and across phoneme boundaries. *Journal of Experimental Psychology, 54,* 358–368.

Liberman, A. M., & Mattingly, I. G. (1985). The motor theory of speech perception revised. *Cognition, 21,* 1–36.

Libkuman, T. M., Nichols-Whitehead, P., Griffith, J., & Thomas, R. (1999). Source of arousal and memory for detail. *Memory & Cognition, 27,* 166–190.

Lindsay, P. H., & Norman, D. A. (1977). *Human information processing: An introduction to psychology.* New York: Academic Press.

Lindsley, J. R. (1975). Producing simple utterances: How far ahead do we plan? *Cognitive Psychology, 7,* 1–19.

Linek, J. A., Kroll, J. F., & Sunderman, G. (2010). Losing access to the native language while immersed in a second language: Evidence for the role of inhibition in second-language learning. *Psychological Science, 20,* 1507–1515.

Liszkowski, U., Schäfer, M., Carpenter, M., & Tomasello, M. (2010). Prelinguistic infants, but not chimpanzees, communicate about absent entities. *Psychological Science, 20,* 654–660.

Litman, D. J., & Allen, J. F. (1987). A plan recognition model for subdialogues in conversation. *Cognitive Science, 11,* 163–200.

Livesey, E. J., Harris, I. M., & Harris, J. A. (2009). Attentional changes during implicit learning: Signal validity protects target stimulus from the attentional blink. *Journal of Experimental Psychology: Learning, Memory, and Cognition, 35,* 408–422.

Lockridge, C. B., & Brennan, S. E. (2002). Addressees' needs influence speakers' early syntactic choices. *Psychonomic Bulletin & Review, 9,* 550–557.

Logan, G. D. (1990). Repetition priming and automaticity: Common underlying mechanisms? *Cognitive Psychology, 22,* 1–35.

Logan, G. D. (2003). Executive control of thought and action: In search of the wild homunculus. *Current Directions in Psychological Science, 12,* 45–48.

Logan, G. D., & Crump, M. J. C. (2009). The left hand doesn't know what the right hand is doing: the disruptive effects of attention to the hands in skilled typewriting. *Psychological Science, 20,* 1296–1300.

Logan, G. D., & Etherton, J. L. (1994). What is learned during automatization? The role of attention in constructing an instance. *Journal of Experimental Psychology: Learning, Memory, and Cognition, 20,* 1022–1050.

Logan, G. D., & Klapp, S. T. (1991). Automatizing alphabet arithmetic: I. Is extended practice necessary to produce automaticity? *Journal of Experimental Psychology: Learning, Memory, and Cognition, 17,* 179–195.

Logie, R. H., Zucco, G., & Baddeley, A. D. (1990). Interference with visual short-term memory. *Acta Psychologica, 75,* 55–74.

Long, D. L., & De Ley, L. (2000). Implicit causality and discourse focus: The interaction of text and reader characteristics in pronoun resolution. *Journal of Memory and Language, 42,* 545–570.

Long, D. L., Oppy, B. J., & Seely, M. R. (1997). Individual differences in readers' sentence- and text-level representations. *Journal of Memory and Language, 36,* 129–145.

Lozano, S. C., & Tversky, B. (2006). Communicative gestures facilitate problem solving for both communicators and recipients. *Journal of Memory and Language, 55,* 47–63.

Lu, S., & Zhou, K. (2005). Stimulus-driven attentional capture by equiluminent color change. *Psychonomic Bulletin & Review, 12,* 567–572.

Luchins, A. S. (1942). Mechanization in problem solving. *Psychological Monographs, 54* (Whole no. 248).

Lustig, C., & Hasher, L. (2001). Implicit memory is vulnerable to proactive interference. *Psychological Science, 12,* 408–412.

Lutz, M. E, & Radvansky, G. A. (1997). The fate of completed goal information. *Journal of Memory and Language, 36,* 293–310.

Maass, A., & Köhnken, G. (1989). Simulating the "weapon effect." *Law and Human Behavior, 13,* 397–408.

Mackworth, N. H. (1948). The breakdown of vigilance during prolonged visual search. *Quarterly Journal of Experimental Psychology, 1,* 6–21.

MacLean, K. A., Ferrer, E., Aichele, S. R., Bridwell, D.

A., Zanesco, A. P., Jacobs, T. L., et al. (2010). Intensive meditation training improves perceptual discrimination and sustained attention. *Psychological Science, 21,* 829–839.

MacLeod, C. M. (1988). Forgotten but not gone: Savings for pictures and words in long-term memory. *Journal of Experimental Psychology: Learning, Memory, and Cognition, 14,* 195–212.

MacLeod, C. M. (1991). Half a century of research on the Stroop effect: An integrative review. *Psychological Bulletin, 109,* 163–203.

MacLeod, C. M. (1992). The Stroop task: The "gold standard" of attentional measures. *Journal of Experimental Psychology: General, 121,* 12–14.

MacLeod, C. M. (2011). I said, you said: The production effect gets personal. *Psychonomic Bulletin & Review, 18,* 1197–1202.

MacLeod, C. M., Gopie, N., Hourihan, K. L., Neary, K. R., & Ozubko, J. D. (2010). The production effect: Delineation of a phenomenon. *Journal of Experimental Psychology. Learning, Memory, and Cognition, 36,* 671–685.

MacLeod, M. D., & Macrae, C. N. (2001). Gone but not forgotten: The transient nature of retrieval-induced forgetting. *Psychological Science, 12,* 148–152.

MacLeod, M. D., & Saunders, J. (2008). Retrieval inhibition and memory distortion. *Current Directions in Psychological Science, 17,* 26–30.

MacPherson, S. E., Phillips, L. H., & Sala, S. D. (2002). Age, executive functioning, and social decision making: A dorsolateral prefrontal theory of cognitive aging. *Psychology and Aging, 17,* 598–609.

MacQueen, G. M., Tipper, S. P., Young, L. T., Joffe, R. T., & Levitt, A. J. (2000). Impaired distractor inhibition on a selective attention task in unmedicated, depressed subjects. *Psychological Medicine, 30,* 557–564.

Madigan, S., & O'Hara, R. (1992). Short-term memory at the turn of the century: Mary Whiton Calkins's memory research. *American Psychologist, 47,* 170–174.

Magliano, J. P., Miller, J., & Zwaan, R. A. (2001). Indexing space and time in film understanding. Applied *Cognitive Psychology, 15,* 533–545.

Magliano, J. P., Taylor, H. A., & Kim, H. J. (2005). When goals collide: Monitoring the goals of multiple characters. *Memory & Cognition, 33,* 1357–1367.

Magliano, J. P., Trabasso, T., & Graesser, A. C. (1999). Strategic processing during comprehension. *Journal of Educational Psychology, 91,* 615–629.

Mahmood, D., Manier, D., & Hirst, W. (2004). Memory for how one learned of multiple deaths from AIDS: Repeated

exposure and distinctiveness. *Memory & Cognition, 32,* 125–134.

Maier, N. R. F. (1931). Reasoning in humans: II. The solution of a problem and its appearance in consciousness. *Journal of Comparative Psychology, 12,* 181–194.

Maloney, E. A., Ansari, D., & Fugelsang, J. A. (2011). The effect of mathematics anxiety on the processing of numerical magnitude. *Quarterly Journal of Experimental Psychology, 64,* 10–16.

Malt, B. C. (1985). The role of discourse structure in understanding anaphora. *Journal of Memory and Language, 24,* 271–289.

Malt, B. C., Sloman, S. A., & Gennari, S. P. (2003). Universality and language specificity in object naming. *Journal of Memory and Language, 49,* 20–42.

Mandler, G. (1967). Organization and memory. In K. W. Spence & J. T. Spence (Eds.), *The psychology of learning and motivation* (Vol. 1, pp. 327–372). New York: Academic Press.

Mandler, G. (1972). Organization and recognition. In E. Tulving & W. Donaldson (Eds.), *Organization of memory* (pp. 139–166). New York: Academic Press.

Manwell, L. A., Roberts, M. A., & Besner, D. (2004). Single letter coloring and spatial cuing eliminates a semantic contribution to the Stroop effect. *Psychonomic Bulletin & Review, 11,* 458–462.

Marian, V., & Neisser, U. (2000). Language-dependent recall of autobiographical memories. *Journal of Experimental Psychology: General, 129,* 361–368.

Markman, A. B., Taylor, E., & Gentner, D. (2007). Auditory presentation leads to better analogical retrieval than written presentation. *Psychonomic Bulletin & Review, 14,* 1101–1106.

Markovits, H., & Doyon, C. (2004). Information processing and reasoning with premises that are empirically false: Interference, working memory, and processing speed. *Memory & Cognition, 32,* 592–601.

Marler, P. (1967). Animal communication signals. *Science, 35,* 63–78.

Marsh, E. J. (2007). Retelling is not the same as recalling. *Current Directions in Psychological Science, 16,* 16–20.

Marsh, E. J., Roediger, H. L., Bjork, R. A., & Bjork, E. L. (2007). The memorial consequences of multiple-choice testing. *Psychonomic Bulletin & Review, 14,* 194–199.

Marsh, R. L., Cook, G. I., Meeks, J. T., Clark-Foos, A., & Hicks, J. L. (2007). Memory for intention-related material presented in a to-be-ignored channel. *Memory & Cognition, 35,* 1197–1204.

Marslen-Wilson, W. D., & Welsh, A. (1978). Processing interactions and lexical access during word recognition in continuous speech. *Cognitive Psychology, 30,* 509–517.

Mason, R. A., Just, M. A., Keller, T. A., & Carpenter, P. A. (2003). Ambiguity in the brain: What brain imaging reveals about the processing of syntactically ambiguous sentences. *Journal of Experimental Psychology: Learning, Memory, and Cognition, 29,* 1319–1338.

Masson, M. E. J. (1984). Memory for the surface structure of sentences: Remembering with and without awareness. *Journal of Verbal Learning and Verbal Behavior, 23,* 579–592.

Masson, M. E. J. (1995). A distributed memory model of semantic priming. *Journal of Experimental Psychology: Learning, Memory, and Cognition, 21,* 3–23.

Masters, R. S. W. (1992). Knowledge, knerves and knowhow: The role of explicit versus implicit knowledge in the breakdown of a complex motor skill under pressure. *British Journal of Psychology, 83,* 343–358.

Mather, M., & Sutherland, M. R. (2011). Arousal-based competition in perception and memory. Perspectives on *Psychological Science, 6,* 114–133.

Mayr, S., & Buchner, A. (2006). Evidence for episodic retrieval of inadequate prime responses in auditory negative priming. *Journal of Experimental Psychology: Human Perception and Performance, 32,* 932–943.

Mazzoni, G., & Cornoldi, C. (1993). Strategies in study time allocation: Why is study time sometimes not effective? *Journal of Experimental Psychology: General, 122,* 47–60.

McCabe, D. P. (2010). The influence of complex working memory span task administration methods on prediction of higher level cognition and metacognitive control of response times. *Memory & Cognition, 38,* 868–882.

McCandliss, B. D., Posner, M. I., & Givon, T. (1997). Brain plasticity in learning visual words. *Cognitive Psychology, 33,* 88–110.

McCarthy, R. A., & Warrington, E. K. (1984). A two route model of speech production: Evidence from aphasia. *Brain, 107,* 463–485.

McCarthy, R. A., & Warrington, E. K. (1990). *Cognitive neuropsychology: A clinical introduction.* San Diego: Academic Press.

McClelland, J. L. (1979). On the time relations of mental processes: An examination of systems of processes in cascade. *Psychological Review, 86,* 287–330.

McClelland, J. L., & Elman, J. L. (1986). The TRACE model of speech perception. *Cognitive Psychology, 18,* 1–86.

McCloskey, M., Wible, C. G., & Cohen, N. J. (1988). Is there a special flashbulb-memory mechanism? *Journal of Experimental Psychology: General, 117,* 171–181.

McDaniel, M. A., Maier, S. F., & Einstein, G. O. (2002). "Brain-specific" nutrients: A memory cure? *Psychological Science in the Public Interest, 31,* 12–38.

McDaniel, M. A., Roediger, H. L., & McDermott, K. B. (2007). Generalized test-enhanced learning from the laboratory to the classroom. *Psychonomic Bulletin & Review, 14,* 200–206.

McDonald, J. L., & MacWhinney, B. (1995). The time course of anaphor resolution: Effects of implicit verb causality and gender. *Journal of Memory and Language, 34,* 543–566.

McGeoch, J. A. (1932). Forgetting and the law of disuse. *Psychological Review, 39,* 352–370.

McKoon, G., & Macfarland, T. (2002). Event templates in the lexical representations of verbs. *Cognitive Psychology, 45,* 1–44.

McKoon, G., & Ratcliff, R. (1986). Inferences about predictable events. *Journal of Experimental Psychology: Learning, Memory, and Cognition, 12,* 82–91.

McKoon, G., & Ratcliff, R. (1989). Inferences about contextually defined categories. *Journal of Experimental Psychology: Learning, Memory, and Cognition, 15,* 1134–1146.

McKoon, G., & Ratcliff, R. (1992). Inference during reading. *Psychological Review, 99,* 440–466.

McKoon, G., & Ratcliff, R. (2007). Interactions of meaning and syntax: Implications for models of sentence comprehension. *Journal of Memory and Language, 56,* 270–290.

McNamara, D. S., & McDaniel, M. A. (2004). Suppressing irrelevant information: Knowledge activation or inhibition? *Journal of Experimental Psychology: Learning, Memory, and Cognition, 30,* 465–482.

McNeill, D. (1992). *Hand and mind: What gestures reveal about thought.* Chicago: University of Chicago Press.

Medin, D. L., Lynch, E. B., Coley, J. D., & Atran, S. (1997). Categorization and reasoning among tree experts: Do all roads lead to Rome? *Cognitive Psychology, 32,* 49–96.

Mehler, J., Morton, J., & Jusczyk, P. W. (1984). On reducing language to biology. *Cognitive Neuropsychology, 1,* 83–116.

Melton, A. W. (1963). Implications of short-term memory for a general theory of memory. *Journal of Verbal Learning and Verbal Behavior, 2,* 1–21.

Metcalfe, J. (1986). Feeling of knowing in memory and problem solving. *Journal of Experimental Psychology: Learning, Memory, and Cognition, 12,* 288–294.

Metcalfe, J. (2002). Is study time allocated selectively to a region of proximal learning? *Journal of Experimental Psychology: General, 131,* 349–363.

Metcalfe, J., & Finn, B. (2008). Evidence that judgments of learning are causally related to study choice. *Psychonomic Bulletin & Review, 15,* 174–179.

Metcalfe, J., & Kornell, N. (2003). The dynamics of learning and allocation of study time to a region of proximal learning. *Journal of Experimental Psychology: General, 132,* 530–542.

Metcalfe, J., & Wiebe, D. (1987). Intuition in insight and non-insight problem solving. *Memory & Cognition, 15,* 238–246.

Metzing, C., & Brennan, S. E. (2003). When conceptual pacts are broken: Partner-specific effects on the comprehension of referring expressions. *Journal of Memory and Language, 49,* 201–213.

Meyer, A. S., & Bock, K. (1992). The tip-of-the-tongue phenomenon: Blocking or partial activation? *Memory & Cognition, 20,* 715–726.

Miller, G. A. (1956). The magical number seven, plus or minus two: Some limits on our capacity for processing information. *Psychological Review, 63,* 81–97.

Miller, G. A. (1973). Psychology and communication. In G. A. Miller (Ed.), *Communication, language, and meaning: Psychological perspectives* (pp. 3–12). New York: Basic Books.

Miller, G. A. (1977). Practical and lexical knowledge. In P. N. Johnson-Laird & P. C. Wason (Eds.), *Thinking: Readings in cognitive science* (pp. 400–410). Cambridge, England: Cambridge University Press.

Miller, G. A., Galanter, E., & Pribram, K. H. (1960). *Plans and the structure of behavior.* New York: Holt.

Miller, G. A., & Isard, S. (1963). Some perceptual consequences of linguistic rules. *Journal of Verbal Learning and Verbal Behavior, 2,* 217–228.

Millis, K. K., & Graesser, A. C. (1994). The time-course of constructing knowledge-based inferences for scientific texts. *Journal of Memory and Language, 33,* 583–599.

Millis, K. K., & Just, M. A. (1994). The influence of connectives on sentence comprehension. *Journal of Memory and Language, 33,* 128–147.

Milner, B., Corkin, S., & Teuber, H. L. (1968). Further analysis of the hippocampal amnesic syndrome: 14–year follow up study of H. M. *Neuropsychologia, 6,* 215–234.

Mitchell, D. C., & Holmes, V. M. (1985). The role of specific information about the verb in parsing sentences with local structural ambiguity. *Journal of Memory and Language, 24,* 542–559.

Mitterschiffthaler, M. T., Williams, S. C. R., Walsh, N.

D., Cleare, A. J., Donaldson, C., Scott, J., et al. (2008). Neural basis of the emotional Stroop interference effect in major depression. *Psychological Medicine, 38,* 24–256.

Miyake, A., Friedman, N. P., Emerson, M. J., Witzki, A. H., Howerter, A., & Wager, T. D. (2000). The unity and diversity of executive functions and their contributions to complex "frontal lobe" tasks: A latent variable analysis. *Cognitive Psychology, 41,* 49–100.

Miyake, A., Just, M. A., & Carpenter, P. A. (1994). Working memory constraints on the resolution of lexical ambiguity: Maintaining multiple interpretations in neutral contexts. *Journal of Memory and Language, 33,* 175–202.

Miyake, A., & Shah, P. (Eds.). (1999). *Models of working memory: Mechanisms of active maintenance and executive control.* New York: Cambridge University Press.

Monaghan, P., & Shillcock, R. (2004). Hemispheric asymmetries in cognitive modeling: connectionist modeling of unilateral visual neglect. *Psychological Review, 111,* 283–308.

Moore, A. B., Clark, B. A., & Kane, M. J. (2008). Who shalt not kill? Individual differences in working memory capacity, executive control, and moral judgment. *Psychological Science, 19,* 549–557.

Moray, N. (1959). Attention in dichotic listening: Affective cues and the influence of instructions. *Quarterly Journal of Experimental Psychology, 11,* 56–60.

Moreno, S., Bialystok, E., Barac, R., Schellenberg, E. G., Cepeda, N. J., & Chau, T. (2011). Short-term music training enhances verbal intelligence and executive function. *Psychological Science, 22,* 1425–1433.

Morrow, D. G., Greenspan, S. L., & Bower, G. H. (1987). Accessibility and situation models in narrative comprehension. *Journal of Memory and Language, 26,* 165–187.

Morton, J. (1979). Facilitation in word recognition: Experiments causing change in the logogen models. In P. A. Kolers, M. E. Wrolstad, & H. Bouma (Eds.), Processing of visible language (Vol. 1, pp. 259–268). New York: Plenum.

Moscovitch, M. (1979). Information processing and the cerebral hemispheres. In M. S. Gazzaniga (Ed.), Handbook of behavioral neurobiology: Vol. 2. Neuropsychology (pp. 379–446). New York: Plenum.

Most, S. B., Scholl, B. J., Clifford, E. R., & Simons, D. J. (2005). What you see is what you set: Sustained inattentional blindness and the capture of awareness. *Psychological Review, 112,* 217–242.

Mueller, S. T., Seymour, T. L., Kieras, D. E., & Meyer, D. E. (2003). Theoretical implications of articulatory duration, phonological similarity, and phonological complexity in verbal working memory. *Journal of Experimental Psychology: Learning, Memory, and Cognition, 29,* 1353–1380.

Murdock, B. B., Jr. (1962). The serial position effect of free recall. *Journal of Experimental Psychology, 64,* 482–488.

Murphy, G. L. (1985). Processes of understanding anaphora. *Journal of Memory and Language, 24,* 290–303.

Murphy, M. C., Steele, C. M., & Gross, J. J. (2007). Signaling threat: How situational cues affect women in math, science, and engineering settings. *Psychological Science, 18,* 879–885.

Murray, D. J. (1967). The role of speech responses in short-term memory. *Canadian Journal of Psychology, 21,* 263–276.

Myers, E. B., Blumstein, S. E., Walsh, E., & Eliassen, J. (2009). Inferior frontal regions underlie the perception of phonetic category invariance. *Psychological Science, 20,* 895–903.

Nairne, J. S., Pandeirada, N. S., & Thompson, S. R. (2008). Adaptive memory: The comparative value of survival processing. *Psychological Science, 19,* 176–180.

Nairne, J. S., Thompson, S. R., & Pandeirada, N. S. (2007). Adaptive memory: Survival processing enhances retention. *Journal of Experimental Psychology: Learning, Memory, and Cognition, 33,* 263–273.

Navon, D. (1984). Resources: A theoretical soup stone? *Psychological Review, 91,* 216–234.

Nee, D. E., & Jonides, J. (2008). Dissociable interference control processes in perception and memory. *Psychological Science, 19,* 490–500.

Neill, W. T. (1977). Inhibition and facilitation processes in selective attention. *Journal of Experimental Psychology: Human Perception & Performance, 3,* 444–450.

Neill, W. T., Valdes, L. A., & Terry, K. M. (1995). Selective attention and the inhibitory control of cognition. In F. N. Dempster & C. J. Brainerd (Eds.), *New perspectives on interference and inhibition in cognition* (pp. 207–261). New York: Academic Press.

Neisser, U. (1982). *Memory observed: Remembering in natural contexts.* San Francisco: Freeman.

Nelson, K. (1993). The psychological and social origins of autobiographical memory. *Psychological Science, 4,* 7–14.

Nelson, T. O. (1978). Savings and forgetting from long-term memory. *Journal of Verbal Learning and Verbal Behavior, 10,* 568–576.

Nelson, T. O. (1985). Ebbinghaus's contribution to the measurement of retention: Savings during relearning. *Journal of Experimental Psychology: Learning, Memory, and Cognition, 11,* 472–479.

Nelson, T. O. (1988). Predictive accuracy of the feeling of knowing across different criterion tasks and across different subject populations and individuals. In M. Gruneberg, P. Morris, & R. Sykes (Eds.), *Practical aspects of memory: Current research and issues* (Vol. 1, pp. 190–196). New York: Wiley.

Nelson, T. O., & Leonesio, R. J. (1988). Allocation of self-paced study time and the "labor-in vain effect." *Journal of Experimental Psychology: Learning, Memory, and Cognition, 14,* 676–686.

Newell, A., Shaw, J. C., & Simon, H. A. (1958). Elements of a theory of human problem solving. *Psychological Review, 65,* 151–166.

Newell, A., & Simon, H. A. (1972). *Human problem solving.* Englewood Cliffs, NJ: Prentice Hall.

Nickerson, R. S. (2001). The projective way of knowing: A useful heuristic that sometimes misleads. *Current Directions in Psychological Science, 10,* 168–172.

Noice, H., & Noice, T. (1999). Long-term retention of theatrical roles. Memory, 7, 357–382.

Noice, H., & Noice, T. (2001). Learning dialogue with and without movement. *Memory and Cognition, 29,* 820–827.

Norman, D. A. (1981). Categorization of action slips. *Psychological Review, 88,* 1–15.

Norman, D. A., & Rumelhart, D. E. (Eds.). (1975). *Explorations in cognition.* San Francisco: Freeman.

Norris, D., McQueen, J. M., Cutler, A., & Butterfield, S. (1997). The possible-word constraint in the segmentation of continuous speech. *Cognitive Psychology, 34,* 191–243.

Novick, L. R. (1988). Analogical transfer, problem similarity, and expertise. *Journal of Experimental Psychology: Learning, Memory, and Cognition, 14,* 510–520.

Nyberg, L., Cabeza, R., & Tulving, E. (1996). PET studies of encoding and retrieval: The HERA model. *Psychonomic Bulletin & Review, 3,* 135–148.

Nyberg, L., McIntosh, A. R., & Tulving, E. (1998). Functional brain imaging of episodic and semantic memory with positron emission tomography. *Journal of Molecular Medicine, 76,* 48–53.

O'Brien, E. J., Albrecht, J. E., Hakala, C. M., & Rizzella, M. L. (1995). Activation and suppression of antecedents during reinstatement. *Journal of Experimental Psychology: Learning, Memory, and Cognition, 21,* 626–634.

O'Brien, E. J., & Myers, J. L. (1987). The role of causal connections in the retrieval of text. *Memory & Cognition, 15,* 419–427.

O'Brien, E. J., Plewes, P. S., & Albrecht, J. E. (1990). Antecedent retrieval processes. *Journal of Experimental Psychology: Learning, Memory, and Cognition, 16,* 241–249.

Öhman, A., Flykt, A., & Esteves, F. (2001). Emotion drives attention: Detecting the snake in the grass. *Journal of Experimental Psychology: General, 130,* 466–478.

Olafson, K. M., & Ferraro, F. R. (2001). Effects of emotional state on lexical decision performance. *Brain and Cognition, 45,* 15–20.

Oosterwijk, S., Winkielman, P., Pecher, D., Zeelenberg, R., Rottveel, M., & Fischer, A. H. (2012). Mental states inside out: Switching costs for emotional and nonemotional sentences that differ in internal and external focus. *Memory & Cognition, 40,* 93–100.

Oppenheim, G. M., & Dell, G. S. (2010). Motor movement matters: The flexible abstractness of inner speech. *Memory & Cognition, 38,* 1147–1160.

O'Seaghdha, P. G. (1997). Conjoint and dissociable effects of syntactic and semantic context. *Journal of Experimental Psychology: Learning, Memory, and Cognition, 23,* 807–828.

Osterhout, L., Allen, M. D., McLaughlin, J., & Inoue, K. (2002). Brain potentials elicited by prose-embedded linguistic anomalies. *Memory & Cognition, 30,* 1304–1312.

Osterhout, L., & Holcomb, P. J. (1992). Event-related brain potentials elicited by syntactic anomaly. *Journal of Memory and Language, 31,* 785–806.

Özyürek, S. (2002). Do speakers design their cospeech gestures for their addressees? The effects of addressee location on representational gestures. *Journal of Memory and Language, 46,* 688–704.

Paivio, A. (1971). *Imagery and verbal processes.* New York: Holt.

Palermo, D. S. (1978). *Psychology of language.* Glenview, IL: Scott, Foresman.

Pashler, H. (1994). Dual-task interference in simple tasks: Data and theory. *Psychological Bulletin, 116,* 220–244.

Pashler, H., & Johnson, J. C. (1998). Attentional limitations in dual-task performance. In H. Pashler (Ed.), *Attention* (pp. 155–189). Hove, England: Psychology Press.

Pashler, H., Rohrer, D., Cepeda, N. J., & Carpenter, S. K. (2007). Enhancing learning and retarding forgetting: Choices and consequences. *Psychonomic Bulletin & Review, 14,* 187–193.

Paul, S. T., Kellas, G., Martin, M., & Clark, M. B. (1992). Influence of contextual features on the activation of ambiguous word meanings. *Journal of Experimental Psychology: Learning, Memory, and Cognition, 18,* 703–717.

Payne, J. D., & Kensinger, E. A. (2010). Sleep's role in the consolidation of emotional episodic memories. *Psychological Science, 19,* 290–295.

Pearlmutter, N. J., Garnsey, S. M., & Bock, K. (1999). Agreement processes in sentence comprehension. *Journal of Memory and Language, 41,* 427–456.

Pedone, R., Hummel, J. E., & Holyoak, K. J. (2001). The use of diagrams in analogical problem solving. *Memory & Cognition, 29,* 214–221.

Pell, M. D. (1999). Fundamental frequency encoding of linguistic and emotional prosody by right hemisphere-damaged speakers. *Brain and Language, 69,* 161–192.

Penfield, W., & Milner, B. (1958). Memory deficit produced by bilateral lesions in the hippocampal zone. *Archives of Neurology and Psychiatry, 79,* 475–497.

Perea, M., Duñabeitia, J. A., & Carreiras, M. (2008). Masked associative/semantic priming effects across languages with highly proficient bilinguals. *Journal of Memory and Language, 58,* 916–930.

Perfect, T. J., Andrade, J., & Eagan, I. (2011). Eye closure reduces the cross-modal memory impairment caused by auditory distraction. *Journal of Experimental Psychology: Learning, Memory, and Cognition, 37,* 1008–1013.

Peterson, R. R., Burgess, C., Dell, G. S., & Eberhard, K. M. (2001). Dissociation between syntactic and semantic processing during idiom comprehension. *Journal of Experimental Psychology: Learning, Memory, and Cognition, 27*(5), 1223.

Peterson, L. R., & Peterson, M. J. (1959). Short-term retention of individual items. *Journal of Experimental Psychology, 58,* 193–198.

Pickering, M. J., & Traxler, M. J. (1998). Plausibility and recovery from garden paths: An eye-tracking study. *Journal of Experimental Psychology: Learning, Memory, and Cognition, 24,* 940–961.

Piercey, C. D., & Joordens, S. (2000). Turning an advantage into a disadvantage: Ambiguity effects in lexical decision versus reading tasks. *Memory & Cognition, 28,* 657–666.

Pinker, S. (1994). *The language instinct: How the mind creates language.* New York: Morrow.

Pitt, M. A., & Samuel, A. G. (1995). Lexical and sublexical feedback in auditory word recognition. *Cognitive Psychology, 29,* 149–188.

Polk, T. A., & Farah, M. J. (2002). Functional MRI evidence for an abstract, not perceptual, word-form area. *Journal of Experimental Psychology: General, 131,* 65–72.

Pollack, I., & Pickett, J. M. (1964). Intelligibility of excerpts from fluent speech: Auditory vs. structural context. *Journal of Verbal Learning and Verbal Behavior, 3,* 79–84.

Polya, G. (1957). *How to solve it.* Garden City, NY: Doubleday/Anchor.

Posner, M. I., & Cohen, Y. (1984). Components of visual orienting. In H. Bouma & D. G. Bouwhuis (Eds.), *Attention and performance X* (pp. 531–556). Hillsdale, NJ: Erlbaum.

Posner, M. I., Kiesner, J. Thomas-Thrapp, L., McCandliss, B., Carr, T. H., & Rothbart, M. K. (1992, November). *Brain changes in the acquisition of literacy.* Paper presented at the meetings of the Psychonomic Society, St. Louis.

Posner, M. I., Nissen, M. J., & Ogden, W. C. (1978). Attended and unattended processing modes: The role of set for spatial location. In H. L. Pick & I. J. Saltzman (Eds.), *Modes of perceiving and processing information* (pp. 137–157). Hillsdale, NJ: Erlbaum.

Posner, M. I., & Rothbart, M. K. (2007). Research on attention networks as a model for the integration of psychological science. *Annual Review of Psychology, 58,* 1–23.

Posner, M. I., & Snyder, C. R. R. (1975). Facilitation and inhibition in the processing of signals. In P. M. A. Rabbitt & S. Dornic (Eds.), *Attention and performance V* (pp. 669–682). New York: Academic Press.

Posner, M. I., Snyder, C. R. R., & Davidson, B. J. (1980). Attention and the detection of signals. *Journal of Experimental Psychology: General, 109,* 160–174.

Postman, L., & Underwood, B. J. (1973). Critical issues in interference theory. *Memory & Cognition, 1,* 19–40.

Pratt, J., Radulescu, P. V., Guo, R. M., & Abrams, R. A. (2010). It's alive! Animate motion captures visual attention. *Psychological Science, 21,* 1724–1730.

Protopapas, A., Archonti, A., & Skaloumbakas, C. (2007). Reading ability is negatively related to Stroop interference. *Cognitive Psychology, 54,* 251–282.

Radvansky, G. A., & Copeland, D. E. (2006a). Memory retrieval and interference: Working memory issues. *Journal of Memory and Language, 55,* 33–46.

Radvansky, G. A., Zwaan, R. A., Federico, T., & Franklin, N. (1998). Retrieval from temporally organized situation models. *Journal of Experimental Psychology: Learning, Memory, and Cognition, 24,* 1224–1237.

Rafal, R. D. (1997). Hemispatial neglect: Cognitive neuropsychological aspects. In T. E. Feinberg & M. J. Farah (Eds.), *Behavioral neurology and neuropsychology* (pp. 319–336). New York: McGraw-Hill.

Ranganath, C. (2010). Binding items and contexts: The cognitive neuroscience of episodic memory. Current Directions, 19, 131–137.

Ranganath, C., & Pallar, K. A. (1999). Frontal brain activity during episodic and semantic retrieval: Insights from event-related potentials. *Journal of Cognitive Neuroscience, 11,* 598–609.

Rapp, B., & Goldrick, M. (2000). Discreteness and interactivity in spoken word production. *Psychological Review, 107,* 460–499.

Rayner, K. (1998). Eye movements in reading and information processing: 20 years of research. *Psychological Bulletin, 124,* 372–422.

Rayner, K., Carlson, M., & Frazier, L. (1983). The interaction of syntax and semantics during sentence processing: Eye movements in the analysis of semantically biased sentences. *Journal of Verbal Learning and Verbal Behavior, 22,* 358–374.

Rayner, K., & Clifton, C., Jr. (2002). Language comprehension. In D. L. Medin (Ed.), *Steven's handbook of experimental psychology* (Vol. X, pp. 261–316). New York: Wiley.

Rayner, K., & Duffy, S. A. (1988). On-line comprehension processes and eye movements in reading. In M. Daneman, G. E. MacKinnon, & T. G. Waller (Eds.), *Reading research: Advances in theory and practice* (pp. 13–66). New York: Academic Press.

Rayner, K., & Frazier, L. (1989). Selection mechanisms in reading lexically ambiguous words. *Journal of Experimental Psychology: Learning, Memory, and Cognition, 15,* 779–790.

Rayner, K., Pollatsek, A., & Binder, K. S. (1998). Phonological codes and eye movements in reading. *Journal of Experimental Psychology: Learning, Memory, and Cognition, 24,* 476–497.

Rayner, K., Warren, T., Juhasz, B. J., & Liversedge, S. P. (2004). The effect of plausibility on eye movements in reading. *Journal of Experimental Psychology: Learning, Memory, and Cognition, 30,* 1290–1301.

Rayner, K., & Well, A. D. (1996). Effects of contextual constraint on eye movements in reading: A further examination. *Psychonomic Bulletin & Review, 3,* 504–509.

Rayner, K., White, S. J., Johnson, R. L., & Liversedge, S. P. (2006). Raeding wrods with jumbled letters: There is a cost. *Psychological Science, 17,* 192–193.

Reason, J. (1990). *Human error.* New York: Cambridge University Press.

Reed, S. K., & Hoffman, B. (2004). Use of temporal and spatial information in estimating event completion time. *Memory & Cognition, 32,* 271–282.

Reeves, L. M., & Weisberg, R. W. (1993). Abstract versus concrete information as the basis for transfer in problem solving: Comment on Fong and Nisbett (1991). *Journal of Experimental Psychology: General, 122,* 125–128.

Reichle, E. D., Carpenter, P. A., & Just, M. A. (2000). The neural bases of strategy and skill in sentence–picture verification. *Cognitive Psychology, 40,* 261–295.

Reichle, E. D., Pollatsek, A., Fisher, D. L., & Rayner, K. (1998). Eye movements during mindless reading. *Psychological Science, 21,* 1300–1310.

Reichle, E. D., Reineberg, A. E., & Schooler, J. W. (2010). Toward a model of eye movement control in reading. *Psychological Review, 105,* 125–157.

Reingold, E. M., Charness, N., Pomplun, M., & Stampe, D. M. (2001). Visual span in expert chess players: Evidence from eye movements. *Psychological Science, 12,* 48–55.

Rips, L. J. (1998). Reasoning and conversation. *Psychological Review, 105,* 411–441.

Roberson, D., Davies, I., & Davidoff, J. (2000). Color categories are not universal: Replications and new evidence from a Stone-Age culture. *Journal of Experimental Psychology: General, 129,* 369–398.

Robertson, D. A., Gernsbacher, M. A., Guidotti, S. J., Robertson, R. R. W., Irwin, W., Mock, B. J., et al. (2000). Functional neuroanatomy of the cognitive process of mapping during discourse comprehension. *Psychological Science, 11,* 255–260.

Roediger, H. L. III, & Crowder, R. G. (1976). A serial position effect in recall of United States presidents. *Bulletin of the Psychonomic Society, 8*(4), 275–278.

Roediger, H. L., & Karpicke, J. D. (2006). The power of resting memory: Basic research and implications for educational practice. Perspectives on *Psychological Science, 1,* 181–210.

Roediger, H. L. III, Marsh, E. J., & Lee, S. C. (2002). Kinds of memory. In D. Medin (Ed.), *Stevens' handbook of experimental psychology, Vol. 2* (3rd ed., pp. 1–42). New York: Wiley.

Roediger, H. L. III, Stadler, M. L., Weldon, M. S., & Riegler, G. L. (1992). Direct comparison of two implicit memory tests: Word fragment and word stem completion. *Journal of Experimental Psychology: Learning, Memory, and Cognition, 18,* 1251–1269.

Rogers, T. B., Kuiper, N. A., & Kirker, W. S. (1977). Self-reference and the encoding of personal information. *Journal of Personality and Social Psychology, 35,* 677–688.

Rosch-Heider, E. (1972). Universals in color naming and memory. *Journal of Experimental Psychology, 93,* 10–21.

Rosen, V. M., & Engle, R. W. (1997). The role of working memory capacity in retrieval. *Journal of Experimental Psychology: General, 126,* 211–227.

Rosler, F., Pechmann, T., Streb, J., Roder, B., & Hennighausen, E. (1998). Parsing of sentences in a language with varying word order: Word-by-word variations of processing demands are revealed by event-related brain potentials. *Journal of Memory and Language, 38,* 150–176.

Ross, B. H. (1987). This is like that: The use of earlier problems and the separation of similarity effects. *Journal of Experimental Psychology: Learning, Memory, and Cognition, 13,* 629–640.

Roy, M., Shohamy, D., & Wager, T. D. (2012). Ventromedial prefrontal-subcortical systems and the generation of affective meaning. *Trends in Cognitive Sciences, 16,* 147–156.

Rubin, D. C. (2007). A basic-systems model of episodic memory. Perspectives on *Psychological Science, 1,* 277–311.

Rubin, D. C., Schrauf, R. W., & Greenberg, D. L. (2003). Belief and recollection of autobiographical memories. *Memory and Cognition, 31,* 887–901.

Ruff, C. C., Kristkjánsson, Á., & Driver, J. (2007). Readout from iconic memory and selective spatial attention involve similar neural processes. *Psychological Science, 18,* 901–909.

Rundus, D. (1971). Analysis of rehearsal processes in free recall. *Journal of Experimental Psychology, 89,* 63–77.

Rundus, D., & Atkinson, R. C. (1970). Rehearsal processes in free recall: A procedure for direct observation. *Journal of Verbal Learning and Verbal Behavior, 9,* 99–105.

Russo, J. E., Johnson, E. J., & Stephens, D. L. (1989). The validity of verbal protocols. *Memory & Cognition, 17,* 759–769.

Sachs, J. S. (1967). Recognition memory for syntactic and semantic aspects of connected discourse. *Perception & Psychophysics, 2,* 437–442.

Sacks, H., Schegloff, E. A., & Jefferson, G. (1974). A simplest systematics for the organization of turntaking for conversation. *Language, 50,* 696–735.

Sacks, O. (1970). *The man who mistook his wife for a hat.* New York: Harper & Row.

Safer, M. A., Christiansen, S-A., Autry, M. W., & Österlund, K. (1998). Tunnel memory for traumatic events. Applied *Cognitive Psychology, 12,* 99–117.

Sakaki, M., Niki, K., & Mather, M. (2012). Beyond arousal and valence: The importance of the biological versus social relevance of emotional stimuli. *Cognitive Affective & Behavioral Neuroscience, 12,* 115–139.

Salame, P., & Baddeley, A. D. (1982). Disruption of short-term memory by unattended speech: Implications for the structure of working memory. *Journal of Verbal Learning and Verbal Behavior, 21,* 150–164.

Salthouse, T. A., & Pink, J. E. (2009). Why is working

memory related to fluid intelligence? *Psychonomic Bulletin & Review, 15,* 364–371.

Saltz, E., & Donnenwerth-Nolan, S. (1981). Does motoric imagery facilitate memory for sentences? A selective interference test. *Journal of Verbal Learning and Verbal Behavior, 20,* 322–332.

Samuel, A. G. (2001). Knowing a word affects the fundamental perception of the sounds within it. *Psychological Science, 12,* 348–351.

Sanchez, C. A. (2012). Enhancing visuospatial performance through video game training to increase learning in visuospatial science domains. *Psychonomic Bulletin & Review, 19,* 58–65.

Sanchez, C. A., & Wiley, J. (2006). An examination of the seductive details effect in terms of working memory capacity. *Memory & Cognition, 34,* 344–355.

Sattler, J. M. (1982). *Assessment of children's intellectual and special abilities* (2nd ed.). Boston: Allyn & Bacon.

Sayette, M. A., Reichle, E. D., & Schooler, J. W. (2009). Lost in the sauce: The effects of alcohol on mind wandering. *Psychological Science, 20,* 747–752.

Sayette, M. A., Schooler, J. W., & Reichle, E. D. (2010). Out for a smoke: The impact of cigarette craving on zoning out during reading. *Psychological Science, 21,* 26–30.

Schab, F. R. (1990). Odors and the remembrance of things past. *Journal of Experimental Psychology: Learning, Memory, and Cognition, 16,* 648–655.

Schacter, D. L. (1987). Implicit memory: History and current status. *Journal of Experimental Psychology: Learning, Memory, and Cognition, 13,* 501–518.

Schacter, D. L. (1989). Memory. In M. I. Posner (Ed.), *Foundations of cognitive science* (pp. 683–725). Cambridge, MA: MIT Press.

Schacter, D. L. (1996). *Searching for memory.* New York: Basic Books.

Schacter, D. L. (1999). The seven sins of memory: Insights from psychology and cognitive neuroscience. *American Psychologist, 54,* 182–203.

Schank, R. C. (1977). Rules and topics in conversation. *Cognitive Science, 1,* 421–441.

Schilling, H. E. H., Rayner, K., & Chumbley, J. I. (1998). Comparing naming, lexical decision, and eye fixation times: Word frequency effects and individual differences. *Memory & Cognition, 26,* 1270–1281.

Schmader, T. (2010). Stereotype threat deconstructed. *Current Directions in Psychological Science, 19,* 14–18.

Schmeichel, B. J. (2007). Attention control, memory updating, and emotion regularity temporarily reduce the capacity for executive control. *Journal of Experimental Psychology: General, 136,* 241–255.

Schmidt, S. R. (1985). Encoding and retrieval processes in the memory for conceptually distinctive events. *Journal of Experimental Psychology: Learning, Memory, and Cognition, 11,* 565–578.

Schmidt, S. R. (2004). Autobiographical memories for the September 11th attacks: Reconstructive errors and emotional impairment of memory. *Memory & Cognition, 32,* 443–454.

Schmolck, H., Buffalo, E. A., & Squire, L. R. (2000). Memory distortions develop over time: Recollections of the O. J. Simpson trial verdict after 15 and 32 months. *Psychological Science, 11,* 39–45.

Schneider, V. I., Healy, A. F., & Bourne, L. E., Jr. (2002). What is learned under difficult conditions is hard to forget: Contextual interference effects in foreign vocabulary acquisition, retention, and transfer. *Journal of Memory and Language, 46,* 419–440.

Schneider, W., & Shiffrin. R. M. (1977). Controlled and automatic human information processing: I. Detection, search, and attention. *Psychological Review, 84,* 1–66.

Schnorr, J. A., & Atkinson, R. C. (1969). Repetition versus imagery instructions in the short- and long-term retention of paired associates. *Psychonomic Science, 15,* 183–184.

Schooler, J. W., Ohlsson, S., & Brooks, K. (1993). Thoughts beyond words: When language overshadows insight. *Journal of Experimental Psychology: General, 122,* 166–183.

Schrauf, R. W., & Rubin, D. C. (2000). Internal languages of retrieval: The bilingual encoding of memories for the personal past. *Memory & Cognition, 28,* 616–623.

Schustack, M. W., Ehrlich, S. F., & Rayner, K. (1987). Local and global sources of contextual facilitation in reading. *Journal of Memory and Language, 26,* 322–340.

Searle, J. R. (1969). *Speech acts.* Cambridge, England: Cambridge University Press.

See, J. E., Howe, S. R., Warm, J. S., & Dember, W. N. (1995). Meta-analysis of the sensitivity decrement in vigilance. *Psychological Bulletin, 2,* 230–249.

Sehulster, J. R. (1989). Content and temporal structure of autobiographical knowledge: Remembering twenty-five seasons at the Metropolitan Opera. *Memory & Cognition, 17,* 590–606.

Serences, J. T., Shomstein, S., Leber, A. B., Golay, X., Egeth, H. E., & Yantis, S. (2005). Coordination of voluntary and stimulus-driven attentional control in human cortex. *Psychological Science, 16,* 114–122.

Sereno, S. C., Brewer, C. C., & O'Donnell, P. J. (2003). Context effects in word recognition: Evidence for early interactive processing. *Psychological Science, 14,* 328–333.

Shallice, T., Fletcher, P., & Dolan, R. (1998). The functional imaging of recall. In M. A. Conway, S. E. Gathercole, and C. Cornoldi (Eds.), *Theories of memory* (Vol. II, pp. 247– 258). Hove, England: Psychology Press.

Shallice, T., & Warrington, E. K. (1970). Independent functioning of the verbal memory stores: A neuropsychological study. *Quarterly Journal of Experimental Psychology, 22,* 261–273.

Shand, M. A. (1982). Sign-based short-term coding of American Sign Language signs and printed English words by congenitally deaf signers. *Cognitive Psychology, 14,* 1–12.

Sharkey, N. E., & Mitchell, D. C. (1985). Word recognition in a functional context: The use of scripts in reading. *Journal of Memory and Language, 24,* 253–270.

Sharot, T., Martorella, E. A., Delgado, M. R., & Phelps, E. A. (2007). How personal experience modulates the neural circuitry of memories of September 11. *Proceedings of the National Academy of Science, 104,* 389–394.

Shelton, A. L., & McNamara, T. P. (2001). Visual memories from nonvisual experiences. *Psychological Science, 12,* 343–347.

Shelton, J. T., Elliott, E. M., Matthews R. A., Hill, B. D., & Gouvier, W. D. (2010). The relationships of working memory, secondary memory, and general fluid intelligence: Working memory is special. *Journal of Experimental Psychology: Learning, Memory, and Cognition, 36,* 813–820.

Shepard, R. N., & Metzler, J. (1971). Mental rotation of three-dimensional objects. *Science, 171,* 701–703.

Sherman, G., & Visscher, P. K. (2002). Honeybee colonies achieve fitness through dancing. *Nature, 419,* 920–922.

Shiffrin, R. M., & Schneider, W. (1977). Controlled and automatic human information processing: II. Perceptual learning, automatic attending, and a general theory. *Psychological Review, 84,* 127–190.

Shintel, H., & Keysar, B. (2007). You said it before and you'll say it again: Expectations and consistency in communication. *Journal of Experimental Psychology: Learning, Memory, and Cognition, 33,* 357–369.

Siegler, R. S. (2000). Unconscious insights. *Current Directions in Psychological Science, 9,* 79–83.

Siegler, R. S., & Stern, E. (1998). A microgenetic analysis of conscious and unconscious strategy discoveries. *Journal of Experimental Psychology: General, 127,* 377–397.

Simon, H. A. (1975). The functional equivalence of problem solving skills. *Cognitive Psychology, 7,* 268–288.

Simon, H. A. (1979). *Models of thought.* New Haven, CT: Yale University Press.

Simon, H. A. (May, 1995). *Thinking in words, pictures, equations, numbers: How do we do it and what does it matter?* Invited address presented at the meeting of the Midwestern Psychological Association, Chicago.

Simpson, G. B. (1981). Meaning dominance and semantic context in the processing of lexical ambiguity. *Journal of Verbal Learning and Verbal Behavior, 20,* 120–136.

Simpson, G. B. (1984). Lexical ambiguity and its role in models of word recognition. *Psychological Bulletin, 96,* 316–340.

Simpson, G. B., Casteel, M. A., Peterson, R. R., & Burgess, C. (1989). Lexical and sentence context effects in word recognition. *Journal of Experimental Psychology: Learning, Memory, and Cognition, 15,* 88–97.

Singer, M. (1990). *Psychology of language: An introduction to sentence and discourse processes.* Hillsdale, NJ: Erlbaum.

Singer, M., Andrusiak, P., Reisdorf, P., & Black, N. L. (1992). Individual differences in bridging inference processes. *Memory & Cognition, 20,* 539–548.

Singer, M., Graesser, A. C., & Trabasso, T. (1994). Minimal or global inference during reading. *Journal of Memory and Language, 33,* 421–441.

Sitton, M., Mozer, M. C., & Farah, M. J. (2000). Superadditive effects of multiple lesions in a connectionist architecture: Implications for the neuropsychology of optic aphasia. *Psychological Review, 107,* 709–734.

Slamecka, N. J. (1968). An examination of trace storage in free recall. *Journal of Experimental Psychology, 4,* 504–513.

Slamecka, N. J. (1985). Ebbinghaus: Some associations. *Journal of Experimental Psychology: Learning, Memory, and Cognition, 11,* 414–435.

Slamecka, N. J., & Graf, P. (1978). The generation effect: delineation of a phenomenon. *Journal of Experimental Psychology: Human Learning and Memory, 4,* 592–604.

Smallwood, J., Fishman, D. J., & Schooler, J. W. (2007). Counting the cost of an absent mind: Mind wandering as an unrecognized influence on educational performance. *Psychonomic Bulletin & Review, 14,* 230–236.

Smallwood, J., McSpadden, M., & Schooler, J. W. (2007). The lights are on but no one's home: Meta-awareness and the decoupling of attention when the mind wanders. *Psychonomic Bulletin & Review, 14,* 527–533.

Smallwood, J., & Schooler, J. W. (2006). The restless mind. *Psychological Bulletin, 132,* 946–958.

Smilek, D., Carriere, J. S. A., & Cheyne, J. A. (2010). Out of mind, out of sight: Eye blinking as indicator and embodiment of mind wandering. *Psychological Science, 21*, 786–789.

Smith, E. E. (2000). Neural bases of human working memory. *Current Directions in Psychological Science, 9*, 45–49.

Smith, E. E., & Jonides, J. (1999). Storage and executive processes in the frontal lobes. *Science, 283*, 1657–1661.

Smith, S. M. (1995). Getting into and out of mental ruts: A theory of fixation, incubation, and insight. In R. J. Sternberg & J. E. Davidson (Eds.), *The nature of insight* (pp. 229–251). Cambridge, MA: MIT Press.

Snow, C. (1972). Mother's speech to children learning language. *Child Development, 43*, 549–565.

Snow, C., & Ferguson, C. (Eds.). (1977). Talking to children: Language input and acquisition. Cambridge, England: Cambridge University Press.

Solso, R. L. (1998). Cognitive psychology (5th ed.). Boston: Allyn & Bacon.

Son, L. K. (2004). Spacing one's study: Evidence for a meta-cognitive control strategy. *Journal of Experimental Psychology: Learning, Memory, and Cognition, 30*, 601–604.

Son, L. K., & Metcalfe, J. (2000). Metacognitive and control strategies in study-time allocation. *Journal of Experimental Psychology: Learning, Memory, and Cognition, 26*, 204–221.

Spelke, E., Hirst, W., & Neisser, U. (1976). Skills of divided attention. *Cognition, 4*, 215–230.

Spellman, B. A., & Holyoak, K. J. (1996). Pragmatics in analogical mapping. *Cognitive Psychology, 31*, 307–346.

Spence, C., & Read, L. (2003). Speech shadowing while driving: On the difficulty of splitting attention between eye and ear. *Psychological Science, 14*, 251–256.

Spivey, M. J., Tanenhaus, M. K., Eberhard, K. M., & Sedivy, J. C. (2002). Eye movements and spoken language comprehension: Effects of visual context on syntactic ambiguity resolution. *Cognitive Psychology, 45*, 447–481.

Squire, L. R. (1986). Mechanisms of memory. *Science, 232* (4578), 1612–1619.

Squire, L. R. (1987). *Memory and brain*. New York: Oxford University Press.

Squire, L. R. (1993). The organization of declarative and nondeclarative memory. In T. Ono, L. R. Squire, M. E. Raichle, D. I. Perrett, & M. Fukuda (Eds.), *Brain mechanisms of perception and memory: From neuron to behavior* (pp. 219–227). New York: Oxford University Press.

Stallings, L. M., MacDonald, M. C., & O'Seaghdha, P. G. (1998). Phrasal ordering constraints in sentence production: Phrase length and verb disposition in heavy-NP shift. *Journal of Memory and Language, 39*, 392–417.

Stefanucci, J. K., & Storbeck, J. (2009). Don't look down: Emotional arousal elevates height perception. *Journal of Experimental Psychology: General, 131*, 131–145.

Sternberg, R. J. (1996). *Cognitive psychology*. Fort Worth, TX: Harcourt Brace.

Sternberg, S. (1966). High-speed scanning in human memory. *Science, 153*, 652–654.

Sternberg, S. (1969). The discovery of processing stages: Extensions of Donder's method. In W. G. Koster (Ed.), *Attention and performance II. Acta Psychologica, 30*, 276–315.

Sternberg, S. (1975). Memory scanning: New findings and current controversies. *Quarterly Journal of Experimental Psychology, 27*, 1–32.

Storm, B. C. (2011). The benefit of forgetting in thinking and remembering. *Current Directions in Psychological Science, 20*, 291–295.

Strayer, D. L., & Drews, F. A. (2007). Cell-phone-induced driver distraction. *Current Directions in Psychological Science, 16*, 128–131.

Strayer, D. L., & Johnston, W. A. (2001). Driven to distraction: Dual-task studies of stimulated driving and conversing on a cellular phone. *Psychological Science, 12*, 462–466.

Stroop, J. R. (1935). Studies of interference in serial verbal reactions. *Journal of Experimental Psychology, 18*, 643–662.

Suh, S. Y., & Trabasso, T. (1993). Inferences during reading: Converging evidence from discourse analysis, talk-aloud protocols, and recognition priming. *Journal of Memory and Language, 32*, 279–300.

Svartvik, J., & Quirk, R. (Eds.). (1980). *A corpus of English conversation*. Lund, Sweden: CWK Gleerup.

Symons, C. S., & Johnson, B. T. (1997). The self-reference effect in memory: A meta-analysis. *Psychological Bulletin, 121*, 371–394.

Tabor, W., & Hutchins, S. (2004). Evidence for self-organized sentence processing: Digging-in effects. *Journal of Experimental Psychology: Learning, Memory, and Cognition, 30*, 431–450.

Takahashi, M., Shimizu, H., Saito, S., & Tomoyori, H. (2006). One percent ability and ninety-nine percent perspiration: A study of a Japanese memorist. *Journal of Experimental Psychology: Learning, Memory, and Cognition, 32*, 1195–1200.

Talarico, J. M., LaBar, K. S., & Rubin, D. C. (2004). Emotional intensity predicts autobiographical memory experience. *Memory & Cognition, 32*, 1118–1132.

Talarico, J. M., & Rubin, D. C. (2003). Confidence, not consistency, characterizes flashbulb memories. *Psychological Science, 14,* 455–461.

Talmi, D., & Garry, L. M. (2012). Accounting for immediate emotional memory enhancement. *Journal of Memory and Language, 66,* 93–108.

Talmi, J. M., Schimmack, U., Paterson, T., & Moscovitch, M. (2007). The role of attention and relatedness in emotionally enhanced memory. *Emotion, 7,* 89–102.

Tamplin, A. K., Krawietz, S. A., Copeland, D. E., & Radvansky, G. A. (in press). Event memory and moving in a well-known environment. *Memory & Cognition.*

Taraban, R., & McClelland, J. L. (1988). Constituent attachment and thematic role assignment in sentence processing: Influences of content-based expectations. *Journal of Memory and Language, 27,* 597–632.

Taylor, S. F., Liberzon, I., & Koeppe, R. A. (2000). The effect of graded aversive stimuli on limbic and visual activation. *Neuropsychologia, 38,* 1415–1425.

Thapar, A., & Greene, R. L. (1994). Effects of level of processing on implicit and explicit tasks. *Journal of Experimental Psychology: Learning, Memory, and Cognition, 20,* 671–679.

Thiede, K. W. (1999). The importance of monitoring and self-regulation during multitrial learning. *Psychonomic Bulletin & Review, 6,* 662–667.

Thomas, J. C., Jr. (1974). An analysis of behavior in the hobbits–orcs problem. *Cognitive Psychology, 6,* 257–269.

Thomas, M. H., & Wang, A. Y. (1996). Learning by the keyword mnemonic: Looking for long-term benefits. *Journal of Experimental Psychology: Applied, 2,* 330–342.

Thomson, D. M., & Tulving, E. (1970). Associative encoding and retrieval: Weak and strong cues. *Journal of Experimental Psychology, 86,* 255–262.

Thorndike, E. L. (1914). The psychology of learning. New York: Teachers College.

Tipper, S. P. (1985). The negative priming effect: Inhibitory priming with to be ignored objects. *The Quarterly Journal of Experimental Psychology, 37A,* 571–590.

Tourangeau, R., & Rips, L. (1991). Interpreting and evaluating metaphors. *Journal of Memory and Language, 30,* 452–472.

Treccani, B., Argyri, E., Sorace, A., & Della Salla, S. (2009). Spatial negative priming in bilingualism. *Psychonomic Bulletin & Review, 16,* 320–327.

Treisman, A. M. (1960). Contextual cues in selective listening. *Quarterly Journal of Experimental Psychology, 12,* 242–248.

Treisman, A. M. (1964). Monitoring and storage of irrelevant messages in selective attention. *Journal of Verbal Learning and Verbal Behavior, 3,* 449–459.

Treisman, A. M. (1965). The effects of redundancy and familiarity on translating and repeating back a foreign and a native language. *British Journal of Psychology, 56,* 369–379.

Treisman, A. (1982). Perceptual grouping and attention in visual search for features and for objects. *Journal of Experimental Psychology: Human Perception and Performance, 8,* 194–214.

Treisman, A. (1988). Features and objects: The Fourteenth Bartlett Memorial Lecture. *Quarterly Journal of Experimental Psychology, 40A,* 201–237.

Treisman, A. (1991). Search, similarity, and integration of features between and within dimensions. *Journal of Experimental Psychology: Human Perception and Performance, 17,* 652–676.

Treisman, A., & Gelade, G. (1980). A feature integration theory of attention. *Cognitive Psychology, 12,* 97–136.

Tuholski, S. W., Engle, R. W., & Baylis, G. C. (2001). Individual differences in working memory capacity and enumeration. *Memory & Cognition, 29,* 484–492.

Tulving, E. (1962). Subjective organization in free recall of "unrelated" words. *Psychological Review, 69,* 344–354.

Tulving, E. (1972). Episodic and semantic memory. In E. Tulving & W. Donaldson (Eds.), *Organization of memory* (pp. 381–403). New York: Academic Press.

Tulving, E. (1983). *Elements of episodic memory.* Oxford, England: Clarendon.

Tulving, E. (1989). Remembering and knowing the past. *American Scientist, 77,* 361–367.

Tulving, E. (1993). What is episodic memory? *Current Directions in Psychological Science, 2,* 67–70.

Tulving, E., & Pearlstone, Z. (1966). Availability versus accessibility of information in memory for words. *Journal of Verbal Learning and Verbal Behavior, 5,* 381–391.

Tulving, E., & Thompson, D. M. (1973). Encoding specificity and retrieval processes in episodic memory. *Psychological Review, 80,* 352–373.

Turner, M. L., & Engle, R. W. (1989). Is working memory capacity task dependent? *Journal of Memory and Language, 28,* 127–154.

Tyler, L. K., Voice, J. K., & Moss, H. E. (2000). The interaction of meaning and sound in spoken word recognition. *Psychonomic Bulletin & Review, 7,* 320–326.

Underwood, B. J. (1957). Interference and forgetting. *Psychological Review, 64,* 49–60.

Underwood, B. J., & Schulz, R. W. (1960). *Meaningfulness and verbal learning.* Philadelphia: Lippincott.

Ungerleider, L. G., & Haxby, J. V. (1994). "What" versus "where" in the human brain. *Current Opinion in Neurobiology, 4,* 157–165.

Unsworth, N. (2007). Individual differences in working memory capacity and episodic retrieval: The dynamics of delayed and continuous distractor free recall. *Journal of Experimental Psychology: Learning, Memory, and Cognition, 33,* 1020–1034.

Unsworth, N., & Engle, R. W. (2007). The nature of individual differences in working memory capacity: Active maintenance in primary memory and controlled search from secondary memory. *Psychological Review, 114,* 104–132.

Unsworth, N., Heitz, R. P., & Parks, N. A. (2008). The importance of temporal distinctiveness for forgetting over the short-term. *Psychological Science, 19,* 1078–1081.

Unsworth, N., & Spillers, G. J, (2010). Working memory capacity: Attention control, secondary memory, or both? A direct test of the dual component model. *Journal of Memory and Language, 62,* 392–406.

Unsworth, N., Spillers, G. J., & Brewer, G. A. (2012). Dynamics of context-dependent recall: An examination of internal and external context change. *Journal of Memory and Language, 66,* 1–16.

Vachon, F., Hughes, R. W., & Jones, D. M. (2012). Broken expectations: Violation of expectancies, not novelty, captures auditory attention. *Journal of Experimental Psychology: Learning, Memory, and Cognition, 38,* 164–177.

Vallar, G., & Baddeley, A. D. (1984). Fractionation of working memory: Neuropsychological evidence for a phonological short-term store. *Journal of Verbal Learning and Verbal Behavior, 23,* 151–161.

Vallée-Tourangeau, F., Euden, G., & Hearn, V. (2011). Einstellung defused: Interactivity and mental set. *Quarterly Journal of Expermental Psychology, 64,* 1889–1895.

Van Berkum, J. J. A. (2008). Understanding sentences in context: What brain waves can tell us. *Current Directions in Psychological Science, 17,* 376–380.

Van Dijk, T. A., & Kintsch, W. (1983). *Strategies in discourse comprehension.* New York: Academic Press.

van Hell, J. G., & Dijkstra, T. (2002). Foreign language knowledge can influence native language performance in exclusively native contexts. *Psychonomic Bulletin & Review, 9,* 780–789.

VanLehn, K. (1989). Problem solving and cognitive skill acquisition. In M. I. Posner (Ed.), *Foundations of cognitive science* (pp. 527–579). Cambridge, MA: MIT Press.

Vecera, S. P., Behrmann, M., & McGoldrick, J. (2000). Selective attention to the parts of an object. *Psychonomic Bulletin & Review, 7,* 301–308.

Vergauwe, E., Barrouillet, P., & Camos, V. (2010). Do mental processes share a domain-general resource? *Psychological Science, 21,* 384–390.

Verfaille, K., & Y'dewalle, G. (1991). Representational momentum and event course anticipation in the perception of implied motions. *Journal of Experimental Psychology: Learning, Memory, and Cognition, 17,* 302–313.

Verhaeghen, P., Cerella, J., & Basak, C. (2004). A working memory workout: How to expand the focus of serial attention from one to four items in 10 hours or less. *Journal of Experimental Psychology: Learning, Memory, and Cognition, 30,* 1322–1337.

Virtue, S., van den Broek, P., & Linderholm, T. (2006). Hemispheric processing of inferences: the effects of textual constraint and working memory capacity. *Memory & Cognition, 34,* 1341–1354.

Vivas, A. B., Humphreys, G. W., & Fuentes, L. J. (2006). Abnormal inhibition of return: A review and new data on patients with parietal lobe damage. *Cognitive Neuropsychology, 23,* 1049–1064.

von Frisch, K. (1967). *The dance language and orientation of honeybees.* Cambridge, MA: Harvard University Press.

von Restorff, H. (1933). Über die Wirkung von Bereichsbildungen im Spurenfeld [On the effect of sphere formations in the trace field]. *Psychologische Forschung, 18,* 299–342.

Vredeveldt, A., Hitch, G. J., & Baddeley, A. D. (2011). Eyeclosure helps memory by reducing cognitive load and enhancing visualization. *Memory & Cognition, 39,* 1253–1263.

Vu, H., Kellas, G., Metcalf, K., & Herman, R. (2000). The influence of global discourse on lexical ambiguity resolution. *Memory & Cognition, 28,* 236–252.

Vuilleumeir, P. (2005). How brains beware: Neural mechanisms of emotional attention. *Trends in Cognitive Sciences, 9,* 585–594.

Vuilleumeir, P., & Huang, Y-M. (2009). Emotional attention: Uncovering the mechanisms of affective biases in perception. *Current Directions in Psychological Science, 18,* 148–152.

Vul, E., & Pashler, H. (2007). Incubation benefits only after people have been misdirected. *Memory & Cognition, 35,* 701–710.

Waltz, J. A., Lau, A., Grewal, S. K., & Holyoak, K. J. (2000). The role of working memory in analogical mapping. *Memory & Cognition, 28,* 1205–1212.

Warm, J. S. (1984). An introduction to vigilance. In J. S. Warm (ed.), *Sustained attention in human performance* (pp. 1–14). Chichester, England: Wiley.

Warm, J. S., & Jerison, H. J. (1984). The psychophysics of vigilance. In J. S. Warm (ed.), *Sustained attention in human performance* (pp. 15–60). Chichester, England: Wiley.

Warren, R. M. (1970). Perceptual restoration of missing speech sounds. *Science, 167,* 392–393.

Warren, R. M., & Warren, R. P. (1970). Auditory illusions and confusions. *Scientific American, 223,* 30–36.

Warrington, E. K., & Shallice, T. (1969). The selective impairment of auditory verbal short-term memory. *Brain, 92,* 885–896.

Warrington, E. K., & Weiskrantz, L. (1970). The amnesic syndrome: Consolidation or retrieval? Nature, 228, 628–630.

Wassenburg, S. I., & Zwaan, R. A. (2010). Readers routinely represent implied object rotation: The role of visual experience. *Quarterly Journal of Experimental Psychology, 63,* 1665–1670.

Waugh, N. C., & Norman, D. A. (1965). Primary memory. *Psychological Review, 72,* 89–104.

Weaver, C. A. III. (1993). Do you need a "flash" to form a flashbulb memory? *Journal of Experimental Psychology: General, 122,* 39–46.

Weinstein, Y., Bugg, J. M., & Roediger, H. L. (2008). Can the survival recall advantage be explained by basic memory processes? *Memory & Cognition, 36,* 913–919.

Weisberg, R. (1995). Prolegomena to theories of insight in problem solving: A taxonomy of problems. In R. J. Sternberg & J. E. Davidson (Eds.), *The nature of insight* (pp. 157–196). Cambridge, MA: MIT Press.

Wenger, M. J., & Payne, D. G. (1995). On the acquisition of mnemonic skill: Application of skilled memory theory. *Journal of Experimental Psychology: Applied, 1,* 194–215.

West, R. F., & Stanovich, K. E. (1986). Robust effects of syntactic structure on visual word processing. *Memory & Cognition, 14,* 104–112.

Wharton, C. M., Grafman, J., Flitman, S. S., Hansen, E. K., Brauner, J., Marks, A., et al. (2000). Toward neuroanatomical models of analogy: A positron emission tomography study of analogical mapping. *Cognitive Psychology, 40,* 173–197.

Whitney, P. (1998). *The psychology of language.* Boston: Houghton Mifflin.

Whorf, B. L. (1956). Science and linguistics. In J. B. Carroll (Ed.), *Language, thought, and reality: Selected writings of Benjamin Lee Whorf* (pp. 207–219). Cambridge, MA: MIT Press.

Wickelgren, W. A. (1974). *How to solve problems.* San Francisco: Freeman.

Wickens, D. D. (1972). Characteristics of word encoding. In A. W. Melton & E. Martin (Eds.), *Coding processes in human memory* (pp. 191–215). New York: Winston.

Wickens, D. D., Born, D. G., & Allen, C. K. (1963). Proactive inhibition and item similarity in short-term memory. *Journal of Verbal Learning and Verbal Behavior, 2,* 440–445.

Wiener, E. L. (1984). Vigilance and inspection. In J. S. Warm (ed.), *Sustained attention in human performance* (pp. 207–246). Chichester, England: Wiley.

Wiggs, C. L., Weisberg, J., & Martin, A. (1999). Neural correlates of semantic and episodic memory retrieval. *Neuropsychologia, 37,* 103–118.

Wiley, J. (1998). Expertise as mental set: The effects of domain knowledge in creative problem solving. *Memory & Cognition, 26,* 716–730.

Wiley, J., & Rayner, K. (2000). Effects of titles on the processing of text and lexically ambiguous words: Evidence from eye movements. *Memory & Cognition, 28,* 1011–1021.

Williams, J. M. G., Mathews, A., & MacLeod, C. (1996). The emotional Stroop task and psychopathology. *Psychological Bulletin, 120,* 3–24.

Willems, R. M., Hagoort, P., & Casasanto, D. (2010). Body-specific representations of action verbs: Neural evidence from right- and left-handers. *Psychological Science, 21,* 67–74.

Willems, R. M. Labruna, L., D'Espisito, M., Ivry, R., & Casasanto, D. (2011). A functional role for the motor system in language understanding: Evidence from theta-burst transcranial magnetic stimulation. *Psychological Science, 22,* 849–854.

Williamson, V. J., Baddeley, A. D., & Hitch, G. J. (2010). Musicians' and nonmusicians' shortterm memory for verbal and musical sequences: Comparing phonological similarity and pitch proximity. *Memory & Cognition, 38,* 163–175.

Wilkes-Gibbs, D., & Clark, H. H. (1992). Coordinating beliefs in conversation. *Journal of Memory and Language, 31,* 183–194.

Wilson, M., & Emmorey, K. (2006). Comparing sign language and speech reveals a universal limit on short-term memory capacity. *Psychological Science, 17,* 682–683.

Wilson, M., & Fox, G. (2007). Working memory for language is not special: Evidence for an articulatory loop for novel stimuli. *Psychonomic Bulletin & Review, 14,* 470–473.

Wilson, M., & Wilson, T. P. (2005). An oscillator model of the timing of turn-taking. *Psychonomic Bulletin & Review, 12,* 957–968.

Wingfield, A., Goodglass, H., & Lindfield, K. C. (1997). Separating speed from automaticity in a patient with focal brain atrophy. *Psychological Science, 8,* 247–249.

Winograd, E., & Killinger, W. A., Jr. (1983). Relating age at encoding in early childhood to adult recall: Development of flashbulb memories. *Journal of Experimental Psychology: General, 112,* 413–422.

Wixted, J. T. (2004). On common ground: Jost's (1897) law of forgetting and Ribot's (1881) law of retrograde amnesia. *Psychological Review, 111,* 864–879.

Wixted, J. T. (2005). A theory about why we forget what we once knew. *Current Directions in Psychological Science, 14,* 6–9.

Wixted, J. T., & Ebbesen, E. B. (1991). On the form of forgetting. *Psychological Science, 2,* 409–415.

Wood, N. L., & Cowan, N. (1995a). The cocktail party phenomenon revisited: Attention and memory in the classic selective listening procedure of Cherry (1953). *Journal of Experimental Psychology: General, 124,* 243–262.

Wood, N., & Cowan, N. (1995b). The cocktail party phenomenon revisited: How frequent are attention shifts to one's name in an irrelevant auditory channel? *Journal of Experimental Psychology: Learning, Memory, and Cognition, 21,* 255–260.

Wraga, M., Swaby, M., & Flynn, C. M. (2008). Passive tactile feedback facilitates mental rotation of handheld objects. *Memory & Cognition, 36,* 271–281.

Wright, A. A., & Roediger, H. L. III. (2003). Interference processes in monkey auditory list memory. *Psychonomic Bulletin & Review, 10,* 696–702.

Wurm, L. H. (2007). Danger and usefulness: An alternative framework for understanding rapid evaluation effects in perception. *Psychonomic Bulletin & Review, 14,* 1218–1225.

Wurm, L. H., & Seaman, S. R. (2008). Semantic effects in naming and perceptual identification but not in delayed naming: Implications for models and tasks. *Journal of Experimental Psychology: Learning, Memory, and Cognition, 34,* 381–398.

Yantis, S. (2008). The neural basis of selective attention. *Current Directions in Psychological Science, 17,* 86–90.

Yantis, S., & Jonides, J. (1984). Abrupt visual onsets and selective attention: Evidence from visual search. *Journal of Experimental Psychology: Human Perception and Performance, 10,* 601–621.

Yonelinas, A. P. (2002). The nature of recollection and familiarity: A review of 30 years of research. *Journal of Memory and Language, 46,* 441–517.

Yuille, J. C., & Paivio, A. (1967). Latency of imaginal and verbal mediators as a function of stimulus and response concreteness-imagery. *Journal of Experimental Psychology, 75,* 540–544.

Zacks, J. M., Braver, T. S., Sheridan, M. A., Donaldson, D. I., Snyder, A. Z., Ollinger, J. M., et al. (2001). Human brain activity time-locked to perceptual event boundaries. *Nature Neuroscience, 4,* 651–655.

Zacks, J. M., Speer, N. K., Swallow, K. M., Braver, T. S., & Reynolds, J. R. (2007). Event perception: A mind/brain perspective. *Psychological Bulletin, 133,* 273–293.

Zbrodoff, N. J., & Logan, G. D. (1986). On the autonomy of mental processes: A case study of arithmetic. *Journal of Experimental Psychology: General, 115,* 118–130.

Zechmeister, E. B., & Shaughnessy, J. J. (1980). When you think that you know and when you think that you know but you don't. *Bulletin of the Psychonomic Society, 15,* 41–44.

Zeelenberg, R., Wagenmakers, E., & Rotteveel, M. (2006). The impact of emotion on perception: Bias or enhanced processing? *Psychological Science, 17,* 287–291.

Zola-Morgan, S., Squire, L., & Amalral, D. G. (1986). Human amnesia and the medial temporal region: Enduring memory impairment following a bilateral lesion limited to field CA1 of the hippocampus. Journal of Neuroscience, 6, 2950–2967.

Zwaan, R. A. (1996). Processing narrative time shifts. *Journal of Experimental Psychology: Learning, Memory, and Cognition, 22,* 1196–1207.

Zwaan, R. A., Langston, M. C., & Graesser, A. C. (1995). The construction of situation models in narrative comprehension: An event-indexing model. *Psychological Science, 6,* 292–297.

Zwaan, R. A., Magliano, J. P., & Graesser, A. C. (1995). Dimensions of situation model construction in narrative comprehension. *Journal of Experimental Psychology: Learning, Memory, and Cognition, 21,* 386–397.

Zwaan, R. A., & Radvansky, G. A. (1998). Situation models in language comprehension and memory. *Psychological Bulletin, 123,* 162–185.

Zwaan, R. A., Stanfield, R. A., & Yaxley, R. H. (2002). Language comprehenders mentally represent the shapes of objects. *Psychological Science, 13,* 168–171.

INDEX

The letter *f* following an entry indicates a page with a figure
The letter *t* following an entry indicates a page with a table